Soldiers in Black:
The History, Organization, and Personnel of the SS

ANTHONY O. HUGHES

To my children

CONTENTS

PREFACE

In the history of the Second World War, no other group is as well-known or as infamous as the Nazi Party's elite "SS". Even in the second decade of the twenty first century, over seventy years after the close of World War II, the German Schutzstaffel - the SS - continues to be a well-known organization responsible for the vast majority of Nazi war crimes and atrocities.

The SS began as a small bodyguard formation in 1925, and during its twenty years of existence grew into a vast European empire under the command of its most well-known leader, Heinrich Himmler. The influence of the SS encompassed nearly every aspect of the Nazi state from the operation of the German security forces, the administration of concentration camps, military campaigns under the authority of the Waffen-SS, as well as the deliberate extermination of over six million Jews, five million Slavs, and other "undesirables" of the Third Reich.

Through a study and analysis of the SS, a story like none other may be told. A story of a bureaucratic and administrative machine, responsible for such a level of death and destruction as the world has ever known, as well as the story of the men who ran and operated the SS with a calculating cold vision.

This work attempts to examine and explain the intricate and complex organization which was the SS. From its initial formation as a bodyguard unit, to an elite Nazi Party organization in the 1930s, and finally to a genocidal agency which perpetrated the Holocaust of the Second World War, a picture emerges of how this organization was structured and how it operated. The records of the SS also show historians the careers of the men who led this organization and who were responsible for its many crimes.

Less than three percent of German men served in the SS during the Second World War, nevertheless this group's legacy is still well known to this day. The SS will forever be remembered as an anti-Semitic organization which relentlessly persecuted the Jews and other peoples deemed inferior to Adolf Hitler's vision of the Aryan master race.

This is the story of the SS, how it was formed, how it operated, and how it came to be known as one of the most infamous organizations in history.

Part One
The History of the SS

CHAPTER ONE: ORIGINS AND EARLY HISTORY

The origins of the SS may be traced to the early 1920s with the birth of the Schutzstaffel directly interconnected with the Nazi Stormtroopers of the Sturmabteilung, commonly known as the SA. The concept of storm trooper detachments – specially trained troops skilled in assault tactics, had originated during the First World War within the German Army. With Germany's defeat in 1919, several paramilitary groups known as "Freikorps" were founded by disillusioned, unemployed, and sometimes radical ex-veterans. Two of the more notorious Freikorps were the Ehrhardt Naval Brigade and the Stahlhelm, both of which would later contribute to the formation of the Nazi storm trooper units of the SA.

Origins of the SA and SS

The creation of the first storm trooper detachments by the early Nazi Party occurred in February of 1920; the first such group was known as the "Saalschutz Abteilung", or Hall Defense Detachment. The Nazi Party, less than a year old at this point, had formed the Hall Defense Detachment to protect key speakers at major Nazi Party meetings, chief among them Adolf Hitler. By August of 1921, Adolf Hitler had begun referring to the growing number of Nazi defense troops as the "Turn und Sportabteilung", or Gymnastics and Sports Division of the Nazi Party. By September of that same year, the final name for the storm troopers, that of the Sturmabteilung, was adopted. The early SA was commanded under the leadership of Emil Maurice who was an early member of the Nazi Party and later one of the founding members of the SS.

Early Nazi storm troopers were loosely organized with few formal ranks and no established insignia; most storm troopers donned themselves in World War I era uniforms with various accoutrements such as kepi caps, jack boots, and daggers. Only in 1925, after the Nazi Party had been reformed after a failed attempt to take over the Bavarian government, did the first formal uniform and insignia regulations of the SA come about. At the same time, Adolf Hitler ordered the creation of a special bodyguard company within the SA – this new group would become the Schutzstaffel, or more simply known as the SS.

Hermann Ehrhardt, founder of the "Ehrhardt Naval Brigade". His model for paramilitary organizations inspired the creation of the SA
(Federal German Archives)

In March of 1923, Adolf Hitler established a select group of storm troopers whose mission was to protect Hitler at major Nazi Party meetings and rallies. The very first group, recognized as a precursor of the SS, was known as the "Stabswache" and was a twelve-man company led by Emil Maurice. By November of 1923, when Adolf Hitler and his Nazi Party attempted to seize control of the Bavarian government by force, Hitler's personal bodyguard unit had grown to one hundred men and was known as the "Stosstrupp Adolf Hitler" or Adolf Hitler's Shock Troops. The commanders of Hitler's bodyguard in 1923 were Julius Schreck and Joseph Berchtold, both of whom would eventually serve as head of the SS in the late 1920s.

The men who founded the SS: Emil Maurice, Julius Schreck, Joseph Berchtold, and Julius Schaub (Federal German Archives)

After a short prison sentence for his failed Bavarian revolt, Hitler re-founded his personal bodyguard unit in April of 1925. Emil Maurice organized this new group as the "Schutzkommondo". Julius Schreck was appointed the first commander with Julius Schaub as his deputy. By that summer, the Schutzkommondo had been renamed the "Sturmstaffel" (Storm Squadron). On the 9th of November 1925, upon the suggestion of World War I fighter ace and now leading Nazi Hermann Göring, the Sturmstaffel took on its final name as the Schutzstaffel, or SS.

> ### *Predecessor Groups to the Schutzstaffel*
>
> * Stabswache (March 1923)
> * Stosstrupp Adolf Hitler (November 1923)
> * Schutzkommondo (April 1925)
> * Sturmstaffel (June 1925)

By April of 1926, the Munich based Nazi Party had begun to expand its influence into other parts of Germany. Local Nazi leaders in the northeast had begun to organize in Berlin while western Germany saw regional Nazi cells appearing in the industrial areas of the Ruhr and the Rhineland. Only in northwest Germany, in the areas around Kiel and Bremen, was the Nazi Party still relatively unknown.

The purpose of the Nazi Party in the late 1920s was to secure power through elected means. To that end, the Nazis established several regional administrative units, known as "Gaus", in order to organize election districts as well as host Nazi leaders during election touring and campaigns.

The role of the SS, under its second leader Joseph Berchtold, was to provide personal bodyguard protection to Adolf Hitler and other senior Nazi Party leaders at major rallies and gatherings. In Munich this was not a problem, since this was the headquarters of the Nazi Party with followers ever present who were loyal to Adolf Hitler. Yet in other regions of Germany, Nazis swore allegiance to local strongmen and the ideals of National Socialism - not the person of Hitler.

To protect Hitler and his Munich based leadership when traveling to other regions of Germany, Berchtold set about establishing a number of SS-Regions which would pair up with a corresponding Nazi Gau. Whenever a Nazi leader traveled to a region outside of Munich it was Berchtold's intent that there would be SS men available who were completely loyal to Hitler. To cope with the administration of expanding the SS outside of Munich, Berchtold introduced a new command structure, as well as the first recognizable series of SS ranks and insignia. To himself, Berchtold was appointed as the National Leader of the SS, or SS-Reichsführer[i].

Leaders of the local SS regions were known by the title SS-Gauführer, while within each region there existed a number of SS-Squadrons, or "Staffeln", each commanded by an SS-Staffelführer. The rank and file of the SS were known simply by the title SS-Mann (SS-Trooper). Each SS-Squadron was to comprise no more than ten troopers each, while all applicants were to be screened for their loyalty, discipline, and obedience to Adolf Hitler. To also initiate command and control of the SS, in 1926 Berchtold organized a senior command office, known as the SS-Oberleitung. Situated in Munich, this office oversaw twelve local SS-Squadrons. Answering to this office were also the SS Regional Commands in other parts of Germany, each of which commanded its own number of SS squadrons.

SS ORGANIZATION IN 1926

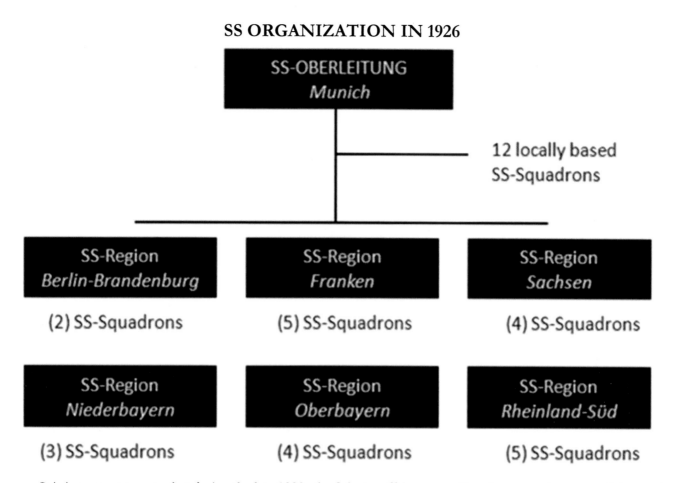

It is important to note that during the late 1920s the Schutzstaffel was considered a mere minor part of the much larger Sturmabteilung – the Nazi storm troopers. SS members were considered to be storm troopers first, and SS men second, while the leadership of the SS was completely regulated to the SA Supreme Command. Even under such conditions, Joseph Berchtold saw in the SS the makings of an elite organization, and to that end began efforts to separate the SS from SA oversight. This would eventually spell disaster for the SS, since SA leaders saw no need for a splinter organization within their own ranks.

By the start of 1927, the SS numbered one thousand members with approximately seventy-five SS-Staffeln established across Germany. The SS had also been chosen by Hitler to take possession of the much revered "Blutfahne" – the blood-spattered Nazi flag which had been carried during the failed Bavarian putsch of 1923. With discussions amongst Nazi leaders to make the SS a separate organization from the SA, the SA leadership quickly took action. Under Supreme SA Commander Franz von Salomon, measures were enacted to disband the SS and merge its duties into local SA detachments. Beginning with relegating the SS to menial tasks, such as passing out Nazi leaflets at rallies, the SA command then began to shut down several SS squadrons in an attempt to decrease SS membership throughout Germany. Joseph Berchtold, unable to stop the SA designs on the SS, resigned as the SS National Leader in March of 1927. He would later serve in various Nazi posts during the 1930s and 40s and eventually live to survive World War II. Berchtold was in fact the only holder of the rank of Reichsführer-SS to do so.

Heinrich Himmler and the SS

Berchtold's successor Erhard Heiden fared little better in keeping the SS from going under to SA designs. As the new Reichsführer-SS, Heiden watched as SS membership sunk to no more than two hundred and eighty members throughout all of Germany, while the SS leadership was reduced to having little authority except within its own tiny command office in Munich. It was a member of Heiden's staff who would then change the fate and destiny of the SS forever - his name was Heinrich Himmler. Himmler had joined the Nazi Party in 1925 as a secretary to Nazi leader Gregor Strasser, and by 1926 Himmler was serving as head of Nazi Propaganda, as well as the Nazi Gauleiter for Lower Bavaria, in addition to duties as the local SS-Leader. In March of 1927, Himmler was appointed as deputy Reichsführer with the rank of SS-Oberführer. In January of 1929, with Heiden dejected and under relentless pressure from the SA to disband the SS, Heiden resigned his position and Heinrich Himmler became the fourth Reichsführer-SS.

There was little in Himmler's background to indicate that he would rise to become one of the most powerful men in Nazi Germany. Born on the 7th of October 1900, Himmler had served in the First World War as an Officer Cadet but had never seen combat. He had also backed the Nazis during the 1923 Munich Putsch, as part of a Freikorps detachment, but had spent the mid-1920s studying to earn an agricultural degree and working as a chicken farmer while other Nazi leaders had struggled to reform the Nazi Party. When hired by Heiden as his deputy, Himmler was described as a "keen young clerk" but without any real signs of leadership potential. He was further described as "sly and unmilitary" and presented the physical appearance of a scrawny and weak sort of man. Nevertheless, Himmler was connected to Hitler and knew the Führer personally. Himmler also, in the same manner as Berchtold, saw in the SS the makings of an elite Nazi Party organization, one free and clear of SA designs.

A film still of Heinrich Himmler (standing on the left) in early 1929, shortly after Himmler's takeover of the SS (Bavarian State Archives)

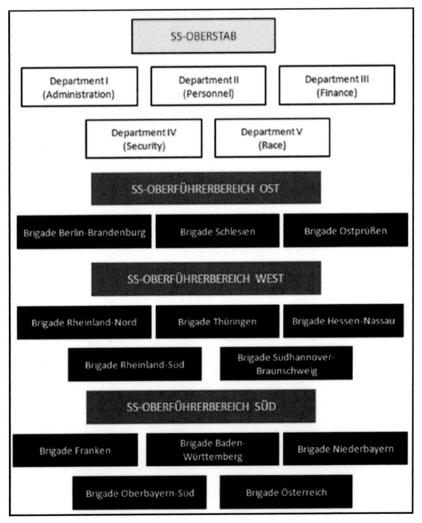

Himmler's first task as the new National Leader of the SS was to set up a command nexus for the SS in Munich. Replacing the Oberleitung was a new "SS-Oberstab" consisting of five separate departments. The old SS-Gau were then consolidated into three Senior Leadership Districts (SS-Oberführerbereich), each of which containing several SS-Brigades. The old SS-Squadrons were then reconsolidated into SS-Regiments, known as "Standarten", while regimental commanders were known by the title "Standartenführer" with this rank further divided into two separate grades, Standartenführer (I) and (II). The first grade of the rank commanded the regiment sized Standarten while the second grade commanded the SS–Brigades. The highest rank in the SS was that of SS-Oberführer with this rank held by the commanders of the Senior Leadership Districts and also by Himmler himself; his position of Reichsführer-SS was at this time completely titular.

Left: SS organization in 1930

Under Himmler's leadership, the SS began to expand rapidly and by the fall of 1930 was approaching a membership of nearly five thousand. By the spring of 1931, the SS abandoned the SS-Brigade system and adopted a new type of unit known as the "Oberführer-Abschnitt". These units would later become known simply as "SS-Abschnitt" (SS-District).

Between August of 1930 and April 1931, an event occurred which significantly allowed Heinrich Himmler to expand SS influence across all of Germany. Known as the "Stennes Revolt", the SA storm trooper detachment in the German capitol of Berlin, under the command of SA-Oberführer Walter Stennes, twice seized control of local Nazi Party offices due to policy disagreements with Nazi Party leaders, chief among them Joseph Goebbels. The Stennes Revolt served as a catalyst for several major changes to the SS, beginning with the removal of one of the organization's greatest threats – the Commander of the SA. As a result of Stennes's actions, Hitler fired SA Supreme Commander Franz Pfeffer von Salomon, who had been a major advocate of disbanding the SS in favor of local SA bodyguard units. In von Salomon's place, Hitler appointed himself as the SA Supreme Commander, thereby ensuring that all Nazi storm troopers throughout Germany would thereafter swear loyalty directly to the Nazi Party Führer.

Walter Stennes, whose attempted SA revolt in Berlin led to the firing of SA leader Von Salomon (Federal German Archives)

To facilitate the day-to-day running of the SA (a task Hitler himself had little interest in performing), Hitler recruited German Army Captain and longtime Nazi Party supporter Ernst Röhm. Röhm, who had been serving as a military advisor in Bolivia since 1928, returned to Germany to assume command as the SA Chief of Staff and operational commander of all the Nazi storm troopers.

When Röhm took over the SA in January of 1931, the Nazi storm troopers numbered over one million in membership but were fractured and divided amongst local commanders. Röhm's position as SA Chief of Staff, a title which had previously been held without any real authority by Otto Wagener, placed Röhm in a position to restructure and reorganize the SA along more stringent military lines. While Röhm was occupied with his SA reforms, Heinrich Himmler and his SS were given a free hand to continue expansion efforts of their own. By January of 1932, the SS numbered over fifty thousand in membership with Himmler now appointed as the Personal Security Chief of the NSDAP (Nazi Party) Headquarters in Munich. By that summer, the former SS Senior Leadership Districts had been expanded into five new SS-Groups, commanded by SS officers in the new rank of "SS-Gruppenführer". Himmler himself was also promoted to this rank, serving now as both National Leader of the SS and Commander of the SS Senior Staff in Munich.

SS ORGANIZATION IN 1932

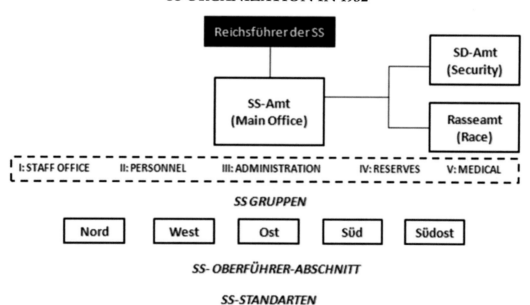

For the remainder of 1932, the Nazi Party focused on achieving their primary aim of securing political power in Germany. After existing as only a barely known political party in the late 1920s, Nazi popularity had soared in 1930 after a world financial crisis had caused a major economic depression. The Nazi promise of "New Order in Old Chaos" appealed to many Germans, including the upper class which had up to that point had little to do with the paramilitary and anti-Semitic Nazi ideology and rhetoric.

DEVELOPMENT OF SS GROUPS (1926 – 1932)

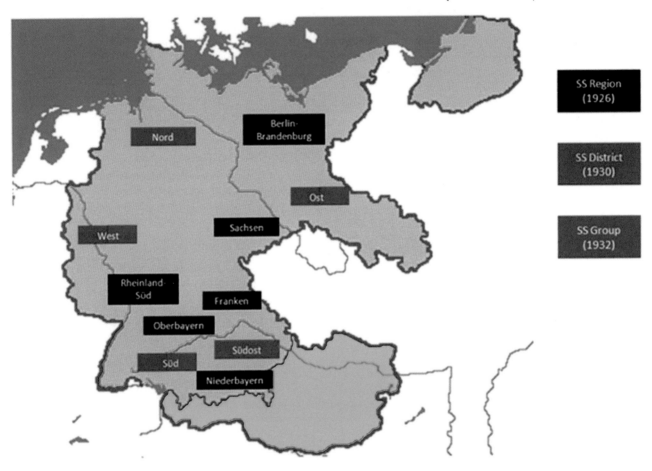

Emboldened with political success, in the summer of 1932 Adolf Hitler attempted to secure election as German President and ran against incumbent Field Marshal Paul von Hindenburg and Communist Party leader Ernst Thälmann. Hindenburg emerged triumphant in the election, which was a serious blow to Hitler and his Nazi Party. This was followed by an even greater defeat in November 1932 when parliamentary elections saw the loss of thirty-four Nazi seats in the German parliament, while the Communist Party gained eleven. The Nazis, however, were not disheartened by the political failures of 1932 and attempted to reverse these political misfortunes. As early as February, open political warfare had erupted on the streets of Germany with the Nazi SA storm troopers routinely clashing against the Communist Red Front. The SS, drawn into the conflict through their duties as bodyguards to top Nazis, lost thirteen SS men killed and hundreds more wounded in street fights with the Communists and police. The situation became so serious that in April of 1932 the German Chancellor Heinrich Brüning outlawed the wearing of political uniforms entirely; this decree was lifted two months later when Brüning was replaced as Chancellor by Franz von Papen.

In the fall of 1932, Army General Kurt von Schleicher was appointed as Chancellor by President Hindenburg in an effort to curtail the rampant political instability and violence throughout Germany. Less than a month later von Schleicher was dismissed due to the failure of his government to obtain a consensus in the Reichstag parliament for cooperation between the various warring political factions. With no other option remaining, Hindenburg offered Adolf Hitler the post of Chancellor of Germany. The Nazi Party was now in power.

Early uniforms of the SS

When the SS was first founded in 1925, Nazi storm trooper uniforms had been developing slowly since 1921. In that year the traditional swastika armband had been invented for use on paramilitary uniforms. The first armbands contained the black "Hakenkreuz" (swastika) within a white circle, centered on a red background. Other than this standard armband, early Nazi Party uniforms held little standardization and most early Nazi storm troopers simple wore World War I vintage paramilitary uniforms as their standard attire.

The swastika armband was invented in 1921 and would become a standard insignia item for nearly every organization of the Nazi Party

The Nazi Party was officially banned between 1923 and 1925, during which time there were no recognized Party uniforms, although several underground Nazi groups still maintained makeshift uniforms of their own. Upon the Nazi Party's re-founding after Hitler's release from prison, it was SA commander Gerhard Roßbach who suggested using a large war surplus of tropical brown denim shirts to outfit the reborn storm trooper movement.

The Nazi brownshirt uniform thus came into being, although still without any real form of standardized rank or uniform insignia. By the fall of 1925, the infant SS had adopted a similar uniform of a brown storm trooper shirt worn with a swastika armband and a black kepi cap. Per a directive issued on September 29th 1925, SS men began wearing a Totenkopf (Death's Head) insignia centered below a cockade centered on their cap.

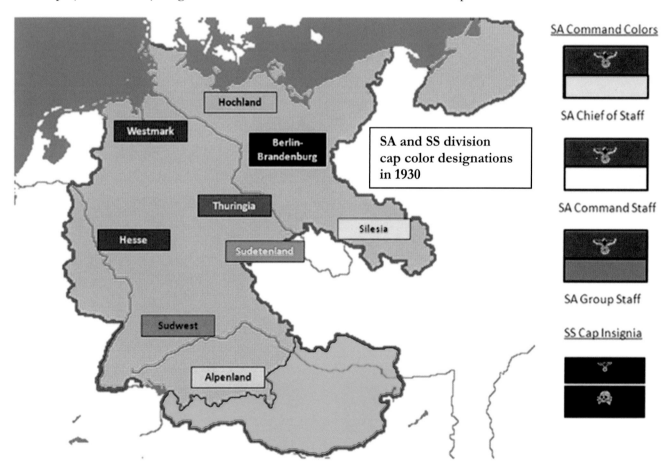

In August of 1929, the Sturmabteilung designated that individual SA divisions (known as "Gruppen") should begin wearing colored cap bands and collar patches displaying individual unit numbers. The SS at this point was considered a stand-alone storm trooper battalion, with black as their unit color. The black kepi cap was also now standardized with a Nazi Party eagle and death's head, while senior SS leaders were entitled to wear silver trim on their headgear. In the fall of 1929, the SS briefly experimented with an early collar tab system to denote positional authority. This system seems to have been very short lived, replaced by a more standardized and permanent collar patch system in 1930.

SS RANK INSIGNIA (1929)

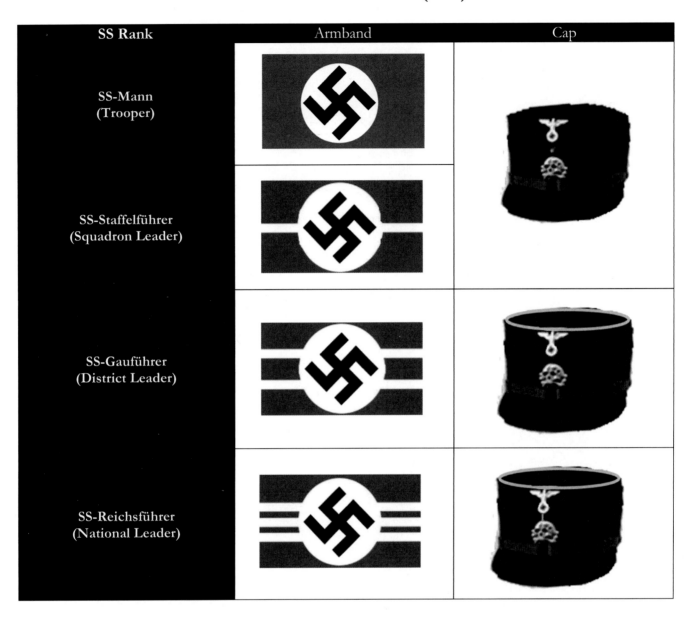

SS Rank	Armband	Cap
SS-Mann (Trooper)		
SS-Staffelführer (Squadron Leader)		
SS-Gauführer (District Leader)		
SS-Reichsführer (National Leader)		

SS-Leader   SS-Adjutant

Above: Early SS collar insignia

SS RANK INSIGNIA (1930)

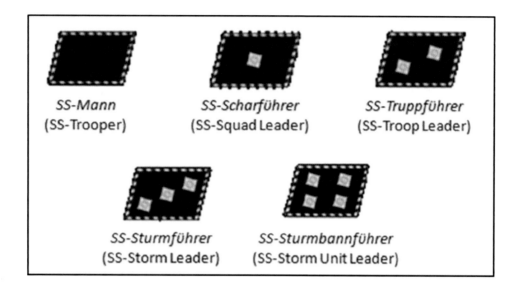

The earliest form of SS collar rank insignia consisted of silver pips worn on the left uniform collar, opposite a unit designator of either a bare patch for headquarters staff, or a Roman numeral to denote SS regiment affiliation.

Rank insignia for SS-Standartenführer and SS-Oberführer wore oak leaves on both collars

By 1930, SS uniforms had become standardized with a new insignia system using oak leaves on collar patches to denote senior rank. The rank of "SS-Staffelführer" was now shortened to simply "SS-Führer" (SS-Leader). By November of 1930, the SS uniform now consisted of a storm trooper brown shirt, with plain swastika armband, worn with rank denoted on the upper left collar patch through the use of silver pips and oak leaves. Early SS ranks mirrored those of the SA, which by now included squad, troop, company, and battalion leader positions. The highest rank in the SS at this time was that of SS-Oberführer, or "Senior Leader". The lower rank of SS-Standartenführer was divided into two separate grades (one for regiment leaders and the other for commanders of SS-Brigades) known as Standartenführer (I) and Standartenführer (II) - both grades displayed a single oak leaf as their insignia.

SS uniforms would undergo a further change in early 1932, as a result of expansion of the SS, necessitating the addition of several new ranks. The new ranks added "Senior" and "Head" (Ober and Haupt) designators to existing rank titles, which were denoted by aluminum piping added to rank badges. The ranks of SS-Standartenführer (I) and (II) were then consolidated into a single grade, the result of the discontinuation of the SS-Brigade system in favor of new SS-Districts. The SS also created a new rank of "SS Group Leader" (SS-Gruppenführer) which was presented to Heinrich Himmler as well as several other senior SS leaders. In the fall of 1932, perhaps one of the most significant SS uniform changes would occur – the creation of the black uniform which would forever become a symbol of the SS.

SS RANK INSIGNIA (1932)

SS-Mann
(SS-Trooper)

SS-Scharführer
(SS-Squad Leader)

SS-Oberscharführer
(SS-Senior Squad Leader)

SS-Truppführer
(SS-Troop Leader)

SS-Obertruppführer
(SS-Senior Troop Leader)

SS-Sturmführer
(SS-Storm Leader)

SS-Regiment Patch
(Right Collar)

SS-Sturmhauptführer
(SS-Storm Head Leader)

SS-Sturmbannführer
(SS-Storm Unit Leader)

SS-Standartenführer
(SS-Regiment Leader)

SS-Oberführer
(SS-Senior Leader)

SS-Gruppenführer
(SS-Group Leader)

CHAPTER TWO: THE NAZI STATE AND THE SS

When Adolf Hitler became Chancellor of Germany in January of 1933, the Schutzstaffel numbered sixty-five thousand members, yet the SS itself was still considered a sub-unit of the now two million strong SA storm troopers. The SS was also considered strictly as a Nazi paramilitary organization and, on the day that Hitler took office, the SS had no formal function in the new government. The bulk of the SS remained a part time mustering formation, had no weapons or arms, nor did SS Chief Heinrich Himmler hold any type of governmental position. This, however, was soon to change.

The Makings of a Police State

On Monday, January 30th 1933, Germany awoke to Adolf Hitler's first day in office as Chancellor of Germany. Prior to Hitler's assumption of power, Germany had existed as a tenuous democracy known as the "Weimar Republic", named after the German city in which the post-World War constitution had been signed. The country was in the midst of an economic crisis and still under the strain of heavy war repatriations dictated by the Treaty of Versailles. As for Hitler, the average German saw the Nazi leader as merely another politician, albeit a somewhat popular one, and many wondered how long his Chancellorship would last.

By this point, the SS had existed for nearly eight years, serving faithfully as a bodyguard unit for Hitler and other top Nazis, yet with Hitler now in power it seemed as if there was little else for the SS to do. Heinrich Himmler, National Leader of the SS, had served in his post since 1929 and during that time had massively expanded the SS throughout the country. In 1931, Himmler had also hired an ex-Naval Officer named Reinhard Heydrich to form an SS Security Service whose purpose was to spy and report on Hitler's political rivals. Politically speaking, however, the SS was still a weak organization in 1933. The group had no standing in the new government and was still considered merely a part of the much larger SA. Himmler was little known outside of his native Bavaria, and even within the SS there were some serious rivalries to Himmler's authority as Reichsführer-SS.

Heinrich Himmler, in his command capacity as Reichsführer-SS, operated with a personal staff from the Nazi Party headquarters office in Munich, Bavaria, as did the fledging SS Security Service known as the "Sicherheitsdienst" or SD. In the north, within the German capitol of Berlin, a different faction of the SS was forming around SS-General Kurt Daluege. Daluege, who had put down the Stennes Revolt of 1930, saw the SS troops in the German capitol as separate and distinct from the SS in Munich. Daluege seldom communicated with Himmler and referred to the Reichsführer-SS as "that chicken farmer", in reference to Himmler's earlier career in agriculture. Envoys from Himmler were dejected as well, as evidenced by a 1932 trip to Berlin by Reinhard Heydrich who was threatened by local SS leaders and told to leave Berlin immediately.

Yet it was Himmler who had the ear of Adolf Hitler and the plan in 1933 was a simple one – transform Germany into a police state. As for the SS, the organization would be expanded to encompass not only the security of the Nazi Party but also the entire German state itself. However, before any of this could occur, Hitler first had to become master within his own house. On February 25th 1933, less than a month after Hitler had become Chancellor, the German Parliament building of the Reichstag was set ablaze, apparently by a Dutch communist named Marinus van der Lubbe. The next day Adolf Hitler signed an Executive Decree known as the "Law for the Protection of People and State". The decree enabled the police to arrest without warrant and imprison "radical opponents" of the Nazi regime. Forty thousand SA and SS men were granted emergency police powers as "Hilfspolizei" (Auxiliary Police), issued firearms, and began to patrol the German streets arresting communists, socialists, and other political opponents of the Nazis. While there were also some spontaneous attacks against Jews, this future target of Nazi anti-Semitism were themselves not yet a primary concern of the government.

By March of 1933, nearly thirty thousand Germans had been arrested as enemies of the Nazi state. To circumvent the German court system, which was overwhelmed by such vast numbers of arrests, Hitler ordered the creation of several labor camps across Germany to house, or "concentrate", enemies of the state in a semi-permanent status of "protective custody", meaning such persons could be held indefinitely without trial.

These new camps, initially run by the SA in a somewhat disorganized manner, were known as "Konzentrationslager" – Concentration Camps. It would not be until 1934, under the leadership of an SS officer named Theodor Eicke, that the Concentration Camps were seen as a symbol of the SS.

On March 23rd 1933, nearly one month to date after the Reichstag Fire, President Hindenburg signed the "Law to Remedy the Distress of the People and the Nation". More commonly known as the "Enabling Act", the new law gave the Chancellor of Germany emergency powers to include changing the constitution and introducing new laws without parliamentary approval. Civil liberates were also suspended and all political opponents of the Nazi government were subject to arrest and imprisonment without trial. The transformation from democracy to dictatorship was complete.

An SS Auxiliary Policeman in March of 1933. The white armband denotes status as "Hilfspolizei" (Bavarian State Archives)

The SS versus the SA

As early as 1931, two years before Adolf Hitler had become Chancellor of Germany, Heinrich Himmler had determined that the SS would have to become separate from its masters in the SA in order to survive. Reinhard Heydrich, and his Nazi Party security service the SD, began this task by spying and collecting information on top SA leaders. By 1932, Heydrich had amassed several impressive dossiers on senior SA personnel with scandals ranging from corruption, embezzlement, to open homosexuality. Himmler then further widened the gap between the SA and the SS by introducing a new all black SS uniform, distinct and separate from the Nazi brown shirts of the storm troopers, although the traditional SA brown shirt uniform was used by some local SS commands until 1935.

Left: Heinrich Himmler and Ernst Röhm in the spring of 1933. The relationship between the SA and SS had by this time deteriorated to essentially a stand-off (Federal German Archives)

By the time Adolf Hitler had become Chancellor in 1933, Ernst Röhm had developed the SA into a two million strong "People's Militia" ready for a violent "Second Revolution" in order to purge the German government of the traditional conservatives and monarchists from the time of the Kaiser a generation before. The relationship between the SS and the SA further deteriorated in the spring of 1933 when Hitler promoted Heinrich Himmler to the new rank of "SS-Obergruppenführer", thereby placing Himmler on equal footing with the Supreme Command of the SA. Himmler then began to totally separate his command staff from SA control, while Hitler further gave orders that no SA commander would be permitted to issue direct orders to the SS. The line of distrust between the SS and SA had clearly been drawn.

For the remainder of 1933, Röhm and his SA began to make more and more fervent demands of Hitler and the Nazi Party leadership. First and foremost, Röhm demanded a formal post in the German government as the Minister of Defense, effectively replacing the German Army High Command with an SA Militia Leadership under Röhm. The SA Chief of Staff further insisted that the SA should be merged with the German Army, something which the honor bound traditionalist minded Army leadership found horrifying. Adolf Hitler was thus placed in a precarious position, since the loyalty of the Army was essential to his control over Germany. In addition, even though Hitler was now dictator of Germany through the Enabling Act, he still answered to President Paul von Hindenburg. Nazi leaders were concerned that, should Hitler lose control of Röhm and his SA storm troopers, the very real possibility existed of Hindenburg declaring martial law and Hitler losing the Chancellorship.

By the spring of 1934, Röhm's SA numbered four a half million men. The SS had reached a strength of eighty thousand while the German Army stood at one hundred thousand active duty soldiers. With Röhm unrelenting from his demands to replace the Army with a storm trooper militia, Hitler had no choice but to act against his old Nazi Party comrade. Röhm was to be eliminated and the instrument of his demise was to be the SS.

However, the SS in early 1934 was essentially still a paramilitary Nazi Party organization and had no powers of arrest. SS units were also not armed, nor did the SS hold control of any local and state military arsenals and barracks. Himmler knew that for the SS to move against the SA, the SS would need to be granted executive arrest powers and also maintain its own armed force to deal with enemies of the state. The process had already begun in March 1933 when Himmler became the Police President of Munich, his first official governmental post. The next month Himmler was appointed the Political Police Commissioner for all of Bavaria; this followed with all the other German states following suit until Himmler had been appointed to police command positions in every German state except Prussia.

Prussia was the largest state in Germany and encompassed the German capitol of Berlin. After the Nazi seizure of power, Prussia fell quickly under the domination of one man - Hermann Göring. Göring was a former World War I flying ace who had served in combat with the famous Manfred von Richthofen, also known as the Red Baron. In 1922, still serving as a Captain in the German Army, Göring had joined the Nazi Party and a year later had served as commander of the SA during the failed Munich Putsch. After the Nazi Party had been re-founded in 1925, Göring had remained on the SA rolls but had focused his efforts on becoming a top leader for the entire Nazi Party. When Adolf Hitler became Chancellor in 1933, Göring was essentially the second in command of the Nazi Party. After becoming Speaker of the Reichstag, Göring seized the top position in the state government of Prussia, naming himself Minister President of Prussia in April of 1934.

The political police force of Prussia, founded in 1848 and known as the "Prussian Secret Police", was responsible for reporting and suppressing political opponents to the German government. Under Göring's influence, the mission of this group was changed, and the organization was renamed as the "Gestapo". When the Gestapo was first created in April of 1933, the group's stated aim was to locate, investigate, and suppress enemies of the Nazi government by any and all means available. Göring appointed as head of the Gestapo the Prussian Political Police Chief Rudolf Diels who was a long time protégé and Göring supporter. In the early days of the Gestapo, the group was not connected to the SS and was in fact a serious rival to Himmler's authority and plans for further SS expansion.

By the beginning of 1934, a showdown had developed with Himmler controlling the political police forces of Bavaria and the other German states, while Göring and Diels operated the Gestapo in Prussia. Göring was lobbying Adolf Hitler to extend the Gestapo control outside of Prussia while Minister of the Interior Wilhelm Frick wanted Himmler to control all political police forces within Germany.

At the same time that Himmler and Göring were battling out who would control the political police forces of Germany, Röhm and his SA were becoming a far greater danger than either Göring or Himmler could pose to one another. Seeing the SA as a common enemy, both Himmler and Göring agreed to place aside their differences and for Himmler to command the Gestapo. On April 20th 1934, Göring handed over control of the Gestapo to Himmler; two days later, Himmler appointed Reinhard Heydrich as Chief of the Gestapo.

On April 20th 1934, Heinrich Himmler was granted command of the Gestapo from Hermann Göring in an effort to combat the growing threat of the SA (Federal German Archives)

Heydrich expanded the Gestapo's authority to every state in Germany and began to staff top Gestapo positions with members of the SS. The command offices of the SS were then relocated from Munich to Berlin with both Himmler's and Heydrich's headquarters occupying the same building at Number 8 Prinz Albrecht Strasse in the south of the German capitol. Further SS offices began to relocate to Berlin as well with the SS now regarded not only as a Nazi Party organization but also as an established agency of the German government.

With the executive arrest powers of the Gestapo now at his disposal, Himmler's next task was to empower the SS with an armed force in order to deal with its enemies. When Adolf Hitler came to power in 1933, the only full-time armed SS detachment was a group in Munich known as the SS-Stabswache. The Stabswache was commanded by Josef "Sepp" Dietrich and considered Hitler's personal protection force. Although nominally under Himmler's command as the Reichsführer-SS, Dietrich had made it abundantly clear that he answered solely to Adolf Hitler. In the fall of 1933, Dietrich transferred his force to Berlin to take up duties as the Chancellery Guard; the name of the group was at that time changed to the "Leibstandarte Adolf Hitler". Although Dietrich saw himself as independent from Himmler, the two SS leaders saw in the SA a common threat. Thus, when the time came to move against the storm troopers, Himmler had his armed force in the strength of the Leibstandarte.

The Night of the Long Knives

The downfall of Ernst Röhm and the destruction of the Nazi storm troopers took place between June 30th and July 2nd 1934. Known historically as the "Night of the Long Knives", the SS code for the operation was "Hummingbird". The goal of the Night of the Long Knives was to neutralize the growing threat of the SA by arresting and executing the top leadership of the organization; this included all senior SA generals as well as Röhm himself. The planning for the operation, which Hitler had at last authorized after persuasion by Hermann Göring and Propaganda Chief Joseph Goebbels, began in early 1934 during a period when Röhm and his storm troopers were at the height of excess, openly advocating for a second revolution and the merger of the SA with the German Army. By mid-June, the Gestapo had prepared death lists to be used for arrests and executions, while the mustering formations of the SS throughout Germany had been placed on high alert.

The first victims of the Night of the Long Knives were a series of kidnappings of various anti-Nazis (who were later killed) between June 21st and the 25th. Following these covert actions, Hitler contacted Ernst Röhm and issued the SA Chief of Staff an order to gather all senior SA generals at a hotel in southern Bavaria located on the lake of Bad Wiessee. A separate order was then issued to Sepp Dietrich and the Leibstandarte to mobilize with directives to arrest and execute the SA leadership. Reinhard Heydrich, from his Gestapo headquarters in Berlin, then began to issue commands to various SS units across Germany, distributing death lists and ordering various arrests.

At Bad Wiessee on the morning of June 30th, Adolf Hitler arrived with an entourage of armed SS troopers and Gestapo personnel. Exact accounts of what occurred vary, but Hitler is said to have personally arrested Röhm who may have been found in bed with another man. Meanwhile, various teams of SS troops either arrested or outright killed the other SA leaders who were present, most of whom were still sleeping in the early morning hours. Meanwhile across Germany, anyone considered a danger to the Nazi regime was rounded up and either then taken away for execution or killed immediately outright. The list of enemies of the state officially topped off at eighty-five persons, but more than two hundred were in fact killed. Most were executed at Stadelheim prison in Munich or at the Lichterfelde barracks in Berlin. Home invasions and brutal killings were also common, such as the case of former Reich Chancellor Kurt von Schleicher who was gunned down in his home along with his wife.

As for Röhm himself, the SA leader's fate was delayed somewhat as discussions were held at the highest levels of the Nazi Party as to the former storm trooper commander's disposition. Hitler apparently valued Röhm's early friendship and debated sparing his life. Most other top Nazis wanted Röhm out of the way, with this view voiced by Göring, Himmler, and Goebbels. Finally, Hitler gave the order to execute Ernst Röhm with the job of carrying out the actual execution falling to the SS commander of the Dachau Concentration Camp, a former mental patient and now SS-Brigadier named Theodor Eicke. Theodor Eicke, along with his aide Michel Lippert, traveled to Stadelheim from Dachau to find Röhm in cell #474 of the prison. Per Hitler's strict instructions, a newspaper was placed in front of Röhm detailing the downfall of the SA while on top of the paper was placed a pistol. Eicke then stated to Röhm: "You have forfeited your life. The Führer will give you one last chance to draw your conclusions." Röhm was then left alone in his cell with the loaded weapon while Eicke and Lippert stood out in the hallway. Fifteen minutes later, failing to hear a shot, the two SS officers reentered Röhm's cell, finding the SA leader still alive. Röhm was then shot point blank in the chest by Lippert and killed instantly.

Senior SS leadership during the Night of the Long Knives

SS Officer	Duties in the SS	Photograph
Heinrich Himmler	National Leader of the SS (Reichsführer-SS). Under orders from Adolf Hitler, Himmler directed the SS to move against the SA. From June 30th to July 2nd, Himmler also provided various status reports of the arrests, executions, and killings to senior Nazis such as Hitler, Göring, and Goebbels.	
Reinhard Heydrich	Commander of the Gestapo. Heydrich served as operational commander over the killing teams and death squads sent to deal with the designated enemies of the Nazi state. Devised a numbering system where victims of the blood purge were assigned a numerical designator to ensure secrecy when distributing death lists to local SS units.	
Josef "Sepp" Dietrich	Commander of the Leibstandarte-SS, an armed bodyguard formation loyal to Hitler. Dietrich led a militarily armed SS unit to perform executions of SA leaders at the Lichterfelde barracks in Berlin and at Stadelheim prison in Munich. Other victims were killed by less formally organized teams of Gestapo and SS men under Heydrich's command.	
Theodor Eicke	Commander of Dachau Concentration Camp. Under orders from Heinrich Himmler and Adolf Hitler, Theodor Eicke personally oversaw the execution of Ernst Röhm in his cell at Stadelheim prison, after the latter's refusal to commit suicide under Hitler's direction.	
Arthur Nebe	A professional Berlin detective and also an early SS member. One of the few SS leaders who opposed the blood purge executions, in particular the slaying of Gregor Strasser. Nebe would later become head of the Criminal Police and would himself be executed after becoming involved in a plot to assassinate Adolf Hitler in 1944.	

Elsewhere in Germany, the murders and executions continued unabated. From Gestapo headquarters in Berlin, Reinhard Heydrich directed the killings using a coded numbering system to identify victims. For instance, reports would pass to Heydrich that "Number 7 has been arrested, Number 18 has been killed, Number 32 is missing" and so forth. Executions were normally carried out by firing squad, but personalized murders took place as well. Gregor Strasser, an early Nazi rival of Hitler's, was shot in the basement of Gestapo headquarters and left in his cell to bleed to death from a head wound. Gustav Ritter von Kahr, the retired State Commissioner of Bavaria who had been a major figure in quelling the 1923 Nazi Munich revolt, was kidnapped from his home and hacked to death with pick axes near Dachau. Franz von Papen, the Vice Chancellor under Hitler, was initially to be a victim but was spared at the last minute. Members of von Papen's staff were not so fortunate with at least two deaths occurring as SS troopers stormed von Papen's office.

The purges during the Night of the Long Knives formally came to an end on the afternoon of July 2nd. Hitler then made a national radio address informing the German people that a rebellion against the government, led by Ernst Röhm and Kurt von Schleicher, had been put down by the Army and the SS. The next day, Hitler and his cabinet passed an emergency decree legalizing the actions of the Night of the Long Knives and justifying the extra-judicial killings which had occurred. Leadership of the SA was then handed to Viktor Lutze who became the new SA Chief of Staff. SA membership was then trimmed down to one million and the group was permanently prohibited from stockpiling weapons or bearing arms. Most significant of all was that the SS was separated from the SA and declared an independent organization of the Nazi Party effective July 1st 1934. Promotions within the SS quickly followed, with the senior SS leaders who had participated in the purges being advanced in rank. As for Himmler, his title of Reichsführer-SS was elevated to the status of the highest actual SS rank, complete with a new form of insignia. The SS rank system itself was then changed, with several older titles renamed to eliminate any similarity and connection with the SA. Himmler and his deputies then looked to the future, seeing the SS as an organization with limitless potential.

Reforming the SS

On August 2nd 1934, President Paul von Hindenburg died at the age of eighty-six. His death had been expected for some time, since the aged Field Marshal had begun to show serious signs of illness and senility earlier that year. With Hindenburg now dead, Adolf Hitler made his move to secure absolute power in Germany.

Although Germany was by this point already a Nazi dictatorship, Hitler's position as Chancellor was still technically subordinate to the President of Germany. After Hindenburg died, Hitler declared that the offices of President and Chancellor would be merged. Hitler was now to be "Führer und Reichskanzler", with this new title by its very nature combining Hitler's position as Nazi Party Leader with that of German Chief Executive and Head of State. To present some form of legality to Hitler's act, a vote was held where the German people were asked if they supported Hitler's assumption of both the offices of President and Chancellor. With a 90% vote in favor, Hitler had gained total power in Germany. Hitler next had the Army swear personal loyalty to him, rather than the German state, and then began a process known as "Gleichschaltung" in which Nazi officials were appointed to key governmental positions in state and local offices. Once Nazi headmen were entrenched in government, various decrees then stripped the German local and state governments of nearly all remaining executive and legislative powers.

Hitler next set about to dismantle the hated Treaty of Versailles from the First World War. In March of 1936, the German Army occupied the Rhineland, which although part of Germany was also demilitarized under treaty provisions. To both Germany and Hitler's surprise, the French and British took absolutely no action, seemingly ignoring this blatant violation of international law. By the end of 1936, Germany had also re-founded its Air Force (yet another treaty violation) and had sent the first Luftwaffe troops to be tested in combat during the Spanish Civil War. The year 1938 then saw the merger of Germany and Austria into the "Greater German Reich", followed by the occupation of the ethnic German Sudetenland from Czechoslovakia in September of 1938. Less than six months later, what remained of Czechoslovakia was split into two halves with the Germans occupying the Czech Republic in the west and a new puppet state of Slovakia established in the east.

Heinrich Himmler – Reich Leader of the SS

Born in 1900 as the godson of a Bavarian Prince, Heinrich Himmler served as an officer cadet during the First World War and studied agriculture to become a chicken farmer in the early 1920s. He joined the Nazi Party in 1923 and the SS two years later. While serving as a Nazi propaganda chief in Bavaria, Himmler became an SS district leader and in 1927 became the Deputy National Leader for the entire SS. In January 1929, he succeeded his superior Erhard Heiden as the new Reichsführer-SS and began a meteoric rise to power within the Nazi Party inner circle.

In July 1934, after executing the top leadership of the SA (Himmler had also overseen the murder of his former boss Heiden one year earlier), Himmler's title as Reich Leader became an actual rank which he would hold for the next eleven years. In April 1945, after Hitler learned Himmler was secretly negotiating surrender with the western allies, the former chicken farmer was stripped of his SS rank, all of his other party and government titles, and declared a traitor. Himmler survived the end of the war, but was captured by the British and committed suicide in a prisoner-of-war camp on May 23, 1945.

In the aftermath of the Night of the Long Knives, Heinrich Himmler began to reorganize and reform the SS. Himmler first set about "cleaning house", expelling over 40,000 SS members who had either been connected with the SA, or had been recruited under "less than ideal" circumstances which included all SS members who were known alcoholics, criminals, or homosexuals. What remained of the SS was a force which was totally loyal to Nazi Germany and completely obedient to Himmler. Under his new rank of Reichsführer-SS, Himmler's authority over the SS was undisputed at least outwardly. Personal agendas were still ever-present amongst the ranks of the SS leadership, and some SS senior officers would never come to trust or respect Himmler entirely.

The fall of 1934 was a hub of activity for Himmler as he initiated and ordered several far reaching and sweeping changes to the organization of the SS. First, Himmler formed a new command staff known as the Reichsführung-SS; attached to this command nexus was Himmler's personal staff as well as an executive branch known as the Kommandostab-RfSS. Himmler next reconsolidated the local SS units, doing away with the old SS groups and creating new senior districts, known as SS-Oberabschnitt. In the summer of 1935, another reconsolidation was made with the creation of a new SS Headquarters Office, known as the SS-Hauptamt (SS Head Office) which replaced the older command offices of the SS-Amt. On equal footing with the Head Office was the SS Security Office, run by Reinhard Heydrich who was also Chief of the Gestapo, as well as a new Race and Settlement Office which had been formed from the older "Rasseamt" (Race Office), established in 1931.

In March of 1935, as part of his plan to rebuild Germany's military, Adolf Hitler ordered the reintroduction of conscription for all able-bodied German males. At the same time, Hitler authorized Himmler to create an entirely new branch of the SS which was to be known as the SS-Verfügungstruppe, or the SS-VT. The SS-VT was to be created from pre-existing "Political Readiness Detachments" (Politische Bereitschaften) which were armed units assigned full time to military barracks under the authority of local SS leaders – many of these detachments had in fact been mobilized during the Night of the Long Knives. The new SS-VT was to be organized into military battalions, incorporating the older Politische Bereitschaften, in much the same way as the Leibstandarte had been formed in Berlin.

SS organization in 1935

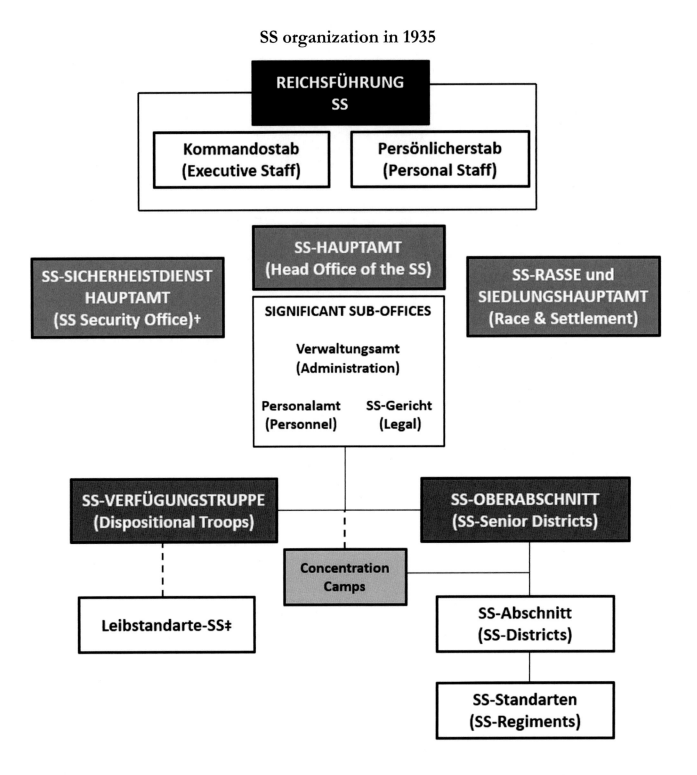

When the SS was reorganized in 1935, Reinhard Heydrich served as both head of the Sicherheitsdienst (SD) and also commanded the Gestapo, which was a political police agency under the jurisdiction of the Prussian Interior Ministry. Sepp Dietrich and his Leibstandarte were also technically under the control of the SS-VT, but in practice the Leibstandarte routinely answered directly to Hitler, bypassing all other SS chains of command including Himmler.

Another major administrative endeavor which occurred between 1934 and 1936 was the takeover of all German concentration camps by the SS. In the months following the Night of the Long Knives, several smaller and temporary camps run by the SA were shut down in favor of more permanent facilities under the control of the SS. The concentration camp at Dachau, under the command of Theodor Eicke, was used as a model for other camps; by the summer of 1935 there existed six major concentration camps in Germany.

For his part in overseeing the SS takeover of all concentration camps, Theodor Eicke was promoted to the rank of SS-Gruppenführer and named as "Inspekteur der Konzentrationslager und SS-Wachverbände" (Inspector of Concentration Camps and Guard Units). Eicke was administratively attached to Himmler's personal staff, but the concentration camps were operationally under the direct authority of the SS district leaders. On April 1st 1936, Himmler issued an order which separated Concentration Camp personnel from the control of local SS leaders and a new organization was then created known as the SS-Totenkopfverbande, or SS-TV. Eicke was then appointed Inspector of the SS-TV, technically subordinate to the SS-Head Office but now granted independent authority over the Concentration Camps. Further administrative reorganization of the camp service followed, including a 1938 directive which stated that the SS-TV would serve as a reserve to the SS-Verfügungstruppe in the event of war.

The main gate of Dachau Concentration Camp. The slogan "Arbeit Macht Frei" (Works Makes Freedom) was first coined by Thedor Eicke (Bavarian State Archives)

By the fall of 1936, with the Night of the Long Knives now two years past, the SS had solidified into a structure which would remain relatively unchanged until Germany found itself at war three years later. At the top of the SS was Himmler, but ironically Himmler had actually lost some administrative control of the two newest branches of the SS, the Totenkopfverbande and the Verfügungstruppe, since the both the SS-TV and SS-VT were considered to be performing state services to Germany and separate from the original SS which was considered a paramilitary organization of the Nazi Party. Both the camp service formations of the SS-TV, and the troops of the SS-VT, received funding directly from the Reich Finance Ministry, and not the Nazi Party proper. This left Himmler with a lack of control over certain logistical elements of these organizations, made even more apparent by the independent nature in which Theodor Eicke and Paul Hausser, respective inspectors of the SS-TV and SS-VT, displayed in their daily actions and relationships with Himmler.

There is no denying, however, that both the SS-VT and SS-TV were integral parts of the SS as confirmed by a directive from Adolf Hitler in August of 1938 that neither group was to be considered part of the Army or police, but rather as independent SS formations under Himmler's command. The only remaining significant SS group not totally dominated by Himmler was the Leibstandarte, under the command of Josef "Sepp" Dietrich. Dietrich had long asserted that his corner of the SS answered to Hitler alone, and had resisted and refused any attempts of subordination to Himmler. This had even extended to Dietrich refusing to receive Himmler at the Leibstandarte barracks in Berlin and instructing sentries that the Reichsführer was to be denied entry to the facility. In the end, it was financial incentive which persuaded Dietrich to give in to Himmler's authority. The Leibstandarte was under-funded and badly trained, in contrast to the SS-VT which was receiving a higher budget and better equipment. In early 1938, Dietrich formally acknowledged that the Leibstandarte was to be regarded as a regiment of the SS-Verfügungstruppe and thus subordinate to Himmler.

Former Army Lieutenant General Paul Hausser was appointed Inspector of the SS-Verfügungstruppe on October 1st 1936. He would later found the Waffen-SS (National Archives)

Defenders of the State

By mid-1936 the combined strength of the SS numbered approximately half a million men, now divided into three distinct groups. The main body of the SS, which included the headquarters offices, the SS districts, and the mustering SS formations, was now known as the Allgemeine-SS, or "General SS". Reinhard Heydrich served as both head of the SD (an SS and Nazi Party organization) and as Chief of the Gestapo which was a political police position attached to the Prussian Interior Ministry. Theodor Eicke's camp service now numbered some 50,000 personnel, while Paul Hausser and Sepp Dietrich had expanded the capabilities of the Verfügungstruppe by creating new regiment sized formations.

The SS in the summer of 1936 must have seemed an impressive organization to Himmler and others, with the ideals of National Socialism firmly entrenched. With such a mindset, Himmler next set out on his greatest endeavor yet – that of gaining total control of Germany's regular police forces. The police forces of Germany in the 1930s were a decentralized group of local and state organizations, as well as a federal branch of internal security known as the Reich Interior Ministry. Discussion had been raised as early as 1933 for the formation of a national German police force, but such efforts had never moved beyond the initial planning stages.

For Himmler, having a security organization as large as the German police out of his control was unacceptable. Himmler already controlled Germany's political police forces, chief among them the Gestapo, but the day-to-day running of law enforcement was still handled by local and state authorities outside of SS jurisdiction.

Himmler's chief rival for control of the German police was Reich Interior Minister Wilhelm Frick. Frick, a longtime ally and supporter of Himmler's old SS rival Kurt Daluege, had wanted Daluege, who already commanded the Prussian State Uniformed Police, to control all of Germany's police forces under one centralized command. When Himmler learned of these intentions, he made his move in June of 1936 when his security deputy Reinhard Heydrich personally met with Adolf Hitler to make a case for Himmler assuming command of all German police forces and replacing Frick as Minister of the Interior. After meeting with Heydrich, Hitler was in fact prepared to dismiss Frick and appoint Himmler in his place; however, Frick countered this move by stating that Himmler should not be allowed to assume such an awesome amount of responsibility and would in fact become a dangerous man to Hitler's authority. In a very uncharacteristic move, Hitler agreed with Frick. As a compromise, it was decided that Himmler would be appointed as Chief of the German Police, but under Frick's authority as Minister of the Interior.

Reich Minister of the Interior Wilhelm Frick. He would eventually lose the power struggle for the German police to Heinrich Himmler who replaced him as Minister of the Interior in 1943.
(Federal German Archives)

On June 17th 1936, Heinrich Himmler was appointed to the new position of "Chef der Deutschen Polizei in Reichsministerium des Innern" (Chief of the German Police in the Reich Ministry of the Interior). A massive overhaul and reorganization of German law enforcement followed, and by the end of 1936 a new federal police force had emerged known as the Order Police (Ordnungspolizei), commonly abbreviated as the "Orpo". At the same time, Germany's professional detective service was consolidated into the Criminal Police, known as the "Kriminalpolizei" and abbreviated as "Kripo". Both the Kripo and the Gestapo were then combined into a single overseeing force known as the Sicherheitspolizei (Secret Police), abbreviated as "Sipo". To appease Frick, Kurt Daluege was appointed as Commander of the Ordnungspolizei, while long time conservative SS member and professional detective Arthur Nebe commanded the Criminal Police.

Reinhard Heydrich was the logical choice to command the Security Police, and he was appointed as "Chef der Sicherheitspolizei und SD". Meanwhile, the day to day running of the Gestapo fell to an SS officer named Heinrich Müller. By the end of 1936, the transition to a centralized national police force in Germany was relatively complete with most of the German states, cities, and towns now having no domestic police forces of their own. A notable exception was Prussia, in which Hermann Göring asserted his authority and ensured the continued existence of a Prussian uniformed police force which was known as the Landespolizei. This police force of Prussia, under total control of Göring and not Himmler, would go on to provide internal Prussian security and would even field a military unit during the Second World War called the "Landespolizeigruppe General Göring".

Under Himmler's new authority as Reich Leader of the SS and Chief of the German Police, which was awkwardly abbreviated as "RfSSuChdDtPol", two things quickly became apparent. First, Himmler immediately began to act independently from the wishes of Wilhelm Frick, leaving the Reich Minister as Himmler's superior in name only. Secondly, with the exception of the Gestapo, none of the new police agencies under Himmler's command contained a high percentage of SS members. There was also the problem of the SD which was bundled under Heydrich's authority as Chief of the Security Police but was not actually a police agency within its own rights. Indeed, many of the professional police looked down upon the Sicherheitsdienst and saw the group as a relic from the early days of the SS with no real purpose in the new police organization of the Reich.

German police organization in 1936

Reich Minister Of The Interior
(Wilhelm Frick)

Reich Leader of the SS and Chief of the German Police
(Heinrich Himmler)

Security Police
Sicherheitspolizei - SIPO
(Reinhard Heydrich)

Order Police
Ordnungspolizei - ORPO
(Kurt Daluege)

Secret State Police
Gestapo
(Heinrich Müller)

Criminal Police
Kripo
(Arthur Nebe)

Following the creation of the Ordnungspolizei, Himmler embarked on the next stage of his plan for the German police, that of total union with the SS. In Himmler's vision of the future, all police forces in Germany were to be totally consolidated into a pure SS organization known as the Staatsschutzkorps, or the "State Protection Corps". This vast organization would not only encompass police functions, but also all other areas and agencies of the SS. The task would not be a simple one with initial estimates placing the full activation of the Staatsschutzkorps sometime in the early 1950s.

The first action in Himmler's plan for a State Protection Corps was the creation of a new Security Police position in August of 1936. Known by the title "Inspekteur des Sicherheitspolizei und SD", this new office was an attempt to eliminate the animosity between the professional security police forces and the SS members of the SD. The Gestapo, Kripo, and SD were now to be organized into districts under a unified commander known as the Security Police and SD Inspector. The next year, by directive of the Reich Interior Ministry dated November 13, 1937, the first of the SS and Police Leaders were appointed. This new post, existing in unison with the Allgemeine-SS Senior District Leaders, unified all SS and police forces under a single authority, with that authority answerable solely to Heinrich Himmler. The post of SS and Police Leader, especially after the beginning of World War II, would become an extremely powerful position and encompass all SS, police, Concentration Camp, and Waffen-SS personnel under a single jurisdiction.

With SS command now firmly established over both the security and uniformed police, Himmler next engaged in an effort to transition the Ordnungspolizei from a politically neutral force into one which was dominated and infiltrated by the SS. A key first measure took place on June 26th 1938 when Himmler introduced the "Rank Parity Decree" which outlined the procedure for Orpo and Sipo police officers to become members of the SS. At the same time, the SS Head Office launched a major recruiting campaign, encouraging SS members to seek a career in the police.

Heinrich Himmler in 1938. By this point, Himmler held undisputed control of both the SS and the German Police (Federal German Archives)

By the summer of 1939 Heinrich Himmler's vision for the creation of an all-powerful SS organization was proceeding exactly according to plan. All levels of the police were now dominated by the SS and all police and SS units were answerable to the SS and Police Leaders. The Criminal Police and the Uniformed Police still had a fair percentage of non-SS members in their ranks, and even within the Gestapo one would occasionally find an officer serving without SS rank. On the whole, however, the SS and the German police had become virtually synonymous.

Himmler's vision of the Staatsschutzkorps then suddenly faded from reality when Germany invaded Poland on September 1st 1939 and the Second World War began. It became quickly obvious that the SS could not fully absorb the German police while Germany was at war and Himmler was thus forced to alter his plans. Himmler then developed an even grander dream inspired by Germany's increasing military conquests, especially in the east. In the lands of Poland and then Russia, Himmler saw the makings for an entire nation run by the SS. A land ruled by SS Lords, protected by SS Legions, and lived on and worked by SS Peasant Warriors. First, however, a mortal enemy had to be destroyed – that enemy was the Jew.

The war against the Jew

The exact historical point at which the SS became an agency devoted to the persecution of the Jewish people is a matter open to some debate. In the 1920s, with the SS primarily existing as a small bodyguard unit, most SS members would not have considered themselves employed to harass or attack Jews. This in contrast to the storm troopers of the SA, who as far back as the founding of the SA in 1920 were known to openly detest Jews and commit spontaneous attacks against Jewish persons, property, and businesses. By 1930, the platform of the Nazi Party was well known as one of Anti-Semitism, and anyone joining a Nazi organization would have been aware of this fact. With Himmler in command of the SS, accompanied by the founding of the SS Race Office in 1931, SS members were indoctrinated into the belief of themselves as an Aryan-Nordic elite, with hatred of the Jew as a centerpiece of this ideology.

The early 1930s saw persecution of the Jews mostly as an unorganized affair committed primarily by the SA. SS units were seen as above such behavior and it was rare (but not unheard of) to see uniformed SS men beating up Jews in the streets. It was, however, clear by 1932 that the Jews of Germany were to be a target of the Nazis. That year, the first official boycotts were organized by the SA and sometimes even assisted by the SS. On April 1st 1933, with Hitler now entrenching himself as a dictator, the first officially sanctioned government boycotts of Jewish businesses were organized across Germany. Armed SA men stood in front of Jewish businesses in all major German cities, urging passers-by to avoid purchasing goods from Jewish owned stores. To the surprise of the Nazis, there was little support for the boycott and the measure was called off after only one day.

The first Anti-Semitic exclusion laws followed, with a law passed in the summer of 1933 barring Jews from serving in certain professions of civil service, farming, law, and medicine. State governments enacted similar measures, and Jewish judges, lawyers, and doctors were stripped of their certifications and prohibited from further practice. In response to these harsh measures, the Jews in fact gained a highly placed ally in the person of President Hindenburg. In early 1934, Hindenburg issued a Presidential decree protecting certain Jewish veterans of the First World War from the more stringent measures of Jewish persecution. With Hindenburg's death, however, this protection became meaningless and was rescinded.

The Jews of Germany experienced a sort of relief in the summer of 1934 as the Night of the Long Knives created a sense that the Nazis were turning on themselves. Many Jews hoped that the destruction of the SA leadership would bring about a lessening of anti-Jewish measures in Germany, and for a time this appeared to be the case. The relief was only temporary, and any hope of tolerance towards the Jews was shattered with the passing of the Nuremberg Laws in 1935. The Nuremberg Laws were enacted on September 15th 1935 and consisted of two separate measures known as the "Law for the Protection of German Blood and German Honor" and the "Reich Citizenship Law". The first measure defined who in Germany would be considered a Jew and forbade marriages or sexual relationships between Jews and Gentiles. A sub-set of the measure prohibited Jews from working as domestic servants in German households. The Reich Citizenship Law further defined who would be considered a German national and effectively stripped German Jews of all rights and declared them non-citizens. Jews were now open to legal persecution and segregation, and it is at this point that the involvement of the SS in anti-Jewish measures truly began.

With the SS already in control of Germany's secret police forces, it fell upon the SS to enforce the Nuremberg Laws and investigate suspected violations.

By 1937, governmental measures had been introduced to not only exclude the Jewish people from all spheres of German life, but to forcible expel Jews from the country. The task was first begun by deporting Jewish foreign nationals, with deportation lists created by the SS Security Police while the physical deportations were handled by the Ordnungspolizei. Deportation measures were next extended to German born Jews of foreign origin, meaning those Germans with family or ancestral ties to other countries. Again, the SS and the Gestapo were responsible for preparing deportation lists and rounding up those German Jews so affected. One such deportation occurred on October 27th 1938, resulting in Zindel and Rivka Grynszpan being deported from their home in Hannover and sent to the German-Polish border. Once there, the refusal of the Polish government to accept German refugees led to over two thousand deportees living unsheltered in the cold and rain for several days. During this time, the Grynszpans succumbed to the elements and perished. The deaths of these two Jewish Germans would spark a chain of events which would lead to one of the most well-known persecutions of the Jews under the Nazi regime – the action known as Kristallnacht.

When the Grynszpans died along the Polish border in 1938, their son Herschel was residing in Paris, France. Upon hearing the news of the death of his parents, Herschel Grynszpan traveled to the German embassy in Paris with the intent of killing the Ambassador. Grynszpan entered the German embassy on the morning of November 7, 1938 and promptly shot the first German official that he was able to find. A junior German diplomat named Ernst vom Rath was Grynszpan's victim, shot five times in the chest and abdomen, dying of his wounds two days later. Herschel Grynszpan was immediately arrested by the French police; he would be held in French custody until 1940 when the chaos surrounding Germany's invasion of France allowed for his temporary escape. Grynszpan would later turn himself over to Vichy French authorities, who promptly extradited him to Germany. He was arrested by the Gestapo and held until the end of the war when he was presumed to have been executed shortly before Germany's capitulation in 1945.

Herschel Grynszpan and Ernst vom Rath. Vom Rath's assassination at Grynszpan's hands would spark "Kristallnacht" (Crystal Night), also known as "The Night of Broken Glass" (Federal German Archives)

When vom Rath died on November 9th 1938, the event was seen by the Nazi government as the perfect excuse to enact a program of terror against Germany's entire Jewish population. Joseph Goebbels, who now served as the Gauleiter of Berlin and also as Propaganda Minister in the German government, issued the first orders for an action against German Jews and called for the destruction of Jewish homes and businesses across the country. Ironically, it was the SS leadership who called for some measure of restraint. Realizing that mobs of uniformed Nazis attacking Jews in the streets would cause not only public support for the Jews but also international outrage, instructions were quickly dispatched to SS commands instructing on proper procedures for measures against the Jews. Reinhard Heydrich, in his capacity as head of the Security Police, issued a directive on the night of November 9th calling for local Nazi regional leaders to avoid spontaneous acts of violence against Jews in favor of a more organized plan. By 2AM that morning, further instructions had been issued to local SS commanders who in turn passed them on to regional Nazi cells to include the SA.

Teams of SS and SA men were then sent to attack Jewish homes and business, wearing only civilian clothes and armed with hand weapons. Strict instructions were in place to avoid damaging non-Jewish property and directives were also in place to avoid any attacks or violence against foreign Jews (especially those with diplomatic ties). Excessive looting and open acts of murder were also prohibited. Jewish synagogues were to be a prime target of Kristallnacht, with instructions issued that these houses of Jewish worship were to be searched by special teams of Sicherheitsdienst personnel for any Jewish religious valuables and documents prior to their destruction. In cases were synagogues where set ablaze, local fire brigades were instructed to contain the arson (but not extinguish it) to the point that adjacent German property was not put at risk. Massive arrests were also ordered, especially of any able-bodied male Jews. Such Jews were to be transported to local jails and then transferred to Concentration Camps. By the conclusion of Kristallnacht, over 30,000 arrests of Jewish males had been made, many of whom were transported to Buchenwald Concentration Camp.

The riots of Kristallnacht were called off after two days of violence. Over seven thousand Jewish businesses had their storefronts shattered, leading to the name given to the riots drawn from the broken glass in the streets shimmering as if crystal. Two hundred synagogues were destroyed, some of which were centuries old. Jewish cemeteries were also vandalized and defaced, while those Jews now in the concentration camp system would suffer further abuse and death. Three months after Kristallnacht, a general amnesty released most of those still incarcerated. The Nazi government attempted to portray Kristallnacht as a spontaneous uprising of the German people against "World Jewry", however most in Germany, as well as the international community, saw the riots for what they were – organized government persecution against the Jews. It was clear that Jews had no future or place in Germany and that they should escape while there was still time. But leaving Germany was an obstacle within itself, beginning with numerous bureaucratic obstacles accompanied by emigration laws in other countries curtailing the large numbers of German Jews wishing to escape from Nazi persecution. It was the SS, as the primary enforcer of Germany's racial edicts, which saw the need to provide a solution for German Jews wishing to quickly leave Germany. As one SS official was quoted: "Why not make it easier for these people? We want the Jews to leave and they want to leave of their own accord." Yet the solution was not to be found in Germany, but rather in Austria.

In March of 1938 Germany's southern neighbor Austria was annexed into the "Greater German Reich" in an event known as the Anschluss. The SS played a key role in the Austrian transfer of power, contributing units of the Verfügungstruppe to the initial occupation force, as well as establishing the first "Special Action Unit" (Einsatzkommondo) to enter government buildings and seize Austrian documents and archives. By the fall of 1938, the underground Austrian-SS had been incorporated into the rank and file of their German counterpart, as well as the SS having established a new concentration camp near the northern Austrian village of Mauthausen. That August, the Gestapo established a large office in Vienna, with the aim being to enforce the Anti-Semitic measures now firmly encompassing Austrian Jews.

Arthur Seyys-Inquart was a Nazi politician and also the head of the Austrian branch of the SS. (Federal German Archives)

It was the disposition of the Austria Jews which gave the SS their most formidable power base. After taking over Austria, the new Nazi leadership, led by Arthur Seyss-Inquart, promptly introduced modified versions of the Nuremberg Laws to strip Austrian Jews of citizenship and basic civil rights. These actions thus relegated the Austrian Jews to the status of second-class citizens. Whereas in Germany, the purpose of the Nuremberg Laws had been to isolate the Jewish population from all aspects of public and civil life, within Austria the Nazis adopted a new strategy which would shift Nazi policy towards the forcible expulsion of Jews from that country.

SS-Captain Adolf Eichmann, a self-proclaimed "Jewish Expert" of the Gestapo, was sent to Austria in 1938 with the task of forming an agency known as the Central Office for Jewish Emigration.

The function of this office would be to serve as a central hub for all departments of the Reich to which a Jew must report in order to emigrate. The office would also serve to confiscate all Jewish property, collect exorbitant emigration fees, and then expel Jews from Austria with little to no property or assets. Those Jews who could not afford immigration fees were provided funds from the finances of their wealthier counterparts in the Jewish community. Eichmann also attempted to form a type of alliance between the SS and various Zionist organizations as an effort to speed up the emigration of Austrian Jews through the use of pre-existing Jewish networks. A year prior to the annexation of Austria, the SS had sponsored Eichmann to visit Palestine in order to meet both Jewish and Arab leaders concerning Jewish immigration to the region. The trip produced little tangible results, with Eichmann and an assistant forced to leave the country by the British after a stay of only a few weeks.

In the fall of 1938, Germany annexed the Sudetenland region of Czechoslovakia, followed by a takeover of the remainder of the Czech Republic the following March. Eichmann was then ordered by his Gestapo superiors to expand the Central Office for Jewish Emigration outside of Austria – a counterpart office was first established in Prague followed by a headquarters office (known as the "Reich Office for Jewish Emigration") in Berlin on January 24th 1939. Eichmann remained in his operational role as head of these new offices while Reinhard Heydrich became the titular commander for all Jewish emigration from the Reich. By the fall of 1939, the Jews of the German Reich had been stripped of citizenship, were subject to harsh discrimination laws, and were now being forcibly compelled to flee to other countries.

Ideology of the Elite

When the SS was first created in 1925, the organization was far removed from the anti-Semitic organization which the SS would eventually become. Early SS members were selected for their physical prowess as bodyguards, rather than strict adherence to Nazi ideology. Personal loyalty to Adolf Hitler was mandatory and this trait remained with the SS for the duration of the group's existence. Even so, Anti-Semitism was ever present in the early days of the Nazi Party and many of Hitler's early speeches in Munich were full of attacks against Jews and other minorities. Indeed, a main platform of the Nazi Party focused upon "purging the German blood" of "vermin and parasites" which Hitler directly attributed to the Jews.

However, in the early years of the Nazi Party, this concept of "racial purity" was sometimes overlooked when it became inconvenient. Emil Maurice, co-founder of the SS, was himself of Jewish descent having a great grandfather (Charles Maurice Schwartzenberger) who was a full practicing Jew. Erhard Heiden, the third Reichsführer-SS, was rumored to have had several Jewish business associates including his tailor. Even Hitler had a personal connection to a Jew – that of Hugo Gutmann who was Hitler's Lieutenant during the First World War and the man responsible for awarding Hitler the Iron Cross. Nevertheless, anti-Semitism and hatred of the Jewish people were a cornerstone of Nazi philosophy as far back as one could trace Hitler's personal views on the subject. The early inner circle of the Nazi Party also claimed to share Hitler's views - that of an Aryan "super race" who were meant to cleanse Germany of impure and unwanted blood, with the Jews seen as the enemy of all that was German. To what extent top Nazis actually ascribed to the theory of the "Master Race" has been debated heavily in historical circles. Hermann Göring, for instance, was quoted as saying "I decide who is a Jew" and protected certain close associates and allies who were rumored to be of Jewish heritage. Even Himmler, who would become one of the most devote adherents to Nazi ideology, was forced on one occasion to make an important "exception to the rule", that of Reinhard Heydrich when rumors surfaced that Heydrich had Jewish ancestry on his father's side.[ii]

Insofar as the SS was concerned, the transition between bodyguard unit to an elite corps of the Aryan race developed between 1929 and 1931 after Heinrich Himmler had become the Reichsführer-SS. When Himmler assumed command of the SS, he had already developed deep rooted ideals of Social Darwinism and genetic purity, originating from his work breeding chickens in the 1920s. In 1931, Himmler founded the Race Office of the SS (Rasseamt) and appointed Richard Walther Darré as its' first commander. Darré, slightly older than Himmler, held a PhD in agriculture and had worked as an animal farm breeder. It was Darré who fine-tuned the racial policy of the SS, bringing in ideals of the Artaman League, which was a "back to the land" movement advocating a return to a simple life of farming, hard work, and community spirit. Darré also incorporated certain elements of the Thule Society, in particular Germanic history and a belief in Aryan superiority over other "inferior races".

By the time the Nazi Party had come to power in 1933, Himmler had developed the SS into an organization which he saw as a Germanic Order adhering to ancient Nordic values. Since the start of 1932, Himmler had also required SS men to obtain his permission before marriage; dossiers on the potential brides were to be screened personally by Himmler for adherence to the prescribed standards of racial purity and Germanic appearance.

Richard Walther Darré defined the early racial policies of the SS (National Archives)

Following the Night of the Long Knives, the SS Race Office was expanded to headquarters status and renamed as the SS Race and Settlement Office (SS-Rasse und Siedlungshauptamt) or the "RuSHA". The function of the RuSHA was now not only to adhere to racial standards within the SS, but to expand SS racial values throughout Germany as well as investigate the history and genetic make-up of the German people. A key element of this research was vilification of the Jew, seen as an "anti-race" and an enemy of the pure Germanic people.

Darré eventually fell out of favor with Himmler and was dismissed as head of the RuSHA in 1938. The RuSHA still survived, and during World War II the group would engage in the displacement of populations, kidnapping of ethnic German children, and assist in the perpetration of genocide against the Jewish peoples of Europe.

In addition to values of racial purity, Himmler also prescribed a great deal of importance to researching the history of the Aryan race. Under offices of his personal staff, Himmler sponsored numerous archeological projects throughout Germany in order to trace the earliest origins of the Germanic people. Himmler was particularly interested in the tribes of Northern Germany who had fought the Romans, as well as Germanic values held during the time of the Holy Roman Empire.

Without a doubt, the farthest-reaching archeology project sponsored by Himmler was the restoration of the castle of Wewelsburg. Located in Westphalia, southwest of Paderborn, Wewelsburg was constructed in the early 1800s upon the ruins of a 12th century fort. The castle had fallen into disrepair by the 1820s, with the first serious restoration work begun in 1907. Wewelsburg was then acquired by the SS in November of 1933, and for the next two years a major renovation took place in order to turn the decrepit fortress into an SS citadel. Administratively, Wewelsburg was listed as an "SS Race School" and under the dual command of the RuSHA as well as a special office of Himmler's personal staff. Wewelsburg was also known as Himmler's personal castle and a center for SS racial ideology and Germanic destiny. In Himmler's view of the future, Wewelsburg would be expanded

The castle at Wewelsburg, which Himmler saw as the future centerpiece for an SS capitol city (Federal German Archives)

as the center point of an SS city stretching outward from the castle in the shape of a giant spear of destiny. An archeological center for Germanic research was established at Wewelsburg in 1934, with numerous excavations conducted in the surrounding countryside for evidence of early Germanic peoples. Himmler often visited Wewelsburg and a large amount of funding was channeled into the Wewelsburg treasury for future projects and further renovations of the castle. The Second World War drew a halt to Himmler's plans at Wewelsburg, and he ordered restoration work suspended with plans to resume the project in the 1950s. During World War II, the castle was utilized as a leadership school and visited by Himmler less and less as the war progressed. In 1945, the castle was dynamited by a special team of SS demolition experts but was later rebuilt and stands again to this day as a museum.

The Road to War

The image of the SS in the mid-1930s was one of fear and respect. All of Germany's police forces were now under the control of Heinrich Himmler, while black uniformed columns of the Allgemeine-SS paraded through the streets. The Concentration Camps were ever present under SS control and the SS was seen as an established branch of the Nazi Party and the Reich government. Outside of Germany, the first world presentation of Nazism occurred in August of 1936 during that year's Summer Olympics. With Germany having won the Olympic bid in 1931, Adolf Hitler saw the 1936 Olympics as a grand opportunity to showcase Nazi accomplishments to a worldwide audience. The Summer Olympics took place for two weeks in the capitol of Berlin, an event which was documented from every possible perspective by German newsreels, as well as in a complete motion picture documentary created by filmmaker Leni Riefenstahl. The role of the SS during the 1936 Olympics was one of order and security – mainly to ensure that the Olympic celebrations were accomplished free of protest or incident. Reinhard Heydrich, in his capacity as head of the Security Police, was designated as Security Chief for the Olympic Games.

By the time of the Olympics, German Jews had suffered heavy segregation and discrimination for over three years due to the 1935 Nuremberg Laws. Nazi leaders were nevertheless concerned that overt anti-Jewish appearances would cause foreign visitors at the Olympics to experience a negative impression of the Nazi state. To avoid this, Berlin was white-washed of all anti-Jewish signs, written slogans, as well as any signs of segregation. Across the German capitol, "Aryan Only" placards were removed from park benches, restaurants, and other public areas to offer the impression that German Jews were treated just as any other citizen. As for the Jews themselves, most choose to simply stay indoors for the duration of the Olympic Games so not to draw unwanted attention or scrutiny.

The 1936 Summer Olympics were a masterpiece of both deception and order for the Nazis, due in large part to the efforts of the SS. Visitors to Germany saw a well-ordered society free of crime with a united population; the oppression of the Secret Police, the Concentration Camps, and the persecution of the Jews were conveniently hidden from outside view. For their part in the preparation and security of the 1936 Summer Olympics, several high-ranking members of the SS were awarded a special medal known as the "Olympic Games Decoration". Presented not for actual participation in the Olympics, but rather for the behind the scenes efforts, SS members presented this award included both Himmler and Heydrich.

Segregated park benches, with their distinctive "Only for Aryans" placards, were removed from Berlin during the 1936 Olympic Games and promptly restored after the end of the festivities (Federal German Archives)

By 1938, Himmler appeared to be master within his own house, full of plans for further expansion of the SS with his organization now a personal instrument of racial purity and Nazi terror. The 1938 annexation of Austria brought even more power to Himmler, but by 1939 perhaps even the Reichsführer himself was wondering what would come next. Adolf Hitler had made it clear, as early as November of 1938, that Germany would be involved in a major war by the start of 1940. The Sudetenland Crisis had nearly brought Germany to this end, causing the Army Chief of Staff Ludwig Beck to resign out of what he saw as Nazi dominance of the military and the increasing power of the SS.

With the exposure of anti-Nazi elements in the leadership of the German Army, Hitler began dismissing and re-organizing the top levels of the German military. By the summer of 1939, Germany's armed forces were now organized under the command of the "Oberkommando der Wehrmacht", which was overseen by unquestioned Nazi supporter Colonel General (later Field Marshal) Wilhelm Keitel. As German posed to strike against Poland in September 1939, the SS was preparing for war as well. The next six years would bring about a new era for Himmler's elite corps, one which would cause the deaths of millions and bring infamy to the name of the SS.

Uniforms of the Elite - the Black Jacket of the SS

The most commonly associated uniform of the SS, the iconic black jacket with swastika armband (see right), was created in the summer of 1932 while the first wide spread issuance of the uniform was during the following January of 1933. The SS black jacket was designed by SS officer Karl Diebitsch, with the black uniform intended to convey fear, intimidation, and respect. From a more practical standpoint, the black SS tunic was designed to clearly separate the SS from its brown shirted masters in the SA. The first black SS uniforms were issued to senior officers of the SS command offices and within the leadership of the SS senior districts. The early design of the black jacket retained SA insignia patterns but would later adopt additional uniform features such as shoulder boards and cuffbands. The jacket was also worn with a brown shirt (as a minor homage to the SA) and black neck tie.

At the start of 1933, with the SS still considered a part time Nazi Party organization, the black uniform was slow to be adopted by the members of local SS regiments who continued to wear the traditional brown shirt of the SA. By 1934, all top SS leaders were now adorned in the new black uniform, but it was not until well into 1935 that the traditional brown uniform had been completely replaced with the new black SS uniform design. The next major SS uniform change occurred in March of 1933 when new regulations expanded SS rank titles, introduced uniform shoulder boards, and created a new series of sleeve

insignia to denote the expanded offices of the SS. By this time, a standard black SS cap had also been adopted which would remain unchanged in appearance until 1938.

The aftermath of the Night of the Long Knives brought about another significant change to the SS uniform, mainly in its rank system. In July 1934, as part of an effort to completely establish the SS as an independent formation, several SS rank titles were changed in order to remove older SA titles from the SS rank hierarchy. While the post 1934 SS rank insignia remained relatively the same, new SS ranks included several modified titles as well as a supreme rank for Heinrich Himmler. As a reward for his service to the Nazi state, Heinrich Himmler's title of Reichsführer-SS was established as an actual SS rank, complete with its own insignia consisting of a wreathed oak leaf triad, accompanied by a special SS general's shoulder cord. Himmler would hold this rank for the remainder of the SS's existence until 1945 when the organization collapsed upon the defeat of Nazi Germany in World War II.

Left: A photograph of an SS man taken in early 1935. The traditional brown shirt uniform is still in use; however, the SS man also wears the new black styled SS cap along with a unit cuffband on the lower left sleeve. The brown shirt SS uniform would be phased out entirely by 1936.
(Federal German Archives)

In this rare photograph, taken in the fall of 1932, a prototype black SS uniform shows the jacket with no shoulder cord worn with the SA style cap.
(Bavarian State Archives)

Enlisted and officer caps of the SS. Officer caps were denoted by a silver chin strap. The cap in the center is adorned with the smaller Nazi Party Eagle, replaced by a larger national eagle insignia in 1938

SS UNIFORMS IN 1933

SS uniforms in 1933 mixed both the traditional brown shirt SA uniform with the new SS black jacket. Rank was displayed on the left collar, opposite a unit numeral. Shoulder cords denoted the grade of the wearer while cuffbands on the lower sleeve indicated sub-units or specific offices

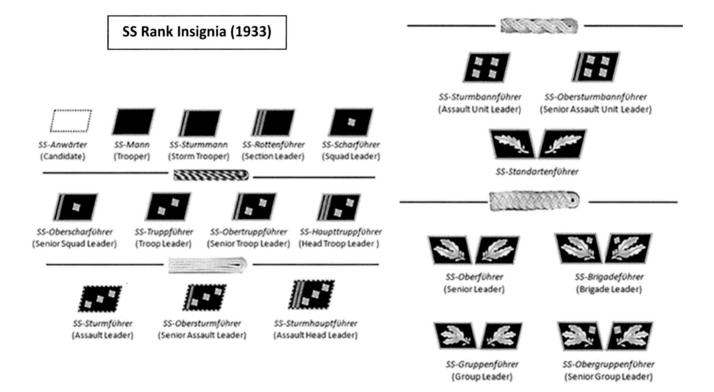

SS regulations were expanded in 1935 to also include uniform accessories, covering a variety of extra uniform items such as overcoats, cloaks, and all-weather jackets. The SS was also the first of the Nazi Party paramilitary organizations to formalize a "dinner dress" uniform, with both an SS dinner jacket and "mess dress" created for wear on formal occasions.

By the fall of 1935, the SS now operated three main branches, these being the General-SS, the SS-Death's Head units, and the political action (armed) troops of the SS-VT. It became obvious that the day to day operations of both the armed SS units and the concentration camp staffs were not practical for the "spit and polish" black SS uniforms worn by General-SS. To this end, a new "drill jacket" was adopted, first by the SS-VT and soon afterwards by the concentration camp service. The SS drill jacket was of the same design as the black service tunic, but with a much more durable fabric for practical field wear. The same insignia was displayed as with the black uniform, however during day to day wear the swastika armband was often removed. The drill jacket was worn in an earth grey color by the SS-VT with a similar light brown colored jacket worn within the concentration camps.

In 1936, the SS adopted a summer white tunic while certain General-SS commands also began authorizing a "Field Service Uniform" which was a light grey jacket extremely similar to the drill jacket of the armed SS. The various color patterns of the field and drill uniforms varied depending upon the specific branch of the SS in which a member served.

The grey colored SS drill jacket was one of the first SS duty uniforms worn by members of the armed SS and camp service in the mid-1930s. The swastika armband was typically excluded as an impractical uniform item, but was most likely worn in this photograph for the benefit of the camera (Federal German Archives)

The black SS tunic, which has so often been associated as a symbol of the entire SS, was ironically one of the shorter lived SS uniforms as a whole. By 1936, the same year in which the black uniform had been completely adopted by all branches of the SS, Heinrich Himmler and the SS leadership were already seeking to replace the uniform with a much more practical design for everyday wear. The result was the creation of the "feldgrau" uniform, prototyped in 1935 and first distributed a year later. By 1938, the grey uniform was being worn by all members of the SS engaged in full time duties, with the black uniform reserved for ceremonial functions and for use by the part time members of the General-SS. Changes between the black and grey SS uniforms included shoulder cords on both shoulders as well as replacing the swastika armband with a national eagle emblem. The first pattern eagle was a larger version of the later standardized eagle insignia worn for the remainder of the SS's existence. A grey SS cap would be introduced in 1937 followed by military type shoulder boards after the start of World War II in 1939.

Left: The prototype grey SS uniform was first designed in early 1935 and worn with a black SS cap, along with standard SS shoulder boards (National Archives)

By the summer of 1938, both a grey SS cover and garrison cap had been introduced for wear with the grey service uniform. The black SS uniform continued to exist, although only in the part time General-SS mustering units. The last formal display of SS units wearing the black uniform was in 1940 during victory parades following the fall of France. By 1942, the black SS tunic had effectively been phased out of the SS, although some photographs show the uniform being worn as late as 1944, mainly by General-SS reservists. Ironically, at that late stage of World War II, publicly wearing the black SS uniform was a mark of non-military service and often viewed as a sign of military shirking – this was a far cry from the fear and terror which the black uniform had once bestowed during the earlier years of the SS.

SS UNIFORMS IN 1938

First Pattern Sleeve Eagle
(1935)

Second Pattern Sleeve Eagle
(1937)

Above: SS sleeve eagles replaced the swastika armband for use on the grey uniform. Shown also is a comparison between the black uniform shoulder cords and the grey service shoulder boards

SS Rank (Pre-1933)	Revised SS Rank (1934)
SS-Scharführer	SS-Unterscharführer
SS-Oberscharführer	SS-Scharführer
SS-Truppführer	SS-Oberscharführer
SS-Obertruppführer	SS-Hauptscharführer
SS-Hauptruppführer	SS-Sturmscharführer
SS-Sturmführer	SS-Untersturmführer
SS-Sturmhauptführer	SS-Hauptsturmführer

Following the Night of the Long Knives, seven SS rank titles were renamed to differentiate from the SA; however, the SS insignia remained the same. By this time, the SS had also adopted a standard belt buckle for all uniforms, emblazoned with the term "Meine Ehre heißt Treue" (Loyalty is my Honor). A final result of the Night of the Long Knives was the creation of the special rank of Reichsführer-SS, turning Himmler's former position into now the highest SS rank with its own special insignia (see right). In addition, Hitler maintained a special title of **Oberste Führer der Schutzstaffel** (Supreme Commander of the SS) which did not entail any special insignia.

CHAPTER THREE: THE SS AT WAR

On September 1st 1939, Germany invaded the neighboring country of Poland, plunging Europe into war. The attack on Poland had resulted from a diplomatic crisis concerning a narrow strip of Polish territory separating the main part of Germany from East Prussia. Known in the vernacular as "the corridor", Adolf Hitler had demanded that Poland cede this territory, as well as the independent city of Danzig, lest Nazi Germany seize both by force. When Poland did not comply, the German military struck east. Two days later on September 3rd, Britain and France declared war on Germany. The Second World War had begun.

From the beginning of the war, Heinrich Himmler's SS was ever present and in fact had played a major role in the events leading up to the formal opening of hostilities. On August 31st a small group of Gestapo and SS personnel stormed a German radio station in the border town of Gleiwitz, posing as Polish saboteurs, and took over the radio transmitters. After broadcasting an inflammatory anti-German message, a handful of previously executed Concentration Camp inmates (who had been dressed in Polish military uniforms, poisoned by lethal injection, then shot with bullet holes) were left at the scene to create the appearance of a repulsed incursion by Polish soldiers. The Gleiwitz raid was part of a much larger effort by both the SS and Wehrmacht military intelligence (the Abwehr) to provide various justifications for attacking Poland. In all, twenty-one separate border incidents were staged, giving Adolf Hitler justification to launch the formal attack on Poland, codenamed "Case White" by the German military high command.

The start of World War II would bring about a new period of terror for the SS, one which would spread death and destruction across all of Europe as well as establish the SS as one of the most powerful forces within the Nazi state. By the time the Second World War ended, the SS would be responsible for the displacement of entire populations, the theft and robbery of property from all over Europe, as well as mass genocide on a scale heretofore unknown in history.

Organizing for War

At the start of 1939, the SS had existed in relatively the same form for nearly five years. Comprised as three main branches, the SS consisted of the general membership of the Allgemeine-SS, concentration camp personnel assigned to the SS-Totenkopfverbande, as well as armed SS troops of the SS-Verfügungstruppe. The SS by this point also had total control of the German police, divided into regular law enforcement under the authority of the Ordnungspolizei, as well as the Secret Police forces (the Sipo) comprised of the Gestapo and the Criminal Police. The original SS intelligence service, the Sicherheitsdienst (SD), was commanded by Reinhard Heydrich through his title as Commander of both the Sipo and SD.

Following the invasion of Poland, Heinrich Himmler undertook the first major effort to reorganize the SS into a wartime organization, beginning with the SS security forces. On September 27th 1939, Himmler directed the formation of a new office within the SS – the Reich Central Security Office (Reichssicherheitshauptamt) or RSHA under the command of Reinhard Heydrich. All security forces of both the state and the Nazi Party were now to be controlled as one institution. The dividing line between the secret police forces of the Gestapo, the criminal detectives of the Kripo, and the SS security agents of the SD, were now abolished. In addition, although the RSHA was technically seen as a governmental agency of the German state, in practice the office was considered one and the same with the SS. The RSHA would go on to oversee brutal actions in Poland against Jews and other "undesirables", as well as set the stage for organized genocide in the years to come.

Since the summer of 1937, Theodor Eicke had sought to form his concentration camp personnel into a capable fighting force equal in prowess to the armed SS units of the SS-VT. To that end, the SS-Totenkopfverbande (SS-TV) had been formed on military lines, complete with armed regiments, albeit with older equipment and less formal training. During the invasion of Poland, with the exception of an SS militia formed in Danzig under the SS-TV's control, none of Eicke's Death Head's units participated[iii].

Beginning in October 1939, the SS-Totenkopfverbande underwent a massive restructuring. The SS-TV organization was reformed as a fully equipped military division, while the guarding of Concentration Camps fell to older SS-TV personnel and reservists unfit for front line duty. While both camp guards and military personnel still wore the Death's Head collar insignia, the two formations were now viewed as completely separate.

SS ORGANIZATION IN 1939

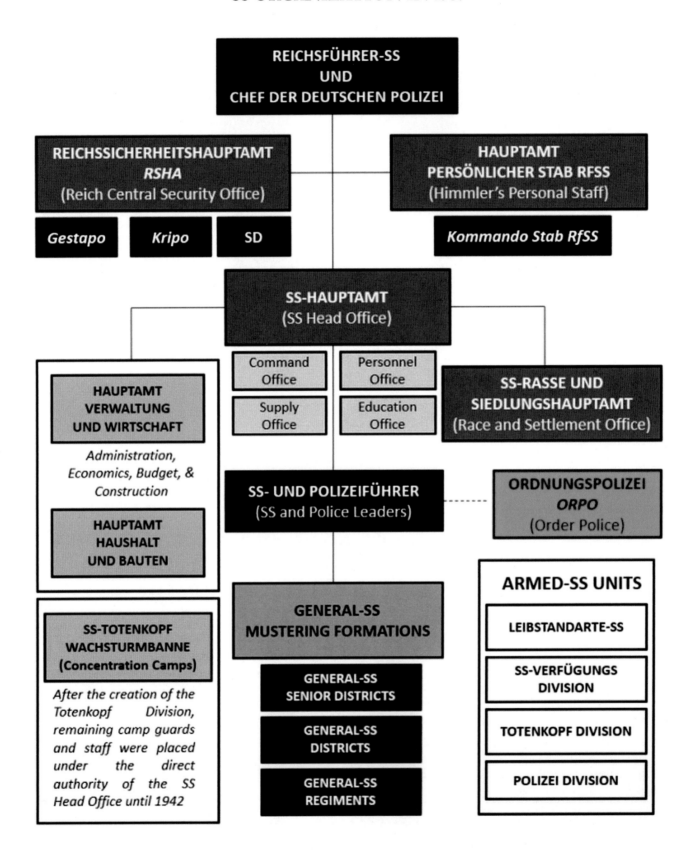

REICHSFÜHRER-SS UND CHEF DER DEUTSCHEN POLIZEI

REICHSSICHERHEITSHAUPTAMT *RSHA* (Reich Central Security Office)

Gestapo | Kripo | SD

HAUPTAMT PERSÖNLICHER STAB RFSS (Himmler's Personal Staff)

Kommando Stab RfSS

SS-HAUPTAMT (SS Head Office)

Command Office | Personnel Office

Supply Office | Education Office

SS-RASSE UND SIEDLUNGSHAUPTAMT (Race and Settlement Office)

HAUPTAMT VERWALTUNG UND WIRTSCHAFT

Administration, Economics, Budget, & Construction

HAUPTAMT HAUSHALT UND BAUTEN

SS-TOTENKOPF WACHSTURMBANNE (Concentration Camps)

After the creation of the Totenkopf Division, remaining camp guards and staff were placed under the direct authority of the SS Head Office until 1942

SS- UND POLIZEIFÜHRER (SS and Police Leaders)

ORDNUNGSPOLIZEI *ORPO* (Order Police)

GENERAL-SS MUSTERING FORMATIONS

GENERAL-SS SENIOR DISTRICTS

GENERAL-SS DISTRICTS

GENERAL-SS REGIMENTS

ARMED-SS UNITS

LEIBSTANDARTE-SS

SS-VERFÜGUNGS DIVISION

TOTENKOPF DIVISION

POLIZEI DIVISION

Elsewhere in the SS, additional administrative reorganizations were underway as a result of the outbreak of war. The first such effort, dating from June of 1939, had been the creation of two new SS offices dealing specifically with construction endeavors as well as financial institutions under the control of the SS. Known respectively as the "Hauptamt Verwaltung und Wirtschaft" (Main Office for Administration and Economy) and the "Hauptamt Haushalt und Bauten" (Main Office of Budget and Construction), these two organizations were under the control of SS-Obergruppenführer Oswald Pohl. Pohl would eventually combine both offices into the massively powerful Main Office of Economics Administration (Wirtschafts-Verwaltungshauptamt or WVHA) which would oversee the financial and logistical side of Germany's Concentration Camps, including profits from looting the bodies of gas chamber victims for gold, cash, and other valuables.

Oswald Pohl, who oversaw the profits of slave labor and genocide, was executed for war crimes after the close of the Second World War (National Archives)

Following the capitulation of Poland in October 1939, the units of the SS-Verfügungstruppe were consolidated into a single armed formation known as the SS-Verfügungs Division. In February of 1940, the SS underwent the largest reorganization to date, with the formal founding of the Waffen-SS which combined the Verfügungs Division, Leibstandarte, and Theodor Eicke's Totenkopf division into one single armed force. To accommodate the logistics and personnel requirements of what would become the largest branch of the SS, several new headquarters offices were created, mostly from pre-existing offices of older SS commands. In April of 1941, mainly for administrative and pay reasons, the guard and staff formations of the old SS-Totenkopfverbande were incorporated into the Waffen-SS. The following year the entire Concentration Camp service was placed under Oswald Pohl's new economic organization, the WVHA.

Protecting the Führer

The primary mission of the SS remained first and foremost safeguarding the life of Adolf Hitler. As the SS expanded in the 1930s, to assume additional duties encompassing the security police, concentration camps, and as an armed force, this original purpose remained; mainly that the SS, above all else, existed to protect Hitler. Prior to Adolf Hitler becoming Chancellor of Germany, his personal protection was formally provided by the 1st SS-Standarte in Munich, tasked with providing security at the Nazi Party headquarters (known as the "Brown House") as well as posting personal security details at Hitler's apartment located at Prinzregentenplatz 16 in downtown Munich. Yet, whenever Hitler traveled, his security was dependent upon local SS commands to which Hitler trusted only for routine security matters.

Left: Erich Kempka, Hitler's chauffeur, and early member of the Führer's bodyguard company (Federal German Archives)

In February of 1932, Hitler ordered the formation of a special eight-man company of SS men who would serve as personal bodyguards. These men would live, work, and travel with Hitler at all times, answering solely to the Führer and to no other authority, including Reichsführer-SS Heinrich Himmler. Most of the men selected for Hitler's personal guard were early SS members from the 1920s, whom Hitler described as "toughs from the old days", handpicked for physical prowess and personal loyalty. These men were assigned to a unit known as the "SS-Begleitkommando des Führers" which was a personal bodyguard protection group for Hitler. A second group, formed to protect other Nazi leaders besides Hitler, was known as the "SS-Begleitkommando".

When Hitler was appointed Chancellor of Germany, the seat of Nazi power was relocated to Berlin, and with it Hitler's SS protection formations quickly replaced the traditional police and Army forces assigned to guard the German Chancellery. For security in and around the Berlin government quarter, Josef "Sepp" Dietrich led a cadre of the 1st SS-Standarte to form what would eventually become the "Leibstandarte Adolf Hitler". Hitler's personal bodyguard protection remained with the eight-man SS-Begleitkommando, while a third SS group, formed in March 1933 as the "Führerschutzkommando", existed to investigate any potential threats to Hitler's life and also to gather intelligence on anti-Nazi factions who may attempt to assassinate the German leader.

In mid-1935, the Führerschutzkommando was renamed as the "Reichssicherheitsdienst" or RSD (similar in name, but of no relation to, the SS security service the SD). Under the command of Johann Rattenhuber, the RSD was primarily an intelligence gathering agency while Hitler's overall protection was provided by the Leibstandarte and the Begleitkommando. In 1937, all RSD personnel were commissioned as reserve offices in the Army and for a brief period this group was known by the cumbersome title "Reichssicherheitsdienst Gruppe Geheime Feldpolizei z. b. V". Upon the outbreak of the Second World War, the mission of protecting Hitler became far more complicated due to Hitler's new position as Supreme Commander of the Armed Forces. Hitler's status as a military commander necessitated security arrangement at several military command posts spread throughout Europe. Furthermore, Hitler frequently traveled throughout both Germany and other occupied

Johann Rattenhuber commanded the RSD through most of its existence (Federal German Archives)

countries onboard a special train known as the "Führersonderzug". Hitler also flew onboard specially designed Luftwaffe transport planes, each accompanied by a fighter squadron for his safety.

HITLER'S COMMAND INSTALLATIONS (1944)

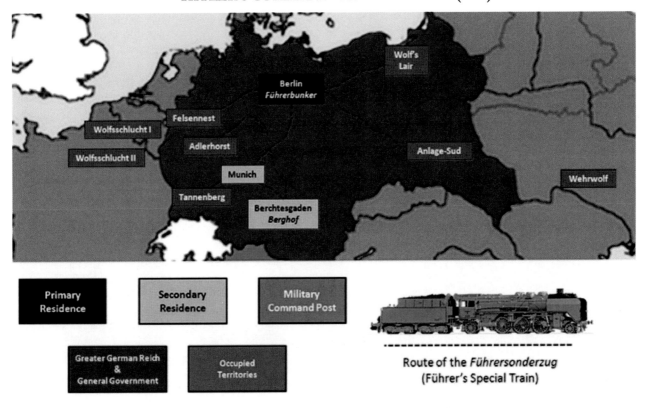

The Leibstandarte, which had served as Hitler's original bodyguard formation since the 1930s, had by 1940 lost most of its significance in the daily affairs of Hitler's security. Even so, until nearly the end of the war, the Leibstandarte continued to maintain a company at both the Berlin Reich Chancellery and at Hitler's private retreat of the Berghof, Austria for ceremonial duties as well as parade formations, domestic work, and routine security. The remainder of the Leibstandarte was from 1941 on considered a front-line division of the Waffen-SS and therefore uninvolved with Hitler's daily security.

Throughout the Second World War, the overall security of Hitler's command posts, personal trains, and transport aircraft was overseen by members of the Reichssicherheitsdienst. Several departments were formed within the RSD to deal with matters concerning Hitler's daily schedule, as well as intelligence gathering regarding any potential threats to the Führer from both external and internal sources. The most important department of the RSD was "Abteilung I", concerned with Hitler's direct personal safety. It was members of this department who provided security and guard platoons accompanying Hitler to his many headquarters facilities. The RSD operated by employing a "cordon defense" surrounding Hitler, with security circles becoming tighter and stricter the closer one came to the Führer. Hitler's broad security, which included perimeter defense of his headquarters facilities as well as patrolling railroad tracks upon which the Führer train would travel, was detailed to a Regular Army unit known as the "Führer-Begleit-Bataillon". Formed in 1938 from two companies of the Großdeutschland Infantry Regiment, the Begleit Battalion was not under the command of the SS and therefore only supplied personnel for the outermost cordon of the RSD's security ring around Hitler. Hitler's inner security ring was patrolled by RSD security platoons, with any person seeking a meeting with Hitler subject to screening and removal of any weapons. This included Wehrmacht general officers, who were treated no differently with regards to gaining access to Hitler. Once past inner security, a final barrier existed to protect Hitler; this consisted of personally picked RSD men who were always in close proximity to Hitler in order to protect him from physical harm.

By the end of World War II, the RSD had effectively replaced the original security unit, the SS-Begleitkommando, in all of its duties with regards to protecting Hitler. Although still existing as a separate entity, the SS-Begleitkommando had lost all of its original functions as Hitler's personal guard and its members were relegated in the last years of Nazi Germany to serving as personal valets and aides to Hitler. By 1944, most of the SS leadership saw the SS-Begleitkommando as an unnecessary relic of an earlier time and there were several calls for the RSD to absorb its predecessor organization, although this never formally occurred. By the end of the war, the Begleitkommando was referred to as an "escort platoon" of the Waffen-SS with SS-Obersturmbannführer Franz Schädle serving as its last commander.

Heinrich Himmler greatly resented both the RSD and the Begleitkommando, since these SS men typically bypassed Himmler's authority and reported directly to Hitler in all affairs. Two of Hitler's personal security guards, who early on came afoul of Himmler, were Christian Weber and Bruno Gesche.

Right: Christian Weber and Bruno Gesche were two of Hitler's early SS bodyguards. Both had joined the SS before Himmler and were considered "old comrades" of Hitler, much to the dismay of the Reichsführer-SS (Bavarian State Archives)

Weber, who had been in charge of security at the 1939 Bürgerbräukeller Rally, publicly humiliated the SS with slipshod security, allowing Georg Elser to plant a bomb in the Beer Hall which nearly killed Hitler. Although enraged, Himmler was unable to act against Weber who had served in the Nazi Party and the SS from the very beginning. Bruno Gesche, a long time SS member and also chronic alcoholic, was a different case and Himmler was eventually able to supplant Hitler's trust in his early comrade, demoting Gesche to the rank of SS-Private, and assigning him to duty on the Eastern Front. Gesche would still outlive Himmler, surviving both combat and the war, living a long life and dying as an old man in 1980.

During Hitler's reign as Chancellor and Führer of Nazi Germany, there were over two dozen major attempts on his life. Dozens of additional plots and counter-plots were also discussed and formulated between 1933 and 1945, although many of these never went beyond the initial planning stages. Adolf Hitler's life would finally end by his own hand in 1945 when he committed suicide in his Berlin bunker by simultaneously shooting himself and ingesting cyanide.

The earliest known attempts on Hitler's life were in 1921 and 1923 when shots were fired at him during two separate Nazi Party rallies. The shooters were never identified, and the incidents never seriously investigated by police. In 1932, while dining at the Hotel Kaiserhof in Berlin, Hitler was delivered poisoned food which was spotted and intercepted by the hotel staff. In March of 1932, just a few months prior to Hitler becoming Chancellor, two unidentified men shot at Hitler's train as it passed between Munich and Weimar – the shooters were never apprehended. During Hitler's first year in office as Chancellor of Germany there were ten recognized attempts on his life, mostly ill-conceived and many were aborted due to security measures placed around the Führer by the SS.

Would be assassin Beppo Römer in 1932 (Federal German Archives)

Perhaps the most significant early attempt on Hitler's life was committed by Beppo Römer, an anti-Nazi Freikorps veteran who attempted to enter the Reich Chancellery in mid-1933 in order to kill Hitler. Arrested by the Gestapo and confined to the Dachau Concentration Camp, Römer was released in 1939 but rearrested in 1942 and executed in 1944. Another noteworthy attempt occurred in the summer of 1933 when a man in an SA uniform infiltrated Hitler's mountain retreat at the Berghof Obersalzburg and broke into Hitler's personal residence. Unable to draw close to Hitler due to SS security forces, the would-be assailant attempted to escape but was later apprehended by local police and handed over to the Gestapo.

Major pre-war attempts on Hitler's life (1934 – 1938)

DATE	LOCATION	EVENT
June 1934	Bad Wiessee	In response to the purges of the Night of the Long Knives, a group of SA men set up a machine gun nest in order to ambush Hitler's automobile convoy. Hitler selects a different route back to Berlin and escapes.
Summer 1935	Berlin	Helmuth Mylius, an ex-radical and former member of the Ehrhardt Naval Brigade, succeeds in infiltrating Hitler's security with 160 loyal supporters. Before the group can move against the Führer, they are arrested.
Summer 1935	Berghof	An SA man fires a single point-blank shot at Hitler, missing the German dictator by inches before being immediately killed by return fire from Hitler's security forces.
December 1936	Nuremberg	A Jewish student named Helmut Hirsch, backed by Nazi exile Otto Strasser, attempts to place a bomb at the Nuremberg stadium. He is arrested and executed in 1937.
Fall 1937	Berlin	A member of the SS plants a bomb under Hitler's podium. The bomb fails to explode when the SS man excuses himself and is inadvertently locked in a restroom.
November 1938	Munich	Maurice Bavaud, a Swiss citizen, spends most of the year stalking Hitler, intent on shooting him. He is arrested at a Nazi rally when he attempts to approach the Führer.
September 1938	Berlin	Wehrmacht Colonel Hans Oster engages in the most far reaching plot to date, organizing a potential military coup against Hitler should Nazi Germany invade Czechoslovakia. At the last minute, the Western Allies negotiate the Munich Pact, and the coup is called off.

The first major attempt on Hitler's life, following the outbreak of the Second World War, occurred in November 1939 when Communist Party member Georg Elser constructed a bomb and hid the weapon within a pillar at the Bürgerbräukeller, a beer hall in Munich. Adolf Hitler, and several other leading Nazis, attended a Nazi Party rally at the beer hall, to which end Elser had hoped to kill Hitler and the top Nazi leadership. However, Hitler left the speech early, missing the bomb blast by thirteen minutes, although seven others were killed, and dozens wounded in the subsequent explosion. Elser was later arrested and accused of being a member of a British assassination team, in which the SS had also captured two British secret agents as part of the "Venlo Incident" along the German border with Holland. Combining Elser's act with the capture of the British agents, Germany would later justify its invasion of the neutral Low Countries.

As early as 1941, a wide scale anti-Hitler resistance had formed within the German military, initially led by General Erwin von Witzleben, whose staff had planned to kill Hitler when the Führer visited Western Army Command headquarters following the invasion of France. Hitler would cancel this initial trip, and security during later visits made an attack against him impossible. Later that year, Major General Henning von Tresckow planned to shoot Hitler outright, but was thwarted after new security measures prevented any non-SS members from carrying weapons around the Führer. Several months later, Tresckow planted a bomb (disguised as a bottle of Cointreau) on Hitler's plane at Smolensk; however, near freezing temperatures in flight caused the firing circuits to malfunction and the bomb failed to explode.

By 1943, with security considered virtually impregnable around Hitler, military resistance members saw a suicide bombing as the only remaining option to kill the Führer. The first attempt was made in March 1943 when General von Gersdorff planned to himself denote a bomb standing next to Hitler but was unable to get close enough to the Führer in order to make the attempt. Several months later, Lieutenant Axel von dem Bussche attempted to commit a suicide bombing during a military uniform presentation to Hitler, but the event was cancelled.

The plot to kill Hitler in the summer of 1944 is generally regarded as the "high water mark" of all the attempts on Hitler's life and also the only attempt in which Hitler's security forces completely failed in preventing or even foreseeing the attack. The primary culprit of the assassination attempt was Army Colonel and German Count Claus von Stauffenberg. After months of planning and several trial runs, including an aborted bombing attempt at Berchtesgaden on July 11th, Stauffenberg planted a briefcase bomb in Adolf Hitler's military field headquarters on July 20th 1944. The bomb exploded, injuring and killing several people, but had previously been moved by a staff aide to the opposite side of a table from where Hitler was standing. Thus, the bomb blast was deflected away from Hitler, leaving the German leader with only minor burns and bruises.

Claus von Stauffenberg, who perpetrated what is arguably the most successful attempt on Hitler's life. (Federal German Archives)

Following the bombing, Stauffenberg and several other Army officers attempted to seize control of the German government. After news began to be verified that the bomb had not killed Hitler, the plan fell apart and Stauffenberg and his inner ring of conspirators were arrested by the Berlin Home Guard, under the command of Army Major Ernst Remer. Stauffenberg's immediate superior General Fromm then ordered Stauffenberg shot on the morning of July 21st, his plan being to quickly execute anyone who could link him to the conspiracy. Fromm was halted from further executions by SS-Lieutenant Colonel Otto Skorzeny, acting under orders from Ernst Kaltenbrunner. Heinrich Himmler then personally took over Fromm's posting as Commander of the Home Army[iv], while the foreign intelligence section of the Sicherheitsdienst took over all functions of the military intelligence arm, known as the Abwehr. As a result of the July 20th plot the SS had significantly increased its power.

Education, Training, and Recruitment

The traditions and demeanor of the SS, which viewed itself as an elite guard of the Nazi Party, are largely attributable to SS programs of indoctrination, training, and continued education. SS training stressed that the SS member was a pure Aryan existing to serve both Hitler and Germany above all else. However, the specifics of training varied greatly and were mostly determined by the particular branch of the SS in which a member served. In the early years of the SS, training was very much an ad hoc affair left up to local commanders who would occasionally receive vague instructions from the senior SS leadership. SS members in the late 1920s were typically employed for brawn, not brains, leaving the need for a formal training curriculum at a minimum.

In 1931, two years into Heinrich Himmler's tenure as Reich Leader of the SS, the first orders regarding training curriculum were issued to the entire SS. The SS Head Office (SS-Hauptamt) was designated as the official command authority over all SS education, with directives issued concerning physical, academic, and racial instruction. For training within the Concentration Camp formations of Theodor Eicke's SS-Totenkopfverbande, Eicke developed a curriculum based upon his days as an enlisted Army paymaster during the First World War. Eicke's ideas of training rejected formal education, since Eike himself despised officer style military education, and instead focused on training based solely from Eicke's own directives and motivations. The result was the creation of a brutal mindset which instilled hatred of camp prisoners along with torture and murder as acceptable practices of discipline.

"There is no room in the SS for men of soft hearts, and any such should retire to a monastery"
–Theodor Eicke (1934)

Eicke's views on SS values would continue into the Second World War, when the SS men of the Totenkopf division were involved in numerous acts of genocide and war crimes. The brutality of the concentration camp training also carried over to the battlefield in other ways, with Eicke's military formations known for their fanatical will to fight and die to the last man.

As early as 1935, the Inspector of the armed SS (the SS-VT – later the Waffen-SS) had instituted a specific training regimen for SS combat units, one which emphasized tactical awareness over drill proficiency as well as the ability of every SS man to think independently and act in a command position for any given military situation. In contrast to the German Army, which operated basic training at recruit depots, recruits of the Waffen-SS were initially enlisted directly to an armed SS regiment, within which they would receive basic training from a seasoned cadre of veterans. Physical training was the most stressed area, as was battlefield tactical knowledge and small unit combat engagement. Field training was conducted frequently, often with live ammunition to include artillery barrages, leading to an SS soldier being very self-reliant under fire and accustomed to handling a variety of combat scenarios.

Officer training was considerably more difficult, with aspiring Waffen-SS cadets requiring eighteen months of prior enlisted service before acceptance to one of the SS officer training schools, known as the "SS-Junkerschulen". Officer training was administered on a strict curriculum of both classroom and field instruction, with those succeeding in obtaining an SS officer's commission gaining the respect of both superiors and subordinates alike.

In the mid to late 1930s, during what may be seen as the "golden years" of the Allgemeine-SS, it was the SS members of the General-SS mustering formations which had the most to gain from SS training and education programs. Every local SS command also served simultaneously as a sports club, with SS members eligible to receive the standard SA and German Sports Badges, as well as several additional sports decorations such as the Motor Sports Badge and Heavy Athletics

Waffen-SS cadets receive instruction at the Bad Tölz SS officer candidate school (Federal German Archives)

Badge. The SS also placed a particular emphasis on the sport of fencing, with several SS Fencing Schools (SS-Fechtschule) established for this purpose. For those SS members with equestrian aspirations, the General-SS maintained its own cavalry corps which operated some of the best riding instruction schools in all of Germany.

Within the realm of racial and ideological instruction, the Allgemeine-SS was perhaps the most thoroughly indoctrinated into the ideals of Anti-Semitism and racial superiority. Weekly meetings of local SS units often included readings from Hitler's autobiography "Mein Kampf" as well as discussions regarding the threat of Judaism and the superiority of the German race. It is therefore of little surprise that many General-SS members, who later transferred to other SS branches involved in genocide, committed war crimes with little hesitation and no remorse.

Recruitment was an ever-present concern to the SS both in the early years of its existence as well as during the course of the Second World War. The very first SS recruits of the 1920s and early 30s were drawn from the ranks of the SA, with such recruits screened for loyalty to Hitler above all else. After 1934, when the SS became an independent formation separate from the SA, recruitment became more standardized and regulated by specific directives both within the Allgemeine (General) and Waffen (Armed) branches of the SS. Within the General-SS, it was the SS-Hauptamt which was responsible for recruiting, with the actual recruiting activities left up to the various SS-Senior District (Oberabschnitt) commands throughout Germany. Recruitment officers from the local SS-districts (Abschnitt) and regiments (Standarten) were the front-line recruiters, seeking out potential SS recruits from all levels of society and walks of life.

Recruitment within the Waffen-SS was even more regulated, first by the Inspector of the SS-VT and later the SS Operations Head Office (SS-Führungshauptamt). In the early days of the SS-Verfügungstruppe, individual regiments carried out their own recruiting, most often at Nazi Party rallies or at sports festivals which were held annually throughout Germany. After the expansion of the SS-VT into the Waffen-SS, recruiting was conducted on a divisional level with each division containing a dedicated recruiting department. Divisional recruiting officers would typically tour Germany, oftentimes establishing recruiting offices in major German cities such as Munich, Hamburg, Leipzig, or Berlin.

In the 1930s, Concentration Camp guards and staff members were recruited from those already serving in the SS. Theodor Eicke, head of the Camp Service, typically sought young unmarried men and preferred those with criminal backgrounds due to their predisposition towards brutality. After the founding of the Totenkopf division, camp guards were often seen as "behind the lines" soldiers, with recruitment standards allowed to grow lax. The camp service of the 1940s primarily consisted of veteran camp service officers, wounded soldiers, and older men unfit for military service. By the end of 1944, in order to keep the camps up and running, camp service recruitment began to include non-SS members who were formed into an organization referred to as the "Auxiliary SS". Auxiliary SS members were issued SS uniforms with a unique tri-swastika insignia and were barely trained, badly equipped, and recruited solely for the purpose of guarding concentration camps while SS members of the camp service proper escaped the coming end of the war. This led to the Auxiliary-SS personnel bearing the unfortunate distinction of being the "last ones in the camp" upon their liberation by the Soviets or the Allies.

**A rare photograph of an Auxiliary SS member
(Federal German Archives)**

More often than not, the SS recruited from other Nazi Party paramilitary groups, in particular the Hitler Youth which was seen as a "breeding ground" for future SS leaders. The Hitler Youth was nearly as old as the Nazi Party itself, having been established as the "Jugendbund der NSDAP" in 1922. A spin-off group was the "Jungsturm Adolf Hitler" created solely for recruitment into the SA. By 1926, both groups had been merged into the "Hitler Jugend" (Hitler Youth) or the "HJ". By the mid-1930s the Hitler Youth was regarded as a direct pipeline for service in the SS and Hitler Youth boys were encouraged to begin the application process to become General-SS candidates upon their seventeenth birthday. In 1936, the Hitler Youth was also granted the single Sig Rune parade flag, with the resemblance to the SS runes abundantly clear.

Left: A recruiting poster from the 12th SS Division showing a young Hitler Youth volunteer in SS uniform. (Federal German Archives)

By 1941, the purpose of the Hitler Youth had shifted from a mission of indoctrination and training towards one of war time support. Hitler Youth members were frequently deployed to military support duties and also served in front line combat. The SS was not ignorant of the manpower potential of the Hitler Youth volunteers and had begun efforts in 1942 to create an SS combat unit comprised entirely of Hitler Youth members. The result was the creation in February 1943 of the 12th SS Panzer Division, which was issued the honor title "Hitler Jugend", and formed with a cadre of SS personnel from the Leibstandarte division. The 12th SS division eventually grew to a membership of over twenty thousand and was known for ferocity in tactics. The division fought at the Battle of Normandy in 1944 before retreating into Belgium and ending the war in Hungary.

The SS also made an attempt to recruit German nobility, with the formation of the "Riding SS" serving as an equestrian social club for Germany's upper class. These early SS horse units were eventually formed into the "Reiterabschnitt" of the General-SS; although, by the outbreak of World War II, the Waffen-SS had gained control over all SS cavalry units and personnel, while the General-SS cavalry faded into obscurity.

Recruitment from universities and higher centers of learning was another aim of the SS, and by 1934 the SS had begun to infiltrate the Nazi Teachers League as well as offering a plethora of honorary SS ranks to high ranking officials, deans, and professors from all of Germany's major universities and centers of academic study. The greatest success in this area was SS control of the National Political Educational Academies, which were preparatory schools from which could be recruited the most elite of Germany's youth. Known by the abbreviation NPEA, or more informally as the "Napola", the National Political Educational Academies were founded in 1933 originally under the authority of the Reich Ministry of Science, Education, and Culture. By 1935, a total of sixteen academies were in operation throughout Germany and operated out of converted Army barracks, monasteries, or castles.

NATIONAL POLITICAL EDUCATIONAL ACADEMIES (1933 – 1939)

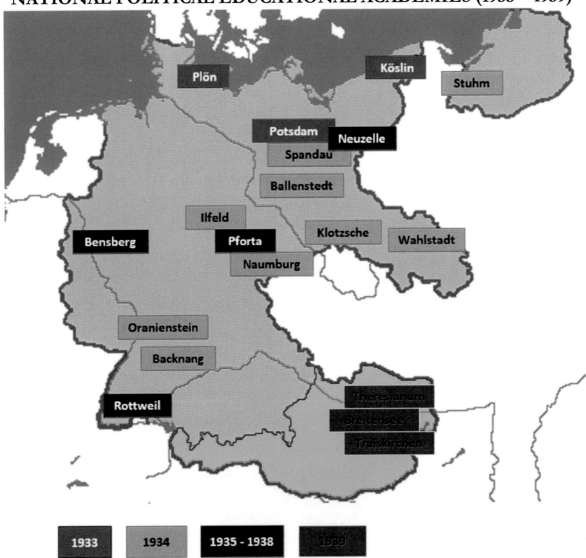

In addition to the schools shown above, eighteen more schools would be opened between 1940 and 1945, including three in Czechoslovakia and one in France.

The National Political Educational Academies were focused on producing future leaders of Germany. Some academies specialized in science, others in the arts, while all of the NPEA schools stressed physical training and sports. Combined with a rigorous curriculum of academics, only twenty five percent of those applying were accepted as students. Students entered the National Political Educational Academies from all walks of life and, while tuition was required, several government programs existed for scholarship payments and financial aid.

By 1934, leadership of the National Political Educational Academies had passed into the hands of the SA who quickly went about militarizing the schools, issuing uniforms to students, and organizing each NPEA academy into the likeness of a military regiment. Students lived in platoon barracks of thirty members, with platoons forming several company sized units known as "Hundertschaften". The students also held paramilitary ranks ranging from "Jungmannen" (ordinary students) to "Hundertschaftsführer" held by a student company commander. After the Night of the Long Knives, SA command of the Napolas was transferred to the German Labor Front under Doctor Robert Ley. From the onset, Ley was opposed in his leadership of the NPEA schools by Bernard Rust of the Science, Education, and Culture Ministry. Ley eventually relinquished control of the NPEAs and founded his own political academies which became known as the "Adolf Hitler Schools". With a power vacuum in who was to continue running the National Political Educational Academies, the SS saw their opportunity and moved in to seize control.

At the start of 1935, the NPEAs were placed under the control of Himmler's command office, the Reichsführung-SS. The SS paid off all debts, introduced a new clothing allowance for students, and instituted a recruiting plan to attract ethnic Germans to the Napolas. On March 9, 1936, SS-Obergruppenführer August Heissmeyer was appointed the head of all NPEAs throughout Germany. Heissmeyer then proceeded to form his own headquarters, known as the "Hauptamt Dienststelle Heissmeyer", to deal with NPEA administration. This office was coincidentally the only SS main office ever directly named after its commander. By 1940, Heissmeyer had completely solidified SS control of the Napolas, including the issuance of SS type ranks to faculty members (i.e. NPEA-Hauptsturmführer). New student application criteria were also introduced to mirror the selection process used by the SS. Life in NPEA's was now based entirely on SS service to include the removal of all contemporary religious aspects, replaced by a focus on Germanic-Nordic heritage, as well as an emphasis on pagan beliefs. Racial indoctrination and Anti-Semitism were also core curriculum as was personal loyalty to Himmler and Hitler.

August Heissmeyer, the SS commander of all NPEAs in Germany (National Archives)

During World War II an attempt was made by Himmler to establish NPEA equivalents in occupied countries, this leading to the creation of three "NPEA-Reichschulen" in Belgium and the Netherlands. Each Reichschulen was paired with a "sister school" in Germany and a regular exchange program quickly developed. Himmler also formed one all-female NPEA, known as the "Reichsschule Niederlande für Mädchen", in the Dutch city of Heithuijsen. Fewer than eight hundred foreign students were ever enrolled in these foreign academies.

Himmler and Heissmeyer next sought to gain authority over education at German colleges and universities. As far back as 1926, Nazi student organizations had been forming in all of Germany's universities, with the largest national group being the National Socialist Students League. Under Nazi guidance, each major university also formed an "NSDAP-Stamm-Mannschaft" which were student companies of political leaders who had already signed up with a major Nazi group such as the SS, SA, or the National Socialist Motor Corps (NSKK). In an effort to gain exclusive control of Nazi activities at German centers of higher learning, Himmler lobbied for the appointment of an SS general officer to the position of "Reichstudentenführer", a post which would hold control of all Stamm-Mannschaft in Germany. SS-Obergruppenführer Dr. Gustav-Adolf Scheel assumed the position of Reichstudentenführer in 1936 and thereafter the SS held control over all student affairs at German universities. Scheel further went on to establish a Nazi alumni organization which was known as the "NS-Altherrenbund der Deutschen Studenten". Members were issued dark blue uniforms in a similar fashion to the SS black jacket and charged financial dues which were channeled through a special office known as the "Altherrenbund".

The single hold-outs to SS control at the universities were Catholic alumni groups who refused to contribute to the SS university funds or its associations. These groups were promptly declared illegal and their Catholic leadership arrested and imprisoned in Concentration Camps. Two additional youth groups, which bear mention insofar as SS recruiting is concerned, were the "HJ-Streifendienst" and the "HJ-Landdienst", both components of the Hitler Youth. The Streifendienst served as an internal security and police group and was seen as a type of SS training and preparatory organization. The Landdienst served to promote agricultural training of Hitler Youth members and was expanded in 1940 to become part of the much larger "Siedlernachwuchsstelle Ost" (Eastern Young Settlers Office) which was run by the SS and focused on training "Wehrbauern" (Peasant Warriors) for eventual SS colonization of conquered eastern territories.

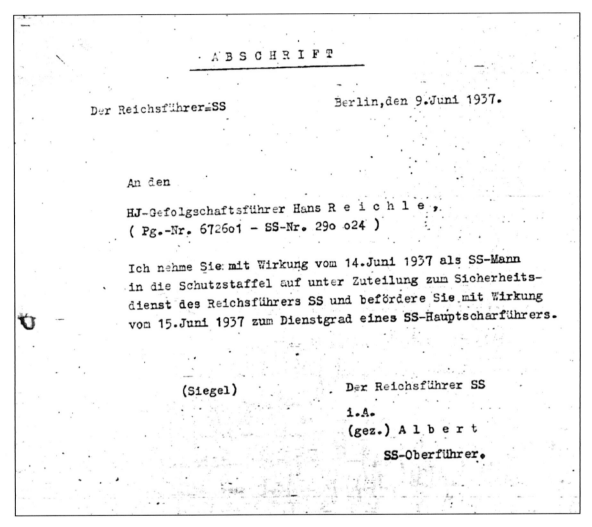

A personnel order transferring a Hitler Youth member into the ranks of the SS. By the start of World War II, the Hitler Youth had come to be seen as a direct pipeline towards membership in the SS (National Archives)

As late as 1944, Himmler had begun plans to extend SS influence into both secondary and elementary schools with the aim being the complete SS control over all education in Germany. The constraints of war prevented Himmler from achieving this aim, although the SS legacy of corrupting the minds of Germany's youths had by this time all but been established.

Occupation and Terror

When World War II began in September of 1939, the SS had existed for fourteen years, six of which the Nazi Party had held power in Germany. The secret police forces of the Gestapo, Kripo, and SD were now consolidated into the Reich Central Security Office, while Theodor Eicke's Concentration Camps continued to operate unabated and feared throughout Germany. The start of the war gave the armed SS its first chance for actual combat, with both the SS-Verfügungstruppe and the Leibstandarte deployed to serve in the initial Polish invasion. Eicke's fledgling Totenkopf division was held in reserve and it would not be until the Battle of France in which the SS Death's Head units demonstrated their full ferocity in combat.

By the spring of 1940, the armed SS was now formally known as the Waffen-SS, and it was this fighting force which would serve in the invasion of Russia as well as holding the West against Allied invasion forces four years later. As country after country fell before the armies of Nazi Germany, occupation regimes began to form along with implemented policies put forth by Adolf Hitler's vision of a Germanic Europe free of undesirables to the German race. In nearly all cases, the enforcement of Hitler's vision fell to Heinrich Himmler and his SS.

Poland was the first victim, falling quickly to a German invasion and then existing briefly under a military occupation government before being divided into several new territories, the largest of which became known as the General Government. Nazi rule in Poland was based on ruthless terror and murder, with the SS tasked to ensure complete subjugation of the Polish population to their German masters. SS Special Action Units, the "Einsatzgruppen", were deployed to execute the Polish intelligentsia and upper class, thus ensuring that no resistance force would form to challenge the authority of Nazi Germany. Jews, Gypsies, Slavs, and other minorities were seen as targets of opportunity, with several massacres occurring in the fall of 1939. By 1940, the western half of Poland had been completely annexed into the Third Reich while the east languished under occupation by the Soviet Union.

The partition of Poland (December 1939)

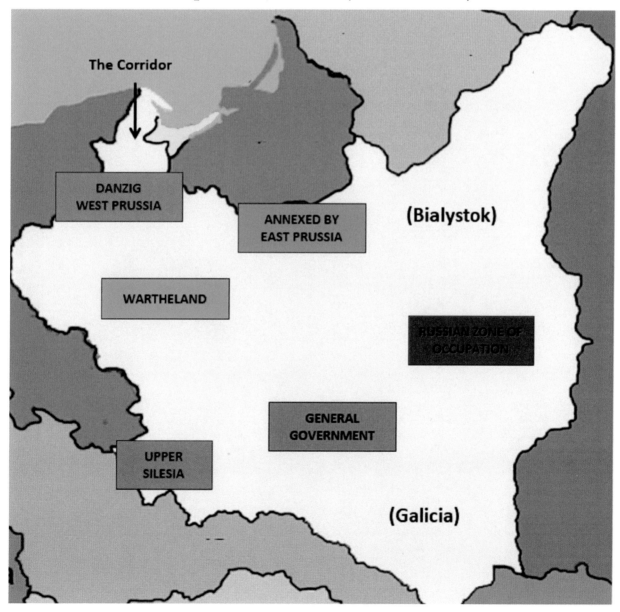

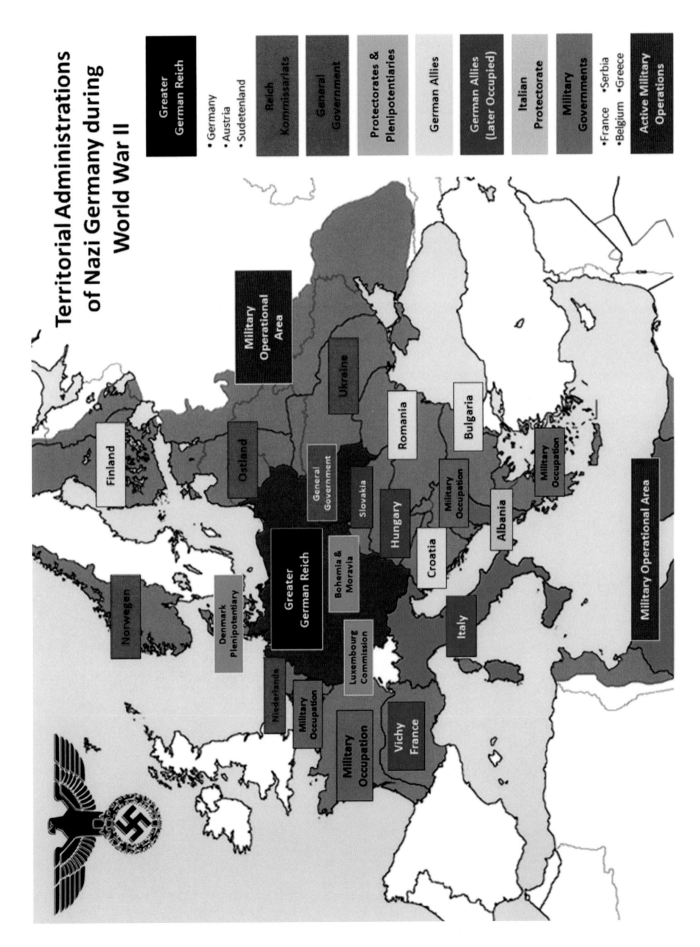

Territorial Administrations of Nazi Germany during World War II

Under the Ribbentrop-Molotov Pact, Germany entered into a non-aggression treaty with the Soviet Union, shocking the world with the ideological differences between Nazism and Communism conveniently forgotten. Under a secret clause of the pact, both parties agreed to attack Poland from either side once hostilities began. The campaign against Poland lasted from September 1st to October 5th 1939, with a military administration briefly existing until December, at which time the western areas of Poland were annexed by Germany. East Prussia absorbed most of Northern Poland while the city of Danzig and "the Corridor" became part of a new Nazi region called Danzig-West Prussia. Central Poland was formed into a region called Wartheland, intended to be a Germanic area suitable for colonization, while the remainder of occupied Poland was formed into the General Government.

With Germany's attack on Poland came declarations of war from both England and France, leading to plans by Germany for an attack in the west. That attack came in the spring of 1940 when German forces charged through the Low Countries of Belgium and the Netherlands, in an action known as the Blitzkrieg, and then smashed through the French Army, captured Paris, and forced a general surrender. Germany also used the opportunity to attack neutral Denmark and Norway, the latter putting up some resistance while Denmark surrendered in under two hours. Nazi rule in the west was less harsh than in Poland, although some atrocities were still committed. Only a single Einsatzgruppen was deployed during the annexation of Luxembourg, with France spared the round-ups and executions which had previously been seen in the east. The Germans solidified their positions, established occupation governments, and encouraged collaborationist groups. Volunteer military formations began to form which led to the creation of the Waffen-SS Foreign Legions. Local collaborationist SS movements were also founded, eventually forming an organization known as the Germanic-SS.

Occupation authorities of Nazi Germany (1939 – 1941)

Nation	Annexed	Occupation Authority
Poland	1939	Military Administration in Poland (Oct - Dec 1939)
		General Government of Poland (1939 – 1945)
Belgium	1940	Military Administration in Belgium and Northern France
France		Military Government in France
Netherlands		Reich Commission of the Netherlands
Luxembourg		Governmental Commission
Denmark		Plenipotentiary Administration
Norway		Reich Commission Norway
Greece	1941	Military Administration in Greece
Serbia		Military Command of Serbia

The governmental commission and plenipotentiary administrations of Luxembourg and Denmark operated with near self-government ability but were still puppet states under German control. Northern France was overseen entirely by a military government, although in 1944 portions of eastern France and Belgium were designated as a Reich commission. The military government of Greece was jointly overseen by Germany, Italy, and Bulgaria.

In 1941, after failing to invade Great Britain the previous fall, German military efforts focused on southeastern Europe. Yugoslavia and Greece were both attacked to support Italian war efforts, followed by the formation of pro-Nazi governments. The result was the creation of new military administrations as well as the formation of a new German ally state known as the "Independent State of Croatia", or more informally as Ustaše Croatia. This Croatian state would rival the Germans in massacre and genocide, founding an independent extermination camp at Jasenovac and murdering thousands of Jews and ethnic Serbians. From 1941 to 1943, Germany also deployed combat troops to North Africa in a fighting force famously known as the "Afrika Korps". This one theater of the war was devoid of any SS combat activity and there were no Waffen-SS units deployed in Africa during the entire course of the German North African campaign.

Had German forces reached Palestine, a plan existed for the deployment of SS troops to murder Jews in the historic Israeli areas. As a prelude, Germany solicited diplomatic relations with many Middle Eastern nations and encouraged pro-German movements in Palestine, Syria, and Iraq. Haj Amin al-Husseini, the Grand Mufti of Jerusalem, was granted honorary rank as an SS-Gruppenführer and later helped to recruit Muslim soldiers into the Waffen-SS, as well as supplying intelligence to German agents with regards to British military activities.

By the summer of 1941, Germany had either conquered or allied every significant nation in Europe. Some hold-outs existed, such as Liechtenstein, Switzerland, and Spain, the latter of which having previously received German aid during the Spanish Civil War. Portugal was another strictly neutral country, although both the Germans and her enemies made use of this coastal nation for espionage, military intelligence gathering, and black-market arms smuggling.

In June of 1941, Adolf Hitler made a decision which would alter the course of World War II when he ordered an attack on the Soviet Union. Hitler had always seen the vast lands of Russia as "Lebensraum" (Living Space) for the German people and, as far back as the 1920s, had foretold prophecies in his book Mein Kampf regarding the necessity of Germany waging a war and conquering eastern lands. As the German Army launched a massive invasion into Russia, more territory fell under control of

Grand Mufti al-Husseini meets Heinrich Himmler in 1942 (Federal German Archives)

the Reich. In eastern Poland, the General Government absorbed the District of Galicia while East Prussia administered the northern district of Bialystok. After Germany captured the Baltic nations (Latvia, Lithuania, and Estonia), the German government formed the "Reich Ministry for the Occupied Eastern Territories" which was headed by Nazi Governor Alfred Rosenberg.

Rosenberg then formed two new German states, known respectively as the "Reichskommissariat Ostland", encompassing the Baltic States and parts of north western Russia, as well as the "Reichskommissariat Ukraine" which, as the name implied, consisted of the territory formerly belonging to the state of the Ukraine. As before with Poland, SS special action units were sent into Russia to suppress resistance but also with a much more sinister purpose in mind. Whereas previous actions against Jews and other minorities had been spontaneous, the Einsatzgruppen of Russia were formed primarily for the mission of Jewish extermination. As the German Army advanced into Russia, the SS followed to commit vast numbers of atrocities and acts of mass murder. It was this shift in policy from isolating and displacing the Jews, to now active and open extermination, which would make Russia the stage for wholescale genocide which would eventually develop into the Holocaust.

Colonization and Germanization

A cornerstone of Nazi ideology was the concept of an Aryan Master Race from which the modern-day German peoples were all descended. It was the aim of Nazism to incorporate into the German Reich all Germanic peoples, both native born and ethnic Germans who lived in foreign countries. Nazi philosophy further stated that the Aryan race was to face a great war in the East, in which the Slavic and "Untermensch" (sub-humans) would be eradicated. The final stage of this conflict was "Germanization" in which the German people would colonize the east and form a new Germanic nation.

From a practical point of view, the outbreak of war had given Hitler the pretext to act on his racial ideas, with the fall of Poland serving as a testing ground for the concept of Germanization. The Poles themselves had no right to inhabit their own country, so believed Hitler, as this area was to serve as a colony for Germany. To accomplish this mission, the native population would be displaced, while ethnic Germans living in Poland would be identified and repatriated while the rest of the population would eventually be deported. As with previous racial decrees and policies, the SS was the agency entrusted to enact Germanization. The two groups most directly responsible for Germanization were the SS Race and Settlement Office (RuSHA) as well as the Department for the Repatriation of Racial Germans (Hauptamt Volksdeutsche Mittelstelle) abbreviated as the VOMI.

Functionally, the RuSHA was responsible for classifying ethnic Germans in conquered lands while the VOMI was in charge of repatriating these ethnic Germans to the German Reich. The VOMI technically began as a civilian organization, unconnected with the SS, but from the very beginning Himmler had staffed VOMI offices with a plethora of SS personnel. In 1941, the VOMI was declared as an SS Head Office and placed under the command of a new SS department known as the "Reichskommissariat für die Festigung deutschen Volkstums" (Reich Commission for the Consolidation of Germanism), more commonly known as the RKFVD. It was the RKFVD which was responbile for the actual logisitics and mechanics of resettlement and relocation, while also holding authority to identify Germanic populations and forcibly remove all non-German peoples from conquered lands. These eastern territories would then be resettled with both settlers from Germany and ethnic Germans as identified by the RuSHA. Heinrich Himmler was himself appointed head of the RKFVD, integrating this complex web of racial offices into the formal command structure of the SS. Both the VOMI and RKFVD were then adminsitratively subordinated to the SS Legal Office (Hauptamt SS Gericht) while the Race and Settlement Office remained an independent head office of the SS.

SS RACIAL OFFICES ORGANIZATION

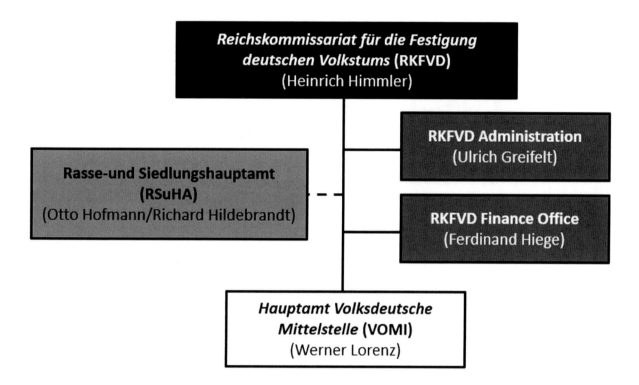

When Germany invaded Poland in 1939, the theory of Germanization was first put into practice. Once a Nazi administration had been established, SS race experts would arrive to set up VOMI field offices, after which the local population would be screened for ethnic Germans. Those so located would be processed for repatriation to Germany while Poles and other "undesirables" of mixed racial background were slated for deportation. In these first days of Nazi conquest, the General Government of Poland was seen as the logical place for non-Germans to live, leading to the region becoming a type of "racial garbage can" much to the dismay of Hans Frank who was by then the Governor General of Poland. Frank and his Nazi minions argued that the General Government should also be Germanized, leading to plans for a future Reich state known as Beskidenland (named after the Beskid Mountains), intended to encompass southern Poland and parts of Czechoslovakia. Frank's aims never came to fruition and the General Government continued to be the site of racial deportations as well as hosting some of the largest ghettos and death camps within the Nazi regime.

Right: Hans Frank, Governor-General of Poland. Outraged by Nazi plans to turn his region into a "racial dumping ground", Frank attempted to resign his position in 1942 (Federal German Archives)

Organization of the Hauptamt Volksdeutsche Mittelstelle (VOMI)

HEADQUARTERS AND STAFF DEPARTMENTS

AMT I
Führungsamt
(Operations Office)

AMT II
Organisation und Personal
(Personnel Office)

AMT III
Finanzen, Wirtschaft und Vermögensverwaltung
(Finance Office)

PUBLIC INFORMATION OFFICE

AMT IV
Informationen
(Press Office)

AMT V
Deutschtumserziehung
(Germanic Education Office)

GERMANIC WELFARE OFFICE

AMT VI
Sicherung Deutschen Volkstums im Reich
(Ethnic German Affairs – Reich)

AMT VII
Sicherung Deutschen Volkstums in den neuen Ostgebieten
(Ethnic German Affairs – East)

GERMANIC LEADERSHIP OFFICE

AMT IX
Politische Führung Deutscher Volksgruppen
(Germanic Political Office)

AMT X
Führung der Wirtschaft in den Deutschen Volksgruppen
(Germanic Operations Office

OTHER DEPARTMENTS

AMT VIII
Kultur und Wissenschaft
(Culture & Science Office)

AMT XI
Umsiedlung
(Resettlement Office)

By the time of the German invasion of Russia in 1941, the policies and practices of Germanization had been well formalized. When the German Army first advanced into new territory, the area was declared an Eastern Operational Zone (Operationszone Ost) until pacification by German forces. At that point, the region became a Rear Army Area (Rückwärtige Heeresgebieten) after which time SS Special Action Groups (Einsatzgruppen) would enter in order to identify Jews, Slavs, and other racial undesirables of the Reich. SS forces in this capacity were under standing orders to annihilate racially undesirable populations.

By the time a civil occupation administration had been established, the local population of ethnic Germans would be designated for "population transfer" and relocated to Germanic colony areas set up in the east. A small percentage of those so relocated were also repatriated to Germany. As well as identifying ethnic Germans, the SS racial experts were responsible for the selection of foreign citizens for slave labor. Russian prisoners-of-war, Poles, and ethnic Slovakians were prime targets as well as the local populations of the Baltic countries and the Ukraine. The RKFVD was further responsible for investigating cases of sexual intercourse between Eastern Races and Germans and worked closely with Einsatzgruppen and other SS commands to segregate populations deemed fit for eradication.

SS-General Richard Hildebrandt, under whose leadership most of the SS racial policies in the east were enacted. (National Archives)

Perhaps one of the more sinister results of SS racial policy was the identification of eastern born children deemed suitable for Germanization. SS Race and Settlement Office experts in Russia, Poland, and other eastern countries were first tasked with seeking out Slavic descent children who outwardly appeared German. If so located, the children would be kidnapped from their parents (who were most often then killed) before being taken to Germany as foster children in Aryan homes. The children would be raised thereafter as Germans, exposed also to Nazi education and ideology in order to erase any trace of their original origins.

In the spring of 1942, Heinrich Himmler announced his views on the end goal of Germanization. In Himmler's vision, Germanization would extend throughout all of Europe, in particular the lands of Czechoslovakia and Eastern Europe, which would then be cleansed of all ethnic minorities and incorporated into the Greater German Reich. In the east, Himmler envisioned the formation of three vast new states, all of which were to be governed by SS appointed leaders and populated with SS veterans and their families.

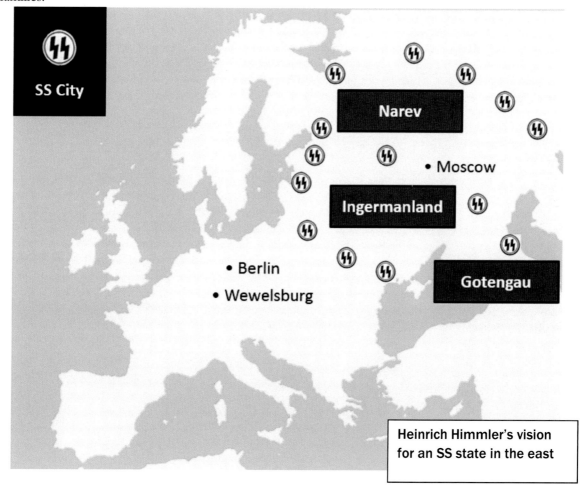

Heinrich Himmler's vision for an SS state in the east

In each state there were to be constructed several SS fortress cities surrounded by farms worked and lived on by "peasant warriors" of the SS. The three states were to comprise a greater SS nation in the east, a future country which Himmler referred to as the "SS-Baueinsatz-Ost". The development of an SS sovereign state was assigned to SS-Oberführer Konrad Meyer, a professor and doctor attached to the RKFVD, who drew out the first plans for an SS nation and estimated that a colonization period of twenty-five years would see a population of fifty percent German.

Right: Alfred Rosenberg, who opposed Himmler's plan for an SS nation in the east (Federal German Archives)

As bold as Himmler's plan was, others in the Nazi leadership scoffed at the idea of an SS nation, in favor of a more practical administration of the conquered eastern territories. Chief among Himmler's critics was Alfred Rosenberg, head of the Reich Ministry for Occupied Eastern Territories, who saw all German states in the east as temporary, serving as a prelude to either incorporation into the German Reich or independent as pro-German Nazi satellite states run by local autonomous and collaborationist governments. As World War II progressed, and the defeat of Nazi Germany grew near, neither Himmler nor Rosenberg's vision would come to pass.

The Path to Genocide

When Adolf Hitler took power in 1933, the Jewish population of Germany stood at approximately half a million, 0.8% of the total population of 62 million Germans. Germany would eventually annex an additional one hundred seventy-eight thousand Jews from Austria and thirty-five thousand from Czechoslovakia. Nearly forty thousand Roma Gypsies also lived in the territory of the Greater German Reich, with this group classified as "undesirable" in the same manner as the Jews under the Nuremberg Laws of 1935.

By the start of the Second World War, Germany's forcible Jewish emigration policies had resulted in 432,000 Jews fleeing the German Reich for other countries[v]. Approximately ninety thousand refugees had fled to the United States while sixty thousand had emigrated to the British Mandate of Palestine. Tragically, some Jews choose to seek refuge in countries which Nazi Germany would later invade such as France, Poland, Norway, and the Low Countries of Belgium and the Netherlands. For these unfortunate numbers, relief in these refuges was sadly only temporary.

After the invasion of Poland, Germany would find over three million Jews, comprising nearly 10% of the overall Polish population. The tried methods of harassment and emigration, which had worked fairly well in the Reich, were of little consequence in Germany's newly conquered possession due to such large numbers of Jews. The Jews of Poland were also "unassimilated", meaning they were part of the Eastern races which Nazism had pledged to wipe out and thus had no place in German society.

The first Jewish casualties in Poland were as a result of both the Einsatzgruppen SS special action groups, as well as certain units of the Waffen-SS which murdered Jews, assisted by components of the German Army. Although at this early stage in the war there was not yet an established program of genocide, SS units in Poland were brutal to the Jewish population and committed several atrocities and massacres in the last months of 1939.

By October 1939, the first official measures had been put into place to deal with the Jews of Nazi occupied Poland. Of the original three million, two million Jews fell within the German occupation zone while the remainder were living in areas of Poland claimed by the Soviet Union. For those Jews living under the Nazi regime, the first sign of oppression began with Jewish registration. In all major cities, government officials began to register the Jewish population, with edicts passed requiring Jews in rural areas to migrate to the cities in order that a proper count of the Jewish population could be conducted. In spring of the following year, German officials began to announce measures to relocate all Jews into special areas of major Polish cities, which were to be known as "Jewish Residential Districts". On October 16th 1940, the first such district was established in the city of Warsaw, to be known thereafter as the Warsaw Ghetto. Jews from both Warsaw and the surrounding countryside were ordered to move into the ghetto which was then walled off and its inhabitants made prisoners. In Warsaw, nearly half a million people would be crammed into an area of just under sixteen square blocks. Conditions in the ghetto were appalling, with nearly one hundred thousand deaths in the first few months attributed to disease, starvation, and murder by German and SS authorities. Additional ghettos were then created in other Polish cities such as Lodz, Krakow, and Lublin, all using the Warsaw ghetto as a model.

Accompanying the creation of Jewish ghettos were further measures to identify Jews outwardly, thus making them susceptible to segregation, discrimination, and abuse. On November 23rd 1939, German authorities in Poland enacted what became known as the "Jewish Star Decree" which ordered all Jews over the age of twelve to wear a Star of David emblem in the form of an armband on the lower sleeve. When Germany invaded the Soviet Union in 1941, thus annexing the remainder of Poland, Jewish measures were extended to the remainder of Poland's Jews, along with more ghettos being set up in Eastern Poland in such cites as Lvov, Rovno, and Brest-Litovsk.

Administration of Jewish Ghettos in the General Government of Poland

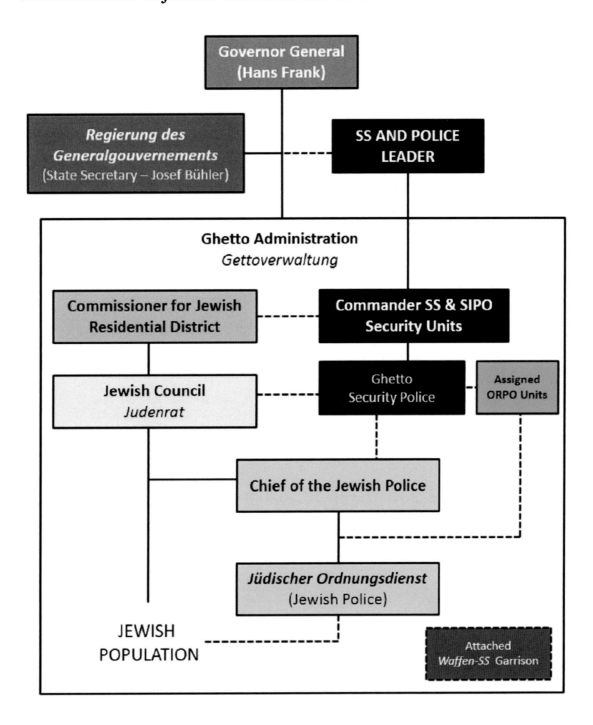

From their first inception, the ghettos of Poland were to exist under a facade of legal framework. In each ghetto, a Jewish council was established which answered to a German commissioner who would pass orders and edicts from the German occupation force. The ghettos were to be administrated by the Jews themselves, with business, culture, and the arts allowed to continue – at least outwardly. In reality, black market and corruption was rampant in the ghetto, with the SS quickly establishing a presence both through external German police guards and internal security police personnel, both of which were known for murder of the Jewish population.

A Jewish police officer poses with two ghetto residents, along with a member of the German Order Police.
By 1940, each ghetto had established its own unarmed Jewish police force. These Jewish police officers were often seen as collaborators and hated by the local Jewish population (Polish State Archives)

At the same time in which the Jews of Poland were being segregated inside walled ghettos, Nazi and SS officials were devising another program of terror and extermination against Germany's mentally ill and handicapped population. In a project known as "Aktion T4", officials in German hospitals and institutions began to target children born with disabilities and recommending that such persons be euthanized. The T4 program officially began in September 1939, the same month Germany invaded Poland, with the killing of several disabled children near Leipzig. The victims of T4 were at first killed through lethal injection, their bodies cremated, and their families notified that death had occurred due to pneumonia. By the end of 1939, the T4 program was expanded to adults and a system developed to identify the disabled, senile, and mentally handicapped, then arrange for euthanasia at one of several special medical facilities. Lethal injection was seen as too expensive and time consuming for mass killings, thus leading to the idea of killing patients with carbon monoxide gas.

By 1940, there were five facilities in Germany for use in the killing of the infirmed. Within each special hospital was an air tight room designed for patients to be sealed inside and killed by monoxide gas pumped in through pipes from an external motor engine. By 1941, a sixth facility had been opened at Hadamar, and by 1942 a total of 70,000 Germans had been killed in the various German euthanasia centers.

Right: Hadamar, where over 10,000 mentally ill and handicapped patients were killed (Federal German Archives)

By the time of the German attack on Russia in June of 1941, the purpose of the euthanasia centers had become known to the German public, largely in part to the vast numbers of unexplained deaths of otherwise healthy individuals who were patients in these various facilities. Once word of the T4 program had spread, opposition began to mount especially within the Protestant and Catholic Church. Several high-ranking bishops and church officials, such as Bishop Galen of Münster, publicly attacked the euthanasia program as immoral and anti-German. At first, Reich officials sought to deal with opposition to T4 by arresting and detaining critics in Concentration Camps. Even so, many officials in the Nazi state knew that a conflict with the church could lead to mass public unrest and possibly riots. Germany had also signed a Concordant with the Vatican in 1933, guaranteeing the rights of Roman Catholics under the Nazi state, with similar edicts issued to various Protestant and Lutheran sects as well.

After one of the first and only public demonstrations against the Nazi government[vi], Reich officials called for the mass arrest of protestors against T4. Plans were made to imprison Bishop Galen and other church leaders, but the arrests were called off by Joseph Goebbels who stated that such an act would lead to open rebellion amongst the German public. In a move uncharacteristic of the Nazi regime, Hitler backed down and declared an end to the T4 euthanasia program on August 24th 1941. Isolated killings of the mentally ill and handicapped would still continue until the end of World War II.

While the T4 program was never managed by the SS, several SS doctors and other administrators did participate in T4 implementation. The program was known for its cumbersome bureaucracy, with literarily thousands of doctors, nurses, and other medical personnel having knowledge of T4 and thus compromising the ability to keep the program of euthanasia a secret. The failure of T4 also demonstrated to the Nazi government that even in a dictatorship there were limits, and that the German public would voice open discontent regarding policies of murder. Insofar as the SS was concerned, T4 would serve as an excellent testing ground for killing methods later employed to murder the Jews of Europe. The SS also recognized that such a program should remain secret, and for this reason the death camps, which later exterminated the Jews, were constructed in isolated regions. Their SS commanders and staff were also sworn to secrecy, and the Jews themselves deceived of the true purpose of the camps until the last possible moment before death.

Agents of Extermination – The Einsatzgruppen of the SS

By the summer of 1941, Poland had existed under Nazi rule for two years, while France had fallen to invasion a year prior. German forces and her allies now occupied nearly all of western and central Europe, with oppression and terror commonplace in the German Reich. Thousands were imprisoned in Germany's concentration camps, while thousands more languished and died in the Jewish ghettos of Poland. With both Germany and the world wondering what to expect next, Hitler then ordered a full-scale invasion of Soviet Russia.

Russia, which had briefly been Germany's ally during the invasion and partition of Poland, held a European based population of nearly seventy-five million. Of these, some 2.5 million were Jews. Two million Jewish Poles had also fallen under the Soviet sphere in 1939, when eastern Poland was invaded by the USSR, as well as Jews from the Baltic states which numbered over two hundred and fifty thousand[vii]. With a combined total of nearly five million Jews, neither emigration nor Ghettoization would serve the German needs with regards to the Jewish populations of the east.

Immediately prior to the invasion of Russia in June of 1941, senior SS leaders were ordered by Hitler to reactivate the Special Action Groups which had served previously in Poland. The Einsatzgruppen were now to accompany the Third Reich's armies into the Soviet Union with a stated mission to murder Jews, Gypsies, Communists, and other undesirables of the German state. The first Einsatzgruppen of the SS had been established in March of 1938 to assist with the annexation of Austria into the German Reich. In these early days of the SS Special Action Groups, the organization's stated aim was to enter annexed territory, take control of government offices, and seize vital documents and archives. The operational authority of the Einsatzgruppen was the Commander of the Security Police, with these groups later falling under the Reich Central Security Office (the RSHA). In both cases, the organizer and supreme leader of the Einsatzgruppen was Reinhard Heydrich, with the Einsatzgruppen themselves staffed by members of the Gestapo, the Criminal Police, and the Sicherheitsdienst (SD).

The Einsatzgruppen were not considered permanent units and membership in these groups was temporary only for the duration of the group's existence. Once an Einsatzgruppen was disbanded, its members returned to their permanent duties in the SS. Between 1938 and 1939 there were three main Einsatzgruppen established to deal respectively with the annexation of Austria, the Sudetenland, as well as the remainder of the Czech Republic. The Einsatzgruppen were activated again for the invasion of Poland, with seven special action groups following in the wake of the German Army.

Reinhard Heydrich – Chief Secret Policeman of the Third Reich

Reinhard Heydrich joined the SS in 1931 after resigning from the German Navy under scandal following an adulterous love affair. Himmler, thinking Heydrich's background had been with naval intelligence, offered Heydrich a position as head of the SS Intelligence Service which Heydrich then formed as a small group called the "Ic-Dienst". The next year, the group was renamed the Sicherheitsdienst (SD). In 1934, Heydrich was named head of the Gestapo and two years later became Commander of the SS Security Police (the Sipo). In 1939, Germany's SS security forces were consolidated into the Reich Central Security Office (RSHA) which Heydrich also commanded. In September 1941, he was appointed Deputy Reich Protector of Bohemia and Moravia and in 1942 chaired the infamous Wannsee Conference, where the decision was formally made to exterminate all the Jews of Europe. Heydrich was killed by British sponsored Czech partisans a few months later in June of 1942.

The height of the Einsatzgruppen came about during the invasion of the Soviet Union, when four large special action groups were formed, each with a number of smaller Einsatzkommondo. These battalion sized units were deployed to enforce Nazi racial ideology, murder Jews, and eradicate other subject peoples in accordance with both Himmler's and Hitler's wishes. As before, these Einsatzgruppen were to be temporary, but nevertheless remained active in Russia until late 1943. The last Einsatzgruppen were converted to Combat Commands (Kampfkommando) in early 1944.

The method in which the Russian based Einsatzgruppen were organized and operated had developed through practical experience in Poland two years earlier. When the German Army advanced into new territory, the Einsatzgruppen would establish a headquarters in a rear area. The Special Action Group would then dispatch its smaller Einsatzkommondos into local towns and villages, ordering all Jews and other targeted groups (such as Communist functionaries and Gypsies) to report for "registration" in a central area, usually a square or other public place within a larger city. While waiting for its victims to report for registration, the Einsatzgruppen would gather together the necessary manpower in order to implement its agenda of killing.

In addition to the SS leadership of the Einsatzgruppen, most of which were SS security police officers, various other SS commands would contribute officers and men to facilitate with executions. Each Einsatzgruppen was also automatically allocated one company of the Waffen-SS, which was randomly selected from nearby armed-SS units, to assist in the killing. The German Army was also advised of Einsatzgruppen actions and further contributed personnel to augment manpower needs as requested. Finally, the SS made use of local collaborationist security forces.

Two SS members of a Polish based Einsatzkommondo. The donning of full medals and ceremonial sword suggests the photograph may have been staged. (Polish State Archives)

Distribution of the Special Action Groups from 1938 through 1944

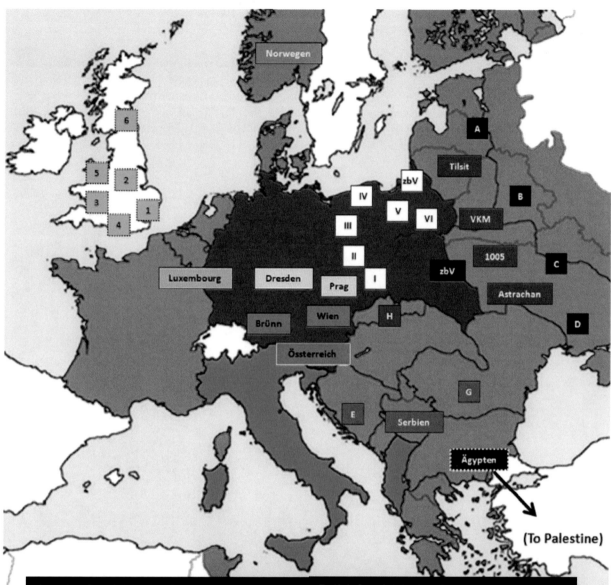

Austrian Special Action Groups
Einsatzgruppe Wien
Einsatzgruppe II Brünn
Einsatzkommando Össterreich

Sudetenland Special Action Groups
Einsatzgruppe Dresden

Czech Special Action Groups
Einsatzgruppen I Prag

Additional Special Action Groups
Einsatzgruppe Norwegen (Norway)
Einsatzgruppe E (Balkans)
Einsatzgruppe Serbien (Serbia)
Einsatzgruppe G (Romania)
Einsatzgruppe H (Slovakia)
Einsatzkommando Luxembourg (Luxemburg)

Polish Special Action Groups
Einsatzgruppe I, II, III, IV, V, & VI
Einsatzgruppe z.b.V. von Woyrsch

Soviet Union Special Action
Einsatzgruppe A, B, C, & D
Einsatzgruppe z.b.V.
Einsatzkommando Tilsit
Vorkommando Moscow (VKM)
Sonderkommando 1005
Sonderkommando Astrachan

Planned Special Action Groups
British Isles (6 Einsatzgruppen)
Einsatzkommondo Ägypten (Palestine)

Those victims reporting for "registration" would be forcibly placed on transport trucks and driven to isolated areas, usually in nearby forests or quarries. Once there, the victims would be unloaded, told to undress, with their clothing and valuables collected by the SS. Victims would then be led in a single file line to the site of execution; this area was almost always concealed from the unloading and undressing area to avoid the disrobing victims from witnessing killings already in progress.

Once at the area of execution, victims would be lined up in front of an open ditch and killed by firing squad. In many cases, where large numbers of killings took place, the Germans would employ the so called "sardine can method" where victims of one shooting would fall onto the previous victims of another. In each firing squad was also a designated soldier to check for any survivors; if so located, the survivor would be shot in the back of the head with a pistol. Although under regulations to conduct their activities in a military and professional manner, the Einsatzgruppen often degenerated into a mixture of corruption and drunkenness. SS soldiers would routinely pillage from the belongings of their victims and often times could only perform mass executions while intoxicated.

From the photographic records of the Einsatzgruppen: A German police officer taking aim at a mother and her child. In another widely publicized photo, an SS sergeant shoots a victim in the head while a large group of spectators looks on. In a third photo, a group of women pose for the camera while undressing. These victims were most likely killed within minutes of this photo being taken.

(Holocaust Memorial Museum)

By December of 1941, the death toll of Einsatzgruppen victims was already in the tens of thousands. Even with such results, SS leaders soon began to express concern regarding the mental strain in which the mass killings were taking on the officers and soldiers conducting the executions. To that end, proposals began to develop "gentler" methods of extermination, with discussions ranging from the use of poison gas to killing victims with dynamite blasts. After considering several "alternate methods", the Reich Central Security Office ordered that each Einsatzgruppen be issued modified trucks which had been converted into mobile gas chambers.

Victims would be sealed inside, the truck driven a distance of a few miles, and exhaust fumes channeled back into the truck's compartment to

A gas van in the Ukraine, in a photo dated from 1942 (Federal German Archives)

kill the victims trapped within. Gas vans were considered successful to such a degree that Himmler and Heydrich ordered their use specifically to kill women and children, thus avoiding the hardship of the Einsatzgruppen personnel executing such defenseless persons. However, the use of gas vans was expensive and also consumed gasoline and oil which were considered a vital war commodity. SS leaders therefore began to seek other ways to murder and sought methods which were considered cheaper to implement yet more efficient.

By the summer of 1942, German military defeats in Russia had caused the forces of the Third Reich to begin a retreat. The Einsatzgruppen had by this point murdered close to one million victims, leaving behind a trail of death and destruction. As the German military began to pull back over the site of some of the worst massacres, concern was raised that surrendered land would reveal evidence of Nazi atrocities. To this end, Reinhard Heydrich ordered the establishment of "Action 1005" whose purpose was to dispose of evidence relating to mass murder and genocide. In early 1942, "Sonderkommando 1005" was established under the command of SS-Standartenführer Paul Blobel.

The unit was comprised of approximately fifty SS officers and guards, as well as approximately two hundred Concentration Camp prisoners designated as "Leichenkommandos" (corpse units). Action 1005 began full operations in June of 1942, visiting concentration camps in Poland and experimenting with the best method for disposal of bodies. Paul Blobel tested various exhumation methods, eventually developing a system of burning large heaps of corpses on top of railway tiers drenched with gasoline. The remaining ashes and bones were then pounded down into dust, thus leading to the invention of a "bone crusher" machine to assist in the process. The prisoner members of the corpse units would themselves then be killed, their bodies often disposed of by a new group of camp internees selected to continue the unit's work.

A bone crushing machine from 1944 in Poland. (Federal German Archives)

Had German plans for conquest succeeded, the Einsatzgruppen may very well have been deployed to murder the Jews of Palestine as well as those Jews living in Great Britain. The British Einsatzgruppen were to be organized into six units under the overall command of SS-Brigadeführer Franz Six, and were not only to murder Jews but also round up government officials and the British upper class. Neither the Palestine nor British Special Action Groups were ever formed, since by 1943 the German forces had begun to retreat on all fronts.

Figures from Einsatzgruppen Operational Reports in the Soviet Union
(December 1941 – June 1943)

EINSATZGRUPPEN	COMMANDER	OPERATIONAL AREA	VICTIMS
A	Franz Walter Stahlecker	White Russia	206,942
A	Franz Walter Stahlecker	Baltic Nations	274,605
B	Arthur Nebe	Central Russia	134,000
B	Arthur Nebe	Belarus	67,722
C	Otto Rasch	Ukraine	269,855
D	Otto Ohlendorf	Caucasus	91,728
TOTAL			1,044,852

One of the largest executions attributed to the Einsatzgruppen occurred at the ravine of Babi Yar, located a few miles to the northwest of Kiev in the vicinity of a Jewish cemetery. Kiev was a major Soviet city and stronghold, with German forces occupying this area on September 19th 1941 after nearly a month of heavy fighting. SS special action groups then moved into the city, following several partisan attacks against German occupied areas in Kiev, and then began genocide actions under the guise of "suppressing resistance".

All Jews in the city were at first ordered to report for "registration" at a large square located on the main thoroughfare of Melnik Street in central Kiev. From here, the Jews were marched by SS guards out of the city towards the Babi Yar ravine. The system of death at Babi Yar then followed standard Einsatzgruppen procedure. Victims were marched to undressing areas, where they were stripped of all clothing and valuables, then led over a hill towards the ravine of Babi Yar itself. The victims were then lined up in front of open graves followed by SS firing squads commencing the execution. Mothers with children were shot in pairs, normally by firing a rifle through the body of the child into the chest of its mother. Follow-up teams of SS personnel then moved through the corpses, firing into the head of anyone who appeared to have survived.

Women await execution next to bodies at Babi Yar (Polish State Archives)

Selected command officers of the Einsatzgruppen

SS Officer	Rank	Special Action Command	Biography	Photograph
Lothar Beutel	SS-Brigadeführer und Generalmajor der Polizei	Einsatzgruppe IV (Poland)	A Gestapo officer from Munich, Beutel led Special Action Group 4 during the early months of the Polish campaign. He supervised the capture of Warsaw and was shortly afterwards relieved of his duties by Arthur Nebe, after evidence of corruption. Beutel survived the war and died in 1986.	
Paul Blobel	SS-Standartenführer	Einsatzkommondo 4a (Russia), Sonderkommando 1005	An SD officer from Düsseldorf, Blobel commanded a Special Action Command during the invasion of Russia. He was later selected to lead Action 1005, responsible for exhuming and burning bodies of Einsatzgruppen victims. Arrested at the end of the war, he was executed by hanging in 1951.	
Otto Bradfisch	SS-Obersturmbannführer	Einsatzkommondo 8 (Russia)	Bradfisch joined the SS in 1938 and became an SD officer, serving in the city of Neustadt. After the invasion of Poland, he commanded SD forces in Lodz, later deploying to command a Special Action Command in Russia. He served six years of a fifteen year sentence after the war.	
Ernst Damzog	SS-Brigadeführer und Generalmajor der Polizei	Einsatzgruppe V (Poland)	A Gestapo officer during the 1930s, Damzog was deployed as a Special Action leader in Poland, later serving as Inspector of Security Police in the city of Posen. In 1940, he assisted with the establishment of the first Jewish death camps. Transferred back to Germany, he was killed in action in 1945.	
Erich Ehrlinger	SS-Oberführer	Einsatzgruppe B, Einsatzkommondo 1b & 4a (Russia)	A lawyer in the 1930s, Ehrlinger was an SA officer who transferred to the SS in 1935. After joining the SS, he served in the SD offices of Vienna and Prague until recruited into the Einsatzgruppen in 1939. He later served in police and SD positions in Central and Western Russia. Sentenced to 12 years in prison, he died in 2004.	

Photograph	SS Officer	Rank	Special Action Command	Biography
	Lothar Fendler	SS-Sturmbannführer	Einsatzkommondo 4b (Russia)	A dentist, Fendler joined the SS in 1933 and by 1935 had transferred to the SD. He served in the SS Foreign Intelligence (Ausland-SD) until 1941 when he was deployed to Russia to lead an Einsatzkommondo. He was found guilty after the war of war crimes and sentenced to ten years.
	Wilhelm Füchs	SS-Oberführer und Oberst der Schutzpolizei	Einsatzgruppe III (Poland), Einsatzgruppe A & E (Russia), Einsatzgruppe Serbien (Yugoslavia)	An SD officer from the city of Braunschweig, Füchs held a doctorate from the University of Leipzig prior to joining the SS in 1932. He served in a Polish Einsatzgruppen before appointed to two separate Russian based units in 1941. In 1944, he was deployed to Serbia; after the war, Füchs was executed.
	Helmut Glaser	SS-Sturmbannführer	Einsatzgruppe I (Poland)	Holding a PhD from the University of Vienna, Glaser joined the SS in 1930, later entering the SD as a legal officer. During the invasion of Poland, he was deployed to lead a Special Action Command and later commanded the SD forces in Krakow. He survived the war free of prosecution.
	Heinz Jost	SS-Brigadeführer und Generalmajor der Polizei	Einsatzgruppe Dresden (Czechoslovakia), Einsatzgruppe A (Russia)	A lawyer and Nazi Party member since 1928, Jost joined the SS in 1934 after briefly serving as a police official. He rose to become head of SD Foreign Intelligence until replaced after a falling out with Reich Security Chief Reinhard Heydrich. Jost commanded two Special Action groups during the war and was later found guilty of war crimes. He died in 1964.
	Waldemar Klingelhöfer	SS-Sturmbannführer	Vorkommando Moscow (Russia), Einsatzgruppe B (Russia)	A World War I veteran and professional singer, Klingelhöfer joined the SS in 1933 and the SD two years later. He served as an SD staff officer in the district of Fulda-Werra, joining SD foreign intelligence in 1939. He served in two Special Action groups and was later sentenced to death; his sentence was commuted in 1956.

SS Officer	Rank	Special Action Command	Biography	Photograph
Josef Kreuzer	SS-Standartenführer und Oberst der Schutzpolizei	Einsatzgruppe G (Romania)	A lawyer and Nazi Party member since 1933, Kreuzer joined the SS in 1933 and served as a Gestapo officer in Cologne and also as a police official in Hamburg. He joined the Einsatzgruppen in 1944, posted to Romania and later southern Russia. He died in 1958.	
Rudolf Lange	SS-Standartenführer	Einsatzgruppe A (Poland), Einsatzkommondo 2 (Russia)	A lawyer fluent in English and French, Lange was a Gestapo officer in the 1930s, deployed during World War II as an SD commander in Latvia and Lithuania. He served as an SD commando leader in the Einsatzgruppen and was present at the Wannsee Conference of 1942. He was killed in action in Poland in 1945.	
August von Meyszner	SS-Gruppenführer und Generalleutnant der Polizei	Einsatzgruppe Serbien (Yugoslavia)	An Austrian by birth, Meyszner was a World War I veteran of the Austrian Army and career police officer. He joined the SS in 1935 and during World War II served in various SS and Police Leader posts as well as commanding a Special Action Unit in Yugoslavia. After the war, he was executed for war crimes.	
Arthur Nebe		Einsatzgruppe B (Russia)	A career police detective during the 1920s, Nebe joined both the SA and SS, becoming head of the Criminal Police (Kripo) in 1936. He served as an Einsatzgruppen leader in Russia in 1941 and recommended "gentler methods" to the carnage of mass shootings. Implicated in a plot to kill Hitler, he was executed in 1945.	
Otto Ohlendorf		Einsatzgruppe D (Russia)	A lawyer and economist, Ohlendorf joined the SS in 1936. Appointed head of SS and SD Internal Intelligence in 1939, he later served as an Einsatzgruppen leader in Russia. Arrested after the war, his frank and uncensored testimony was used to convict both himself and fellow Nazis. He was executed in 1951.	

Photograph	SS Officer	Rank	Special Action Command	Biography
	Otto Rasch	SS-Brigadeführer und Generalmajor der Polizei	Einsatzgruppe Prag (Czech Republic), Einsatzgruppe z.b.V. von Woyrsch (Poland), Einsatzgruppe C (Russia)	An early member of the Special Action Groups, Rasch joined the SS in 1933 and was an SD and Sipo officer, deployed in early SS actions in the Czech Republic and Poland. He commanded an Einsatzgruppen in 1941, shortly afterwards being placed on the inactive SS list. He died from illness in 1948.
	Udo von Woyrsch	SS-Obergruppenführer und General der Polizei und Waffen-SS	Einsatzgruppe z.b.V. von Woyrsch (Poland)	An early SS and Nazi Party member, von Woyrsch held senior Allgemeine-SS positions in the 1930s and was a military district leader in the 1940s. Appointed to command his own personally named Einsatzgruppen in Poland, which engaged in the first concentrated efforts of Jewish extermination, von Woyrsch was known for his brutality and was sentenced to prison after World War II. He died in 1983.

The Babi Yar massacre claimed the lives of 33,771 victims, nearly a third of which were women and children. The overall commander of the Babi Yar massacre, SS-Standartenführer Paul Blobel, would return to Babi Yar two years later, when the bodies of massacre victims were exhumed and burned to destroy evidence of genocidal crimes.

The ravine at Babi Yar in 1943. The persons seen in the photograph are engaged in exhuming the bodies of victims in order to conceal evidence of genocide. Most of those assigned to this detail were themselves then killed (Polish State Archives)

Although the massacre at Babi Yar remains one of the worst atrocities perpetrated by the SS-Einsatzgruppen, it was certainly not the only such act committed. The city of Kamenets-Podolski, in the south western Ukraine, experienced a similar massacre of over twenty thousand Jews murdered. Further mass killings took place in several other well-known Russian cities such as Vilna, Grodno, Bialystok, Smolensk, and Minsk. Most SS officers and men who served in the Einsatzgruppen would later be folded into combat units, and many of the perpetrators of genocide would themselves be killed against advancing Allied and Russian forces. For those SS men who did survive the war, justice would be dealt out to only a few, with many of the junior Einsatzgruppen soldiers fading into history without having to answer for their crimes.

Formalizing Extermination

The years of 1939 thru 1941 had been practically brutal on Poland, which by 1942 was little more than a slave labor colony of Germany. While the Poles suffered under German rule, the Jews interned within the Polish ghettos experienced even further hardship with rampant disease, starvation, and brutality at the hands of their German overseers. On the broader front, by the winter of 1941 the German war machine had at last met its match in the wintered expanses of Russia. As the German Army stalled just outside the gates of Moscow, Adolf Hitler personally assumed command of the German Army as Commander-in-Chief, dismissing and replacing Field Marshal Walther von Brauchitsch. To add even further to Germany's dilemma, Hitler declared war on the United States on December the 11th, countering the United States' similar declaration to Japan two days earlier in response to the attack on Pearl Harbor.

The ghettos of Poland had always been seen as merely a temporary measure for Jewish internment. A "final solution" to the question of the Jews had yet to be reached by German leaders officially; although, in the killing fields of Eastern Europe, the Einsatzgruppen had been slaughtering Jews in what many of the SS leadership saw as a viable program of annihilation. Even so, the steppes of rural Russia were quite a different environment from the cities of Germany and Western Europe, and so for Jews living in those areas, such harsh tactics had yet to be imposed. The formation of Ghettos outside of Poland had been discussed for some time by SS leaders, with several new Ghettos established in 1941 in areas of occupied Russia. These ghettos, in contrast to their Polish counterparts, were seen as registration and collection centers as a prelude for extermination, rather than permanent living facilities.

A scene from a Polish ghetto in 1942. By this point, thousands of Jews had died due to poor conditions and deliberate abuse (Holocaust Memorial Museum)

Indeed, in contrast to the false sense of administrative legality which the Polish ghettos seemed to employ through Jewish government, the ghettos in Russia were run entirely by the SS and were periodically liquidated by the Einsatzgruppen by way of mass killings.

One significant ghetto established outside of Poland was located in the German Protectorate of Bohemia and Moravia (formerly Czechoslovakia) and was known as "Terezín". It was here that the Germans established a combined Ghetto and Concentration Camp which became known to the outside world as Theresienstadt. Originally a Czech military fortress, Theresienstadt began its existence as a prison for use by the Gestapo. On June 14th 1940, the first inmates arrived and were imprisoned in a citadel known as the "Small Fortress" across the Ohře River from the main Terezín fort.

In November 1941, the SS began to convert the Terezín fort into a large concentration camp which was subsequently organized as a ghetto yet classified as a "KZ" (concentration camp) in addition to designation as a transit camp.

MAJOR JEWISH GHETTOS OF EUROPE (1941 - 1944)

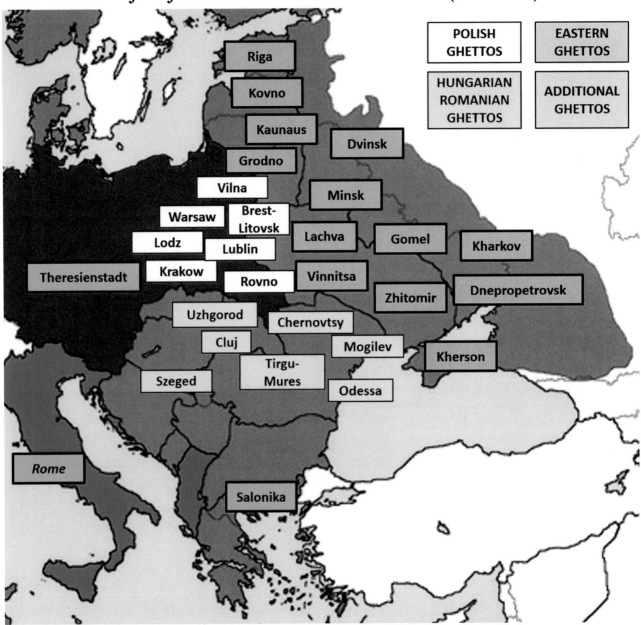

The Jewish ghettos of Europe as they existed from 1942 through 1944.
The Jewish quarter of Rome was a previously existing community before German occupation in 1943

The Theresienstadt ghetto was originally intended to house Czech Jews, but eventually became a holding area for famous and prominent Jewish persons from all over Europe. These were Jews whom the Nazi government either wanted to protect for propaganda reasons or who were considered useful due to their background and skills. The ghetto at Terezín was also used for the "retirement" of elderly Jews, over the age of sixty-five, who were either decorated war veterans or who held some other sort of special exemption under the Nazi racial laws and policies.

The Theresienstadt Ghetto was under the overall administration of the Reich Central Security Office, instead of the Concentration Camp Directorate, with the ghetto commandants all having backgrounds in Adolf Eichmann's Central Office for Jewish Emigration[viii]. SS guards of the Theresienstadt ghetto were mainly recruited from the Waffen-SS and assisted by local Czech police of the Gendarmerie.

By 1943, there were forty thousand inhabitants of Theresienstadt. A governmental "Judenrat" was allowed to exist (officially known as the "Cultural Council") and it was this body which was responsible for the day to day running of the Ghetto as well as the implementation of orders and directives received from German authorities. The Ghetto also maintained a Jewish police force, fire brigade, as well as its own currency system.

The main gate of the Theresienstadt "Little Fortress" at the Terezín Concentration Camp-Ghetto (Holocaust Memorial Museum)

In the summer of 1944, partly due to the somewhat better conditions in which Theresienstadt inmates allegedly lived, the camp was the site of a propaganda film entitled "A Documentary Film from the Jewish Settlement Area". This documentary, of which only twenty-two minutes still survive today, describes the "pleasant conditions" in which ghetto inhabitants lived. In preparation for the film, the SS administration of Theresienstadt undertook several weeks of a "beautification project" in which the ghetto was made to outwardly appear civilized with well-dressed and nourished inhabitants. The finale of the project was a visit to the ghetto by the Danish Red Cross, who were escorted through Theresienstadt on a carefully guided tour.

The corresponding documentary film was produced by the Jews themselves, headed by famous German Jewish actor and director Kurt Gerron. Within weeks of the film's completion, Gerron and most of those who had appeared in the documentary were themselves deported from Theresienstadt and killed in extermination centers. Theresienstadt was then completely evacuated in May of 1945 with all remaining inmates placed in the custody of the International Red Cross. Theresienstadt was liberated by the Soviet Red Army on May 8th 1945.

Elsewhere in Western Europe, where no ghettos had been established nor any Einsatzgruppen deployed, Jews experienced the tried and tested methods of registration, segregation, and oppression. Every country occupied by Nazi Germany was required to enact modified versions of the Nuremberg Laws designed to eliminate Jews of all their rights and citizenship. In countries which were allied to Germany (such as Italy, Bulgaria, Norway, and Romania) German diplomatic pressure encouraged these nations to pass their own anti-Semitic laws to oppress their national Jews. In 1940, to make Western European Jews outwardly and easily identifiable, German authorities began implementing regulations for Jewish identification badges to be worn at all times in public. These "Jewish Star Decrees", based on similar regulations passed earlier in Poland, were eventually implemented throughout Germany, Austria, Czechoslovakia, as well as all countries either allied with or occupied by Germany.

By the fall of 1941, after thousands had died under Einsatzgruppen actions, SS leaders had been tasked with finding more efficient methods to murder and exterminate Jews as well as deal with overcrowding in the Polish ghettos. In the long term, the SS hoped to enact a continent-wide policy to deal with all Jews of the Greater German Reich and Western Europe. The actual decision to kill all the Jews of Europe had been in the mind of Adolf Hitler for years beforehand, yet it was not until a verbal directive was made to Luftwaffe Commander Hermann Göring, in the summer of 1941, that Hitler formally sanctioned complete Jewish extermination. Göring in turn directed the implementation of such measures to the Reich Leader of the SS, Heinrich Himmler, who then designated the actual implementation of extermination to the head of SS security services Reinhard Heydrich.

Upon receiving the order to kill all Jews in Europe, Heydrich looked to the expertise of the Einsatzgruppen, which had by this point been engaging in wholescale murder for several months. While it was clear that mass shootings were impractical for murder on the scale of millions, the Einsatzgruppen had also experimented with other killing methods such as dynamite and most important of all poison gas. Carbon monoxide was the most promising, as it had already been used effectively in the T4 euthanasia program and also by the gas vans of the Einsatzgruppen.

In October of 1941, Reinhard Heydrich ordered the surveying of sites in Poland for possible extermination centers. These centers would consist of a permanent gassing facility, designed to kill prisoners with carbon monoxide gas, as well as an attached concentration camp for prisoner trustees who would assist in the killing process and dispose of the bodies. The following month, SS-Sturmbannführer Herbert Lange (no relation to Einsatzkommondo leader Rudolf Lange) located an abandoned manor house on the outskirts of the Polish town of Chełmno. With adequate land in the surrounding estate grounds, Lange proceeded to construct Nazi Germany's first death camp. The manor house was converted into a gas chamber while SS and prisoner facilities were built in the surrounding estate grounds. The camp was officially named "Kulmhof" and was staffed and managed entirely by members of the Security Police and SD, in the same manner as an Einsatzgruppen.

JEWISH IDENTIFICATION BADGES OF NAZI EUROPE

Country	Implementation	Emblem
Occupied Poland	November 23rd 1939	
Eastern Poland, Baltic Countries, Occupied Russia	July 13th 1941	
Luxembourg	August 1st 1942	
Hungary	March 31st 1944	
Romania	August 8th 1941	
Germany, Austria, Protectorate of Bohemia & Moravia	September 1st 1941	
Slovakia	September 9th 1941	
The Netherlands	April 29th 1942	
Belgium	June 3rd 1942	
France	June 7th 1942	
Bulgaria	August 12th 1942	

*Jewish identification badge graphics recreations based
on original images courtesy of the Holocaust Memorial Museum*

The SS unit assigned to Chełmno was first known as the "SS-Sonderkommando Lange" (named after its first commander) later changing its name to the "Sonderkommando Kulmhof". The first on-site killings took place in December 1941, when Jews evacuated from the nearby Lodz Ghetto were murdered by gassing. To facilitate body disposal, a second camp (known as Waldlager) was constructed two miles away from Kulmhof in a small forest enclosure where bodies were buried in mass graves.

The primary purpose of Chełmno was to exterminate all Jews living in the Wartheland District of German occupied Poland. In March of 1943, with this mission considered complete, the Chełmno camp was shut down with many of the victims' bodies exhumed and burned by the Action 1005 Einsatzgruppen. In April of 1944, to murder some 70,000 Jews from the Lodz Ghetto who had previously been considered essential to war production, Chełmno was reopened and was now known as the "SS-Sonderkommando Bothmann". The killings finally ended on January 18th 1945 when Chełmno was closed permanently and the last of the Jewish inmates were shot. By this time, nearly three hundred and fifty thousand victims had died at Chełmno.

Right: One of the only known photographs of the manor house at Chełmno. Victims were taken to gassing facilities fifty at a time, their bodies later removed after death by other Jewish inmates (Holocaust Memorial Museum)

While Chełmno had served to exterminate Jews locally in the Wartheland District, the goal to eliminate all the Jews of Europe would require much grander plans involving larger extermination facilities, millions of victims, and a vast array of logistics and bureaucracy. In December of 1941, Reinhard Heydrich called for a meeting of top Nazi Party, SS, and German officials to discuss these issues. The meeting would outline Nazi plans for the extermination of the Jews, discuss the exact procedures and methods to be used, and (most importantly) establish the SS as the primary agency which would oversee the killings. With the entry of America into World War II, as well as the retreat of the German Army before the gates of Moscow, the meeting called by Heydrich was postponed for one month until January 20th 1942. On that day, at a lake side mansion converted into an SS conference center in the Berlin suburb of Wannsee, Heydrich and other Nazi leaders met to discuss what would become known as the "Final Solution of the Jewish Question", an action which would formally begin the Holocaust and genocide of all Jews throughout Europe.

The Wannsee Conference

By the end of 1941, the SS-Einsatzgruppen had been murdering victims for several months and the Chełmno extermination camp had been in operation since the previous fall. The SS leadership had further enacted a plan to exterminate the Jews of Poland in what would be known as "Operation Reinhard" (named after Reinhard Heydrich). The purpose of the Wannsee Conference, held in January 1942, was therefore not to make the actual decision to exterminate the Jews of Europe (a decision which had already been made) but rather to assert that the SS would control the genocide actions and to outline a plan by which other Nazi government agencies would operate.

There were fifteen persons in attendance at the Wannsee Conference, which lasted just over ninety minutes. The conference was chaired by SS-Obergruppenführer Reinhard Heydrich, with nearly half of the attendees members of the SS. Half the participants were also lawyers, while the ages of the conference participants ranged from thirty-five to fifty-one years of age. Conspicuously absent from the Wannsee Conference were any members of the German armed forces, although some of the participants were reserve military officers. The Waffen-SS was also un-represented and, most surprisingly of all, there were no attendees from the Concentration Camp service, which was to be the agency designated to carry out the actual genocide of the Jews in the death chambers of such camps as Auschwitz, Treblinka, Majdanek, Belzec, and Sobibor.

PARTICIPANTS OF THE WANNSEE CONFERENCE

Photograph	Name	Agency	Rank	Age	Education
	Reinhard Heydrich	Reich Central Security Office (RSHA)	SS-Obergruppenführer und General der Polizei	37	Naval College
	Josef Bühler	General Government of Poland	State Secretary		Law School
	Adolf Eichmann	Gestapo Jewish Affairs Office (RSHA IV-B4)	SS-Obersturmbannführer	35	Secondary School
	Roland Freisler	Reich Ministry of Justice	Chairman and Secretary of the Peoples Court	48	Law School
	Otto Hofmann	SS Race and Settlement Main Office (RuSHA)	SS-Gruppenführer	45	Vocational School
	Gerhard Klopfer	Nazi Party Chancellery	NSDAP-Befehlsleiter, Permanent Secretary, SA-Obergruppenführer	36	Law School

Name	Agency	Rank	Age	Education	Photograph
Friedrich Wilhelm Kritzinger	Reich Chancellery	Permanent Secretary	51	Law School	
Rudolf Lange	Commander SS Security Forces Latvia	SS-Sturmbannführer	31		
Georg Leibbrandt	Reich Ministry for the Occupied Eastern Territories	Reichs-Amtsleiter	42	Philosophy Doctorate	
Martin Luther	Reich Foreign Ministry	Under Secretary	46	Vocational School	
Alfred Meyer	Reich Ministry for the Occupied Eastern Territories	NSDAP-Gauleiter, State Secretary, Deputy Reich Minister	50	Doctorate of Political Science	
Heinrich Müller	Chief of the Gestapo	SS-Gruppenführer und Generalleutnant der Polizei	41	Secondary School	

Photograph	Name	Agency	Rank	Age	Education
	Erich Neumann	Office of the Four Year Plan	State Secretary	49	University Degree (Economics)
	Karl Eberhard Schöngarth	Commander SIPO and SD forces in the General Government of Poland	SS-Oberführer	38	Law School
	Wilhelm Stuckart	Reich Interior Ministry	State Secretary	39	

Wannsee conference participant images courtesy of the National Archives and Federal German Archives

The Wannsee conference was formally opened by Reinhard Heydrich, addressing the participants in a greeting, and then stating that the "Final Solution to the Jewish Question" (in some texts, this has been translated as the "Complete Solution") had been directed by Reich Marshal Hermann Göring. Heydrich also clarified that Heinrich Himmler, as head of the SS and Chief of the German Police, had been tasked with implementing the specifics. An overview was then provided of anti-Jewish measures thus far, including a somewhat lengthy description of the Central Office for Jewish Emigration which had been established in the 1930s to emigrate Jews from Germany and Austria. Heydrich then stated that emigration from the Reich had been permanently suspended as of December 1941 due to war time restrictions, particularly due to the entry of America into the conflict and the dangers of European Jews immigrating into enemy countries.

The second segment of Heydrich's oratory included a phrase which would be used widespread in the Holocaust to avoid the mention of genocide in official documents. Coined as "Evacuation to the East", Heydrich explained that the new Jewish policy would involve relocating all European Jews to resettlement camps in the eastern lands of conquered Russia, where such Jews would be put to work in rural labor projects such as building construction works and paving roads. The scope of such a relocation was then discussed, at which time Adolf Eichmann provided statistics for the number of Jews living in Europe which tallied at over eleven million persons. In Eichmann's description, he also indicated that these numbers included some Jews living in countries not controlled or occupied by Germany, and also that there was a distinction between "racial Jewry", meaning persons physically identified as Jews based on their outward appearance, as compared to Jews who were classified as such simply by following the stated religion.

Heydrich next shifted the discussion to Jews living in the Soviet Union. Of the five million Jews living in the European portion of the Soviet Union, Adolf Eichmann provided percentages for Jews based on occupation; specific numbers were provided for agriculture, urban employees, trade workers, state employees, as well as a catch all category for "other occupations". The interest in the Russian Jewish population was based on the large-scale extermination actions which had already taken place by the SS-Einsatzgruppen. There was also a general interest in Russian Jews from the conference participants, given that four of those in attendance were Russian language speakers while two of them

(Freisler and Leibbrandt) had traveled and lived extensively in Russia. During the course of the discussion, Reinhard Heydrich gave the first official definition of the term "evacuation", thus setting an official policy, insofar as what measures would await those resettled in the east.

> *"Able bodied Jews, separated according to sex, will be taken in large work columns to those areas for work on roads, in the course of action doubtless a large portion will be eliminated by natural causes. The possible final remnant will, since it will undoubtedly consist of the most resistant portion, have to be treated accordingly." –Reinhard Heydrich (1942)*

Heydrich next stated that all the Jews of Europe would eventually be evacuated to the east under the definition previously provided. The conference attendees knew perfectly well what truly awaited any Jew transported east, with Rudolf Lange (who had commanded a death squad in the Baltic region) commenting that his Einsatzkommondo had already "evacuated" several thousand Jews by shooting them. Heydrich apparently let the comment pass, moving into the next topic of the conference which was the reaction of German allies to the resettlement and evacuation programs against the Jews.

Specifically mentioned were Slovakia, Croatia, Italy, France, Romania, and Hungary. Finland and Norway were referenced simply as "Scandinavian countries" while other nations were referred to by their geographical region of Europe. The attendees at the Wannsee Conference saw no difficulty implementing German policies in puppet states and firmly controlled allies, yet some concern was raised regarding Scandinavia, with a suggestion made by Nazi diplomat Martin Luther that these countries be excluded from the Final Solution. A type of "power struggle" then occurred when speaking of Hungary, a nation which was then still a sovereign state and ally to Germany (Hungary would later be occupied by German forces in 1944), when Otto Hofmann, head of the SS Race and Settlement Office, stated that the best way to implement German policies in Hungary was to send an SS liaison from his office to that nation. Reinhard Heydrich immediately countered that any such liaison should be appointed from the Reich Central Security Office and not the SS Race and Resettlement Office. Heydrich, possibly through intimidation, quickly secured Hofmann's understanding that Heydrich's personnel would oversee implementing Jewish policies in Hungary.

Throughout the Wannsee Conference, a great deal of emphasis was placed on the specific classification method to determine who in Europe would be regarded as a Jew. Using the Nuremberg Laws as a basis, the status of Jews from mixed marriages was also discussed, as well as who would ultimately be subject to the evacuation orders of the Final Solution. The ghetto at Theresienstadt was designated as a possible location for Jews exempt from evacuation measures, a decision which brought about a debate amongst the conference participants. Specifically, using sterilization rather than deportation was discussed as a means to prevent Jews from bearing more children to the Jewish race. Otto Hofmann was one such proponent of sterilization, and further favored a non-voluntary sterilization medical procedure against the German Jewish population.

Wilhelm Stuckart, who had been one of the primary authors of the Nuremberg Laws, stated that splitting up Aryan and Jewish married couples would create an administrative burden with regards to divorce petitions filed by deserted German spouses. Stuckart suggested a national divorce declaration, nullifying all mixed Jewish and Aryan marriages in Germany, but was mostly opposed to this idea by the other conference participants, many of whom simply recommended sterilizing Jews in mixed marriages and allowing them to remain living in Germany. Heydrich apparently ended the debate by declaring that evacuation directives would stand as discussed and that most mixed Jews would be treated as full members of the race, unless extreme cases for exemption were approved.

The last twenty minutes of the Wannsee Conference were occupied by a "discussion of methods and solutions to be used with regards to evacuation". It is at this point that the written record fails to describe the uncensored conversation which took place; however, from verbal accounts of those conference members who survived the Second World War, the participants spent the last half of the meeting openly speaking about genocide and various means which could be employed to kill the Jews of Europe. It was at this point that Rudolf Lange gave accounts of mass shootings, gas vans, and other atrocities in Russia. Adolf Eichmann further shared information regarding successful experiments with poison gas, including carbon monoxide poisoning, and then revealed plans to convert the concentration camp of Auschwitz into a mass killing center. When Eichmann further revealed that the construction of three smaller death camps in Poland was already underway (referencing Sobibor, Treblinka, and Belzec), the conference attendees from the General Government of Poland and Eastern Territories Ministry were markedly upset as they saw this as a usurpation of their authority.

Jewish Racial Classifications

FULL JEWISH

Parents and any children evacuated

CHILDLESS MIXED MARRIAGES

Jewish spouse evacuated on a case by case basis

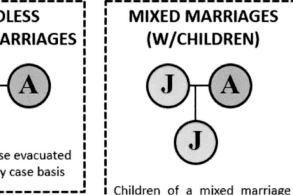

MIXED MARRIAGES (W/CHILDREN)

Children of a mixed marriage to be considered as Jews and evacuated. If the children were married to an Aryan spouse, exemptions may apply

SECOND DEGREE MIXED JEWISH CHILDREN

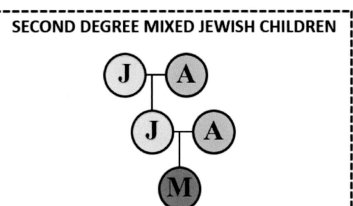

Children of a mixed marriage where the parent was themselves a mixed Jew (1st degree mixed) would be considered as "2nd degree mixed Jews" and declared exempt from evacuation. Exceptions would be made for those persons who outwardly appeared or acted as a Jew or who had an unreliable police or political record. In those cases, the 2nd degree mixed Jew would be evacuated.

EXEMPTIONS

Exemptions from evacuation were to be made for Jewish spouses of full Aryans on a case by case basis. Exemptions would also be made for Jews over the age of 65, those Jews already granted exemption by the Nazi government, or highly decorated Jews from the First World War. In such cases, the Jews would be relocated to the Theresienstadt Ghetto.

Jewish racial classifications as defined by the Wannsee Conference. In the depicted table, (J) indicates Jewish ancestry, (A) for Aryan, and (M) indicates mixed Jewish & Aryan heritage.

Heydrich called the Wannsee Conference to a close after an hour and a half, and offered the participants one last round to voice concerns before the meeting was adjourned. None of the conference participants voiced any objections to what had been discussed, with only one comment made regarding exemption of Jewish workers in essential war industries (a stipulation to which Heydrich agreed) as well as a plea from the Eastern Territories Ministry to enact the Final Solution in Poland first (rather than Germany) due to severe overcrowding of the ghettos. The participants of the Wannsee Conference then departed the meeting and returned to their various offices and responsibilities, seemingly accepting what was to come with regard to the fate of the Jews of Europe.

Heydrich, who was now the self-proclaimed architect behind the Final Solution extermination program, was killed just five months later by Czech partisans in Prague. The task of implementing the Final Solution then fell to Adolf Eichmann, who had kept the minutes of the Wannsee Conference, and was thereafter appointed as "Transportation Administrator" in charge of deporting the Jews of Europe to extermination camps in Poland. Eichmann would survive the Second World War, escape to Argentina, where he was eventually kidnapped by Israeli agents. He was then flown to Jerusalem, put on trial for crimes against humanity, and sentenced to death by hanging. Eichmann was executed in Israel on June 1st 1962, just over twenty years from the time of the Wannsee Conference.

The only participant of the Wannsee Conference who attempted to actively oppose the measures put forth was Friedrich Kritzinger. Following the conference, Kritzinger attempted to resign his position at the Reich Chancellery, but his resignation was disapproved by Hitler. Kritzinger died in 1947 after giving testimony against fellow Nazis at the Nuremberg war crimes trial. Post war death and prison sentences awaited many of the Wannsee Conference participants, with both Josef Bühler and Karl Schöngarth executed for war crimes and crimes against humanity. Otto Hofmann served five years in prison, Georg Leibbrandt and Wilhelm Stuckart four years each, while Erich Neumann was sentenced to time served in 1949 after spending three years in Allied captivity. Both Nazi Judge Roland Freisler and SS death squad commander Rudolf Lange did not live to see the end of the Second World War, both being killed in February 1945 by an air raid and enemy action respectively. Alfred Meyer committed suicide in April of 1945, while Gestapo Chief Heinrich Müller disappeared (and was later presumed dead) as Berlin was surrounded by Soviet forces in May 1945.

Nazi diplomat Martin Luther was perhaps the unluckiest of the Wannsee Conference participants, in that he was arrested and sent to a Concentration Camp in 1943 after a falling out with his superior Joachim von Ribbentrop. Liberated in 1945, he was re-arrested by Allied authorities and scheduled for trial, yet died of a heart attack in 1946. It is however Gerhard Klopfer who remains the greatest ambiguity of Wannsee. A dedicated Nazi Party official, as well as a close associate to Reichsleiter Martin Bormann, Klopfer was reported to have opposed the Wannsee measures, thinking the mass extermination directives to be excessive[ix]. While never voicing his discontent publicly, Klopfer did little to promote the Final Solution directives. He was arrested and investigated following the Second World War, but released due to lack of evidence. He also was the last of the Wannsee Conference participants to die, passing away in 1987.

At the conclusion of the Wannsee Conference, Heydrich had directed all participants to maintain secrecy with regards to what had been discussed. The conference minutes were classified as Top Secret and participants advised that they could discuss what had occurred only with superiors. Many senior Nazis, such as Hermann Göring, Heinrich Himmler, and Martin Bormann, already had full knowledge of the Jewish extermination directive, while Hans Frank, Governor General of Poland, was reportedly told of the Wannsee conference after the

Franz Walter Stahlecker, who served as an Einsatzgruppen and SD commander, was briefed by his subordinate Rudolf Lange following the conclusion of the Wannsee Conference in January 1942. (Federal German Archives)

fact and was outraged that the SS had come up with a plan to conduct genocide in his jurisdiction without any forewarning. The same anger was not to be found within the various Reich Ministers to which many of the Wannsee Conference participants reported, as many of these government officials simply accepted what had occurred at Wannsee without debate or protest. In the end, Wannsee was most effective in dealing with the Jews of Central and Western Europe, for which no firm measures had yet been developed as of 1942. In Poland and Eastern Europe, genocide continued unabated with Wannsee simply confirming the actions which had already taken place.

Enacting Genocide

Even before the events the Wannsee Conference, the SS leadership had decided to enact the genocide of Jews in Poland, mainly to alleviate massive ghetto crowding, disease, and black-market activities. The process of killing the Jews of Poland was to be known as "ghetto liquidation" which would involve systematically closing down the Polish ghettos, separating able bodied Jews for slave labor, and then exterminating all who remained either by summary execution or through the use of death camp extermination facilities.

The first organized killing of Polish Jews took place in December of 1941 at the Chełmno Concentration Camp. Chełmno developed the first permanent system to kill Jews through carbon monoxide poisoning and also enacted a method of deception, by convincing Jews they were about to take a shower, then sealing them inside a disguised bathing room, after which the room was filled with poison gas. This system served as a model for Jewish murder and was later enacted at all Nazi death camps.

In January 1942, at the same time of the Wannsee Conference, the SS leadership enacted "Operation Reinhard" which was a code name for the plan to exterminate all Polish Jews interned within ghettos. Operation Reinhard was to make use of three death camps situated in eastern Poland, whose purpose would be to collect, process, and exterminate all Jews living in nearby ghettos. The first permanent death camp of Operation Reinhard was opened at Belzec in March of 1942. At the same time, construction began on two additional extermination death camp facilities at Sobibor and Treblinka. By the summer of 1942, the three main Operation Reinhard camps were in full operation. Mass extermination would continue until October 1943 when the camps were closed after two revolts by the inmates, as well as the impending advance of the Soviet Army. By that time, half a million Jews had died at Belzec with an additional two hundred thousand killed at Sobibor. Treblinka possessed the highest killing number of all the Operation Reinhard camps, with nearly nine hundred thousand deaths attributed to extermination operations.

OPERATION REINHARD ORGANIZATION

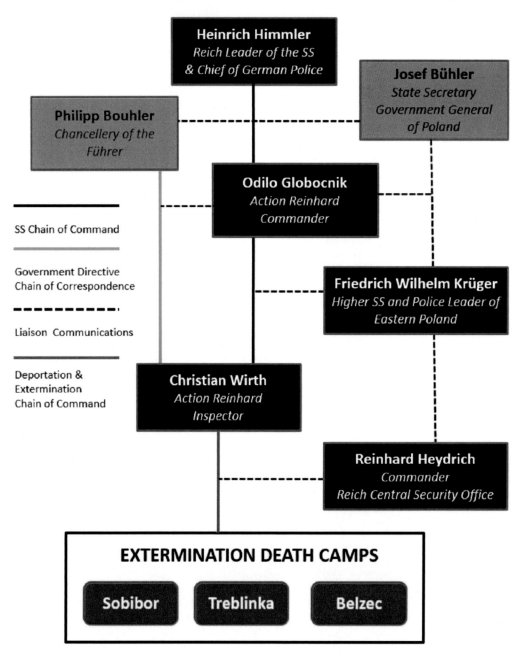

COMMAND AND LEADERSHIP OF OPERATION REINHARD

Name	Rank	Position	Duties	Photograph
Reinhard Heydrich	SS-Obergruppenführer und General der Polizei	Chief of the Reich Central Security Main Office	The mastermind behind the Jewish extermination program, Heydrich oversaw the upper administration of round-ups and deportations to the extermination centers. These duties were often tasked to subordinates, mainly Adolf Eichmann who served as transportation administrator for deportations to the death camps of Poland.	
Friedrich Wilhelm Krüger	SS-Obergruppenführer und General der Polizei und Waffen-SS	Higher SS and Police Leader (Eastern Poland)	As the highest ranking SS officer in eastern Poland, Krüger oversaw several subordinate SS and Police Leaders responsible for ghettos in Polish cities, as well as Jewish evacuations to the death camps in eastern Poland as well as Auschwitz.	
Odilo Globocnik	SS-Gruppenführer und Generalleutnant der Polizei	Action Reinhard Commander	A ruthless SS officer from Austria, Globocnik (known by the nickname "Globus") was the operational commander of the death camp extermination facilities in Poland. He supervised the construction of the three primary death camps and was the immediate superior to the death camp commanders.	
Christian Wirth	SS-Sturmbannführer	Action Reinhard Inspector	The primary deputy of Globocnik, Wirth's duties entailed the implementation of administrative procedures surrounding the Death Camp program, as well as standardization with regards to extermination measures. He was also a Death Camp commander twice himself, commanding at one point both Chełmno and Belzec.	

Images courtesy of the National Archives and Federal German Archives

An often overlooked extermination camp, operating at the same time as the Operation Reinhard facilities, was Maly Trostenets located outside the Soviet city of Minsk. Originally opened in 1941 as a prisoner-of-war-camp, in May 1942 the camp had been converted into an extermination facility, using gas vans and exterminating mostly German Jews deported east. The camp also assisted the local Einsatzgruppen with the extermination of Jews in the surrounding regions. Over sixty-five thousand Jews perished at Maly Trostenets before the camp was closed in October 1943; the camp was then destroyed by Action 1005 personnel. Maly Trostenets is unique amongst other extermination camps since it was run primarily by the Sicherheitsdienst and seen as an extension of the Einsatzgruppen actions, rather than as a formal extermination camp. The facility was also very small and commanded by a non-commissioned officer titled as "Administrator" rather than "Commandant" as other death camps were. For this reason, Maly Trostenets is often excluded from lists of the major Nazi death camps of the Second World War.

Apart from the Operation Reinhard camps, the SS also upgraded two previously existing concentration camps to incorporate extermination facilities. The first was at Majdanek, a concentration camp located on the outskirts of Lublin, which was outfitted with carbon monoxide gas chambers in September 1942. The second was the concentration camp of Auschwitz.

An elderly Jewish woman being abused sometime in 1942. By the fall of 1943, Heinrich Himmler had ordered all Polish ghettos be closed and the remaining Jews exterminated (Holocaust Memorial Museum)

Following the conversion of these two camps, on June 21st 1943 Heinrich Himmler issued a decree ordering the dissolution of all Polish ghettos and ordered all remaining Jews to either be exterminated or imprisoned in concentration camps. By that November, the gas chambers at Majdanek were refitted for use of the more potent poison "Zyklon-B", and then began mass killings as part of "Aktion Erntefest" (Operation Harvest Festival) aimed at killing all remaining Jews in Poland. In the first week of extermination, over twenty thousand Jews were eliminated with a total of sixty thousand dead by the end of 1943. The camp at Majdanek was liberated by the Soviet Army in July of 1944, nearly completely intact, offering the first irrefutable evidence of Nazi and SS extermination actions.

Of all the Nazi death camps, it is Auschwitz which has become most infamously associated with the Holocaust. Originally a concentration camp for Polish political prisoners and Russian prisoners-of-war, Auschwitz was expanded to become one the largest camps in the Nazi system as well as the primary camp in which Jewish exterminations were conducted. In all, over a million Jews were killed by gassing at Auschwitz while countless more died as a result of maltreatment, disease, and starvation. The camp was further known for brutality, slave labor, and medical experimentation. First opened in 1940, the camp was evacuated in January 1945 and captured by the Red Army shortly thereafter.

While Operation Reinhard was designed to exterminate the Jews of Poland, Auschwitz was used for the extermination of all remaining Jews in Europe, specifically from the western and southern regions of the continent. Deportation directives were issued to various occupied and allied countries, in accordance with the design of the Wannsee Conference, and specified that Jews should be rounded up and detained at a central location then "evacuated east" for extermination. This design led to the creation of the Transit Camp - a make shift concentration camp whose sole purpose was to collect Jews for deportation east to Auschwitz. Two of the most notorious transit camps were at Drancy in France and Westerbork in the Netherlands. Both French and Dutch collaborationist authorities arrested Jews for confinement in these facilities, which were themselves known for brutality, starvation, and disease, before ultimately transporting the Jewish prisoners east to Auschwitz. In all, over a hundred thousand were deported from Westerbork while sixty-eight thousand were deported from Drancy. Deportees were crammed into cattle car rolling stock for the journey east, often without food or water, and forced to endure a journey of several days with no sanitary facilities. Deaths on the trip were common, and upon arrival at Auschwitz those surviving were quickly gassed on site at the Auschwitz extermination facilities.

Jewish ghettos, concentration camps, and death camps of Poland

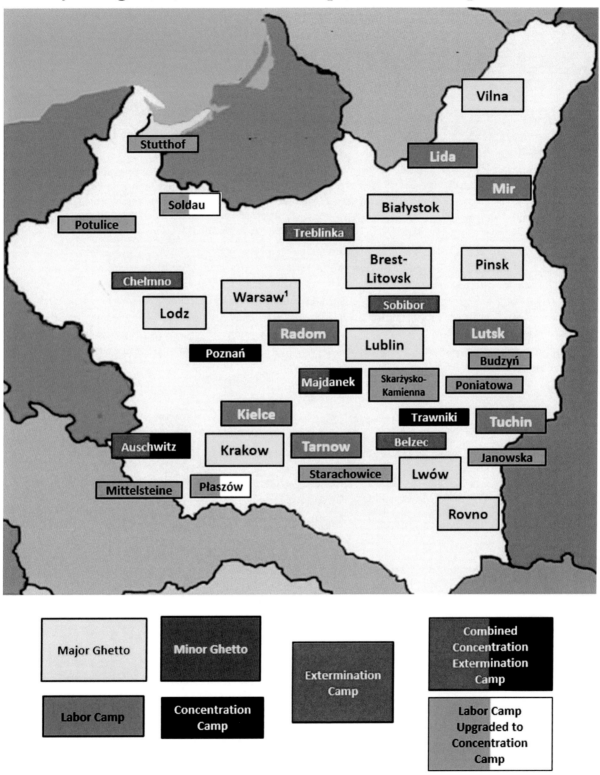

¹ The city of Warsaw contained six internal camps, collectively referred to as the "Warsaw Concentration Camp"

The mass deportations of Jews across Europe created a large administrative burden on German bureaucracy, which was already overwhelmed with the logistical requirements of wartime. Adolf Eichmann, who had served as Heydrich's deputy at the Wannsee Conference and as transportation administrator for Jewish deportations, was ultimately responsible for chartering trains to deport Jews to Auschwitz, as well coordinating deportation schedules with local officials.

A cattle car converted for the transport of Jews to Auschwitz. Dozens of persons would be crammed inside without food, water, or adequate ventilation and sanitary facilities. (Graphical recreation based on photograph courtesy of Holocaust Memorial Museum)

At first, few Polish Jews were killed at Auschwitz since Poles were mainly sent to the smaller death camps of Sobibor, Treblinka, and Belzec as part of Operation Reinhard. The German Jews, with a wartime population of nearly two hundred and fifteen thousand, were typically deported first to one of the major Polish Ghettos (mainly at Lodz) and then killed in one of the smaller death camps. After 1942, German Jews were sent further east to ghettos in Riga, Kaunas, and Minsk, where they were immediately shot or worked to death. In 1943, the last of Germany's Jews were deported directly to Auschwitz.

In some nations, such as France and the Low Countries, authorities participated whole heartedly with the registration, round-up, and deportation of Jews. Other countries were not so forthcoming, such as Denmark which managed to avoid any significant deportations as well as the Scandinavian countries which outright refused to deport Jews. Areas under direct German control were not as fortunate, such as Greece in which two thirds of the Jewish population were sent to Auschwitz and slaughtered, as well as Slovakia (a German puppet state) which deported over fifty percent of its Jews.

A steam locomotive of the German Reichsbahn (Federal Rail Service), of which several hundred railway employees participated in deportations to Auschwitz. After the war, there was no serious effort to prosecute these persons. Railway conductors and engineers, who had participated in the Holocaust, frequently claimed to have held little knowledge of their "cargo's" final destination.
(Graphical recreation based on photograph courtesy of Polish State Archives)

Italian deportations to Auschwitz only began after that country's occupation by German forces following the overthrow of Benito Mussolini in 1943. Initially resistant to German calls for Jewish deportations, this changed under the new "Italian Social Republic" when the fascist government cooperated with SS and Nazi officials to round-up and deport several thousand Jews, mostly from Rome.

The Slavic countries of Serbia and Croatia deserve special mention, in that the Jewish population in these regions were not only subject to German extermination directives, but also ethnic cleansing and anti-Semitic programs enacted by the local population. In Serbia, some sixty thousand Jews were deported and killed in Auschwitz. In Croatia, the Ustaše government regime enacted their own Jewish extermination program to rival even the Germans. Croatian authorities formed their own death squads, committed mass executions, and even operated an independent death camp (Jasenovac) in which torture and brutality were commonplace. The German authorities briefly considered using Jasenovac as a "back-up camp" for Auschwitz extermination action, but abandoned these plans when the level of barbarity and cruelty at Jasenovac exceeded even the tolerance of the SS.

Romanian and Hungarian Jewish ghettos and labor camps

Of all the major German allies, Finland was the least cooperative with the Jewish deportation directives, with only eight Jews reported as deported to Auschwitz during the Second World War. Bulgaria was resistant as well, since the Jewish population of that country was well integrated, and the local citizens were mostly outspoken against anti-Semitic directives and policies. This still did not prevent Bulgaria from deporting several thousand Jews (mostly Greek and Macedonian refugees) before halting all deportations in 1944.

The nations of Romania and Hungary were considered extremely important allies of Germany against the Soviet Union, and as such these two nations were initially permitted to retain relative autonomy regarding Jews. Beginning in 1942, at the behest of the German authorities and due to existing anti-Jewish policies in both nations, Romania and Hungary began establishing Jewish ghettos and soon afterwards had converted some of these into labor camps. Actual deportations of Jews to Nazi death camps were still resisted, and Heinrich Himmler ceased asking these two countries to deport Jews in the spring of 1943. Jews in Hungary were to suffer a harsh reprisal in March 1944 when Germany occupied the country after the Hungarian government attempted to negotiate an armistice with the Soviet Union. Adolf Eichmann, who had served as an SS liaison in Hungary a year earlier, returned to that country and began a massive deportation program now fully supported by the pro-German government. Nearly half a million Hungarian Jews were deported to Auschwitz until Himmler ordered a cessation of extermination actions in November 1944. Eichmann then continued his deportation directives for another month against orders, later admitting his zeal was fueled by his hatred of the Jews.

By the end of 1944, knowledge of Germany's extermination program was becoming fairly well known both by Allied governments and even the German populace. As Soviet and Allied forces invaded Germany itself, the liberation of the Concentration Camps offered vast evidence of Nazi and SS crimes. By this time, the death camps of Operation Reinhard had been deliberately destroyed to conceal evidence of genocide; however, both Majdanek and Auschwitz were liberated by the Red Army in 1944 and 1945.

JEWISH HOLOCAUST STATISTICS OF THE SECOND WORLD WAR

Country	Jewish Population	Percentage Population	Extermination Method	Death Toll	Percentage Killed
Germany Austria	240,000	0.35%	Chełmno & Treblinka (1942) / Maly Trostenets (1942 – 1943) / Auschwitz (1943 – 1944)	210,000	90%
Czechoslovakia	357,000	3.4%	Maly Trostenets (1942) / Treblinka & Majdanek (1943)	180,000	50%
Poland	3,300,000	9.5%	Chełmno & Majdanek (1941 – 1943) / Belzec, Sobibor, & Treblinka (1942-1944) / Auschwitz (1944)	3,000,000	90%
Latvia Lithuania Estonia	255,000	5%	Einsatzgruppen Executions (1941 – 1943)	187,000	73%
White Russia	375,000	8.2%		245,000	65%
Central Russia	975,000	3.4%		107,000	11%
Ukraine	1,500,000	5.4%	Maly Trostenets (1942 - 1944)	900,000	60%
Belgium	65,000	0.7%	Auschwitz (1942-1944)	40,000	
France	350,000	0.8%		90,000	26%
Netherlands	156,000	1.8%		105,000	67%
Luxembourg	5,000	1.6%		1,000	20%
Hungary	650,000	5.1%		450,000	70%
Romania	600,000	3%		300,000	50%
Bulgaria	64,000	0.9%		14,000	21%
Croatia	40,000	0.5%	Jasenovac (1943-1944)	31,000	77%
Serbia	80,000	1.7%	Einsatzgruppen Executions (1942 – 1944)	60,000	75%
Albany	200	0.02%	Auschwitz (1942-1944)	192	96%
Italy	48,000	0.11%		8,000	16%
Greece	70,000	1.2%		54,000	77%
Norway	2,170			890	41%
Finland	2,000	0.05%	Eight foreign Jewish refugees were extradited in 1942 and later killed at Auschwitz		
Denmark	5,700	0.94%	470 Jewish deportees were sent to Theresienstadt of which fifty-two died of disease and starvation		
Channel Islands	16	0.02%	Auschwitz (1943)	3	18%

Prior to the Second World War, Europe's Jewish inhabitants stood at nine and half million, which was approximately two percent of the continental population and over fifty percent of all Jews living in the world. During Germany's conquests, sixty five percent of Europe's Jews were exterminated, with a combined death total of approximately six million victims. While over half of Europe's Jews were killed during the Holocaust, nearly as many Gypsies and other "undesirables" (approximately five million in all) perished alongside them under similar extermination directives. Several thousands more Slavs, homosexuals, and political prisoners were also killed. In all, over eleven million people died at the hands of the Nazis and the SS as part of extermination directives during the course of World War II.

Resistance and Security

Since its original inception, the SS served to provide security to the leadership of the Nazi Party and later expanded this role to the protection of the German state. During the 1930s, the SS security apparatus grew from the Nazi Party Sicherheitsdienst (SD) to a state-run security police apparatus; this included both uniformed and plain clothes police officials as well as the secret police forces of the Gestapo. During the Second World War, the SS security services served in a dual role both maintaining order within the German Reich as well as enforcing Nazi doctrine and crushing dissent in occupied territories. Within Germany, the crime of "defeatism" was punishable by death and a special "People's Court" existed to deal with charges against German citizens who were denounced as disloyal to the German state or who otherwise spoke out against the Nazi regime. The People's Court was chaired by Roland Freisler, who had also been present at the Wannsee Conference.

One of the most well-known cases before the People's Court was that of Sophie Scholl, her brother Hans Scholl, and other members of a student resistance group known as the "White Rose". From the summer of 1942 until February 1943, the White Rose distributed anti-Nazi leaflets throughout Munich University; on February 18th 1942, Sophie and Hans were arrested by the Gestapo after a janitor observed the two dropping leaflets from the top floor of a Munich university hall. The chief interrogator of the Scholl siblings was SS-Sturmbannführer and Police Major Robert Mohr. A trained tailor, Mohr had served in the German Army during the First World War and afterwards joined the Bavarian State Police. By 1935, he had risen through the ranks to become the Police Chief of Frankenthal, before transferring to the Gestapo and the SS in 1938. His main assignment for most of the Second World War was as a Gestapo interrogator; between 1939 and 1940 Mohr also was deployed to serve with an Einsatzgruppen.

Sophie Scholl and her brother Hans. The two were sentenced to death by the People's Court for treason, sedition, and aiding the enemy. Robert Mohr, who served as a professional detective under the title "Regierungs-Kriminalrat und SS-Sturmbannführer", supervised the arrest and interrogation of the Scholl siblings and subsequently delivered them to the People's Court for prosecution. After the war, he was briefly detained by French authorities for his administration of a Gestapo post in Alsace, but was never prosecuted. He died in 1977. (Federal German Archives)

As the arresting officer of the Scholl siblings, Mohr was at first sympathetic to Sophie and initially recommended her release. Her brother Hans then made a full confession which implicated Sophie and many others. Afterwards, Sophie freely admitted her guilt to Mohr and her fate was sealed. After a trial before the People's Court, both Sophie Scholl and her brother Hans were executed by guillotine decapitation on February 22nd 1943.

One of the greatest threats to security outside of Germany were partisan and resistance forces in occupied territories. The SS formed numerous paramilitary formations to deal with partisans and even tasked some combat units of the Waffen-SS to perform anti-guerilla actions. Partisans in the east were dealt with swiftly, without mercy, and often through armed military force. This in contrast to Western Europe in which security forces of the Gestapo, aided by the German police and local authorities, investigated and arrested suspected resistance fighters. Towards the end of the war, partisan forces in Southern Europe, particularly Greece and Yugoslavia, became an even larger problem as these forces were often professionally organized and equipped as military units, often directly combating the German Army and in many cases causing German retreats from occupied areas.

The French Resistance was seen as one of more significant threats to German order in the west, with German security forces in occupied France tasked with routing and destroying any suspected French resistance cells. Gestapo agents in France arrested without warrant, tortured and brutalized prisoners, and often committed summary executions of any suspected members of the French Resistance. For a French resistance fighter to fall into German hands was almost a guaranteed death sentence, but only after a long period of abuse and torture.

After the war, French survivors of Gestapo interrogations related stories of beatings, burnings, castrations, the slicing of women's breasts, and even more grisly interrogation methods. Another common tactic of Gestapo agents was to infiltrate resistance cells with spies, then draw out all of the cell's members through staged operations in which German forces would be lying in wait. While this method was highly successful in destroying several French resistance cells, the overall operation of the French resistance was unaffected, and this force became an extremely effective asset to Allied intelligence.

Elsewhere in Europe, partisan groups formed in Greece, the Low Countries, and in Poland. In all cases, both German security forces and armed units of the Waffen-SS were deployed to deal with acts of sabotage, insurrection, and sedition. In Scandinavia, resistance forces in Norway were able to inflict the most damage against the SS, with several assassinations of SS officers occurring between 1942 and 1945. The group most largely responsible was the "Milorg" (militær organisasjon) which took orders from the Norwegian government in exile in England.

It was however in Czechoslovakia in which the most significant resistance attack of the Second World War took place on May 27, 1942. While traveling in an open car from his home to the center of Prague, Reinhard Heydrich was attacked by Czech partisans, all of which had been specially trained in England specifically to kill Heydrich. Heydrich died from his wounds a week later, setting into motion a massive wave of reprisals against the Czech population as well as a manhunt for Heydrich's assassins.

Heydrich was eventually succeeded in all of his offices by Ernst Kaltenbrunner, a far less capable man who was seen as less of a threat to Himmler and the SS leadership. Had Heydrich lived, rumors indicated he would have eventually been posted to Paris in order to oversee the SS suppression of all French Resistance. Even broader speculation has stated Heydrich may have led an underground SS movement after the war against Allied occupation forces, a plan which in reality never materialized due to a lack of will and leadership from surviving SS members and the German public.

Ernest Kaltenbrunner in 1943. Before succeeding Heydrich, Kaltenbrunner had served as head of the SS in Austria (National Archives)

Heydrich's successor Kaltenbrunner did survive the war and was put on trial at Nuremberg as a major Nazi war criminal as well as the highest SS member arrested for war crimes. Kaltenbrunner thus took the brunt of blame for the extermination of Jews, minorities, and other undesirables of the Third Reich. Kaltenbrunner had also been a major SS figure in the annexation of Austria and was responsible for the establishment of the Mauthausen Concentration Camp, in which countless Austrians had died of abuse and starvation. For these and other crimes, Kaltenbrunner was found guilty at Nuremberg and executed by hanging on October 16th 1946.

When Heydrich was assassinated on May 27th 1942, he was acting as the Deputy Reich Protector of Bohemia and Moravia, a post which was the de facto governor of occupied Czechoslovakia. Reinhard Heydrich lived in a mansion north of Prague (known as the Panenské Břežany), along with his family, and his daily commute into the city took approximately forty minutes. Heydrich often made the drive in an open toped Mercedes with no escort, save for a single driver and occasionally a motorcycle guard. On the morning of May 27th, Heydrich had left his home shortly after 9:30 and began his daily commute into the city. The assassination attempt against him occurred in the suburbs of northern Prague, where Heydrich was wounded in a bomb attack on his car, and subsequently died of his injuries on June 4th 1942. In the aftermath of the attack, the Germans launched both a manhunt for Heydrich's assassins as well as reprisals against Czech citizens. This included the razing of two Czech villages, accompanied by the murder and deportation of the inhabitants. Heydrich's attackers were eventually cornered in an Eastern Orthodox Church where, after hours of fighting with SS forces, they committed suicide rather than face capture.

Timeline of the Heydrich Assassination

DATE	TIME	EVENT
30 Sep 1938		The Munich Agreement cedes the border regions of Czechoslovakia (known as the Sudetenland) to Germany. Germans dismantle Czech border stations and completely occupy the region by October 10th.
15 Mar 1939		German troops invade the western portion of Czechoslovakia, with the eastern half of the country breaking away to become the German puppet ally of Slovakia. In Prague, the Protectorate of Bohemia and Moravia is declared.
1 Sep 1939		World War II begins when Germany invades Poland. In England, a Czech government in exile forms under President Edvard Beneš.
27 Sep 1941		Reinhard Heydrich is appointed Deputy Reich Protector of Bohemia and Moravia, serving as the Acting Governor of Czechoslovakia.
20 Oct 1941		The British Special Operations Executive formulates a plan to assassinate Reinhard Heydrich. Two Czech soldiers (Jan Kubiš and Jozef Gabčík) are recruited for the mission which is codenamed "Operation Anthropoid".
1 Nov 1941		Training for Operation Anthropoid begins. Gabčík and Kubiš are cycled through five separate training schools operated by the Special Operations Executive.
28 Dec 1941		Gabčík and Kubiš are parachuted into Czechoslovakia by the British Royal Air Force. They land east of Prague, near the town of Nehvizdy. The two move to the nearby town of Pilsen and make contact with the Czech underground resistance.
20 Jan 1942		Reinhard Heydrich attends the Wannsee conference in Berlin where the decision is formalized to exterminate all the Jews of Europe.
15 Feb 1942		Having made contact with Lieutenant Adolf Opálka, and the Czech Resistance Cell "Out Distance", Gabčík and Kubiš begin to develop a plan to kill Heydrich. After conducting surveillance on both his home and headquarters in Prague, the men agree that Heydrich is too well guarded, and he must be attacked outside of these locations, most practically when he is traveling.
1 Mar 1942		A plan to kill Heydrich on a train with a sniper rifle is aborted after the timing of the operation fails to achieve success.
13 Mar 1942		A second plan to stop Heydrich's car with a wire across a road is called off after Heydrich changes his route and the would-be assassins wait three hours before returning to Prague.
20 Apr 1942		A third plan is devised to attack Heydrich in the northern suburbs of Prague, in an area where his driver will be forced to reduce speed at a very sharp turn near a tram station. Gabčík and Kubiš begin a month long surveillance of this area.
27 May 1942	10:30 AM	While proceeding from his home outside of Prague, Heydrich's Mercedes is attacked when Jozef Gabčík steps in front of the vehicle and attempts to shoot Heydrich with a Sten machine gun. The gun jams, Heydrich stands up in the Mercedes, and yells at his driver to stop. Jan Kubiš then throws a hand-held bomb which explodes near the car's right rear bumper.

Left: Site of the May 1942 attack against Heydrich at a tram station in Prague 8-Libeň.
Right: The official crime scene photo of Heydrich's bombed car (Federal German Archives)

DATE	TIME	EVENT
27 May 1942	10:37 AM	In the aftermath of the bomb explosion, Gabčík and Kubiš use hand pistols to fire at Heydrich who stumbles from his car, returning fire from his own pistol before collapsing. Kubiš then mounts a bicycle and escapes down a steep hill while Gabčík flees on foot.
	10:45 AM	Heydrich's driver, SS-Oberscharführer Johannes Klein[x], pursues Gabčík. The SS man chases Gabčík around a corner and into a local butcher shop. With no rear exit, Gabčík turns on Klein and fires twice, hitting the SS-Sergeant in the thigh and leg. Gabčík then escapes from the area by boarding a local tram.
	10:52 AM	After noticing the commotion and the wounded Heydrich in the street, a Czech woman flags down a passing delivery truck and several bystanders help Heydrich into the cab. After Heydrich complains of intense pain, he is transferred to the bed of the truck which then drives him to the nearby Na Bulovce Hospital.
	11:00 AM	Heinrich Himmler is informed of the attempt on Heydrich's life. He immediately orders SS security units in Prague to mobilize and a half hour later informs Hitler of the attack. Hitler is outraged and orders massive reprisals against the Czech people. Himmler in the meantime sends instructions to Heydrich's second in command, Karl Hermann Frank, ordering the scene of the attack to be cordoned off and an investigation commenced into the identity of the attackers.
	11:15 AM	Heydrich arrives at the emergency room of Na Bulovce Hospital and is treated for his immediate wounds. The attending physicians are two Sudeten Germans listed in hospital records as Dr. Slanina and Dr. Walter Diek. Heydrich is diagnosed with severe injuries to his left side with major trauma to the diaphragm, spleen, and lung. He also has suffered a fractured rib.
	12:30 PM	German authorities in Prague declare martial law throughout the city while SS and police patrols begin to round up citizens who were in the vicinity of the attack on Heydrich.
	12:45 PM	Heydrich enters surgery after Dr. Hollbaum, a Silesian German and chairman of surgery at Charles University in Prague, arrives to treat him. In an operation which lasts several hours, Heydrich's collapsed left lung is re-inflated, the tip of his fractured rib is extracted, his diaphragm sutured, and his spleen removed. Throughout the operation, the doctors also insert several catheters and debride Heydrich's internal organs of splinters, grenade fragments, and upholstery material which was embedded into Heydrich from the seat of his car.

DATE	TIME	EVENT
27 May 1942	5:00 PM	In post-operative care, Heydrich is administered large amounts of morphine. He develops a temperature which ranges from 100.4 to 102.2 °F for the next several days.
	9:00 PM	SS and police forces in Prague begin raiding homes of any and all suspected Czech resistance members, as well as those which the Gestapo had placed under surveillance for suspicion of disloyal activities. Over the course of the next week, over twenty thousand security troops are deployed to Prague, with over thirty-five thousand Czech homes raided. Arrests would reach a total of over three thousand, of which 1,357 were summarily executed.
	11:30 PM	Karl Gebhardt, Heinrich Himmler's personal physician, arrives in Prague to assume medical care of Reinhard Heydrich. From this point, Heydrich is placed completely under the medical supervision of SS doctors.
28 May 1942		SS-Major General Arthur Nebe, head of the Criminal Police, is appointed as lead investigator in the case of the attack on Reinhard Heydrich. Arriving in Prague, Nebe is reportedly disturbed that local authorities seem more concerned with reprisals rather than seeking out those actually responsible for the attack.
31 May 1942		After hiding in two resistance safe houses, Gabčík and Kubiš are granted refuge in an Eastern Orthodox Church (the Cyril and Methodius Cathedral) under the protection of Bishop Gorazd. With them are members of two additional resistance groups. The men live in the crypt below the cathedral and are brought food and water daily by the cathedral priests.
1 Jun 1942		The German authorities in Prague, having failed to locate Heydrich's attackers, begin additional roundups and executions. The authorities further publish daily lists of reprisal victims shot at the Kobylisy Shooting Range.
2 Jun 1942		Arthur Nebe concludes his investigation, reporting that the attack on Reinhard Heydrich was mostly likely carried out by a Czech partisan team trained in England. As evidence, Nebe presents the British manufactured Sten gun left at the scene of the attack as well as British anti-tank grenade fragments found in the wreckage of Heydrich's car.
3 Jun 1942		Having seemingly recovered from the worst of his wounds, Reinhard Heydrich suddenly collapses while taking his noon day meal in his hospital room.
4 Jun 1942		After falling into a coma, Heydrich dies at 4:10 AM on June 4th 1942, coincidently the same day as the Japanese decisive defeat at the Battle of Midway in the Pacific. His official cause of death is listed as a massive pulmonary embolism and septicemia (blood poisoning) most likely caused by the horsehair upholstery of his car which was embedded into his internal organs at the time of the bomb blast.

Right: Heydrich's deputy, Karl Hermann Frank, who oversaw the initial investigation and reprisal actions into Heydrich's death. Shown also is the death mask of Reinhard Heydrich. (Federal German Archives)

DATE	EVENT
7 – 9 Jun 1942	After lying in state in Prague, Heydrich's body is taken to Berlin for a state funeral. He is buried with national honors at the Invalidenfriedhof military cemetary. His grave is marked with a temporary wooden memorial, with plans to construct a grand tomb at the conclusion of World War II[xi].
10 Jun 1942	In retaliation for Heydrich's death, the SS select the village of Lidice for a massive reprisal. SS-Obersturmführer Max Rostock leads a battalion of SS and police troops to Lidice where they round up all the inhabitants; 173 men are taken to a nearby barn and shot while 203 women are detained for deportation to concentration camps. The village is then burned and razed to the ground.
13 Jun 1942	Eighty-one children detained at Lidice are screened by the SS Race and Settlement Office. Less than ten are selected for Germanization while eighty-eight are held in a make shift concentration camp constructed within a converted textile factory in Lodz. On the 2nd of July these children are deported to the Chelmno Extermination Camp where they are killed.
14 Jun 1942	With no leads in the Heydrich assassination plot, the Germans have by now arrested over six thousand Czechs, half of which have been executed. Karl Herman Frank offers a pardon to anyone who comes forward with new information and further offers a bounty of 500,000 Reichmarks for anyone who assists the Germans in capturing Heydrich's killers.
16 Jun 1942	Karel Čurda, a former resistance member of the "Out Distance" partisan group, turns himself in to Gestapo authorities in Prague. Čurda had fled to his mother's house after the assassination, instead of with his fellow partisans, and became distraught over the heavy reprisals and killings of Czech citizens. Čurda provides the Gestapo with the location of resistance safe houses as well as the names of his partisan contacts in Prague. Raiding one such home, and after torturing the mother and son who live there, the Gestapo learn that Heydrich's killers are hiding in the Cyril and Methodius cathedral.

The traitor Karel Čurda is shown along with Karl von Treuenfeld, who was responsible for capturing and ultimately killing the Czech partisans who assassinated Heydrich. (Federal German Archives)

DATE	TIME	EVENT
18 Jun 1942	3:45 AM	SS-Brigadeführer Karl von Treuenfeld orders the mobilization of seven hundred Waffen-SS soldiers to surround the Cyril and Methodius Cathedral. The majority of the soldiers are members of the Reserve Replacement Battalion for the Regiment Deutschland, augmented by troops assigned from the police and security forces already in Prague.
	4:15 AM	The SS cordon off the area around the Cyril and Methodius Cathedral. There are seven partisans inside.
	5:00 AM	SS and police enter the Cyril and Methodius Cathedral. They first search the outer sanctum and the church warden's apartment, within which is an unscrewed grate and ladder, later suspected to have been a makeshift escape route from the crypt below.
	6:15 AM	Entering the inner sanctum of the cathedral, the SS troops are fired upon by three partisans located in a choir loft above the church gallery. The partisans are armed with small pistols, one rifle, as well as a 7.92mm machine gun. In what would become known as the "Battle of the Choir Loft", the partisans manage to wound between twelve to twenty SS soldiers while killing at least five.
	8:45 AM	After pinning the partisans down in the church gallery, three Czech resistance fighters commit suicide after suffering critical wounds and running out of ammunition. The SS troops then search the chapel area of the cathedral and discover the main entrance to the cathedral crypt where four more partisans are well entrenched with rifles, machine guns, and pistols.
	9:15 AM	As SS troops are fired upon from the resistance fighters in the church crypt, Karel Čurda arrives at the scene and attempts to convince his former comrades to surrender. The partisans respond by firing at Čurda from their positions in the crypt.
	9:45 AM	The Prague Fire Brigade is called to the Cyril and Methodius Cathedral in order to pump water into the church crypt. The Germans also throw tear gas into the enclosure in an effort to force out the partisans.
	10:15 AM	Out of ammunition, wounded, and drowning, the last surviving partisans shoot themselves rather than face capture by the Germans. The bodies of all seven resistance fighters are then dragged from the church into the street where they are identified by Karel Čurda.

The Choir Loft inside Cyril and Methodius Cathedral, where Heydrich's assassins died during a last stand. Outside, water was pumped into the cathedral crypt by the Prague fire brigade (Federal German Archives)

Czech partisans killed by German forces on June 18, 1942

PHOTOGRAPH	NAME	RANK	AGE IN 1942	PLACE OF DEATH
	Josef Bublík	Cadet Officer	22 years old (February 12, 1920)	Choir Loft
	Jozef Gabčík	Warrant Officer	30 years old (April 8, 1912)	Church Crypt
	Jan Hrubý	Sergeant	27 years old (March 4, 1915)	
	Jan Kubiš	Warrant Officer	29 years old (June 24, 1913)	Choir Loft
	Adolf Opálka	First Lieutenant	27 years old (January 4, 1915)	

NAME	RANK	AGE IN 1942	PLACE OF DEATH	PHOTOGRAPH
Jaroslav Švarc	Staff Sergeant	28 years old (May 11, 1914)	Church Crypt	
Josef Valčík	Second Lieutenant	27 years old (November 2, 1914)		

Service record photographs courtesy of Federal German Archives

With Heydrich's assassins dead, Karel Čurda was provided a bounty reward by Nazi authorities and given a new identity. He later married and spent the remainder of the war in Prague working as a Gestapo informant. The priests and bishop of Cyril and Methodius, where the partisans had concealed themselves and ultimately had died fighting, were arrested and executed.

On June 24th 1942, after further investigation into the background of the partisans killed at Cyril and Methodius, the Gestapo determined that the village of Ležáky, southeast of Prague, was the possible location of an additional resistance cell. Five hundred SS troops were sent to the small hamlet, where thirty-three adults were executed with most of the surviving children deported and later exterminated. Only a handful of children were deemed worthy of Germanization and were subsequently sent to live with families in Germany.

International reaction to the German reprisals in the Czech Protectorate was swift. On August 5th 1942 the British government formally declared the Munich Agreement of 1938 nullified and void. A pledge was then stated to reunite Czechoslovakia at the conclusion of the Second World War. By this time, Kurt Daluege (who had enacted most of the reprisal orders in the Protectorate) had resigned from his duties due to ill health. In October 1943 Wilhelm Frick became the last Reich Protector of Bohemia and Moravia. Both Frick and Daluege were executed for war crimes after the conclusion of World War II while Karel Čurda, who had betrayed Heydrich's assassins to the Germans, was executed by Czechoslovak authorities on April 29th 1947.

Uprisings and Revolt

At the height of the Second World War, disloyalty and defeatism were considered capitol offenses within the German Reich. However, to those under Nazi occupation, it was obvious by 1943 that the tide of war had turned and that the reign of Nazi Germany was coming to an end. In the last two years of the war, malcontent grew amongst the subjugated nations, and it was the SS which sought to suppress any rebellion and crush all dissent.

The first major acts of rebellion came from Jewish special action teams within the concentration camps, tasked with assisting in the extermination process, who rose up and caused revolts to occur at three of the major death camps. Ghetto revolts soon followed, led by young men and women who knew the truth regarding "resettlement" and "relocation to the east". As the tide of war turned even further against the Germans, entire cities revolted and eventually entire nations.

Significant concentration camp uprisings
(1943 – 1944)

Date		Description
August 2, 1943	Treblinka	700 Jewish prisoners attack the main gate of Treblinka. Many are killed by sentry guards, with 200 escaping. Most are caught soon afterwards. A total of 70 would live to survive the war.
October 14, 1943	Sobibor	A group of Russian prisoners-of-war, along with an internal camp resistance, organize a mass escape attempt. Prisoners secretly kill several SS and Ukrainian guards before the plot is discovered. Over 600 prisoners then storm the camp gate and fences, with 300 escaping into the nearby forest. Approximately 60 would survive the war.
October 7, 1944	Auschwitz	Jewish prisoners assigned to Crematorium 3 attack and kill their SS overseers then set makeshift explosives to destroy the gassing installations. Prisoners from Crematoria 2 and 4 also join the revolt, with nearly 300 killed while fighting back against German reinforcements from the main Auschwitz camp. By nightfall, the revolt has been suppressed and the SS execute all Jews captured in the rebelling crematorium. Jewish prisoners in Crematorium 5, as well as a handful of trustees and prisoners who were elsewhere in the camp, are spared.

One of the most successful attempts at armed uprising took place between April and May 1943 by Jewish resistance fighters in Warsaw. Between April 19th and May 16th, over one thousand Jewish insurgents faced off against nearly twice as many SS solders under the command of SS-Brigadeführer Jürgen Stroop, the SS and Police Leader of the Warsaw area. By the spring of 1943, organized Jewish deportations to death camps had been occurring for over a year. Between July and September 1942, in what the Germans designated as "Grossaktion Warsaw", three hundred thousand Warsaw Ghetto inhabitants were deported to the death camp at Treblinka.

By the end of 1942, two well established Jewish underground groups had formed to combat the German aims. These were the Jewish Combat Organization ("Żydowska Organizacja Bojowa" or ŻOB), and the Jewish Military Union ("Żydowski Związek Wojskowy" or the ŻZW). The respective commanders of these groups were Mordechai Anielewicz and Paweł Frenkiel. Under their leadership, the Jewish underground had first begun to stockpile arms and ammunition within the Ghetto in anticipation of an uprising. At the start of 1943, the underground began to target and kill known German collaborators, including all members of the Żagiew (Jewish Freedom Guard) which was a collaborationist militia set up by the German authorities to spy on Jewish Ghetto resistance.

The first armed conflict between German and Jewish forces took place on the 18th of January 1943 when a roundup to the Umschlagplatz (the central deportation area of the ghetto) was attacked by Jewish forces. The Jewish underground then began constructing bunkers throughout the ghetto, all the while continuing to attack and harass German patrols until the Germans had withdrawn from the ghetto entirely.

Chronology of the Warsaw Ghetto Uprising

22 Jul 1942: The Germans initiate "Action Warsaw" to deport the majority of the Jews in the Warsaw Ghetto. Adam Czerniakow, head of the Warsaw Judenrat, commits suicide the following day.

12 Sep 1942: Deportations from Warsaw number 265,000. Sixty thousand Jews remain.

18 Jan 1943: German forces enter the Warsaw Ghetto for a new round of deportations. They are attacked by Jewish forces; in the ensuing battle most of the Jews are killed. Five thousand Jews are rounded up for deportation.

19 Apr 1943: German forces assault the Warsaw Ghetto and are repulsed by heavily fortified Jewish defenders.

29 Apr 1943: A number of the Ghetto fighters escape through underground sewer tunnels. Organized resistance collapses.

8 May 1943: The Germans destroy the last major Jewish command bunker.

16 May 1943: The Germans declare the Warsaw Ghetto Uprising at an end.

During January and February of 1943, the Germans had only managed to deport five thousand ghetto inhabitants, far below the demanded quota, leading to reports to the SS leadership and a call for action against Jewish resistance.

The city of Warsaw was located within the territory of the General Government of Poland, while security in the region was under the authority of the Higher SS and Police Leader "Ost" who was headquartered in Krakow. The SS command in the area held considerable power, including control of locally garrisoned Waffen-SS units as well as both the SS and police security formations. The Higher SS and Police Leader "Ost" was veteran Nazi and SS officer Friedrich-Wilhelm Krüger. Subordinated to Krüger were various SS and Police Leaders, with the city of Warsaw under the authority of SS-Oberführer Ferdinand von Sammern-Frankenegg. On April 19th 1943, after German troops were repulsed from the Warsaw Ghetto following the first large scale engagement against Jewish resistance, von Sammern-Frankenegg was relieved of his position and replaced by SS-Brigadeführer Jürgen Stroop.

SS leadership during the Warsaw Ghetto Uprising: Ferdinand von Sammern-Frankenegg and Jürgen Stroop (Polish State Archives)

Whereas von Sammern-Frankenegg had attempted to assault the ghetto with locally assigned SS security troops, Jürgen Stroop mustered the full force of the SS to include Waffen-SS units, German Police commands, auxiliary Wehrmacht troops, as well as units of the Polish Police and Fire Brigades. 2,054 troops of the SS and other commands fought in the Warsaw Ghetto between April 19th and May 16th. Seventeen SS members were killed, with an additional ninety-three wounded. Jewish casualties were much higher with 13,000 killed as well as an additional 56,885 deported after the suppression of the uprising.

Nearly half a million Jews resided in the Warsaw Ghetto at the start of 1942 and were forced to live in an area of less than two square miles. When German forces attacked the ghetto in April 1943, the majority of the fighting took place on the northern ghetto perimeter. Hundreds of underground bunkers had also been established throughout the ghetto which then required the Germans to advance block by block to combat the entrenched Jewish forces.

In addition to the Warsaw Ghetto revolt, the entire city of Warsaw fell into rebellion on August 1, 1944 when fighting broke out between German forces and the Polish Home Army. The city rebellion lasted two months, the suppression of which was overseen by the regular German military[xii], although SS units did assist. Similar revolts in Slovakia and Hungary were likewise suppressed, although the victories of the Germans were short-lived. By the start of 1945, the Soviet Red Army was advancing across Eastern Europe towards the German border, while both the regular German Army and Waffen-SS were in full retreat.

German order of battle during the Warsaw Ghetto Uprising and layout of the Warsaw Ghetto

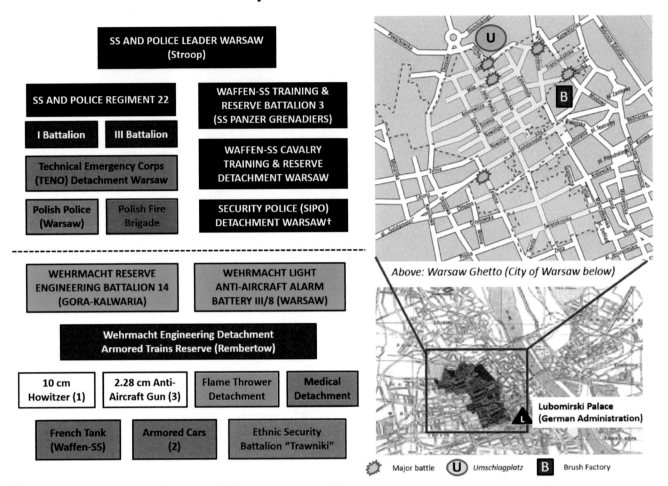

Above: Warsaw Ghetto (City of Warsaw below)

Lubomirski Palace (German Administration)

Major battle | U Umschlagplatz | B Brush Factory

† The Security Police (Sipo) detachment in Warsaw was on standby, but did not participate in the actual fighting.

Map image courtesy Holocaust Memorial Museum

Profit and Industry

Throughout its existence, the SS remained first and foremost a paramilitary agency of the Nazi Party, and as such its primary source of funding was through Nazi Party appropriations and budgeting. With the rise of the Waffen-SS, the armed branch of the SS was funded by the Reich Finance Ministry, although this channel of budget applied only towards military arms and equipment. To supplement the SS treasury, Himmler ordered an SS finance department to begin investing in businesses and work projects whose profits could be added to SS income.

The first SS office to be concerned with budget and income was Department III of the "SS-Oberstab", founded in 1930. This early SS office was mainly concerned with membership dues and minor funding matters, since the Nazi Party had yet to seize political power and the SS was still considered subordinate to the SA. By 1935, the SS was an independent Nazi Party formation with its budget and finance managed by the "Verwaltungsamt" (Administration Office) which was considered a sub-office of the SS headquarters command, the SS-Hauptamt. Oswald Pohl was the first leader of the Verwaltungsamt and would use his experience as an SS administrator to expand his power into a massive enterprise of business, industry, and slave labor. During the Second World War, the SS came to amass a literal fortune, and further become highly corrupt with bribery and embezzlement commonplace, especially in occupied territories where oversight was minimal, and brutality was common.

Oswald Pohl had first begun to expand his economic empire in 1939 when Germany began the Second World War. As Poland fell under Nazi rule, the SS quickly moved into that nation and began seizing property, assets, as well as instituting a forced labor program among the population. Pohl then became the combined commander of two separate offices: the SS Administration & Economics Office and the SS Office of Budget and Construction.

While the administration office retained most of the clerical functions associated with SS finances, it was the Office of Budget and Construction which was put in charge of establishing a slave labor system in occupied Poland.

Organization of the "Hauptamt Haushalt und Bauten"
(SS Head Office for Budget and Contraction)

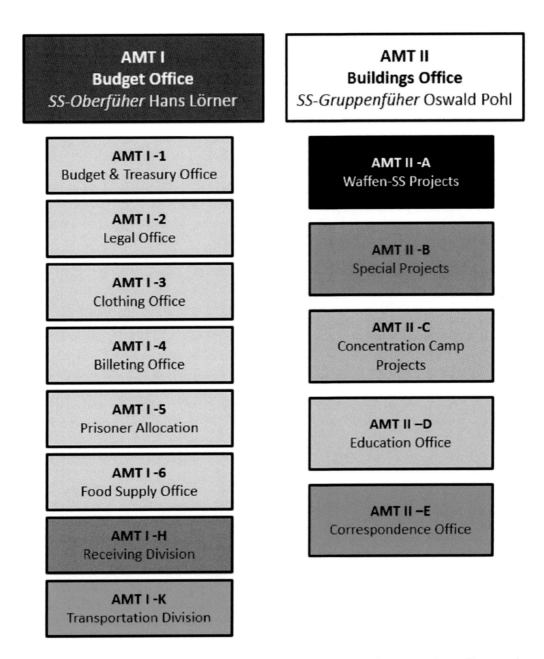

In early 1942, as part of an effort to consolidate all SS economic, labor, and construction efforts under one authority, the SS offices of Budget, Construction, Administration, and Economics were merged into one large headquarters office known as the "SS-Wirtschafts-Verwaltungshauptamt" (SS Economics and Administration Main Office), abbreviated as the WVHA. The creation of the WVHA also effectively ended the SS Concentration Camp service as a separate recognized branch of the SS. The independent Totenkopf guard units had been absorbed into the camp staffs by 1940, while the camp service members were then transferred to the administrative control of the Waffen-SS in April 1941. By a directive from the SS Operations Main Office in March 1942, the Office of the Inspector of Concentration Camps was absorbed by the WVHA and renamed as "Department D". In conjunction with "Department W", these two offices administrated all concentration camp and slave labor projects of the SS.

Within occupied Poland, and to a certain extent the Czech Republic as well as France and Belgium, the SS indirectly operated private industries through the use of regulatory fees and service charges for German businesses operating in occupied countries. By far, this system was most predominant in Poland where German firms and businesses made use of both the subjugated Polish population as well as Jewish skilled labor for the accomplishment of immense profit. Any German business operating in an occupied country had to pay an initial start-up fee, as well as a plethora of permit and certification costs in order to begin business operations. The work force for such businesses were either very low paid employees or slave labor supplied by the SS. In the case of skilled labor Jews, the worker was required to obtain a permit from the SS stating that the skills which the worker held were considered essential for German industry. The issuance of a valid work permit was a highly sought-after commodity, with an entire network of black market and forgery developed to provide these work documents to ghetto inhabitants.

A Jewish work card from the Krakow Ghetto (Polish State Archives)

By 1942, with extermination directives issued against the Jewish populations of occupied countries, the SS began disregarding previously established regulations concerning Jewish skilled labor and in turn began deporting more and more Jews to extermination centers. With Department D of the WVHA controlling the concentration camps, while Department W oversaw the use of skilled labor, the SS leadership faced a dilemma as German business owners filed petitions and grievances against the loss of skilled workers while the SS, the very agency receiving the complaints, was also responsible for deportations and mass killings. In a very significant loop hole of Nazi bureaucracy, SS members who arbitrarily killed Jews in ghettos and labor camps were held accountable for the "loss of skilled labor" if the Jew was under employ by a German business. SS members were eligible to be fined for such acts and, in some extreme cases, imprisoned although there are no records of an SS member ever being incarcerated for the murder of a Jewish worker. SS directives of extermination eventually took precedence over any interest of German business, and most skilled Jewish workers were eventually deported to extermination camps.

Jewish ghetto leaders further attempted to forestall deportations by bribing German officials or by conveying the impression that Jewish skilled labor was still needed for the war effort. One of the most successful efforts was led by Jewish Council leader Chaim Rumkowski, of the Lodz Ghetto, who effectively turned the Jewish ghetto population into a gigantic slave labor force for the SS. Rumkowski was able to keep the Lodz Ghetto intact longer than any other ghetto in Poland by convincing the Nazi government that the labor and production provided was too valuable to ignore. Even so, by 1944 the SS had ordered the ghetto closed with Rumkowski himself deported to Auschwitz that August and killed.

Above: Chaim Rumkowski (white hair, left side of photo) meets with Heinrich Himmler in 1943. After waiting several hours to see Himmler, Rumkowski's conversation took less than a minute after Himmler simply stated for Rumkowski to continue the encouragement of hard work by the Lodz ghetto populous. (Polish State Archives)
FOLLOWING PAGE: Organization of the SS Economics and Administration Main Office, commonly known as the WVHA

AMTSGRUPPE A
Finance, Law, & Administration

AMT A I
Budget & Savings

AI-1: *Waffen-SS* Budget
AI-2: *Allgemeine-SS* Budget
AI-3: Savings Treasury

AMT A II
Salary & Funds

AII-1: Salary Office
AII-2: Accounts Treasury
AII-3: Pay & Allowances

AMT A III
Law Office

AIII-1: Tax & Contract Office
AIII-2: Land & Building Permits

AMT A IV
Inspections Office

AIV-1: Cash & Accounting Audits
AIV-2: Military Economics Inspections

AMT A V
Personnel Office

AV-1: Replacement Acquisitions
AV-2: Promotions & Transfers
AV-3: Education & Training
AV-4: Command Appointments

AMTSGRUPPE B
Supply, Administration, & Equipment

AMT B I
Catering Supplies

BI-1: Food Acquisition
BI-2: Troop Administration
BI-3: Culinary Education

AMT B II
Clothing Supplies

BII-1: Clothing & Equipment
BII-2: Clothing Manufacturing
BII-3: Uniform Distribution

AMT B III
Berthing Office

BIII-1: Berthing Planning
BIII-2: Berthing Assignment
BIII-3: Berthing Liaison

AMT B IV
Raw Materials

BIV-1: Commodities Office
BIV-2: Clothing Procurement
BIV-3: Price Comparisons
BIV-4: Foreign Labor Procurement

AMTSGRUPPE C
Works & Buildings

AMT C I
General Construction

CI-1: *Waffen-SS* Construction
CI-2: POW & Concentration Camps
CI-3: Police Facilities
CI-4: *Allgemeine-SS* Construction

AMT C II
Special Facilities

CII-1: Food & Clothing Plants
CII-2: Weapons & Ammunition Plants
CII-3: Hospital Facilities
CII-4: NPEA Board Schools
CII-5: Emergency Housing
CII-6: Special Facility Funding

AMT C III
Technical Office

CIII-1: Engineering Office
CIII-2: Irrigation & Drainage
CIII-3: Machinery Office
CIII-4: Surveying Office

AMT C IV
Artistic Office

CIV-1: Urban Development Office
CIV-2: Landscape & Interior Design

AMT C V
Building Inspection

CV-1: Construction & Building Projects
CV-2: Budget & Accounting Office
CV-3: Structural Inspection Office
CV-4: Inspection Liaison Office

AMT C VI
Building Maintenance

CVI-1: *Waffen-SS* Properties
CVI-2: *Allgemeine-SS* Properties
CVI-3: Construction Site Selections

AMTSGRUPPE D
Concentration Camps

Department D was formed in March of 1942 from the previous Concentration Camp Inspectorate office. Commanded by SS-Major General Richard Glucks, Department D oversaw administration of all political prisoner camps, labor camps (*Arbeitslager*), and extermination centers.

AMTSGRUPPE W
Economic Enterprises

Department W was the administrative center for the manufacture of SS goods and wares, most of which were created through the use of slave labor provided from Concentration Camps. As such, Department W worked closely with Department D. SS-General Oswald Pohl, who served as overall commander of the WVHA, also served as head of Department W.

Concentration Camp Administration
(WVHA Department D)

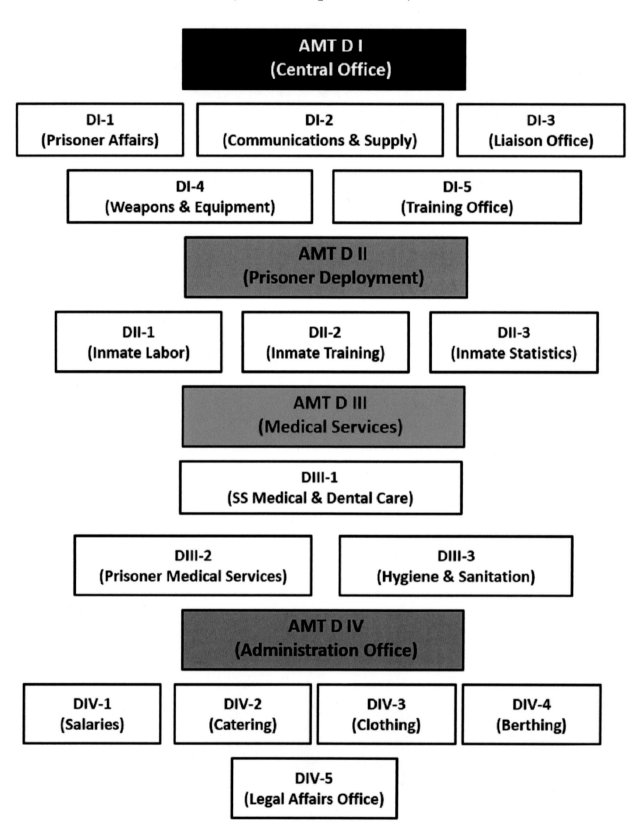

AMT D I
(Central Office)

DI-1
(Prisoner Affairs)

DI-2
(Communications & Supply)

DI-3
(Liaison Office)

DI-4
(Weapons & Equipment)

DI-5
(Training Office)

AMT D II
(Prisoner Deployment)

DII-1
(Inmate Labor)

DII-2
(Inmate Training)

DII-3
(Inmate Statistics)

AMT D III
(Medical Services)

DIII-1
(SS Medical & Dental Care)

DIII-2
(Prisoner Medical Services)

DIII-3
(Hygiene & Sanitation)

AMT D IV
(Administration Office)

DIV-1
(Salaries)

DIV-2
(Catering)

DIV-3
(Clothing)

DIV-4
(Berthing)

DIV-5
(Legal Affairs Office)

SS Commercial and Enterprises Office
(WVHA Department W)

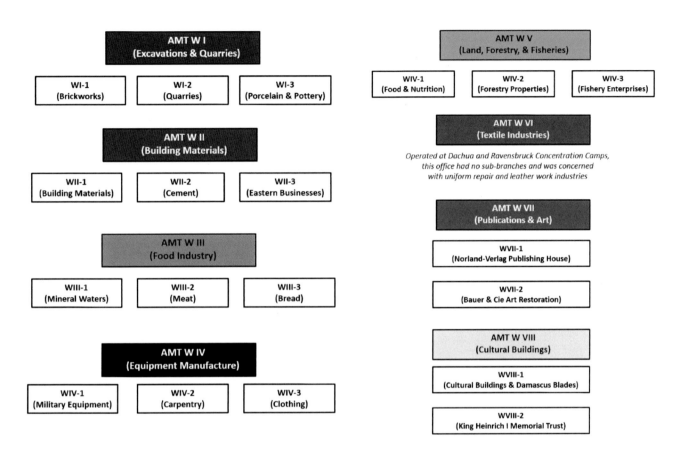

Apart from Jewish labor employed from ghettos, the SS made extensive use of Concentration Camp inmates for the manufacture of goods, products, and services. By 1942, the SS had established a vast labor camp system throughout both the Greater German Reich and within the occupied territories. In September 1942, the SS formed the first "SS Construction Brigade" to facilitate an even greater use of slave labor. Construction Brigades were a type of mobile concentration camp comprising one thousand inmates who would deploy to various areas of Europe for work on large construction projects. There were five SS Construction Brigades (SS-Baubrigade), originally created under the authority of the WVHA Department C (Works and Buildings), with each brigade headquartered at a parent Concentration Camp.

SS Construction Brigades (1943)

DESIGNATION	ACTIVATED	HEADQUARTERS
SS-Baubrigade I	October 1942	Sachsenhausen
SS-Baubrigade II	April 1943	Neuengamme
SS-Baubrigade III	September 1942	Buchenwald
SS-Baubrigade IV	August 1943	Buchenwald
SS-Baubrigade V	January 1943	Sachsenhausen

A total of nine SS construction brigades had been established by 1944, the last of which (SS-Baubrigade IX) activated in November 1944 at the Sachsenhausen Concentration Camp. That same year the SS began establishing Railway Construction Brigades (Eisenbahnbaubrigaden) which traveled by train to various areas of Germany in order to construct fortifications, gun emplacements, and to repair bombed out train tracks.

The first SS Railway Construction Brigade was established on September 12th 1944 and headquartered from the Buchenwald Concentration Camp. On September 19th a second brigade was established out of Auschwitz, and by January of 1945 a total of thirteen Railway Brigades were in existence. The last brigade was established on January 18, 1945 headquartered at Sachsenhausen.

Another critical function of the SS Economics and Administration Main Office was to oversee the supply chains by which both the Armed and General-SS received equipment. Allocation of weapons and military equipment was authorized through the Reich Ministry for Weapons, Munitions, and Armaments, while the purchase and shipment of the physical weaponry was overseen by the SS Operational Headquarters (SS-Führungshauptamt). Similar measures existed within the SS Operational Headquarters for the shipment of clothing, food, and supplies to various SS units.

The WVHA maintained two types of supply depots for distribution of weapons, clothing, and equipment to SS commands. The first type was known as a "Headquarters Depot" (HWL) and distributed supplies to major commands such as Waffen-SS divisions and corps. A smaller type of depot, the "Local Depot" (TWL), handled supply requisition requests from the regimental and battalion level. To maintain stock supplies, as well as keep track of supply inventories transported to various SS units, the WVHA maintained a control document known as the "Ausstattungssoll" (Issuance Schedule) as well as Supply Liaison Officers (SS-Wirtschafter) attached to all major SS commands.

SS SUPPLY COMMANDS

Nordabschnitt (Riga, Latvia)

Mittelabschnitt (Mogilev, West Russia)

Südabschnitt (Krim, Crimea)

Supply Command	SS-Rank
WVHA Office Group	SS-Gruppenführer
Regional Supply Commander	SS-Brigadeführer
Regional Supply District Leader	SS-Oberführer
Headquarters Depot Commander	SS-Oberführer
Sub-Office Command	SS-Standartenführer
Local Supply Depot Commander	SS-Sturmbannführer
Supply Liaison Officer	SS-Hauptsturmführer
Supply Station Commander	SS-Hauptsturmführer

Supply distribution on the eastern front was further organized into three major WVHA supply commands, known collectively as the "Versorgungsstützpunkte der Waffen-SS und Polizei". These commands held authority to regulate all supply and approve all local contracts in their geographical regions.

Left: Supply command levels and commander ranks

The eastern front supply districts were collectively under the command of a special WVHA office known as the "SS-Nachschubkommandantur", with each subordinate district able to fully supply three divisions with clothing, arms, and equipment. The SS also employed smaller "Supply Stations", known as "SS-Stützpunkte", which were ad hoc supply units established on the front lines of Russia. German Police units assigned to combat duties also utilized the SS supply system, of which an SS depot was usually capable of supplying a police command of ten thousand men.

The supply system in the west was essentially the same used on the eastern front, modified slightly in 1944 for combat operations in France following the invasion of the Allies at the Battle of Normandy. The WVHA supply responsibility covered the entirety of the Waffen-SS and (after 1942) also the SS members assigned to the Nazi Concentration Camp system. The Allgemeine-SS received funding strictly through Nazi Party channels, with the WVHA providing administrative oversight but not actual purchasing power. The Reich Central Security Office (RSHA), which operated the Secret Police forces and Special Action Groups (Einsatzgruppen), operated its own supply system and received funding for weapons and equipment via the Reich Ministry of the Interior.

At the height of its power, the WVHA had secured contracts with some of the largest manufacturing and business firms in Germany, among them Volkswagen and the chemical firm I.G. Farben, which supplied poison gas to the SS in order to exterminate Jews. The clothing firm Hugo Boss held the contract for the manufacture of all SS uniforms, although the SS itself operated its own clothing issuance through Concentration Camp workshops known as "SS-Bekleidungswerke". Other large firms in contract with the SS included the conglomerate "German Equipment Works, Ltd" as well as "Eastern Industries" which made heavy use of Concentration Camp slave labor.

One of the surviving legacies of SS industry are the works of Damascus Blades and Allach Porcelain. Both corporations were managed by Department W of the WVHA, with Damascus Blades providing all ceremonial daggers and swords to the SS. Allach Porcelain further manufactured plates and dinnerware bearing Nazi and SS symbols, as well as creating the "SS-Julleuchter" decoration, which was a type of clay candle holder, for use during solstice celebrations.

Even seventy years after the close of the Second World War, artifacts manufactured by Damascus Blades and Allach Porcelain are still sought after by collectors. The Allach Company was disbanded after World War II, but its equipment and molds were later acquired by the current German porcelain company Efchenbach. The art of producing Damascus steel is still practiced by many manufactures in Germany, although no one company claims to be a successor to the SS Damascus Blades industry.

Downfall of the Elite

By the winter of 1944, the armies of the Third Reich were in full retreat on two fronts, with many in the Nazi government knowing full well that the end was drawing near. This was most obvious from a November 1944 directive when Heinrich Himmler ordered a halt to all extermination measures against Jews. Jewish prisoners were now to be viewed as hostages used as potential leverage with the Allies, and perhaps even the Soviets, the latter of which whose armies were now beginning to overrun Poland and approach the eastern border of Germany.

By the end of the Second World War, awareness of SS genocide against the Jews had spread throughout Europe, with knowledge commonplace amongst the German public that the "resettled" Jews had in fact been killed. For some, this knowledge promoted personal action, and several brave Germans risked their livelihood and sometimes even their lives in order to shelter and assist Jews. One of the more well-known examples was the story of Oskar Schindler, a German industrialist who had established an enamelware factory in Poland in 1940. Originally concerned solely with profit, Schindler later protected over one thousand Jewish workers after it became clear that the Nazi government planned to exterminate the Jews of Poland. By the end of World War II, Schindler had relocated 1,200 Jews to Czechoslovakia where he operated a false front armaments factory in which the produced shells and ammunition were in fact purchased from other sources. Through bribery and black-market dealings, Schindler protected his Jewish workers until the end of the war and was later harbored and sheltered by those same Jews he had once protected, who also helped him escape Czechoslovakia at the end of the war. For his heroic efforts, Schindler was declared a Righteous Person in Israel. He died poverty stricken and penniless in 1974.

**Oskar Schindler in 1939
(Polish State Archives)**

Some Jewish rescue efforts came from a very unlikely source, this being the SS itself. Such was the case of SS-Obergruppenführer Werner Best, who was the Chief Nazi administrator in Denmark during most of the Second World War. After issuing an order in October 1943 to round-up Danish Jews for deportation, Best allowed word of the operation to be leaked to Jewish support organizations and further ordered that the German military take no action against Danish Jews fleeing to Sweden. As a result, over 7,200 Jews escaped from Denmark; a few hundred more were deported to Theresienstadt, but were eventually freed as the Germans abandoned that ghetto. Another unusual attempt to spare Jews came in March of 1944 from SS-Obersturmbannführer Adolf Eichmann who was the top SS administrator for deportation and extermination in accordance with the "Final Solution" directive.

Left: Joel Brandt (Federal German Archives)

After Germany invaded Hungary, Eichmann approached Joel Brand, head of the Jewish Relief Agency in Budapest. After two meetings in April and May, Eichmann and Brand worked out a plan where Brand would contact the Allies and present a German offer to release a million Jews in exchange for war materials comprised mostly of trucks, foodstuffs and other wartime essentials. This "Jews for Trucks" deal involved Brand traveling to the Middle East in a clandestine Cloak and Dagger type operation. In the end, the offer was rejected by British authorities and Brand was detained in Syria and later moved to Cairo for detailed interrogation. His failure to return to Hungary led to a continuation of Hungarian Jewish deportations to Auschwitz.

SS Organization in 1944

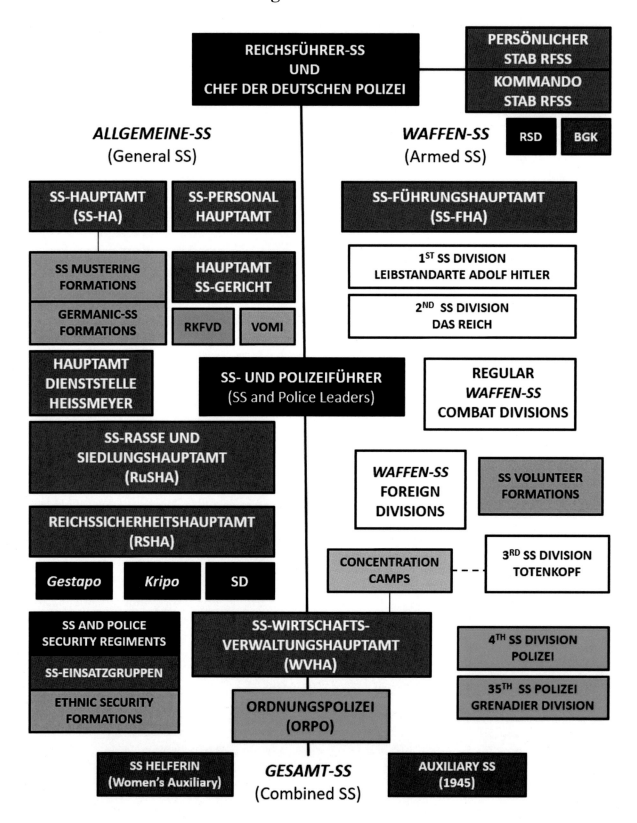

The SS in 1944 was divided between the Allgemeine (General) and Waffen (Armed) SS. Offices overlapping both branches were said to be part of the "Combined SS" (Gesamt-SS). Commonly used SS abbreviations included the SD (Sicherheitsdienst), RSD (Reichssicherheitsdienst), BGK (Begleitkommando), VOMI (Volksdeutsche Mittelstelle) and the RKFVD (Reichkommisar für die Festigung Deutschen Volksstrum).

The Auschwitz Concentration Camp was liberated by the Soviet Army in January 1945, thus revealing for the first time the vast extent of Nazi atrocities and genocidal programs. In the west, following the German defeat at the Battle of the Bulge, Allied forces invaded Germany and were now poised to strike at the very heart of the Reich. The SS leadership in 1945, albeit comprised of some fanatical Nazis who would fight to the bitter end, knew full well that the war was essentially over. Perhaps in an effort to provide documentary evidence on his own behalf, in March 1944 Himmler published an odd memo to senior SS leaders, stating that "the evacuation and isolation of the Jewish and Roma people is complete", seemingly to encourage a cessation of harsh measures and a halt to wide spread killing actions.

By the end of 1944, Himmler had amassed a tremendous amount of power and was viewed as a possible successor to Adolf Hitler after Hermann Göring. Himmler was also serving as Reich Minister of the Interior, Reich Leader of the SS, Chief of the German Police, Reich Commissioner of German Nationhood, and Commander of the German Home Army. Himmler was further a Reichsleiter in the Nazi Party (the senior most political rank other than Hitler himself) and had been posted as an operational military commander in late 1944.

Towards the end of the war, Himmler was operating from a field headquarters at Schneidemühl in western Poland. He spent most of his time on a special command train, known as the "Sonderzug Steiermark", which was a highly inefficient headquarters possessing little command and control capability. Himmler himself avoided any sort of operational responsibility for the forces under his command, seldom met with subordinates, and insisted on uninterrupted afternoon naps and lengthy visits with his personal masseuse Felix Kersten. It is thought that in their private conversations, Kersten first suggested to Himmler that Germany would lose the war and Himmler could perhaps become Hitler's successor and save the Third Reich from total collapse. Himmler's SS Chief of Foreign Intelligence, Walter Schellenberg, had expressed similar views in late 1944. Perhaps with the knowledge that Germany was in fact doomed, Himmler became withdrawn and in March of 1945 abandoned his command post to register as a patient in a sanatorium at Hohenlychen, Germany. Himmler formally resigned from his military posts on March 16th 1945 and on March 29th Hitler declared that Himmler was to have no further role in military operations.

The very next month, with the Red Army now poised to strike Berlin, Himmler ordered special SS teams to patrol the front and execute any German soldier who failed to hold their position against the enemy. In April 1945, with Allied forces just days away from liberating several Concentration Camps within Germany, Himmler signed an order to execute Concentration Camp inmates at Dachau, rather than abandon them to the Allies; the order was transmitted but never carried out. The first Concentration Camp in Germany was liberated on April 4th 1945.

Himmler made his final visit to Berlin on April 20th 1945, when he met with Adolf Hitler on the occasion of the Führer's fifty sixth birthday. Unknown to Hitler was that for the past two months Himmler had been in contact with a Swedish diplomat, Count Folke Bernadotte, with the intention of surrendering Germany to the Western Allies.

The end of Nazi Germany

By the spring of 1945, most of Europe's occupied and German allied countries had either been liberated or had switched sides against the Germans. The Soviet Union had liberated the Baltic countries, Poland, and the Ukraine, while in the west the countries of France, Belgium, Luxembourg, and the Netherlands had all fallen into Allied hands by the start of the year. Bulgaria and Romania, two of Germany's staunchest allies, had declared an armistice with the Soviet Union and in turn had declared war on Germany.

In Southern Europe, partisan uprisings had caused German forces to begin retreating from Greece, Croatia, and Yugoslavia, while in Hungary and Slovakia German forces had invaded those countries to prevent national uprisings. Finland had signed an armistice with the Soviet Union in September 1944 and promptly had forcibly expelled German troops in an action known as the Lapland War.

Germany's primary ally Italy had in fact surrendered to the Allies in September 1943, and declared war on Germany, but had in turn been occupied by German forces with a puppet state (under a restored Benito Mussolini) established in Rome. Italy was subsequent invaded by the Allies and Rome was liberated in 1944. The only two remaining countries which Germany held in 1945 were Denmark, liberated by Allied forces in May 1945, and Norway which had been partially invaded by the Soviet Army in 1944, but mostly remained under German control until the end of the Second World War.

Himmler's plan of surrender to the Allies called for Himmler becoming Germany's next leader, with German forces then mobilized alongside the Allies to fight against the Soviet Army. Himmler also had aims to use the SS as a post-war police force, with Himmler himself appointed as "Minister of Police" in a post-war occupation government run by the Allies.

Right: Felix Kersten, Himmler's masseuse, who was possibly one of the first people to learn of Himmler's plan to surrender to the Allies. (Federal German Archives)

Himmler's surrender plan was already well in motion when he meet Hitler in Berlin in April 1945. The day after meeting Hitler, both Himmler and Hermann Göring relocated to Berchtesgaden where Himmler attempted to ally himself with Göring who was still recognized as Hitler's legitimate successor and heir apparent. In post war interrogations, Göring reported that Himmler had nominated himself as Chancellor of Germany under a Göring government, to which Göring comically dismissed as impractical since Hitler was still living and technically the office of Führer encompassed both the titles of Chancellor and President. Himmler then asked if Göring would decline his position as Hitler's successor, stating:

"Sir, if something should prevent you from becoming successor, can I have the job then?"
—Heinrich Himmler (1945)

On April 23rd 1945, after Göring sent a telegram to Hitler notifying the Führer that he intended to take power in Germany should Hitler die, Hitler ordered Göring's arrest and declared him a traitor. Himmler ordered SS guards to hold Göring at Berchtesgaden, yet Himmler's own denouncement was soon to follow. Five days later Hitler learned of Himmler's negotiations with the Allies and, after flying into a rage, expelled Himmler from both the SS and the Nazi Party, ordered his arrest, and further had Himmler's adjutant Hermann Fegelein executed for desertion.

Himmler next departed Berchtesgaden for northern Germany, with Göring having been previously relocated by the SS to a castle in Mauterndorf, Austria. Göring would later be released to the custody of a retreating Air Force unit on May 5, 1945. After Germany's surrender, he would voluntarily turn himself over to Allied forces and later would face trial for war crimes at Nuremberg.

After departing from Göring, Himmler established an SS headquarters in the naval port city of Flensburg where he held two important meetings in the first week of May 1945. The first, as recounted by Auschwitz commander Rudolf Höss, was a meeting with SS security and concentration camp personnel in which Himmler encouraged the surviving SS to "disappear into the armed forces". A second, seemingly contradictory meeting, was apparently held two days later in which Himmler told an inner circle of SS generals that he intended to establish a new SS nation with its capitol in Northern Germany.

Folke Bernadotte, who served as an intermediary for Himmler's plan to surrender Germany to the Allies (Federal German Archives)

Himmler's future in post war Germany was to amount to very little since, even before Hitler's death, Himmler had no further power in the Nazi state. After Adolf Hitler had formally expelled Heinrich Himmler from both the SS and the Nazi Party, these actions were then made official in Hitler's will, signed at 4AM on April 29th, in which Karl Hanke, the Nazi governor of Lower Silesia, was appointed as Himmler's successor in both the office of Reich Leader of the SS and Chief of the German Police. In Himmler's former role as Minister of the Interior (an office which Himmler had at last secured in August of 1943), Hitler appointed SA-Obergruppenführer Paul Giesler.

Karl Hanke, who had joined the SS in 1934 as an Allgemeine-SS staff officer, had little to do with the SS since 1938. His full-time government post was as a member of Josef Goebbels's Propaganda Ministry; however, after falling out of favor with Goebbels, Hanke joined the German Army as a reserve officer and served in both Poland and France. Eventually obtaining the rank of Captain in 1941, he began a rise in the Nazi Party political leadership corps and was appointed a Gauleiter (Governor) while at the same time granted rank as an SS-Gruppenführer.

Hanke came to the notice of Adolf Hitler in 1944, after Hanke was appointed the "Battle Commander of Breslau" (in Western Poland) to defend the city against invasion by the Soviet Army. Hanke was awarded the German Order (the highest decoration in Nazi Germany) for his fanaticism in defending the city, which eventually fell in any event on May 6th 1945. The day before, Hanke had been notified that he was now the new Reichsführer-SS, and he flew from the city of Breslau in order to join the 18th SS Division "Horst Wessel". Hanke wore the uniform of an SS-Schütze (Private) and surrendered to Czech partisans in early June 1945. On June 5th, while being marched to a more secure prisoner-of-war camp, Hanke and two other SS men attempted to escape by jumping onboard a passing train. Accounts vary as to exactly what happened next, however Hanke was most likely shot and then beaten to death by Czech soldiers.

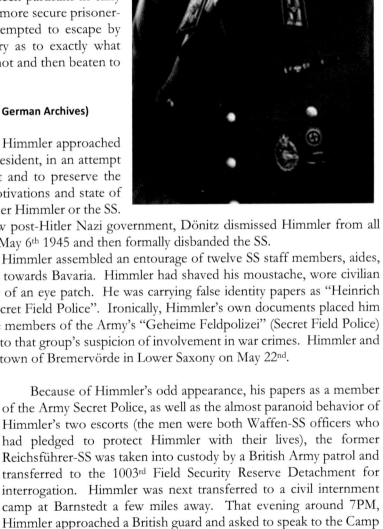

Right: Karl Hanke, the last Reichsführer-SS (Federal German Archives)

After Hitler committed suicide on April 30, 1945, Himmler approached Grand Admiral Karl Dönitz, the new German President, in an attempt to obtain a position in the German government and to preserve the existence of the SS. Regardless of Himmler's motivations and state of mind at this point, Karl Dönitz had no use for either Himmler or the SS. In one of his first official acts as head of the new post-Hitler Nazi government, Dönitz dismissed Himmler from all political, military, and governmental positions on May 6th 1945 and then formally disbanded the SS.

On May 10th 1945, now dejected by Dönitz, Himmler assembled an entourage of twelve SS staff members, aides, and medical personnel and then proceeded south towards Bavaria. Himmler had shaved his moustache, wore civilian clothes, and had removed his eye glasses in favor of an eye patch. He was carrying false identity papers as "Heinrich Hitzinger" of the "Special Armored Company, Secret Field Police". Ironically, Himmler's own documents placed him in an automatic arrest category by the Allies, since members of the Army's "Geheime Feldpolizei" (Secret Field Police) were now being rounded up for interrogation due to that group's suspicion of involvement in war crimes. Himmler and two members of his original SS party reached the town of Bremervörde in Lower Saxony on May 22nd.

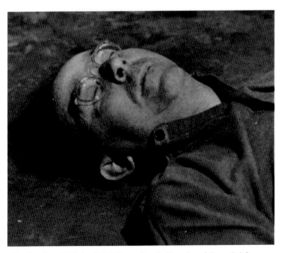

The body of Heinrich Himmler following his suicide on May 23rd 1945 (National Archives)

Because of Himmler's odd appearance, his papers as a member of the Army Secret Police, as well as the almost paranoid behavior of Himmler's two escorts (the men were both Waffen-SS officers who had pledged to protect Himmler with their lives), the former Reichsführer-SS was taken into custody by a British Army patrol and transferred to the 1003rd Field Security Reserve Detachment for interrogation. Himmler was next transferred to a civil internment camp at Barnstedt a few miles away. That evening around 7PM, Himmler approached a British guard and asked to speak to the Camp Commander (Captain Thomas Selvester) at which point Himmler openly confessed as to his true identity. A message was then sent to the 2nd Army Headquarters which then quickly dispatched an intelligence officer to verify Himmler's identify and conduct a preliminary interrogation. Once the British had confirmed that they had in custody none other than Heinrich Himmler, he was transferred to Lüneburg and placed in the custody of the 2nd British Army Intelligence Unit, under the command of Colonel Michael Murphy.

At 10:45 on the night of May 23rd, an Army doctor arrived to conduct a medical examination. When the doctor examined Himmler's mouth, Himmler bit down and cracked a vile of cyanide between his teeth. Himmler was dead within ten minutes; his body was later buried in an unmarked grave at Lüneburg on May 25th 1945.

The end of the SS had been well in sight even before Himmler had been declared a traitor by Adolf Hitler. Following a long retreat along the Eastern Front, the Waffen-SS ended its existence fighting desperate battles in Hungary and Eastern Germany before the remnant divisions fled into Germany and Austria, where they surrendered to the Allies.

The top SS commander in Italy (Karl Wolff) had been in negotiations with Allied forces since February 1945, using the American Office of Strategic Services[xiii] as an intermediary between the Germans and Allied command. In the beginning of May 1945, Wolff finalized a formal surrender agreement and all German forces in Italy capitulated. Meanwhile, in the German capitol of Berlin, several elite SS guard formations, such as the "Begleit-Bataillon Reichsführer-SS" and the "Führer-Begleit-Kompanie", defended Adolf Hitler's bunker until the surrender of the city on May 2, 1945.

Following the suicide of Adolf Hitler, with the German government now taken over by Grand Admiral Karl Dönitz, Germany unconditionally surrendered to the Western Allies and Soviet Union on May 8th 1945. The so called "Flensburg Government" (named after the city in which Dönitz maintained his headquarters) lasted until May 23rd (the same day Himmler committed suicide) when all of its members were arrested by the Allies. Germany was technically a nation without a government until June 5th when the country was formally placed under occupation following the signing of the "Declaration Regarding the Defeat of Germany and the Assumption of Supreme Authority by Allied Powers". From that moment on, Germany fell under the government of an agency known as the Allied Control Council.

Karl Wolff in 1944. Born in 1900, Wolff served as a World War I infantry officer, and later was Chief of Staff to Himmler as well as Supreme Commander of SS forces in Italy. After World War II, his elegant manner and cooperation with the Allies spared Wolff from any serious prosecution. He received minor prison terms both in the 1940s and 1960s, and had retired from the public eye by the 1970s. He died in Rosenheim, Germany on July 17th 1984. (National Archives)

In the last days of World War II, as well as into the beginning of the occupation, there was some fear that the SS would devolve into an underground guerilla movement intent on preserving the Nazi regime. The first indications of such misgivings were in the spring of 1945 when American military units were diverted towards the Bavarian Alps under the belief that SS units were intending a last stand at the "National Redoubt".

Fear existed that if Hitler escaped Berlin, he would set up a stronghold in Bavaria, supported by heavily fortified SS units, and further urge the German people to fight on. Following Hitler's death, a new concern developed that Himmler had ordered the creation of SS guerilla units for a similar purpose of terrorism and sabotage.

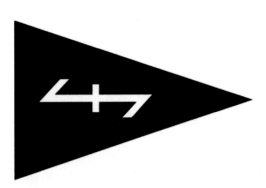

The flag of the Werwolf-SS. Fears existed by both Allied and Soviet forces that an SS sabotage group would arise after the cessation of formal hostilities. In reality, the actual effectiveness and even the existence of the Werwolf-SS is questionable.

Himmler had in fact conceived of a plan for post war SS sabotage groups in a project known as "Operation Werwolf". The order to create SS guerilla teams was first issued in August 1944 when Himmler created the "Generalinspekteur für Spezialabwehr" (Inspector General for Special Defense) which was initially headed by veteran SS commando Otto Skorzeny. Hans-Adolf Prützmann was then designated as the Inspector General of all Werwolf commands.

In March and April of 1945, the Werwolf claimed to have assassinated several American military officers as well as high ranking Germans who had surrendered to the Allies. The Werwolf also performed at least one recognized sabotage operation behind enemy lines, although all twenty-five men of this operation were captured. A propaganda radio program, known as "Radio Werwolf", was also broadcast for a few weeks in April of 1945 from a transmitter in Berlin. The radio announcements encouraged resistance and acts of violence against the Allied and Soviet forces and proclaimed that Germany would never surrender.

By the time Germany did surrender in May 1945, the Werwolf organization was only two hundred strong and Otto Skorzeny was actively attempting to disband the group. As of June 1945, there were still a handful of suspected Werwolf actions occurring against the occupation forces; however, whether the Werwolf was truly to blame was never confirmed. In September 1945 the Second World War came to an end, after Germany's ally Japan surrendered unconditionally. By this point, fanaticism for Hitler had disappeared, along with any active or remnant SS groups, with the war weary population of what had once been Nazi Germany now to face a new era of history.

Justice to the SS

By the fall of 1945, with Allied and Soviet armies now in complete control of occupied Germany, the desire of the victors turned towards justice against those who had caused the Second World War and the horror which the conflict had wrought upon civilization. With the Concentration Camps liberated, and German records now open to investigation, it was obvious that the vast majority of war crimes perpetrated in the name of the Nazi regime had been carried out by the SS.

In an attempt to bring SS members responsible for war crimes to justice, the occupation authorities devised a system by which war criminals would be identified, arrested, tried, and punished. The prosecution of the SS had already begun as early as 1944, when the advancing Soviet Red Army had adopted a policy to summarily execute any SS personnel caught fleeing west. Such summary justice was often overlooked by both the Soviet leadership and the Western Allies, with a general feeling that SS men captured by the Communists deserved their respective fates.

SS men captured in the west were placed in prisoner-of-war camps, albeit in segregated sections away from members of the regular German armed forces. In the east, the murder of captured SS personnel was commonplace, as well as kangaroo courts in which SS officers captured by the Soviets would be tried, convicted, and executed sometimes within just a few hours. The Soviets attempted to justify such measures by pointing out the brutality of the SS and how such persons did not deserve due process. The Soviets offered wide spread evidence of SS atrocities, even attempting to cover up some Soviet actions by blaming them on the SS[xiv].

By the fall of 1945, with the Western Allies preparing for their first trial of major war criminals, the Soviet Union begrudgingly came into line and began to generally follow the same legal procedures for dealing with captured SS men. This factor was not so much a Soviet wish to conform, but rather that most major SS war criminals were being held in the west, and the Soviet Union desired the opportunity to participate in SS prosecutions through cooperation with the Allies.

Heinrich Himmler in 1934. By 1945, the SS which he had forged lay destroyed and its members hunted for war crimes. (Bavarian State Archives)

The first step in bringing SS war criminals to trial was to identify, amongst the chaos of the post war demobilizing German military, who amongst the millions of prisoners-of-war had served in the SS. The task began by publishing the

CROWCASS list, which was an abbreviation for the "Central Registry of War Criminals and Security Suspects". Complied after months of investigation, the list specified specific persons, as well as specific groups, which were to be considered eligible for war crimes prosecution. The Allies also developed a system in which suspected war criminals were classified by levels, depending upon the severity of their crimes. The most serious designation (Category I) dealt with major Nazi war criminals such as top government officials and senior SS personnel.

By agreement amongst the Allies and Soviet Union, Category I war criminals would be tried by an International Tribunal established at Nuremberg. The first such trial, lasting from November 1945 to October 1946, dealt with the top leadership of Nazi Germany. In all, twenty-three defendants were prosecuted, including Ernst Kaltenbrunner who had commanded the SS security forces after the death of Reinhard Heydrich. Between 1946 and 1949 the Allies also conducted twelve additional war crimes tribunals, collectively known as the "Subsequent Nuremberg Trials". Four of these trials dealt specifically with crimes committed by the SS.

SS personnel prosecuted at the Nuremberg War Crimes Trial and Doctor's Trial

Defendant	SS Rank	Position	Trial	Sentence
Martin Bormann	Obergruppenführer	Head of the Nazi Party Chancellery	Trial of Major War Criminals	Death
Viktor Brack	Oberführer	Chancellery Medical Officer	Doctor's Trial	Death
Karl Brandt	Gruppenführer	Hitler's Personal Physician	Doctor's Trial	Death
Rudolf Brandt	Standartenführer	Himmler's Chief Medical Officer	Doctor's Trial	Death
Fritz Fischer	Sturmbannführer	Assistant to Karl Gebhardt	Doctor's Trial	Life in prison
Karl Gebhardt	Gruppenführer	President of the German Red Cross	Doctor's Trial	Death
Karl Genzken	Gruppenführer	Surgeon General of the Waffen-SS	Doctor's Trial	Life in prison
Rudolf Hess	Obergruppenführer	Deputy Führer	Trial of Major War Criminals	
Waldemar Hoven	Hauptsturmführer	Buchenwald Chief Medical Officer	Doctor's Trial	Death
Ernest Kaltenbrunner	Obergruppenführer und General der Waffen-SS und Polizei	Commander Reich Central Security Office (RSHA)	Trial of Major War Criminals	Death
Helmut Poppendick	Oberführer	Chief of SS and Police Medicine	Doctor's Trial	10 years imprisonment
Joachim Mrugowsky	Oberführer	Commander SS Hygiene Institute	Doctor's Trial	Death
Joachim von Ribbentrop	Gruppenführer	Nazi Foreign Minister	Trial of Major War Criminals	Death
Arthur Seyss-Inquart	Gruppenführer	Reich Minister without Portfolio	Trial of Major War Criminals	Death
Wolfram Sievers	Standartenführer	Head of SS Research	Doctor's Trial	Death

During the trial of major war criminals, much discussion focused on whether Albert Speer, who had served as Hitler's Minister of Armaments, had ever served in the SS. Under testimony, Speer stated that he had never been a member of the SS and had in fact turned down the honorary rank of SS-Oberst-Gruppenführer when offered the title by Himmler. In reality, Speer had served in the SS in 1931, as a member of its transport corps, but had been discharged as a private (SS-Mann) to pursue higher Nazi posts.

The so called "Doctor's Trial", held from December 1946 to August 1947, brought twenty-three defendants (ten of them former SS members) to account for medical crimes, chief among them human experimentation. Seven death sentences were passed with two life prison terms and one sentence of ten years. The life sentences were later commuted, and both SS members were released in 1957.

In the spring of 1947, while the Doctor's Trial was still proceeding, the Allied authorities began the prosecution of personnel assigned to the SS Economics and Administration Main Office (the WVHA) which had been the primary command authority for the Concentration Camps, as well as the overseeing administrative body for SS slave labor policies. The "Pohl Trial", named after WVHA Chief Oswald Pohl, lasted from April to November 1947 and tried eighteen members of the SS for war crimes. Richard Glücks, who had commanded Department D of the WVHA overseeing the Concentration Camps, had committed suicide in May 1945 leaving only three living department heads and Oswald Pohl to stand trial. The defendants also included various sections chiefs and administrative underlings, with an indictment issued on four charges of crimes against peace, war crimes, the operation of a slave labor system, and membership in the SS.

Oswald Pohl at his trial in 1947. Pohl was sentenced to death and executed in 1951. (Federal German Archives)

The court convicted fourteen of the WVHA SS members on all charges, while one was convicted on three charges and three more were acquitted. Georg Lörner and Oswald Pohl, the latter of which had served as head of Department W in charge of slave labor projects, were both given death sentences while August Frank, head of the WVHA administration, received a life sentence. The remaining convicted SS members were sentenced to prison terms ranging from ten to twenty years. An appeals court in August 1948 upheld most of the convictions, but spared Lörner from the death penalty and changed his sentence to life imprisonment. In 1951, an amnesty board further commuted all the remaining sentences to lesser prison terms except for Oswald Pohl who was executed on June 8, 1951.

From October 1947 to March 1948, the Allied authorities held the "RuSHA Trial" which prosecuted SS members involved in implementing and enforcing SS racial policies. Defendants included surviving top officers of the SS Race and Settlement Main Office as well as SS personnel assigned to the RKFDV and VOMI which had dealt with relocation and repatriation of ethnic Germans in the conquered eastern territories. Richard Hildebrandt, head of the RuSHA, was the highest-ranking SS officer prosecuted at the RuSHA trial. Ulrich Greifelt, acting head of the RKFVD, and Werner Lorenz, head of the VOMI, were co-defendants. Otto Hofmann, who had been present at the Wannsee Conference, was also prosecuted as were ten other lesser ranking SS officers. The court convicted all but one defendant on charges of war crimes, mainly organizing the deportations of ethnic groups to include the kidnapping of children deemed suitable for Germanization under adopted families. Five of the convicted men were released with time served while the remainder received prison sentences. By 1955, all sentences had been commuted with all those still imprisoned released.

One of the final Nuremberg trials, involving a significant number of SS personnel, was the Einsatzgruppen Trial which took place between September 1947 and April 1948. Twenty-four SS members were indicted on charges of war crimes and genocide, including the commanders of all four of the major Einsatzgruppen. All of the defendants at the Einsatzgruppen Trial, with one exception[xv], were convicted on all counts and sentenced to death. Only three of the defendants would actually be executed, with the remainder of the sentences commuted.

Left: Otto Ohlendorf, one of the more notorious Einsatzgruppen trial defendants, led an Einsatzgruppen where he was accused of murdering tens of thousands of people. Ohlendorf admitted to most of his crimes during frank and open testimony as a witness at the trial of major war criminals. He was subsequently tried himself and sentenced to death. He was executed, along with co-defendant Paul Blobel who had commanded the Babi Yar massacre, on June 7, 1951. (Photo courtesy National Archives)

The last prosecution of SS personnel at Nuremberg occurred between January 1948 and April 1949 during the "Ministries Trial" where twenty-one government bureaucrats were tried for crimes committed during the Nazi regime. Four of the accused were SS members, two of which had held active SS positions while the remainders were holders of honorary SS rank in addition to their standard governmental positions.

SS personnel prosecuted at the Nuremberg Ministries Trial

Defendant	Rank	Position	Photograph
Gottlob Berger	SS-Obergruppenführer und General der Waffen-SS	Head of the SS Main Office	
Hans Kehrl	SS-Brigadeführer	Planning Office of the Ministry of Armaments	
Paul Körner	SS-Obergruppenführer	Prussian Secretary of State	
Walter Schellenberg	SS-Brigadeführer und Generalmajor der Polizei und Waffen-SS	Head of the Ausland-SD and head of the Abwehr military intelligence	

Images courtesy National Archives and Federal German Archives

As compared to other Nuremberg trials, sentences at the Ministries Trial were relatively light. Prison sentences were issued between ten to fifteen years, and all of the convicted SS were released in 1951. The Nuremberg Trials had set an important legal precedence, this being that not only could individuals be held accountable for personal crimes, but also that membership in a particular organization, in this case the SS which had committed countless criminal acts, was also grounds for prosecution. Nuremberg also declared that the entire SS was a criminal organization and that to merely be a member of the SS was in itself a crime. Similar indictments were issued for the Gestapo as well as the SS intelligence service the Sicherheitsdienst (the SD).

The defense attorneys at Nuremberg argued that there were obviously members of the SS who were not criminals and had merely joined an organization which had been associated as a whole with dreadful criminal acts. Prosecutors countered that any member of the SS would have known that the organization was founded on a philosophy of racial superiority and Anti-Semitism, and that most every branch of the SS had in one way or another been connected with war crimes and crimes against humanity. Within the SS, blame was also cast about as members of the Allgemeine-SS claimed to have simply been desk bound paper pushers, with the crimes on the front lines of the Second World War attributable to the Waffen-SS. Members of the Waffen-SS countered that they were simply soldiers doing their duty, and that high ranking decisions involving extermination and genocide had been beyond the level of the front-line SS trooper. The SS even turned on itself, admitting that Gestapo and Concentration Camp personnel were guilty of criminal acts, but that this blame should not be cast upon the more "innocent" members of the SS such as foreign intelligence officers, who simply decrypted enemy messages for the duration of the war, or the part time Allgemeine-SS members who simply met at mustering formations and had never harmed or killed anyone.

In the end, Nuremberg declared that the entire SS was a criminal organization with special emphasis on the Secret Police forces which were to share full guilt as well. The only portion of the SS which was deemed not guilty was the General-SS cavalry formations, which had existed in the 1930s but had been phased out of the SS by 1938. The General-SS Cavalry, which had been seen as a something of a social equestrian riding club, coincidently held membership of the German upper class and nobility. By declaring this group of the SS innocent of wrong doing, Nuremberg had effectively closed the door on prosecution of German high society solely for membership in the SS.

Apart from the Nuremberg war crimes trials, lesser SS personnel faced prosecution from several additional sources. For members of the Waffen-SS charged with war crimes, both the Allied and Soviet authorities held military courts martial proceedings empowered to pass the death sentence. In the east, such trials were a swift and harsh affair, however western military tribunals did offer the accused SS some measure of defense. One of the more famous trials was that of the SS men who had participated in the Malmedy Massacre during the Battle of the Bulge.

Seventy-five members of the Waffen-SS, including SS-Colonel General Josef "Sepp" Dietrich and SS-Colonel Joachim Peiper, were brought to trial for the murder of Allied prisoners of war. The trial lasted between May and July 1946, during which time allegations arose that SS men had been beaten and tortured by Allied interrogators in order to coerce confessions. An American military tribunal convicted seventy-three of the defendants and ordered forty-three death sentences; the remainder of the SS men were given various degrees of prison sentences. Joachim Peiper was sentenced to death while Sepp Dietrich received life in prison. Appeals followed, including a United States Senate investigation which concluded that unlawful prosecutorial and interrogation tactics had been used to obtain convictions.

Sepp Dietrich was paroled in 1955[xvi] while Joachim Peiper walked free a year later. Dietrich was later re-arrested by West German authorities and tried in 1956 for murder due to his role in the 1934 Night of the Long Knives.

Joachim Peiper in a photo dated from 1944 as compared to a personal photograph taken in 1972 (Federal German Archives)

Convicted of manslaughter by the West German government, Sepp Dietrich spent nine months in prison and was released due to ill health. He lived off of a pension contributed to by former SS soldiers and died in 1966. Joachim Peiper spent the 1950s working as a car salesman in Germany, first with Porsche and later Volkswagen. Peiper's notoriety followed him throughout the 1960s and he was the subject of several investigations but never rearrested. He retired to France in 1972 and lived a quiet life until he was tracked down by French Communists in 1976. Peiper's home was firebombed and he was shot to death in July of that year.

In the immediate aftermath of the Second World War, SS personnel captured in Concentration Camps were either tried by the liberating Allied military authority or handed over to the nation in which the Concentration Camp had been located. The camp at Bergen-Belsen, which the British liberated on April 15th 1945, was the site of the first independent Concentration Camp trial in the west. Upon arriving within the Bergen-Belsen camp, the British forces found piles of dead bodies, mass starvation amongst the surviving prisoners, and horrific sanitary conditions. All of the remaining SS personnel in the camp were immediately arrested, including the camp commander Josef Kramer. In September 1945, in the city of Lüneburg, the British prosecuted Kramer and forty-four other SS personnel who had served at Bergen-Belsen. Eleven death sentences were handed down and all of the condemned defendants (including Josef Kramer) were hung on December 13th 1945.

Right: Josef Kramer, the final commander of the Bergen-Belsen Concentration Camp, is shown here shortly after his arrest by the British in May 1945. (Federal German Archives)

In Poland, which had been the site of some of the worst Nazi atrocities of the Second World War, the newly established Republic of Poland created the Supreme National Tribunal which was granted authority by the Soviet government to carry out war crimes trials against Nazi and SS personnel. This communist sponsored legal body replaced several unofficial courts which had been operated by the Polish government-in-exile. The National Tribunal held seven separate trials between June 1946 and July 1948, three of which dealt specifically with the SS. Both Rudolf Höss (Commander of Auschwitz) and Płaszów Concentration Camp commander Amon Göth

were sentenced to death and executed. The tribunal also held a trial of forty-one SS personnel who had served at Auschwitz; in this trial, twenty-three death sentences were passed with the remainder receiving various prison terms. The tribunal also acquitted one SS officer (Doctor Hans Münch) who had served as a physician at Auschwitz and had been known to aide and assist prisoners.

Left: Amon Göth, commander of the Płaszów Concentration Camp, and one-time friend to German industrialist Oskar Schindler, shown in a photo from 1946 (Polish State Archives)

As the 1940s drew to a close, the more formal war crimes tribunals began to conclude in favor of prosecution of Nazi and SS war criminals by local authorities. France held numerous trials of SS personnel, in particular members of the Gestapo, as did Belgium and the Netherlands. In 1947, Italian authorities sentenced Herbert Kappler, who had served as the Security Police Chief of Rome, to life imprisonment.

Kappler would spend thirty years in prison before, after being diagnosed with terminal cancer, he was smuggled from a prison hospital by his wife and died in Soltau, Germany in 1978. Kappler's deputy, SS-Hauptsturmführer Erich Priepke, would fare much better than his superior and would escape to Argentina after the war via falsified Vatican travel papers. He would live in Argentina until 1996 when he was finally extradited to Italy to stand trial for war crimes. Initially found not guilty, a string of appeals and re-trials placed Priepke under house arrest in Italy. He died in October 2013 at the age of 100.

By the 1950s, the prosecution of major SS war criminals had generally subsided, with the last significant SS trial occurring in July 1951 when Jürgen Stroop, who had commanded the Warsaw Ghetto Uprising suppression, was indicted by the Warsaw Criminal District Court and extradited to Poland by American authorities. Stroop was found guilty on four counts of war crimes and crimes against humanity and was executed by hanging in March 1952.

By the late 1950s, the Cold War between the Soviet Union and Western Allies had so solidified that the prosecution of Nazis and former SS personnel became a low priority on both sides of the Iron Curtain. Indeed, past service in the

Nazi regime was sometimes overlooked if the skills and knowledge of a former SS member would be of benefit to either Communist Russia or the Western Allies. By 1958, both the Soviet Union and the western powers were actively recruiting former SS personnel with specialized skills and experience. A well-known incident of overlooking SS membership was the case of Wernher von Braun, who had served as head of Nazi Germany's V-2 rocket program, and was now sought after by the Americans to assist in the space race against the Soviet Union. Von Braun had served as an SS-Sturmbannführer in the Allgemeine-SS, a posting which he would claim in later life was honorary and to which he performed no actual duties.

The case of von Braun was mirrored in several other situations of high profile or highly skilled Germans who had once served in the SS, and who now were being recruited for their skills by a major superpower. The intelligence communities of the American Central Intelligence Agency (CIA), British MI6, and Soviet KGB even went so far as to overlook the past of known war criminals and recruited former Gestapo and Security Service personnel as espionage and intelligence agents. Klaus Barbie, who had served as a Gestapo agent in France and had been responsible for the deportation of children to death camps, was recruited by the U.S. Army Counterintelligence Corps in 1947 and was later granted safe passage to Bolivia by the CIA in the 1950s. Barbie was known to have supplied intelligence information to American, British, and West German agencies and was eventually appointed a Bolivian intelligence officer with the rank of Lieutenant Colonel. Under pressure from France, Barbie was extradited in 1984 and sentenced to life in prison. He died in September 1991 at the age of seventy-seven.

The world would receive a harsh remainder of Nazi history in 1962 when an Israeli Secret Service team, acting on the highest orders of the Israeli government, kidnapped former SS-Lieutenant Colonel Adolf Eichmann who had been present at the Wannsee Conference and had also served as administrator for the Final Solution Jewish extermination program. Eichmann was put on trial in Jerusalem for crimes against humanity, with the court proceedings against him broadcast around the world. After a trial lasting four months, Eichmann was convicted of war crimes and crimes against humanity and sentenced to death; he was executed by hanging on May 31, 1962.

The capture and prosecution of Adolf Eichmann generated a new surge of "Nazi Hunters" around the world; these men and women combed the globe looking for former members of the SS in order to bring such persons to justice. Several international organizations were also founded which sought to bring former SS members to answer for their crimes. One was the Simon Wiesenthal Center, founded in 1977 and named in honor of Jewish Concentration Camp survivor Simon Wiesenthal. Wiesenthal had assisted in the location of Adolf Eichmann and complied lists and dossiers of all known SS personnel still at large, in an effort to assist in their capture.

Renewed interest in Nazi war crimes also led to a new generation of Germans seeking justice against the old guard of the Nazi regime. In December 1963, West Germany charged twenty-two defendants with war crimes, all of whom had been minor SS functionaries at the Auschwitz Concentration-Death Camp between 1941 and 1945. In what became known as the "Frankfurt Auschwitz Trial", a prosecution team led by the Hessian State Attorney Fritz Bauer attempted to prove culpability in war crimes, in particular the selection of prisoners for gas chamber extermination. In defiance, most of the SS defendants at the Frankfurt trial refused to testify, nor would any SS member incriminate another.

One exception was Robert Mulka, who had served as an SS-Captain and adjutant at the Auschwitz camp, and who was one of the very few to take the stand at Frankfurt in his own defense. Under prosecution cross-examination, Mulka denied all knowledge of genocide activities at Auschwitz and claimed that senior officers at the camp were completely unaware that gassings were occurring. In testimony which shocked the world, Mulka angrily shouted to the prosecutor that he himself, as adjutant of the Auschwitz Concentration Camp, had absolutely no knowledge of gassing operations. Despite Mulka's assertions, he was found guilty of war crimes and sentenced to fourteen years in prison. After attempting suicide in 1968, Mulka was released on humanitarian grounds and died of natural causes a year later.

Adolf Eichmann testifies from a bullet proof booth during his Israeli trial in 1962. Eichmann was charged with seventeen separate counts of war crimes and crimes against humanity. He was found guilty and executed by hanging. (Holocaust Memorial Museum)

With the death penalty abolished in West Germany, the defendants at the Frankfurt Auschwitz Trial were in no danger of a capitol sentence, although many still faced the prospect of several years in prison. At the conclusion of the trial, the court handed down six life sentences, mostly to those SS personnel who had been directly involved with the murder of prisoners by gassing or for those who had been members of the camp Gestapo. Former Gestapo officer Wilhelm Borger, who had been identified by camp survivors as a brutal murdering sadist, was sentenced to "Life plus five years" ensuring under German law that he would never be released or paroled. Borger died in prison in 1977.

At the same time as the Frankfurt Auschwitz Trial, the West German government had revisited the case of SS-General Karl Wolff, who had served as both Heinrich Himmler's Chief of Staff and as the Supreme Commander of SS forces in Italy in the last months of World War II. Wolff, who had escaped any serious prosecution after the war, was sentenced by West Germany in 1963 to fifteen years in prison for war crimes. He was released in 1969 due to poor health and his conviction partially vacated in 1971. He died in 1984.

As the 1970s drew to a close, many former SS members began to succumb to old age and escaped justice ironically through death. One such SS member, who was never brought to trial for his crimes, was Doctor Josef Mengele who had conducted medical experiments on children and had further selected thousands for extermination in the Auschwitz gas chambers. Mengele died of a stroke in São Paulo, Brazil in 1979; his remains were exhumed from a Brazilian cemetery in 1985 in which his identity and death were confirmed.

Left: Karl Wolff, shortly before his death in 1984. After being released from prison for a final time in 1969, Wolff lived in quiet retirement and would occasionally lecture or give interviews regarding his time in the SS (Federal German Archives)

The 1980s saw a shift in Nazi hunting from major war criminals towards those who had served as minor functionaries in the SS machine of extermination. A handful of trials occurred through-out the decade, mostly focusing on low level SS guards and other SS personnel who had been involved in genocide administration. For those which justice still could not reach, active vigilante groups continued to seek them out. Gustav Wagner for instance, First Sergeant of the Sobibor Extermination Camp, was found stabbed to death in his Brazilian home in 1980.

As the 20th century drew to a close, the crimes of the SS gradually began to fade from judicial interest. However, in the 1990s this would drastically change with the collapse of the Soviet Union and the opening of Russian archives. After the fall of the USSR, a new wave of interest was sparked concerning Russian and Ukrainian collaborators who had been posted as guards at extermination centers or for those who had served in the Foreign Legions of the Waffen-SS. As late as 2010, there were still active investigations into some of these men who were only in their teens during World War II but were now living unremarkable lives in their 80s and 90s.

Legacy of the SS

There were over one million Germans who served in some capacity within the SS, both before and during the Second World War. Over twenty-two thousand members of the SS served directly in Germany's Concentration Camps while the German Police, including those who served in front line military formation such as the 4th SS-Police Division, comprised just under 150,000 personnel. Over two hundred thousand foreigners also served in the SS, both in the foreign volunteer formations and in the Germanic-SS collaborationist groups in occupied countries.

SS service components and personnel

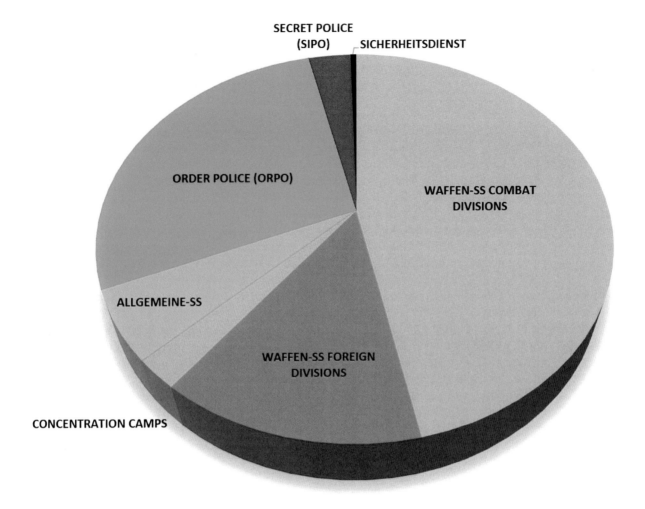

SERVICE COMPONENTS OF THE SS (1944)		
Waffen-SS	SS Officers	18,000
	SS Non-Commissioned Officers	52,000
	SS Enlisted Personnel	640,000
	Foreign Legions and Volunteers	200,000
	TOTAL	**910,000**
Allgemeine-SS	Main Office Personnel	14,500
	Mustering Formations	29,200
	Inactive & Honorary	4,900
	Germanic-SS	35,000
	TOTAL	**83,600**
Police and Security	Ordnungspolizei (Orpo)	401,500
	Sicherheitspolizei (Sipo)	44,800
	Sicherheitsdienst (SD)	6,500
	TOTAL	**452,800**
Total membership of the SS and Police		**1,446,400**

Concentration camp personnel were considered part of the Waffen-SS and numbered approximately 25,000 in strength

The two main branches of the SS, the Allgemeine (General) and Waffen (Armed) SS, existed in a tandem relationship, where SS members could hold separate ranks in either group, while members of the police could hold both SS and police rank simultaneously. A special category was created in 1944 for a select few SS Generals who had been granted simultaneous rank in all three main services of the SS: "SS-Obergruppenführer und General der Polizei und Waffen-SS". Members of the Gestapo and Criminal Police could also hold professional detective and investigator titles, in addition to SS rank, or even serve in the Security Police as non-SS members. During the height of the Second World War, the Gestapo held over thirty-two thousand members while the Criminal Police (Kripo) maintained just under thirteen thousand personnel.

The vast majority of SS members were soldiers of the Waffen-SS, an organization which even to the present day maintains a reputation as one of the fiercest fighting forces in German military history. Concentration camp personnel, of which over twenty thousand served in the SS, were technically part of the Waffen-SS after the year 1942. The smallest branch of the SS was the Sicherheitsdienst (the SD) of which just over six thousand members were serving as of 1944.

The SS officially was disbanded on May 6th 1945, yet many former SS members would find life in post war Germany to be difficult. In the immediate aftermath of the Second World War, membership in the SS was not a fact which many wished to advertise, and for this reason many former SS members choose to abandon their homeland of Germany for a new future abroad. Seeking a place where the past would perhaps fail to follow them, many in the SS sought haven in South America, where several of that continent's governments were sympathetic to the Nazi cause and operated fascist and military dictatorships similar to the now fallen Third Reich. Through escape routes known as "ratlines", former SS members traveled to various sea ports throughout Europe in the hopes of booking passage off the continent. Indeed, even before the outbreak of World War II, South America had been home to several German communities and it was in these settings to which the former SS membership attempted to immerse.

The SS also formed assistance groups to help those trapped in Germany escape the Allies, the first being "Die Spinne" (the Spider) which is thought to have operated until 1950 from a base in Austria. The Spider organization was led by former SS commando Otto Skorzeny and reportedly assisted over six hundred former SS members escape to the South American countries of Argentina, Paraguay, Chile, and Bolivia. The group is also thought to have smuggled a small number of former SS members into Spain. By 1960, reports had surfaced of an even larger SS organization, known as the "Organisation der ehemaligen SS-Angehörigen" (Organization of Former SS Members), abbreviated as "Odessa". The Odessa was suspected to have not only assisted SS members to flee Germany after World War II, but also in having established an underground network of SS operatives, with agents all over the world, many of whom had infiltrated the governments and intelligence services of various nations. The antagonistic relationship between the Arab Middle East and Israel was said to work in favor of Odessa, and the group was further stated to have funding from international businesses as well as ties with terrorist organizations. In truth, while there was most likely an escape network of SS personnel operating similar to Odessa, the international intrigue of such a group is today largely regarded as fiction[xvii].

One SS assistance group which operated fairly openly was "Stille Hilfe" (the full name being "Die Stille Hilfe für Kriegsgefangene und Internierte" or "Silent assistance for prisoners of war and interned persons"). The group operated at its height between 1955 and 1974 and assisted former members of the SS who were accused of war crimes. Stille Hilfe collected funds for defense attorneys and also assisted Nazis accused of war crimes seeking to avoid prosecution. One the main leaders of Stille Hilfe was Heinrich Himmler's daughter, Gudrun Burwitz. As with Odessa, Stille Hilfe was rumored to have operated an underground network of SS throughout the world; however, in reality, the group was mainly a welfare aid association with modest membership.

One organization which sought recognition of SS service was the "Hilfsgemeinschaft auf Gegenseitigkeit der Angehörigen der ehemaligen Waffen-SS" (Mutual Assistance Association of Former Waffen-SS Members), better known as the HIAG. The HIAG was founded in 1959 by former SS-Major General Otto Kumm and sought the recognition of Waffen-SS soldiers as combat soldiers entitled to military pensions. By the mid-1960s there were a quarter of a million former Waffen-SS soldiers living in West Germany, of which twenty thousand were members of the HAIG. While the organization had some success at military recognition of the Waffen-SS, by the 1970s the group had been classified as a far-right political group. HAIG was formally disbanded in the 1980s, although attempts to obtain pensions for Waffen-SS veterans continued into the 21st century. Today, the government of Germany does grant war pensions to disabled Waffen-SS soldiers, provided that the service member was not directly involved with war crimes nor assigned to a unit which was known to have participated in genocidal atrocities during the Second World War.

One lasting legacy of the SS, which is seen in Germany to this very day, is the impact in which Heinrich Himmler's black corps exerted upon the German police. By the close of the Second World War, the German Police had been completely infiltrated by the SS, fielding two full police divisions within the Waffen-SS, and further maintaining hundreds of police paramilitary units for the purposes of occupation and atrocities along the Eastern Front. In war torn Germany, both the Allied and Soviet occupation authorities required police services to maintain order, and subsequently the German police were quickly put to work throughout the broken and defeated country. While there was some prosecution of high-ranking police officials for war crimes, the ordinary rank and file German policemen mostly escaped notice by both war crimes investigators and the de-Nazification courts, established in the late 1940s to prevent former Nazis for reassuming positions within the civil service. By the 1950s, both East and West Germany had established new police forces, with many of the police officers recruited from the former ranks of the Ordnungspolizei. Veteran detectives of the Criminal Police (Kripo) were also highly sought after, while security personnel of the Sicherheitspolizei were occasionally offered police positions within the communist run secret police force of East Germany, known as the "Stasi"[xviii]. The regular East German Police (Volkspolizei or "People's Police") was also established using organizational structures very similar to the Nazi Ordnungspolizei.

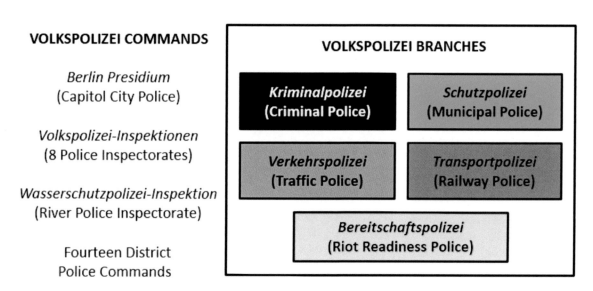

Above: The organization of the East German police forces.
Many of the phrases, terms, and office names for this organization were direct carry overs from the Ordnungspolizei of Nazi Germany

The East German Police was originally commanded by a senior police official known as the "Chef der deutschen Volkspolizei", a phrase very similar to Himmler's title as Chief of the German Police. Command of the East German police was later merged with the Interior Ministry Director, and became known by the single title "Minister of the Interior and Chief of the German Police" (Minister des Innern und Chef der deutschen Volkspolizei). The East German Police ceased to exist in 1990, with the defunct Volkspolizei merged with their West German counterparts and the Secret Police of the Stasi abolished.

In West Germany, the police were re-founded in the late 1940s as a decentralized force within each German state, and known collectively as the "Landespolizei". In the modern age, there are currently sixteen separately legislated Landespolizei in Germany, with each one delegating further authority to city and town police, collectively known as the Ordnungsdienst. In some of the larger German cities (such as Hamburg and Berlin) independent self-regulating police forces exist known as the Stadtpolizei. The German federal government, under the authority of the Minister of the Interior, also maintains several police organizations which deal with national law enforcement issues. In both the case of East and West Germany, as well as the modern day police of 21st century Germany, many of the regulations, uniforms, and organizational structures may be attributed to the Order Police of the 1930s.

Wartime uniforms of the SS

Beginning in 1942, when wartime publications of both the Americans and British attempted to familiarize their military personnel with the confusing array of SS titles and insignia, SS uniforms have captured the interest of both professional historians and enthusiasts alike.

By 1939, the field grey SS tunic had been adopted as a standard uniform by both the armed SS units of the SS-Verfügungstruppe as well as the concentration camp staffs of the SS-Totenkopfverbande. Within the General (Allgemeine) SS, full time office and headquarters staff members had been issued the grey jacket as well, while the black uniform survived within the part time SS mustering formations.

Regulations enacted in the summer of 1939 provided for a more militaristic look to the SS grey jacket uniform. A closed collar was adopted, replacing the shirt and tie with a generic undershirt, while the older SS shoulder cords were replaced with Army style insignia. For non-commissioned officers, white collar piping was worn in the same practice as NCOs of the German Army. The first military SS uniforms were then issued to the SS-VT, with concentration camp staffs receiving the military jacket shortly thereafter. To differentiate between the various branches of the armed SS, as well as to distinguish SS-VT troops from Concentration Camp personnel, shoulder boards were worn with a colored underlay. This coloring was also displayed in the piping worn along the edges of the SS field cap.

The grey uniforms of the General-SS never adopted wartime Army style insignia, but rather continued to display the thinner shoulder cords worn on SS uniforms prior to 1939. General SS uniforms also could be worn with either a closed or open collar, although most uniforms of the Allgemeine-SS were worn open collared with a shirt and tie. All SS uniforms displayed rank and unit insignia on opposite color lapels, while SS-Colonels and SS-General officers wore rank on both collars.

An SS non-commissioned officer in 1942. The Army style shoulder boards and NCO piping were first adopted in 1939 (Federal German Archives)

By 1941, several of the pre-war unit insignia patches had been discontinued, and within the armed SS a generic "SS" runes had been adopted as a standard insignia for most of the Waffen-SS. A standard Death's Head insignia was also now in use by the SS-Totenkopf formations. All military SS uniforms were worn with Army style shoulder boards – in some cases, the SS personnel would not display collar rank, but rather a "double" version of the unit insignia. This style of wear was common mostly to the SS-Death's Head's units, but also occasionally encountered in other branches of the SS.

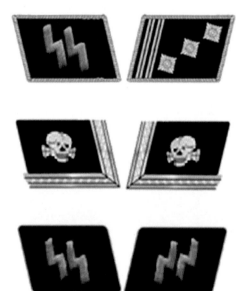

Throughout World War II, SS headgear developed to match the particulars of the various wartime uniforms. In addition to the standard grey SS cap, an SS helmet was commonly worn by enlisted soldiers, as was a field cap known as an "Einheitsmütze", or more technically known as the M43. A "Crusher Cap" also existed which was essentially a standard SS cap with the visor cord removed. An SS garrison cover could also be used for field duty.

Left: Collar insignia style of the war time SS. SS runes displayed with rank pips (top example) was the most common method of rank display. Within the Totenkopf Division, the double Death's Head insignia (middle example) was worn on both collars. Rarest of all was the reversed SS runes (bottom example), of which very few examples survive.

Enlisted SS soldiers displayed SS rank collar insignia accompanied with a bare black shoulder strap. For the Senior Private and Corporal ranks, an Army style sleeve chevron was worn on the left shoulder. SS non-commissioned officers displayed SS rank collar insignia accompanied by a corresponding Army style sergeant shoulder strap.

For SS enlisted soldiers serving in the Corporal grades, who were under consideration for promotion to non-commissioned officer status, a special title of "SS-Unterführer-Anwärter" (Junior Leader Candidate) was used in lieu of a standard rank.

SS officers displayed silver trimmed rank collar patches, along with corresponding Army style shoulder boards. Within the armed units of the SS-VT (later the Waffen-SS), the rank of SS-Oberführer possessed no military equivalent in the German Army and thus was regarded as a Senior Colonel position. Within the Allgemeine-SS, this rank was seen as the first general officer position. Those holding the rank of Oberführer were entitled to wear the grey overcoat lapels of a general officer, but still wore the shoulder boards of an SS-Colonel. For this reason, Oberführer is often equated to a type of Brigadier position, although its exact status and parity has remained dubious.

At the beginning of the Second World War, SS general officers attached to military commands still displayed the older styled silver SS shoulder cords. In the first year of the war, SS generals attached to the SS-Verfügungstruppe also were known by the suffix "General der SS-VT" in addition to their SS rank. In 1940, with the formal creation of the Waffen-SS, the suffix "der Waffen-SS" replaced the older SS-VT title for all SS generals attached to armed SS units.

An SS soldier in 1943. This soldier displays the "SS" runes and wears an M43 Field Cap (National Archives)

An M40 SS helmet. The helmet bore the runes of the SS on one side with a swastika crest displayed on the other.

In 1942, the SS created a new general officer rank known as SS-Oberst-Gruppenführer, which was the equivalent to Colonel General. To incorporate the new rank into the SS hierarchy, collar insignia for SS generals was modified to a new design displaying a three leafed collar insignia with additional pips based upon the rank of the SS-General in question. The 1942 upgrade of SS general officer insignia also encompassed a slight change to the insignia for Standartenführer and Oberführer, mainly to conform the collar rank design to the same straight leaf pattern used for general officer insignia.

The collar leaf design of the SS-Colonel ranks was also changed within the General-SS; however, Allgemeine-SS Oberführer were still entitled to display the thick shoulder boards of an SS general, whereas Waffen-SS personnel of this rank wore a standard military colonel's board, the same as a Standartenführer.

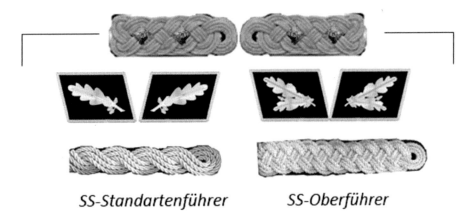

SS-Standartenführer   SS-Oberführer

Post-1942 insignia for SS-Standartenführer and Oberführer. Waffen-SS Oberführer wore shoulder boards of an Army Colonel (top example) while Allgemeine-SS personnel continued to wear the thick silver boards of an SS-General.

SS Membership Numbers

The SS membership number system was designed as a parallel seniority method to SS rank, and also served as an SS member's service number within the overall structure of the SS. The holding of a low membership number identified an SS member as an "Old Fighter" and often entitled such persons to rapid promotions, choice assignments, and the receipt of various other benefits. All members of the Allgemeine-SS were assigned an SS membership number as were most members of Waffen-SS.

Adolf Hitler, in his capacity as Supreme Commander of the SS, held SS membership number 1, as well as a special title known as the "Oberste Führer der Schutzstaffel". SS membership number 2 was held by Emil Maurice, who also served in the 1920s as the Supreme Commander of the Nazi Stormtroopers.

Heinrich Himmler, who ultimately became the most powerful leader of the SS, held SS membership #168. Himmler was known to dislike those SS members with earlier numbers than his, since many were considered early Nazi Party fighters with close ties to Hitler. Himmler was further known to actively attempt to discredit early SS members, in particular Emil Maurice whom Himmler accused of being Jewish, as well as Christian Weber who was one of Hitler's first bodyguards and later declared incompetent after failing to stop an assassination attempt against Hitler in 1939. Karl Hanke, the last Reichsführer-SS, held SS membership number #203,013.

Chronology of SS membership numbers

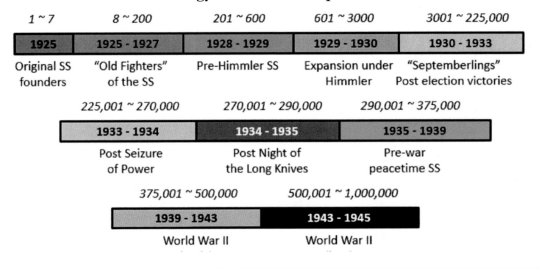

A special SS rank of administrative significance, created in 1942, was that of "SS-Rottenführer (2. Gehaltsstufe)". Created as an equivalent to the German Army's "Stabsgefreiter" rank (see right for comparison), this cumbersome title was used for pay purposes and was bestowed upon any Rottenführer with over five years of SS service. Two other SS ranks of unique history are those of the entry level probationary titles "Bewerber" and "Anwärter". The rank of SS-Anwärter (translated as "Candidate") had existed as a title dating  back to the 1920s, but first appeared as a formal SS rank in 1933. SS Candidates within the Allgemeine-SS underwent a challenging probationary and training period of six months, only after which were they fully accepted into the SS with the rank of SS-Mann.

The rank of SS-Bewerber (Applicant) first appeared within the SS hierarchy in 1934, and was primarily used for members of the Hitler Youth who had reached the age of 18 and now sought to become members of the SS. Both

Anwärter and Bewerber were only apparently used within the General-SS, and did not exist within the military formations of the SS-VT and later the Waffen-SS.

Under a system devised in November of 1935, the term SS-Anwärter ceased to be an SS rank and instead became a generic title for any member of the SS who had yet to complete a probationary period of three years membership in the Allgemeine-SS. SS members in a probationary status were known by the prefix "Staffel", instead of "SS". For instance, an SS member with the rank of Sturmmann would be known as a "Staffel-Sturmmann", until having served three years in the SS, after which time the SS member would be referred to by the full title of SS-Sturmmann. Full SS members were collectively referred to by the title "SS-Mann", which itself survived as a rank, but only in the General-SS. Within the counterpart Waffen-SS, this rank was generically known as SS-Schütze

The Armed-SS inducted members under different enlistment criteria from their General-SS counterparts, with SS recruits commonly referred to by the standard "SS" prefix before their ranks. In the case of the lowest rank of Private (SS-Schütze), the rank was known by a variety of titles depending upon the career field of the SS man in question. The rank of SS-Schütze was the generic and most common rank; after 1942, Concentration Camp personnel were considered full members of the Waffen-SS, and used the rank of SS-Schütze instead of SS-Mann.

After six months of service in the armed SS, personnel were automatically promoted to the rank of Senior Private, designated by the prefix "Ober" in front of the standard rank title. The insignia for this designation was a silver diamond worn on the left sleeve above the national eagle insignia (see example right).

The Senior Private rank was apparently unique to the armed SS – historical connotations of the existence of an "SS-Obermann" rank within the General-SS remain unconfirmed.

Several special SS uniforms were also created for use in alternate weather climates, including fur lined overcoats and caps, as well as a khaki uniform for use in tropical climates. The SS also maintained a summer white tunic as well as a rare "summer shirt" uniform worn with open collar and shoulder boards.

Examples of alternate SS uniforms. Left to right: Summer SS service uniform, tropical SS jacket, along with the rare white duty shirt uniform (Images courtesy Federal German Archives and Holocaust Memorial Museum)

SS ranks and insignia (1942)

Enlisted Rank Insignia

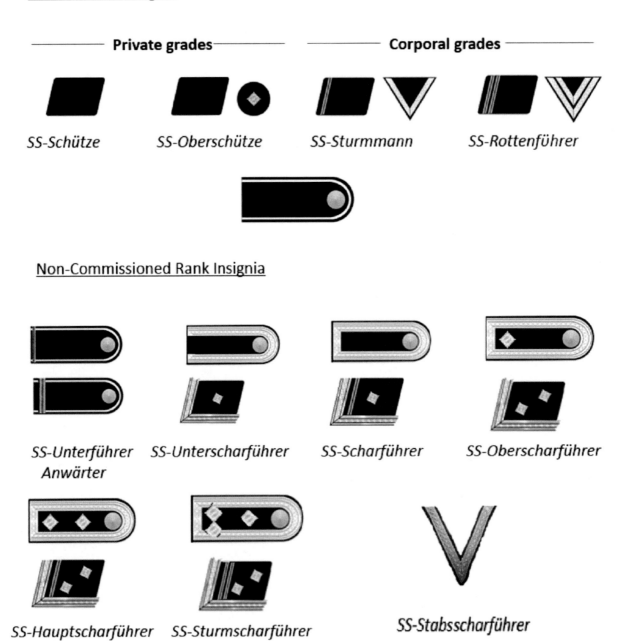

———— Private grades ———— **———— Corporal grades ————**

SS-Schütze   SS-Oberschütze   SS-Sturmmann   SS-Rottenführer

Non-Commissioned Rank Insignia

SS-Unterführer   SS-Unterscharführer   SS-Scharführer   SS-Oberscharführer
Anwärter

SS-Hauptscharführer   SS-Sturmscharführer   SS-Stabsscharführer

In 1942, the rank of SS-Private was known by various names depending upon the career field of the soldier. For those SS soldiers aspiring for promotion to non-commissioned officer, two different insignia existed for NCO candidates, depending upon years of service (above and below 12 years). A special insignia of SS-Stabsscharführer, worn as a chevron on the right arm, denoted the first sergeant of an entire company, battalion, or regiment. This chevron was later replaced by silver cuffbands, commonly known as "pistons", worn on the lower sleeves.

Officer Rank Insignia

Company grades

SS-Untersturmführer   SS-Obersturmführer   SS-Hauptsturmführer

Field grades

SS-Sturmbannführer   SS-Obersturmbannführer

SS-Standartenführer   SS-Oberführer

Waffen-SS officers during the Second World War wore Army style shoulder boards, coupled with rank insignia on one collar and an SS unit insignia on the other. Officers ranked Standartenführer and above wore rank insignia on both collars. Prior to 1940, generals in the Armed-SS wore a single grade thick silver shoulder cord and were known by the suffix "der SS-VT" (SS-Verfügungstruppe). After 1941, generals of the armed SS were known by the suffix "der Waffen-SS" and began wearing golden laced general officer shoulder boards.

General Officer Rank Insignia (SS-VT)

SS-Brigadeführer   *SS-Gruppenführer*   *SS-Obergruppenführer*
und Generalmajor   *und Generalleutnant*   *und General*
der SS-VT   *der SS-VT*   *der SS-VT*

General Officer Rank Insignia (Waffen-SS)

SS-Brigadeführer
und Generalmajor
der Waffen-SS

SS-Gruppenführer
und Generalleutnant
der Waffen-SS

SS-Obergruppenführer
und General
der Waffen-SS

SS-Oberst-Gruppenführer
und Generaloberst
der Waffen-SS

SS military branch colors

Artillery	Veterinary	Tank & Anti-Tank
Support & Garrison Troops	Cavalry & Reconnaissance	Signal & Propaganda
Panzer Grenadiers	Mountain Troops	Administration & Reserve
Infantry	Engineers	Legal Personnel & Smoke Units
Medical	Supply & Field Administration	Motorcycle Units
SS Generals		
Military Geologists		

Non-Military SS Branch Colors

General-SS	Concentration Camps

Members of the SD and Security Police wore white uniform piping with green piped shoulder boards

SS-Private rank designations

FORMATION	TITLE	BRANCH DESIGNATION
Infanterie	SS-Schütze	Infantry Units
Panzerjäger		Tank Units
Kradschützen		Motorcycle Units
Radfahrer		Bicycle Units
Sanitäts Einheit		Medical Units
Werkstatt Einheit		Construction Units
Wehrgeologen		Geology Units
Kriegsbericht		Correspondence Units
Konzentrationslager(*)		Concentration Camps
Artillerie	SS-Kanonier	Artillery Units
Gebirgs-Artillerie		
Sturmgeschütz		Assault Guns
Flak Einheit		Anti-Aircraft & Rocket Units
Werfer Einheit		
Panzer Regiment	SS-Panzerschütze	Tank Units
Panzer Späh Einheit		
Panzer Grenadier	SS-Panzergrenadier	
Grenadier	SS-Grenadier	Mortar Units
Gebirgsjäger	SS-Jäger	Mountain Units
Karstwehr		
Reiter Regiment	SS-Reiter	Cavalry & Reconnaissance Units
Pionier Einheit	SS-Pionier	
Nachrichten	SS-Funker	Communications Units
Nachschub Einheit	SS-(Kraft)fahrer	Supply Units
Veterinär Einheit	SS-Reiter	Veterinary Units
Feldgendarmerie	SS-Feldgendarm	Military Police & Penal Battalions
Bewährungs Einheit	SS-Bewährungsschütze	

* After 1942, Concentration Camp personnel were considered full members of the Waffen-SS and used the rank of SS-Schütze as the lowest Concentration Camp SS rank. Prior to this, concentration camp privates held the rank of SS-Mann.

Part Two
Organization and Personnel

CHAPTER FOUR: THE ALLGEMEINE-SS

The German term "Allgemeine", meaning "general, common, or universal" was first applied to members of the Schutzstaffel in the summer of 1934. The very first utterance of the phrase "Allgemeine-SS" appears to have been made by members of the Leibstandarte to differentiate between themselves, as armed SS soldiers attached to the Chancellery Guard in Berlin, and the regular SS troopers who mustered throughout all of Germany.

The General-SS was declared an official component of the SS in August 1935, primarily to separate the mustering SS units from the full-time personnel of the SS-Verfügungstruppe. Concentration camp staffs and guards were at this time also considered part of the Allgemeine-SS, but in 1936 the operation of the camps was removed from the administrative control of regional SS leaders and placed under control of the SS-Totenkopfverbande. While the Concentration Camps would technically remain part of the Allgemeine-SS until 1942, the camp service maintained a separate identity from the General-SS formations throughout Germany.

The secret police apparatus of Nazi Germany, eventually totally dominated by the SS, was technically never officially part of the Allgemeine-SS. Those SS members who served in such organizations as the Criminal Police and the Gestapo were in fact state employees of the Ministry of the Interior. The one exception was the Sicherheitsdienst, which remained a Nazi Party sponsored SS group throughout its existence, and whose members were considered regular personnel of the Allgemeine-SS. After 1939, all of the secret and state police forces of Germany were administered through the Reich Central Security Office, which was a joint command between the SS and the German Interior Ministry. What remained of the Allgemeine-SS became a mixture of full and part time SS groups, all of which were considered Nazi Party organizations unconnected to either the governmental or military forces of the Third Reich. The General-SS in this capacity was originally as it had always been intended to be- a fraternal organization of Aryan men serving the cause of the Nazi Party for the promotion of a Germanic nation and race.

The General-SS formations

In January of 1933, when the SS was still considered part of the Sturmabteilung, most of the SS unit and office titles mirrored their SA counterparts. After the Night of the Long Knives, the SS organization was overhauled by Heinrich Himmler, causing many older SS designations and offices to either be renamed or disbanded.

Most members of the SS in 1934 were part of mustering formations located in major German towns and cities. These groups were voluntary organizations whose members served without pay and usually meet once or twice a week in SS uniform to attend training and discuss Nazi doctrine. When Nazi Party officials visited the local area, these SS units would mobilize to serve as ad hoc body guard units.

The SS units in Germany were organized in a hierarchal manner, at the top of which were the SS Senior Districts and extending downwards to the level of the local SS regiments. Each command level of the SS had its own leader and staff, along with various sub-offices. By 1936, this SS chain of command had solidified into what would remain its final form until the end of the Second World War.

The SS-Senior Districts (SS-Oberabschnitt) were first formed in August of 1934 from the older SS Groups. These original groups had evolved from earlier SS regions based on SA commands. Within the hierarchy of the SS Senior Districts, it was the "Oberabschnitt Führer" (Senior District Leader) who was seen as the direct representative of Heinrich Himmler in all SS matters. As the SS went on to absorb more and more security and police functions, these senior SS officials would inherit the title of SS and Police Leader. By the time of the Second World War, it was standard practice for SS-Senior District Leaders and SS and Police Leaders to be the same person.

The Chief of Staff was second in command to the Oberabschnitt Führer and oftentimes served as acting Senior District Leader when the regular leader was engaged elsewhere or otherwise deployed to other SS posts outside of Germany. The Chief of Staff was also the direct superior to the Chief of Personnel who in turn oversaw the headquarters staff officers of administration, training, medical, and communications.

Right: Senior commands of the General-SS. Within the SS regiments existed smaller units of SS battalions, companies, squads, and teams. The SS company was the level at which most SS troopers would be associated on a daily basis.

Every SS Senior District maintained a Sports Office in charge of physical training of SS men and the certification for sports decorations. A Family Welfare Office also existed which served to assist the next-of-kin of SS members who were ill, had suffered injuries, or who had died while serving on active duty in the armed forces.

The SS Family Welfare Offices were subordinated to the larger SS Family Office (Sippenamt), considered part of the SS Race and Settlement Office (RuSHA). Subordinate SS-Districts were further required to maintain a collateral duty position known as "Fürsorgereferent", whose function was to monitor the health and welfare of all SS members in the lower districts and regimental commands. The health and welfare officer was most often a senior SS-non-commissioned officer.

SS-Oberabschnitt organization

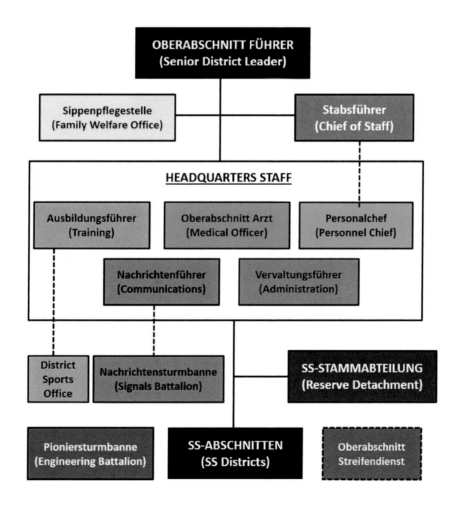

129

The SS Senior Districts further maintained a number of independent engineering and signal battalions. These units were often deployed throughout the district in order to deal with matters involving large SS gatherings, where communications between various lower commands was required. These units also responded to civil alert situations such as flooding or emergency construction work. A further component of the Senior Districts was the "SS-Streifendienst", formed on an as-needed basis to serve as an internal SS police force.

The SS-Streifendienst uniform brassard. These SS troopers were specially selected for high profile security duties and protected top SS and Nazi leaders (Graphical recreation based upon original photograph courtesy Federal German Archives)

Within each SS-Oberabschnitt were maintained between three to four subordinate SS districts (known as "SS-Abschnitten"). Each district in turn maintained a staff and headquarters compliment. SS districts, in contrast to their Senior District counterparts, were designated by Roman numerals rather than proper names. Each district was also allocated a medical office, as well as a transportation company, to coordinate the movement of senior SS personnel throughout the district. Within each SS district existed between three to five "SS-Standarten", which were regimental sized formations of approximately two thousand SS men. By the outbreak of the Second World War, many Standarten had lost their members to wartime conscription, and other war essential duties, which precluded regular SS service and downsized these units significantly.

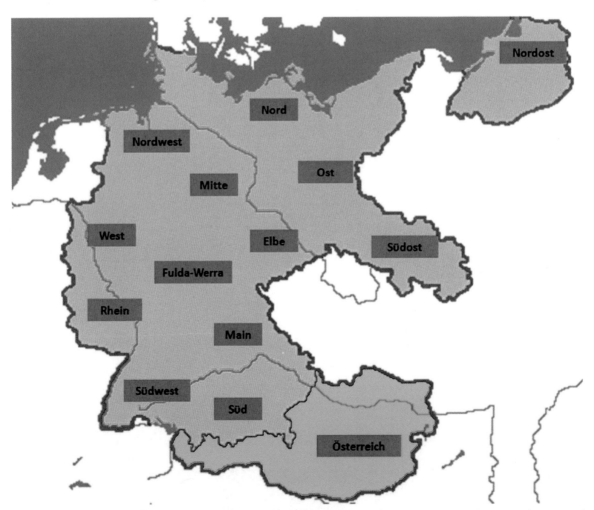

SS senior districts of Germany and Austria in 1937. The Austrian SS senior district, originally considered a foreign SS formation, had existed since 1934. In 1938, following the Anschluss with Germany, this district was renamed "Donau".

130

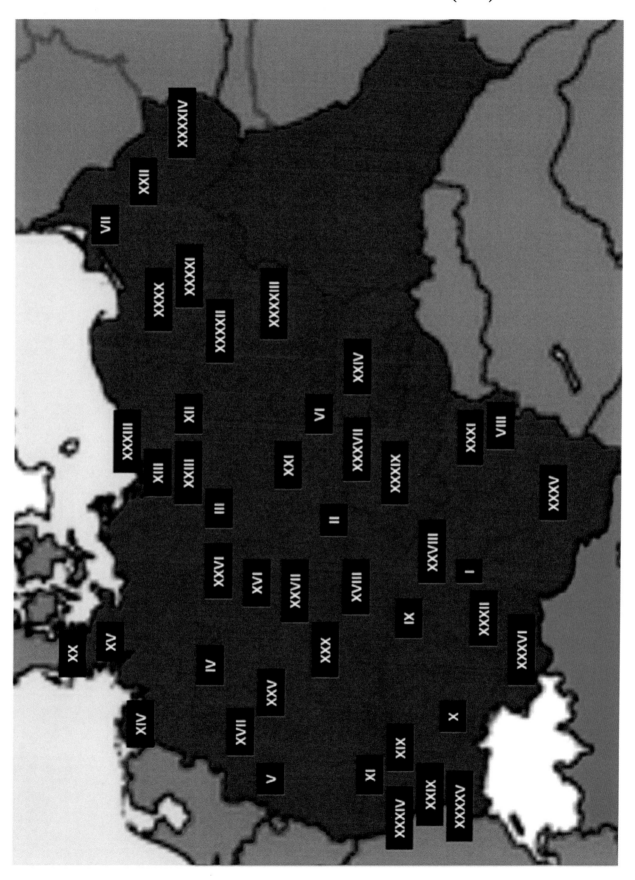

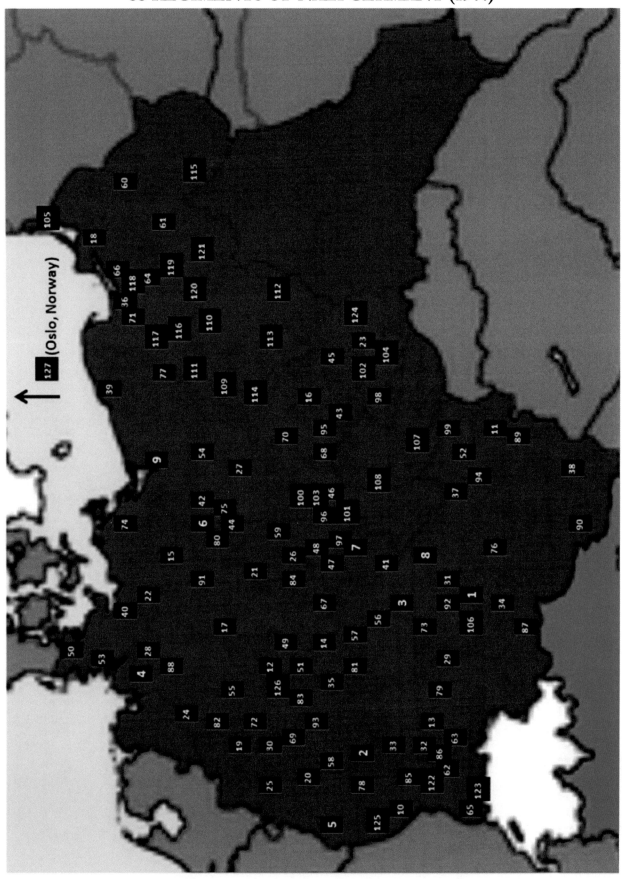

SS-District organization

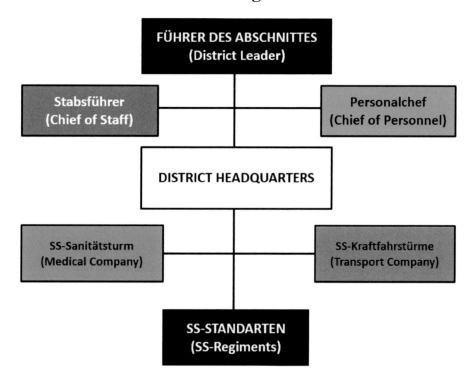

The SS-Standarten were the core Allgemeine-SS formations, with a headquarters situated in a major German city with subordinate units located in the surrounding geographical area. Each Standarten had its own commander and headquarters staff, as well as various specialty and staff units. There were eventually over one hundred SS-Standarten established in Germany, as well as an additional SS regiment founded at the end of the Second World War in Norway.

Manpower strength of the General-SS regiment

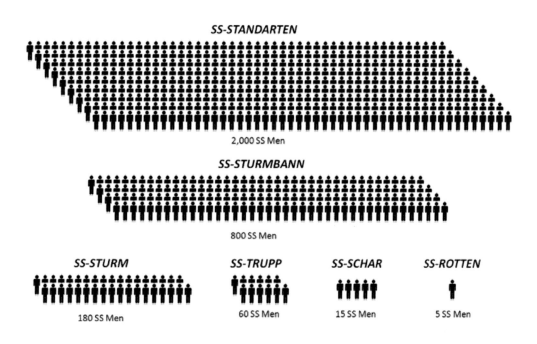

The SS-battalion (SS-Sturmbann) was the basic operational unit of the General-SS and was designed to act independently of its parent Standarten should the need arise. A single Sturmbann numbered approximately eight hundred SS men and was comprised of four line companies (SS-Sturm) as well as a medical squad and a music company for parade functions. The designation for SS battalions was through the use of roman numerals, paired with the numeric designation of a SS trooper's company and regiment. For instance, an SS soldier assigned to the 5th company of the 3rd battalion in the 77th SS regiment would have their assignment designator "5/III/77".

The SS-company was the primary unit in which an SS member held day to day contact. Companies were further divided into two or three platoons (known as "SS-Truppen") which were themselves divided into three or four squads (SS-Scharen) of fifteen men a piece. The smallest SS unit was the "Rotten" (team) which contained four or five SS men under the command of an SS-Rottenführer.

SS-Standarten organization

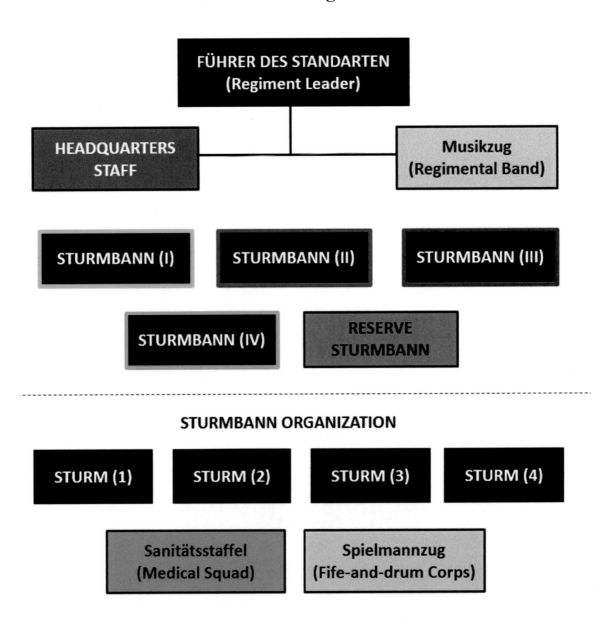

Staff and specialty units

Each SS Senior District possessed a signals and engineering battalion, while the subordinate SS-districts contained an independent transportation company. The General-SS also possessed its own medical corps, beginning with the "Sanitätsstaffel" which were medical squads attached to each SS battalion. These medical units were in turn subordinated to an SS District Medical Company (SS-Sanitätsturm) with all such companies collectively referred to as the "SS-Sanitätsabteilung" (SS Medical Detachment).

The ultimate authority for all medical units in the Allgemeine-SS was the Chief Medical Office of the SS, originally designated as Department Five of the SS headquarters in 1932, later becoming a sub-office of the expanded SS Main Office (the SS-Hauptamt). By 1940, the position of "Surgeon General of SS and Police" (Reichsarzt SS und Polizei) had been established and was subordinated to the Chief of the SS Main Office.

While most SS medical units were integrated into SS line commands, an independent SS medical unit known as the "Röntgensturmbann SS-HA" (SS X-Ray Battalion of the SS Main Office) existed between 1934 and 1939. Comprised of three hundred and fifty full time SS medical personnel, this unit toured Germany and offered physical exams and X-ray screening to the membership of the General-SS. The SS X-Ray Battalion was first commanded by SS-Obersturmbannführer Konrad Perwitzschky and later transferred to the leadership of Dr. Hans Holfelder who was a Professor of Medicine at the University of Frankfurt and also an SS-Oberführer in the General-SS. The services of the SS X-Ray Battalion were utalized not only by the SS, but also the Nazi political districts (Gauleitung) and by the German Labor Front. In 1940, the SS X-Ray Battalion was disestablished and its members transferred into other medical positions within the Waffen-SS.

Perhaps the most significant of the SS speciality units were the SS cavalry commands of the General-SS. First created in 1934, a total of twenty three Allgemeine-SS cavalry regiments were eventually established, grouped into seven riding districts. The riding commands were essentially equistrian sport clubs intended to intice the German nobility and upper class towards SS membership, with the majority of these riding commands operating in smaller towns and throughout the countryside of Germany. A headquarters for the SS Cavarly Corps was established in 1935 as the "Inspector of SS Cavalry Training" under the command of veteran SS officer Christian Weber. Weber further formed an SS Cavalry School (SS-Hauptreitschule) which was commanded by Hermann Fegelein. It was Fegelein who shaped the SS Cavalry into a force which would go on to serve in combat during World War II.

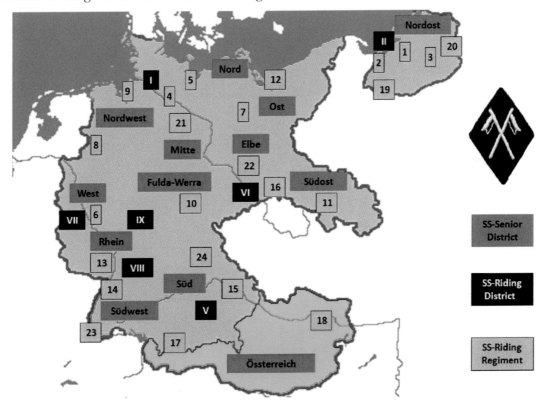

SS cavalry formations in 1938. Riding Districts III and IV were authorized but never formed.

Hermann Fegelein – Cavalry Master of the SS

Hermann Fegelein, a native of Bavaria, joined the Bavarian State Police in 1927; three years later, he joined both the Nazi Party and the Sturmabteilung (SA). A proficient horse rider, he transferred to the SS and in 1934 joined the original SS Cavalry Corps (Reiter-SS). In 1935, Fegelein became head of the SS Cavalry School and in 1938 supervised the equestrian events at the Berlin Summer Olympics. In 1939, Fegelein formed the SS Death's Head Cavalry Regiment, responsible for suppressing resistance in Warsaw, and in 1941 commanded the newly formed SS Cavalry Brigade. He spent the next two years performing Jewish round-ups and executions in the Soviet regions of the Pripyat marshes. A year later, the SS Cavalry Brigade was upgraded to a division and in 1944 was designated as the 8th SS Cavalry Division "Florian Geyer". In 1944, Fegelein was assigned as Himmler's adjutant to Adolf Hitler and in June 1944 married the sister of Eva Braun, Hitler's future wife. In 1945, Fegelein followed Hitler to Berlin; that April he attempted to desert the city but was captured by an SS patrol and executed on Hitler's orders.

SS-Riding Regiment organization

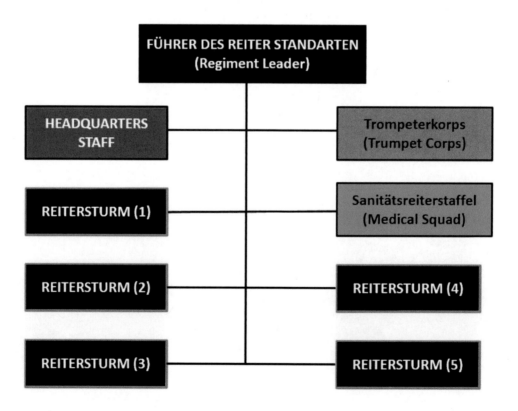

In 1939, the SS riding commands were significantly downsized, with the majority of their members conscripted into Army cavalry commands. A high portion of SS cavalry members were also transferred into the SS Death's Head Cavalry Regiments which were themselves later consolidated into the SS Cavalry Brigade of the Waffen-SS. By 1942, an SS Cavalry Division had been formed, which would later be designated as the 8th SS Cavalry Division "Florian Geyer" in the Waffen-SS.

In addition to cavalry and medical units, the Allgemeine-SS maintained several signals, engineering, and transportation commands. Signals and engineering personnel were organized into battalions while the smaller transport units operated as companies. The Allgemeine-SS generally positioned the support units geographically to augment several line SS regiments and other senior commands.

Allgemeine-SS staff units

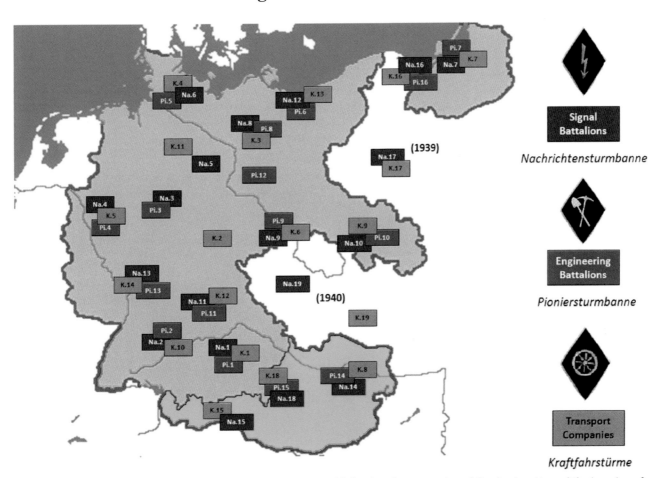

SS specialty units in 1938. Four additional units would be created following the annexation of Czechoslovakia and the invasion of Poland. The transportation companies were originally known as the "SS-Motoreinheiten".

The rarest SS unit ever established, and shortest lived, was the SS Flying Corps created in November 1931 as the "SS-Fliegersturm". The SS Flying Corps was recruited from the membership of the National Socialist Motor Corps (NSKK) and consisted of a single company of SS men who were tasked with air transportation of high-ranking Nazi leaders throughout Germany. The SS Flying Corps existed for less than two years and was disbanded in September 1933. Its members were then either transferred to the SA or to the newly formed Reichsluftschutzbund (Air Defense Service). During the Second World War, the Luftwaffe (German Air Force) was primarily responsible for the air transportation of the Nazi leadership.

SS training schools

To provide technical training to its membership, the General-SS maintained a number of training schools and technical academies to which SS members could receive specific education. The most coveted of these, attendance at which was mandatory for most SS senior officers, was the Leadership School of the SA to which SS officers could also attend. Successful completion of the leadership school curriculum entitled an SS officer to both advanced preference for command selection as well as a special arrow shaped badge for wear on the black SS jacket. After the downfall of the SA in 1934, the leadership school was still attended by some SS officers but had been shut down by 1938.

The SS also maintained training schools to teach administrative skills, trade education, business management, medical certification, as well as musical skills. Successful completion of an SS training academy entitled SS members to wear a specialty badge on their uniform and further provided the SS member with a preference in promotion and assignments. The use of technical schools also extended into the SS Security Services, with members of both the Gestapo and Sicherheitsdienst (SD) eligible to attend their own versions of leadership, technical, and administrative training academies.

One of the lesser known training establishments of the SS were the "SS Men's Halls" (SS-Mannschaftshäuser). Essentially civil service training academies, the Men's Halls began as ad hoc institutions where university students who were also SS members began living together in common dorms. By the mid-1930s, there were three hundred and fifty registered SS members of the Men's Halls, prompting Heinrich Himmler to appoint a "Chief of the Mannschaftshäuser" and organize the Men's Halls in the same manner as a General-SS Standarten. Life in the Men's Halls included combined study sessions, SS and Nazi party indoctrination, as well as group social occasions.

SS Men's Hall locations (1938 – 1944)

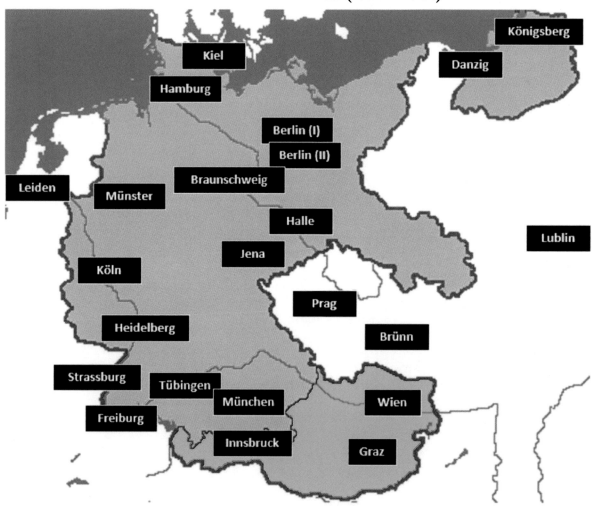

Field exercises of Men's Hall members were also conducted, which mostly included country and mountain marches as well as special training, offered each summer, alongside the military SS officer candidates of the SS-Verfügungstruppe. By 1938, there were over a dozen SS Men's Halls throughout Germany; this number would rise to twenty-two by the end of the Second World War. After 1939, SS Men's Hall membership drastically decreased as most of the part time SS were drafted to serve in the regular German military. What remained of the Men's Hall membership were mostly SS reservists, SS personnel who had been discharged from military duty due to wounds in combat, or SS men who were exempted from military service due to a civilian occupation deemed critical to the war effort.

The SS also utilized the existing trade education system of Germany as a method of recruitment, drawing on centuries old practices of guilds and apprenticeships to entice recruits into the SS. Youth training academies, known as the "SS-Berufsoberschulen", were established under the authority of the SS Main Office as trade and technical training schools. These SS run youth centers accepted candidates between fourteen and seventeen years of age who could then receive education towards a state certificate of technical training (known as a "Reifeprüfung"). Basic training was also provided in economics, trade skills, and agriculture, while advanced studies were offered in law, history, politics, forestry, mining, and engineering. Those students graduating were offered SS membership while many others were sponsored to further studies at a university, after which they would become officers in the SS.

The SS considered continued political education as an important factor in any SS member's career, and political education and training was a cornerstone of SS curriculum. Every major SS training school was appointed an Education Officer (SS-Schulungsoffiziere) who would ensure that training and education adhered to SS designs. One of the constant themes in all SS training was the concept that the SS was a Germanic Men's Organization which existed to maintain the purity of the German nation. The SS Main Office, in charge of all recruiting into the General-SS, promulgated this recruiting ideology through such publications as "Dich ruft die SS" (The SS Needs You) as well as through SS educationial pamphlets known as "SS-Schlungshefte". Two news periodicals were also published by the General-SS, known as the "SS-Informationsdienst" and the "SS-Leitheft", as well as a professional magazine known as "Der Schwarze Korps".

In its purest form, the SS was considered both an elite group of the Nazi Party as well as a brotherhood of Germanic men who supported the aims of the Aryan race. In Heinrich Himmler's vision, the SS was considered the "Deutsche Männerorden" (Order of German Men) to which only the most dedicated and racially pure would be admitted.

The original cadre of SS members from the 1920s had been recruited for brawn, rather than brains, during a period when the group was solely considered a bodyguard regiment for Hitler and other leading Nazis. After Nazi election victories in the early 1930s, the prospect for opportunity and advancement encouraged a mixture of the unemployed, anti-social, and delinquent to all join the SS. Himmler promptly went about expelling these elements from the SS, beginning in the spring of 1933 with a major purge of the organization. Himmler then instituted strict admission requirements into the SS, which remained relatively unchanged until the end of the Second World War, and also specified that the armed SS (later known as the Waffen-SS) would independently develop its own recruitment criteria; these prerequisites were even more demanding than the rest of the SS.

A potential SS man's career began with an initial political screening in order to establish a clean police record, as well as political reliability towards the aims of the Nazi Party; an SS applicant's family members were also investigated. The SS recruit was then required to establish Aryan ancestry to the year 1800 and further pass a medical examination which verified Aryan traits. A special "SS Race Commission" then certified the prospective member for SS service, with the recruit then entered into the SS rolls with the probationary rank of SS-Bewerber (SS-Candidate). The SS-Candidate was then required to attend basic indoctrination training followed by appointment as an "SS-Anwärter" (SS-Applicant); at this time, the applicant would be issued an SS uniform without insignia. The SS-Applicant was then called upon to swear an oath of loyalty to Hitler, which usually took place in an elaborate torchlight ceremony on November 9th, symbolic as the anniversary of the failed Nazi Munich Putsch of 1923. The SS oath was designed by Himmler and was used by both the General and Armed SS.

"I swear to you, Adolf Hitler, as Führer and Chancellor of the Reich, loyalty and bravery. I promise to you, and to those you have appointed to have authority over me, obedience unto death." –SS Oath of Loyalty

After formal induction into the SS, the SS-Anwärter was returned to a local SS unit where further training and indoctrination would occur. Over the next three to six months, the applicant was also expected to earn both the SA Sports Badge and German National Sports Badge. After presentation of both awards, the SS member was assigned to six months compulsory duty in the Reich Labor Service (RAD) followed by a further two-year conscription into the German Army[xix].

Right: From a 1934 propaganda poster, describing the "Ideal SS Man" (Federal German Archives)

After an SS member's return to civilian life from military and labor service, the final stage of indoctrination began. This consisted of intensive physical and ideological instruction, followed by final certification to become a full SS member. In another elaborate nighttime ceremony on November 9th, the applicant was sworn in as a full member of the SS, repeating his oath to Hitler, and further pledging the loyalty of his family to the ideals of the SS.

Members of the Allgemeine-SS were expected to serve on active mustering duties until the age of thirty-five after which time they were eligible for an honorable discharge or transfer to a reserve battalion of a local SS unit. At the age of forty-five, the SS member was eligible to retire with assignment to the Supplementary Reserve (Stammabteilung) until the age of sixty at which time they were released from all further service obligations.

The path to becoming a member of the SS was significantly changed by the outbreak of the Second World War. By 1940, recruitment into the Allgemeine-SS had drastically decreased with over seventy percent of the existing General-SS members drafted into the German armed forces. By 1944, total membership in the Allgemeine-SS (to include full time, mustering, and honorary members) had dropped to 40,000 as compared to a pre-war strength of over twice as many members.

Components and Manpower

At its height, the Allgemeine-SS held a membership of nearly eighty-five thousand full time members. Twenty percent of that number served as salaried members, while the remainder were considered part time or inactive members whose service in the SS was voluntary without pay. To differentiate the distinction between the full and part time General-SS, members were assigned to one of three major SS components. SS officers were also assigned into one of four groups.

COMPONENT	DEFINITION
Hauptamtlich-SS	Full time salaried members of the General-SS
Nebenamtlich-SS	Part time SS members of mustering units and regional staffs
Ehrenamtlich-SS	Honorary SS members with inactive duties and rank
Aktive SS Führer	These SS officers were assigned to either full or part time duties within the SS and were regularly engaging in SS duties. This distinction extended to both full time headquarters SS personnel and part time mustering formations.
Zugeteilte Führer bei den Stäben	This category was reserved for regular members of the SS who could not perform regular duties due to obligations in the German government, armed forces, or for those who held other political postings in the Nazi Party.
Führer in der Stammabteilung	Known as the "Supplementary Reserve", this component of the SS was reserved for elderly or infirmed SS officers who could no longer perform regular duties. Such officers were administratively attached to an SS unit and wore a distinct white SS collar patch to distinguish from regular SS personnel. After the start of World War II, the Supplementary Reserve was also used as a component for police officers who were dual members of the SS.
Führer zu Verfügung	A special category for officers under disciplinary action was known as "Officer On-Call". Such SS officers were removed from active duties as a result of the sentence of an SS court and placed on probation for a maximum of two years.

In the early days of the SS, Heinrich Himmler reserved the right to appoint and promote all SS officers himself. As the SS grew in size, this method became impractical and, by the mid-1930s, the General-SS had adopted a tier system for the delegation of promotion authority. The highest of SS ranks could only be appointed by Hitler, while lower ranks could be bestowed by any mid-level or local commander.

SS PROMOTION AUTHORITIES

RANK	AUTHORITY
SS-Gruppenführer & above	Personally appointed by Adolf Hitler with the recommendation and endorsement of the Reichsführer-SS.
SS-Sturmbannführer to SS-Brigadeführer	Promotions above the rank of SS-Major were technically to be granted only by Heinrich Himmler. As the SS grew in size, this duty was delegated to a promotion office within the SS-Hauptamt.
SS-Untersturmführer to SS-Hauptsturmführer	The promotion of company level SS officers was delegated to the SS-Hauptamt, which could authorize routine promotions to these ranks without higher approval.
SS-Hauptscharführer	Promotions to SS-First Sergeant were authorized by the SS-Oberabschnitt commander in which the member served.
SS-Unterscharführer to SS-Oberscharführer	The promotion of SS non-commissioned officers was authorized by the local Abschnitt commander.
SS-Sturmmann & below	Promotions to junior SS ranks were delegated to the local level of the SS-Standarten in which the member served.

The General-SS also maintained a reserve force consisting of at least one reserve battalion maintained within each Allgemeine-SS regiment. Each Reserve Sturmbann also maintained a small battalion staff as well as two companies and a medical squad.

General-SS reserve battalion organization. Each reserve battalion consisted of two reserve companies and one medical unit

Prior to the Nazi seizure of power in 1933, the SS was regarded as simply a paramilitary organization of the Nazi Party with all of its members enlisted on a voluntary basis without pay. For this reason, the SS placed a special emphasis on SS members who had served in the organization before 1933, as compared to members who had joined after the Nazis had come to power. The "Alter Kämpfer" chevron, worn with pride on the right sleeve of the SS jacket, was the outward identifier of this status.

After 1933, the SS become an institution of the Nazi government, although the SS was still regarded as an organ of the Nazi Party and not a civil service branch of the German state. Early SS salaries were drawn from the coffers of the Nazi Party itself, with federal funds only granted after 1936 when Himmler become Chief of the German Police and later Minister of the Interior. The early armed SS received funding through the Reich Finance Ministry, although Concentration Camp staffs were still considered Nazi Party formations and thus unfunded through governmental channels. This would finally change in 1942 when the entire camp service was absorbed into the Waffen-SS and received pay books out of that SS branch. The Allgemeine-SS leadership and mustering formations remained as part time institutions with only the senior most levels receiving a salary. Commanding the entire SS were the main SS offices, of which twelve primary office eventually existed. These offices were considered part of the "Gesamt-SS" (entire SS) as they held authority over both the Allgemeine and Waffen branches of the SS.

HAUPTAMT PERSÖNLICHER STAB RFSS
(Head Office of the Personal Staff of the Reich Leader SS)

Office Information

Created: 1935

Function: Command and administration of Heinrich Himmler's personal staff

Predecessor Agency

Persönlicherstab RfSS (1933 – 1935)
(Sub office of the *Reichsführung-SS*)

Headquarters

8 Prinz-Albrecht Strasse, Berlin

Commanders

1935-1942

SS-Obergruppenführer und
General der Waffen-SS
Karl Wolff[1]

1942 – 1945

SS-Obergruppenführer und
General der Waffen-SS
Maximilian von Herff

[1] *Also served as head of predecessor agency*

OFFICE HISTORY AND OPERATION

As a formal office, the personal staff of Heinrich Himmler was the creation of SS officer Karl Wolff, who served as Himmler's adjutant for over nine years before being replaced after a falling out with Himmler. The personal staff was part of a much larger organization known as the "Reichsführung-SS" which consisted of an executive staff as well as a personal headquarters overseeing any SS special projects under Himmler's direct control. The personal staff also maintained a mobile command headquarters, known as the Feldkommandostelle RfSS.

Right: Karl Wolff, who served as the head of Himmler's personal staff from its inception in 1933 until 1942. (Federal German Archives)

HIMMLER'S PERSONAL STAFF ORGANIZATION

Chef des Persönlicher Stab
(Chief of the Personal Staff)

Personalhauptabteilung
(Personnel Affairs Office)

Chef des Amtes Stabsführung
(Chief of the Leadership Office)

Stabsabteilung der Waffen-SS
(Waffen-SS Staff Department)

Abteilung Presse
(Press Department)

Abteilung Schriftgutverwaltung
(Record Department)

Rohstoffamt
(Office of Raw Materials)

Kommando Stab RfSS

Executive Staff responsible for issuing directives and orders from Himmler to SS commands

Feldkommandostelle RfSS

Field Command Staff.
A fourteen carriage train for tours was also maintained, known as the **Sonderzug Heinrich**

Escort Battalion	Escort Battalion
Signals Section	Flak Unit
Motor Pool	Post Office

Persönlicher Stab RfSS

Persönliches Referat Reichsführer-SS
(Personal Branch of the Reich Leader)

SS-Adjutantur RF-SS
(SS Adjutant to the Reich Leader)

Auszeichnung und Orden
(Decorations and Awards Office)

Verwaltung Hauptabteilung
(Head Office of Administration)

Wirtschaftliche Hilfe
(Office of Economic Aid)

Hauptabteilung SS Richter
(Head Office of Legal Affairs)

Polizei Adjutantur
(Police Adjutant Office)

ATTACHED OFFICES OF THE PERSONAL STAFF

Amt Wewelsburg
Operated the Wewelsburg Castle, which by 1944 served as an SS leadership school

Amt Ahnenerbe
Scientific research staff, mostly involved in researching the history of Nordic myths and legends

Amt Lebensborn
Administration of the *Lebensborn* program, providing financial aid and maternity assistance to SS wives

Amt Volsumfragen
Central Office established for answering all pertinent race questions which may have affect on SS policy and orders

Amt München
Artistic and architectural advisory office, providing information of interest to Heinrich Himmler

Zentralinstiut für optimale Menschenerfassung
The "Central Institute for the Total Survey of the Population" was involved in census taking of all SS and Police personnel

Der Beauftragte für das Diensthundewesen beim Reichsführer-SS
The "Commission for the Canine Corps of the Reich Leader SS" dealt with matters concerning police and military dogs

The attached offices of Himmler's headquarters were independently maintained but subordinated to Himmler's personal staff. Most such offices dealt with special projects of interest to Himmler, usually concerning Germanic history or Aryan racial matters.

SS-HAUPTAMT
(SS Head Office)

Office Information

Created: 1935

Function: Overall SS administration

Predecessor Agency

SS-Amt (1932 – 1935)

Headquarters

7-11 Douglasstrasse, Berlin-Grünewald

Commanders

1935-1938

SS-Gruppenführer Kurt Wittje[1]

1938 – 1940

SS-Obergruppenführer
August Heissmeyer

1940 – 1945

SS-Obergruppenführer
Gottlob-Chrstian Berger

[1] *Also served as head of predecessor agency*

OFFICE HISTORY AND OPERATION

The SS head office, under a variety of older titles, had served as an administrative headquarters for the entire SS since as early as 1928. From 1935 to 1940, the Head Office was the largest and most significant command within the bureaucratic make-up of the SS. In 1940, the office was significantly downsized and lost a significant amount of its operational importance. In 1942, the Head Office was put in charge of recruitment and administration of all non-German SS formations in occupied countries, later designated as the Germanic-SS.

Right: Gottlob Berger, who commanded the SS Head Office during the latter half of the Second World War.
(National Archives)

SS HEAD OFFICE ORGANIZATION
(1935 – 1940)

Zentralkanzlei
(Central Chancellery)

Führungsamt
(Command Office)

Personnelamt
(Personnel Office)

Amt Nachrichten Verbindungen
(Communications)

Amt Sicherungsaufgaben
(Security)

Verwaltungsamt
(Administration Office)

Amt Gericht
(Legal Office)

Sanitatamt
(Medical Office)

Versorgungs und Fursorgeamt
(Welfare and Supply)

Schulungsamt
(Education Office)

Erfassungsamt
(Requisitioning)

Amt Leibsubungen
(Physical Training)

Erganzungsamt
(Reenforcements)

In 1940, the Personnel Office, along with its subordinate Legal Office, were separated to become their own main offices. At the same time, the Communications Office was transferred to the authority of Himmler's personal staff.

Beschaffungsamt
(Procurement)

SS HEAD OFFICE ORGANIZATION
(1940 – 1945)

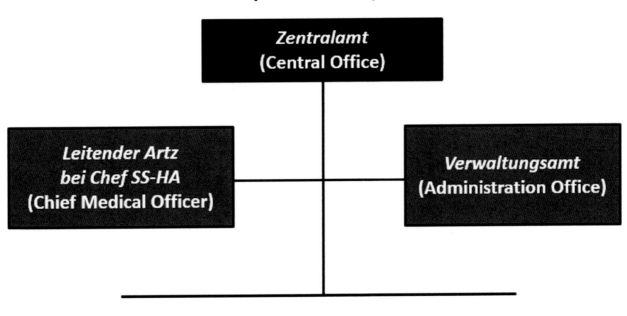

Zentralamt
(Central Office)

**Leitender Artz
bei Chef SS-HA**
(Chief Medical Officer)

Verwaltungsamt
(Administration Office)

SUPPLY DEPARTMENTS

Erfassungsamt
(Requisitioning Office)

**Erganzungsamt
der Waffen-SS**
(Waffen-SS Reenforcements)

GERMANIC-SS OFFICES

Germanische Leitstelle
(Germanic Control)

Germanische Erganzung
(Germanic Recruitment)

TRAINING DEPARTMENTS

**Amt fur
Weltanschauliche Erziehung**
(Ideological Training)

Amt fur Leibeserziehhung
(Physical Training)

Amt fur Berufserziehung
(Trade Training)

Germanische Erziehung
(Germanic Education)

SS-FÜHRUNGSHAUPTAMT
(SS Operations Head Office)

Office Information

Created: 1940

Function: Operational administration of the Waffen-SS

Predecessor Agency

SS-Hauptamt (1935 – 1940)
(Established from various sub-offices)

Headquarters

188 Kaiserallee, Berlin-Wilmersdorf

Commanders

1940-1943

Reichsführer-SS Heinrich Himmler

1943 – 1945

SS-Obergruppenführer und
General der Waffen-SS
Hans Jüttner

OFFICE HISTORY AND OPERATION

Created from a merger of several SS departments of the SS-Hauptamt, the SS Operations Office was established in 1940 as a result of the formal creation of the Waffen-SS. Primarily concerned with Waffen-SS logistics, supply, and recruiting, the Operations Office was commanded directly by Himmler during the first two and half years of its existence. By 1944, the Operations Office had reached a staffing level of over 40,000 personnel and held near total control of both the Allgemeine (General) and Waffen (Armed) SS branches.

Right: Hans Jüttner, commander of the SS Operations Head Office during the last two years of World War II (Federal German Archives)

SS OPERATIONS OFFICE ORGANIZATION

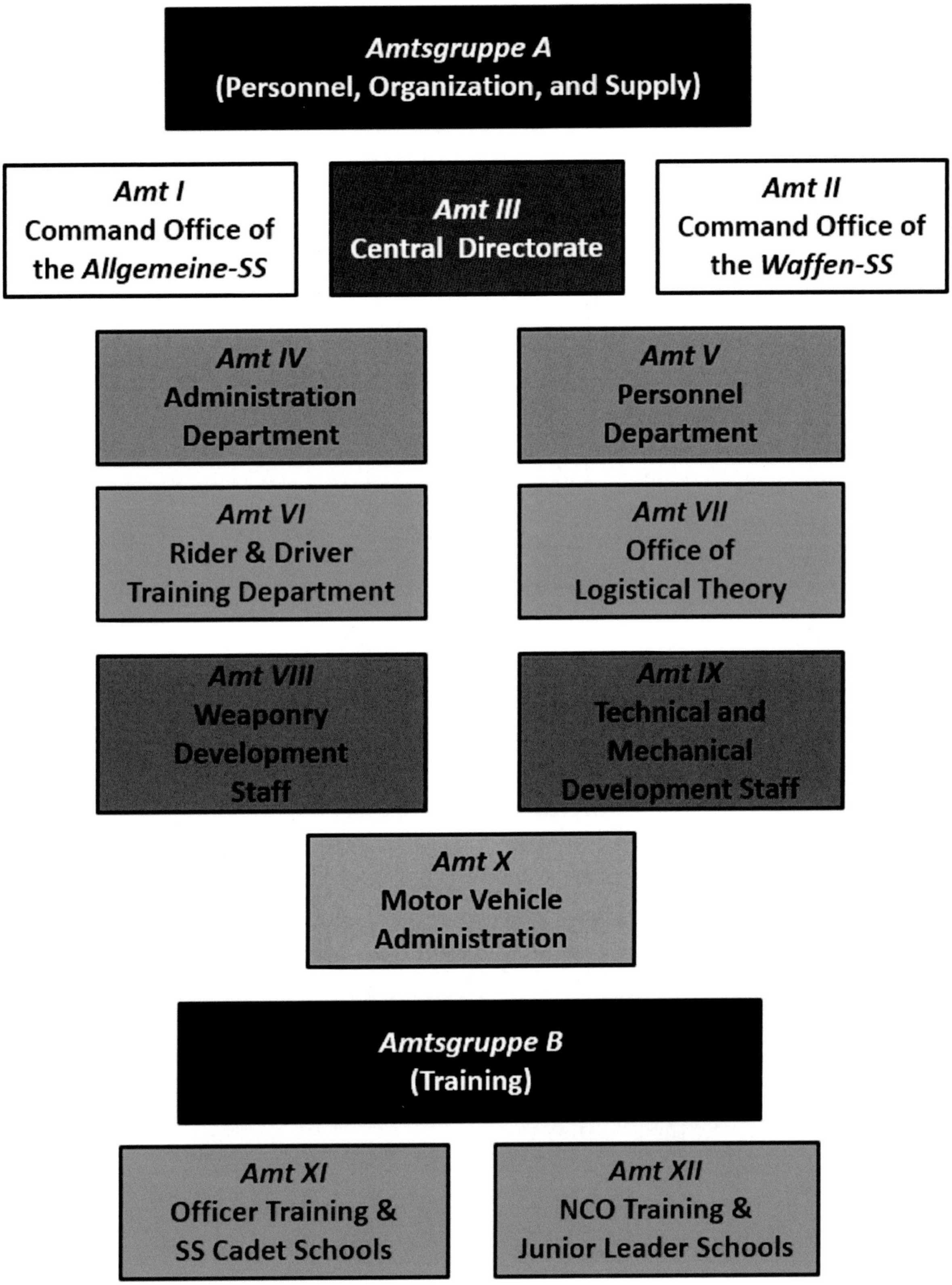

Amtsgruppe A
(Personnel, Organization, and Supply)

Amt I
Command Office of
the *Allgemeine-SS*

Amt III
Central Directorate

Amt II
Command Office of
the *Waffen-SS*

Amt IV
Administration
Department

Amt V
Personnel
Department

Amt VI
Rider & Driver
Training Department

Amt VII
Office of
Logistical Theory

Amt VIII
Weaponry
Development
Staff

Amt IX
Technical and
Mechanical
Development Staff

Amt X
Motor Vehicle
Administration

Amtsgruppe B
(Training)

Amt XI
Officer Training &
SS Cadet Schools

Amt XII
NCO Training &
Junior Leader Schools

Amtsgruppe C
(Inspection)

Abteilung 1 Inspector General	Abteilung 2 Infantry & Mountain Troops	Abteilung 3 Cavalry Troops
Abteilung 4 Artillery Troops	Abteilung 5 Engineering Troops	Abteilung 6 Panzer Troops
Abteilung 7 Signal Troops	Abteilung 8 Field Maintenance Troops	Abteilung 9 Service Support Troops
Abteilung 10 Motor Pool Troops	Abteilung 11 Miscellaneous Formations	Abteilung 12 Technical Training
	Abteilung 13 Anti-Air Artillery Units	

Amtsgruppe D
(Medical Office of the *Waffen-SS*)

Amt XIII Administration	Amt XIV Dental Treatment	Amt XV Medical Supply
	Amt XVI Medical Treatment	

SS-PERSONALHAUPTAMT
(SS Personnel Head Office)

Office Information

Created: 1940

Function: Personnel liaison office and maintenance of officer service records

Predecessor Agency

Personalamt (1935 – 1940)
(Sub-office of the *SS-Hauptamt*)

Headquarters

98-9 Wilmersdorferstrasse, Berlin-Charlottenburg

Commanders

1940-1942

SS-Obergruppenführer Walter Schmitt

1942 – 1945

SS-Obergruppenführer und General der Waffen-SS Maximilian von Herff

OFFICE HISTORY AND OPERATION

Until 1940, the personnel department of the SS had existed as a bureau of the much larger SS Head Office, after which time most personnel functions were reorganized into a separate office. Concerned with administrative liaison and officer service records (enlisted records were still maintained by the SS Head Office), the personnel office also published the highly significant SS Officer Seniority List. In 1942, the SS personnel office was taken over by Maximilian von Herff, who also served as Himmler's Chief of Staff until 1945.

Above: Maximilian von Herff, the final director of the SS personnel office. Prior to serving in the SS, von Herff had been a member of the German Army's Africa Corps with the rank of Colonel (Federal German Archives)

SS PERSONNEL DEPARTMENT ORGANIZATION

Amt für Führerpersonalien
(Office of Officer Personnel Records)

Amtsgruppe A Administration	**Amtsgruppe B** General-SS Personnel	**Amtsgruppe C** Waffen-SS Personnel
Amt I Central Records	**Amt IV** Administration	**Amt VI** Administration
Amt II Awards & Schooling	**Amt V** Allgemeine-SS Records	**Amt VII** Waffen-SS Records
Amt III Discipline & Honors		

Amt für Führernachwuchs
(Office of Potential Officer Recruits)

The potential officer records section of the SS personnel department pertained to SS personnel enrolled in either Waffen-SS officer candidate schools or those General-SS personnel under consideration for an officer's commission. Actual officer appointment was not a function of the personnel office, but rather resided with Heinrich Himmler, although Himmler frequently delegated these tasks to subordinates.

HAUPTAMT SS-GERICHT
(SS Legal Office)

Office Information

Created: 1940

Function: SS Legal Office and oversee the SS regional court system

Predecessor Agency

SS-Gericht (1935 – 1940)
(Sub-office of the *SS-Hauptamt*)

Headquarters

10 Karlstrasse, Munich

Commanders

1940-1942

SS-Obergruppenführer
Paul Scharfe[1]

1942 – 1945

SS-Obergruppenführer und
General der Waffen-SS
Franz Breithaupt

[1] Also served as head of predecessor agency

OFFICE HISTORY AND OPERATION

The SS Legal Office was first created in the mid-1930s as a means to remove SS personnel from the jurisdiction of the regular German civilian courts. By decree of the Reich Ministry of Justice, the SS was empowered with its own court system, effectively placing all SS members above regular law. For infractions considered even by the SS to be illegal, judgment was dispensed through a series of SS courts under the overall command of the SS Legal Office. Penalties could range from simple reprimands, disciplinary duty, expulsion from the SS, or (in extreme cases) even death.

Above: Paul Scharfe, the SS lawyer who commanded the SS Legal Office through most of its early existence. He died of natural causes in 1942 at the age of sixty-two. (Federal German Archives)

SS COURT SYSTEM ADMINISTRATION

Amtsgruppe I
(Legal Affairs)

Abteilung Ia Legal Procedure	**Abteilung Ib** Civil Law	**Abteilung Ic** Judge Assignment
Abteilung Id Administration	**Abteilung Ie** Appeals & Review	**Abteilung If** Investigations

Amtsgruppe II
(Disciplinary Review)

Amtsgruppe III
(Sentences & Punishment)

Amtsgruppe IV
(Legal Liaison Office)

Verwaltungsamt
(Administration)

Ausbildungsamt
(Training)

SS AND POLICE COURTS

SS- und Polizeigericht
(Regional SS & Police Courts)

Oberstes SS- und Polizeigericht
(Supreme SS & Police Courts)

SS- und Polizeigericht z.b.V
(Special SS & Police Courts)

Feldgerichte der Waffen-SS
(Waffen-SS Courts Martial)

SS-RASSE UND SIEDLUNGSHAUPTAMT
(SS Race and Settlement Head Office)

Office Information

Created: 1935

Function: Investigating genealogy of SS members, issuing marriage licenses, and enforcing SS racial standards

Predecessor Agency

SS-Rasseamt (1932 – 1935)

Headquarters

24 Hedemannstrasse, Berlin

Commanders

1935-1938

SS-Obergruppenführer Richard Walther Darré[1]

1938 – 1940

SS-Gruppenführer Günther Pancke

1940 – 1943

SS-Gruppenführer Otto Hofmann

1943 – 1945

SS-Obergruppenführer und General der Waffen-SS Richard Hildebrandt

[1] *Also served as head of predecessor agency*

OFFICE HISTORY AND OPERATION

One of the oldest offices of the SS, the primary function of the Race and Settlement Office was to research the lineage of potential SS members as well as approve marriages of SS personnel to Aryan brides. During the Second World War, the office became involved in the forcible expulsion of subject populations from conquered lands, with plans in place to colonize subject countries with Germans, once ultimate victory had been achieved.

Right: Otto Hofmann, who served as the representative of the Race and Settlement Office during the Wannsee Conference of 1942. (Federal German Archives)

RACE AND SETTLEMENT OFFICE ORGANIZATION

Organisation und Verwaltungsamt
(Organization & Administration)

Verwaltungsamt Administration	*Organisationsamt* Organization	*Personalwesen* Personnel

Amt fur Bevolkerungspolitik
(Office of Population Policy)

Rassenamt Race Office	*Siedlungsamt* Settlement Office	*Schulungsamt* Education Office
District Office *(Litzmannstadt)*	District Office *(Prag)*	District Office *(Südost)*

Sippen und Heiratsamt
(Marriage and Family Office)

Heiratsamt
Hereditary Office

Amt fur Archiv und Zeitungswesen
(Office of Records and Press Relations)

SS-WIRTSCHAFTS-VERWALTUNGSHAUPTAMT
(SS Economics and Administration Head Office)

Office Information

Created: 1942

Function: Serve as a command administrative office for all SS supply, finance, and business matters

Predecessor Agencies
(1939 – 1942)
Hauptamt Verwaltung und Wirtschaft
Hauptamt Haushalt und Bauten

Headquarters

126-35 Unter den Linden
Berlin-Lichterfelde

Commanders

1942-1945

SS-Obergruppenführer und
General der Waffen-SS
Oswald Pohl[1]

[1] *Also served as head of predecessor agency*

OFFICE HISTORY AND OPERATION

The Economics and Administration Office was created at the height of World War II, primarily to coordinate SS business projects and oversee the Nazi slave labor program through the use of Concentration Camp prisoners. Commanded by Oswald Pohl, the WVHA was sub-divided into five major departments, the fifth of which Pohl personally commanded, as well as serving as commander of the WVHA as a whole.

Below: The heads of the various offices of the WVHA in 1943. From left to right - Richard Glücks (Dept D), August Frank (Dept A), Oswald Pohl (WVHA and Dept W), Georg Lörner (Dept B), and Hans Kammler (Dept C) – (Federal German Archives)

MAIN OFFICE OF ADMINISTRATION AND ECONOMY
(1939 – 1942)

Office of the Economic Examiner (Division W)

Administration Department	*Amtsgruppe A* Enterprises	*Amtsgruppe B* Production
Legal Office	Amt A-I German Enterprises	Amt B-I Mineral Waters
Personnel Department	Amt A-II Foreign Enterprises	Amt B-II Porcelain Manufacturing
	Amt A-III Building Projects	Amt B-III Patent Office
Amtsgruppe S Special Projects	Amt A-IV Material Plants	
Amt S-I Cultural Monuments	*Amtsgruppe C* Publishing & Supply	*Amtsgruppe D* Exterior Works
Amt A-II Memorial Funds	Amt C-I Picture Publishing	Amt D-I Agriculture
Amt A-III Racial Research	Amt C-II Literature Publishing	Amt D-II Forestry
Amt A-IV Buildings Office	Amt C-III Equipment Supplies	Amt D-III Merchendising

The "Hauptamt Verwaltung und Wirtschaft" (Office of Administration and Economy) was one of the predecessor offices of the WVHA which, along with the Budget and Construction Office, merged in 1942 to become the Economics and Administration Head Office[xxi].

SS-REICHSSICHERHEITSHAUPTAMT
(SS Reich Security Head Office)

Office Information

Created: 1939

Function: Command all SS and Security Police security agencies throughout Germany and all occupied territories

Predecessor Agencies

Created from a merger of the *Gestapo, Kripo,* and *Sicherheitsdienst,* each of which became a sub-office of the larger RSHA

Headquarters

8 Prinz-Albrecht Strasse, Berlin

Commanders

1939-1942

SS-Obergruppenführer und General der Polizei Reinhard Heydrich

1942 – 1943

Reichsführer-SS Heinrich Himmler

1943 – 1945

SS-Obergruppenführer und General der Polizei und Waffen-SS Ernest Kaltenbrunner

OFFICE HISTORY AND OPERATION

The RSHA was created at the start of World War II to consolidate all of Germany's internal and external security forces under one single command. Overseeing the actions of the Einsatzgruppen death squads, the operation of extermination camps, as well as the arrest and torture of thousands of innocent victims, the RSHA reached the height of its power in 1944 when it absorbed the military intelligence arm of the Abwehr.

Right: Ernest Kaltenbrunner was chosen to succeed Reinhard Heydrich as head of the RSHA in 1943. Kaltenbrunner's selection by Himmler was specifically due to Kaltenbrunner's slightly inept and incompetent nature, as Himmler did not want a successor to the RSHA Chief position who could in turn threaten Himmler's own authority.
(Federal German Archives)

Following page: SS main office locations in Berlin (Original map courtesy Federal German Archives)

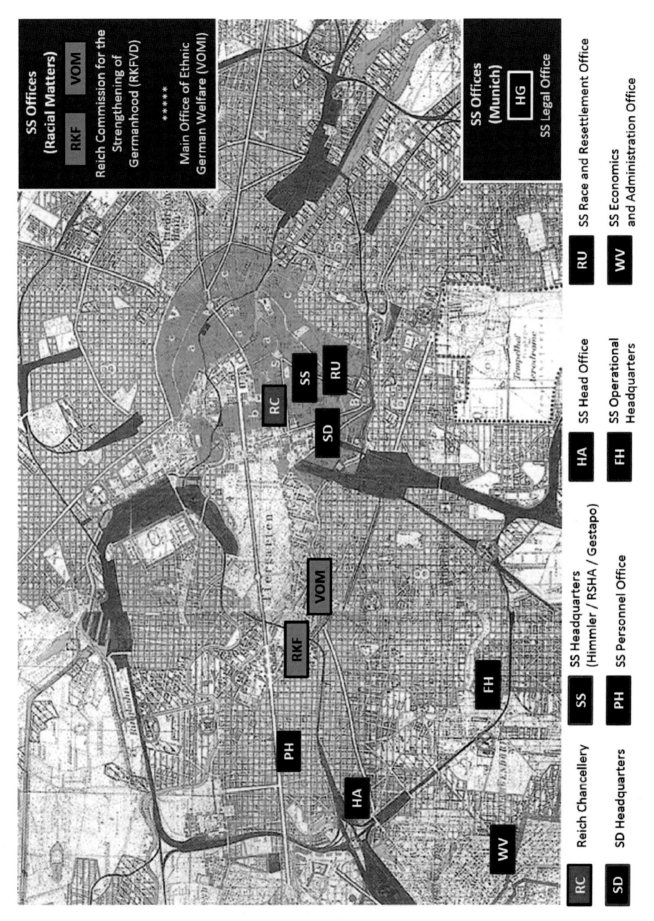

SS Offices
(Racial Matters)

RKF   VOM

Reich Commission for the
Strengthening of
Germanhood (RKFVD)

*****

Main Office of Ethnic
German Welfare (VOMI)

SS Offices
(Munich)

HG

SS Legal Office

RU   SS Race and Resettlement Office

WV   SS Economics
       and Administration Office

HA   SS Head Office

FH   SS Operational
       Headquarters

SS   SS Headquarters
       (Himmler / RSHA / Gestapo)

PH   SS Personnel Office

RC   Reich Chancellery

SD   SD Headquarters

After 1935, the Allgemeine-SS had solidified into its final form which would remain relatively unchanged until the end of the Second World War. At the top of the organization was Heinrich Himmler, his personal staff, and as well as the leaders and staff personnel of the SS Main Offices. Twelve such offices would eventually exist, one of which (the Reich Security Main Office) was recognized as an official agency of the German government under the Ministry of the Interior. The senior leaders of the Oberabschnitt and Abschnitt, as well as certain members of their staffs, were considered full time SS members and received a salary through the Nazi Party Treasury. Upon the outbreak of World War II many of the SS district leaders were granted equivalent positions as SS and Police Leaders, awarded equivalent police rank, and thereafter regarded as employees of the German Interior Ministry. The part time mustering formations remained unpaid and voluntary for the entirety of the SS existence. After the outbreak of war many of these formations existed on paper only, as their members were lost to military conscription, service in the Waffen-SS, or postings to other branches of the German government. By 1944 very few of the mustering formations remained active, although most such units technically continued to exist until May of 1945.

One unique aspect of SS manpower were Austrian SS members, who comprised nearly fifteen percent of all SS membership, and held numerous significant roles in both the SS leadership as well as the German police. The term "Austrian SS" was not an actual branch of the SS, but was used informally to distinguish those SS members hailing from Germany's southern neighbor. The history of the Austrian SS may be divided into two periods, mainly the time frame from before the Anschluss with Germany in 1938 and the period following when both Germany and Austria were combined into the Greater German Reich.

Austrian National Socialism pre-dated Germany by over a decade, with the first recognized Austrian Nazi group originating in 1903 as the "Deutsche Arbeiterpartei in Österreich", more commonly known as the DAP. In 1918, after the close of the First World War, the group changed its name to the Deutsche Nationalsozialistische Arbeiterpartei, which was known as the DNSAP. While never confirmed, it is believed Adolf Hitler studied the manifesto of the DNSAP and used some of its elements to form the German Nazi Party.

**Theodor Habicht in 1934
(Federal German Archives)**

The Austrian Nazi Party split into two separate factions in 1923, the more radical of which was known as the "Deutschsozialen Verein" (German Social Association) led by extremist Anti-Semite Walter Riehl. Riehl lost most of his influence with the Austrian Nazis after 1930, who in turn then looked to Germany for leadership. In 1931, Hitler appointed Theodor Habicht as "Landesinspekteur" of the Austrian Nazi Party and instructed Habicht to consolidate all Austrian National Socialist movements into one group which would then be subordinate to Germany. In 1932, with the Austrian Nazis now considered merely a branch of the Nazi Party of Germany, Heinrich Himmler ordered the establishment of an Austrian branch of the SS, and sent former naval officer Alfred Rodenbücher to Vienna, in order to organize Austrian SS men. Rodenbücher established the SS Senior District of Austria (SS-Oberabschnitt Österreich) which quickly took root with five SS regiments in Austria by the summer of 1934.

An event which nearly destroyed the Austrian Nazi movement was the assassination of Austrian Chancellor Engelbert Dollfuss, followed by an attempted coup against the Austrian government, organized by members of the SS.

**Austrian SS men in 1935. During this period, the SS was illegal in Austria with SS groups meeting in secret without uniforms.
(Original photograph - Author's Collection)**

On July 25th 1934 several Austrian Nazis, most of whom were serving members of SS-Standarten 84, entered the Austrian Chancellery building, shot and killed Chancellor Dollfuss, then barricaded themselves inside and announced the formation of a new Austrian Nazi government. In a surprising move, Hitler expressed outrage at the attack, denounced the assassins, and left them to their own devices.

The Austrian plotters eventually surrendered to the Austrian Army and were tried and executed for murder. In the aftermath of the Dollfuss assassination, the Austrian government launched a massive crackdown of Austrian Nazis and declared both the Nazi Party and the SS illegal. Rodenbücher fled to Germany, leaving his deputy Karl Taus in charge of the now underground Austrian SS movement. Meanwhile, the Austrian authorities imprisoned hundreds of Austrian Nazis and placed SS members in concentration camps.

In 1935, the Austrian Nazi Party and SS were reformed under the leadership of two men, both of whom would eventually lead that nation to the Anschluss with Germany in 1938. Arthur Seyss-Inquart became the de facto leader of the Austrian Nazi Party, while Ernst Kaltenbrunner became commander of the Austrian SS. Back in Germany, Alfred Rodenbücher continued to support the Austrian SS by creating an office known as the SS-Sammelstelle. Subordinated to the SS Head Office, the Sammelstelle (literally meaning "collection point") assisted SS men who fled Austria by housing them in training camps along the German-Austrian border. The Sammelstelle further trained SS personnel on matters of subterfuge, espionage, and sabotage, with the intent being to support covert actions in Austria to influence a union with Germany.

In March 1938, the Austrian Chancellor Kurt Schuschnigg resigned after failed diplomatic negotiations with Germany, accompanied by looming threats from Hitler to invade the country. Schuschnigg was replaced by Arthur Seyss-Inquart who had previously served as the Austrian Minister of the Interior. Seyss-Inquart had been appointed by the Austrian President Wilhelm Miklas as part of a political maneuver to staff the Austrian cabinet with pro-Nazis, thus discouraging Hitler from invading Austria and overthrowing the government. As Chancellor, Seyss-Inquart called for a plebiscite for union with Germany and opened the borders to German troops who promptly occupied the Austrian nation.

By the end of March 1938, Austria was for all intents and purposes now a province of Germany. In the first few months after the German union, the Austrian SS reformed itself with many underground cells emerging to create active SS units of the Allgemeine-SS. Meanwhile, the SS security forces moved into Austria and began enforcing Nazi doctrine, Anti-Semitic policies, and conducting arrests both of dissidents and Jews. An early version of the Einsatzgruppen was deployed to Vienna to seize governmental records, while a Concentration Camp was established at Mauthausen-Gusen under the authority of the Totenkopf units.

The General-SS in Austria would be consolidated under a single regional district which was renamed in 1939 as the SS-Oberabschnitt Donau. Alfred Rodenbücher returned to Austria in 1939 and afterwards headed Oberabschnitt Alpenland, which was formed in eastern Austira and consisted of SS mountain units. Several members of the Austrian SS would thereafter rise to promience as Waffen-SS officers, Concentration Camp commanders, police leaders, and Gestapo personnel.

The General-SS at War

During the Second World War, the SS became regarded as the enforcement agency of the Nazi regime, and as such was involved in a vast number of war crimes and atrocities committed in the name of National Socialism. The secret police forces of the Gestapo, Kripo, and the SD were consolidated under the Reich Security Main Office, which was itself an institution of the Reich Interior Ministry and not technically part of the SS, but without a doubt was completely overshadowed and integrated with SS personnel.

On the battle fronts of the Second World War, the Waffen-SS was regarded as the premiere fighting force of the Third Reich, as well as the elite of Germany's armed forces. The Concentration Camp service, originally considered part of the Allgemeine-SS, was administratively transferred to the control of the Waffen-SS in 1942. By that same year, the German Police had become nearly one and the same with the SS. Police generals automatically were granted SS rank and the wearing of SS collar insignia with green police backing became compulsory after 1943.

In such a wartime environment, the original concept of the part time Allgemeine-SS mustering units became impractical. Conscription into the German armed forces was still obligatory for most General-SS members, meaning that nearly all part time Allgemeine-SS personnel soon found themselves drafted into the German military. Those SS personnel who remained were either draft exempt, due to service in some other branch of the German government or were too old or infirmed for front line duty. Local Nazi Party authorities then saw a way to make use of these skeleton Allgemeine-SS units, grouping what remained of the mustering formations into local civil defense units.

The higher levels of the General-SS battalion and regimental commands remained relatively unchanged during the war, although with far less full-time personnel. On the Abschnitt and Oberabschnitt district levels, most of the assigned SS personnel were considered to be performing essential duties and were therefore draft exempt. This was particularly the case for those SS district officers who overlapped as SS and Police Leaders.

Allgemeine-SS Wartime Battalion Organization

SS COMPANY	DESIGNATION	DUTIES
First Stürme	SS-Wachkompanie	Protection of important buildings and bridges
Second Stürme	SS-Alarmsturm	Civil response to air raids and ground attacks
Third Stürme	SS-Streifedienst	General patrol duties
Fourth Stürme		

During the Second World War, a significant number of General-SS personnel were conscripted into the "Hilfsgrenzangestellte" (Auxiliary Frontier Service, also known as the HIGA) which comprised reserve border guards nominally under the control of the Gestapo. For mustering SS units in coastal cities, a formation known as the "SS-Hafensicherungstruppen" (Harbor Security Service Troops) was formed to protect coastal and harbor facilities from sabotage.

For most of the rank and file members of the Allgemeine-SS, military service during the Second World War meant either front line duty in the Waffen-SS or conscription into the regular German armed forces. In the latter case, SS membership was often a negative aspect, since most Army soldiers were suspicious of Allgemeine-SS reservists in their midst, often viewing such persons as informers spying for any sign of anti-Nazism or defeatism. The vast majority of part time SS members served in the German Army, however a significant portion also served as reservists in the German Air Force. Reinhard Heydrich, commander of the Reich Central Security Service and all of its attached security agencies, was himself a reserve officer in the German Air Force rising to the rank of Major and serving as both a reconnaissance and fighter pilot.

Right: Reinhard Heydrich poses in his Luftwaffe uniform in front of his BF-109 during the Russian campaign of 1941. (Federal German Archives)

Having received training in a BF-109, Heydrich spent most his reserve duty attached to Jagdgeschwader 77, which was a fighter squadron first stationed in Norway and later Romania. Heydrich flew missions in both Poland and Russia, before being shot down behind enemy lines and narrowly avoiding capture. He was forbidden to engage in further front-line duties on personal orders from Hitler, who feared that Heydrich's capture as a prisoner of war would be a major security breach for Germany.

The German Navy (Kriegsmarine) saw the least number of SS members serving as reservists, although there were some notable examples. One such naval reservist was Alfred Rodenbücher, founder of the Austrian branch of the SS, who served as a Lieutenant Commander and performed sea duty onboard a destroyer.

Left: The only known photograph of an SS member wearing the Blockade Runner War Badge, which was issued to German merchant seaman during the Second World War (Federal German Archives)

The German U-Boat arm, considered one of the more politically reliable branches of the German armed forces, saw almost no SS members serving amongst its crews. The famed U-Boat War Badge, a symbol of the Battle of the Atlantic, is one of the few decorations which has never been photographed as worn on an SS uniform. Fewer still were merchant seaman enlisted into the SS, although a small number of SS personnel are known to have served onboard German commerce raiders.

During the Second World War, an attempt was made to expand the Allgemeine-SS into other areas of occupied Europe, albeit with limited success. There were six foreign based SS-Oberabschnitt established in occupied territories, with the Böhmen-Mähren district, located in the Czech protectorate, becoming the only district comparable to SS formations in Germany.

The SS senior districts in the occupied east were considered paper commands to the office of the SS and Police Leader, with the senior SS officer in command intended to hold both posts simultaneously. The single General-SS district in the west was organized as a liaison command for foreign volunteers of the Waffen-SS and never held any subordinate Allgemeine-SS units. The only foreign General-SS regiment ever established outside of Germany was in Norway as the 127th SS-Standarten under the command of "Oberabschnitt Nord". The regiment was founded in December 1944 and existed for less than six months. It is unknown if the Standarten ever actually mustered any active General-SS troops.

Below: SS senior districts (Oberabschnitt) and German military war districts in 1943

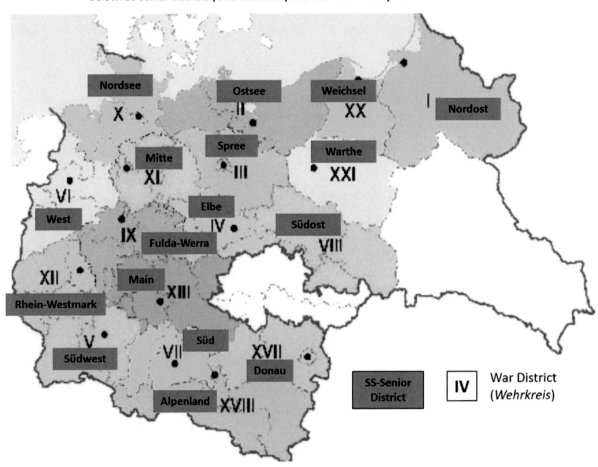

(Original NSDAP district map courtesy Federal German Archives)
Below: SS-senior districts located outside of Germany. The Ukraine district was the only Oberabschnitt named after its subject country

SS-OBERABSCHNITT	GEOGRAPHICAL REGION	SUBORDINATE SS UNITS
Böhmen-Mähren	Czech Protectorate	SS Abschnitt XXXIX
		Standarten 107 & 108
Nord	Norway	Standarten 127
Nordwest	Netherlands	None
Ost	Poland	Five SS Districts (Proposed but never formed)
Ostland	Baltic countries (Estonia, Latvia, Lithuania)	None
Ukraine		

Allgemeine-SS Senior Districts

SS-Oberabschnitt Alpenland

Established	1 June 1939	Headquarters	Salzburg
Cuffband	Alpenland		
Previous Commands	Formed from a portion of the territory previously comprising SS-Oberabschnit Donau		
SS and Police Command	HSSPF Alpenland	War District	Wehrkreis XVIII
Subordinate Units			

SS-Abschnitt XXXV
- SS-Standarten 38
- SS-Standarten 90
- SS-Standarten 94

SS-Abschnitt XXXVI
- SS-Standarten 76
- SS-Standarten 87

- Nachrichtensturmbann 15
- Nachrichtensturmbann 18
- Pioniersturmbann 15
- Kraftfahrsturm 15
- Kraftfahrsturm 18

The second of two main SS divisions in Austria, the Alpenland Senior District was considered the "Mountain Corps" of the General-SS. Members of the district (including subordinate Abschnitt and Standarten) were entitled to display a unique Edelweiss collar device as a distinct unit insignia. (right)

SS-Oberabschnitt Böhmen-Mahren			
Established	1 April 1944	**Headquarters**	Prague
Cuffband	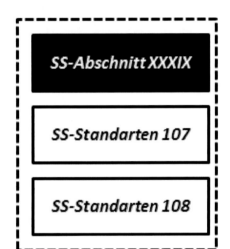		
Previous Commands	Formed in the Reich Protectorate of Bohemia and Moravia using Abschnitt XXXIX as an initial cadre		
SS and Police Command	HSSPF Böhmen und Mahren	**War District**	N/A
Subordinate Units			

SS-Abschnitt XXXIX

SS-Standarten 107

SS-Standarten 108

Nachrichtensturmbann 19

Kraftfahrsturm 19

Formed in the occupied Czech Republic, Senior District Böhmen Mähren was the only major extension of active SS mustering formations into an occupied territory. Administratively, the district was a parallel command to the Higher SS and Police Leader of Bohemia and Moravia, with the two posts intended to be held by the same person. For the duration of the senior district's existence, its commander was Karl Hermann Frank (right – Federal German Archives). In the last months of the war, Frank delegated command to his deputy SS-Oberführer Emanuel Saldek.

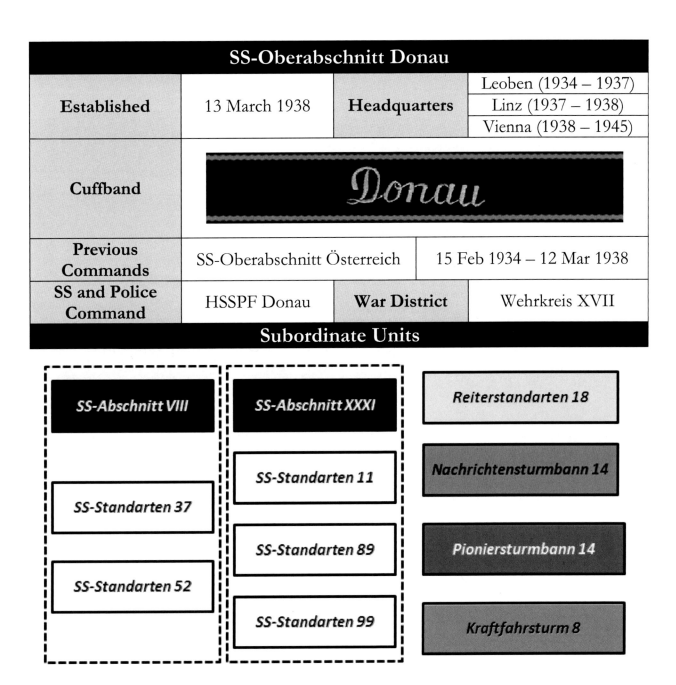

SS-Oberabschnitt Donau			
Established	13 March 1938	**Headquarters**	Leoben (1934 – 1937)
			Linz (1937 – 1938)
			Vienna (1938 – 1945)
Cuffband			
Previous Commands	SS-Oberabschnitt Österreich	15 Feb 1934 – 12 Mar 1938	
SS and Police Command	HSSPF Donau	**War District**	Wehrkreis XVII
Subordinate Units			

SS-Abschnitt VIII

SS-Standarten 37

SS-Standarten 52

SS-Abschnitt XXXI

SS-Standarten 11

SS-Standarten 89

SS-Standarten 99

Reiterstandarten 18

Nachrichtensturmbann 14

Pioniersturmbann 14

Kraftfahrsturm 8

The primary Allgemeine-SS division in Austria, this Senior District was known by the title "Österreich" and existed as an underground headquarters for the Austrian SS from 1934 to 1938. The district's first commander was Alfred Rodenbücher.

Above: Conjectural design for the original cuffband for "SS-Oberabschnitt Österreich".
No known photographs exist of this cuffband displayed on an SS uniform

SS-Oberabschnitt Elbe

Established	4 April 1936	Headquarters	Dresden

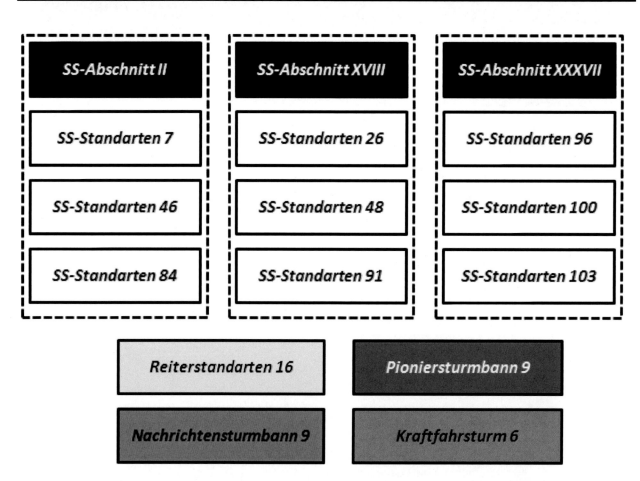

Cuffband			

Previous Commands	SS-Gruppe Ost	1932 – 15 Nov 1933	
	SS-Oberabschnitt Elbe	16 Nov 1933 – 14 Jun 1934	
	SS-Oberabschnitt Mitte	15 Jun 1934 – 3 Apr 1936	

SS and Police Command	HSSPF Elbe	War District	Wehrkreis IV

Subordinate Units

SS-Abschnitt II
- SS-Standarten 7
- SS-Standarten 46
- SS-Standarten 84

SS-Abschnitt XVIII
- SS-Standarten 26
- SS-Standarten 48
- SS-Standarten 91

SS-Abschnitt XXXVII
- SS-Standarten 96
- SS-Standarten 100
- SS-Standarten 103

Reiterstandarten 16

Pioniersturmbann 9

Nachrichtensturmbann 9

Kraftfahrsturm 6

The Elbe senior district of the Allgemeine-SS was formed from one of the original SS groups first created in 1932. The district took the name of "Elba" after the Nazi seizure of power in 1933, but a year later was designated as the "Mitte" (Central) district of the Allgemeine-SS. In 1936, the name reverted to "Elba" after a new central district was created in the city of Braunschweig.

SS-Oberabschnitt Fulda-Werra

Established	1 January 1937	Headquarters	Arolsen

Cuffband	 **Fulda-Werra**

Previous Commands	Formed from a portion of the territory previously comprising SS-Oberabschnit Rhein (renamed in 1943 to Rhein-Westmark)

SS and Police Command	HSSPF Fulda-Werra	War District	Wehrkreis IX

Subordinate Units

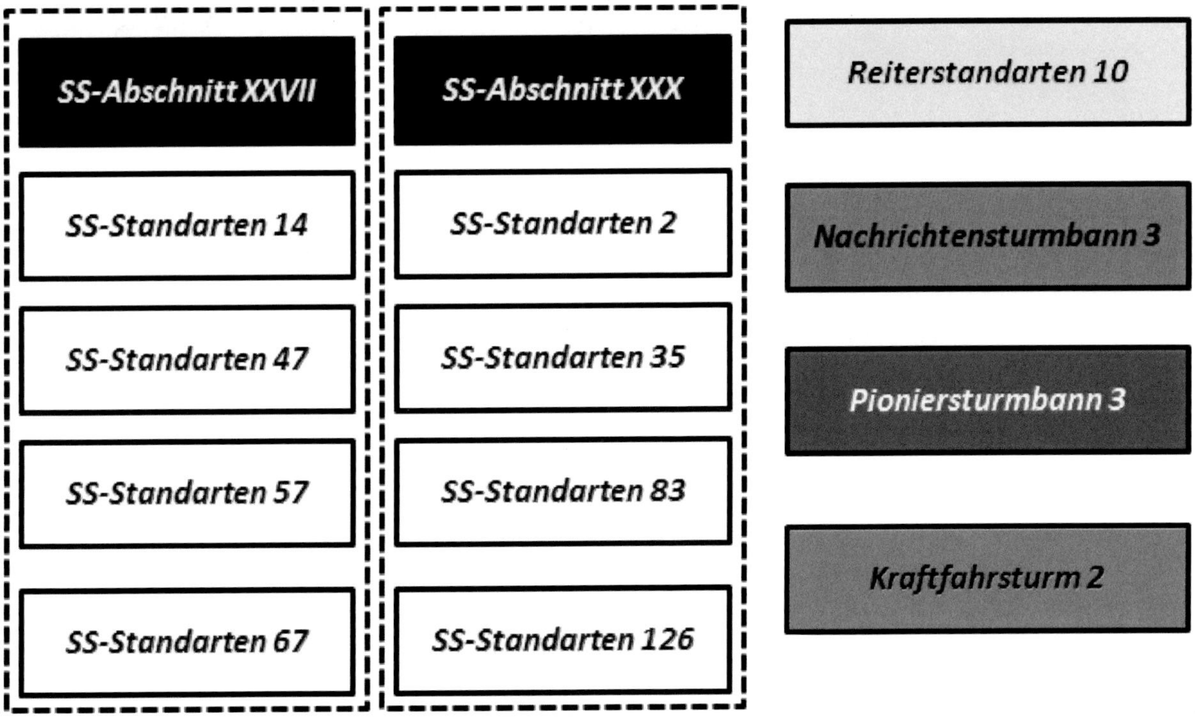

SS-Abschnitt XXVII
- SS-Standarten 14
- SS-Standarten 47
- SS-Standarten 57
- SS-Standarten 67

SS-Abschnitt XXX
- SS-Standarten 2
- SS-Standarten 35
- SS-Standarten 83
- SS-Standarten 126

- Reiterstandarten 10
- Nachrichtensturmbann 3
- Pioniersturmbann 3
- Kraftfahrsturm 2

Formed from a cadre of the Abschnitt XXVII staff, the Senior District Fulda-Werra's territory was drawn from SS Senior District "Rhein". Fulda-Werra's sole commander from 1937 through 1945 was SS-Obergruppenführer und General der Polizei und Waffen-SS Prince Josias Erbprinz zu Waldeck-Pyrmont.

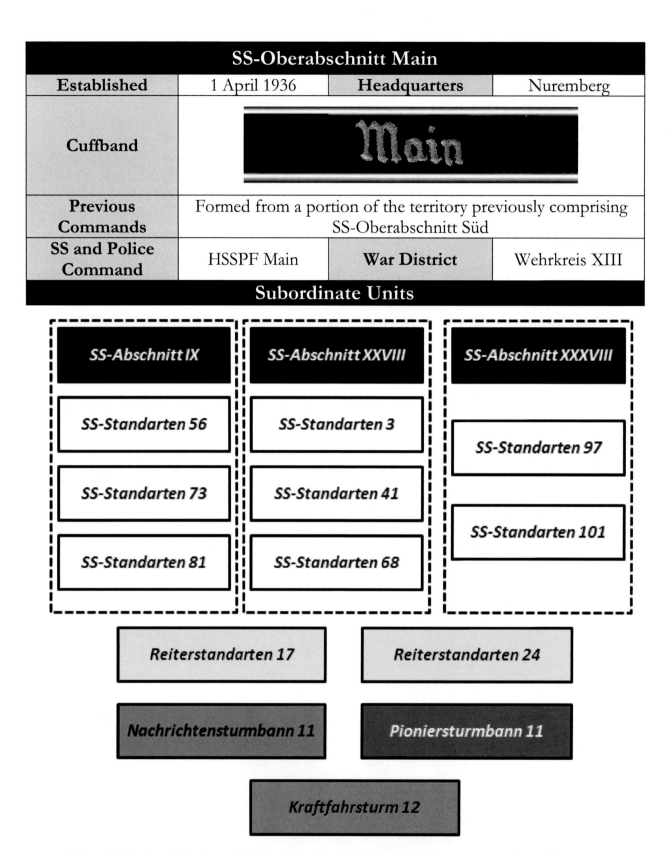

SS-Oberabschnitt Main			
Established	1 April 1936	**Headquarters**	Nuremberg
Cuffband			
Previous Commands	Formed from a portion of the territory previously comprising SS-Oberabschnitt Süd		
SS and Police Command	HSSPF Main	**War District**	Wehrkreis XIII
Subordinate Units			

SS-Abschnitt IX
- SS-Standarten 56
- SS-Standarten 73
- SS-Standarten 81

SS-Abschnitt XXVIII
- SS-Standarten 3
- SS-Standarten 41
- SS-Standarten 68

SS-Abschnitt XXXVIII
- SS-Standarten 97
- SS-Standarten 101

Reiterstandarten 17

Reiterstandarten 24

Nachrichtensturmbann 11

Pioniersturmbann 11

Kraftfahrsturm 12

The SS-Senior District "Main" was one of the largest units in the Allgemeine-SS, encompassing three subordinate districts, eight SS-regiments, two cavalry commands, and three support units. Operating from the city of Nuremberg, which was the ceremonial seat of the Nazi Party, the senior district was one of the more important General-SS commands.

SS-Oberabschnitt Mitte

Established	4 April 1936	Headquarters	Braunschweig

Cuffband	Mitte

Previous Commands	SS-Gruppe Nordwest	10 Aug 1933 – 15 Nov 1933
	SS-Oberabschnitt Nordwest	16 Nov 1933 – 31 Mar 1936

SS and Police Command	HSSPF Mitte	War District	Wehrkreis XI

Subordinate Units

SS-Abschnitt IV
- SS-Standarten 12
- SS-Standarten 49
- SS-Standarten 51

SS-Abschnitt XVI
- SS-Standarten 17
- SS-Standarten 21
- SS-Standarten 59

- Reiterstandarten 21
- Nachrichtensturmbann 5
- Pioniersturmbann 12
- Kraftfahrsturm 11

Formed from a portion of SS-Group West, this was the last of the original SS-Groups to be formed before the SS changed the nomenclature of the original SS groups into SS-Senior Districts. Known originally as "Nordwest", the unit's first commander was Friedrich Jecklen. After the unit was renamed "Mitte" in 1936, the designation of "Nordwest" would be recycled and used as the designation for several other SS units.

SS-Oberabschnitt Nord			
Established	20 April 1940	**Headquarters**	Oslo
Cuffband	**Nord**		
Previous Commands	Formed in occupied Norway. The last of three SS-Oberabschnitt to hold the designation "Nord".		
SS and Police Command	HSSPF Nord	**War District**	N/A
Subordinate Units			

SS-Standarten 127

The SS designation of "Nord" traces its origins to SS Group North first formed in 1932. In 1933, the first SS-Oberabschnitt Nord was formed and existed until 1936, when the territory was split between a new SS Senior District North and Northwest. The smaller version of the SS-Oberabschnitt Nord then existed until 1940 when the territory was renamed as SS-Oberabschnitt Ostsee, with the designation of Nord transferred to a newly formed SS command in Norway.

The Norwegian version of Senior District Nord was essentially a paper command meant to exist in tandem with the office of the Higher SS and Police Leader of occupied Norway. The Allgemeine-SS office of the Oberabschnitt Führer was intended to be held by the SS and Police Leader, although a separate office of General-SS Chief of Staff did exist.

Two men held the position of Senior District Leader, these being Fritz Weitzel and Wilhelm Rediess, both holding the rank SS-Obergruppenführer und General der Polizei (Rediess was also a General in the Waffen-SS). The Chief of Staff position was held by SS-Standartenführer Erdmann Skudlarek, although in the very last days of the war this posting was transferred to Norwegian control and held by Lief Schjoren, a Norwegian National Socialist. The Senior District had one subordinate unit, which was an SS Regiment formed for administrative reasons with few actual members.

SS-Oberabschnitt Nordost

Established	16 November 1933	Headquarters	Konigsberg

Cuffband	 **Nordost**		

Previous Commands	Formed from a portion of the territory previously comprising SS-Gruppe Nord.		
SS and Police Command	HSSPF Nordost	**War District**	Wehrkreis I

Subordinate Units

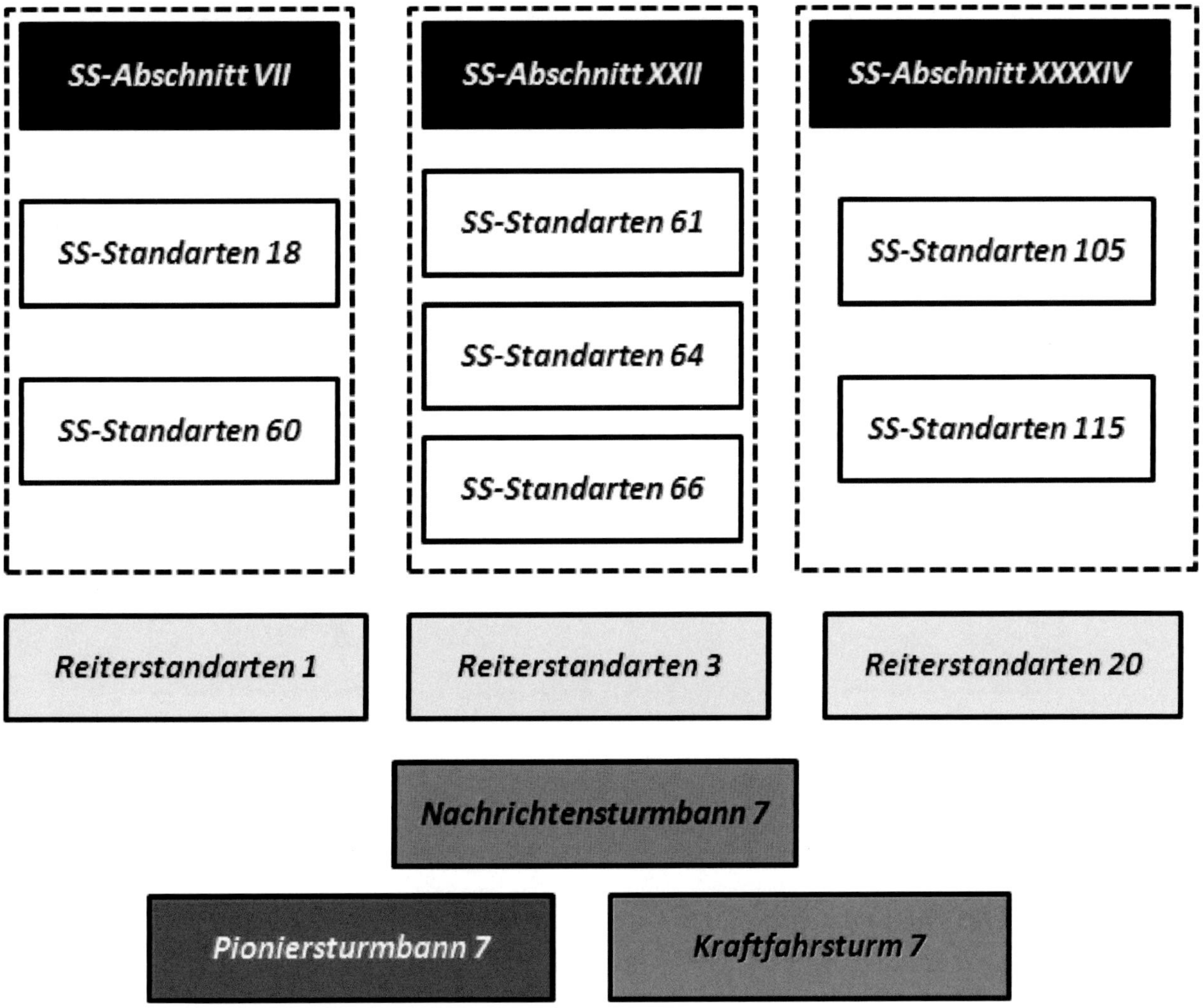

SS-Abschnitt VII

SS-Standarten 18

SS-Standarten 60

SS-Abschnitt XXII

SS-Standarten 61

SS-Standarten 64

SS-Standarten 66

SS-Abschnitt XXXIV

SS-Standarten 105

SS-Standarten 115

Reiterstandarten 1

Reiterstandarten 3

Reiterstandarten 20

Nachrichtensturmbann 7

Pioniersturmbann 7

Kraftfahrsturm 7

Formed from a portion of the original SS Group North, the Nordost senior district contained the largest numbers of General-SS cavalry commands, as well as seven SS regiments organized into three separate districts.

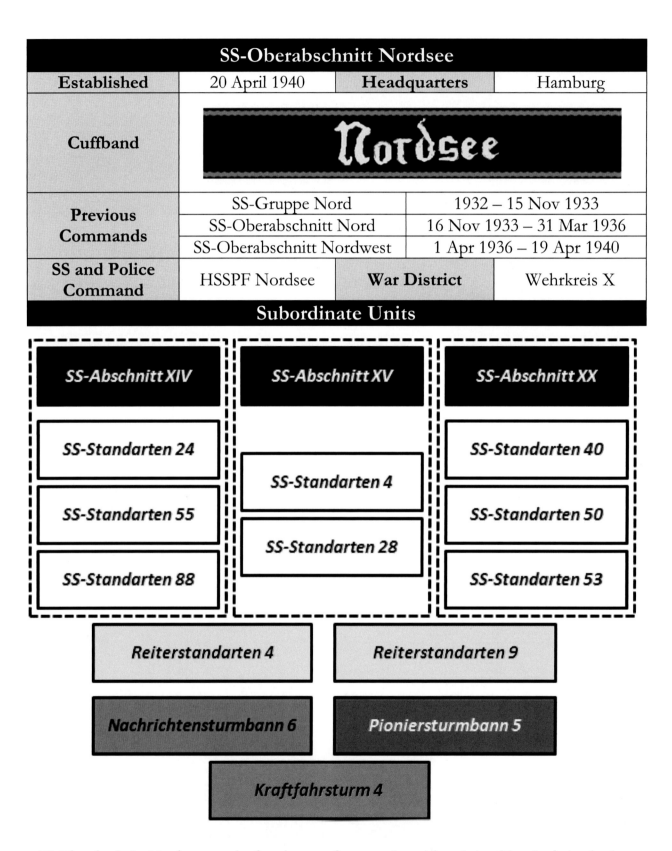

SS-Oberabschnitt Nordsee

Established	20 April 1940	Headquarters	Hamburg
Cuffband	Nordsee		
Previous Commands	SS-Gruppe Nord	1932 – 15 Nov 1933	
	SS-Oberabschnitt Nord	16 Nov 1933 – 31 Mar 1936	
	SS-Oberabschnitt Nordwest	1 Apr 1936 – 19 Apr 1940	
SS and Police Command	HSSPF Nordsee	War District	Wehrkreis X

Subordinate Units

SS-Abschnitt XIV
- SS-Standarten 24
- SS-Standarten 55
- SS-Standarten 88

SS-Abschnitt XV
- SS-Standarten 4
- SS-Standarten 28

SS-Abschnitt XX
- SS-Standarten 40
- SS-Standarten 50
- SS-Standarten 53

Reiterstandarten 4
Reiterstandarten 9
Nachrichtensturmbann 6
Pioniersturmbann 5
Kraftfahrsturm 4

SS-Oberabschnitt Nordsee was the fourth name for a continuously existing SS unit, dating back to 1932, when the unit was known as SS Group North. The Nordsee senior district contained eight SS regiments, two cavalry commands, and three support units.

SS-Oberabschnitt Nordwest			
Established	23 May 1940	**Headquarters**	The Hague
Cuffband	 **Nordwest**		
Previous Commands	Formed in occupied Holland. The second of two SS-Oberabschnitt to hold the designation "Nordwest"		
SS and Police Command	HSSPF Nordwest	**War District**	N/A

The second of two SS Senior Districts to hold the designation "Nordwest" was formed in occupied Holland as a direct equivalent to the posting of the Higher SS and Police Leader of the Netherlands. The posting was intended to be held by the same person and, for the five years of the district's existence, its commander was SS-Obergruppenführer und General der Polizei Hans-Albin Rauter. Rauter's Chief of Staff was SS-Obersturmbannführer Wilhelm Montel. The Senior District never held any subordinate units and was primarily a paper command for the corresponding post of the Higher SS and Police Leader.

Right: Hans Albin Rauter, who served as the senior most SS officer in the occupied Netherlands from 1940 to 1945. Shortly before the end of the war, he was seriously wounded by Dutch partisans and later arrested in his hospital bed by the British Army. He was tried and found guilty of war crimes and executed by firing squad in 1949.

(Image courtesy of Federal German Archives)

SS-Oberabschnitt Ost			
Established	15 September 1942	**Headquarters**	Krakau
Cuffband	Ost		
Previous Commands	SS-Sondersturmbann Ost	3 Mar 1941 – 14 Sep 1942	
SS and Police Command	HSSPF Ost	**War District**	N/A
Subordinate Units			

Führer der Allgemeine-SS

SS-District Radom   **SS-District Krakau**   **SS-District Lublin**

SS-District Warsaw   **SS-District Lemberg**

Created as an Allgemeine-SS counterpart for SS forces in occupied Poland, the position of the senior district commander was intended to be the same person as the Higher SS and Police Leader of the General Government in Poland. In theory, the senior district office was to maintain a special staff position, known as the "Führer der Allgemeine-SS", who would oversee five SS districts encompassing all General-SS units in occupied Poland. The intent being that, once Germany had won the Second World War and had purged Poland of racial inferior populations, this would lead to the formation of new SS-Standarten in a Germanized Poland. This vision never came to pass, and no SS officer was ever assigned to the Allgemeine-SS staff leader position.

SS-Oberabschnitt Ostland			
Established	1 December 1941	**Headquarters**	Riga
Cuffband	Ostland		
Previous Commands	Formed in occupied Latvia as an Allgemeine-SS equivalent to the office of Higher SS and Police Leader.		
SS and Police Command	HSSPF Ostland und Rußland-Nord	**War District**	N/A

Formed as an Allgemeine-SS equivalent to the posting of the Higher SS and Police Leader in occupied Latvia, this Senior District was a paper command and had no assigned units or a General-SS Chief of Staff. The sole commander of SS-Oberabschnitt Ostland was SS-Obergruppenführer und General der Polizei und Waffen-SS Friedrich Jecklen.

Jecklen held the posting of the SS and Police Leader, as well as Senior District Leader, from December 12, 1941 until the command was dissolved in March 1945.

Right: Friedrich Jecklen in the late 1930s. A career officer of the Allgemeine-SS since 1930, Jecklen had served as a Standarten, Abschnitt, and Oberabschnitt commander before being appointed to police duties in Russia. Considered one of the more brutal SS commanders in the east, he coordinated Einsatzgruppen activities in his region with ruthless efficiency, leading to the deaths of tens of thousands of innocent victims. After the war, he was put on trial by a Soviet military tribunal and executed for war crimes. (Image courtesy National Archives)

SS-Oberabschnitt Ostsee			
Established	1 February 1940	**Headquarters**	Stettin
Cuffband	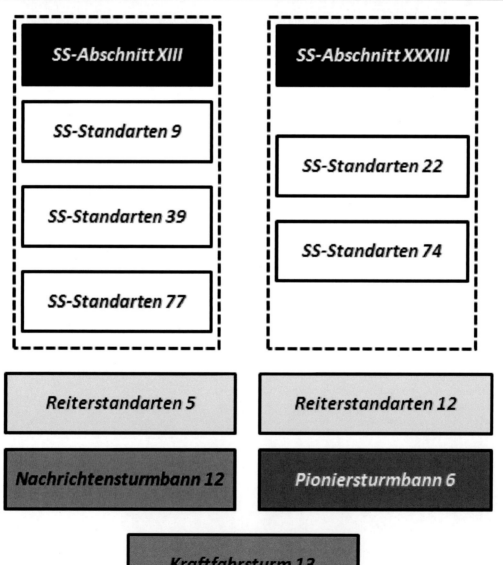		
Previous Commands	SS-Oberabschnitt Nord	1 Apr 1936 – 31 Jan 1940	
SS and Police Command	HSSPF Ostsee	**War District**	Wehrkreis II
Subordinate Units			

SS-Abschnitt XIII

SS-Standarten 9

SS-Standarten 39

SS-Standarten 77

SS-Abschnitt XXXIII

SS-Standarten 22

SS-Standarten 74

Reiterstandarten 5

Reiterstandarten 12

Nachrichtensturmbann 12

Pioniersturmbann 6

Kraftfahrsturm 13

SS-Oberabschnitt Rhein-Westmark

Established	11 September 1943	Headquarters	Wiesbaden

Cuffband	**Rhein-Westmark**

Previous Commands	SS-Oberabschnitt Rhein	1 Jan 1934 – 10 Sep 1943
	SS-Oberabschnitt Lothringen-Saarpfalz	August 1940 – October 1941
	SS-Oberabschnitt Westmark	1 Oct 1941 – 10 Sep 1943

SS and Police Command	HSSPF Rhein-Westmark	War District	Wehrkreis XII

Subordinate Units

SS-Abschnitt XI	SS-Abschnitt XXXIV	
SS-Standarten 5	SS-Standarten 10	Reiterstandarten 13
SS-Standarten 33	SS-Standarten 32	Reiterstandarten 23
SS-Standarten 78	SS-Standarten 85	Nachrichtensturmbann 13
SS-Standarten 93	SS-Standarten 125	Pioniersturmbann 13
		Kraftfahrsturm 14

Rhein   **Westmark**

Above: The original cuffbands for the Rhein and Westmark SS districts, which were combined in 1943 to form the SS-Oberabschnitt Rhein-Westmark[xxii].

SS-Oberabschnitt Spree			
Established	14 November 1939	**Headquarters**	Berlin
Cuffband	 Spree		
Previous Commands	SS-Oberführerbereich Ost	1 Aug 1930 – 1 Mar 1932	
	SS-Gruppe Ost	1 Mar 1932 – 15 Nov 1933	
	SS-Oberabschnitt Ost	16 Nov 1933 – 13 Nov 1939	
SS and Police Command	HSSPF Spree	**War District**	Wehrkreis III
Subordinate Units			

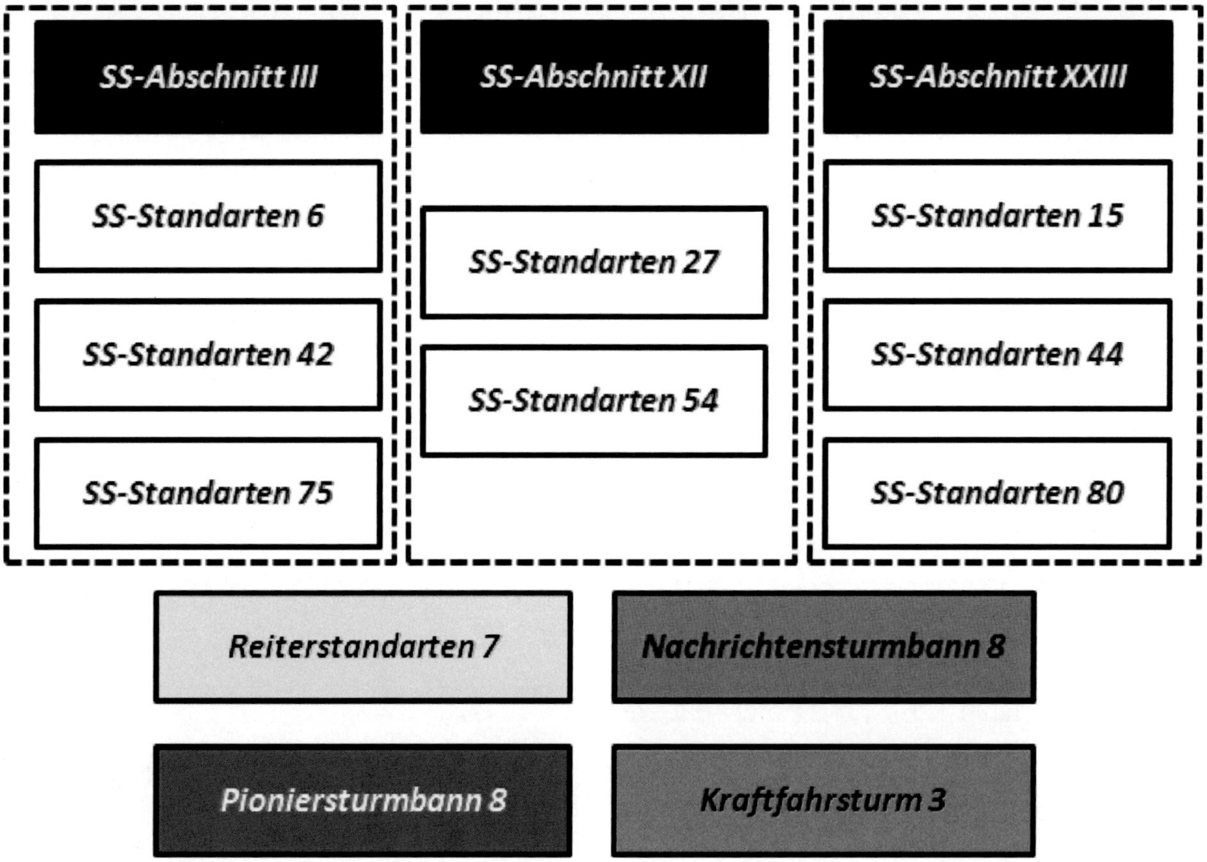

SS-Abschnitt III
- SS-Standarten 6
- SS-Standarten 42
- SS-Standarten 75

SS-Abschnitt XII
- SS-Standarten 27
- SS-Standarten 54

SS-Abschnitt XXIII
- SS-Standarten 15
- SS-Standarten 44
- SS-Standarten 80

Reiterstandarten 7

Nachrichtensturmbann 8

Pioniersturmbann 8

Kraftfahrsturm 3

The Spree SS senior district was originally known as "Ost" (East) and was headquartered in the German capitol of Berlin. As such, it was one of the more important districts of the Allgemeine-SS

SS-Oberabschnitt Süd			
Established	16 November 1933	**Headquarters**	Munich
Cuffband			
Previous Commands	SS-Oberführerbereich Süd	1929 - 1931	
	SS-Brigade Süd	1931 - 1932	
	SS-Gruppe Süd	1 Jul 1932 – 15 Nov 1933	
SS and Police Command	HSSPF Süd	**War District**	Wehrkreis VII
Subordinate Units			

SS-Abschnitt I	SS-Abschnitt XXXII	
SS-Standarten 1	SS-Standarten 29	Reiterstandarten 15
SS-Standarten 31	SS-Standarten 92	Nachrichtensturmbann 1
SS-Standarten 34	SS-Standarten 106	Pioniersturmbann 1
		Kraftfahrsturm 1

The oldest continuously operating unit of the Allgemeine-SS, the SS District South (Süd) was founded as one of the original SS leadership areas in 1929. The unit was later the first brigade of the General-SS, later upgraded to a group and then an SS senior district. Notable commanders included Rudolf Hess, Josef "Sepp" Dietrich, Friedrich Jecklen, and Richard Hildebrandt. During Dietrich's tenure, he commanded both the senior district and SS district 1 (Abschnitt I) simultaneously.

SS-Oberabschnitt Südost

Established	16 November 1933	Headquarters	Brieg (1933 – 1936)
			Breslau (1936 – 1945)

Cuffband	Südost

Previous Commands	SS-Brigade Schlesien	1930 - 1931
	SS-Gruppe Südost	1931 – 1933

SS and Police Command	HSSPF Südost	War District	Wehrkreis VIII

Subordinate Units

SS-Abschnitt VI	SS-Abschnitt XXI	Reiterstandarten 11
SS-Standarten 16	SS-Standarten 8	Nachrichtensturmbann 10
SS-Standarten 43	SS-Standarten 70	Pioniersturmbann 10
SS-Standarten 98	SS-Standarten 95	Kraftfahrsturm 9

SS-Abschnitt XXIV	SS-Standarten 23	SS-Standarten 45
SS-Standarten 102	SS-Standarten 104	SS-Standarten 124

The Südost senior district, as one of the original SS groups, was formed from one of the first SS brigades. In November 1933 it was one of the first of the new SS senior districts, created simultaensouly with senior district Südwest.

SS-Oberabschnitt Südwest

Established	16 November 1933	Headquarters	Stuttgart

Cuffband	 Südwest

Previous Commands	Formed from a portion of the territory previously comprising SS-Gruppe West

SS and Police Command	HSSPF Südwest	War District	Wehrkreis V

Subordinate Units

SS-Abschnitt X
- SS-Standarten 13
- SS-Standarten 63

SS-Abschnitt XIX
- SS-Standarten 62
- SS-Standarten 86

SS-Abschnitt XXIX
- SS-Standarten 65
- SS-Standarten 79

SS-Abschnitt XXXV
- SS-Standarten 122
- SS-Standarten 123

Reiterstandarten 14

Nachrichtensturmbann 2

Pioniersturmbann 2

Kraftfahrsturm 10

The Südwest senior district was one of the original SS senior districts, formed from territory prevously a part of SS Group West. The new SS senior district was created simultaensouly with senior district Südost.

SS-Oberabschnitt Ukraine			
Established	1 December 1941	**Headquarters**	Kiev
Cuffband	Authorized for design but never issued		
Previous Commands	Formed in the occupied Ukraine. Existed as a counterpart command to the office of the Supreme SS and Police Leader		
SS and Police Command	HoSSPF Ukraine	**War District**	N/A
Subordinate Units			

The SS Senior District Ukraine was an Allgemeine-SS equivalent to the much more powerful posting of the Supreme SS and Police Leader of the Ukraine, which from 1941 to 1944 was held by SS-Obergruppenführer und General der Polizei und Waffen-SS Hans-Adolf Prützmann.

The Ukraine Senior District was strictly a paper command and held no subordinate units. The unit was authorized a General-SS Chief of Staff, but no officer was ever appointed to this position. The highest active Allgemeine-SS posting in the senior district was that of District Administrative Officer, which appears to have functioned as a liaison between the Ukraine SS command and the Allgemeine-SS offices in Germany.

The posting of administrative officer was held from 1943 to 1944 by Josef Spacil, after which time the position was abolished and the Senior District Ukraine was dissolved.

Above right: Hans-Adolf Prützmann in 1943. Prützmann served as the Supreme SS and Police Leader of the Ukraine and, by default, was also the Allgemeine-SS senior district leader for the region. Due to the high number of SS genocide activities in the Ukraine during his tenure, Prützmann oversaw the murder of hundreds of thousands of innocent victims. He was captured by Allied forces at the war's end and committed suicide on May 21st 1945. (Photo courtesy Federal German Archives)

SS-Oberabschnitt Warthe

Established	26 October 1939	Headquarters	Posen
Cuffband	 Warthe		
Previous Commands	Formed from portions of western Poland annexed into Germany after 1939. Briefly known as SS-Oberabschnitt Posen for the first few weeks of the command's existence.		
SS and Police Command	HSSPF Warthe	War District	Wehrkreis XXI

Subordinate Units

SS-Abschnitt XXXXII
- SS-Standarten 109
- SS-Standarten 110
- SS-Standarten 111

SS-Abschnitt XXXXIII
- SS-Standarten 112
- SS-Standarten 113
- SS-Standarten 114

- Reiterstandarten 22
- Nachrichtensturmbann 17
- Kraftfahrsturm 17

Formed from conquered Polish territory, the first commander of Senior District Warthe was SS-Gruppenführer und Generalleutnant der Polizei Wilhelm Koppe. Koppe commanded the SS district from 1939 to 1943, after which time the district was commanded by Theodor Berkelmann, Heinz Reinefarth, and Willy Schmelcher, all of whom were also police generals.

SS-Oberabschnitt Weichsel

Established	9 November 1939	Headquarters	Danzig

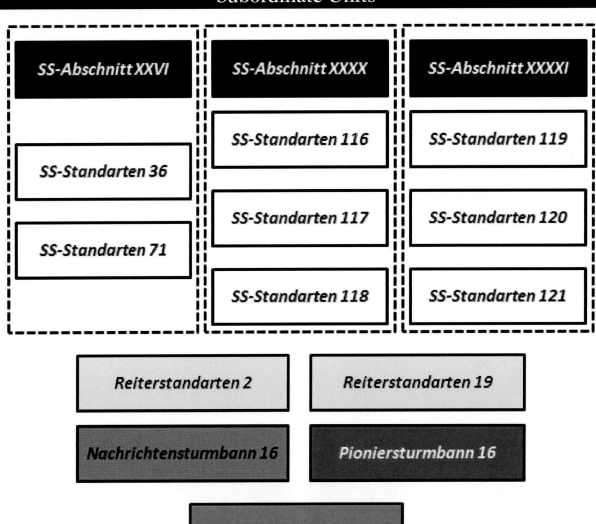

| Cuffband | Weichsel | | |

| Previous Commands | Formed from the western portion of SS-Oberabschnitt Nordost, using Abschnitt XXVI as an initial cadre command | | |

| SS and Police Command | HSSPF Weichsel | War District | Wehrkreis XX |

Subordinate Units

SS-Abschnitt XXVI
- SS-Standarten 36
- SS-Standarten 71

SS-Abschnitt XXXX
- SS-Standarten 116
- SS-Standarten 117
- SS-Standarten 118

SS-Abschnitt XXXXI
- SS-Standarten 119
- SS-Standarten 120
- SS-Standarten 121

Reiterstandarten 2

Reiterstandarten 19

Nachrichtensturmbann 16

Pioniersturmbann 16

Kraftfahrsturm 16

SS-Oberabschnitt West

Established	16 November 1933	Headquarters	Düsseldorf

Cuffband	
	Weſt

Previous Commands	SS-Oberführerbereich West	1930 - 1931
	SS-Gruppe West	1 Apr 1931 – 15 Nov 1933

SS and Police Command	HSSPF West	War District	Wehrkreis VI

Subordinate Units

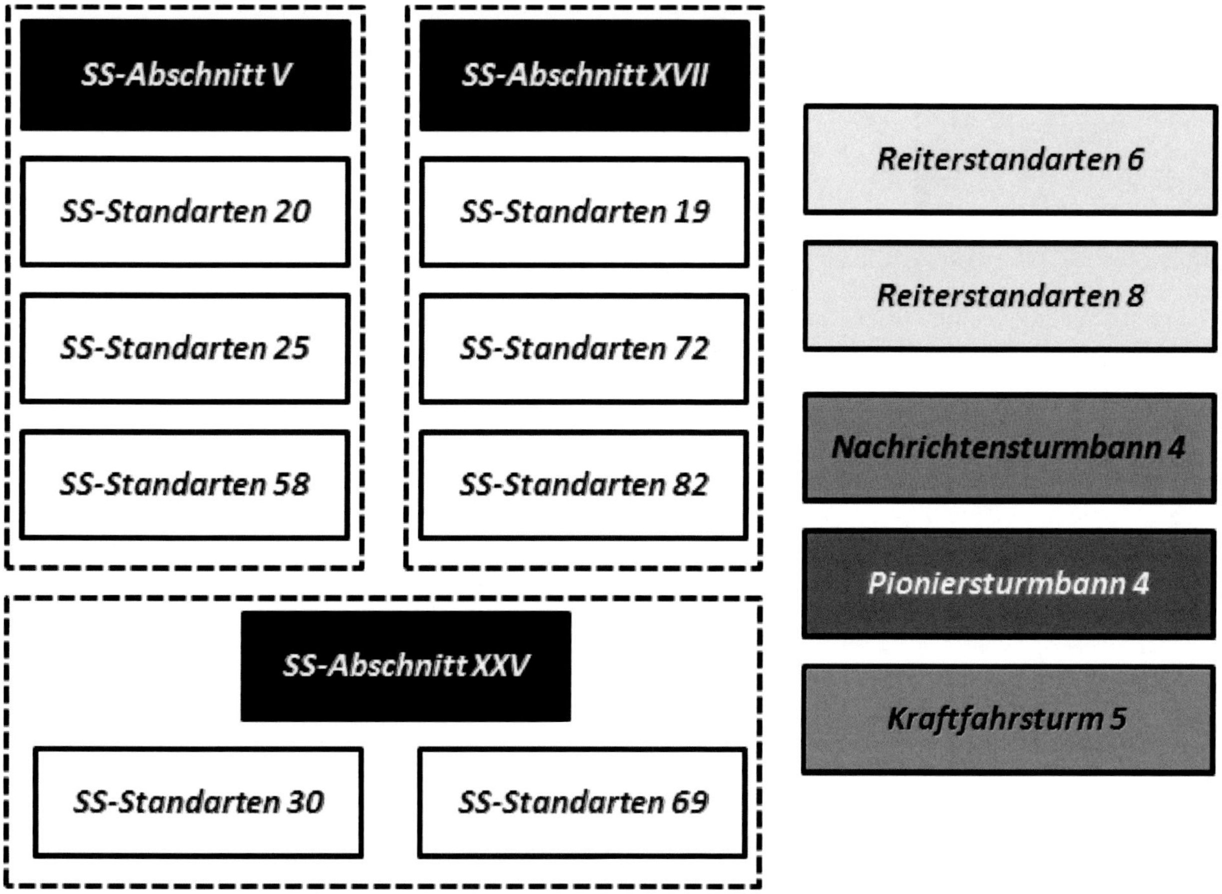

SS-Abschnitt V
- SS-Standarten 20
- SS-Standarten 25
- SS-Standarten 58

SS-Abschnitt XVII
- SS-Standarten 19
- SS-Standarten 72
- SS-Standarten 82

Reiterstandarten 6

Reiterstandarten 8

Nachrichtensturmbann 4

Pioniersturmbann 4

Kraftfahrsturm 5

SS-Abschnitt XXV
- SS-Standarten 30
- SS-Standarten 69

The second oldest SS unit in continuous existence, a majority of its territory was used to form other commands of the General-SS.

Life in the General-SS

During the formative years of the SS, membership in the organization was oftentimes looked down upon, since the group was vastly overshadowed by the stormtroopers of the SA. After the SS became an independent organization in 1934, service in Himmler's black corps took on a new meaning as elite troops of the Nazi Party and an organization which was to be both feared and respected.

For those SS men who served in the Allgemeine-SS during the pre-war years of the 1930s, SS membership offered a lucrative array of opportunities and entitlements. During this time the SS developed into an organization of Aryan men, with SS race experts formulating both ideological and racial policies intent on preserving the best traits of the Germanic race. It was the vision of Heinrich Himmler to transform the SS into an elite society within Germany, accountable only unto itself. One of Himmler's first official acts, after the SS had gained independence from the SA in 1934, pertained to directives which removed SS members from the accountability of German civilian courts. The SS would thereafter police itself with special SS courts, each formed to prosecute and judge those members who had committed transgressions against the black corps. The SS court system was overseen by the Main Office for SS Legal Affairs (Hauptamt SS-Gericht) which codified SS regulations and certified SS lawyers and judges. The SS Legal Office also administered the SS and Police Courts (SS und Polizei Gerichte) of which three main types existed.

SS Court	Jurisdiction	Description	Sentences
SS- und Polizeigericht	Routine court for the prosecution and trial of infractions committed by members of the SS	Attached to Oberabschnitt headquarters with thirty-eight courts in all	Probation, demotion in rank, assignment to SS penal battalion or SS prison, dismissal from the SS
Oberstes SS- und Polizeigericht	Cases of treason, crimes against the state, and espionage. Also held jurisdiction over any trial of an SS-General	Operated in Munich by SS-Oberführer Dr. Günther Reinecke	Same as above to including the death penalty
SS- und Polizeigericht z.b.V	Sensitive or classified matters concerning internal issues of the SS	Attached to the SS Legal Main Office	Same as above, excluding death

The staffing and operation of the three main SS courts were overseen by officers known as "SS-Richter", who were certified lawyers and judges, and were assisted by SS legal aides known as SS-Hilfsrichter. These assistants were usually paralegals possessing higher education in administration and law. The SS also maintained an array of legal protocol officers (SS-Beurkundungsführer und Unterführer) who would assist in trial preparation and proceedings. A final classification of SS legal personnel was the "SS-Untersuchungsführer" who conducted pre-trial interviews with potential witnesses.

The ultimate legal foundation of the SS court system was finalized in 1939, with a decree known as the "SS und Polizeigerichtsbarkeit" (Special Jurisdiction of the SS and Police) which was the final legal measure in a long line of jurisprudence to remove members of the SS from the jurisdiction of civilian courts. All of the SS legal regulations were further published in a document known as the "SS-Disziplinarstraf und Beschwerdeordnung" (SS Disciplinary and Penal Code), known commonly as the DBO. Heinrich Himmler was considered the final appeal authority for the SS courts and held the same appellate power as a Reich Supreme Judge. Himmler also had authority to establish judicial courts of inquiry, known as the SS-Disziplinarhof, although in most cases Himmler would only personally oversee legal proceedings against senior SS officers, ranked Gruppenführer and above. For all other matters Himmler granted review power to the SS Main Office leaders, as well as the SS-Oberabschnitt commanders.

For those SS men found guilty of offenses, several sentences could be meted out by SS judges. In the more serious cases, an SS member could be dismissed from the service and executed by either hanging, shouting, or beheading. In most cases however, SS men found guilty in an SS and Police Court were sentenced to a period of incarceration at one of several SS disciplinary facilities. These camps were staffed by a specially selected group of veteran Concentration Camp personnel with very few records remaining as to who these men were or the exact nature of how the SS prisons operated.

SS disciplinary facilities

Discipline Facility	Classification	Location	Sentence Type
SS-Strafvollzugslager	Prison Camp	Danzig	Standard incarceration
		Ludwigsfelde	
Straflager der SS und Polizei	Labor Camp	Dachau	Heavy Labor
		Karlsfeld	
SS-Strafanstaltquartier	Prison Quarters	Munich	Minor sentences

After the start of the Second World War, convicted SS men were also given the opportunity to serve out sentences attached to an SS penal battalion. The first such unit was known as the "Bewährungs Abteilung" (Rehabilitation Detachment) which was based in Chlum, Bohemia and was intended as a hazardous duty combat formation. A second formation, known as the "Arbeits Abteilung" was engaged in heavy labor projects.

The SS court system also encompassed a form of civil litigation, although with far less power than the regular SS and Police Courts which prosecuted criminal cases. Known as the SS-Schiedshofe (SS Honor Court), this branch of the SS legal system existed to mitigate personal disputes between SS members. The Honor Court had limited arbitration power and existed primarily as a means to mediate between two SS members who held a personal disagreement. The Honor Court also existed to oversee personal challenges and duels, ensuring that dueling was conducted in proper form with swords or pistols. Adolf Hitler discouraged the practice of dueling in any Nazi Party organization, leaving the Honor Court to its original purposes of arbitrating affairs of honor so that the dispute did not escalate. There were two separate types of SS honor courts, these being the Minor Courts of Honor (Kleine Schiedshofe), which dealt with investigations into civil arbitration, and the Major SS Honor Court (Grosse Schiedshofe) which presided over the actual resolution of cases. Honor Courts were formed on an as-needed basis and were not permanent bodies. The formation of an Honor Court could be called by any SS-general at the level of an SS-district commander or above. Heinrich Himmler was the ultimate appeal and final arbitration authority for all SS honor cases.

While the SS dealt harshly with those who violated its rules and regulations, the organization conveniently overlooked such egregious acts as murder, genocide, and oppression insofar as those policies were in line with the actions of the Nazi regime. There were even some SS men who refused to participate in atrocities, leading to a type of "administrative discipline" which was a commonly used means to keep cases out of the SS and Police courts relating to SS men who had refused to carry out a criminal order involving genocide.

The term "transferred to the front" was often used to describe those SS men who were considered unfit for the duties in the SS requiring behind-the-lines atrocities, such as the shooting of women and children or the mass murder of Jews. For members of the Allgemeine-SS, this usually meant transfer into a Waffen-SS combat unit which further entailed a drastic reduction in rank. Wilhelm Höttl, an SS-Sturmbannführer in the Security Police, was ordered transferred to the front after disagreements with Reinhard Heydrich concerning SS policies against Jews and other minorities. Höttl was transferred to the Waffen-SS as a Lance Corporal (Rottenführer), regaining his rank in the General-SS only after front line service had been completed.

One crime which the SS did not tolerate, even against the backdrop of genocide and extermination, was corruption. During the Second World War, one of the most common cases brought before the SS and Police Courts was "theft of state property" which related to SS men who had stolen money or other valuables from extermination victims. The chief investigator for SS corruption cases was SS-Sturmbannführer and lawyer Georg Konrad Morgen. Morgen's primary focus was the prosecution of SS men who had stolen confiscated valuables at German Concentration Camps, with his inquires extending even to camp commanders such as Rudolf Höss of Auschwitz and Karl Otto Koch of Buchenwald. Morgen also attempted to investigate activates at the Treblinka Death Camp; however, he was prohibited from doing so since Treblinka was classified as a secret camp under the extermination directives of Operation Reinhard.

In a legal irony, during his investigations at Auschwitz and Buchenwald, Morgen was prohibited from filing any charges for the mass murder of prisoners, since extermination was an accepted practice and sanctioned by the state. In his corruption cases, Morgen's investigations led to an indictment of the Buchenwald camp commander, resulting in a trial and death sentence against Karl Otto Koch by an SS and Police Court. Auschwitz was to prove a far more difficult case, since Rudolf Höss had prisoners murdered who could be potential witnesses against SS men and was further suspected of orchestrating the disappearance and murder of Morgen's chief legal aid and assistant SS-Hauptscharführer Gerhard Putsch. In the end, Morgen was unable to file any charges against Auschwitz Commandant Höss and was further ordered by Heinrich Himmler to cease further investigations into activities at the concentration camps.

Heinrich Himmler's ultimate aim was for the Allgemeine-SS to serve as an SS state protection corps which would also encompass every aspect of German life and serve as an elite guard from which to propagate the German Master Race. To that end, Himmler established several SS offices tasked with both researching Germany's Aryan heritage as well as promoting the concept of a Germanic racial elite. The scientific research arm of the SS, known as the SS-Ahnenerbe, was an agency of Himmler's personal staff tasked with researching the origins of the German race, collecting artifacts of Aryan heritage, and maintaining museums dedicated to the racial superiority of Germany.

The first effort to form an SS scientific research corps was in 1934 with the founding of the "Abteilung Ausgrabungen", which was an SS archeology department attached to Himmler's personal staff. This was complemented by a branch of the SS Race and Settlement Office, known as the "Abteilung für Vor und Frühgeschichte" which specailized in Germanic pre-history. On July 1ˢᵗ 1935, Himmler founded the "Deutsches Ahnenerbe - Studiengesellschaft für Geistesurgeschichte" (Society for the Study of the History of Primeval Ideas) which had by 1937 become known simply as the Ahnenerbe. The Ahnenerbe was run from a headquarters office in Berlin and was funded entirely through private donations. This was unique as the only branch of the SS which was not financed through either the Nazi Party or with state funds.

The two main functions of the Ahnenerbe were to sponsor Aryan research institutes in Germany as well as scientific expeditions around the world. At its height, the Ahnenerbe sponsored thirty-two institutes of social sciences and nineteen of medicine. The most infamous was the Institute for Military Scientific Research (Institut für Wehrwissenschaftliche Zweckforschung) which was the SS command responsible for directing human experimentation carried out in the Concentration Camps. Among such experiments on human subjects were high altitude pressure tests, prolonged freezing water exposure, as well as a host of other hideous procedures such as vivisections and the submerging of living humans into acid in order to conduct burn experiments. The scientific research institute was also known to preserve the skeletons of its victims for pseudo-anthropological studies.

Right: Wolfram Sievers, head of SS scientific research, who was executed after the war for his role in human medical experiments (National Archives)

Between 1935 and the close of the Second World War, the Ahnenerbe also sponsored over a dozen field expeditions to search for historical artifacts of the German race. Several expeditions took place in Germany and France, while the Ahnenerbe also sent SS historians and archeologists to such far reaches as Tibet and Antarctica. In the latter's case, the German expedition technically founded a Nazi Antarctic colony called "New Swabia". This colony, now known as Queen Maud Land, is today administered by Norway. The SS also sent scientific research teams to Sweden and had planned expeditions to both South America and Iceland. Due to budget restrictions and the onset of World War II, these later expeditions were cancelled.

During the Second World War, the Ahnenerbe became involved with the confiscation of rare art and artifacts in conquered territories. Agents of the Ahnenerbe ransacked Poland for all manner of medieval art works and the Ahnenerbe also occupied the Louvre in Paris in order to gain access to its many treasures. The SS allowed major French artworks (such as the Mona Lisa painting) to remain in the care of the Louvre; however, an attempt was made to transport the Bayeux Tapestry (depicting the Norman conquest of England) to Germany in the last year of the war. The SS officers sent to confiscate the tapestry abandoned their effort due to the French Resistance having occupied the Louvre and expelling its German caretakers.

The actual scientific value of SS expeditions, medical experiments, and other research projects is today considered negligible and even during the Nazi era Adolf Hitler generally scoffed at the idea of Germanic research. Hitler felt that Himmler's efforts in this field were misguided and that the destiny of Germany lay in the future rather than the past. Modern day myths of SS research, including stories of Nazi flying saucers, SS projects to locate the Yeti, the Lost Ark of the Covenant, and the Holy Grail, are mostly in the realm of imagination rather than fact.

A parallel office to the Ahnenerbe, operating with much more concrete implications, was the SS-Lebensborn (Fountain of Life) program which was founded in September of 1936 to promote health and welfare amongst SS families.

The Lebensborn program was originally under the control of the SS Race and Settlement Office, with an aim to provide maternity assistance to women pregnant with the children of SS men. A financial foundation known as the "Lebensborn e.V" was established on September 23rd 1936 and managed a special fund with dues paid by all SS senior officers. By 1938, nearly eight thousand SS members had enrolled in the Lebensborn foundation, with the Lebensborn headquarters office transferred to Himmler's personal staff in 1939. During the pre-war years of the 1930s, the Lebensborn also operated maternity homes for SS wives and women who had become pregnant out of wedlock. This program also ran an adoption service for illegitimate children of German mothers. Once the Second World War began, the Lebensborn became a type of welfare agency for those children whose parents had been killed in bombing raids. In occupied territories, the organization collaborated with the SS Race and Settlement Office to identify suitable native children for "Germanization" and transfer such children to homes in Germany. After the war, the Lebensborn was accused of kidnapping children from their parents, especially in Norway and Poland. The Lebensborn program would state in its defense that the only foreign children relocated to Germany were orphans.

The seal of the Lebensborn program
(Graphical recreation)

The SS also operated a number of hospitals specializing in female and maternity care, collectively known as the "Heim Hochland" with ten such facilities operating in Germany and three in Austria. Norway and Poland also saw the opening of several Lebensborn facilities (nearly ten in each country) while a small number were opened in the western countries of France, Belgium, the Netherlands, and Luxembourg.

Left: A widely publicized photo of Heinrich Himmler speaking to an orphan in Poland in 1940. The Lebensborn program claimed to exist to assist war orphans and children displaced from their families. In reality, such children were usually kidnapped from their parents and relocated to German families. (Polish State Archives)

Following the close of the Second World War, the Lebensborn program was vilified by occupation agencies as a child trafficking ring and SS breeding ground. The Lebensborn facilities were described as brothels, where SS men would impregnate women, to further propagate the master race. The allegations against Lebensborn were later declared untrue, while the Lebensborn chief administrator Max Sollman was acquitted of any war crimes.

General-SS uniforms and insignia

The black uniform of the Allgemeine-SS, designed to project authority and inspire fear, has since became one of the iconic images of the SS. The uniform itself was issued to the SS membership for less than eight years, yet during that time created one of the most complex rank and insignia patterns within the hierarchy of Nazi paramilitary uniforms. Evolving from the brown shirt uniforms of the Sturmabteilung, and utilizing the same rank insignia system, the black SS uniform was first issued in late 1932 and was the standard uniform of the SS until the start of World War II in 1939. Between 1939 and 1942 the uniform was phased out in favor of a grey wartime tunic. Until the year 1935, both the earlier brown shirt SS uniform and the new black jacket were worn side by side by various SS units. The rank insignia remained the same for both uniform types, yet there were isolated examples of insignia badges which were authorized for wear on the brown uniform not intended for display on the black jacket.

The Hilfspolizei armband (used by the Auxiliary Police) was worn in February 1933 by SS units deployed to maintain order after the German Reichstag fire. This armband was worn over the swastika brassard and only displayed on the brown SS shirt. Another insignia item, unique to the brown SS shirt, was the "Medical Training Patch" (see right). This badge was worn above the swastika armband and appeared as a white circle displaying a red cross. The badge was intended to denote those SS personnel who were in training to become medical orderlies but had not yet passed a state medical examination.

Between 1933 and 1938, the SA operated a state sponsored leadership academy (Führungschule), for both SA and SS personnel, whose successful attendance at which was denoted by a runic black arrow with gold and red trim. This arrow insignia was worn above the swastika armband on both the brown SA uniform and black SS jacket. This insignia piece became obsolete upon the outbreak of World War II and was not displayed on the later grey SS tunics issued from 1938 to 1945.

Above: The SA Leadership School Insignia, as worn on the SS black jacket
(Image graphic and photo courtesy of National Archives)

A unique SS insignia which existed until 1934 were those badges and patches worn by SS members assigned to the SA Supreme Command. SS duty officers attached to the SA Supreme Command (Oberste SA-Führung) were denoted by a special cuffband worn on the lower left jacket sleeve. An even rarer form of insignia, displayed on the early SS brown shirt uniforms, was the "double rank insignia", worn by SS officers assigned as aides to SA generals and worn in the color of the SA Group to which the SS officer was attached.

Above: Supreme SA Command cuffband as compared to the "double rank insignia" of an SS-Obersturmbannführer attached to the SA Hochland Group in Northern Germany

Allgemeine-SS uniform pattern

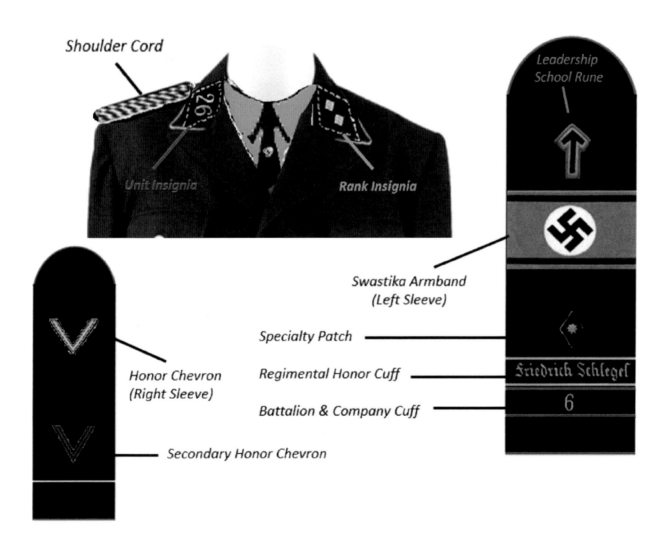

The array of insignia displayed on the black SS jacket was designed to fully denote an SS member's unit affiliation through a variety of collar patches, cuffbands, and other accoutrements. The SS of the 1930s developed a complex system of insignia intending to outwardly show attachments to the highest levels of the SS headquarters and extending downwards to the lowest SS units of the Allgemeine-SS mustering formations.

The insignia pattern used by the black uniform had developed from previous patches and cuffbands first adopted for the SS brown shirt uniform in use since 1929. The rank insignia of the SS, first created in 1930, underwent little change with the exception of renaming certain ranks in 1934 following the Night of the Long Knives. In 1931, Heinrich Himmler also authorized the creation of the first sleeve cuff band for SS headquarters personnel. The insignia was a bare black cuffband which was worn on the lower left sleeve of the SS brown shirt uniform. When the SS transitioned to the black SS jacket, the use of the bare cuffband was adopted by all SS staff attached to the SS main offices. In 1933, Himmler ordered a new series of silver cuffbands to denote senior SS command officers while the bare cuffband continued to be worn by staff officers.

Allgemeine-SS command cuffbands
(1933 – 1938)

Office Title	Cuffband	Usage
Reichsführer-SS		Heinrich Himmler, the office chiefs of the SS main offices, as well as SS district and senior district leaders.
Hauptamtschef und Amtschef		
Oberabschnitt Leiter		
Abschnitt Leiter		
Hauptabteilungsleiter		Chief Department Heads on the staffs of the personnel listed above
Abteilungsleiter		Department Heads in the same manner as described above
Referent im Stab		Adjutants to Himmler and other senior SS commanders
SS Stab des Reichsführer-SS	RfSS	Himmler's personal staff from 1935 to 1939
SS Offizer		SS personnel attached to a major SS headquarters or staff

In 1935, Heinrich Himmler introduced a special cuffband worn solely by members of his personnel staff. The cuffband bore the initials of "RFSS" denoting Himmler's position as Reich Leader of the SS. In 1939, this cuffband was replaced by a slightly modified version displaying the more pronounced sig runes of the SS. In the spring of 1933 Himmler also had enacted a short-lived policy in which both he and members of his immediate staff would wear white backed SS collar tabs in contrast to the black collar insignia displayed by the rest of the SS.

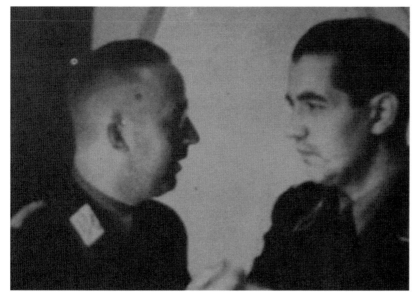

The motivation for this directive stemmed from the black SS jacket becoming more wide spread across Germany, and Himmler's desire to differentiate headquarters personal from the remainder of the SS who served in the mustering formations.

The wearing of white collar tabs by Himmler's staff was ordered discontinued in the fall of 1933; by 1934, all applicable personnel had reverted to regular insignia, but the white tabs would survive for use by the SS Supplementary Reserve until the end of the Second World War.

Left: Himmler shown wearing his unique white SS-Obergruppenführer insignia, which was used briefly in 1933 (Bavarian State Archives)

In 1935, Himmler ordered that all personnel of the SS Main Offices wear unique cuffbands denoting the name of their office. Senior leaders and department heads continued to wear a solid silver cuffband

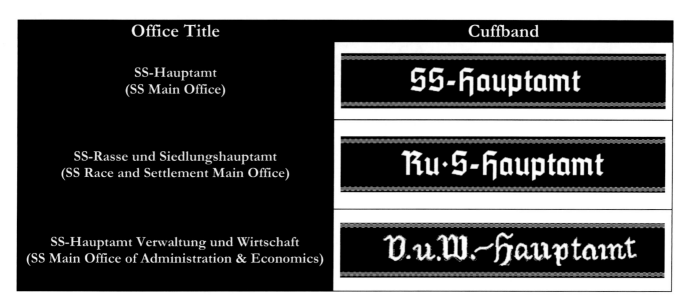

Office Title	Cuffband
SS-Hauptamt (SS Main Office)	SS-Hauptamt
SS-Rasse und Siedlungshauptamt (SS Race and Settlement Main Office)	Ru·S-Hauptamt
SS-Hauptamt Verwaltung und Wirtschaft (SS Main Office of Administration & Economics)	V.u.W.-Hauptamt

Above: Main office cuffbands as designed in 1935. The cuffband used by the SS Main Office of Administration and Economics was later adopted by the SS Office of Budget and Construction

In the fall of 1936, after Heinrich Himmler became Chief of the German Police, a slight uniform modification was ordered concerning the undershirts worn beneath the black SS jackets. When the black jacket was first created, regulations specified that a brown undershirt would be worn with a tie clipped with a swastika pin. The brown shirt was a homage to the original storm trooper uniforms worn by the SA, while the swastika pin denoted the SS as a paramilitary group of the Nazi Party.

Under the 1936 regulations, SS members would wear a white undershirt and tie (without swastika pin) if they held duties which were considered "state service" such as officials of the police, Gestapo, or within the Ministry of the Interior. This included Himmler and most of his top SS generals, as well as SS personnel attached to the secret police. For the remainder of the SS, including the Sicherheitsdienst (SD), the brown undershirt would continue to be worn.

Also, during this period, a small number of General-SS unit insignia and cuffbands were discontinued for wear, mainly as a result of certain SS offices and regions merging or disbanding. The SS Flying Corps, which existed for less than a year between 1931 and the summer of 1932, consisted of a single SS company which was authorized a unique collar patch displaying a wing and propeller. SS pilots were also awarded an extremely rare decoration known as the SS-SA Flyers Badge.

The discontinued SS insignia of the SS-Fliegersturm (Flying Corps), showing collar insignia and the SS-SA Flyers Badge

From 1933 through 1939, the General-SS district encompassing Berlin was entitled to wear a special collar insignia emblazoned with the word "Ost" in gothic script. By 1937, this collar insignia had been changed to match the district's cuffband, and in 1939 the insignia was declared obsolete as the Berlin SS district was renamed as "SS-Oberabschnitt Spree". Another short-lived SS insignia was a cuffband denoting service in the liaison office for Austrian Nazis known as the SS-Sammelstelle (Reception Office). Permanently assigned personnel were entitled to wear a special cuffband denoting the office's name; this insignia was discontinued after Austria was annexed by Germany.

Above: The first and second pattern "SS-Oberabschnitt Ost" collar insignia, as well as the SS Reception Office cuffband used in Austria. Both sets of insignia were discontinued in 1939

On the level of the operational units of the Allgemeine-SS, all SS personnel assigned to an Oberabschnitt staff (and ranked Obersturmbannführer and below) displayed a bare collar patch (see right) as a unit insignia. The two exceptions were the senior district in Berlin (SS-Oberabschnitt Ost), which displayed the district name until 1939, and the Alpenland Senior District which was authorized an Edelweiss patch to denote status as a mountain unit.

Subordinate SS-Districts (excluding the mountain districts) displayed a roman numeral unit insignia, paired up with an identical cuffband. The first seven SS districts were created simultaneously from the older SS brigades in the summer of 1931. The remaining districts were formed between 1932 and 1940.

The core unit of the Allgemeine-SS was the regimental sized SS-Standarten, of which one hundred and twenty-seven such units were eventually founded. The term "Standarten" (referring to a flag which a local SS unit would carry on parade) first appeared in Nazi terminology in 1928. Prior to this time, local SS units were referred to as "Stafflen". By 1929, the use of the term Standarten had standardized throughout the SS, with local units issued a roman numeral patch to denote regimental affiliation. By the summer of 1931 there were ten SS-Standarten in existence.

Left: An SS member in 1929 displays the collar patch for SS-Standarten 4. The Roman numeral system would be adopted by the SS-Abschnitt in 1931, after which time SS regiments were denoted by standard numerals. Twenty-eight SS districts and sixty regiments would exist by the time the Nazis took power in 1933. That number would double by the end of the Second World War. (Image courtesy of Bavarian State Archives)

SS-Abschnitt Formation Dates

1-7	8-17	18-28	29-30	31-33	34	35-38	39	40-45
1931	1932	1933	1934	1936	1937	1938	1939	1940

SS-Standarten Formation Dates

1-2	3	4-6	7-41	42-59	60-73	74-91
1928	1929	1930	1931	1932	1933	1934

92		93-104	105-108	109-125		126-127
1936	~	1938	1939	1940	~	1944

The unit insignia system of the Allgemeine-SS would eventually evolve into one of the most complex series of accoutrements ever designed by the SS. Through a system of collar patches, cuffbands, and colored piping, the black uniform was designed to denote an SS member's affiliation down to the battalion and company level. SS regiments were also known by several different titles: a numerical designation, an "honor title" bestowed for extraordinary deeds, and a popular name by which SS members typically referred to in casual conversation. Individual companies could themselves receive an honor title, for which a special cuffband would be awarded. The honor title cuffbands of the General-SS remain today some of the rarest SS insignia pieces in existence, many of which have never been photographed.

Cuffband insignia of General-SS. From left to right - Cuffband worn by SS-Standarten 20 Regimental Leader, Honor Cuffband worn by Battalion Leader, Bare cuffband worn by Regimental and Battalion staff members. SS-District Five cuffband worn by all personnel.

All members of an SS-Standarten typically wore a numeric collar insignia. Enlisted personnel would wear the insignia framed in black and aluminum pipping, while officers would wear the unit insignia trimmed in solid silver. If the regimental commander was ranked SS-Standartenführer, they would wear rank on both collars, but regardless of rank would display a silver piped cuffband with the unit's regimental number in Arabic script.

Enlisted and officer SS-Standarten unit insignia

If the regiment was issued an honor title, a cuffband displaying the honor name would be worn in lieu. SS battalion commanders, typically ranked as SS-Sturmbannführer, displayed the same unit insignia as the regimental level. All members of the regimental and battalion staffs wore a white piped bare cuffband. SS personnel assigned to the SS-Abschnitt level, both command and staff, wore a similar cuffband with the SS district's Roman numeral. The wear of the district numeral by lower ranked personnel has been speculated, but there are no photographs confirming this practice.

The SS uniforms at the company (Sturm) level possessed one of the more complicated of insignia systems, with both collar patches and cuffbands designed to display an SS member's unit affiliation at the regimental, battalion, and company level. In addition to the standard regimental unit patch worn on the right collar, SS officers assigned as company officers displayed a silver piped cuffband with the company number in Arabic script. Most SS regiments possessed a total of fifteen to twenty regular companies organized into three battalions. SS enlisted personnel wore the company number on a cuffband with different colors to denote battalion affiliation.

SS company cuffbands

Classification	Cuffband Piping	Example
Company officers	SILVER	5
First Battalion members	GREEN	3
Second Battalion members	PURPLE	8
Third Battalion members	DARK BLUE (Before 1935)	11
	RED (After 1935)	15

SS companies were originally numbered independently within each battalion, for instance the 1st company of the 2nd battalion (the 6th in the regiment) would display a numeral "1" on the purple colored cuffband instead of "6". This was changed in 1936 to number companies consecutively across the entire regiment. In cases where the SS company member served in a regiment which had been awarded an honor title, the regimental honor cuff title would be worn above the standard company cuffband. Individual company honor cuffbands bore the honor name beside the company number and were trimmed in silver piping. For cases where an SS member was eligible for both a company and regimental honor cuffband, both were worn simultaneously.

Honor cuffbands of the General-SS. From left to right - Cuffband worn by an SS officer attached to the 6th Company of an SS Regiment; Cuffband worn by a member of the SS 9th Company, 2nd Battalion with the Regimental honor cuffband "Loeper" of the 59th SS Regiment; Company honor cuffband worn by a member of the 1st SS Company "Paul Berch" of the 26th SS Regiment; Company honor cuffband of the 5th SS Company "Franz Hellinger" accompanied by the Regimental honor cuffband "Julius Schreck" of the 1st SS Regiment.

Attached to each SS-Standarten was at least one reserve battalion, to which were assigned older SS members generally over the age of thirty-five. In the early years of the SS, membership in the reserve battalion was denoted by an "R" patch worn on the SS brown shirt opposite both the regimental number and rank insignia. By 1934, some of the larger General-SS regiments held upwards of three reserve battalions.

Right: Early SS insignia for a reserve SS-Scharführer attached to the 28th SS-Standarten (Graphical recreation)

With the introduction of the black SS uniform, reserve members began wearing a cuffband bearing the script "Reserve" piped with coloring in the same manner as the regular SS battalions. Individual reserve companies further displayed a company numeral. By 1936, most of the SS-regiments maintained only a single reserve battalion with a cuffband piped in a unique light blue coloring.

In addition to standard reserve members, each SS regiment was administratively assigned a number of supplementary reservists between the ages of forty-five and sixty. For special occasions, the Supplementary Reserve would muster alongside the regular SS regiment.

In such instances Supplementary Reserve members wore standard SS uniforms with white regimental collar patches.

1ˢᵀ Reserve Battalion Staff

Reserve Battalion Staff (Later pattern)

5ᵗʰ Reserve Company, 3ʳᵈ Battalion

3ʳᵈ Reserve Company (Later pattern)

Above: Reserve and supplementary insignia of the Allgemeine-SS. Upper left displays cuffbands worn by reserve battalion and company members. The white backed insignia was worn by the supplementary reserve, as shown on the right by two SS supplementary reservists (Insignia images graphical recreations, photo courtesy Bavarian State Archives)

After the Nazi Party came to power in 1933, Heinrich Himmler began to actively seek out high profile Germans and other elites to join the SS as honorary members. By 1935, the SS officer rolls included senior Nazi political leaders as well as notable figures in business, science, education, and the arts. Originally, honorary SS members were attached to local SS-Standarten, in a non-mustering capacity, and were issued a complicated insignia system to denote both rank and regimental affiliation. This honorary SS insignia consisted of an oak leaf SS-Standartenführer patch in which rank pips were worn around the insignia to denote overall honorary rank. The member's SS regimental numeral was displayed on the stem of the oak leaf insignia. By 1935, this special insignia system for honorary SS officers had been discontinued, with such members now wearing standard badges of rank.

Most honorary SS officers were administratively attached to a headquarters SS office and displayed a special cuffband denoting their status. Honorary officers ranked Standartenführer and above would be rated as a "Ehrenführer" while lower ranks would be designed "Rangführer". A special honorary cuffband was also reserved for any SS member who had been part of the original pre-SS bodyguard formation (the "Adolf Hitler Shock Troop") founded in 1922.

Honorary SS insignia, attached to the 2nd SS-Standarten (Graphical recreation)

SS-ABSCHNITT UNIT INSIGNIA

SS District	Headquarters	Collar and Cuff Insignia	
One	Munich	I	I
Two	Chemnitz	II	II
Three	Berlin	III	III
Four	Braunschweig	IV	IV
Five	Essen	V	V
Six	Brieg	VI	VI
Seven	Danzig-Mariensee	VII	VII
Eight	Linz	VIII	VIII
Nine	Kulmbach	IX	IX
Ten	Stuttgart	X	X
Eleven	Frankfurt-Main	XI	XI

Twelve	Dühringhof	XII	XII
Thirteen	Stettin	XIII	XIII
Fourteen	Bremen	XIV	XIV
Fifteen	Altona	XV	XV
Sixteen	Zwickau	XVI	XVI
Seventeen	Münster	XVII	XVII
Eighteen	Weimar	XVIII	XVIII
Nineteen	Karlsruhe	XIX	XIX
Twenty	Kiel	XX	XX
Twenty One	Liegnitz	XXI	XXI
Twenty Two	Allenstein	XXII	XXII

Twenty Three	Berlin	XXIII	XXIII
Twenty Four	Neustadt	XXIV	XXIV
Twenty Five	Bochum	XXV	XXV
Twenty Six	Danzig	XXVI	XXVI
Twenty Seven	Gotha	XXVII	XXVII
Twenty Eight	Regensburg	XXVIII	XXVIII
Twenty Nine	Mannheim	XXIX	XIXX
Thirty	Kassel	XXX	XXX
Thirty One	Vienna	XXXI	XXXI
Thirty Two	Augsburg	XXXII	XXXII
Thirty Three	Schwerin	XXXIII	XXXIII

Thirty Four	Neustadt	XXXIV	XXXIV
Thirty Five	Graz		XXXV
Thirty Six	Innsbruck		XXXVI
Thirty Seven	Reichenberg	XXXVII	XXXVII
Thirty Eight	Karlsbad	XXXVIII	XXXVIII
Thirty Nine	Prague	XXXIX	XIXXX
Forty	Bromberg	XXXX	XXXX
Forty One	Thorn	XXXXI	XXXXI
Forty Two	Gnesen	XXXXII	XXXXII
Forty Three	Litzmannstadt	XXXXIII	XXXXIII
Forty Four	Gumbinen	XXXXIV	XXXXIV
Forty Five	Strasbourg	XXXXV	XXXXV

SS-STANDARTEN UNIT INSIGNIA

Regiment	Location	Popular Name	Collar Insignia	Regimental Honor Title	Company Honor Titles
One	Munich		1	Julius Schreck	1. Karl Ostberg 2. Theodor Casella 5. Franz Hellinger 10. Karl Laforce
Two	Frankfurt Main	Hessen	2		4. Josef Bleser
Three	Nuremberg		3		
Four	Altona	Schleswig-Holstein	4		
Five	Trier	Mosel	5		
Six	Berlin	Charlottenburg	6		6. Eduard Felsen 8. Oskar Goll 9. Kurt von Der Ahe
Seven	Plausen		7	Friedrich Schlegel	3. Paul Fressonke 6. Paul Teubner
Eight	Hirschberg	Niederschlesien	8		
Nine	Stettin	Pommern	9		
Ten	Kaiserslautern	Pfalz	10		
Eleven	Wien	Burgenland	11	Planetta	
Twelve	Hannover	Niedersachsen	12		

Thirteen	Stuttgart	Württemberg	13		
Fourteen	Gotha	Thüringen	14		
Fifteen	Neuruppin	Brandenburg	15		
Sixteen	Breslau	Unterelbe	16		
Seventeen	Celle		17		
Eighteen	Konigsberg	Ostpreußen	18		
Nineteen	Münster	Westfalen-Nord	19		
Twenty	Düsseldorf		20	Fritz Weitzel	1. Karl Vobis / 3. Kurt Hilmer / 5.Werner Hannermann / 11. Friedrich Schreiber
Twenty One	Magdeburg		21		
Twenty Two	Schwerin	Mecklenburg	22	Friedrich Graf von der Schulenburg	
Twenty Three	Beuthen	Oberschlesien	23		
Twenty Four	Oldenburg		24	Ostfriesland	
Twenty Five	Essen	Ruhr	25		1. Garthe / 2. Friedrich Karpinski / 4. Arnold Guse / 5. Leopold Paffrath

Twenty Six	Halle		**26**	1. Paul Berck
Twenty Seven	Frankfurt Oder	Ostmark	**27**	
Twenty Eight	Hamburg		**28**	1. Henry Kobert / 9. Hans Cyranka
Twenty Nine	Lindau	Schwaben	**29**	
Thirty	Bochum	Westfalen-Süd	**30**	Adolf Höh — 1. Fritz Borawski / 3. August Pfaff / 11. Adolf Höh
Thirty One	Landshut	Niederbayern	**31**	4. Faust / 12. Andreas Zinkl
Thirty Two	Heidelberg	Baden	**32**	
Thirty Three	Darmstadt	Rhein-Hessen	**33**	
Thirty Four	Weilheim	Oberbayern	**34**	
Thirty Five	Kassel		**35**	
Thirty Six	Danzig		**36**	
Thirty Seven	Linz	Ob der Enns	**37**	
Thirty Eight	Graz			

Thirty Nine	Köslin	Ostpommern	39
Forty	Kiel		40
Forty One	Bayreuth	OberFranken	41
Forty Two	Berlin		42
Forty Three	Frankenstein		43
Forty Four	Eberswalde	Uckermark	44
Forty Five	Oppeln	Neisse	45
Forty Six	Dresden		46
Forty Seven	Jena		47
Forty Eight	Leipzig		48
Forty Nine	Goslar	Braunschweig	49
Fifty	Flensburg	Nordschleswig	50
Fifty One	Göttingen	Harz	51

1. Radke

8. Martens

4. Fritz Scholz

8. Gutsche

Fifty Two	Krems	Unter-Enns	52		
Fifty Three	Heidelberg	Dithmarschen	53		
Fifty Four	Lansberg		54	Seidel-Dittmarsch	
Fifty Five	Lüneburg	Weser	55		
Fifty Six	Bamberg	Franken	56		
Fifty Seven	Meiningen	Thüringer Wald	57		
Fifty Eight	Köln		58		2. Franz Müller
Fifty Nine	Dessau		59	Loeper	
Sixty	Insterburg		60		
Sixty One	Allenstein	Masuren	61		
Sixty Two	Karlsruhe		62		
Sixty Three	Tübingen		63		
Sixty Four	Danzig	Marienburg	64		

Sixty Five	Freiburg	Schwarzwald	65
Sixty Six	Bartenstein	Friedland	66
Sixty Seven	Erfurt	Wartburg	67
Sixty Eight	Regensburg	Oberpfalz	68
Sixty Nine	Hagen	Sauerland	69
Seventy	Glogau		70
Seventy One	Elbing	Weichsel	71
Seventy Two	Detmold	Lippe	72
Seventy Three	Ansbach	Mittelfranken	73
Seventy Four	Greifswald	Ostsee	74
Seventy Five	Berlin	Tempelhof	75
Seventy Six	Salzburg		
Seventy Seven	Schneidmühl		77

12. Fritz Beubler

1. Ernst Ludwig

8. Edmund Behnke

Seventy Eight	Wiesbaden		78	
Seventy Nine	Ulm		79	
Eighty	Berlin	Groß-Beeren	80	
Eighty One	Würzburg		81	2. Hans Purps
Eighty Two	Bielefeld		82	
Eighty Three	Giessen		83	Oberhessen
Eighty Four	Chemnitz	Saale	84	4. Grobe / 9. Steinbach / 11. Ludwig Frisch
Eighty Five	Saarbrücken		85	
Eighty Six	Offenburg	Hanauer Land	86	
Eighty Seven	Innsbruck	Tirol		
Eighty Eight	Bremen	Stedingen	88	
Eighty Nine	Wien		89	Holzweber
Ninety	Klagenfurt	Kärnten		Franz Kutschera

Ninety One	Wittenberg		91
Ninety Two	Ingolstadt	Alt-Bayern	92
Ninety Three	Koblenz		93
Ninety Four	Leoben	Obersteiermark	
Ninety Five	Trautenau		95
Ninety Six	Brüx		96
Ninety Seven	Eger		97
Ninety Eight	Mährisch-Schönberg		98
Ninety Nine	Znaim		99
One Hundred	Reichenberg		100
One Hundred One	Saaz		101
One Hundred Two	Jägerndorf		102
One Hundred Three	Aussig		103
One Hundred Four	Troppau		104

One Hundred Five	Memel	105
One Hundred Six	Augsburg	106
One Hundred Seven	Brünn	107
One Hundred Eight	Prague	108
One Hundred Nine	Posen	109
One Hundred Ten	Hohensalza	110
One Hundred Eleven	Kolmar	111
One Hundred Twelve	Litzmann-stadt	112
One Hundred Thirteen	Kalisch	113
One Hundred Fourteen	Lesslau	114
One Hundred Fifteen	Zichenau	115
One Hundred Sixteen	Bromberg	116
One Hundred Seventeen	Konitz	117
One Hundred Eighteen	Stargard	118

One Hundred Nineteen	Graudenz	119
One Hundred Twenty	Kulm	120
One Hundred Twenty One	Strasbourg	121
One Hundred Twenty Two		122
One Hundred Twenty Three	Kolmar	123
One Hundred Twenty Four	Scharley	124
One Hundred Twenty Five	Metz	125
One Hundred Twenty Six	Marburg	126
One Hundred Twenty Seven	Oslo	127

Battalion Cuffband Colors: First Sturmbann (I)   Second Sturmbann (II)   Third Sturmbann (III)

Note: It is unknown if the final two Standarten (126 & 127) were ever issued numerical collar insignia. Both were created in 1944, when the standard collar insignia for all Allgemeine-SS units was a bare unit collar tab.

Honorary cuffbands of the Allgemeine-SS. The "Ehrenführer" cuffband was commonly displayed with a unit name for any honorary officer attached to an SS regiment, district or senior district. Example "Ehrenführer Ost", "Ehrenführer XII", or "Ehrenführer 7". The use of these special honorary SS cuffbands had generally been discontinued by 1938

Staff and specialty insignia

The cavalry regiments of the General-SS, which existed from 1934 to 1939, displayed a modified form of the standard Allgemeine-SS regimental insignia. All General-SS cavalry officers wore a silver trimmed unit insignia, displaying crossed cavalry lances, while a specialty sleeve insignia was worn by all cavalry ranks. A horseshoe badge, denoting training in hoof care, was worn by SS-Farriers. Cavalry officers attached to the headquarters of the cavalry training command also wore a distinctive cuffband, as did the staff of the main riding school located in Munich.

General-SS cavalry insignia (top to bottom) - Cavalry Sleeve Diamond, Cavalry officer collar insignia, SS-Farrier specialty insignia. Also shown are the cuffbands for the Cavalry Training Inspection Command and the Munich Cavalry School.

Staff officers attached to the short lived "Reiter-Abschnitt" (Cavalry Districts) wore a crossed lances insignia and were apparently never granted a specific cuffband. The rank and file cavalry membership were authorized a unit insignia of crossed lances and regimental number, as well as an orange trimmed cuffband displaying specific cavalry company numbers. Cavalry company and regimental officers apparently wore the same type of cuff insignia, albeit with the regimental number instead of a company. The rarest type of cavalry cuffband pertained to those cavalry companies which were attached directly to the command of an SS senior district for special duty or assignments. In such cases, the cuffband displayed both the company numeral and the name of the senior district

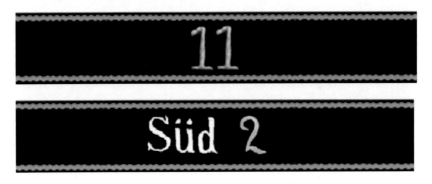

The orange trimmed cuffband of an 11th SS-Cavalry company member.
Also shown is a 2nd cavalry company member attached to the command of SS-Senior District South

The General-SS cavalry wore the standard SS black uniform for most duties, although a summer white riding uniform was also authorized for field training cavalry maneuvers. The white tunic would eventually be adopted by various units of the General-SS "Fuß Standarten" (Foot Regiments) and was also used within the SS Concentration Camp service.

A staff officer of the Allgemeine-SS Cavalry, wearing the black SS uniform, while an enlisted member of the 7th SS Cavalry Regiment is shown in a summer white tunic (National Archives and Federal German Archives)

ALLGEMINE-SS CAVALRY INSIGNIA

Cavalry Regiment	Headquarters	Unit Insignia	Riding District (pre-1938)	Senior District Command
One	Mannheim		Reiterabschnitt II (Insterburg)	Nordost
Two	Marienburg			Weichsel
Three	Lyck			Nordost
Four	Hamburg		Reiterabschnitt I (Hamburg)	Nordsee
Five	Stetten			Ostsee
Six	Düsseldorf		Reiterabschnitt VII (Düsseldorf)	West
Seven	Berlin			Spree
Eight	Münster		Reiterabschnitt VII	West
Nine	Bremen		Reiterabschnitt I	Nordsee
Ten	Arolsen			Fulda-Werra
Eleven	Breslau			Südost
Twelve	Schwerin			Ostsee

Thirteen	Mannheim			Rhein-Westmark
Fourteen	Stuttgart		Reiterabschnitt VI (Dresden)	Südwest
Fifteen	Munich		Reiterabschnitt V (Munich)	Süd
Sixteen	Dresden		Reiterabschnitt VIII (Karlsruhe)	Elbe
Seventeen	Bad Wörishofen			Main
Eighteen	Vienna			Donau
Nineteen	Graudenz			Weichsel
Twenty	Tilsit			Nordost
Twenty One	Hannover			Mitte
Twenty Two	Posen		Reiterabschnitt VIII	Warthe
Twenty Three	Pirmasens			Rhein-Westmark
Twenty Four	*See Note*xxiii			Main

As well as the cavalry units, the General-SS maintained SS-Signal Battalions (Nachrichtensturmbanne), Pioneer Units (Pioniersturmbanne) and the SS Transport Companies (Kraftfahrstürme). Each of these specialty commands displayed a unique collar insignia and sleeve diamond, as well as cuffbands trimmed in specific colors. Enlisted personnel displayed a battalion or company number on both the collar and sleeve cuffband insignia.

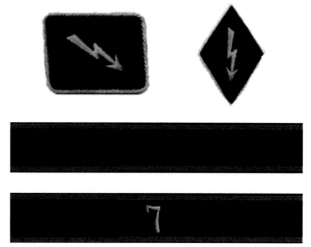

Right: SS signals insignia. From top to bottom –
Signals officer collar patch with signals training sleeve diamond and SS signals staff officer cuffband. A cuffband of an enlisted SS member of the 7th company attached to an SS Signals Battalion is shown below.

Officers of the SS signal battalions wore a jagged arrow collar patch, as well as a bare cuffband with brown colored trim. Enlisted personnel displayed a specific battalion number on the collar insignia with company number on the cuffband. Those who had received training through an approved SS signals course were further entitled to display an SS signals sleeve diamond.

SS personnel of pioneer battalions wore a "pick and axe" collar patch along with a cuffband trimmed in white for officers and black for enlisted personnel. All SS pioneer personnel were required to complete an indoctrination training course, for which a special engineering training company existed at the Eisleben Mining School in Saxony-Anhalt. SS members attached as instructors were authorized a modified "pick-axe-shovel" sleeve diamond. The SS pioneer battalions were also known to maintain a reserve force, typically one reserve pioneer company for each five battalions. Reserve pioneer members displayed a trim-less black "Reserve" cuffband, along with the collar patch of the SS member's assigned pioneer battalion.

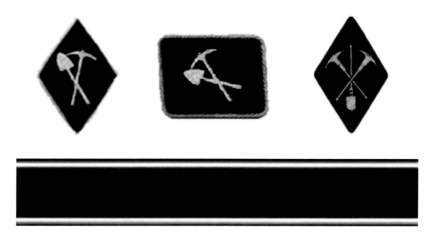

Above: SS-Pioneer sleeve diamond, engineering officer collar patch, and mining school instructor sleeve insignia.
The cuffband shown denotes a pioneer officer. Below: Enlisted cuffband of a member of the 3rd company attached to an SS Pioneering Battalion. The Pioneer Reserve Company cuffband is also shown

SIGNAL BATTALIONS OF THE ALLGEMEINE-SS

SS Signal Battalion	Headquarters	Unit Insignia	Senior District Command
One	Munich	ϟ1	Süd
Two	Stuttgart	ϟ2	Südwest
Three	Arolsen	ϟ3	Fulda-Werra
Four	Düsseldorf	ϟ4	West
Five	Braunschweig	ϟ5	Mitte
Six	Hamburg	ϟ6	Nordsee
Seven	Königsberg	ϟ7	Nordost
Eight	Berlin	ϟ8	Spree
Nine	Dresden	ϟ9	Elbe
Ten	Breslau	ϟ10	Südost
Eleven	Nuremberg	ϟ11	Main
Twelve	Stettin	ϟ12	Ostsee

220

Thirteen	Wiesbaden	⚡13	Rhein-Westmark
Fourteen	Vienna	⚡14	Donau
Fifteen	Graz	⚡15	Alpenland
Sixteen	Danzig	⚡16	Weichsel
Seventeen	Posen	⚡17	Warthe
Eighteen	Salzburg	⚡18	Alpenland
Nineteen	Prague	⚡19	Böhmen Mähren

Left: A highly unusual photograph showing what appears to be an Allgemeine-SS signals officer wearing the unit collar patch of the 2nd signals battalion on the field grey wartime uniform of the SS. By 1941, most Allgemeine-SS grey uniforms displayed a generic blank collar patch. It is possible the officer shown was using left over stock from the General-SS, and may have been serving as a signals officer in the Waffen-SS.

(Personal photograph, Author's collection)

ALLGEMEINE-SS PIONEER UNITS

SS Pioneer Battalion	Headquarters	Unit Insignia	Senior District Command
One	Munich		Süd
Two	Stuttgart		Südwest
Three	Arolsen		Fulda-Werra
Four	Cologne		West
Five	Harburg-Wilhelmsburg		Nordsee
Six	Stettin		Ostsee
Seven	Königsberg		Nordost
Eight	Berlin		Spree
Nine	Dresden		Elbe
Ten	Breslau		Südost
Eleven	Nuremberg		Main
Twelve	Magdeburg		Mitte

Thirteen	Frankfurt	⚒13	Rhein-Westmark
Fourteen	Vienna	⚒14	Donau
Fifteen	Salzburg	⚒15	Alpenland
Sixteen	Danzig	⚒16	Weichsel

Members of the SS transport companies were directly attached to the command of an SS Senior District and provided motorcade transport and escort for high ranking SS members. SS officers attached to the transport companies were considered staff members of the SS Senior District, and as such displayed a bare collar patch along with a transport officer sleeve diamond (see right)[xxiv].

Enlisted transport personnel were divided into squads which were in turn issued grey trimmed cuffbands with a squad numeral. In February 1938, the 3rd squad of the 4th transport company in Hamburg received the honor title "BERND ROSE-MEYER"; however, it is unknown if an honor cuffband was ever produced.

Motor transport unit insignia was displayed by enlisted personnel only; for duties involving special motorcycle escort in the capitol of Berlin, motor transport personnel would display the "Ost" collar insignia of SS-Senior District East. This practice was discontinued in 1939 after the SS Senior District in Berlin was renamed "Oberabschnitt Spree".

Above: Cuffbands used by the General-SS motor transport units. Each motor transport company was authorized upwards of ten to fifteen individual squads, including a reserve unit. Individual squads wore white trimmed cuffbands with individual squad numbers. Shown above is the cuffband of the 9th Motor Transport Squad of an SS Motor Company, as well as the generic machine scripted cuffband used by all Motor Squad reserve units.

MOTOR TRANSPORT UNITS OF THE ALLGEMEINE-SS

SS Motor Companies	Headquarters	Unit Insignia	Senior District Command
One	Munich	M1	Süd
Two	Erfurt	M2	Fulda-Werra
Three	Berlin	M3	Spree
Four	Hamburg	M4	Nordsee
Five	Düsseldorf	M5	West
Six	Dresden	M6	Elbe
Seven	Königsberg	M7	Nordost
Eight	Vienna	M8	Donau
Nine	Breslau	M9	Südost
Ten	Stuttgart	M10	Südwest
Eleven	Hannover	M11	Mitte
Twelve	Nuremberg	M12	Main

Thirteen	Stettin	M13	Ostsee
Fourteen	Frankfurt	M14	Rhein-Westmark
Fifteen	Innsbruck	M15	Alpenland
Sixteen	Danzig	M16	Weichsel
Seventeen	Posen	M17	Warthe
Eighteen	Salzburg	M18	Alpenland
Nineteen	Brünn	M19	Böhmen Mähren

SS sleeve diamonds were the primary method of denoting specialty training within the Allgemeine-SS. Sleeve diamond insignia were worn on the lower left sleeve of the SS uniform and centered above any applicable cuffbands. Sleeve diamonds were most often used to denote additional training, or specialization, to which an SS member had received.

The most commonly issued sleeve diamonds were those to denote formal training completed at an SS school; additional diamonds were issued for prior service in other Nazi organizations as well as an entire series of marksmanship badges issued for proficiency in sharpshooting. One of the rarest sleeve diamonds was the "NSDAP Foreign Organization" insignia (Auslands-Organisation der NSDAP). This insignia was worn by SS members who were full German citizens and lived outside the borders of the Greater German Reich in foreign countries.

With the re-introduction of German conscription in the year 1935, the mustering membership of the Allgemeine-SS became subject to the military draft. By 1937, a significant portion of SS men had performed service in the German Army; for which often involved the earning of weapons qualifications while on active duty. Initially, an unofficial practice developed to display Wehrmacht marksmanship lanyards on SS uniforms; however, this practice was ordered discontinued by Himmler in the year 1937, replaced by a new series of SS marksmanship awards.

Originally, a single SS Marksmanship Badge was issued for all weapons proficiency (see right). The decoration was issued in two classes and was worn as a personal decoration on the left breast pocket of the black SS uniform. In 1938, the SS Marksmanship Badge was discontinued, and Himmler ordered a new series of expanded sleeve diamonds to denote SS weapons qualifications. These badges were issued until 1942, when the use of SS marksmanship insignia fell into disuse for unknown reasons.

GENERAL-SS SLEEVE DIAMOND INSIGNIA

Prior Service	Sleeve Diamond	Special Criteria	Sleeve Diamond
Former Sturmabteilung		Race Expert	
Former Hitler Youth		Agriculture Expert	
Former German Police		Recruiting Officer	
Former National Socialist Motor Corps		Member, NSDAP Foreign Organization	

GENERAL-SS MARKSMANSHIP INSIGNIA

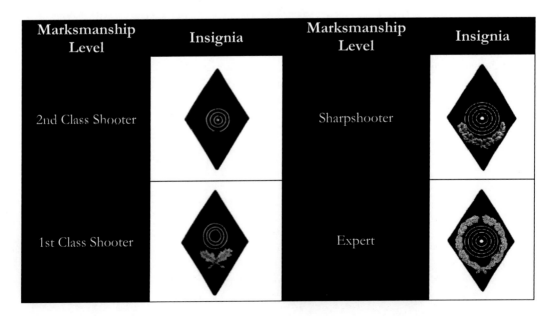

Marksmanship Level	Insignia	Marksmanship Level	Insignia
2nd Class Shooter		Sharpshooter	
1st Class Shooter		Expert	

The Allgemeine-SS also maintained several training schools for its personnel, the staff of which were considered full time salaried SS members while students were assigned temporarily from both active duty and mustering SS formations. SS schools included institutions for cavalry, signals, transportation, and mining training. The SS further maintained an SS medical academy at Graz, Austria as well as an Administration College and Music College at Dachau and Braunschweig respectively. The last two institutions were issued special cuffbands, while music school graduates were further entitled to wear bandsmen shoulder boards (known as "Swallow's Nests") while on parade.

Above- left: SS bandsmen with "Swallow's Nest" shoulder boards (Federal German Archives). Right: The administrative and music school sleeve diamonds and cuffbands. During the Second World War, operation of the administration and music schools was transferred from the Allgemeine to the Waffen-SS.

The SS medical corps

The SS medical service was first created in 1932 with the establishment of an SS Medical Office within the SS headquarters office, the SS-Hauptamt. By 1935, all units of the Allgemeine-SS had been assigned some type of medical staff; Concentration Camp medical personnel were grouped into a separate category with their own insignia system. After 1942, all Concentration Camp medical staff were considered personnel of the Waffen-SS.

By the beginning of the Second World War, the Office of the SS and Police Surgeon General had been established, which was a nominally independent SS formation, yet technically answered directly to Heinrich Himmler as part of his personal staff. The SS medical services also worked closely with the SS Scientific Research Branch (the Ahnenerbe) insofar as human experimentation was concerned.

After Germany's defeat, many SS doctors were implicated in war crimes for medical experiments on Concentration Camp inmates and prisoners of war. The Surgeon General of the SS, Doctor Ernst-Robert Grawitz, is believed to have committed suicide (along with his entire family) in April of 1945. Several other high-ranking SS doctors received either death sentences or lengthy terms in prison following post war prosecutions.

SUBORDINATE OFFICES OF THE SS SURGEON GENERAL

- Personal Physician of the Führer
- Chief Surgeon of the Allgemeine-SS
- Chief Surgeon of the Waffen-SS
- Chief Pharmacist of the SS
- Chief Hygienist of the SS
- President of the German Red Cross

227

ORGANIZATION OF SS MEDICAL COMMANDS
(1940)

Reichsarzt SS und Polizei
SS and Police Surgeon General
SS-Obergruppenführer Prof. Dr. Ernst-Robert Grawitz

Chief SS Medical Quartermaster
SS-Gruppenführer
Dr. Carl Blumenreuter

Chief SS Hygiene Officer
SS-Oberführer
Dr. Prof. Joachim Mrugowsky

Local SS Medical Units

Leitender Artz bei Chef SS-HA
(SS Headquarters Chief Medical Office)

SS and Police Surgeon General Doctor Ernst-Robert Grawitz (left) with Waffen-SS Chief Physican Karl Genzken. Grawitz had risen to prominence within the SS after assisting with the Aktion T4 program, in which the handicap and mentally disabled were systemically exterminated through secret killings. He later authorized human experimentation directives and in the last days of World War II was appointed as Head of the German Red Cross. Seeking to escape from Berlin in April 1945, he was denied permission to leave by Adolf Hitler. On April 24th, Grawitz denotated a hand grenade while sitting down to dinner with his family, killing himself, his wife, and children.

(Photo courtesy of Federal German Archives)

The earliest identifying insignia for SS medical personnel was first issued in 1932 when members attached to the Medical Office of the SS Headquarters were issued a "Sanitation Department" cuffband for wear on the lower left sleeve. In 1934, this cuffband was redesigned to incorporate the logo "SS-HA". By 1935, the SS had also begun issuing a special cuffband for the SS X-Ray Medical Battalion (Röntgensturmbann); this unit was disbanded in 1939 and the cuffband subsequently discontinued.

Early SS medical cuffbands: The original SS medical cuffband (top) was used between 1932 and 1935.
The SS headquarters medical cuffband (center) and the SS X-Ray Battalion insignia (lower)
were issued until the outbreak of the Second World War.

Throughout the 1930s, the SS issued a special collar insignia for all headquarters and special staff medical personnel, as well as a specialty sleeve diamond insignia denoting training in the various medical sciences. A modified medical crest was issued to SS veterinarians, the majority of which were attached to the General-SS Cavalry (Reiter-SS) as veterinary officers.

ALLGEMEINE-SS MEDICAL SLEEVE DIAMONDS

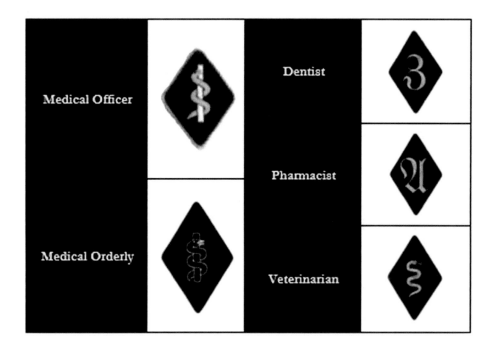

Local SS medical personnel, assigned to the level of the General-SS districts, wore modified medical cuffbands displaying either the senior district name or district numeral. Senior district (Oberabschnitt) medical personnel wore a medical crest collar patch, while district (Abschnitt) personnel further displayed the district numeral. The lowest assigned SS medical units were the Sanitätsstaffel (Medical Squads) of the SS Regiments; in the SS Cavalry Regiments, these formations were similarly known as the SS-Sanitätsreiterstaffel. Members of the SS medical squads were under the operational command of their local units, but administratively accountable to the SS medical headquarters of the SS Main Office. Medical squad personnel wore standard collar patches displaying their regimental numeral, as well as a cuffband indicating assignment to the regiment's medical detachment.

DISTRICT AND LOCAL MEDICAL INSIGNIA OF THE ALLGEMEINE-SS

SS COMMAND	COLLAR INSIGNIA	SLEEVE CUFFBAND
SS Senior District (Oberabschnitt)		
SS District (Abschnitt)		
Local Medical Units	*Local Unit Insignia*	

Note: The examples above are for the SS Senior District (Oberabschnitt) South and District (Abschnitt) Nine.
Other districts displayed appropriate names and numerals according to their own designations

Allgemeine-SS uniforms of the Second World War

Following the example of both the SS-Verfügungstruppe and the Concentration Camp service, in 1938 Himmler ordered that the Allgemeine-SS adopt a grey colored uniform to replace the black jacket design used throughout the 1930s. Prototypes of this new uniform were produced in the fall of 1938, with the first wide scale circulation occurring during the summer of 1939. Upon the outbreak of World War II, Himmler ordered that all full-time members of the Allgemeine-SS, which mainly included the senior district leaders, their staffs, and members of the SS main offices, begin wearing the grey SS jacket. The black jacket was still retained in circulation within the SS mustering formations, but this too was ordered discontinued in 1942.

The Allgemeine-SS wartime uniform used the same insignia as the pre-war black jacket, yet with rank cords on both shoulders and no swastika armband. The grey jacket was intended to be worn with a brown undershirt for SS members assigned to the SS mustering formations, as well as the Sicherheitsdienst (SD), while a white shirt was worn by those SS members involved with state duties. This included Heinrich Himmler, in his capacity as Chief of the German police, as well as most members of the SS main offices and senior commands.

A significant change to the wartime General-SS uniform was the elimination of the complicated and confusing system of regimental unit patches, battalion colored cuffbands, and specialty unit insignia. During the war, the entire Allgemeine-SS adopted a standardized unit insignia of a bare collar patch worn on the right collar, opposite the SS member's badge of rank. This insignia had been used previously by members of Himmler's staff, SS main office personnel, and by staff members of the Allgemeine-SS senior districts. There were isolated cases of pre-war Allgemeine-SS insignia, such as Standarten numerals and certain specialty insignia, appearing on the grey wartime jacket, but these cases were mostly unauthorized and were extremely rare.

Two examples of the wartime Allgemeine-SS uniform. The officer on the left wears the thin shoulder boards of an Allgemeine-SS officer, with the bare collar tab distinctive to the General-SS, as well as a white undershirt denoting full time service on Himmler's personal staff. The group of three Allgemeine-SS personnel on the right wear the closed collar style grey SS tunic, with bare collar patches and thin corded enlisted shoulder boards, as well as the tunic worn open with shirt and tie.
(Photos courtesy Bavarian State Archives and Federal German Archives)

The iconic black SS uniform survived within the mustering formations until 1941, after which time Himmler ordered that the black jacket be completely phased out of the SS. Over the next three years, an effort was made to collect surplus black SS uniforms for re-issuance to other Nazi Party and Germanic paramilitary organizations. Even so, photographic records indicate some mustering SS units continued to wear the black jacket well into 1944. There are also no known photographs of a part time mustering SS unit wearing the grey uniform, with all such photographs restrictive to full time SS members and headquarters office staffs.

Variations to the Allgemeine-SS grey uniform included the "closed collar" style, worn in the same manner as the Waffen-SS, but with General-SS insignia. This style of wear appears to have been confined to SS members who were deployed to duties in countries outside of Germany or for those on the staffs of the SS and Police leaders. The Second World War also brought about a change to General-SS dress uniforms, mainly that the various dress uniforms of the 1930s were phased out of the SS in favor of a standard "full dress" uniform, known unofficially as "Sunday Best", which appeared as an SS jacket worn with an open collar, white shirt and tie, full medals, and a silver SS belt, along with any appropriate SS insignia. For extremely formal occasions, the dress jacket could be worn with an SS sword or dagger.

A comparison between the pre-war and wartime dress uniforms of the SS. The two SS personnel above wear respectively the SS mess dress and walking out uniform, both of which were phased out of circulation after the outbreak of World War II and replaced with the standard full dress grey tunic shown on the left.
(Photos courtesy Bavarian State Archives.
Grey tunic graphical creation)

WARTIME CUFFBANDS OF THE ALLGEMEINE-SS

POSITION	CUFFBAND
Reich Leader of the SS	
Main Office Commanders	
SS District Leaders	
Personal Staff of the Reich Leader of the SS	RFSS
Members of the SS Main Offices	Reichsführung-SS
Members of the SS Head Office	SS-Hauptamt
Members of the SS Economics and Administration Main Office	W.u.V.-Hauptamt
General-SS members on special duty (zur Verfugung)	z.V.

During the Second World War, all of the General-SS regimental, battalion, and company cuffbands were discontinued for use on the new grey uniform; in their place, most members wore a generic bare cuffband. The use of district and senior district cuffbands was also discontinued. Sleeve diamonds of the General-SS remained relatively unchanged, although one addition introduced in 1938 was the Political Leader's sleeve diamond, which was worn by SS members who were also political leaders (Politische Leiter) in the Nazi Party. This sleeve diamond appeared as a Nazi crest with eagle and swastika and was worn on the lower left sleeve (see right).

An extremely rare insignia, worn by some members of the SS Race and Settlement Main Office, pertains to SS field agents who were deployed to the eastern front under assignment to screen the local population for racially suitable children.

Known as the "Umfiedlungskommando" (Special Field Commandos), members wore a golden lettered cuffband and were further authorized a sleeve diamond if qualified as a "Racial Assistance Officer" indicating membership in the German Racial Assistance and Labor Corps.

The SS Race Field Expert cuffband and sleeve insignia

An equally rare cuffband insignia was issued to SS members who had served in the Ehrhardt Naval Brigade, considered one of the original German Free Crops and a predecessor organization to the SA. Prior membership in this organization was recognized by a special "SS" cuffband, as well as a special collar device and badge.

The Ehrhardt Naval Brigade veteran's collar patch, cuffband, and service badge

CHAPTER FIVE: THE WAFFEN-SS

During the Second World War, the Waffen-SS came to be known as one of the most elite fighting forces in history, while the Waffen-SS itself eventually held a manpower strength of nearly one million men from nations all across Europe, including those of Germany's foes. The Waffen-SS would be organized into thirty-eight field divisions, fourteen Army Corps, and two SS Armies. Ferocious on the battlefield, and known for merciless atrocities against its enemies, the officers and men of the Waffen-SS would later claim that they were only soldiers, duty bound to follow orders, and had simply performed their duty on the battlefields of World War II. For years after the close of the Second World War, the dilemma of the Waffen-SS remained as to how classify veterans of this organization, either as soldiers or criminals.

Origins of the Armed-SS

The origins of the Waffen-SS have historically been shrouded in mystery, with many members of the SS itself unaware of exactly how this organization came into being. The first time in which members of the Nazi Party armed themselves was during the Munich Beer Hall Putsch of 1923, albeit with disastrous consequences. Thereafter, in the turbulent 1920s and early 30s, paramilitary political groups were prohibited under German law from stockpiling and openly brandishing weapons. To do so meant confrontations with both the German Army and the police, as well as possible criminal charges ranging from armed assault to the more serious charge of insurrection and treason. Even so, several early storm trooper formations armed themselves with a variety of weapons, leading to clashes with both rival political parties and the German authorities. It was one of these early groups in which the origin of the Armed-SS may be found, this being the guard detachment of the Nazi Party headquarters in Munich.

The earliest known Nazi guard formation was a hand-picked group of Sturmabteilung (SA) troopers who were previously members of the 19th Granatwerfer-Kompanie. These soldiers were organized into a company sized formation and tasked with the protection of Nazi Party leaders in Munich. This group operated from 1923 to 1925, after which time the Nazi Party was disbanded. When Hitler re-formed the Nazi Party in 1925, he tasked protection of senior Nazis to a new group called the Schutzkommondo, which was quickly renamed the Schutzstaffel – the SS. Various local groups of the SS would offer protection to Nazi leaders until the opening of the new Nazi Party headquarters in Munich on January 1st 1931. Hitler then designated that a special group of SS men would serve to guard this facility. Recruited from the 1st SS-Standarten, under the command of Josef "Sepp" Dietrich, the headquarters guard detachment was known as the Stabswache[xxv].

The Stabswache were unpaid SS men who served tours of duty guarding the Nazi headquarters in Munich and were billeted in makeshift barracks located in converted houses and lofts. The open display of weapons was still prohibited by the German authorities, leading to the Stabswache outwardly appearing unarmed while at the same time maintaining caches of hidden weapons for armed conflict should the need arise.

When Hitler became Chancellor of Germany, the SS became a legalized organization, with Sepp Dietrich transferring the Stabswache to Berlin in order to assume duties as the Chancellery Guard. From then on, security at the Munich Nazi headquarters was entrusted again to local SS units; this would remain unchanged until the outbreak of World War II when units of both the German Army and Waffen-SS would station troops in Munich to guarantee the security of top Nazi offices.

The guard formation founded by Sepp Dietrich would undergo a variety of name changes after its move to Berlin, eventually becoming the "Leibstandarte Adolf Hitler" in November 1933. The Leibstandarte would remain relatively independent as an armed SS formation until 1941, when the unit became a full division of the Waffen-SS.

Elsewhere in Germany, the idea of armed SS units seemed appealing, and in the fall of 1933, Hitler ordered Heinrich Himmler to create small units of armed SS personnel who could respond to national emergencies. Himmler began recruiting men from local SS units and forming them into one hundred man "SS-Sonderkommandos" (SS Special Detachments), whose members were initially armed with whatever weapons they personally owned, and loosely organized with an unclear command structure. By the start of 1934, Himmler ordered a more structured approach and the armed units were placed under the direct command of SS Senior District leaders and thereafter lived full time in paramilitary barracks. These units were then renamed the "Kasernierte Hundertschafter" (Barracked Centuries) before assuming their final name as the "Politische Bereitschaften" (Political Readiness Detachments) in the spring of 1934.

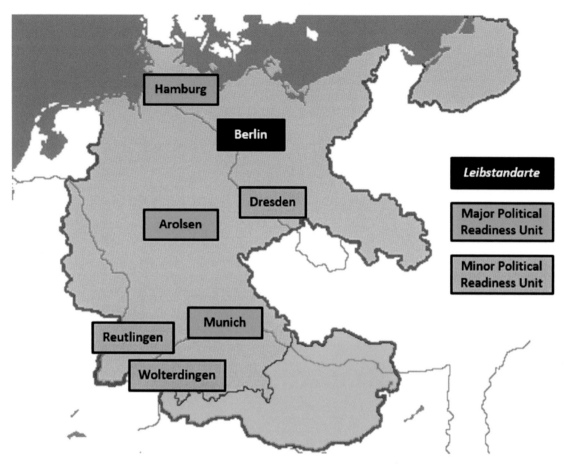

Above: The SS political readiness detachments in July 1934

In June 1934, the Political Readiness Detachments were put to their first operational test when they were deployed to assist with the purge of the SA storm troopers during the Night of the Long Knives. For administrative reasons, the Leibstandarte was at this time also designated as a political readiness detachment, an action which Sepp Dietrich protested. As a measure of defiance, Dietrich ordered his men to remove the swastika armband from their black SS uniforms in the fall of 1934. Dietrich further proclaimed that his SS command was an independent branch of the SS and further forbade any non-Leibstandarte personnel from entering the SS barracks at Berlin-Lichterfelde[xxvi].

Right: Sepp Dietrich in 1934. During this time, Dietrich and the SS troops under his command had removed their swastika armbands to differentiate themselves from members of the General-SS. (Federal German Archives)

In the summer of 1934, based largely on their performance during the Night of the Long Knives, Himmler ordered the Political Readiness Detachments to consolidate into three armed SS regiments, respectively known as the Political Readiness Units Württemberg (PBW), Munich (PBM), and Hamburg (PBH). The Leibstandarte was omitted from this order, although was technically declared as the Political Readiness Detachment stationed in Berlin.

In the fall of 1934, with the SS now a separate and independent organization from the SA, efforts began to create a military arm of the SS using the Political Readiness Detachments as a template. On September 24th 1934, Hitler ordered the Political Readiness Detachments consolidated into an armed SS branch to be known as the "SS-Verfügungstruppe" (SS Dispositional Troops).   In a memo circulated to various government departments and to the German Army, the SS-Verfügungstruppe (SS-VT) was stated to be an armed force under the command of the Reich Leader of the SS, except in times of war when these SS troops would transfer to the command of the Army.   The SS-VT was to exist as three regiments, each containing three battalions.

POLITICAL READINESS UNIT TRANSITIONS TO THE ARMED-SS

Political Readiness Detachment	SS Regiment	Headquarters
Leibstandarte SS Adolf Hitler	SS-Standarte 1 – Leibstandarte	Berlin
PB-Württemberg	SS-Standarte 2/VT	Munich
PB-Munich		
PB-Hamburg	SS-Standarte 3/VT	Hamburg

Attempting to preserve the Leibstandarte as an independent SS formation, Sepp Dietrich appealed directly to Hitler that his troops should not be subordinated to the newly formed SS-VT. In October 1934, Hitler ordered the composition of the SS-VT changed, removed the Leibstandarte from the order of battle, and renamed the remaining SS regiments accordingly. Thus, the second armed SS regiment in Munich now became "SS-Standarte 1/VT" while the Hamburg based troops became designated as the "SS-Standarte 2/VT". By the end of 1934, Himmler had ordered that the armed SS units receive military equipment and transition from status as infantry companies to fully motorized regiments.

ORGANIZATION OF THE LEIBSTANDARTE-SS (NOVEMBER 1934)

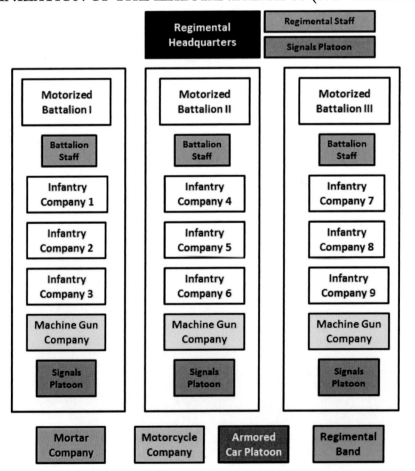

Upon transferring to Berlin, the first company of the Leibstandarte was permanently assigned to ceremonial duties, and as such only performed security duty at the Berlin Chancellery and the Hitler mountaintop residence in the Berghof. In 1938, the Leibstandarte received the addition of an armored car and engineering platoon, and on the eve of the invasion of Poland in 1939 was attached to the German 10th Army based in Silesia. In 1940, the Leibstandarte was upgraded to a brigade and then became a full division of the Waffen-SS in 1941. The basic structure of the Leibstandarte would be used as a guide for other early commands of the SS-Verfügungstruppe.

In these early days of the armed SS, units were haphazardly organized and operated independently from each other, even if assigned to the same SS-VT regiment. In the summer of 1935, the original Political Readiness Detachments had begun the conversion to become battalions of the new SS-VT regiments, although many of these commands lacked both berthing and training facilities. As a solution, many of the early SS-VT battalions were housed in either police barracks or within the SS quarters of Concentration Camps.

Pre-SS/VT command	SS-VT Battalion	Berthing Facility	Training Facility
PB-Munich	I Battalion/ SS-VT Regiment 1	City Police Barracks (Munich, Bavaria)	Königsbrück Training Station (Dresden)
SS Reception Station Schleissheim (HWL)	II Battalion/ SS-VT Regiment 1	Prittlbach, Bavaria	Dachau Concentration Camp
PB-Württemberg	III Battalion/ SS-VT Regiment 1	SS Barracks (Munich-Freimann)	Königsbrück Training Station (Dresden)
	IV Battalion/ SS-VT Regiment 1	Bernhardstrasse 62 (Dresden)	Various Locations

Berthing and training facilities of the 1st Armed SS-Regiment in 1935. This unit would later become the Regiment Deutschland. The "SS-Hilfswerklager (HWL) Schleissheim" was a recruiting center for Austrians who wished to join the SS-Verfügungstruppe.

In the winter of 1935, Himmler ordered the various battalions of the SS-VT to form cohesive regiments, leading to the creation of regimental planning staffs known as the "SS-Arbeitsstab". By 1936, the planning staffs had been converted to regimental headquarters, with SS barracks now existing at Munich, Dachau, and Ellwangen. The 1st SS-Regiment was then enhanced with both a reconnaissance platoon as well as three motor transport columns known as "SS-Kraftfahrkolonnen". On July 1st 1936, the 1st SS Regiment of the SS-Verfügungstruppe was declared fully formed as an infantry unit and re-designated as the "SS-Regiment Deutschland".

The 2nd SS Regiment followed a slightly different development path, beginning in the spring of 1935 when the Hamburg Political Readiness Detachment was designated as the 1st Battalion of the 3rd SS-VT Regiment, later changed to the 2nd SS Regiment following the removal of the Leibstandarte from the SS-VT order of battle. The 2nd Battalion of the 2nd Regiment was recruited mainly from the ranks of the General-SS, in particular SS units stationed in Munich. A third battalion was similarly raised from General-SS personnel in Hamburg.

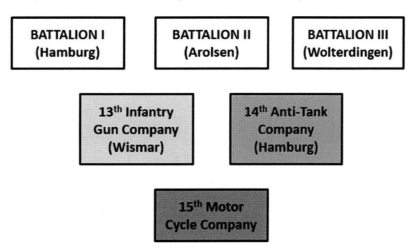

Organization of the 2nd SS-VT Regiment in the fall of 1935

Throughout most of 1935, the 2nd SS Regiment was an unorganized affair, with the battalions acting independently with very little leadership or direction. Even so, the regiment was assigned control of three independent infantry companies and in the summer of 1935 was assigned an armored car platoon. Training facilities for the 2nd SS Regiment were established at the Brunswick Police School and in 1936 a regimental staff was formed. The regiment was officially designated as the "SS-Regiment Germania" in September 1936.

To further promote unity and a higher quality of training amongst SS-VT units, the SS-Hauptamt authorized in 1936 the formation of an SS-VT Inspectorate to oversee all matters relating to the Armed-SS. This new SS Inspectorate was established on October 1st 1936 as the "Inspektion der SS-VT" headed by SS-Brigadeführer Paul Hausser, who had served since 1934 as the Chief of SS-VT Training. Hausser, who was a retired Major General in the German Army, was next appointed as "Inspector of the Armed SS and SS Leadership Schools" by the start of 1937.

Originally, Hausser commanded a relatively small force of two regiments (Germania and Deutschland) as well as the staff and specialty units which the SS-VT had established in 1935. The Leibstandarte was still forbidden territory for Hausser, as Sepp Dietrich would not allow his armed SS formation to fall under SS-VT control. Eventually, Dietrich was persuaded to subordinate himself to the SS-VT, mainly to gain access to SS-VT funding and training. In 1938, the Leibstandarte was consolidated into the SS-Verfügungstruppe, which had by now grown from a few disorganized battalions into a consolidated armed force.

In addition to the regular formations of the SS-Verfügungstruppe, the SS-VT also formed a number of specialty units to augment the armed SS line regiments. By 1940, all of these specialty units had either been disbanded or merged into the regular formations of what would become the Waffen-SS.

The oldest SS-VT specialty unit was the SS-Signals Battalion (SS-Nachrichtensturmbann), which was ordered for creation in December 1934, with a staff formally assembled the following February. By the summer of 1935, the signals unit consisted of a battalion staff, telephone company, wireless company, and a battalion band. The name was thereafter changed to the "SS-Nachrichtenabteilung" (signals detachment) and by 1936 had a permanent garrison headquarters at Berlin-Adlershof. By 1938, the signals unit had transferred to a barracks at Unna, in Westphalia, and had participated in both the annexation of Austria and the takeover of Czechoslovakia. By 1939, the SS-VT signals detachment also included a motor transport company, mechanic platoon, and an equipment fitting shop. Signals training courses were also offered through various communications schools, for which a special sleeve diamond insignia was authorized. By the time of the invasion of Poland in September 1939, the SS signals detachment was a fully motorized battalion attached to an East Prussian Panzer Group. The unit was disbanded the following year.

Another early SS-VT specialty unit was the SS Pioneer Battalion (SS-Pioniersturmbann) which was established in February 1935 with an original cadre of twenty-four SS men based in a barracks at Dresden. By the summer of 1936, the unit had been renamed as the "SS-Pionerbataillon Dresden" and was comprised of three pioneer companies, a battalion band, as well as a medical detachment (SS-Krankenrevier). The battalion further assigned one of its companies to be designated as a motor bridge unit (SS-Brückenkolonne), while internal platoons were designated as either engineering, mechanical, or electrical units. The battalion further maintained one internal signals platoon known as the SS-Nachrichtenzug.

A somewhat odd unit of the SS-VT was known as SS-Sturmbann "N". Founded in September 1936, the unit was at first designated to be a horse drawn infantry battalion with three SS rifle companies (SS-Schützen-Kompanie). Early organizational charts also specify that the unit would possess a band, signals platoon, machine gun company, and motor transport column. In March 1938, just prior to the annexation of Austria, Sturmbann "N" was disbanded but was reformed a few months later in November. At that time, the line companies were reclassified as motorcycle units (Kradschützen-Kompanie) and the battalion gained a light reconnaissance platoon.

The following year, in the summer of 1939, plans were enacted to convert Sturmbann "N" into an anti-tank unit with the battalion gaining a mortar company, anti-tank platoon, and a heavy gun company consisting of two light infantry gun platoons. Just prior to the invasion of Poland, Sturmbann "N" was deployed to a training facility near Dachau. A few weeks later, in July 1939, Sturmbann "N" ceased to exist when its units were reconsolidated into the "Panzerjäger-Abteilung SS-VT", which consisted of three anti-tank companies, a repair detachment (SS-Instandsetzungs-Staffel) as well as a battalion staff, signals platoon, and band. No sooner had the anti-tank battalion been declared operational then the entire unit was disbanded again, with most of the personnel transferred to form a new SS Artillery Regiment. In September 1939, the Panzerjäger-Abteilung SS-VT was again briefly reformed, but finally disbanded two months later in November.

The original armed SS artillery regiment (SS-Artillerie-Standarte/VT) was formed in the summer of 1939 by transferring two thousand SS-VT troops from regular line companies into this first artillery unit of the SS. The regiment was based at Jüterbog, a historic training area for German artillery commands, and by July 1939 had been designated as a motorized artillery regiment with three artillery batteries (SS-Artillerie-Abteilung), as well as an equal number of light artillery columns.

In the fall of 1938, the SS-VT began the process of forming a reconnaissance battalion, beginning with converting the fourth battalion of the Deutschland regiment into a motorcycle unit (SS-Kradschützen Bataillon). A month later, this unit was reconsolidated into two new reconnaissance companies, resulting in the creation of the "Aufklärungsabteilung/SS-VT" which was headquartered at Ellwangen and consisting of two motorcycle companies, an armored car unit, and anti-tank platoon.

During the expansion of the SS-VT in 1938, an all-purpose administrative unit was created, on a strictly temporary basis, in order to control units which were in the process of reforming, reconsolidating, and refitting. Known as the "SS-Regiment z.b.V. Ellwangen", this unit contained two special employment battalions which were based respectively at Dachau and Ellwangen. Upon the outbreak of World War II, the special employment unit was refitted for combat and declared as a motorized dispatch and signals battalion, thereafter known as the "SS-Standarte z.b.V. (mot)". The unit was disbanded in 1940 following the formal creation of the Waffen-SS.

The last SS-VT specialty unit to be created was the "Fliegerabwehr-Maschinengewehr-Abteilung/SS-VT" which was outfitted as an anti-aircraft battalion using cadres from motorcycle battalions in other armed-SS units. The SS anti-aircraft detachment consisted of two anti-aircraft gun companies as well as a battalion staff and band. Upon the outbreak of World War II, the SS anti-aircraft battalion was placed under tactical control of the Deutschland regiment and would later serve as an organizational template for all SS flak units of the Waffen-SS.

Insignia of the SS-Verfügungstruppe

The lightning bolt SS sig runes, which would eventually become the internationally recognizable symbol for the entire SS, were first created in the fall of 1933 when an SS graphic artist, named Walter Heck, drew two Nordic sig runes side by side (see right) and, upon noticing their similarity to the initials of the SS, suggested that this symbol be used as an insignia for the entire organization. The first SS unit to formally adopt the double sig runes insignia was the Leibstandarte-SS on May 5th 1934. On June 1st the same insignia was prescribed for use by the Political Readiness Detachments, but with an Arabic numeral to denote the SS district in which the detachment was located.

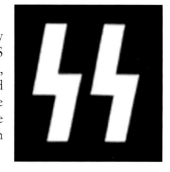

SS UNIT	INSIGNIA	SENIOR COMMAND
Leibstandarte-SS		
Political Regiment One		SS-Oberabschnitt Süd
Political Regiment Two		SS-Oberabschnitt West
Political Regiment Three		SS-Oberabschnitt Mitte

Above: The original insignia of the Armed-SS. The phrase "Political Regiment" was a term used to group the various Political Readiness Detachments together in a geographical area and did not refer to an actual SS command

In December of 1934, armed SS members were issued colored piped cuffbands to denote SS-VT battalion affiliation. Company members further displayed a company number within the cuffband itself. A special cuffband was further reserved for the SS recruiting staff at the Schlessheim Reception Station. During a brief period in the spring of 1935, SS-VT personnel displayed collar insignia of political regiments, paired with battalion cuffbands of the new SS-VT battalions. This practice was discontinued by that fall.

EARLY CUFFBAND INSIGNIA OF THE SS-VERFÜGUNGSTRUPPE

SS-VT UNIT	CUFFBAND PIPING	CUFFBAND EXAMPLE
First Battalion	Green	**2** (Second Company)
Second Battalion	Dark Blue	(Battalion Staff)
Third Battalion	Red	**9** (Ninth Company)
Recruiting & Reception Staff, SS Reception Station Schlessheim		SS-H.W.L. Schleißheim

In the summer of 1935, a larger SS runes insignia was adopted as the collar insignia of the Leibstandarte-SS. At the same time, the SS-VT regiments adopted a new collar insignia which consisted of larger SS runes accompanied by a smaller regimental number. SS officers wore the collar insignia with a solid silver trim while enlisted personnel displayed black and aluminum piping. The following year, after the SS-VT regiments had received official regimental names, individual battalion cuffbands were eliminated and replaced by a regimental cuff title. In late 1936, all SS staff members of the SS-VT Inspectorate were issued a standard cuffband with the script "SS-Inspektion"; prior to this time, the headquarters members had displayed the cuff insignia of the SS Main Office (SS-Hauptamt).

Between 1935 and 1939, the armed SS utilized two primary uniforms: the black SS service jacket and a grey field duty uniform. In 1938, the armed SS began using a modified duty uniform known as the "walking out dress". The walking out uniform consisted of the field grey jacket worn open collar with a tan shirt and black tie. This uniform was typically worn with ribbons, medals, and an SS ceremonial dagger.

Right: A member of the Leibstandarte-SS in the walking out dress uniform. The larger SS runes and cap eagle insignia were used after 1938 (Federal German Archives)

SS-VERFÜGUNGSTRUPPE LINE REGIMENT INSIGNIA (1938)

SS-VT UNIT	REGIMENT CREAST	COLLAR INSIGNIA	CUFFBAND
SS-VT Inspectorate			SS-Inſpektion
Leibstandarte-SS Adolf Hitler			Adolf Hitler
SS-Regiment Deutschland			Deutſchland
SS-Regiment Germania			Germania
SS-Standarte Der Führer			Der Führer

**Above: Insignia series of the armed-SS headquarters and line regiments in 1938.
The regimental crest strap was worn by junior enlisted personnel.**

The Armed-SS also developed specialty unit insignia along the same lines as the regular SS-VT regiments. There is no record of the collar insignia used by the Special Purpose Regiment (SS-Regiment z.b.V. Ellwangen) nor the short-lived SS reconnaissance detachment. Such insignia may have consisted of a bare collar patch or as an SS runes collar patch worn with an unknown specialty crest.

**Right: One of the only known photographs of a SS-VT Inspectorate staff member wearing the bare collar patch as a unit insignia. This same insignia was possibly used by both the SS-VT special purpose regiment as well as the reconnaissance detachment.
(Federal German Archives)**

During the development of armed SS uniform insignia, the SS was also standardizing SS headgear. From 1934 to 1939, different styles of helmets were issued for the Leibstandarte-SS and SS-Verfügungstruppe respectively. The Leibstandarte displayed a helmet with crested SS runes on one side and the German national colors on the reverse. In comparison, the SS-Verfügungstruppe displayed a circular SS runes crest opposite a diamond shaped swastika. In 1940, the SS began to use a standardized helmet crest pattern for all armed units. This new helmet design featured SS runes worn on one side opposite a swastika crest on the other. That same year, with the formal creation of the Waffen-SS, all insignia of the SS-VT was discontinued and consolidated into one SS runes collar patch for all SS combat commands.

SS-VT SPECIALTY UNIT	UNIT TYPE	COLLAR INSIGNIA		SHOULDER CREAST
SS-Artillerie-Abteilung	Artillery Detachment			
SS-Nachrichtenabteilung	Signals Detachment			
SS-Pionerbataillon	Engineering Battalion			
SS-Sturmbann "N"	Battalion "N"			
Panzerjäger-Abteilung SS-VT	Anti-Tank Detachment			
Fliegerabwehr-Maschinengewehr-Abteilung	Anti-Aircraft Detachment	UNKNOWN		

Helmet crest and pattern for the SS-Verfügungstruppe and Leibstandarte-SS. The swastika helmet crest was used by both after 1940

ORGANIZATION OF THE SS-VERFÜGUNGSTRUPPE (1939)

INSPEKTION DER SS-VERFÜGUNGSTRUPPE

LINE REGIMENTS

LEIBSTANDARTE SS "ADOLF HITLER"

SS REGIMENT "DEUTSCHLAND"

SS REGIMENT "GERMANIA"

SS-STANDARTE "DER FÜHRER"

SS-ARTILLERIE-REGIMENT/VT (Artillery Regiment)

SS-REGIMENT z.b.V. "ELLWANGEN"

SPECIALTY BATTALIONS

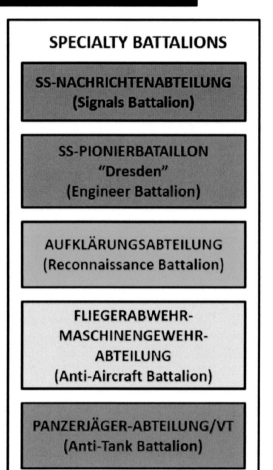

SS-NACHRICHTENABTEILUNG (Signals Battalion)

SS-PIONIERBATAILLON "Dresden" (Engineer Battalion)

AUFKLÄRUNGSABTEILUNG (Reconnaissance Battalion)

FLIEGERABWEHR-MASCHINENGEWEHR-ABTEILUNG (Anti-Aircraft Battalion)

PANZERJÄGER-ABTEILUNG/VT (Anti-Tank Battalion)

INSPEKTION DER SS-JUNKERSCHULEN

SS-JUNKERSCHULE TÖLZ

SS-JUNKERSCHULE BRAUNSCHWEIG

SS-FÜHRERSCHULE DES VERWALTUNGSDIENSTES (SS Administration Leadership School)

SS-ÄRZTLICHE AKADEMIE (Medical Academy)

SS-SANITÄTSABTEILUNG (Medical Corps)

Early SS military actions

The military capability of the Armed-SS was first put to the test in March of 1938 when Adolf Hitler ordered the annexation of Austria into the Greater German Reich. In what became known as the Anschluss, the Germania regiment of the SS-VT was deployed alongside the Leibstandarte to enter Austria and perform initial annexation and occupation duties. While no actual engagements took place, the annexation of Austria was the first true operational deployment of armed SS formations.

Following the Austrian Anschluss. Heinrich Himmler ordered the creation of an Austrian based armed SS unit, and in April 1938 a cadre was assembled to form a new SS-VT regiment. The Austrian armed SS regiment was first organized as "SS-Standarte 3" and was to comprise three battalions stationed at various locations in Austria. The unit would also possess three garrison companies stationed in Vienna[xxvii]. The first armed battalion, under the command of SS-Sturmbannführer Wilhelm Bittrich, recruited Austrian nationals from the previously established "SS-Hilfswerklager Schleissheim" and was based at the Radetzky barracks in Vienna.

The second SS Austrian battalion was based at Tobelbad and recruited from the ranks of the General-SS in Austria. A third and final battalion, based at a military academy in Klagenfurt, recruited from the Austrian general population through SS-VT recruiting centers established in the major cities of Tirol, Vienna, and Salzburg. Smaller recruiting stations were operated at Steiermark, Kürnten, Ober-Österreich, and Burgenland.

In September of 1938, the third armed SS regiment was designated the honor title "Der Führer". In March of 1939, the unit was deployed for the first time to assist in the annexation of the Czech Republic and was thereafter assigned as the garrison occupation force in Prague, where it was known by the cumbersome title "Wach-Regiment des Reichsprotektors von Böhmen und Mähren".

In the final months of peace before the outbreak of World War II, the armed SS briefly experimented with forming its own supply corps known as the SS-Nachschubeinheiten. No formal SS supply commands were ever actually created under this command, and when war began in 1939 the SS-VT supply needs were placed under the command of the German Army. By 1940, all SS logistical matters would be transferred to the control of the Waffen-SS through various offices such as the WVHA and the SS Operations Main Office.

In SS memos dated summer 1938, mention is made of creating a fifth line regiment of the SS-Verfügungstruppe. A cadre was ordered to form a unit known as the "Infanterie-Battalion/SS-VT", with plans to expand this unit into a fully armed regiment by the end of 1939. No record exists of this unit ever having been activated, and by 1940 the idea of a fifth SS-VT regiment had been disregarded. The SS-Verfügungstruppe also had little success in forming an independent cavalry command. In a letter dated October 1934, the armed SS was ordered to create three cavalry battalions based at Soltau, Gardelegen, and Salzwedel. Each battalion was to consist of two mounted companies (Reiterstürme), a bicycle company (Radfahrsturm) as well as a signals unit and a heavy machine gun platoon. Collectively to be known as the "Reiter-Sturmbann Aufklärungs-Abteilung/SS-VT", these armed SS cavalry units found little support amongst SS leadership, in particular due to all equestrian matters jealously controlled by the riding commands of the General-SS. In the end, it would be the Death's Head units of the Concentration Camp service which would form the first armed cavalry commands of the SS. Thereafter, the Waffen-SS would assume control of two main SS cavalry divisions and oversee all further SS cavalry development.

A little known program of the SS-Verfügungstruppe, existing briefly in the 1930s, was the SS Vocational School located at Oberdonau in Austria. Known as the "SS-VT Berufsschule St. Georgen", this trade school offered apprenticeship and trade education to SS members discharged from the SS-VT to occupations in civilian life. Once World War II began, the trade school's importance diminished drastically since all active SS men were expected to serve through the duration of the conflict.

A member of the SS-VT Signals Battalion in the summer of 1939. By this time, the SS-VT had taken its final form which it would remain until the outbreak of war (Federal German Archives)

PRE-WAR MILITARY ACTIONS OF THE SS-VERFÜGUNGSTRUPPE

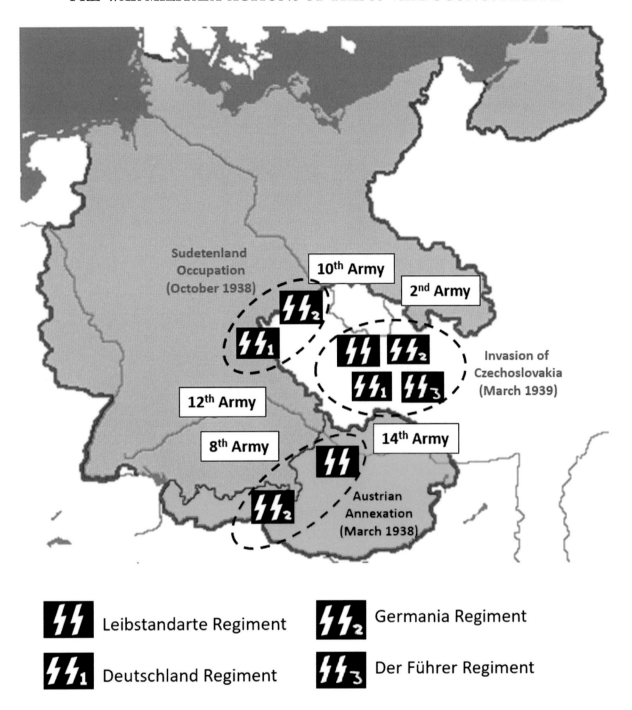

Armed SS operations between 1938 and 1939. SS units attached to military operations in the 1930s were administratively assigned to a corresponding Army command and did not act independently until 1940 when the SS-VT was restructured as the Waffen-SS.

Upon the outbreak of the Second World War in August 1939, the Armed-SS consisted of three regular motorized infantry regiments, several armed SS specialty battalions, and finally the Leibstandarte-SS which still operated relatively independently. The SS forces invading Poland were not grouped as an independent formation, but rather assigned under the tactical control of German Army commands. The Leibstandarte-SS and the SS-Pioneer battalion were attached to the German 10th Army, while the Deutschland regiment, SS reconnaissance battalion, and the SS artillery regiment were attached to the 4th Panzer Brigade. The remainder of SS units in Poland were attached to the 14th Army under the command of General List.

SS MILITARY ACTIONS IN POLAND
(SEP – OCT 1939)

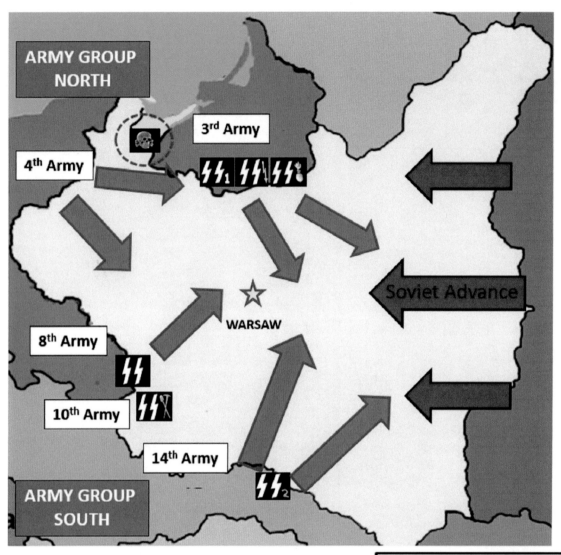

Main Paths of Advance
(1 Sep – 6 Oct 1939)

Reserve Units

Der Führer   *Heimwehr Danzig*

Leibstandarte Regiment

Deutschland Regiment

Germania Regiment

SS Pioneer Battalion

SS Signals Battalion

SS Artillery Regiment

Following the surrender of Poland, German Army commanders complained that the armed SS had operated recklessly, with too much aggression, and had displayed poor training. The German Army was especially concerned of situations where SS units had failed to support Army attacks, resulting in high casualties. Paul Hausser, the Inspector of the SS-VT, was tasked to correct these deficiencies.

In October 1939, with Himmler and Hitler's approval, Hausser separated all armed SS units from Army tactical control and formed the "SS-Verfügungs Division" to which he was named commander. All armed SS units, with the exception of Sepp Dietrich's Leibstandarte and Theodor Eicke's Death's Head formations, were now under a unified command. Hausser next commenced to re-train the armed SS with heavy emphasis on professional military thinking. In order to supply front line regiments with newly trained personnel, the SS further established garrison posts for the armed SS, known as "SS-Standort", which would serve as a base barracks for SS units and also to supply replacement troops due to casualties at the front. The SS garrisons in Germany were organized as military battalions with a special shoulder board crest authorized for the garrison commander (see right).

The older SS unit titles (Standarten, Sturmbann, etc.) were replaced by standard Army terms, such as regiment and battalion, with some SS units even going so far as to abandon the use of SS ranks in preference to Army titles (Lieutenant, Captain, etc.). To this last point, Himmler issued directives that SS personnel would not adopt Army ranks and strictly ordered the continued use of SS titles for armed SS personnel.

By the start of 1940, the armed SS had codified a standard term of service for all of its members, thus preventing the transfer or discharge of SS soldiers during times of war. All members of any armed SS division were obligated to serve in the SS until the end of the war; during peacetime, SS solders were required to complete four years of service, non-commissioned officers twelve, and SS officers a full twenty-five years of service in order to honorably retire.

SS GARRISON COMMANDS (1939)

Barracks	Replacement Unit Title	Composition	Base Regiment
Munich	Infanterie-Panzer-Abwehr-Ersatz-Sturm	Anti-tank replacement company	SS-VT **Anti-tank Battalion**
Berlin	Infanterie-Ersatz-Sturmbann[xxviii]	Infantry replacement battalion with 3 rifle companies & 1 machine gun company	SS-Regiment "Deutschland"
			Leibstandarte-SS "Adolf Hitler"
Hamburg			SS-Regiment "Germania"
	Infanterie-Geschütz-Ersatz-Sturm	Infantry gun replacement company	NONE
Unna	Nachrichten-Sturmbann und Truppen-Nachricten-Züge	Signals replacement company	SS-VT **Signals Battalion**
Dresden	Pionier-Ersatz-Sturm	Engineering replacement company	SS-VT **Engineering Battalion**

Creation of the Waffen-SS

By the summer of 1940, the armed SS had matured into a professional military organization, although the various units continued to act somewhat independently with only marginal joint operational control. By this time, the armed SS also included a division of police personnel, originally known simply as the "Polizei Division", and later to become the 4th Panzer Grenadier Division of the Waffen-SS. The presence of relatively untrained police troops in the same category as the armed SS was disturbing to many, although this was by Himmler's design who saw the merger of the SS and police always as a primary aim.

Paul Hausser – Father of the Waffen-SS

Paul Hausser was born to a military family in Prussia, first becoming a military cadet at the age of twelve and commissioned a lieutenant seven years later in 1899. He served in staff assignments during World War I and was promoted to Colonel in 1927. He was promoted to Major General in 1931 and retired one year later, advanced to the rank of Lieutenant General in 1932. Hausser next became involved in the Stahlhelm, a veteran's group heavily influenced by the Nazi Party. He then joined the Nazi stormtroopers in 1934 and transferred to the SS later that year to form a military arm of the SS which became the SS-Verfügungstruppe. Hausser led the armed SS during its formative years, serving as head of the SS-VT during the Polish invasion of 1939 and later as commander of the SS-Verfügungs Division. In 1940, Hausser's command was upgraded and became the 2nd division of the Waffen-SS. Hausser later served as an SS Corps commander and was one of only two SS officers to ever command an Army. He died in 1972, buried with full military honors.

In May of 1940, Germany struck west and overran the Low Countries of Belgium and the Netherlands, before conquering France. The three primary armed divisions of the SS, with the police division in reserve, were attached to various German armies and performed fiercely in front line combat. As with the Polish campaign, the Army complained with regards to over aggressive SS tactics, especially in the case of the Totenkopf Death's Head units which were accused of committing numerous atrocities.

During the summer and fall of 1940, the German military awaited the anticipated invasion of Great Britain, during which time the Luftwaffe and Royal Air Force battled for control of the skies over England in the Battle of Britain. Meanwhile, the entire SS underwent a vast reorganization in order to accommodate the manpower and logistical requirements of war.

Right: Waffen-SS initial organization

In August 1940, Himmler ordered the creation of the SS Operations Main Office (SS-Führungshauptamt) to which were subordinated two sub-offices in command of the Armed and General-SS respectively. It was at this time that the armed component of the SS was formally renamed as the Waffen-SS.

Kommando Amt der Waffen-SS
(Hans Jüttner)

SS-Division (mot.)
Leibstandarte SS "Adolf Hitler"
(Josef "Sepp" Dietrich)

SS-Infanterie-Division (mot.)
"Reich"
(Paul Hausser)

SS-Division "Totenkopf"
(Theodor Eicke)

Polizei Division
(Karl Pfeffer-Wildenbruch)

SS-Division (mot.)
"Germania"
(Felix Steiner)

SS MILITARY ACTIONS IN FRANCE (MAY – JUNE 1940)

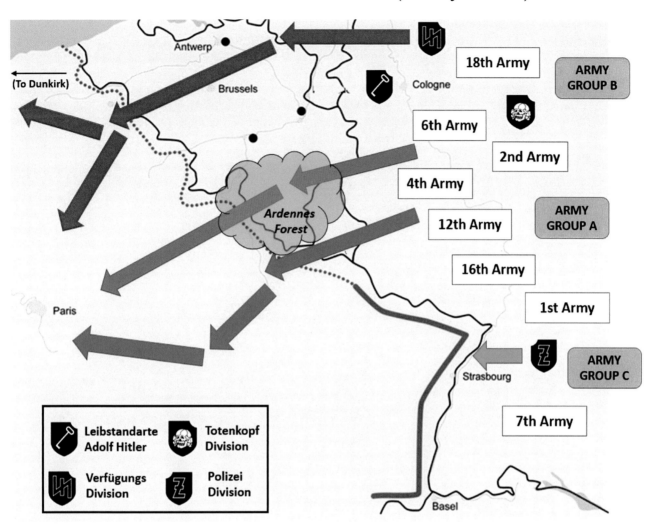

 Invasion of the Netherlands and Belgium by the Leibstandarte and Verfügungs Division, with the Totenkopf Division in reserve. All three divisions later crossed into France and moved to Dunkirk, from which British forces were then evacuated.

 Main thrust by the German Army into Belgium, through the Ardennes Forest, and then followed by the invasion of France. Paris would be overrun and surrendered on June 14th 1940.

 Attack on the Maginot Line (in red) by Army Group C, of which the Polizei Division was attached. After suffering heavy casualties, the Polizei Division was redeployed as a rear-guard formation.

With Paul Hausser now posted as an SS division commander, his previous assignment as Inspector of the SS-VT was renamed as the "Waffen-SS Kommandant" and tasked to Gottlob Berger. After only a few short weeks, Berger was transferred to the SS Main Office and his duties assumed by Hans Jüttner, who was also the head of the SS Operations Main Office. Jüttner set about to expand the Waffen-SS, beginning with the creation of a new pan-Germanic SS division intended to recruit Germanic foreign nationals into the Waffen-SS. Originally known as the "Germania" division, this unit was renamed "Wiking" in 1941.

In the summer of 1941, the Waffen-SS was deployed to fight in the Balkans and Greece, after Germany invaded that region in order to establish a pro-German Yugoslav government and to assist Germany's Italian allies. Only two SS divisions fought in the Balkans, these being the Leibstandarte division under Sepp Dietrich and the Reich division commanded by Paul Hausser. As with previous military operations, SS units were subordinated to Regular Army commands and were deployed as front-line advance shock troops.

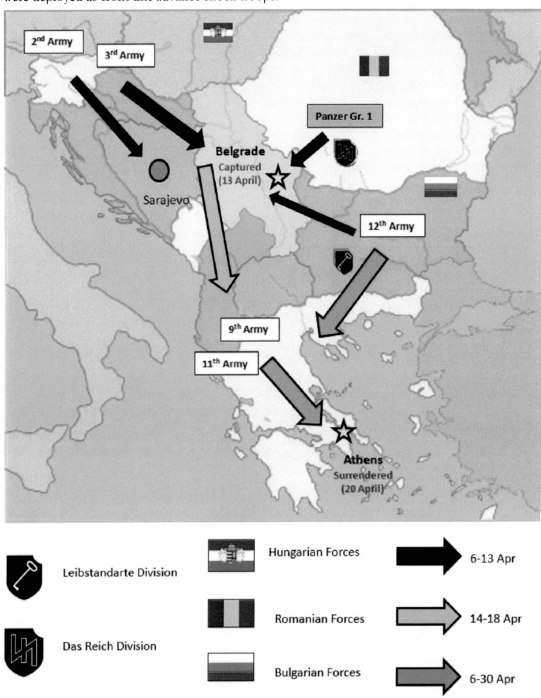

Above: Combat operations and deployment of SS units in the Balkans and Greece in 1941

The Waffen-SS performed tenaciously in the Balkans, with SS troops in the vanguard of several major assaults. In a special point of honor, a small company of SS troops single handedly captured the Yugoslavian capitol without firing a single shot. By the end of April, the German armed forces had also overrun Greece, and that country surrendered on April 30, 1940.

Less than two months later, Adolf Hitler decided to invade Germany's greatest opponent to date – the Soviet Union.

Year	Divisions	Corps	Armies
1940	5		
1941	7		
1942	8		
1943	13	4	
1944	31	11	2
1945	38	14	

Above: Growth of the Waffen-SS

Waffen-SS Foreign Volunteers

In respect to Heinrich Himmler's unquestionable loyalty to Adolf Hitler, there was one area of ideological belief in which these two men significantly differed. In Hitler's vision of Germany's future, all of Europe would eventually become part of a vast Greater German Reich, with individual nations absorbed and assimilated as German provinces. Himmler had quite a different view, especially insofar as Western Europe was concerned. Himmler saw the western nations as inhabited by members of the Aryan race, and therefore these individual countries should be allowed to continue to exist, yet as part of a Confederation of Germanic States in which Germany was the principle nation. In respect to eastern lands, Himmler possessed a more radical approach, one involving exterminating non-Germanic races and setting up German client states which would eventually become part of a vast SS nation.

Himmler's vision of a Pan-Germanic Europe saw its first step within the forces of the Waffen-SS. Once Germany began conquering and occupying nations, Himmler saw local populations as potential recruits into the SS, yet in specially formed foreign volunteer units unique to each nation. In all, over half a million foreign citizens would volunteer for service in the SS; the manner in which foreign units were raised differed greatly depending upon where they were formed and in which nation they were hosted.

Foreign SS units were categorized between those raised in the west, those founded in the east, as well as foreign volunteers from neutral or belligerent countries. The first foreign Waffen-SS unit created was the 5th SS Panzer Division "Wiking", although it was considered a pure SS unit with German SS officers, while the volunteers were from a variety of nations including Denmark, Norway, Sweden, the Netherlands, and Belgium.

The second foreign SS unit established was the 7th SS Mountain Division "Prinz Eugen", created in the fall of 1941 from ethnic Germans from the conquered Balkans. To differentiate foreign volunteers from regular SS personnel, Himmler ordered that the Prinz Eugen division display a unique collar patch, and that all non-German members be addressed with the prefix "Waffen" before their SS rank (for instance Waffen-Unterscharführer, Waffen-Hauptsturmführer, etc.).

The collar tab of the 7th SS Mountain Division "Prinz Eugen". The practice of issuing unique collar tabs to all foreign SS units soon became widespread.

In February 1943, Himmler ordered the creation of a new SS unit which was to be recruited, staffed, and manned entirely by foreign volunteers. Using a cadre from the 5th SS Wiking Division, this unit was originally to be known as "Kampfverband Waräger" but was renamed as the "Germanische-Freiwilligen-Division" (Germanic Volunteer Division) once recruiting began. The new division recruited primarily from Scandinavia but also accepted volunteers from throughout occupied Europe. After expansion into four regiments, the division was declared combat ready and renamed as the 11th SS Volunteer Grenadier Division "Nordland".

Simultaneously with the founding of foreign divisions, Himmler was also seeking to develop "home guard" units within the sphere of the occupied west. The "Landwacht Niederlande", which would eventually become the 34th Volunteer SS Division, was established in 1940 shortly after the surrender of the Netherlands. This home guard system was also used in Denmark, which founded the "Freikorps Denmark" in 1941. In other conquered countries, the SS created a number of foreign legions, which were equipped as small Army Corps, usually with two brigades or divisions. The two largest SS legions were formed in Latvia and Estonia.

FOREIGN SS UNIT NOMENCLATURE

SS Unit Type	Home Guard	Foreign Legion	Waffen-SS Unit
Volunteer Regiment	Landwacht	SS-Standarte	SS-Freiwilligen-Regiment
Volunteer Brigade	Landstorm	SS-Sturmbrigade	SS-Freiwilligen-Brigade
Volunteer Division	Freikorps	SS-Legion	SS-Freiwilligen-Division

Above: A member of the 11th SS Division "Nordland", which was the first SS division to be comprised entirely of foreign volunteers. Below are shown members of the Estonian and Latvian Legions in 1943. The distinctive swastika collar insignia was worn by the 19th Waffen-Grenadier Division. (Images courtesy Federal German Archives and Polish State Archives)

252

INDEX OF FOREIGN SS VOLUNTEERS

Nation	Number	Primary SS unit
Albania	9,000	7th, 13th, and 21st SS Divisions
Armenia	4,000	Caucasus SS Volunteers
Azerbaijan	70,000	Azeri SS Legion
Belgium	22,000	5th, 23rd, 27th, and 28th SS Divisions
Bulgaria	700	Waffen-Grenadier Regiment der SS (Bulgarisches Nr. 1)
Canada	8	33rd SS Division, British Free Corps
Croatia	20,000	7th, 13th, 23rd, and 24th SS Divisions
Czechoslovakia	Czech citizens from the Bohemian Protectorate were enlisted into the SS as German nationals. No numbers were recorded for Slovakians joining the SS.	
Denmark	12,000	Danish Free Corps, 5th & 11th SS Divisions
Estonia	20,000	Estonia Legion, 3rd Volunteer SS Brigade, 20th SS Division (1st Estonia)
Finland	2,500	5th and 11th SS Divisions, Kurt Eggers war correspondence regiment
France	22,000	11th, 17th, 18th, 28th, and 33rd SS Divisions
Georgia	7,000	SS-Waffengruppe Georgien
Hungary	40,000	7th, 11th, 25th, 26th, 31st, 33rd, and 37th SS Divisions
India	2,500	Indian SS Volunteers "Tiger Legion"
Indonesia	1	34th SS Division
Ireland	30	SS Irish Brigade (Never activated)
Italy	18,000	24th, 29th, 31st SS Divisions
Japan	2	33rd SS Division
Latvia	55,000	Latvian Legion, 15th & 19th SS Divisions
Luxembourg	3,000	Unorganized SS Volunteers
Netherlands	55,000	11th, 14th, 23rd, and 34th SS Divisions
New Zealand	1	One New Zealander served as an SS war correspondent
North Caucasus	1,500	SS-Waffengruppe Nordkaukasus
Norway	12,500	Norwegian Legion, 5th, 6th, & 11th SS Divisions; A small number served as war correspondents
Romania	55,000	7th, 8th, 11th, and 17th SS Divisions; 1st and 2nd Volunteer Romania SS Regiments
Russia	25,000	29th, 30th, & 36th SS Divisions
Russian (Cossacks)	23,000	SS-Cossack Cavalry Corps
Russian (Turks)	1,200	Osttürkische Waffen-Verbände der SS; Tatarische-SS; 36th SS Division
Serbia	10,000	7th and 24th SS Divisions
Slovenia	6,000	24th SS Division
Spain	3,000	Blue Legion; 11th, 24th, and 28th SS Divisions; Spanish Volunteer Companies 101 & 102
Switzerland	800	5th, 11th, and 33rd SS Divisions[xxix]
Ukraine	20,000	14th, 24th, 30th, & 36th SS Divisions
United Kingdom	1,500	British Free Corps; 1st, 3rd, and 11th SS Divisions
United States	20	Unorganized SS Volunteers

The Estonian Legion, founded in October 1942, was renamed one year later as the Estonian SS Volunteer Brigade; this unit in turn would expand to a full SS division by 1944. The much larger Latvian Legion was created in 1943, and would exist until 1945 as an administrative command for the 15th and 19th Waffen Grenadier Divisions of the SS. Most veterans of the Latvian Legion, seen even today as heroes against Communism, are still respected in their own country.

All members of the SS Legions were considered foreign volunteers, and thus not entitled to wear the SS runes of the regular Waffen-SS. In addition to specific national insignia, all foreign legion members also prefixed their rank with the term "Legion" (i.e. Legion-Oberscharführer, Legion-Hauptsturmführer, etc.) to differentiate from regular SS soldiers. SS Legions were primarily deployed to the Eastern Front, with both the Estonian and Latvian Legions active in this theater, alongside an SS legion formed in Norway. By 1944, to make up for manpower losses, the Eastern Front legions began to conscript soldiers rather than depend solely on volunteers.

It is perhaps ironic that the greatest number of SS foreign volunteers originated from within Germany's ideological enemy the Soviet Union. As the German Army advanced into the plains and steppes of Russia, local populations welcomed the Nazi forces as liberators and quickly began to form pro-German paramilitary forces. By 1942, both the German Army and the SS were organizing irregular troops, and thereafter deployed these units into combat against the Red Army.

The largest group of Russian collaborationist forces were formed into the Belarusian Home Defense Force (BKA). At twenty thousand strong, this unit was not technically part of the SS, but did receive training and logistical support from SS commands. The first true SS-Russian unit was the "Volunteer Battalion Kaminski" which was formed from a mixture of Russian collaborators and prisoners-of-war who had defected to the German Army. Founded in August 1944, and commonly known as the "Kaminski Brigade" after its commander, the unit was renamed as the "Sturmbrigade RONA" and participated mainly in anti-partisan operations. By 1945, the unit had been declared as the 29th division of the Waffen-SS; a 30th SS division of Belo-Russian volunteers was created shortly afterwards.

As the German military advanced deeper into the Soviet Union, traditionally oppressed ethnic groups began to volunteer to serve in both the German Army and the Waffen-SS. One such group were the Cossacks, who had held immense hatred for the Soviets for years and would eventually form an entire SS Corps of Cossack units. Upon the German Army reaching its farthest advance in the Caucasus, the SS sought to recruit Russo-Turkic and Mongolian minorities for service in the war against the Soviet Union. Simultaneously, the SS began to form combat commands comprised of local Muslim volunteers who were both anti-Communist and anti-Semitic. Previous efforts to recruit Muslims into the SS had met with significant success in the Balkans and Yugoslavia, with the first attempt at recruiting Muslims occurring during 1943 in Croatia. The result was the formation of the 13th SS Volunteer Mountain Division, more commonly known as the Handschar Division. The Handschar Division was authorized a unique collar patch depicting an Arabic scimitar, as well as a special type of SS headgear in the traditional Muslim fashion, known as the SS-Fez.

The Handschar Division initially fought bravely and with distinction; however, by 1944 the unit began to experience mutiny and desertion by Muslim soldiers who knew full well that the Germans were losing the war. Two later Muslim SS divisions (the 21st and 23rd Volunteer Divisions) were formed in 1944 and experienced a similar history of disorganization and sedition. Both units had been disbanded by 1945, but only after becoming notorious for war crimes and atrocities.

The raising of Muslim SS units in the Soviet Union began in November 1943 when Himmler ordered the creation of an SS unit comprised of Muslim prisoners-of-war as well as general volunteers from the Russian Caucasus and the Russian-Turkish border regions. In January 1944, the "Ostmuselmanisches SS-Regiment" was formally created, utilizing soldiers and staff from a former German Army Muslim unit known as the 450th Turkestanisches Battalion. This new SS unit was considered an irregular military formation and was transferred to Poland for security and anti-partisan duties. By the spring of 1944, the SS Muslim regiment consisted of three thousand members divided amongst five infantry companies.

A SS Cossack commander in 1944. The traditional Cossack headdress, known as a Papakha, is worn as standard headgear (Polish State Archives)

In October 1944, after service in both Poland and the Ukraine, the Ostmuselmanisches SS-Regiment was transferred to Slovakia in order to form a completely new type of SS unit known as a "Waffen-Verband". Using the original SS regiment as a cadre, the SS merged several Russian volunteer formations together into two volunteer legions (the Tartar and Volga Legions), originally under the administration of the German Army. These units consisted of various ethnic groups from southern Russia and were collectively referred to as the "SS Caucasus Volunteers". By 1944, these units had been designated as the "Osttürkische Waffen-Verbände der SS". A distinctive wolf head's collar insignia and honor cuffband were issued to all personnel.

Right: Muslim SS soldiers of the 13th Volunteer Mountain Division "Handschar", a unit which would be used as a template for all other SS Muslim formations. The Muslim SS-Fez is worn as headgear, as well as the distinctive scimitar collar patch. (Polish State Archives)

The SS Caucasus Combat Formation was formed in December 1944 under the command of former Russian Army officer and Azerbaijani Muslim Waffen-Standartenführer Magomed Israfilbey. The Caucasus SS units were transferred to northern Italy in January 1945 where they surrendered a few weeks later to British forces. Another Caucasus SS unit was the East Turkish Waffen-SS formation, commanded by Austrian Muslim Wilhelm Hintersatz, who was also known by his Muslim title "Waffen-Standartenführer Harun-el-Raschid-Bey".

CAUCASUS SS VOLUNTEER FORMATIONS

**OSTTÜRKISCHE WAFFEN-VERBÄNDE DER SS
(East Turkish Combat Formations of the SS)**

WAFFENGRUPPE TURKESTAN	WAFFENGRUPPE KRIM	WAFFENGRUPPE IDEL-URAL

**KAUKASISCHER WAFFEN-VERBAND DER SS
(Caucasus Combat Formation of the SS)**

WAFFENGRUPPE ARMENIEN	WAFFENGRUPPE NORDKAUKASUS	WAFFENGRUPPE GEORGIEN

WAFFENGRUPPE ASERBEIDSCHAN

At peak strength, the SS Caucasus formation contained 8,500 soldiers, with each Waffengruppe consisting of a battalion staff with five infantry companies. In January 1945, the "Waffengruppe Aserbeidschan" was renamed as "Waffengruppe Krim", with the former title assigned to a new Waffengruppe in the Caucasus. In March 1945, the last SS Caucasus formations were deployed to Italy, but refused to participate in anti-partisan operations. Instead, these units disarmed themselves and surrendered to American forces of the 1st Armored Division in April 1945.

Right: Wilhelm Hintersatz, commander of the East Turkish SS volunteers, during which time he was known as "Waffen-Standartenführer Harun-el-Raschid-Bey".
(Federal German Archives)

The Waffen-Verband concept was also attempted in the west, but with very limited success. The only significant unit ever raised in France was known as the "Bretonische Waffenverband der Waffen-SS". Consisting of eighty members, and known in French as the "Bezen Perrot", this unit was led by French collaborator Célestin Lainé and was involved primarily in security functions as well as anti-partisan operations against the French resistance. In 1943, Lainé and his unit were declared as an SS combat formation and deployed in 1944 against the Allies.

Later war foreign SS recruitment focused more on the creation of fully equipped SS foreign volunteer divisions. The 33rd and 34th SS divisions were intended to be Pan-Germanic, forming in the west but accepting volunteers from all over Europe. Six divisions of the Waffen-SS were formed entirely from foreign volunteers in the west, mainly from France, Denmark, the Netherlands, and Belgium. Such combat units normally began as SS Legions and were then converted to regular divisions of the Waffen-SS.

Left: An Indonesian volunteer serving in the 34th SS Division, which fought mainly in Holland. According to SS records, the man seen in this photo was the only Indonesian to ever serve in the SS (Federal German Archives)

As well as accepting recruits from conquered countries, Germany's allies in the war were seen as ideal recruitment grounds for service in the SS. Motivated by both fear and hatred of Communism, the countries of Hungary, Romania, and Bulgaria all contributed citizens to serve in the SS.

The nation of Hungary was by far the greatest source of foreign recruits to the SS, with a total of five Waffen-SS divisionsˣˣˣ raised entirely from Hungarian volunteers. Romania and Bulgaria contributed to a lesser degree in the form of "Waffen Regiments", all of which were deployed along the Eastern Front. The Hungarian SS membership also held two of the highest ranking members of the SS foreign volunteers: Waffen-Obergruppenführer der SS Ferenc Feketehalmy-Czeydner and Jenő Ruszkay-Ranzenberger. Both were high ranking Hungarian military officers who were granted SS commissions and further served as SS corps commanders.

BULGARIAN AND ROMANIAN SS UNITS

SS UNIT	DATE FORMED
Waffen Grenadier Regiment of the SS (1st Bulgarian)	September 1944
Waffen Grenadier Regiment of the SS (1st Romanian)	November 1944
Waffen Grenadier Regiment of the SS (2nd Romanian)	January 1945

WAFFEN-SS VOLUNTEER FORMATION INSIGNIA

SS VOLUNTEER FORMATION	FORMED	COLLAR INSIGNIA	CUFFBAND	SLEEVE INSIGNIA
Russo-Turkic SS Volunteers	1944			
SS-Cossack Division				
Ukrainian SS Volunteers				
Caucasus SS Volunteers				
Fascist Italian SS Volunteers				

Estonian SS Legion	1942			
Norwegian SS Legion			Frw. Legion Norwegen	
Finnish SS Volunteers	1941		Finnisches Frw. Bataillon der Waffen SS	
Latvian SS Volunteers				LATVIJA
Danish Free Corps			Freikorps Danmark	
British Free Corps	1944		British Free Corps	
French SS Volunteersxxxi				FRANCE
Italian Army SS Conscripts	1945		Italien	

One of the most unique foreign SS volunteer units was the Indian Legion, which had originally been sponsored by the German Army as the "Indisches Freiwilligen Infanterie Regiment 950". Comprised of Indian prisoners-of-war, and informally known as the "Tiger Legion", the SS took control of the unit in 1944 as part of a general agreement with the Army to transfer all foreign military volunteers to the control of the Waffen-SS. SS insignia was designed but never issued, with most members of the Indian Legion continuing to wear German Army uniforms.

Right: An Indian volunteer wearing a German Army uniform (Imperial War Museum). An SS collar patch was designed for Indian volunteers (far right) but was apparently never issued.

The majority of the Indian Legion was deployed to Europe from 1943 to 1945, originally performing garrison and security duties in Belgium and the Netherlands. Upon the Allied invasion of France, the Indian Legion was deployed to rear areas to serve as a reserve to German forces. Not trusted with front line combat, the Indian Legion was withdrawn from the Western Front in 1944 and transferred to garrison duties in northern Italy. In May of 1945, the Indian Legion retreated towards Switzerland. The unit was captured by British and American forces prior to reaching the Swiss border.

After the war, members of the Indian Legion were extradited to India where the British had planned a series of trials on charges of treason. Few Indians ever saw the inside of a courtroom, since India was demanding independence by this point, and the subject of Indian citizens fighting for the Axis powers was a subject that the British did not wish to publicize. By 1948, charges had been dismissed against all but a handful of Indian SS members; these remaining persons were then sentenced to prison and had all been released by 1950.

In Bulgaria and Romania, SS units were formed primarily from German collaborators and fascists who supported continuing the war against the Soviet Union after their respective countries had either capitulated or surrendered. Very few specific SS insignia or cuffbands were designed for those units, and many of the SS members simply wore uniforms of their own national military. A Romanian SS collar tab has been reported by some sources (see right), but it is unknown how widespread was its issuance.

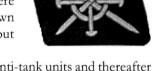

In February 1945, the 1st Bulgarian and 2nd Romanian SS Regiment were reequipped as anti-tank units and thereafter known respectively as "SS Panzer Zerstörer Regiment (Bulgarisches Nr. 1) und (Rumänisches Nr. 2)". Both units were annihilated upon deployment to Hungary in the face of the advancing Red Army.

One of the rarest insignias of the SS foreign volunteer units was the cuffband used by the "Volunteer Legion Netherlands", also known as the SS Dutch Legion. The Dutch Legion was first formed in 1941 and would see service on both the Eastern Front and in Yugoslavia. During this period, the unit wore a unique cuffband, which was replaced in 1943 when the unit became a Panzer Grenadier Brigade; the unit was then reformed as the 23rd Volunteer SS Panzergrenadier Division in February 1945.

**The original cuffband of the Dutch Legion, prior to its reforming as an SS brigade in 1943.
Very few examples of the original Netherlands Legion cuffband survived the Second World War**

Italy was at first slow to contribute volunteers to the SS, and it was not until the founding of the Italian Social Republic (a puppet state under German control) that significant Italians began to join the SS. The first Italian SS soldiers were recruited from the Italian Army and were known respectively as Fascist Conscripts and Volunteers. Distinctive collar insignia was authorized, as well as a special German national eagle which clutched the fascist staff rather than a swastika.

By the fall of 1944, the Italian SS had been formed as a full division of the Waffen-SS and was deployed against American and British forces in southern Italy. To reward the Italian SS for bravery and courage, Heinrich Himmler merged all Italian SS units into an "Italian SS Corps" and authorized Italian SS personnel the wear of standard SS runes worn on a red background. In all, over eighteen thousand Italians would serve in the Waffen-SS, with several hundred more attached to the security and police formations.

Perhaps the most sensational foreign SS units were those formed from citizens of nations at war with Germany. While recruits from the Soviet Union dominated the foreign SS in the east, the western front saw SS troops recruited from the British Isles, America, Canada, as well as several other neutral countries. The most widely publicized SS unit from an enemy country was the British Free Corps, formed from citizens of the United Kingdom.

An Italian SS officer wearing the unique tri-foil collar insignia of the Italian Fascist SS (Federal German Archives)

Originally known as the "Legion of St. George", the British Free Corps was formed in 1944 from disenfranchised British prisoners-of-war who wished to defect to the Nazi cause. Fifty-nine British citizens would eventually comprise the British Free Corps, although nearly 1,500 more Britons would join other units of the Waffen-SS. The British Free Corps was never intended to serve in combat and was primarily assigned to propaganda duties. All of the British members were granted enlisted Waffen-SS rank, although none were ever appointed as SS officers. Instead, the Germans appointed a "Liaison Officer" (Verbindungsoffizier) who oversaw general administration, order, and discipline. Three such SS officers held this position from 1944 to 1945.

Left: A member of the British Free Corps in 1944 (Federal German Archives)

In March of 1945, the members of the British Free Corps were ordered to combat status and integrated into the 11th SS Division "Nordland". Most of the British were attached to the division's armored reconnaissance battalion and deployed to eastern German to attack the advancing Soviets. After one significant engagement against the Red Army at the town of Schoenburg, the 11th SS division was redeployed to Berlin where the British Free Corps was attached to the headquarters of SS-General Felix Steiner. Steiner then began a retreat westward and assigned the British to a motorized transport column.

The British Free Corps was dissolved on May 2nd 1945 when the last of its membership surrendered to the American Army.

Another country in which the SS sought to raise a foreign legion was Ireland. Due to anti-British sentiment amongst many Irish soldiers in the British Army, the Germans began sweeping prisoner of war camps in 1942 with the intent being to create an Irish SS Legion. The Germans later claimed that some 400 Irishmen enlisted in the German Army and Waffen-SS, but an actuality an Irish SS Legion was never formed. Instead, in 1943 the German Army created a special Irish Section of German Military Intelligence, with approximately thirty members. This group was intended to be trained as spies and saboteurs, but only five Irishmen were ever fully certified as intelligence operatives and none were ever returned to Great Britain to participate in clandestine operations. The Irish Section was rather used primarily for propaganda purposes and to recruit other Irish prisoners-of-war into the Germany military. When the SS took over all aspects of military intelligence in 1944, the Irish Section was transferred to SS control, but no official SS designation was given to the group nor were any unique Irish SS uniforms or insignia ever designed.

An American SS Legion was also proposed but never formed. Only twenty Americans served in the Waffen-SS, and all were assigned across a number of previously established SS commands. One of the more well-known cases of an American SS member was that of Martin James Monti, a Second Lieutenant in the U.S. Army Air Forces who stole a plane in Italy and defected to Nazi Germany. Monti was assigned to the SS War Correspondence Regiment and commissioned as an SS-Untersturmführer.

Right: American SS officer Martin James Monti (National Archives)

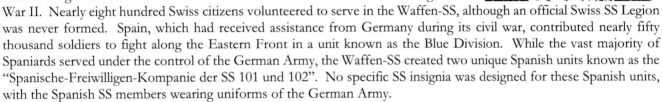

Monti surrendered to Allied authorities after the war, but escaped prosecution and returned to the Army as an enlisted Sergeant. He was rearrested in the 1950s, after the extent of his SS activities became known to the Federal Bureau of Investigation. The FBI had discovered that Monti had used the alias Martin Wiethaupt, during his time in the SS, and he was arrested for treason. Monti was convicted and handed a twenty-five year prison sentence; however, he was paroled in 1960 and died in 2000.

In addition to foreign volunteers from conquered and enemy countries, the SS further sought to recruit SS soldiers from nations which were neutral during World War II. Nearly eight hundred Swiss citizens volunteered to serve in the Waffen-SS, although an official Swiss SS Legion was never formed. Spain, which had received assistance from Germany during its civil war, contributed nearly fifty thousand soldiers to fight along the Eastern Front in a unit known as the Blue Division. While the vast majority of Spaniards served under the control of the German Army, the Waffen-SS created two unique Spanish units known as the "Spanische-Freiwilligen-Kompanie der SS 101 und 102". No specific SS insignia was designed for these Spanish units, with the Spanish SS members wearing uniforms of the German Army.

Following the close of the Second World War, most foreign volunteers of the SS were branded as traitors by their home countries and many were arrested, imprisoned, and executed. In nations which had suffered the harshest under Nazi occupation, vigilante and other citizen groups hunted down former SS volunteers, oftentimes murdering them without a trial. A notable exception was Finland, which had fought as a "co-belligerent" (but not as an ally) of Nazi Germany against the Soviet Union. After the Finnish Army was defeated in the Winter War of 1940, the Germans created the "Finnish Volunteer Battalion of the Waffen-SS", one of whose members was Finnish Army Lieutenant Lauri Törni. Törni attended advanced training in Vienna and was deployed to combat in the last days of the war. After surrendering to the British, and returning to Finland, Törni immigrated to the United States where he became a citizen and changed his name to Larry Thorne. He then joined the United States Army and became a Captain in the Special Forces, training Army personnel in sabotage, counter-insurgency, and alpine combat tactics. In the 1960s, he deployed to Vietnam and was killed in a helicopter accident during a clandestine mission in 1965. Posthumously promoted to the rank of Major, Thorne's remains were located in 1999 and he was interned at Arlington National Cemetery with full military honors.

Lauri Törni, who served as a Lieutenant in the Finnish Army, a Hauptsturmführer in the Waffen-SS and later (under the name Larry Thorne) as a Captain in the United States Army (National Archives)

261

Training programs of the Waffen-SS

By the summer of 1941, the Waffen-SS had completed its transformation from a relatively unorganized and undertrained paramilitary Nazi Party organization into a well hardened and respected military branch of the German armed forces. The Waffen-SS now practically mirrored the Army in both organization and titles, except for SS ranks which were used in lieu of standard military grades. The special rank of SS-Stabsscharführer, which the SS had established in the 1930s, was a positional title for the head SS sergeant of a company or regiment. The rank insignia for this position was significantly modified in 1941 to replace an older sleeve chevron with a new "double piston" cuffband used by First Sergeants in the regular German military. Inherited from the German Army were also a variety of sleeve insignia and other badges to denote specialty training in weapons, alpine warfare, and other military operational areas. The Army Driver's Badge was fully adopted as an SS specialty insignia in 1940 as was the SS-Coxswain Badge, introduced in 1941 and denoting those Waffen-SS soldiers trained in small boat tactics, including river pontoons.

Left: An SS-Hauptscharführer wears the sleeve cuffband insignia of an SS First Sergeant (shown above). The SS-Coxswain Badge, for qualified SS boat crew members is also shown. (Image courtesy Federal German Archives. Insignia graphical recreations)

One of the major shifts between the Waffen-SS and the former SS-Verfügungstruppe was the manner in which SS units were garrisoned and the method by which recruits were enlisted and trained. The SS-VT had originally recruited personnel at the regimental level, who were then trained by active duty cadre members of the same unit. Replacements were then pooled into "Ersatz" battalions located in major German cities. By 1940, with all of the SS divisions contributing to front line combat operations, the ability to recruit and train SS personnel was tasked to a newly formed system of SS depots. Known as the "SS-Truppenübungsplatz", these units were regimental sized formations which also served as garrison posts for SS commands and as stations for replacement troops. The basic training of new recruits was handled by a sub-command of the SS depot which was known as the "Rekruten-Depot der Waffen SS". This basic training unit had its own commanding officer with approximately three recruit companies for newly sworn SS personnel. The SS depots were commanded by an officer ranked either Standartenführer or Oberführer who maintained both a headquarters staff and signals battalion. Most SS depots further contained a medical detachment and well as a permanent garrison unit known as the Wach-Kompanie. Other SS units assigned to the depot were considered replacement troops for commands deployed in the field. The original garrison posts of the SS-Verfügungstruppe were still maintained during World War II[xxxii], while most of the wartime Waffen-SS divisions maintained a headquarters in the home city from which the division was formed[xxxiii].

SS MILITARY DEPOTS (1940 – 1945)

SS DEPOT	GARRISON HEADQUARTERS	ACTIVE YEARS
SS-Truppenübungsplatz Beneschau	Benešov, Czech Republic	1938-1940
SS-Truppenübungsplatz Böhmen		1940-1945
SS-Truppenübungsplatz Debica	Dębica, Poland	1940-1943
SS-Truppenübungsplatz Heidelager		1943-1944
SS-Truppenübungsplatz Kurmark	Brandenburg, Germany	1940-1944
SS-Truppenübungsplatz Moorlager	White Russia	1943-1944
SS-Truppenübungsplatz Ostpolen	Krakow, Poland	1939-1940
SS-Truppenübungsplatz Seelager	Denmark	1941-1944

Building upon lessons learned in Poland and France, the training regimen of the Waffen-SS developed into one of the most effective ever developed in modern military history. The Waffen-SS was forged as a fighting force considered the elite of the German armed forces, with SS men seen as highly effective soldiers, both individually and as a combined whole. SS units frequently served as the vanguard for major German operations and were seen as highly valuable assets by military commanders.

The origins of Waffen-SS training may be traced to the ideas and theories of Paul Hausser, considered to be the SS officer who founded the armed SS and developed the SS-Verfügungstruppe into an elite force which would become the basis for the Waffen-SS. Hausser was himself a retired Major General from the German Army and stressed individual training and military awareness rather than group drill and repetitive exercises.

The earliest training of armed SS units took place in 1934, when Heinrich Himmler established a liaison program where officers of the Political Readiness Detachments could observe tactics of the German Army. Himmler also proposed that the German Army provide personnel to SS units for an exchange of ideas, but this liaison program met with limited success and there are no records of the Army accepting Himmler's invitation to assign Army personnel to SS commands. A small number of SS personnel were assigned to Army training commands, but still too little to serve as an overall benefit to the training program of the armed SS.

In November 1934, with permission from the German Defense Ministry, the armed units of the SS-Verfügungstruppe were recognized as a military force and the SS empowered to train its own personnel with state funding. Paul Hausser was then appointed as head of the Inspectorate of SS Leadership Schools (Inspektion der SS-Führer-Schulen) and proceeded to develop a standardized SS training program. Enlisted personnel of the SS would be trained by their own regiments, through strict guidelines outlined by Hausser, while the SS was also authorized the formation of two officer candidate schools, the first of which was opened at Bad Tölz, Bavaria followed by a second school at Braunschweig.

The first SS leadership course for armed units commenced on April 1st 1935 in a converted hotel previously used as a leadership school by the SS Security Service (Sicherheitsdienst). The new armed SS course lasted for several months, with veteran officer SS-Obersturmbannführer Paul Lettow serving as the lead instructor. On October 1st 1935, the SS-Junkerschule Tölz was formally opened with an entry class of one hundred and ten SS officer candidates. The converted hotel, site of the previous leadership course, was renovated and turned into an SS barracks, while nearby a much larger SS training complex was constructed. The complex at Bad Tölz would be declared completed on October 1st 1937, however continued construction and expansion would continue until 1941.

In February of 1935, Paul Hausser was appointed to command the second SS Officer Candidate School which was opened at Braunschweig, with an initial class of two hundred and forty SS cadets. In the summer of that year, Hausser was promoted to SS-Oberführer and became Inspector of all SS training schools under his new title "Inspektion der SS-Junkerschulen". Under the system designed by Hausser, the SS officer training program took ten months to complete, after an initial four to six months of service in the enlisted SS ranks. SS officer candidates wore special insignia denoting their officer school assignment and were referred to by a series of officer candidate titles with insignia corresponding to equivalent SS non-commissioned officer rank.

The SS training complex at Bad Tölz, Bavaria. This photo was taken in 1945 after the complex had been occupied by American forces (Federal German Archives)

Above: Each officer candidate school was authorized a designated cuffband, as well as a special collar insignia and shoulder crest for wear by both instructors and students. Shown is the prototype cuffband insignia used at the Braunschweig SS-school until 1936, the SS-Junkerschule Bad Tölz cuffband insignia used from 1935 to 1938, and the wartime cuffband insignia for both SS Officer Candidate Schools (with the signature lightning bolt SS runes), used until 1945.

SS OFFICER CANDIDATE INSIGNIA

SS Officer Candidate School	Officer Candidate Collar insignia (Pre-1938)	Officer Candidate Collar insignia (1938 - 1945)	Officer Candidate Shoulder Crest
SS-Junkerschule Tölz			
SS-Junkerschule Braunschweig			

Upon appointment to an SS officer candidate school, the students were assigned an officer candidate rank and issued corresponding SS non-commissioned officer insignia. SS members who were on probationary status wore private and corporal rank badges until full appointment as an officer candidate.

SS Officer Candidate Rank	Collar Insignia	Shoulder Insignia	SS-NCO Equivalent
SS-Junker			SS-Unterscharführer
SS-Oberjunker			SS-Scharführer
SS-Standartenjunker			SS-Oberscharführer
SS-Standartenoberjunker			SS-Hauptscharführer

Once an SS officer candidate was promoted to the highest rank of SS-Standartenoberjunker, they were issued a silver officer's chin strap and assigned to an active SS unit for advanced field training and final evaluation. During peacetime, the SS member would then return to their parent SS academy for final testing and formal commissioning as an SS officer. Upon the outbreak of World War II, the SS began commissioning most Waffen-SS officers directly in the field. After 1942, due to manpower shortages and the growing need for combat officers, field commissions became the norm, although the officer candidate schools continued to operate, producing commissioned officers albeit in smaller numbers.

Right: "A boy and his dog" - An SS-Standartenoberjunker wears the silver chin strap of an SS officer while assigned to final training with the Death's Head units of the 3rd SS Totenkopf Division. (Bavarian State Archives)

One SS uniform style, which was initially designed specifically for SS officer candidates, was the SS physical training gear, consisting of a white shirt (with SS runes logo) worn with black running shorts and shoes. This training attire was eventually adopted by the entire SS.

SS cadets at the Bad Tölz SS Academy run in formation (Federal German Archives)

In addition to the two main SS officer candidate schools, the SS also operated an SS medical officer academy in the city of Graz, Austria. The school was opened in March 1935 as the "SS-Ärztliche Akademie", with the first medical courses held in Berlin before the school was relocated to Austria. The SS medical academy appears to have been a day-course type of school and maintained no barracks nor was any special insignia initially authorized for instructors or students. Originally, medical personnel of the SS-Verfügungstruppe were assigned to an independent SS unit known as the "SS-Sanitätsabteilung/VT". By 1938, medical personnel of the SS-Verfügungstruppe were authorized a special collar patch (see right) as well as a generic cuffband.

Students and staff of the SS medical academy were further authorized a school specific cuffband. In September of 1939, the SS-VT Sanitätsabteilung was disbanded, and all armed SS medical personnel were assigned to regular combat units. Medical personnel permanently based at hospitals were categorized into units known as SS-Lazarette.

The medical insignia of the SS-VT was then discontinued, and armed SS medical personnel issued standard insignia of Waffen-SS. The medical academy cuffband continued to endure until the end of the Second World War.

The SS medical academy cuffband used by the SS medical school in Graz, Austria

For training as a non-commissioned officer in the Waffen-SS, two separate methods for advancement were available. The first was a direct field promotion, usually under combat conditions, to the first non-commissioned officer rank of SS-Unterscharführer. More formally, the SS maintained two non-commissioned officer academies to which prospective NCO candidates could apply for training. The NCO training course lasted several weeks, during which time the SS-NCO candidate was known by the special title "SS-Unterführer Anwärter". Students and instructors were further authorized to display a special cuffband as well as a unique shoulder crest.

SS-NCO Training School	Shoulder Crest
SS-Unterführerschule Radolfzell	
SS-Unterführerschule Lauenburg	

Above: SS non-commissioned officer school shoulder crests, worn on the rank shoulder boards.
Below: Standard cuffband for all SS-NCO school students and staff

In 1936, the SS-Verfügungstruppe assumed control of the SS Administration College, which was based near the Dachau Concentration Camp and previously under the authority of the General-SS. The two main courses taught at the administration college, general administration and legal methods, were recognized with a sleeve diamond insignia upon graduation. By 1938, the armed SS had also assumed authority of the SS Musician Academy at Braunschweig. A special collar patch was thereafter issued to permanently assigned staff, as well as a shoulder crest insignia.

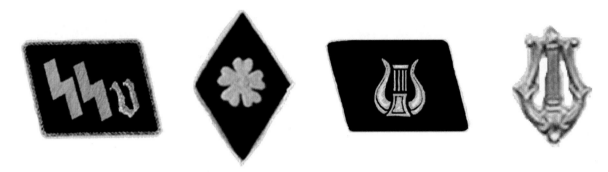

Above: SS specialty school insignia as issued by the SS-Verfügungstruppe. From left to right are the administration school collar insignia, sleeve diamond for administrative service course graduates, collar insignia for the SS music school, as well as the shoulder crest worn by music school instructors and students. Below is shown the administration school cuffband.

The SS also maintained a number of Fencing Schools (known as "SS-Fechtschule") which were jointly under the control of both the General-SS and the SS-VT. While the fencing schools were not authorized any unique uniform insignia, the SS did design a special fencing uniform which was worn by all SS participants at fencing matches.

Another important wartime training school of the Waffen-SS was the SS Motor Vehicle Training Academy (Kraftfahrtechnischen Lehranstalt der SS), more commonly known as the SS-KTL. The academy was established to train professional motor vehicle drivers for SS convoys, personnel escorts, and motorcar chauffeurs. SS members assigned to the KTL were issued both a school cuffband and shoulder board crest.

Above: Reinhard Heydrich wears the SS fencing uniform, which was commonly worn with an SS sleeve diamond. (Federal German Archives) Left: SS cuffband and shoulder rank crest for instructors and students of the SS Motor Vehicle Training Academy

WAFFEN-SS QUALIFICATION INSIGNIA

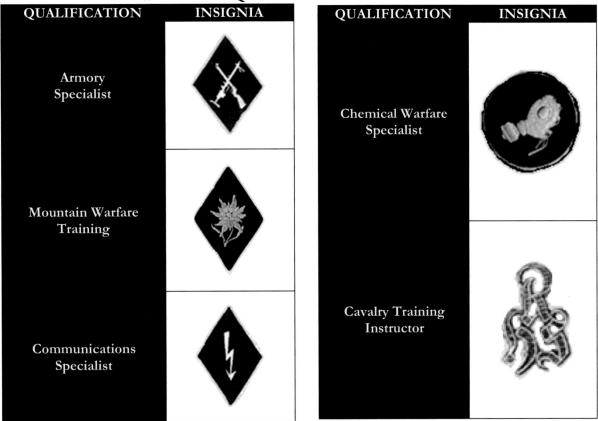

QUALIFICATION	INSIGNIA	QUALIFICATION	INSIGNIA
Armory Specialist		Chemical Warfare Specialist	
Mountain Warfare Training			
Communications Specialist		Cavalry Training Instructor	

The Waffen-SS offered several personal training courses which were either conducted on site, under field conditions, or at a garrison location by visiting SS instructors. Some of the insignia granted for Waffen-SS specialty course completion (see above table) were duplicated in the Allgemeine-SS. Waffen-SS specialty insignia were worn as sleeve insignia with the exception of the cavalry instructor insignia, which was worn as a shoulder board crest.

THE WAFFEN-SS RESERVES

Under a system established in 1938, armed SS reservists would enlist in the SS-VT as an SS-Schütze and attend a basic training course with an SS combat unit. The reserve program then required a number of field training exercises, usually lasting from two to six weeks. The SS reservist would then be granted non-commissioned officer rank as an "SS-Unterscharführer der Reserve". Further advancement in rank occurred after more training exercises and evaluations until reaching the rank of SS-Hauptscharführer. After a final field examination, the SS member was commissioned as an officer in the rank of "SS-Untersturmführer der Reserve (d.R.)". When the Waffen-SS was established in 1940, the reserve program was expanded with only a few minor administrative changes. For instance, reserve ranks were referred to as "der Reserve der Waffen-SS" while regular Waffen-SS officers held a rank title followed by the suffix "der Waffen-SS". An officer reaching the field grade of SS-Sturmbannführer would be augmented to the regular officer rolls of the Waffen-SS. The Waffen-SS reserve program also did not have a permanent enlisted force, with enlisted reserve ranks held only for the purposes of officer training. In 1944, enlisted reserve ranks were done away with entirely and reservists now held the same officer candidate ranks used by the SS-Junkerschule with an additional rank suffix; for instance, "SS-Standartenjunker der Reserve der Waffen-SS" or more commonly as "SS-Standartenjunker (d.R.)". In the spring of 1941, when the Concentration Camp service was transferred to the authority of the SS Economics Main Office, all camp officers were granted rank in the Waffen-SS. Junior officers were granted reserve rank, while all camp commanders and senior staff were granted rank as regular Waffen-SS officers.

Staff and specialty units of the Waffen-SS

Upon the formation of the Waffen-SS in 1940, the SS Operations Main Office issued directives concerning the administrative categorization of all SS personnel into select career fields. Thereafter, all SS members were assigned to one of six career groups. Collectively known as the "SS-Stellengruppen", each officer of the Waffen-SS was assigned a specialty code and designated as either a line or staff officer. General officers of the Waffen-SS occupied a special category and, unlike their counterparts in the Regular German Army, did not technically hold a group classification.

SS SPECIALITY CATEGORY	CLASSIFICATION
B	Battalion Officer
K	Company Officer
Z	Platoon Officer
O	SS-Sergeants
G	SS-Corporals
M	SS-Soldiers

All general officers of the Waffen-SS were addressed by their full SS title followed by an equivalent general officer's rank. For instance, a division commander, who was a Lieutenant General, would be referred to as "SS-Gruppenführer und Generalleutnant der Waffen-SS". Staff officers of the Waffen-SS were further designated by a specific title, in addition to their standard SS rank. For instance, a doctor who held the rank of SS-Hauptsturmführer would be alternatively referred to as an SS-Stabsarzt. In practice, most SS officers simply referred to themselves by their rank, with staff titles only used in written correspondence. The Waffen-SS also made use of a specialty series of shoulder board crest insignia, which were worn centered upon the SS officer's shoulder rank.

WAFFEN-SS STAFF OFFICER INSIGNIA

SS SPECIALTY BRANCH	SS-TITLE	SHOULDER INSIGNIA
Medical Officer	SS-Arzt	
Dental Officer	SS-Zahnarzt	
Pharmacist	SS-Apotheker	
Veterinarian	SS-Veterinär	
Legal Officer	SS-Richter	

Staff officers reaching the rank of SS-Hauptsturmführer would be referenced by the term "Stab" in front of their title, for instance SS-Stabsarzt, SS-Stabsapotheker, etc. Upon reaching field command grade, which was classified as an SS-Obersturmbannführer, the staff officer would be referred as a senior field specialist, such as the title "SS-Oberfeldzahnarzt".

General officers of the staff corps would use titles of the Waffen-SS, such as "SS-Brigadeführer und Generalveterinär der Waffen-SS" or "SS-Gruppenführer und Generalstabsarzt der Waffen-SS". The highest possible rank was known as a senior general staff officer, such as "Generaloberstabsrichter der Waffen-SS" who would also hold the rank of SS-Obergruppenführer. Only two such titles existed, in the SS legal and medical corps respectively[xxxiv].

In 1941, the entire Concentration Camp service was placed under the overall command of the Waffen-SS, with all camp staff and guards thereafter designated as Waffen-SS solders. Doctors and other medical personnel assigned to concentration camps continued to wear standard Waffen-SS staff insignia. A small number of medical staff, mostly those who had served in the camps during the 1930s, wore medical insignia unique to personnel of the SS-Totenkopfverbande. After 1941, most of these personnel were designated as Waffen-SS reservists, but continued to wear concentration camp specific insignia.

It was Waffen-SS doctors and medical personnel who were responsible for combat triage, as well as the staffing of SS hospitals. During the height of the Second World War, the Waffen-SS triage system mirrored the field medical care provided by the German Army. Front line combat medics provided first aid for combat wounds, while SS medical evacuation stations provided emergency care to stabilize more critical wounds. Short term medical care for injuries could be provided at medical field hospitals, while long term care was administered by fully staffed SS hospitals in Germany.

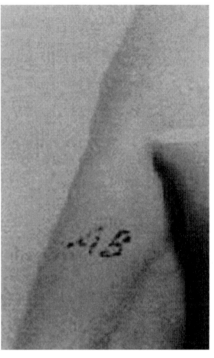

As a means to provide preferential treatment to SS men who were being treated in Regular Army hospitals, Waffen-SS soldiers received tattoos identifying their particular blood type. The premise behind the blood group tattoos was that wounded SS men would be identifiable by medical personnel and would receive blood transfusions before other injured members of the regular armed forces. The blood group tattoos were inscribed on the upper left arm with one of the four primary blood types (A, B, AB, and O). Blood types positive and negative were not outwardly indicated. The Waffen-SS (including those SS men cross assigned to concentration camp duty) were the only SS branch to utilize blood group tattoos and this system was not used in the General-SS or the police and security forces. After the close of the Second World War, the SS blood group tattoos were used as an identifying mark to single out SS men in Allied prisoner-of-war camps. Escaped SS war criminals often went to great lengths (including scarring and burning) to remove the blood group tattoo, since this mark was a means of exposure to post-war authorities and brought risk of arrest, trial, and conviction of war crimes.

An example of a blood type tattoo for the AB group (Federal German Archives)

Interconnected with the SS medical services were SS pharmacists, who provided needed drugs and other medications to field SS medical units, as well as maintaining apothecaries both within SS facilities and German Concentration Camps. SS pharmacists were assigned to local commands but were also accountable to the office of the SS Chief Pharmacist, himself on the staff of the SS and Police Surgeon General. From 1936 to 1945 the SS Chief Pharmacist was SS-Gruppenführer Carl Blumenreuter, who also served as the Chief Sanitation Officer of the SS (SS-Sanitätszuegmeister) until August 1943.

Left: Chief SS Pharmacist Carl Blumenreuter (Federal German Archives)

Blumenreuter was heavily involved with the supply of drugs and poisons to Concentration Camps for medical experimentation purposes, although his direct duties did not entail the acquisition of poison gas. This omission most likely saved him from execution as a war criminal, and he was released after the war to return to his home in Grömitz, Holstein. Blumenreuter thereafter worked as head of a hospital pharmacy until retirement in the late 1950s. He died in 1969.

Staff officers noticeably absent from the Waffen-SS were chaplains, for whom Heinrich Himmler had little use, since the SS ideology absconded organized religion and stressed instead Nordic Aryan supremacy. Himmler instead preferred his SS men to participate in pagan celebrations, rather than formal religious events, and therefore there was never a Chaplain Corps established in the SS.

A lesser known staff branch, but one which was seen of some importance especially during the early years of World War II, was the SS Veterinary Corps. Concerned primarily with the care of horses in SS mounted units, the earliest SS veterinary units were the SS-Veterinärpark (Veterinary Offices) as well as the SS-Pferdelazarett (Horse Hospitals), which were established as part of the SS headquarters staff in 1940.

```
┌─────────────────────────────────────────────┐
│        VETERINÄRUNTERSUCHUNGSAMT             │
│             DER WAFFEN SS                    │
│   (Veterinary Affairs Office – Waffen-SS)    │
└─────────────────────────────────────────────┘
```

HAUPTVETERINÄRPARK DER WAFFEN-SS (Head Veterinary Office – Waffen-SS)	**HEIMATPFERDELAZARETT DER WAFFEN-SS** (Central Horse Hospital – Waffen-SS)
SS VETERINÄR AUSBILDUNGS UND ERSATZ ABTEILUNG (Veterinary Training and Replacements)	**HEIMATPFERDELAZARETT DER WAFFEN-SS OSTLAND** (Central Eastern Hose Hospital – Waffen-SS)

PFERDELAZARETT 105/505 (Horse Care Battalion)	**KORPS PFERDEPARK** *Mobile Animal Clinics*	
VETERINÄRPARK 105/505 (Field Veterinary Office)		**SS PFERDELAZARETT KUUSAMO** (Horse Clinic Kuusamo) *Located in Finland*

SS veterinary units in 1942. The Central Eastern Horse Hospital was later renamed as the "Heimatpferdelazarett der Waffen-SS 2".

Throughout most of the Second World War, the SS Veterinary Corps was headquartered in Warsaw, Poland. Animal treatment facilities were also located in the city of Radom. The chief SS veterinarian was SS-Obersturmbannführer Doctor Walter Hausmann, while the Chief of Veterinary Training and Replacement units was Doctor Wilhelm Kröhle. An SS horse hospital was also maintained in Latvia until 1944, after which time this facility was moved to Senftenberg.

The SS Veterinary Corps of the Waffen-SS was concerned primarily with the upkeep of the SS cavalry units and was originally attached to the SS Cavalry Brigade. This cavalry brigade was formed in 1939, from a cadre of SS-Death's Head mounted units, and in 1942 was renamed as the SS Cavalry Division. From this point on the division maintained a veterinary company (SS Veterinary Company 8) which was responsible for all horse medical care in the division.

The original cuffband of the SS Cavalry Division

In 1943, the SS Cavalry Division was renamed as the 8th SS Cavalry Division "Florian Geyer", but still maintained the original SS veterinary company as part of the divisional order of battle. At the same time, a cadre was formed for the creation of the 22nd SS Volunteer Cavalry Division "Maria Theresia"; but an independent veterinary company was not formed within this new division. In 1944, with the retreat of German forces from Poland, the SS veterinary units effectively ceased to exist. The headquarters offices and horse care facilities were then closed, and the remaining SS veterinarians folded into standard medical units within their respective Waffen-SS commands. In 1945, the 8th SS Cavalry Division was destroyed in the siege of Budapest and the 22nd Volunteer Cavalry Division was disbanded with all remaining personnel transferred to the short lived 37th SS Volunteer Cavalry Division "Lützow".

One of the least known of the SS specialty branches were the Waffen-SS specialist corps, first created in 1941 to grant SS rank to highly specialized technical personnel. Originally, these SS specialists were granted a Waffen-SS position known as "SS-Sonderführer". These SS members were appointed temporarily for wartime needs and were classified as medical, administration, judiciary, or general service technicians.

SS specialists were originally assigned the single rank of SS-Sonderführer and wore SS uniforms with a special type of shoulder cord. It is unknown if such SS specialists also wore collar patches, although most likely a corresponding SS rank was displayed equivalent to the level and seniority of the SS specialist's position.

The original SS specialist insignia used during 1941 and 1942

In 1942, the designation of SS specialists was changed to "SS-Fachführer", with a new type of shoulder board design incorporating standard SS rank. SS specialists were thereafter referred to by a standard SS rank, in one of three categories. Specialist officers would further display collar insignia for the applicable SS rank, as well as an appropriate collar and cuffband insignia. The last SS specialist appointments were made in late 1944.

SS SPECIALIST INSIGNIA (1942 – 1945)

SPECIALIST CATEGORY	SHOULDER INSIGNIA	APPLICABLE SS RANK
Non-Commissioned Specialist		SS-Unterscharführer ~ SS-Hauptscharführer
Junior Commissioned Specialist		SS-Untersturmführer ~ SS-Hauptsturmführer
Senior Commissioned Specialist		SS-Sturmbannführer ~ SS-Standartenführer

Battle Fronts of the Waffen-SS

On June 22nd 1941, the German Army launched a massive invasion of the Soviet Union in what became known as "Operation Barbarossa". Smashing through eastern Poland, the German armed forces liberated the previously Soviet annexed Baltic countries of Latvia, Lithuania, and Estonia, while also quickly capturing Minsk and Kiev. The Germans then moved towards the northern city of Leningrad as well as the Russian capital of Moscow. Six SS divisions, grouped amongst six armies and four Panzer groups, participated in the attack against the Soviet Union. The SS served in the forefront of the invasion, both inflicting and receiving heavy loses.

SS DIVISIONAL DEPLOYMENT – OPERATION BARBAROSSA

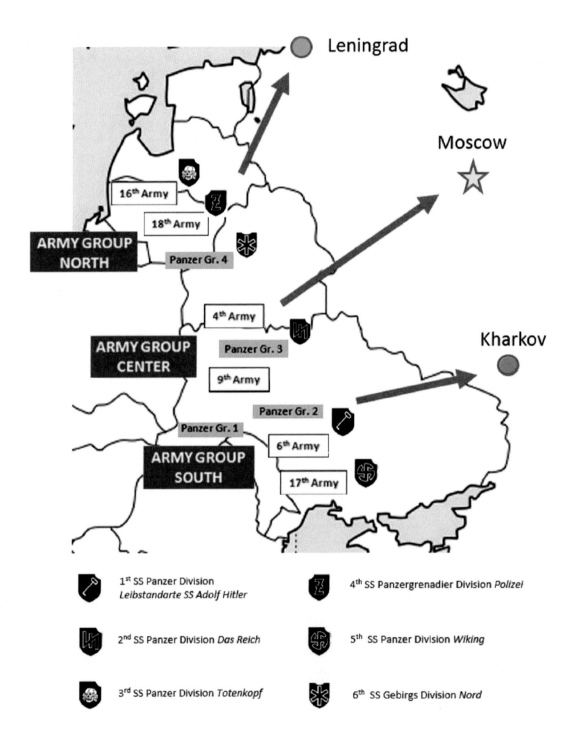

During the invasion of the Soviet Union, the Waffen-SS was active in several major battles at Minsk, Smolensk, and Borodino (where Paul Hausser injured his eye). By the end of 1941, the German advance had stalled, and the SS was ordered to hold the line against Soviet counterattacks. The winter counter offensive of the Red Army, lasting from December 1941 until the following spring of 1942, led to heavy defensive fighting, most notably at the Demjansk Pocket, where Totenkopf forces fought for days in sub-zero temperatures. The Waffen-SS divisions were eventually pulled from the line in early 1942 and then recalled from the front for refit and re-equipping.

By March of 1942, the Soviet counter-offensive had stalemated the Eastern Front, leading to a new German offensive towards the Caucasus that spring. The Caucasus thrust excluded the divisions of the Waffen-SS, with these units being refitted and reformed while the bulk of the German military attacked southern Russia. This omission perhaps spared the Waffen-SS from a scathing defeat, since the entire German 6th Army was later encircled and destroyed during the Battle of Stalingrad, lasting from August 23, 1942 until February 2, 1943.

Elsewhere in the German war effort, the Africa Corps under Field Marshall Rommel faired with great success in 1940, but due to a series of defeats in 1942, Rommel's forces were forced to eventually withdraw from Africa in May 1943. It did not pass unnoticed that Germany's first two major defeats of the war (Stalingrad and North Africa) had occurred without SS participation.

In 1943, now greatly expanded and modernized, the Waffen-SS participated in the battles of Kharkov and Kursk. The city of Kharkov was initially occupied by the Germans in October 1941 and later held against a Soviet counterattack in May 1942. Under occupation, Kharkov was administratively under the German Army, however the remainder of the region was incorporated into the Reichskommissariat Ukraine. The SS Einsatzgruppen were active in this area and a ghetto was established in Kharkov to round up Jews for extermination actions.

THE FOUR BATTLES OF KHARKOV

1st Battle of Kharkov
(20 – 24 Oct 1941):
Initial German capture of Kharkov

2nd Battle of Kharkov
(12 – 28 May 1942):
Soviet attempt to recapture Kharkov, repulsed by the German Sixth Army

3rd Battle of Kharkov
(19 Feb – 15 Mar 1943):
Soviet capture of Kharkov, followed by a counterattack in which the Germans under Erich von Manstein, liberate the city.

4th Battle of Kharkov
(12 – 23 Aug 1943):
The final battle of Kharkov in which German forces retreat from the city.

Left: SS units at the Battle of Kharkov were organized into a single SS Corps under Paul Hausser. The overall commander at Kharkov was Field Marshall Manstein, who commanded Army Group B which also controlled the 1st Panzer Army comprised of the XL and LVII Panzer Corps, and the 4th Panzer Army containing SS units.

4TH PANZER ARMY	
XLVIII PANZER CORPS	**SS PANZER CORPS**
6th Panzer Division	1st SS Panzer Division *Leibstandarte SS Adolf Hitler*
11th Panzer Division	2nd SS Panzer Division *Das Reich*
17th Panzer Division	3rd SS Panzer Division *Totenkopf*

Over 15,000 Kharkov Jews were executed by the SS between 1941 and 1942. By February 1943, following the German defeat at Stalingrad, the Soviet Army began to advance west and recaptured several cities, chief among them Kharkov and Kursk. In what became known as the Third Battle of Kharkov, German forces under the command of Field Marshal Erich von Manstein were able to repulse the Soviet Red Army and recapture the city. The Third Battle of Kharkov was also the first engagement in which Waffen-SS units were grouped together into a single SS Panzer Corps.

The Third Battle of Kharkov lasted for nearly a month and unfolded in three major stages, beginning with the evacuation of the city on February 19th as the Soviet Army broke through German lines. For the remainder of the month, heavy fighting occurred south of the city, in which SS divisions attacked and destroyed several fortified Russian positions. From March 7th to the 10th, the SS Panzer Corps under Paul Hausser conducted an encirclement of the city; Hausser had attempted an assault on the city itself, but his order was countermanded by Army Group headquarters who were concerned about heavy casualties and depleting reserve forces.

The attack on city was thus delayed, but eventually began on March 11th and lasted until the 15th. During this time, SS divisions were at the vanguard of the assault, with the Leibstandarte being the first German formation to reach the center of Kharkov. The Germans then attacked south against retreating Soviet forces, who by this time had withdrawn from Kharkov in what would become one of the greatest German victories of the Second World War. The total losses of the SS Panzer Corps exceeded nearly forty-five hundred troops – nearly 44% of the Corps fighting strength. Total Soviet losses exceeded 80,000 with fifty-two Red Army divisions destroyed. While a tremendous victory for the Germans, Kharkov would be attacked and liberated by Red Army troops in August 1943. This was to coincide with a devastating defeat at the Battle of Kursk (July 5 – 16, 1943) which would see Hausser's Panzer Corps again in combat, accompanied by the 5th SS Wiking division in reserve. In what would become the greatest tank battle of the 20th century, the Germans were unable to hold Kursk and were forced to retreat.

Paul Hausser in 1943, shown wearing the Knight's Cross as an SS-Obergruppenführer und General der Waffen-SS. His victory at the Battle of Kharkov would propel him to the status of a living legend and confirm the role of the Waffen-SS as an elite fighting force in Germany's war effort. (Federal German Archives)

During the retreat from Kursk, SS forces were deployed as "fire brigades" and moved from one area of the front to another wherever a critical situation had developed. There were three SS Corps active during the Eastern Front retreat, the first two being the 3rd and 6th SS Corps. Both were pushed north into the Baltic "Courland Pocket" where they eventually surrendered in 1945 after a battering by Soviet forces. The remaining 4th SS Panzer Corps retreated back through Poland, pausing in August 1944 to help suppress the Warsaw City Uprising, before further retreating into Hungary.

As compared to the eastern front, the Waffen-SS in the west faced less vicious battles but still critically important engagements, such as the defence of France against Allied invasion. The SS was heavily involved in combating the Allied Expeditionary Force at Normandy, and the SS fought fiercely as the Allies pushed inland during the Normandy breakout. During the 1944 invasion of France, the Waffen-SS was known for committing numerous atrocities against enemy soldiers, and in the subsequent Battle of the Bulge was involved in the massacre of Allied prisoners at Malmedy.

During the initial landings at Normandy on June 6th 1944, there were no SS units deployed in the beach defenses, with all of the SS commands instead either awaiting deployment as armored reserves or not yet present in the combat area. The 2nd SS Division Das Reich, stationed in southern France, received deployment orders on June 10th. Before moving north, the 4th SS Panzer Grenadier Regiment "Der Führer" killed over six hundred civilians at Oradour-sur-Glane as reprisal for a suspected partisan attack. By June 20th 1944, most of the SS units at Normandy had been deployed around Caen in order to fight the Allied advance. The 1st SS Division Leibstandarte would remain in reserve at Pas-de-Calais until June 27th.

SS units in France were grouped into two SS Panzer Corps under the 7th and 15th Armies, with SS-General Paul Hausser assuming command of the 7th Army on June 29th. Hausser would later command Army Group G during Operation Dragoon (the Allied invasion of Southern France in August 1944); however, no SS divisions would participate in this operation. The 9th and 10th SS divisions, present at Normandy, would also fight in Operation Market Garden where a British airborne assault was repulsed in Holland.

By September 1944, Allied advances in France had liberated Paris, with front lines stabilized on both sides for the approaching onset of winter. In December 1944, in what would be the last major German western offensive of World War II, German forces launched an all-out assault against Allied forces in an engagement known as the Battle of the Bulge.

SS UNITS ON THE WESTERN FRONT (1944 – 1945)

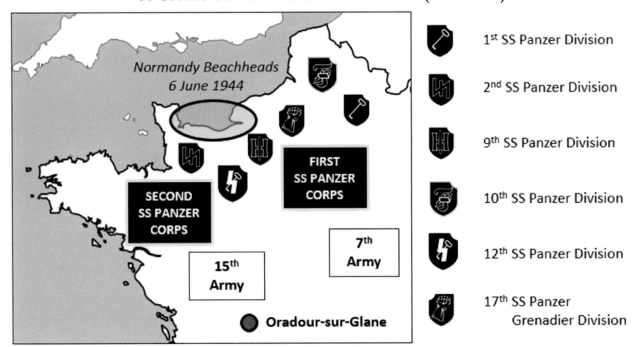

1st SS Panzer Division

2nd SS Panzer Division

9th SS Panzer Division

10th SS Panzer Division

12th SS Panzer Division

17th SS Panzer Grenadier Division

Above: SS units present at Normandy in June 1944
Below: SS, Germany Army and Allied forces during the Battle of the Bulge

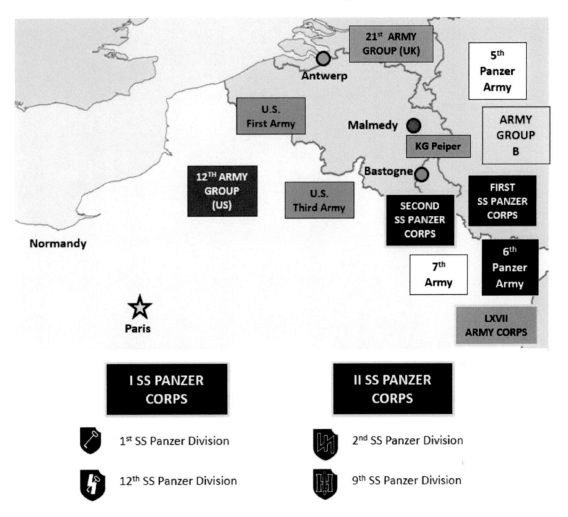

THE COLLAPSE OF THE EASTERN FRONT (1944 – 1945)

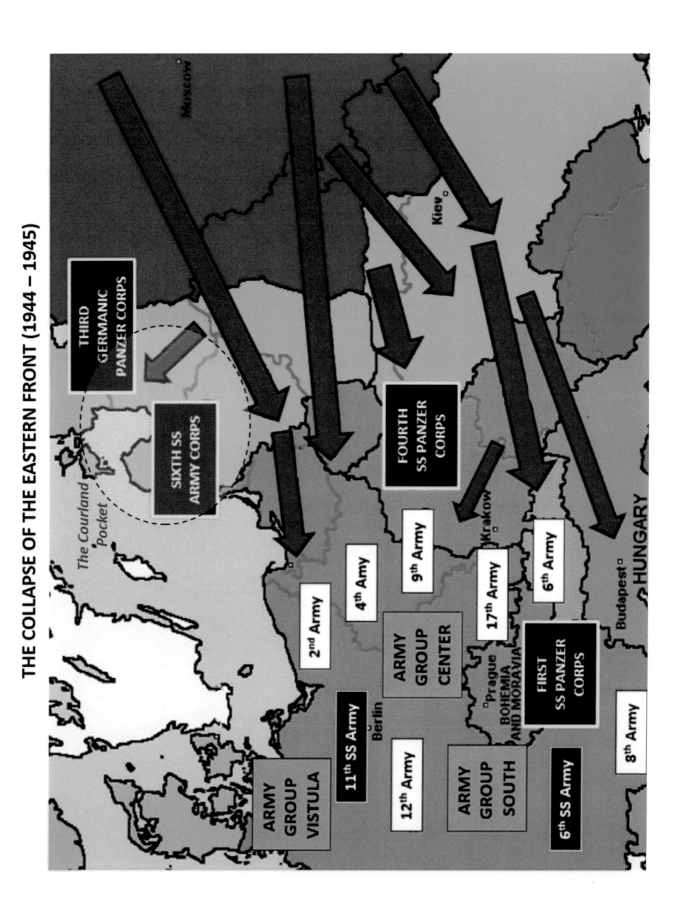

The Battle of the Bulge was the high-water mark for Waffen-SS combat in the west. Four Waffen-SS divisions served in two Corps, under the overall command of the 6th German Army. In a massive strike west, the German forces attacked American and British forces on December 16th. By December 23rd, the German assault had effectively come to a halt. The Allied counter assault lasted until January 25th 1945 with a second failed German attack on January 1st. By February 1945, the German Army was in full retreat. With the German defeat in the Battle of the Bulge, the SS withdrew back into Germany and was thereafter trapped in a pincer between the Allied armies in the west and the Soviet Red Army in the east.

The Battle of the Bulge also saw the first major usage of the SS-Kampfgruppe (Attack Group), intended to be stand-alone combat units, detached from larger divisions on a temporary basis in order to achieve specific military aims. The first such unit formed was an armored formation under SS-Colonel Joachim Peiper, known as the Kampfgruppe Peiper. This unit would achieve infamy after a massacre of eighty-four Allied prisoners of war between 23 and 25 December 1944 in the town of Malmedy.

One ancillary combat theatre, in which the Waffen-SS heavily participated, was Italy. The SS in Italy was mainly involved in security and anti-partisan duties; however, both German SS divisions and Italian SS volunteers deployed against invading Allied armies in 1944.

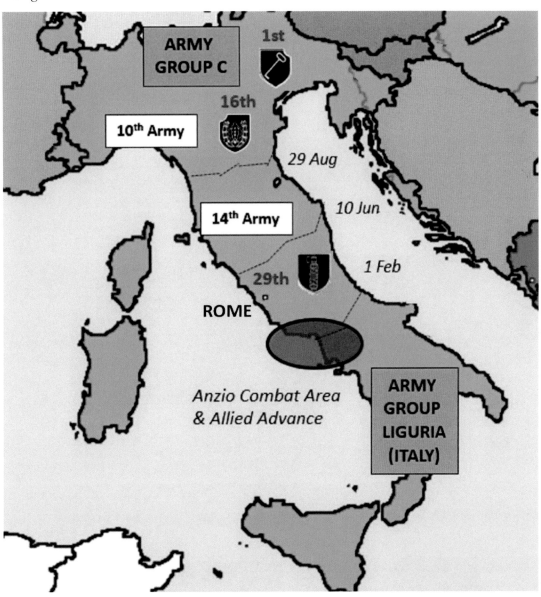

SS units in Italy (marked in red). In September 1943, after Italy surrendered to the Allies and switched sides against the Germans, Adolf Hitler sponsored the formation of a puppet state under Mussolini known as the Italian Social Republic. The SS in Italy was mainly involved in disarming loyalist units of the Italian Army and suppressing partisan actions. In 1944, the Allies invaded Italy and had reached northern Italy, and liberated Rome, by that August.

SS units active in Italy were mainly involved in anti-partisan and security functions, with many such units considered as dual SS-police formations. The only units of the regular Waffen-SS deployed to Italy were the 1st SS Panzer Division Leibstandarte and the 16th SS Panzergrenadier Division Reichsführer-SS. The Italian Social Republic (a puppet Nazi sponsored regime) also formed one SS brigade which was later upgraded to a division as the 29th Waffen-Grenadier Division of the SS. The bulk of SS combat fighting in Italy took place at Anzio in a battle which lasted over four months. The 29th Waffen Division directly participated in the fighting, while both the Leibstandarte and Reichsführer divisions deployed battle groups (Kampfgruppen) in support. To reward Italian SS units which had fought with gallantry, Himmler authorized an "Italian SS Corps" which would wear standard SS sig runes with red backing. Nevertheless, the Germans were unable to hold Italy, and by the end of June 1944 Rome had been liberated. German forces retreated north towards the German border the next month.

Defeat of the Waffen-SS

The final defeat of the Waffen-SS began in earnest in Hungary, specifically the region around Budapest, where the Waffen-SS fought a last stand to prevent the Hungarian capitol from falling to the Soviet Army. The resulting disaster led to the destruction of four German divisions, with nearly all forces in Budapest encircled and destroyed. In one of the last major German offensives of the war, Josef "Sepp" Dietrich led an entire SS army in an attempt to retake Budapest. In what became known as Operation Frühlingserwachen, the SS failed to break the Soviet lines, but did succeed in allowing a limited breakout from the besieged Budapest.

Above: Combat operations and German-Hungarian units during the Siege of Budapest. German forces in Budapest were under the overall command of the Ninth Waffen-SS Mountain Corps. A special unit, known as "SS Detachment 509", was formed specifically for the battle and contained a pioneer, artillery, anti-tank, anti-aircraft, and signals battalion.

COMBAT ACTIONS IN HUNGARY (1945)

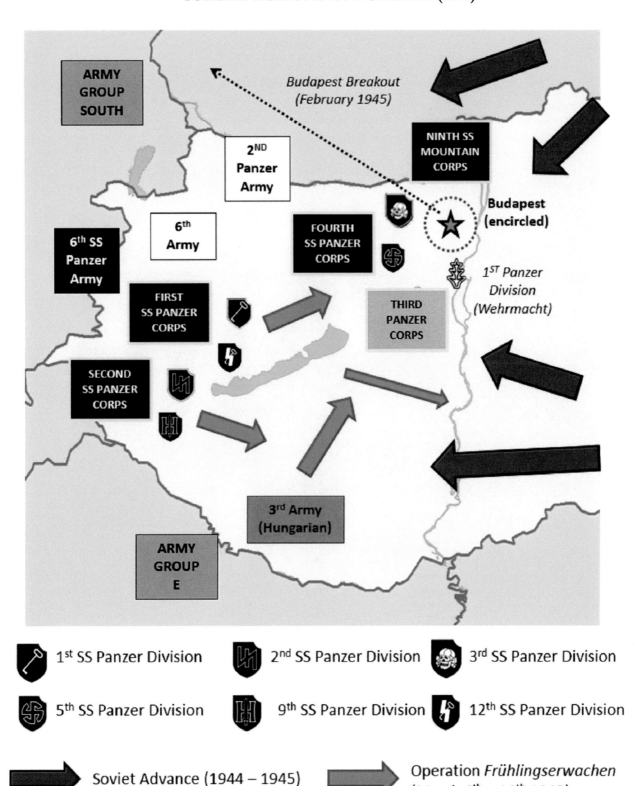

As a result of the SS defeat in Hungary, Adolf Hitler was furious and declared that the SS had lost his confidence. Hitler transmitted to Dietrich the infamous "armband order" which demanded all SS members of the 1st SS Panzer Division remove the "Adolf Hitler" cuffband from their uniforms. Dietrich refused to transmit the order to his troops, although the order was essentially meaningless since, by this time, the standard policy of the SS was to avoid wearing divisional cuffbands, both for camouflage and counter-intelligence reasons.

After the retreat of German forces from Hungary, the remaining Waffen-SS divisions withdrew northward into Austria, where they defended Vienna from a Soviet assault from the 2nd to the 13th of April 1945. Similar efforts were made around Prague which faced a Soviet attack from 6 – 11 May of 1945. In Berlin, the last bastions of the Waffen-SS were assembled to defend the capitol of the Third Reich. Adolf Hitler committed suicide on April 30th 1945, with Berlin surrendering to the Soviet Red Army on May 2nd. A week later, on May 8th 1945, Germany surrendered unconditionally although some sporadic fighting did continue until May 15th.

SS UNITS DURING THE BATTLE OF BERLIN
(April 28 to May 2, 1945)

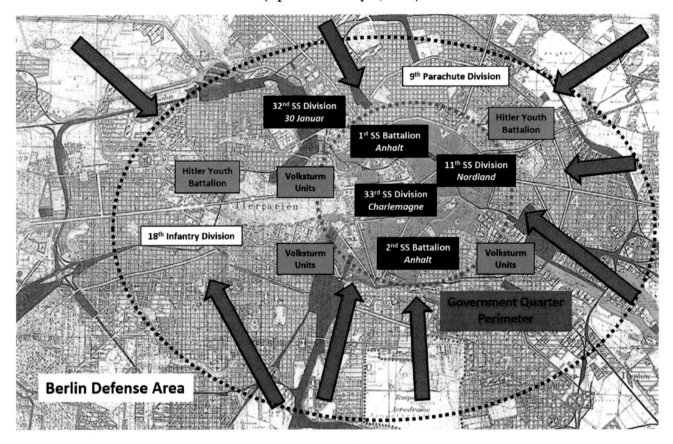

After the capitulation of Germany, the Waffen-SS was immediately identified as an organization directly involved with war crimes, while Waffen-SS solders were categorized in a special class of prisoners-of-war, detained in special prison camps, and oftentimes brought before military tribunals to answer for their crimes. The atrocities of the Concentration Camps, the genocide against whole populations, and brutality of warfare on the Eastern Front were a harsh reality, with little sympathy or reprieve given to those SS members who claimed to be simple front-line combat soldiers only doing their duty. In subsequent investigations, Waffen-SS complicity in war crimes was all but confirmed. The crimes of the Waffen-SS also included support of the Einsatzgruppen, as well as anti-partisan and security operations enacted far behind the lines.

There were some areas of the Second World War in which the Waffen-SS was notable absent. During the defense at the bridge of Remagen, which was captured by the Allies to facilitate an invasion of the German homeland, no SS units were present. Absent too was the SS at the Battle of Stalingrad, and Waffen-SS units were likewise never deployed to North Africa. The Waffen-SS also never created a naval corps (unlike the SA, which founded the SA-Marine) nor was an SS air force ever considered, although several SS members did serve in the Luftwaffe reserve.

Combat units of the Waffen-SS

Since its original inception, the Waffen-SS was organized along military styled lines in the same manner as the professional German Army. The SS regiment was the primary fighting unit of the Waffen-SS, consisting of between three to five thousand soldiers and commanded by an SS-Standartenführer or Oberführer. Regiments of the Waffen-SS were categorized by type of unit, regimental number, and (if applicable) an honor title displayed on a regimental cuffband (for instance SS-Panzergrenadier Regiment 3 "Deutschland").

REGIMENTAL DESIGNATORS OF THE WAFFEN-SS

SS-Panzergrenadier: Panzergrenadier units consisted of motorized and mechanized infantry and were the most common unit of the Waffen-SS. The Panzergrenadiers were highly sought after by Regular Army commanders due to their motorized capabilities, in contrast to the bulk of the German Army which relied primarily on horseback.

SS-Panzer: SS tank regiments were organized along the same lines as the German Army and used the same models of tanks in battle. Tank crews of the Waffen-SS, like their Army counterparts, wore an all-black uniform. At the conclusion of World War II, some Army tank crews were summarily executed by partisans, and sometimes even by Allied soldiers, due to the similarity in appearance between the German Army and Waffen-SS tank uniforms.

SS-Artillery: Artillery units of the Waffen-SS were assigned as support elements to a division. There were three separate classifications for artillery battalions: SS-Artillerie (regular), SS-Panzerartillerie (anti-tank), and SS-Gebirgsartillerie (mountain guns).

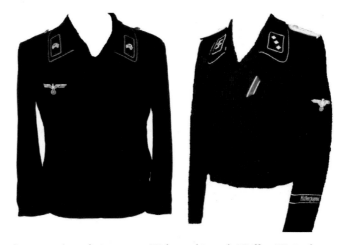

A comparison between a Wehrmacht and Waffen-SS tank uniform. The similarity between the two resulted in many German Army tank crews mistaken for members of the SS.

SS-Sturmgeschütz: Assault gun formations, typically abbreviated as "StuG", were deployed as lightly armored mobile artillery vehicles, whose mission was to provide close fire support for infantry, tank, and anti-tank units.

SS-Gebirgsjäger: SS-mountain troops were elite units of alpine rifleman, trained for close quarters combat in mountainous or snow-covered terrain. Paired up with mountain artillery, these troops also specialized in entrenchment and fortification.

SS-Kavallerie: SS cavalry regiments were some of the oldest units within the arsenal of the Waffen-SS. Originally formed from mounted units of the Death's Head concentration camp guard detachments, the Waffen-SS cavalry had replaced the older General-SS riding regiments by the start of World War II.

SS-Panzerjäger: The tank hunter units of the Waffen-SS were specialized in anti-tank warfare and utilized the same tactics and equipment as their Regular Army counterparts.

Within each regiment were upwards of three to five battalions, which were the primary operational unit to which the average SS soldier would be associated. Commanded by an SS-Sturmbannführer or Obersturmbannführer, battalions were specialized depending upon the type of regiment (infantry, tank, artillery, etc.) and were designated by a roman numeral written before the regimental designation.

WAFFEN-SS REGIMENTAL AND BATTALION ORGANIZATION

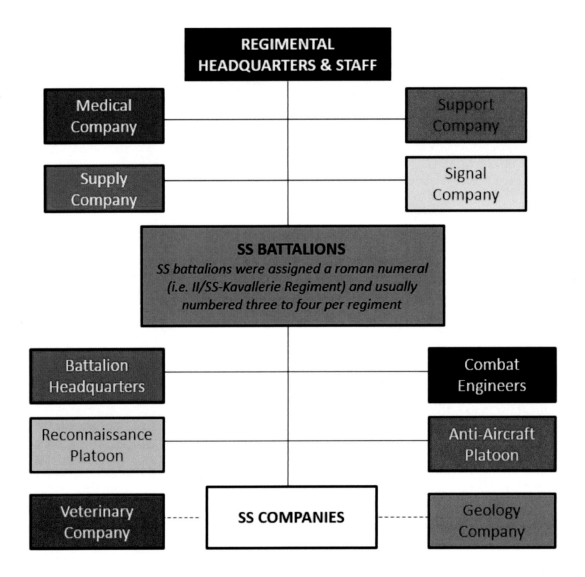

The SS regiment contained a headquarters staff as well as several support companies attached at the regimental level. SS battalions consisted of a headquarters company as well as several specialized sub-units such as anti-aircraft troops, engineers, and reconnaissance platoons. Below the battalion level were the SS-companies, usually commanded by an SS-Hauptsturmführer, and generally numbering one hundred soldiers.

Within each company were several platoons (Zug), each containing a number of squads, known in the Waffen-SS as "Gruppen"xxxv. The smallest unit of the Waffen-SS was the section, commanded by a junior soldier, most often an SS-Rottenführer, and numbering between six to eight men.

**Waffen-SS soldiers on the Eastern Front in 1942
(Federal German Archives)**

In addition to the SS regiments, at the start of the Second World War the Waffen-SS had also formed a number of SS brigades. These units were often formed for either specific military actions or for occupation and anti-partisan duties. Some SS brigades developed a highly notorious reputation, and many were involved in war crimes and genocidal activities. Most of the SS brigades were eventually phased out of the Waffen-SS, in favor of the more permanently established SS divisions.

There were eight numbered SS brigades authorized between 1941 and 1944, but only seven were formed. The eighth SS brigade, which was to be known as the 7th Volunteer SS Brigade, was planned in Norway but was never officially created. In addition to the numbered SS brigades, several additional brigade formations were considered "stand alone" and assigned to anti-partisan and security duties behind the lines in occupied territory.

WAFFEN-SS BRIGADES

SS BRIGADE	OPERATIONAL YEARS	MAIN ACTIVITIES	SUCCESSOR UNIT
1st SS Infantry Brigade	Apr 1941 – Jan 1944	Anti-partisan duties in the USSR	18th SS Division "Horst Wessel"
2nd SS Infantry Brigade	May 1941 – Jan 1944	Combat support of Army Group North	2nd Latvian Brigade (1943) 19th SS Division (1944)
3rd Estonian Volunteer Brigade	May 1943 – Jan 1944		20th SS Estonian Division
4th SS Panzer Grenadier Brigade	Feb 1941 – May 1945		23rd SS Division
5th SS Volunteer Sturm Brigade	Aug 1941 – Jan 1944	Supported the Das Reich division	28th SS Grenadier Division
6th SS Volunteer Sturm Brigade	Apr 1941 – Sep 1944	Combat near Leningrad and later with Army Group South	27th SS Volunteer Panzer Grenadier Division
8th SS Volunteer Sturm Brigade	Jun 1944 – Apr 1945	Assigned to the eastern front and then Berlin in 1945	33rd Waffen Grenadier Division of the SS
SS Cavalry Brigade	Sep 1939 – Mar 1942	Internal security duties in Poland. Later served in combat in the USSR	8th SS Cavalry division "Florian Geyer"
SS Brigade Westfallen	Mar – Apr 1945	Mixed SS unit, assembled in the Ruhr Pocket	Reorganized as a Regular Army unit.
SS-Sturm Brigade "Reichsführer-SS"	Feb – Oct 1943	Garrison duty in France and Italy before fighting in action on Corsica	16th SS Panzer Grenadier Division "Reichsführer-SS"
SS-Sturm Brigade "Dirlewanger"	Jun 1940 – Feb 1945	Anti-partisan duties in Poland	36th Waffen-SS Grenadier Division
Schutzmannschaft Brigade "Siegling"	Jul – Aug 1944	Auxiliary police duties in Prussia	30th Waffen-SS Grenadier Division
Volunteer Grenadier Brigade "Landstorm Nederland"	Oct 1943 – Feb 1945	Combat actions in Belgium and the Netherlands	34th SS Volunteer Grenadier Division

Towards the end of World War II, as Germany's armed forces began suffering massive losses, the SS formed several irregular combat groups, nominally organized as brigades. The most common were the "Kampfgruppe" (Combat Groups) which were ad hoc mixed units comprised of various subordinate SS commands. The first significant combat group was "Kampfgruppe Peiper", deployed in December of 1944 under the command of SS-Obersturmbannführer Joachim Peiper. Peiper's command was a mixture of armored vehicles, smaller tanks, and held a compliment of five thousand men. The Peiper Battle Group became notorious in the Ardennes forest after committing a massacre at Malmedy, France. Over eighty Allied prisoners of war were executed by the SS, a crime which was later prosecuted, with Joachim Peiper and several other Kampfgruppe personnel sentenced to death[xxxvi].

SIGNIFICANT WAFFEN-SS KAMPFGRUPPE

BATTLE GROUP	COMMANDER	FORMED	PARENT COMMAND	ACTIONS
Kampfgruppe Ameiser	SS-Sturmbannführer Anton Ameiser	September 1944	22nd SS Cavalry Division	Battle of Debrecen (Romania)
Kampfgruppe Beyersdorff	SS-Obersturmbannführer Friedrich Beyersdorff	September 1944	14th Waffen Grenadier Division	Slovak Uprising
Kampfgruppe Dörner	SS-Standartenführer Helmuth Dörner	December 1944	9th SS Mountain Corps	Siege of Budapest
Kampfgruppe Peiper	SS-Obersturmbannführer Joachim Peiper	December 1944	1st SS Panzer Division	Battle of the Bulge
Kampfgruppe Skanderbeg	SS-Brigadeführer August Schmidhuber	October 1944	7th SS Mountain Division	Evacuation of Kosovo
Kampfgruppe Wiedemann	SS-Hauptsturmführer Karl Wiedemann	September 1944	22nd SS Cavalry Division	Battle of Debrecen (Romania)

In the last year of the war, the SS also established two numbered units to serve as replacement regiments which were later expanded to brigade status. Both of these units, known respectively as **SS Panzergrenadier Brigade 49** and **SS Panzergrenadier Brigade 51**, were formed in June 1944 and incorporated members of the regular German military who were drafted to serve into the SS. These two brigades performed combat actions in France, Denmark, and Belgium before they were destroyed in action and the survivors transferred to the 17th SS Panzergrenadier Division.

As the military situation deteriorated, the SS battle groups were formed with less personnel and inferior equipment. One of the last significant combat groups to take the field was "Armeeabteilung Steiner" (Army Detachment Steiner), under the command of SS-Obergruppenführer Felix Steiner, tasked with relieving a besieged Berlin in April of 1945. Steiner's command consisted of two under strength divisions supported by three independent battalions. In the city of Berlin, "Kampfgruppe Mohnke" was deployed with two SS battalions under the command of SS-Standartenführer Günther Anhalt. Also present in Berlin were remnants of the SS divisions Nordland and Charlemagne, supported by a scattering of SS security forces defending Adolf Hitler in his Berlin bunker.[xxxvii]

ARMY DETACHMENT STEINER

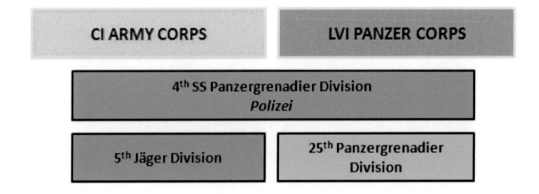

All SS forces in Berlin were commanded by SS-Brigadeführer Wilhelm Mohnke, a veteran office of the Waffen-SS. Mohnke's forces were deployed as part of the "Berlin Defense Area" under the overall command of General Helmuth Weidling. Weidling was the last Regular German Army commander to lead SS troops in combat. In the end, neither Steiner nor Mohnke could save Berlin, and Adolf Hitler committed suicide on April 30th 1945. The Battle of Berlin ended two days later on May 2nd.

Senior commands of the Waffen-SS

The mainstay of the Waffen-SS order of battle was the SS division, of which a total of thirty-eight SS divisions were created during World War II[xxxviii]. At full strength, a Waffen-SS division numbered close to 20,000 soldiers and was commanded by either an SS-Brigadeführer or Gruppenführer. Divisional strengths were often considerably lower, especially later in the war when many of the divisions never rose above regimental or even battalion strength.

Directly above the level of the Waffen-SS division were the SS corps, considered an operational combat command consisting of two or more divisions, as well as possessing its own headquarters staff and support elements. The divisions assigned to an SS corps were not permanently based, and many divisions rotated through several different corps during their period of existence. The first official corps of the Waffen-SS was formed in the summer of 1942, when two eastern front divisions were merged to become the "SS-Panzer-Generalkommando". The SS-Panzer-Generalkommando was placed under the command of Paul Hausser and renamed shortly thereafter simply to "SS Panzer Corps". In July 1943, a second SS Panzer Corps was formed (although designated as the First SS Corps), after which the SS corps were indicated by Roman numerals (i.e. III SS Panzer Corps). The Waffen-SS established a total of eighteen corps; towards the end of the war some corps were considered paper commands and never possessed fully active combat divisions.

Corps of the Waffen-SS were themselves intended to be incorporated into larger SS armies, in much the same manner as the regular military forces of the Wehrmacht. The only SS Army which was ever fully formed was known as the 6th SS Panzer Army, under the command of Josef "Sepp" Dietrich. The 6th SS Panzer Army was formed in August of 1944 and was originally designated simply as the 6th Army before receiving its SS specific name in December, following the Battle of the Bulge.

Right: 6th SS Panzer Army organization

The parent command of the 6th SS Panzer Army was **Army Group B**. The 6th SS Panzer Army fought in two major theaters: the Ardennes Forest in 1944 and Hungary in 1945. In May 1945, the various subordinate units surrendered to American forces. The last unit of the 6th SS Panzer Army formally surrendered on May 12th 1945.

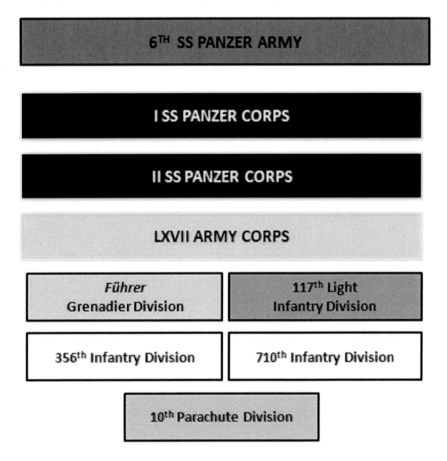

Another SS Army was known as the 11th SS Panzer Army, originally known as "SS-Panzer-Armeeoberkommando 11". The 11th SS Panzer Army was formed in November of 1944, originally under the direct command of Reichsführer-SS Heinrich Himmler, in his capacity as commander of Army Group Vistula. The 11th SS Army began as little more than a paper command, until expansion in February 1945 under the command of SS-Obergruppenführer Felix Steiner. At that time, the 11th SS Army was augmented with three full corps and two mechanized groups. The 11th SS Army participated in one significant engagement during Operation Solstice, which was an attack east of the Oder River in an effort to stop the Soviet advance towards Berlin. After failing in that offensive, the 11th SS Army was transferred to the command of Western Army Command (OB West), stripped of its subordinate units, and left with only a headquarters staff.

Right: The 11th SS Army in February 1945

In April of 1945, the 11th SS Army was reformed with regular Army military units (the IX, LXVI, and LXVII Army Corps). Now known by its final name as the 11th SS Panzer Army, the unit was deployed to the Harz Mountains to defend against the advance of Allied forces from the west. After a handful of engagements at the Weser River, the 11th SS Panzer Army surrendered to American and British forces on April 21, 1945.

11TH SS PANZER ARMY

III SS (GERMANIC) PANZER CORPS

X SS ARMY CORPS

XIXXX PANZER CORPS
4th SS Panzergrenadier Division *Polizei*
10th SS Panzer Division *Frundsberg*
28th SS Freiwilligen-Panzergrenadier Division *Wallonien*

TETTAU CORPS GROUP	MUNZEL CORPS GROUP
Führer Grenadier Division	*Führer Begleit* Division

Headquarters War District II	163rd Infantry Division

The Waffen-SS was never large enough to justify the formation of larger SS Army Groups; however, Paul Hauser did command Army Group G, comprised of regular German military commands, from January 28th to April 3rd 1945. Hausser was one of the few SS leaders who was ever granted such broad control over the regular German Army, in contrast to the majority of SS-generals who spent their careers commanding SS divisions and corps.

Right: Paul Hausser's official photograph as an *SS-Oberst-Gruppenführer und Generaloberst der Waffen-SS*. Hausser received his promotion on August 1, 1944. The promotion photo was intentionally doctored to restore Hausser's damaged right eye. (National Archives)

Heinrich Himmler would himself command both Army Group Upper Rhine and Army Group Vistula; however, Himmler eventually abandoned his military posts and was relieved of further duties by Hitler due to Himmler's incompetence as a military commander.

WAFFEN-SS CORPS HISTORIES

I SS PANZER CORPS

The First SS Panzer Corps was formed in July 1943 and was initially assigned only the 1st SS Division Leibstandarte Adolf Hitler as a cadre element. Josef "Sepp" Dietrich was the corps first commander; although designated as the "first" corps, the unit was actually the second SS corps to be formed.

The first action of the corps was a deployment to Italy in August 1943, assisting in the disarming of Italian troops following Italy's capitulation to the Allies. By the following June, the corps was at full strength and now held the 1st, 12th, and 17th SS divisions as its primary elements, along with the 101st Heavy Panzer Battalion and the German Army's Panzer Lehr Division.

By the time of the Battle of the Bulge, the First SS Corps had been restructured with the 1st and 12th SS divisions, augmented by the German Army's 277th Infantry Division, 3rd Parachute Division, and 12th Volksgrenadier Division. In December 1944, a special unit known as the 501st SS Heavy Panzer Battalion was added to the corps order of battle. In 1945, the First Corps fought in Hungary as part of Operation Frühlingserwachen. After retreating into Austria, the Corps fought in Vienna before surrendering on May 8th 1945.

II SS PANZER CORPS

The Second SS Panzer Corps was actually the first to have been created, and was formed in July 1942, originally as the SS-Panzer-Generalkommondo, before changing its name to simply the SS Panzer Corps. The cadre division was the 2nd SS division Das Reich, while the 9th SS division Hohenstaufen was attached as a reserve.

The first major action of the corps was during Case Anton, when Germany occupied Vichy France in November 1942. The corps was then sent to the eastern front and reorganized at Kursk, as the 2nd SS Panzer Corps, assigned the first through third SS divisions. In the fall of 1943, the corps was reformed on the western front containing the 9th and 10th SS divisions. The corps participated in the defense against the Allied invasion of France, Operation Market Garden, and also fought during the Battle of Bulge.

In 1945, the 2nd SS Panzer Corps was reorganized for the last time, with the 2nd SS division Das Reich and the 9th SS division Hohenstaufen as its primary elements. The corps was then deployed to Hungary where it engaged Soviet forces before retreating into Austria. After fighting in Vienna, the corps then surrendered to American forces on May 8th 1945.

III SS PANZER CORPS

The Third (Germanic) SS Panzer Corps was the first SS corps to be comprised entirely of foreign volunteers. The corps was formed in April 1943, with the 5th SS division Wiking as a cadre, and the 11th SS division Nordland in reserve. During the first months of its existence, under the command of Felix Steiner, the third corps was deployed against partisans in Yugoslavia.

In June 1944, the corps was deployed to Narva (Estonia) augmented with the 20th and 23rd SS divisions while the Wiking division was detached. In September of that year the corps was expanded to its largest extent and now held the 11th, 23rd, 27th, and 28th SS divisions, as well as the Wehrmacht 11th and 300th infantry divisions. Later that month, the division further gained the 103rd SS Heavy Panzer Battalion for armored support.

In 1944, the third SS Panzer Corps was deployed in the defense of the Courland Pocket. In February 1945, the corps was attached to the 11th SS Panzer Army and ended the war defending the Oder River.

IV SS PANZER CORPS

The Fourth SS Panzer Corps was ordered for creation in April 1943 in France; over a year later, in June 1944, the corps was declared combat ready with the 3rd SS division Totenkopf and 5th SS division Wiking as its primary elements. The Wehrmacht 19th Panzer division and 73rd infantry division were attached as supporting elements, as was the 1st Hungarian Cavalry Division.

The corps was first deployed to Warsaw, Poland and was then forced to retreat to Modlin in the face of the Soviet advance. In January 1945, the corps was ordered to defend Hungry with the Wehrmacht 1st and 3rd Panzer divisions providing armored support. The Fourth SS Panzer Corps then suffered heavy casualties during the fighting as part of Operation Frühlingserwachen. The corps then withdrew to Austria where it surrendered to American forces on May 9th 1945.

V SS MOUNTAIN CORPS

The Fifth SS Mountain Corps was originally formed in October 1943 and deployed against Yugoslavian partisans. The corps main elements were the 32nd, 35th, and 36th divisions of the Waffen-SS. In December 1944, the unit was redeployed to Frankfurt and then, the following year, was the primary SS unit which fought in the Battle of Berlin. The corps was subsequently annihilated in April 1945.

VI SS ARMY CORPS

The Sixth SS Army Corps was formed in October 1943, ostentatiously as a higher command for the SS foreign volunteer units of the Latvian Legion. As such, the corps contained both the 15th and 19th Waffen-Grenadier divisions and was deployed initially as a security force in Latvia.

Throughout 1944, the corps was attached to Army Group North and fought against the Soviet advance into the Baltic countries. The corps eventually withdrew into the Courland Pocket, where it spent the remainder of the war fighting defensive actions against Red Army advances into the region.

VII SS PANZER CORPS

The Seventh SS Panzer Corps was a paper command of the Waffen-SS, ordered for formation in late 1943, but whose main elements were never assembled. In April of that year, the corps ceased to exist with all assigned staff transferred to the Fourth SS Panzer Corps.

VIII SS CAVALRY CORPS

The Eighth SS Cavalry Corps was to be the first attempt of the Waffen-SS to form a higher command comprised entirely of SS cavalry units. The corps was ordered for creation in mid-1944, but a staff was slow to assemble. Although existing on paper, no elements had been assigned to the corps by the time of Germany's defeat in May 1945.

IX SS MOUNTAIN CORPS

The Ninth SS Mountain Corps, originally known as the "IX Waffen Mountain Corps" was formed in June 1944, initially for service in Croatia. The primary elements of the corps were the 7th and 13th SS divisions, supported by the Wehrmacht 118th Jäger Division, with the 369th Croatian Infantry Division in reserve.

In December 1944, the corps was reformed and ordered to Hungary to combat advancing Soviet troops. The new corps elements were the 8th and 22nd SS divisions, with the Wehrmacht 271st Infantry Division in support. The corps had also gained the 13th Panzer Division as well as the elite "Feldhernhalle" Division of the German Army.

The bulk of the Ninth SS Corps was destroyed in Hungary between 17 and 28 January 1945. The few remaining soldiers, approximately 800 in all, surrendered to Soviet forces on February 12th.

X SS ARMY CORPS

The Tenth SS Army Corps was originally formed in late 1944, and consisted of headquarters and staff elements from the disbanded 14th SS Corps. The Tenth SS Corps served entirely without any attached SS units and contained only Regular Army commands. The primary elements were the 163rd and 314th Wehrmacht Infantry Divisions, with the 8th Jäger Division in reserve.

The Tenth SS Corps was one of the only Waffen-SS units to be directly commanded by a Regular Army officer, and for most of its existence the corps commander was Generalleutnant Günther Krappe (see right – Image courtesy Federal German Archives).

In February 1945, the Tenth SS Corps was deployed against Soviet forces near Dramburg, in western Poland. The corps was subsequently obliterated and formally surrendered on March 8th.

XI SS PANZER CORPS

The Eleventh SS Panzer Corps existed for a few months between August 1944 and May 1945. The Corps consisted of a single independent Panzer Battalion (the 502nd), supported by mixed battalion elements of the German Army. The Corps was destroyed while fighting in the Battle of Berlin.

XII SS ARMY CORPS

The Twelfth SS Army Corps was formed in August of 1944 to serve as a combat command for the defense of the Ruhr, and originally consisted of a signals company and headquarters battalion. The Twelfth SS Corps was then assigned three Regular Army units (the 59th, 176th, and 183rd infantry divisions) and was deployed in early 1945. All corps elements had been destroyed in April 1945 and the corps disbanded.

XIII SS ARMY CORPS

The Thirteenth SS Corps was formed in September 1944 and operated its own intelligence, signals, artillery, transport, and military-police company. In late 1944, the corps had gained the 17th and 38th SS divisions as its primary elements and was deployed to Czechoslovakia in January 1945. For most of its existence, the corps commander was SS-Gruppenführer Hermann Priess. The corps surrendered to American forces in May 1945, after retreating into Bavaria.

XIV SS CORPS

The Fourteenth SS Corps was a paper command conceived in late 1944, but never assigned a command staff or any subordinate units. The Corps was officially disbanded in 1945 following an administrative merger into the Tenth SS Army Corps.

XV SS COSSACK CAVALRY CORPS

The Fifteenth SS Cavalry Corps began its existence as a Regular Army unit, authorized in April 1943 as the First Cossack Division. The unit was created from collaborationist Cossack cavalry units, mostly recruited from prisoner-of-war camps. In the summer of 1944, the Cossack Division was expanded to a corps, with its two internal brigades renamed as the 1st and 2nd Cossack Cavalry Divisions.

Right: A German Cossack cavalry officer (Polish State Archives)

In February 1945, the Waffen-SS took over administration of the Cossack Corps, and the unit was renamed as the XV SS Cossack Cavalry Corps. The corps was then deployed to the Western Front where, after facing overwhelming enemy superiority, it surrendered to the British Army.

Despite promises to the contrary, Allied authorities extradited all captured Cossack personnel, including the corps commander Generalleutnant Helmuth von Pannwitz, back to the Soviet Union. In an act which became known as the "Betrayal of the Cossacks", the Soviets promptly declared the Cossacks as traitors and executed or imprisoned anyone who had been involved with the SS cavalry units.

XVI SS CORPS

The Sixteenth SS Corps was created in January 1945, specifically to defend West Prussia and Pomerania from the advance of the Red Army. The Corps was assigned the 32nd Wehrmacht Infantry Division as its primary unit, and was supported by mixed SS units of infantry and grenadiers which had been detached from otherwise destroyed units of the Waffen-SS. The corps survived until the end of the war, when all corps units were disbanded upon the surrender of Germany in May 1945.

XVII WAFFEN CORPS

The Seventeenth Waffen Corps was comprised entirely of Hungarian volunteer units (the 25th and 26th Hungarian Waffen-Grenadier Divisions) and was activated in early 1945 to defend Hungary against a Soviet invasion. After engaging Red Army forces in western Hungary, the corps retreated to the Swiss border where it was disbanded in May 1945.

XVIII SS ARMY CORPS

The Eighteenth SS Army Corps was the last Waffen-SS Corps established during the Second World War, and was first activated in February 1945, stationed along the Upper Rhine. The corps was assigned a defensive position and was also used as a garrison unit to monitor the Swiss broader with Germany.

The Corps possessed an SS headquarters staff and commanded five under strength Regular Wehrmacht divisions with no subordinate SS units. The Corps was first engaged by British and American forces in April of 1945, and formally surrendered on April 26th.

Supporting the various SS corps were a number of independent SS Panzer units, which were formed as stand-alone tank detachments which could be transferred between regiments and divisions depending upon combat needs and tactical situations. Three well known independent SS Panzer units were the 101st, 102nd, and 103rd Heavy SS Panzer Battalions.

The 150th SS Panzer Brigade is another noteworthy formation, comprised of both SS and German Army personnel, deployed during the Battle of the Bulge in late 1944 and early 1945. The brigade was commanded by SS officer Otto Skorzeny and was well known for having inserted English-speaking German personnel behind Allied lines, dressed in American military uniforms, as an effort to cause confusion and commit sabotage. Several members of this brigade were later charged and convicted of espionage, with eighteen executed for war crimes.

In September 1943, Heinrich Himmler ordered the formation of an independent SS Parachute Battalion to be used for special operations and combat assaults. The first SS parachutists reported the following month for indoctrination in Czechoslovakia. The fledging unit was then transferred to Yugoslavia to begin training under Luftwaffe instruction. After operational drop training in Hungary, the 500th SS Parachute Battalion was formally deployed in the spring of 1944.

The only combat operation in which the 500th SS Parachute Battalion participated was "Operation Rösselsprung" in which German forces attempted to destroy Yugoslav partisans by attacking the headquarters of Josip Tito. The operation was a disaster and nearly two thirds of the 500th battalion were killed during the assault. The survivors were then transferred to the newly formed SS-Fallschirmjägerbataillon 600 (Parachute Battalion 600) which was forming in Hungary. An apocryphal story states that the 500th battalion veterans lost the right to display SS collar runes and could only regain this privilege after serving a successful combat mission with the 600th.

The 600th SS Parachute Battalion formally mustered into active combat service in November of 1944, attached as a unit of the 150th SS Panzer Brigade. The unit saw combat against American forces in France and participated in the Battle of the Bulge. The 600th SS Parachute Battalion surrendered in May of 1945 upon Germany's capitulation.

DIVISIONAL ORDER OF BATTLE
OF THE WAFFEN-SS

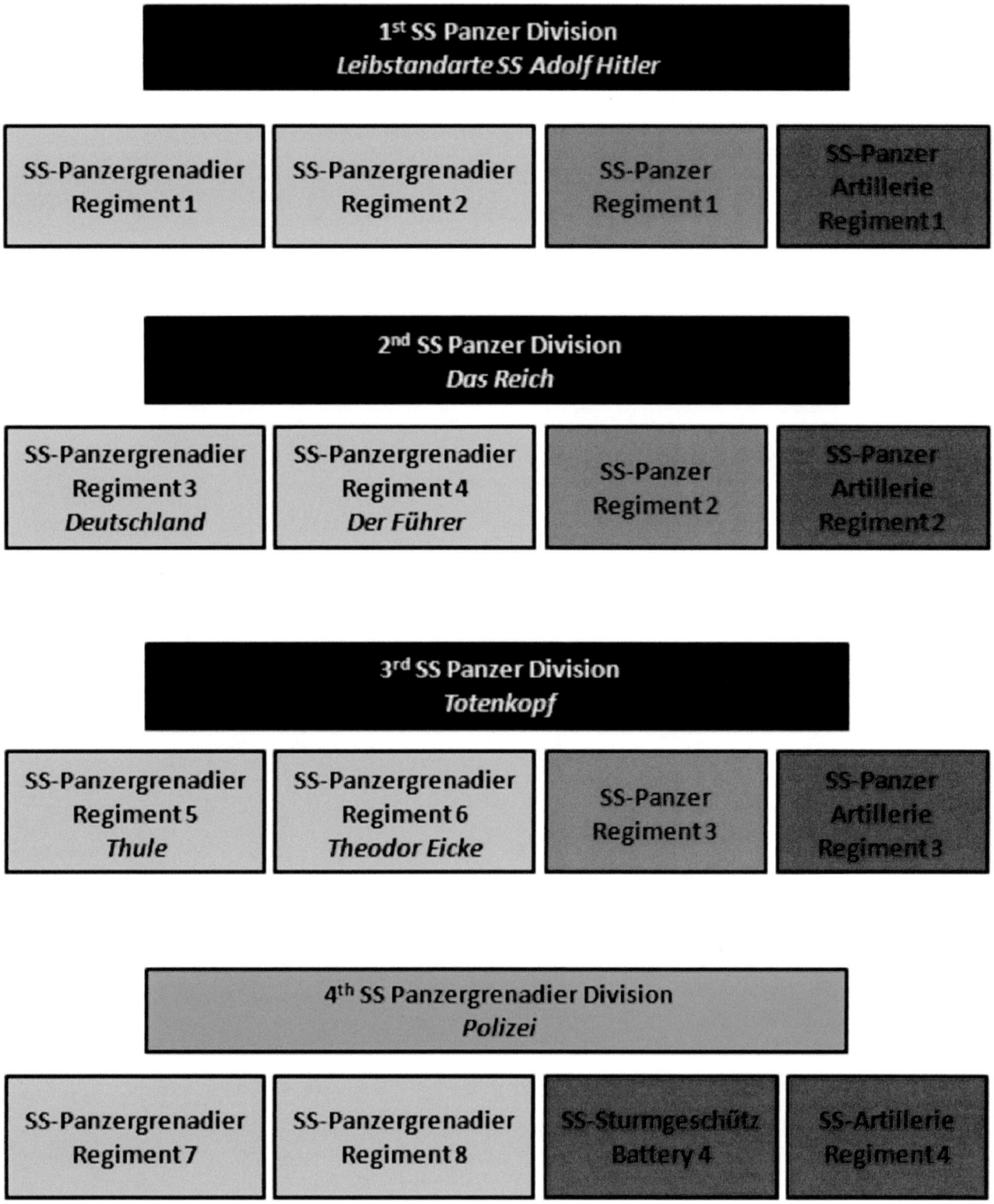

1st SS Panzer Division
Leibstandarte SS Adolf Hitler

| SS-Panzergrenadier Regiment 1 | SS-Panzergrenadier Regiment 2 | SS-Panzer Regiment 1 | SS-Panzer Artillerie Regiment 1 |

2nd SS Panzer Division
Das Reich

| SS-Panzergrenadier Regiment 3 *Deutschland* | SS-Panzergrenadier Regiment 4 *Der Führer* | SS-Panzer Regiment 2 | SS-Panzer Artillerie Regiment 2 |

3rd SS Panzer Division
Totenkopf

| SS-Panzergrenadier Regiment 5 *Thule* | SS-Panzergrenadier Regiment 6 *Theodor Eicke* | SS-Panzer Regiment 3 | SS-Panzer Artillerie Regiment 3 |

4th SS Panzergrenadier Division
Polizei

| SS-Panzergrenadier Regiment 7 | SS-Panzergrenadier Regiment 8 | SS-Sturmgeschütz Battery 4 | SS-Artillerie Regiment 4 |

In addition to the primary regimental elements shown above, all SS divisions contained several support battalions and companies, to include a headquarters staff, medical unit, communications battalion, engineering staff, a replacement garrison, as well as a supply battalion and war correspondence company. Several divisions also contained specialty units, such as anti-aircraft battalions and anti-tank gun companies.

		1st SS Panzer Division _Leibstandarte SS Adolf Hitler_		
Collar Tab		**Divisional Creast**		
		Shoulder Insignia		
Cuffband				

The origins of the Leibstandarte may be traced to the 1st SS-Standarten in Munich, from which a small cadre formed the SS-Stabswache in 1932. In the fall of 1933, Josef "Sepp" Dietrich led the Stabswache to Berlin where the formation took over duties as the Chancellery Guard, thereafter known as the SS-Stabswache Berlin. This followed with the creation of two more Berlin units, the SS-Sonderkommando Zossen and Jüterbog, which were merged with the Stabswache in September of 1933 to form the SS-Sonderkommando Berlin.

In November of 1933 the Berlin guard command was renamed as the Leibstandarte Adolf Hitler. In April of 1934 it was renamed again to the Leibstandarte SS Adolf Hitler and by 1939 was known as the Infanterie-Regiment Leibstandarte SS Adolf Hitler. One company of the Leibstandarte, considered the Chancellery Guard, was permanently based in Berlin while another oversaw security at the Berchtesgaden complex in Austria.

Right: An inspection drill of Leibstandarte troops in the late 1930s (Federal German Archives)

Upon the outbreak of the Second World War, the Leibstandarte was attached to the Wehrmacht 17th Infantry Division. In the summer of 1940, the unit was expanded to brigade strength and attached to the 9th Panzer Division.

Upon the Soviet invasion of June 1941, the Leibstandarte was declared a full division and thereafter fought in Russia, France, Italy, and Hungary before retreating into Austria in the spring of 1945. The division surrendered to American forces in Austria in May 1945 while a small cadre of the ceremonial guard battalion fought in Berlin during the defense of the Führer bunker.

2nd SS Panzer Division *Das Reich*		
Collar Tab		**Divisional Creast**
Divisional Cuffband	Das Reich	
Regimental Cuffbands and Shoulder Insignia		
Deutschland		
„Der Führer"		

The 2nd SS Panzer Division traces its origins to the original armed SS, formed in 1933 as the SS political readiness detachments. In August 1934, these formations were consolidated into the SS-Verfügungstruppe (SS-VT). The original SS-VT was comprised of two regiments: Deutschland, Germania, while a third regiment (Der Führer) was created after the annexation of Austria and Czechoslovakia.

The SS-Verfügungstruppe participated in all of the pre-war annexation actions of Nazi Germany, and afterwards was deployed to fight alongside the German Army during the 1939 invasion of Poland. During the Polish invasion, individual SS-VT formations were attached to Regular Army commands and were not yet an independent military formation. This would change in early 1940, when the three regiments of the SS-VT were consolidated into the SS-Verfügungs-Division.

In the summer of 1940, the SS-Verfügungs-Division served in the vanguard of the attack on France. In 1941, the regiments of the Verfügungs-Division were reorganized, with the Deutschland and Der Führer regiments becoming the cadre for the new "Das Reich" Panzer Division. The Germania regiment was also detached, to form the cadre for the new SS-Wiking division.

The Das Reich division's first major action was in Yugoslavia; thereafter, it was deployed to serve in the invasion of the Soviet Union. In 1942, the division was redesignated as a Panzergrenadier formation and deployed to France, returning to fight again in Russia in 1943. After forming part of the II SS Panzer Corps, the Das Reich Division was sent back to France in 1944 and set against the Allied invasion. The last action of the Das Reich Division was in 1945, when the unit fought in the siege of Budapest followed by a retreat to Vienna, Austria. In May 1945, the last units of the division surrendered to American forces.

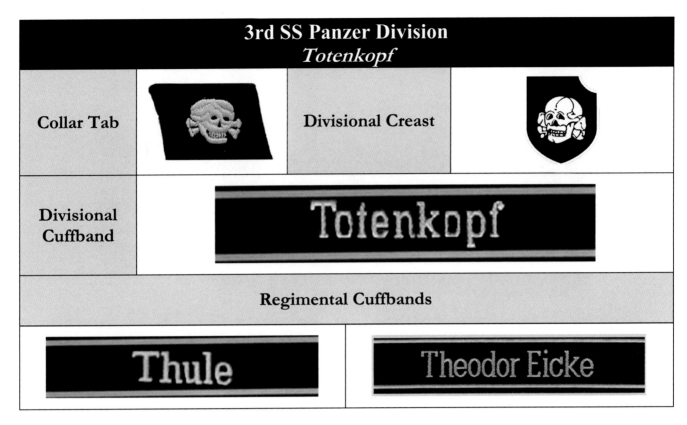

3rd SS Panzer Division
Totenkopf

Collar Tab		Divisional Creast	

Divisional Cuffband — Totenkopf

Regimental Cuffbands

Thule | Theodor Eicke

The creation of the SS Death's Head (Totenkopf) Division was the result of efforts on the part of Theodor Eicke to create an SS military unit formed upon the same training and philosophy as the SS concentration camp service. The SS camp service had been created in 1936 as the SS-Totenkopfverbände (SS-TV) and had quickly been divided into a "camp service proper", consisting of SS personnel who operated the camps and interacted with the prisoners, as well as independent camp guard formations which were formed as military battalions (and later regiments) which answered to their own chain of command.

The camp guard formations were formally separated from the camp service in October 1939 to form the SS Totenkopf Division. Attached to the new division was also an independent death's head combat unit in the city of Danzig, known as the SS Heimwehr Danzig. The Totenkopf Division did not actively participate in the invasion of Poland but was deployed to France in May 1940 and suffered heavy losses while also committing several war crimes and atrocities.

In April 1941, the Totenkopf division was deployed to the east and served in the vanguard of the attack on the Soviet Union. The division served nearly the entire war on the Eastern Front and participated in several major battles at Demjansk, Kharkov, and Kursk. In February of 1943, the division commander Thedor Eicke was killed during a reconnaissance flight near Kharkov. The 6th SS Panzergrenadier regiment was thereafter awarded Eicke's name as its honor title.

Right: Thedor Eicke in 1942 (National Archives)

After Eicke's death, the division was led by a successive number of SS commanders and continued to fight in Russia before retreating to Poland in 1944 and then into Hungary. The division's final action was at the siege of Budapest, after which the last remnants of the Totenkopf Division retreated into Austria, where the unit surrendered to American forces in May 1945.

4th SS Panzergrenadier Division *Polizei*			
Collar Tab		**Divisional Creast**	
Cuffband			

The concept of an armed SS division, comprised entirely of police personnel, arose in the late 1930s as an effort to prevent the conscription of policemen into the regular German armed forces. The Polizei division was formed in October 1939, too late to participate in the invasion of Poland, but nevertheless deployed for security and anti-partisan duties within that conquered nation.

In May 1940, the Polizei division was deployed to France, where the unit engaged in heavy fighting along the Aisne river, and the Ardennes Canal, as part of Army Group C's assault on the Maginot Line. The Polizei divisions suffered relatively high casualties, due in part to the division's second-hand equipment and lack of motorized transport. In June 1940, the Polizei division was redeployed to East Prussia to perform garrison and security duties. In 1941, the division was assigned a supporting role during the attack on the Soviet Union and lost over two thousand of its soldiers, including the division commander, at the Battle of Luga, near Leningrad.

In early 1943, the Polizei division was reformed with new equipment and was then formally renamed as the SS-Polizei-Panzergrenadier Division. Administratively, the division was an integrated part of the Waffen-SS and wore the national eagle crest, instead of the Ordnungspolizei shoulder insignia, although police troops still wore the characteristic Polizei collar tabs.

Right: Polizei division troops in 1942 (Federal German Archives)

In May 1943, the Polizei division was deployed to Greece, to perform anti-partisan duties, and in 1944 fought in Belgrade before retreating into Slovenia.

In May of 1945, what remained of the Polizei division was transferred to Danzig where the unit was assigned as the primary element for Army Detachment Steiner, assigned to relieve besieged forces during the Battle of Berlin. After failing to save the German capitol, the fragmented Polizei division retreated westward and surrendered to American forces in May 1945.

5th SS Panzer Division
Wiking

| SS-Panzergrenadier Regiment 9 Germania | SS-Panzergrenadier Regiment 10 Westland | SS-Panzer Regiment 5 | SS-Panzer Artillerie Regiment 5 |

6th SS Gebirgs Division
Nord

| SS-Gebirgsjäger Regiment 11 Reinhard Heydrich | SS-Gebirgsjäger Regiment 12 Michael Gaißmair | SS-Sturmgeschütz Battery 6 | SS-Gebirgs Artillerie Regiment 6 |

7th SS Freiwilligen-Gebirgs Division
Prinz Eugen

| SS-Freiwilligen Gebirgsjäger Regiment 13 Arthur Phelps | SS-Freiwilligen Gebirgsjäger Regiment 14 Skanderbeg | SS-Sturmgeschütz Battery 7 | SS-Gebirgs Artillerie Regiment 7 |

8th SS Kavallerie Division
Florian Geyer

| SS Kavallerie Regiment 15 | SS Kavallerie Regiment 16 | SS Kavallerie Regiment 18 |

| SS-Artillerie Regiment 8 | SS-Panzerjäger Section 8 |

5th SS Panzer Division
Wiking

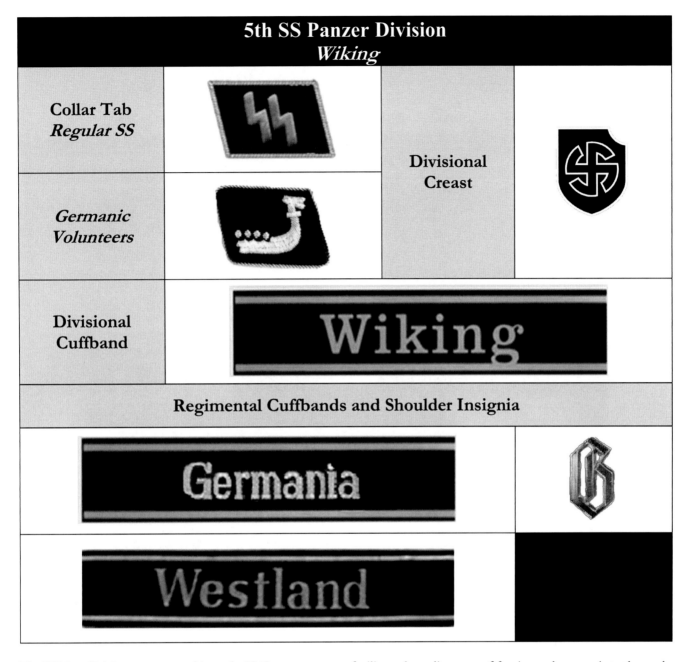

Collar Tab *Regular SS*		**Divisional Creast**
Germanic Volunteers		
Divisional Cuffband	Wiking	

Regimental Cuffbands and Shoulder Insignia

Germania

Westland

The Wiking division was created in early 1940 as a means to facilitate the enlistment of foreign volunteers into the ranks of the Waffen-SS. Originally known as the "Nordische Division (Nr. 5)", the division was led by a cadre from the Germania regiment of the SS-Verfügungs-Division.

In December 1940, the division was briefly referred to as the "SS-Division (mot.) Germania" before adopting its final name as Wiking. After further training in the spring of 1941, the division was deployed east to participate in the summer invasion of the Soviet Union. For the next three years, the Wiking division fought exclusively on the Eastern Front, participating first in Operation Barbarossa and later engaging in several battles within the Caucasus. In November 1942 the division was redesignated as a Panzergrenadier command and deployed to fight at the Battle of Kharkov. The division also fought at Kursk, followed by a retreat in 1944, leading to the division fighting in Warsaw.

In late 1944 the Wiking division retreated into Hungary, and in 1945 fought during the siege of Budapest. In the spring of 1945 the division retreated into Czechoslovakia and then, at the start of May, moved into Austria. The Wiking division was formally disbanded when it surrendered to American forces on May 9, 1945.

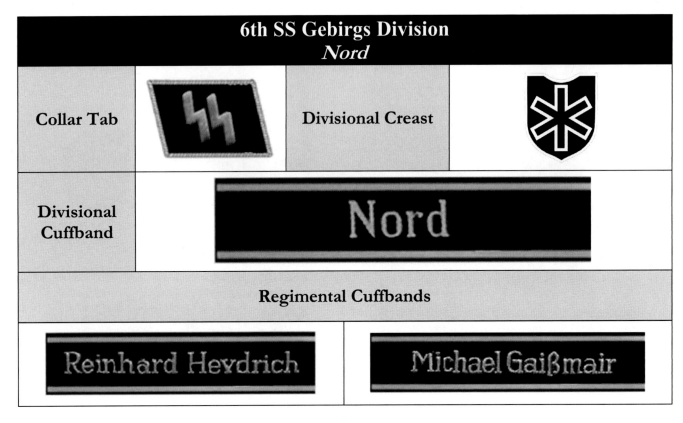

6th SS Gebirgs Division *Nord*		
Collar Tab		**Divisional Creast**
Divisional Cuffband	**Nord**	
Regimental Cuffbands		
Reinhard Heydrich	Michael Gaißmair	

The 6th SS Mountain Division was created in early 1941 as a garrison unit in occupied Norway. The unit was originally known as the "SS Bataillon Reitz", with the first members recruited from the Totenkopf division. By early 1941, the unit included two regiment infantry formations and was subsequently upgraded to a brigade.

Although under equipped and relatively untrained, the Nord brigade was committed to the invasion of the Soviet Union in June 1941, where the brigade was deployed towards the city of Murmansk as part of the 3rd Finnish Corps. The brigade was very nearly destroyed at the Battle of Salla and then pulled from the line at the end of 1941. Reequipped and expanded to divisional strength the following spring, the Nord division then returned to Norway to perform border patrols until 1944. At that time, now known as the 6th SS mountain division, the unit was evacuated from Norway when that nation signed an armistice with the Soviet Union.

Right: A recruiting poster for the SS mountain troops, of which the 6th SS division was mostly comprised (Federal German Archives)

In September of 1944, the Nord division was refitted in Denmark and served as a rear area reserve formation during the Battle of the Bulge. In early 1945, the division was deployed to France and fought against American forces in the vicinity of the Vosges Mountains. In the spring of 1945 the division was attached to the German 7th Army and fought in western Germany before retreating into Austria. In May of 1945, what remained of the division surrendered to the Americans.

The Nord division's two mountain regiments were both granted honor titles, the first in honor of SS-Gestapo Chief Reinhard Heydrich, following his assassination in 1942, while a second regiment bore the name of Michael Gaißmair who was a 15th century secretary to the Bishop of Brixen.

7th SS Freiwilligen-Gebirgs Division
Prinz Eugen

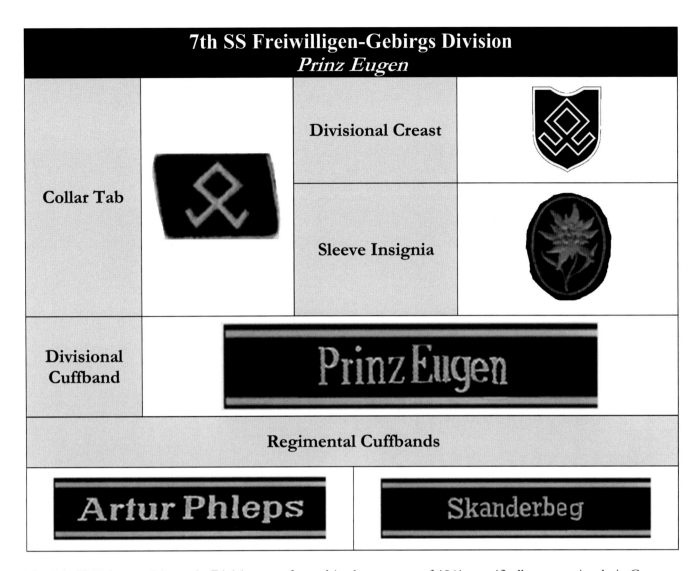

Collar Tab		**Divisional Creast**	
		Sleeve Insignia	
Divisional Cuffband	Prinz Eugen		

Regimental Cuffbands

Artur Phleps	Skanderbeg

The 7th SS Volunteer Mountain Division was formed in the summer of 1941, specifically to recruit ethnic Germans (Volksdeutsche) into the SS from the conquered country of Yugoslavia. When a recruiting center was opened in Belgrade, initial enlistment was low, leading the Germans to adopt conscription of Germanic Croatians. In early 1942, the SS declared the new division combat ready and appointed the Romanian General Artur Phelps as its commander.

The 7th division spent the entire war performing anti-partisan and security duties in Bosnia, Croatia, and Yugoslavia. In mid-1944, the division served as a supporting command to the withdrawal of German forces in Greece. Later that year, the 7th division was ordered to cover a German withdrawal from Yugoslavia. In 1945, the 7th division was attached to Army Group E and commenced a fighting retreat against Yugoslavian partisans. In May of 1945, upon the surrender of all German forces in Europe, the 7th division was in Slovenia where the remnants of the division surrendered to elements of the Yugoslav Army.

**Artur Phelps (right) was a former lieutenant colonel in the Austro-Hungarian Army, later joining the Romanian military and rising to the rank of major general. He was forcibly retired in 1940, after which he traveled to Germany and offered his services to the Waffen-SS. Phelps founded several ethnic Waffen-SS divisions, most of which were involved in anti-partisan actions, as well as war crimes. He was killed by Soviet troops while inspecting a small village along the Romanian front. A regiment of the 7th SS division was later named in his honor.
(Image courtesy National Archives)**

Collar Tab		**Divisional Creast**	
Cuffband			

8th SS Kavallerie Division
Florian Geyer

The concept of an SS cavalry unit was first proposed in the mid-1930s, in the form of the Reiterstandarte cavalry regiments of the General-SS. Upon the outbreak of World War II, the SS formed a single Cavalry Brigade which was used for anti-partisan and security duties; this original cavalry brigade was primarily recruited from Concentration Camp personnel while the General-SS cavalry units were mostly disbanded. In March of 1942, the SS cavalry brigade was upgraded to a division, and augmented with ethnic German volunteers from Transylvania and Serbia. In contrast to other foreign SS units, the 8th Cavalry Division was permitted to retain the SS runes of a pure German SS unit

In the spring of 1943, the 8th division was deployed to assist in the suppression of the Warsaw Uprising. Following this action, the unit was deployed to the Soviet Union for security and anti-partisan duties. Later that year the 8th division was deployed to Hungary and assisted in the German takeover of that nation in 1944. The division was then briefly deployed to Croatia, also for anti-partisan duties, before returning to Hungary in late 1944 to combat advancing Soviet forces. In early 1945, the 8th division was assigned to the forces defending Budapest and formed the primary element of the Ninth SS Mountain Corps. During the siege of the city, the 8th division suffered heavy casualties and was subsequently destroyed after numerous combat engagements.

**Mounted cavalry troops of the 8th SS division Florian Geyer
(Federal German Archives)**

The divisional name "Florian Geyer" was derived from the 16th century Franconia nobleman and knight Florian Geyer. Subordinate regimental honor titles were never issued. Hermann Fegelein, a founder of the SS cavalry units, served as divisional commander on two separate occasions. The final divisional commander was SS-Brigadeführer Joachim Rumohr.

9th SS Panzer Division
Hohenstaufen

| SS-Panzergrenadier Regiment 19 | SS-Panzergrenadier Regiment 20 | SS-Panzer Regiment 9 | SS-Panzer Artillerie Regiment 9 |

10th SS Panzer Division
Frundsberg

| SS-Panzergrenadier Regiment 21 | SS-Panzergrenadier Regiment 22 | SS-Panzer Regiment 10 | SS-Panzer Artillerie Regiment 10 |

11th SS Freiwilligen-Panzergrenadier Division
Nordland

| SS-Panzergrenadier Regiment 23 *Norge* | SS-Panzergrenadier Regiment 24 *Danmark* | SS-Panzer Regiment 11 *Herman von Salza* | SS-Panzer Artillerie Regiment 11 |

12th SS Panzer Division
Hitlerjugend

| SS-Panzergrenadier Regiment 25 | SS-Panzergrenadier Regiment 26 | SS-Panzer Regiment 12 | SS-Panzer Artillerie Regiment 12 |

13th Waffen-Gebirgs Division der SS (kroatische Nr 1)
Handschar

| SS-Waffen Gebirgsjäger Regiment 27 | SS-Waffen Gebirgsjäger Regiment 28 | SS-Panzerjäger Section 13 | SS-Waffen Artillerie Regiment 13 |

9th SS Panzer Division *Hohenstaufen*			
Collar Tab		**Divisional Creast**	
Cuffband	Hohenstaufen		

The 9th SS Panzer Division was named in honor of the Swabian House of Hohenstaufen and was formed in February 1943 from a cadre of personnel from the SS-Leibstandarte. Originally known as "SS-Panzergrenadier-Division 9", the unit spent the majority of 1943 training and equipping, before deploying as a full SS division in early 1944.

The division was first sent to the Ukraine and formed the nucleus of the Second SS Panzer Corps. After suffering heavy casualties against Soviet forces, the division was hastily reequipped and sent to France to fight against the Allied invasion of Normandy in June 1944. After fighting in several engagements against American and British forces, the 9th SS division was pulled from the front lines in September of 1944 and was then sent to the Netherlands for refit and resupply. This respite was short lived, as the division was called back to full combat status during Operation Market Garden and fought against British airborne landings at Arnhem.

In late September 1944, the 9th division was sent to Paderborn where it received new equipment and personnel. In December of that year, the division was attached to the 6th SS Panzer Army and deployed to fight in the Battle of the Bulge. In January 1945, the division began a fighting retreat to the German border and was thereafter sent to Hungary to fight against the Soviet Army. The 9th division was very nearly destroyed participating in the defense of Budapest, before breaking out of the city and moving towards American lines in Austria. In May of 1945, what remained of the division surrendered to American forces.

Right: Hohenstaufen divisional commander Sylvester Stadler (National Archives)

The first divisional commander of the 9th SS division was Wilhelm Bittrich, who also served the longest in the position for four months. The final commander, who had served as acting divisional commander in July 1944, was SS-Brigadeführer und Generalmajor der Waffen-SS Sylvester Stadler. Stadler had joined the armed SS in 1935 and had previously served as regimental commander of the "Der Führer" regiment. Stadler survived the war and died in 1995.

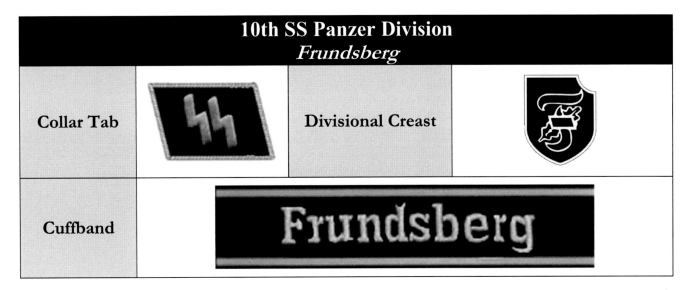

10th SS Panzer Division *Frundsberg*			
Collar Tab		**Divisional Creast**	
Cuffband			

The 10th SS Panzer Division was formed in January of 1943 and designated as a reserve formation to be placed in readiness for the expected Allied invasion of France. The division was originally granted the title "Karl der Große", but this was changed at the end of 1943 to "Frundsberg", named in honor of the 16th century knight and Landsknecht commander Georg von Frundsberg.

The 10th SS division was equipped for combat in 1944 and then deployed to the Ukraine, where the division enjoyed relative success against smaller Soviet forces, as well as participating in the Eastern Front anti-partisan campaigns. In June of 1944, the division was recalled to France to fight against the Allied invasion of Normandy. After suffering heavy casualties, the division retreated into the Netherlands where it subsequently fought against the Allies during Operation Market Garden, a failed airborne invasion of Holland.

After defeating Allied troops at Arnhem, in the fall of 1944 the 10th SS division was withdrawn and stationed as a garrison unit in eastern Germany. In the winter of 1944, the division was deployed back into combat and fought against advancing Soviet forces in the vicinity of Saxony. By the spring of 1945, the division was retreating towards Czechoslovakia and fought in several smaller engagements before reaching the city of Teplice. In May of 1945, just prior to encirclement and certain capture by advancing Soviet troops, the division formally surrendered to American forces.

Right: Frundsberg divisional commander Heinz Harmel poses with two SS soldiers[xxxix] (Federal German Archives)

In addition to the primary elements of two Panzer-Grenadier regiments, the 10th SS division also contained a "Kradschützen-Regiment" (Motorcycle Riflemen Regiment) as well as elements of anti-aircraft, anti-tank, assault-gun, engineering, and communications battalions. The division further contained the standard divisional staff elements covering supply, maintenance, medical, and replacements.

11th SS Freiwilligen-Panzergrenadier Division
Nordland

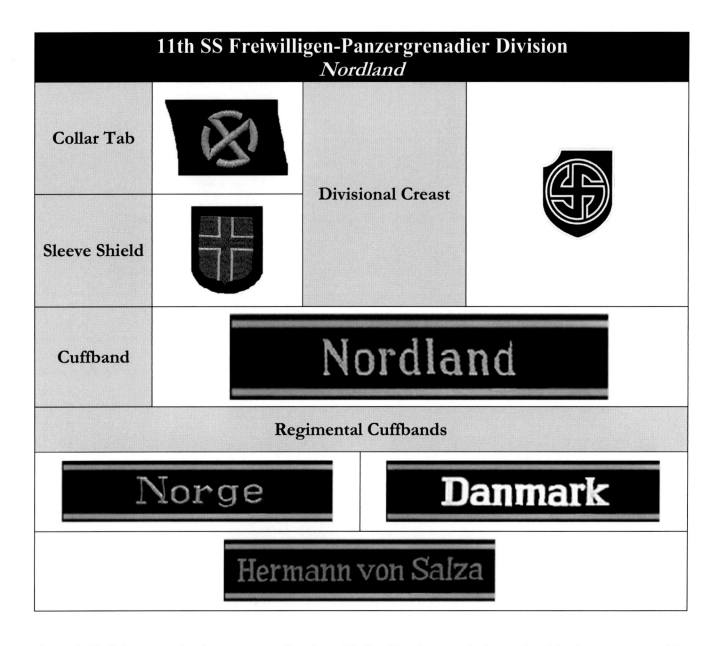

Collar Tab		**Divisional Creast**
Sleeve Shield		
Cuffband	Nordland	

Regimental Cuffbands

Norge

Danmark

Hermann von Salza

The 11th SS division was the first attempt at forming a Waffen-SS unit comprised entirely of foreign volunteers. The unit was first proposed in February 1943 and staffed with a cadre from the Wiking division. Recruitment was primarily from Scandinavia, but the division would eventually have within its ranks nationalities from twelve different nations.

After training in Croatia, the 11th SS division was deployed in January of 1944 to fight in the siege of Leningrad. By February, the division was in retreat after which time the division was engaged by the Soviet Army at Narva in Estonia. The division was then attached to the Third Germanic SS Panzer Corps and began a fighting retreat into Pomerania and eventually East Prussia.

By April of 1945 the 11th SS division had retreated to the outskirts of Berlin and was deployed in a hastily organized defense of the German capitol. The division thereafter engaged in brutal house-to-house fighting in urban Berlin, finally surrendering on May 2nd following the general capitulation of the capitol to the Red Army.

12th SS Panzer Division *Hitlerjugend*			
Collar Tab		**Divisional Creast**	
Cuffband			

An SS division comprised entirely of Hitler Youth members was first proposed in January 1943, with the formation of such a division approved the following February. Commanded by SS-Oberführer Fritz Witt, and staffed with a cadre from the 1st SS Leibstandarte Division, the 12th SS division was originally known as the "Panzergrenadier Division Hitlerjugend" before receiving its final designation as the 12th SS Panzer Division in October 1943.

The division was declared combat ready in March 1944 and moved to France where it was attached to the First SS Panzer Corps. When the Allies invaded Normandy in June of that year, the 12th SS division was one of two Panzer units closest to the landing beaches. Due to a lack of orders from Hitler, the division was not immediately released into combat; however, after receiving orders to engage the enemy, the 12th division fought in several fierce battles before entrenching north of the city of Caen.

Throughout July and August 1944, the division was battered with Allied attacks and was forced to withdraw across the Rhine River on September 6th. In November, the division was sent to Nienburg for refitting and then deployed back into combat. The division then fought in the Battle of the Bulge as part of Kampfgruppe Peiper. By January 1945, the Battle of the Bulge had come to an end and the 12th SS division was redeployed to Hungary. The division next participated in the defense of Budapest before withdrawing towards Vienna at the end of March. On May 8th 1945, the remnants of the division surrendered to American forces.

Right: Kurt Meyer, who both founded and commanded the 12th SS Panzer Division. After the Second World War, he was convicted of war crimes and sentenced to death. His sentence was later commuted, and he was released in 1954 and died in 1961 (National Archives)

Despite its name, the Hitler Youth division was not comprised of child soldiers, with most of the senior divisional members all veteran Waffen-SS personnel, including over two thousand who had served in the Leibstandarte. For the rank and file of the division, active and former Hitler Youth members born before 1926 were preferred, but the division accepted regular enlistments as well. The initial cadre training of the division was stated to be brutal, intent on instilling absolute obedience to orders. Perhaps for this reason, the 12th SS division was involved in several atrocities during the Normandy campaign, most notably at Ascq and at the Ardenne Abbey in which eleven Canadian prisoners were summarily executed.

13th Waffen-Gebirgs Division der SS (kroatische Nr 1)
Handschar

Collar Tab		**Divisional Creast**
Sleeve Shield		
Cuffband		

The 13th SS division was the first Waffen-SS unit to be comprised entirely of ethnic non-Germans. Heinrich Himmler, conveniently overlooking Nazi racial policy, proposed a notion in 1942 to raise an SS unit of Muslim soldiers, whom Himmler saw as fierce warriors and racially pure, since they were neither Jewish nor Slavic.

In February 1943, recruitment for the new SS division began in Zagreb, Croatia. The cadre of the division was staffed from the 6th SS Mountain Division. The division's recruiting officer was SS-Standartenführer Karl von Krempler while the first divisional commander was the retired Romanian Army General Artur Phelps. Originally known as the "Kroatische SS-Freiwilligen-Division", the unit was sent to France in the summer of 1943 to undergo indoctrination and training. In September, while garrisoned at Villefranche-de-Rouergue, several members of the division's pioneer battalion mutinied against their German SS superiors; the mutiny was quickly put down with seventy-eight soldiers disciplined, including fourteen executions.

Right: Muslim SS soldiers of the 13th SS Handschar division. The unique SS-Fez headgear is worn, as is the distinctive scimitar divisional collar insignia (Polish State Archives)

The division was then re-deployed to Silesia and was declared combat ready in October 1943, renamed as the 13th Volunteer Mountain Division of the SS. In February 1944, the 13th SS division was deployed to Bosnia to engage in anti-partisan actions. In August of 1944, with the Germans clearly losing the war, over 2,000 Bosnians deserted from the division with the remainder redeployed to Belgrade to defend against a Soviet attack. In March, the division retreated northwards and entered Austria where it surrendered in May 1945.

14th Waffen-Grenadier Division der SS (ukrainische Nr 1)
Galizien

Waffen-Grenadier Regiment der SS 29	Waffen-Grenadier Regiment der SS 30	Waffen-Grenadier Regiment der SS 31

Waffen-Artillerie Regiment der SS 14

15th Waffen-Grenadier Division der SS (lettische Nr 1)

Waffen-Grenadier Regiment der SS 32	Waffen-Grenadier Regiment der SS 33	Waffen-Grenadier Regiment der SS 34

Waffen-Artillerie Regiment der SS 15

16th SS Panzergrenadier Division
Reichsführer-SS

SS-Panzergrenadier Regiment 35	SS-Panzergrenadier Regiment 36	SS-Panzer Regiment 16	SS-Artillerie Regiment 16

17th SS Panzergrenadier Division
Götz von Berlichingen

SS-Panzergrenadier Regiment 37	SS-Panzergrenadier Regiment 38	SS-Panzerjäger Section 17	SS-Panzer Artillerie Regiment 17

14th Waffen-Grenadier Division der SS (ukrainische Nr 1)
Galizien

Collar Tab		**Divisional Creast**	
Sleeve Shield			
Cuffband			

The Galicia region of Poland, which had previously been part of the Ukraine before the First World War, was annexed by Germany after conquering Soviet occupied Poland in 1941. In April of 1943, recruitment began for an ethnic Galician regiment of Ukraine volunteers. The division was to be used solely on the Eastern Front and commanded by a mixture of German, Austrian, and Ukrainian officers. Training began in the summer of 1943, with the new unit originally known as the "SS-Ausbildungs-Battalion z.b.V" (Special Training Battalion) before being renamed as the SS Schuetzen Division "Galizien".

In August 1943, the division had reached full strength and was renamed as the SS Freiwilligen Division "Galizien". In February 1944, the division was designated for anti-partisan duties, but by July it was engaging regularly with the Soviet Army. On July 22nd 1944, over two thirds of the division was destroyed near the city of Brody, Ukraine. Captured members of the division were either executed on the spot or sent to slave labor camps in the Soviet Union.

In September 1944, the division had been renamed as the 14th Waffen-Grenadier-Division der SS (Galizische Nr.1). The unit was then deployed to Slovakia where it assisted in suppressing a national uprising. Later that fall, the volunteer suffix of the division was changed to "ukrainische Nr.1".

The division was then deployed to the Austrian border, assigned to frontier security and anti-partisan duties, and then retreated towards the city of Graz in March of 1945. In April of 1945, the entire 14th SS division was separated from the German armed forces and became the First Division of the Ukrainian National Army. The separation was more symbolic in nature, since administratively the division still operated as a formation of the Waffen-SS.

In April 1945, the 14th division was deployed to Graz, Austria which was then under attack by Soviet forces. After close quarters fighting, including hand to hand engagements with the elite Soviet 3rd Guards Airborne Division, the Soviet forces temporarily withdrew from Graz, although Vienna had fallen to Soviet forces on April 13th. On May 10, 1945 the division surrendered to Allied forces in Austria.

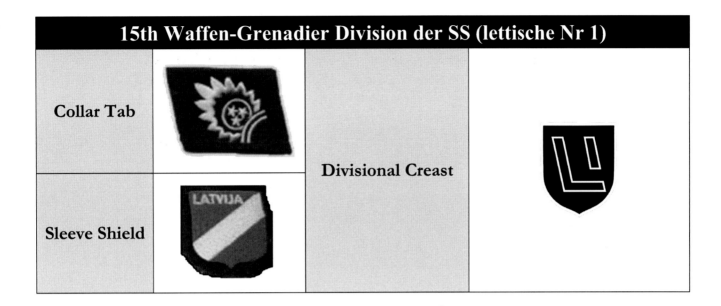

15th Waffen-Grenadier Division der SS (lettische Nr 1)			
Collar Tab		**Divisional Creast**	
Sleeve Shield			

The 15th SS division was formed to recruit SS soldiers from several independent Baltic military formations, all of which had arisen after the German conquest of Latvia, Lithuania, and Estonia. In August of 1942, the first Latvian SS unit had been raised as the "Lettische SS-Freiwilligen-Legion"; this unit would be renamed the SS-Freiwilligen-Division in January of 1943.

After performing homeland security and anti-partisan duties, the Latvian SS division was combined with the 19th Waffen-Grenadier division to form the Latvian Legion. The Legion was subsequently deployed into the advance of the Soviet Army which had begun a campaign to push German forces out of the Baltic countries. By February 1945, after numerous engagements with Soviet forces, the 15th SS division had retreated into Pomerania.

By the time of the Battle of Berlin, the 15th SS division had been fragmented, with only a single battalion actively fighting in the German capitol. The remainder of the division retreated towards the Elbe River and eventually surrendered to American forces on May 2nd. At the time of its surrender, the 15th SS division still maintained both a field post office and a war correspondence branch. For this reason, the records of the division remained largely intact.

The Latvian SS division was considered a foreign volunteer division of the Waffen-SS, and as such was issued a unique collar tab for its membership. Most Latvian SS members, however, ignored the regulations to display a national collar insignia and instead wore SS runes cast in metal and pinned on a blank collar tab[xl]. The metal SS runes of the Latvian SS are today considered one of the rarest SS insignia items in existence.

**Right: A Latvian SS member wearing the metal SS runes pin
(Private photograph on loan to author)**

Since the Latvian Legion was recruited mainly by forced conscription, the group was deemed to be a non-criminal body by both American and Soviet authorities. Even so, reports of war crimes persisted, as well as the Latvian Legion containing at least six hundred members of the Arajs Kommando (Latvian Auxiliary Police). War crimes investigations continued into the 1950s. After the fall of the Soviet Union, the modern-day Russian Republic declared the Latvian Legion to have been a criminal organization while, within Latvia itself, former members are considered by some to be national heroes in the struggle against Communism.

Collar Tab		**Divisional Creast**	
Cuffband			

16th SS Panzergrenadier Division
Reichsführer-SS

Reichsführer-SS

The lineage of the 16th SS division began in the late 1930s, when an escort guard was established for Heinrich Himmler's field command staff. Originally known as the "Feldkommandostelle RfSS", in May 1941 this unit was designated as an armed battalion of the Waffen-SS, exclusively at the disposal of Heinrich Himmler. The unit was renamed as the "Begleit-Bataillon Reichsführer-SS", and in February of 1943 ordered deployed to combat along the Eastern Front. The unit was then expanded to a brigade and renamed as the "Sturmbrigade Reichsführer-SS".

In the summer of 1943, the Reichsführer-SS brigade was deployed to Italy where it was engaged in anti-partisan operations. In November 1943, the unit was upgraded to a division, adopting its final title and numerical designation as the 16th SS Panzergrenadier Division.

In the summer of 1944, the 16th SS division was split into two combat groups (Kampfgruppe) with the first deployed to the Anzio beachhead in Italy while the second combat group assisted in the occupation of Hungary. A single training and replacement battalion was simultaneously established at Arnhem and was deployed in combat during Operation Market Garden, the airborne invasion of the Netherlands.

Right: The final division commander of the 16th SS division was Knight's Cross recipient SS-Oberführer Otto Baum. Baum had begun his career in the Totenkopf divisions where he had participated in the invasion of the Soviet Union. He was severely wounded in 1943, returning to duty as a regimental commander and then appointed as division commander of the 16th SS division. Baum survived the war and died in 1998. (National Archives)

In the spring of 1945, the remnants of the 16th SS division were refitted and redeployed into Austria. In May of that year the division surrendered to American forces.

17th SS Panzergrenadier Division *Götz von Berlichingen*		
Collar Tab		**Divisional Creast**	
Cuffband			

In October 1943, mainly to boost recruitment of ethnic Germans in France and Romania, the SS created the Panzer-Grenadier-Division "Götz von Berlichingen" and staffed the division with cadre from several other SS divisions, as well as replacement and training regiments.

In February 1944, the division received its numerical designation as the 17th SS division and was deemed combat ready, although it had no motorized units. A replacement battalion for the division was also established, known as the "Waffen SS-Ersatz- und Ausbildungsbataillon 5". Support elements included an anti-aircraft battalion, reconnaissance unit, communications company, and medical battalion. Specialty elements included an SS-Panzer Instandsetzungs (Tank Repair Shop) as well an "economics battalion" known as the 17th SS-Wirtschaft battalion. The division also held one tank hunter and assault gun battalion each.

In June 1944, the division fought against the Allied advance at Normandy, engaging both the 82nd and 101st American airborne divisions. In September, after retreating from the Falaise Pocket, the division was strengthened with fresh SS combat troops from various other regiments and battalions, and then sent back into combat near the city of Metz.

In December 1944, the division retreated into Germany and maintained a defensive position during the Battle of the Bulge. Later that month the division was attached to the Thirteenth SS Corps and deployed into heavy fighting. After three weeks of constant assault by Allied forces, the division retreated, before being relieved of combat duties on January 25th 1945. In March 1945, the 17th SS division was sent back in combat defending the German West Wall against advancing American forces attacking east from France. The division fought near Heilbronn, Germany before retreating to Moosburg and then withdrew south into Austria where it continued fighting in the Tyrol until May 5th 1945. The next day, what remained of the division surrendered to troops of the U.S. 101st American Airborne Division.

After the war, several members of the 17th SS division were accused of war crimes, specifically killing prisoners or war, as well as attack on French civilians, in the winter of 1944. The accused SS men were tried by an Allied military tribunal at Dachau, with two convictions as well as several acquittals.

18th SS Freiwilligen-Panzergrenadier Division
Horst Wessel

| SS-Panzergrenadier Regiment 39 | SS-Panzergrenadier Regiment 40 | SS-Panzerjäger Section 18 | SS-Artillerie Regiment 18 |

19th Waffen-Grenadier Division der SS (lettische Nr 2)

| Waffen-Grenadier Regiment der SS 42 *Voldemars Veiss* | Waffen-Grenadier Regiment der SS 44 | Waffen-Grenadier Regiment der SS 43 *Hinrich Schuldt* |

Waffen-Artillerie Regiment der SS 19

20th Waffen-Grenadier Division der SS (estnische Nr 1)

| Waffen-Grenadier Regiment der SS 45 | Waffen-Grenadier Regiment der SS 46 | Waffen-Grenadier Regiment der SS 47 |

Waffen-Artillerie Regiment der SS 20

21st Waffen-Gebirgs Division der SS (albanische Nr 1)
Skanderbeg

| Waffen-Gebirgs Regiment der SS 50 | Waffen-Gebirgs Regiment der SS 51 | Waffen-Gebirgs Artillerie Regiment 21 |

18th SS Freiwilligen-Panzergrenadier Division *Horst Wessel*			

Collar Tab		**Divisional Creast**	
Cuffband			

In late 1943, Heinrich Himmler ordered the formation of a new division to make up for manpower losses which the Waffen-SS had sustained in over two years of constant combat. The First SS Brigade, formed in 1941 from SS Death's Head Regiments, was therefore ordered upgraded to divisional status. Recruitment was begun in France, under the leadership of Paul Marie Gamory-Dubourdeau, a French collaborator holding the rank of Obersturmbannführer in the Waffen-SS.

The 18th SS division was originally formed as an SS Volunteer Sturm Brigade and recruited not only Frenchmen but also ethnic Germans from Hungary. In January 1944, the division received its numerical designation and was also granted the honor title "Horst Wessel" after a Nazi storm trooper martyr killed in 1930 against Communist street fighters.

For most of its existence, the 18th SS division was under the command of Waffen-SS veteran officer SS-Brigadeführer Wilhelm Trabandt. The division was first deployed for anti-partisan duties along the Eastern Front, before committed to combat in Galicia against the advance of the Red Army. After suffering heavy casualties, the division withdrew to Hungary where one regiment was detached in August 1944 to assist in suppressing a Slovakian revolt.

Right: Knight's Cross recipient Wilhelm Trabandt served as divisional commander of the 18th SS division from 1944 through the beginning of 1945. Joining the SS in 1935, Trabandt had fared well in the Leibstandarte SS Adolf Hitler, before he was caught attempting to smuggle stolen goods after the Battle of France. He was thereafter posted to anti-partisan duties with the notorious 1st SS Brigade, regaining a combat assignment in 1943. He spent nine years in Soviet captivity after the war and died in 1968. (Image – Federal German Archives)

In October 1944, the 18th SS division withdrew from Hungary and moved into the Czech Protectorate of Bohemia and Moravia. Josef Fitzthum, an SS Lieutenant General in both the Waffen-SS and police, assumed command of the division in January 1945 but was quickly replaced by a subordinate. The division then formed a defensive line along the approaches to Prague but was destroyed when Soviet forces moved into the region and advanced towards the Czech capital.

19th Waffen-Grenadier Division der SS (lettische Nr 2)			
Collar Tab	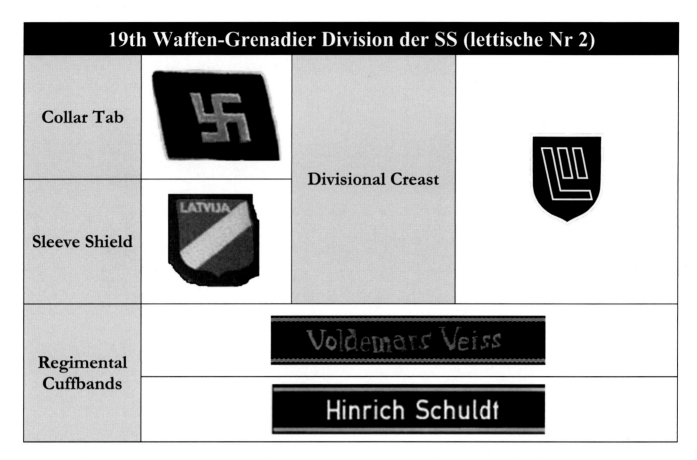	**Divisional Creast**	
Sleeve Shield			
Regimental Cuffbands			

The 19th SS division was formed in January 1944, originally known as the "Waffen Grenadier Regiment 46 (Latvian No. 6)". The leadership of the regiment was provided by German officers from the 2nd SS Brigade, with SS-Oberführer Hinrich Schuldt serving as the first commander.

In September 1944, the originally Latvian regiment was expanded to become the 2nd Latvian SS Brigade. After performing anti-partisan duties in Latvia, the brigade was upgraded to divisional status and thereafter known as the 19th Armed Grenadier Division of the SS. The 19th division was the second component of the Latvian Legion, the other being the 15th SS division.

In October 1944, the 19th division was deployed to Lithuania in the face of the Soviet Red Army advance. The 19th division fought in six separate battles over the next several months, suffering heavy casualties. Due to mounting losses, the Red Army deployed its own Latvian conscript units into battle, these being the 43rd and 308th Latvian Infantry Divisions. After soldiers on both sides refused to fight against each other, both the Germans and Soviets redeployed these units to other areas, in order to avoid direct confrontation between Latvian troops.

After spending nearly all of its existence fighting in the Courland Pocket, the 19th division formally surrendered to the Soviet Army on May 9, 1945. Rumors of summary executions led some Latvian SS members to refuse to surrender and instead found underground partisan forces against the newly established communist regime in the Baltic countries. Known as the "Forest Brothers", these anti-communist groups continued to fight against the Soviet government until the death of Joseph Stalin in 1953. At that time, under a general amnesty, the last of the Latvian partisans laid down their arms. To this day, the majority of Latvian SS veterans are considered as heroes in their country.

The 19th SS division was never issued a divisional title or cuffband, but its two primary regiments were issued regimental titles as "Voldemars Veiss", named after one of the founders of the Latvian volunteer SS units, and "Hinrich Schuldt" after the division's first commander. The regimental cuffbands of the 19th SS division are considered some of the rarest SS insignia to have existed and, in the case of the Hinrich Schuldt cuffband, there are no known photographs of the insignia in actual wear on an SS uniform.

Above: 19th SS division regimental leaders Voldemars Veiss (1899 – 1944) and Hinrich Schuldt (1901 – 1944),
Below: A group of 19th SS division soldiers wearing the unique divisional swastika collar insignia
(Federal German Archives)

20th Waffen-Grenadier Division der SS (estnische Nr 1)

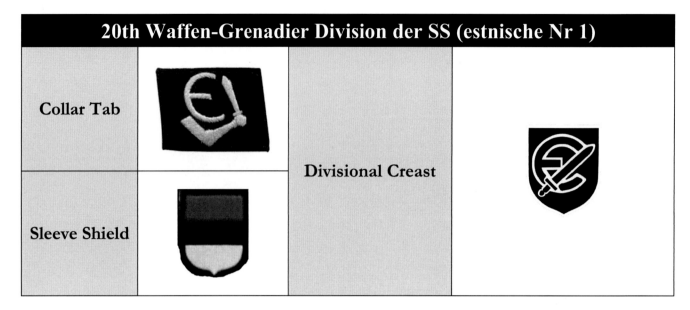

Collar Tab		Divisional Creast
Sleeve Shield		

The recruiting of Estonian soldiers into the Waffen-SS began in August 1942 with the creation of the original Estonian SS Legion, a volunteer regimental sized formation of SS volunteers. In May of 1943, membership had reached 1,280 after which time the unit was renamed as the Estonian SS Brigade.

In November 1943, now known as the 3rd Estonian Brigade, membership of Estonian SS volunteers reached six thousand. The Estonian Brigade was then deployed for anti-partisan duties in Belarus, before deploying to combat against the Soviet Army near Nevel. In January 1944, after withdrawing to Opochka, the brigade was ordered expanded to divisional strength and declared as the 20th Division of the Waffen-SS. The 20th division spent the remainder of 1944 engaged in the defense of Estonia against the Red Army. During this period, the 20th division participated in the Battles of Narva, Tannenberg, and Tartu. In September 1944 the division retreated to Neuhammer.

In February 1945, with a strength of twelve thousand men, the 20th division was deployed into combat against the Red Army attacking the Vistula. The 20th division then retreated across the Oder River towards Prague, where the division mounted a last stand as Soviet forces attempted to capture the Czech capital. In May 1945, the 20th division attempted a breakout from Prague which failed. Left with no choice, the division surrendered to Red Army backed Czech forces which proceeded to summarily execute all SS prisoners-of-war.

Right: SS-Brigadeführer und Generalmajor der Waffen-SS Franz Augsberger, who served as commander of the 20th SS division for most of its existence. Augsberger was an early member of the SS-Verfügungstruppe and had spent the first part of World War II in the 6th SS Mountain Division "Nord". He was then appointed commander of the 20th SS division and was subsequently killed in action on March 19th 1945 (Federal German Archives)

Facing murder at the hands of Czech partisans, a small number of the 20th division managed to escape Czech captivity and reached Austria where they re-surrendered to American forces. The Americans then turned the Estonians back over to Soviet authorities, who summarily executed or deported the prisoners to gulags. A handful of anti-Nazi Estonians were allowed to remain in American custody, where they provided security at the subsequent Nuremberg Trials as part of the 4221st Guard Company.

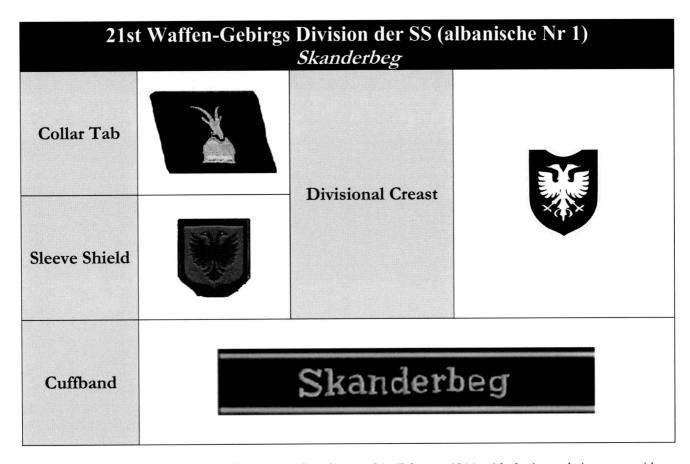

Collar Tab		**Divisional Creast**	
Sleeve Shield			
Cuffband	Skanderbeg		

The formation of an ethnic Albanian SS unit was first discussed in February 1944, with the intent being to provide an anti-partisan force near Kosovo, as well as to recruit Muslim soldiers into the SS. The Albanian SS unit was to be formed in the same manner as the 13th SS Division Handschar and would further contribute towards the establishment of an SS Muslim Corps.

In April 1944, an Albanian battalion of the 13th SS division formed the cadre of the new Skanderbeg unit. The 21st division was formally announced in May 1944 and was attached as a unit of the German XXI Mountain Corps. By June, the division had murdered hundreds of ethnic Serbs and was involved in several incidents of rape and torture. In August 1944, as an effort by German officers to curtail atrocities, the entire division was placed on barracks restriction and guard duty. This led to resentment and the desertion of over one thousand Albanian SS soldiers.

A rare photo of an awards ceremony in the 21st SS division. The Albanian arm shield is clearly visible. The awarding officer also wears the mountain shoulder insignia of the Gebirgs troops (Polish State Archives)

In September 1944, the division suffered a mutiny when Albanian SS soldiers of two battalions attacked and murdered their German officers. SS Chief Heinrich Himmler ordered four thousand German Navy personnel to be transferred into the Waffen-SS in order to fill the ranks and restore order in the 21st division. In October 1944, the division fought in its only significant engagement at Đakovica. The next month the division was formally disbanded. The remaining SS members were folded into local anti-partisan units or attached to the hastily formed Kampfgruppe Skanderbeg, which shortly became involved in atrocities against local populations.

22ⁿᵈ Freiwilligen-Kavallerie Division der SS
Maria Theresia

Freiwilligen-Kavallerie Regiment der SS 52	Freiwilligen-Kavallerie Regiment der SS 53
Freiwilligen-Kavallerie Regiment der SS 54	Freiwilligen-Kavallerie Regiment der SS 55

23ʳᵈ Waffen-Gebirgs Division der SS
Kama

Waffen-Gebirgsjäger Regiment der SS 56	Waffen-Gebirgsjäger Regiment der SS 57	Waffen-Gebirgsjäger Regiment der SS 58

Waffen-Gebirgs Artillerie Regiment 23

(Reconstituted in 1944 as follows)

23ʳᵈ Freiwilligen-Panzergrenadier Division
Nederland

SS-Freiwilligen Panzergrenadier Regiment 48 *General Seyffardt*	SS-Freiwilligen Panzergrenadier Regiment 49 *De Ruiter*

22nd Freiwilligen-Kavallerie Division der SS *Maria Theresia*			
Collar Tab	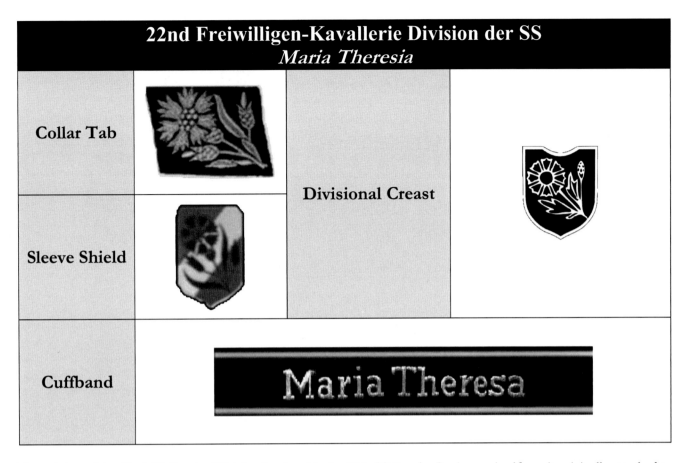	**Divisional Creast**	
Sleeve Shield			
Cuffband	Maria Theresa		

The origins of the 22nd SS Cavalry Division begin with the 17th SS Cavalry Regiment, itself a unit originally attached to the 8th SS Cavalry Division Florian Geyer. In December 1943, the 17th SS Cavalry Regiment was sent to Hungary in order to serve as the cadre for a new cavalry command. With recruits mostly from the Hungarian Army, the 22nd Cavalry Division was declared fully manned in April 1944[xli].

After completing training exercises in the vicinity of Budapest, a portion of the division was assigned to the Kampfgruppe Wiedemann in June 1944, and afterwards deployed to fight against the advancing Soviet Army in Romania. After fighting near Debrecen, this detached unit was then re-designated "Kampfgruppe Ameiser" and attempted a breakout from Soviet encirclement.

By October 1944, only forty-eight survivors had reached Budapest to rejoin the main division. The 22nd SS Cavalry Division spent the remainder of the war in the defense of Budapest. In January 1945, the division was destroyed during Soviet attacks to capture the Hungarian capitol. The survivors of the 22nd SS Cavalry Division were then transferred to the newly formed 37th SS Volunteer Cavalry Division Lützow.

Right: An officer of the 22nd SS Cavalry Division, wearing the distinctive Edelweiss collar insignia (Federal German Archives)

In addition to four primary cavalry regiments, the 22nd SS Cavalry Division also contained an artillery regiment, anti-tank reconnaissance and gun command, signals battalion, medical unit, as well as an engineering battalion. The division further contained both supply and administrative units, known respectively as the SS-Nachschubtruppen und Verwaltungstruppen.

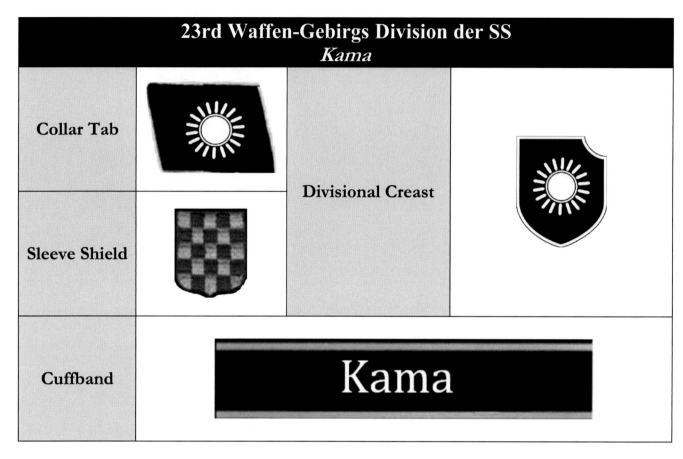

23rd Waffen-Gebirgs Division der SS
Kama

Collar Tab		
Sleeve Shield		**Divisional Creast**
Cuffband	Kama	

The 23rd SS division was the third Muslim SS unit created, the others being the 21st SS division Skanderbeg and the 13th SS division Handschar. Heinrich Himmler had hopes to form a total of four Muslim divisions, which would then form a Muslim SS Corps. This was not to be the case, and the 23rd division was the last of the Muslim SS units created.

In June 1944, a cadre from the 13th SS division was ordered to form a new Muslim SS command. By July, this new division numbered nearly 2,000 in strength and was transferred to Bácska in Serbia for equipment and training. The division was then transferred to southern Hungary in September 1944, and by this time had reached a manpower strength of four thousand.

Right: Two soldiers of the 23rd Waffen division "Kama" in the fall of 1944 (Polish State Archives)

In mid-September 1944, after increased desertions and mutiny amongst Muslim SS soldiers, a decision was made to halt the formation of the 23rd division and cease recruiting Muslim soldiers into the SS. The membership of the 23rd SS division was ordered transferred to Croatia and then merged back into the 13th SS division Handschar. A headquarters staff of the 23rd SS division remained in the city of Vinkovci, Croatia.

During its downsizing, a large number of the Muslim soldiers of the 23rd division mutinied, while a further one thousand deserted. The 23rd division was then disbanded and stricken from the SS order of battle. The numerical designation was reassigned to the 23rd Volunteer Grenadier Division Nederland.

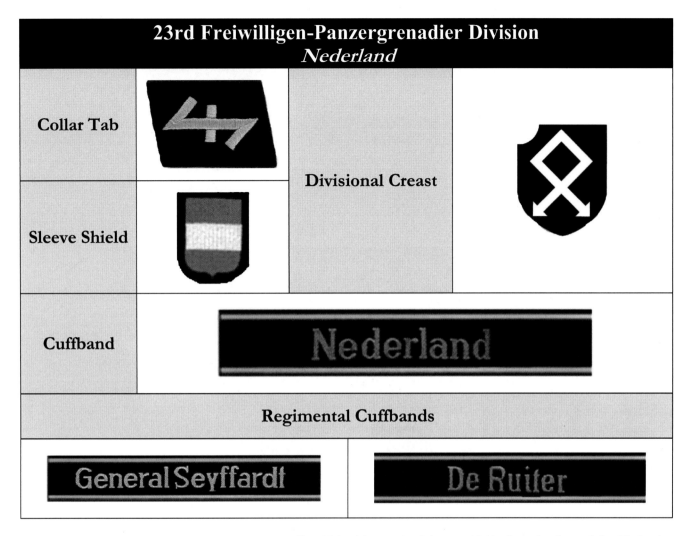

23rd Freiwilligen-Panzergrenadier Division
Nederland

Collar Tab		**Divisional Creast**
Sleeve Shield		
Cuffband	Nederland	

Regimental Cuffbands

General Seyffardt	De Ruiter

The recruitment of Dutch personnel into the Waffen-SS had begun in February 1941 when the first of the SS foreign legions was formed as the SS-Standarte Nordwest. Training of the Dutch SS then began in Hamburg, when the unit was known as the Waffen-SS Regiment "Westland", and by July 1941 the unit had been reformed as the SS Volunteer Legion "Niederlande".

In November 1941, the Netherlands SS Legion was deemed combat ready and deployed to Leningrad as part of Army Group North. The legion was grouped with Norwegian units and fought mostly in the vicinity of Lake Ladoga. In April 1943, after nearly two years deployed on the Eastern Front, the legion was withdrawn from combat for replacements and refitting.

In September 1943, now known as the SS Volunteer Panzer Grenadier Brigade Nederland, the unit was deployed to Yugoslavia for anti-partisan operations. In December of that year, the unit was deployed to Oranienbaum, along the Gulf of Finland, to fight against the Soviet Army. Over the next year the unit was engaged in a fighting retreat towards Estonia.

In September 1944, the Nederland SS Brigade became one of several German commands pinned by the Soviets in the Courland Pocket. In February 1945, the unit was finally upgraded from a brigade to a division but was then almost immediately reduced in strength to two separate combat groups (Kampfgruppe). On May 2, 1945 the division was able to breakout of the Courland Pocket and surrendered to American forces.

24th SS Gebirgs Division
Kartsjäger

Waffen-Gebirgsjäger Regiment der SS 59

Waffen-Gebirgsjäger Regiment der SS 60

Waffen-Gebirgs Artillerie Regiment 24

25th Waffen-Grenadier Division der SS (ungarische Nr 1)
Hunyadi

Waffen-Grenadier Regiment der SS 61

Waffen-Grenadier Regiment der SS 62

Waffen-Grenadier Regiment der SS 63

Waffen-Artillerie Regiment der SS 25

26th Waffen-Grenadier Division der SS (ungarische Nr 2)
Hungaria

Waffen-Grenadier Regiment der SS 64

Waffen-Grenadier Regiment der SS 65

Waffen-Grenadier Regiment der SS 66

SS-Panzer Battalion 26

Waffen-Artillerie Regiment der SS 26

		24th SS Gebirgs Division
		Karstjäger

24th SS Gebirgs Division *Karstjäger*		
Collar Tab		**Divisional Creast**
Sleeve Shield		
Cuffband	Karstjäger	

The 24th SS mountain division traces its origins to the summer of 1942, when the SS created an anti-partisan company trained for patrols in the Alps, with emphasis on mountain anti-guerilla tactics. After initial training at Dachau, the unit was designated as the SS Volunteer Karstwehr Battalion (SS-Freiwilligen-Karstwehr), and for most of 1943 performed security duties in Austria.

In October 1943, the battalion was deployed to Italy to assume roles as an anti-partisan security unit in the German puppet state of the Italian Social Republic. The battalion had reached a strength of one thousand men by 1944 and was known for brutal tactics such as burning villages, summarily murdering suspected partisans, as well as engaging in the rape and torture of civilians.

Right: SS-Sturmbannführer Werner Hahn commanded the Karstwehr Battalion (later a brigade and division) throughout most of its existence. Hahn survived the war and died in 1982 (Polish State Archives)

In July 1944, after the Allies had liberated Rome, Heinrich Himmler ordered the Karstwehr Battalion expanded to divisional status; the unit was then renamed as the 24th SS Mountain Division Karstjäger. Equipment and manpower shortages were chronic, and by December 1944 the 24th SS division had only reached a strength of three thousand, although it was still classified on SS rolls as a full military division.

In early 1945, the 24th SS division was subsequently downsized to a brigade and referred to thereafter as the Karstjäger Brigade. The brigade was then deployed to the Alps where, after fighting against British forces, the Karstjäger Brigade retreated to Trieste and was downsized further to a combat group. In May of 1945, what was left of the Karstjäger unit surrendered to British forces in Austria.

25th Waffen-Grenadier Division der SS (ungarische Nr 1)
Hunyadi

Collar Tab	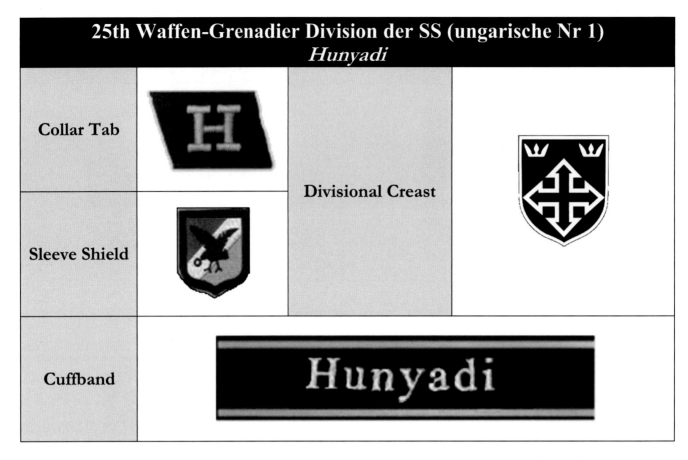	**Divisional Creast**
Sleeve Shield		
Cuffband	Hunyadi	

The creation of the 25th Waffen Division was as a result of Germany's occupation of Hungary, after that country's attempted armistice with the Soviet Union. In October 1944, Admiral Miklós Horthy offered to surrender Hungary to the Soviets, upon which Germany launched Operation Panzerfaust to replace Horthy with pro-German supporter Ferenc Szálasi.

By November 1944, the new Hungarian government was raising ethnic units to incorporate into the German armed forces. The 25th Waffen Division was comprised nearly entirely of Hungarians recruited from the Levente Institution, a paramilitary Hungarian youth organization. The division was formed and trained in Budapest, before being deployed to the Eastern Front in late 1944 to forestall the Soviet invasion of Silesia.

Right: An identification card photograph of a Hungarian SS recruit (Personal photograph)

After fighting at Neuhammer (now Świętoszów in Poland), the 25th division retreated westward and then took up a defensive position in Bavaria. After being overrun by advancing British and American forces, the division retreated into Austria and surrendered to the U.S. Third Army on May 4th 1945, near Lake Attersee.

In addition to three standard infantry regiments, the 25th Waffen Division further contained an artillery regiment as well as a specially trained Waffen-SS ski battalion. The commander of the 25th division for nearly all of its existence was József Grassy, a Ukrainian born Hungarian, and former Hungarian army officer, who in January 1944 was appointed a Waffen-Gruppenführer in the Waffen-SS.

26th Waffen-Grenadier Division der SS (ungarische Nr 2)
Hungaria

Collar Tab	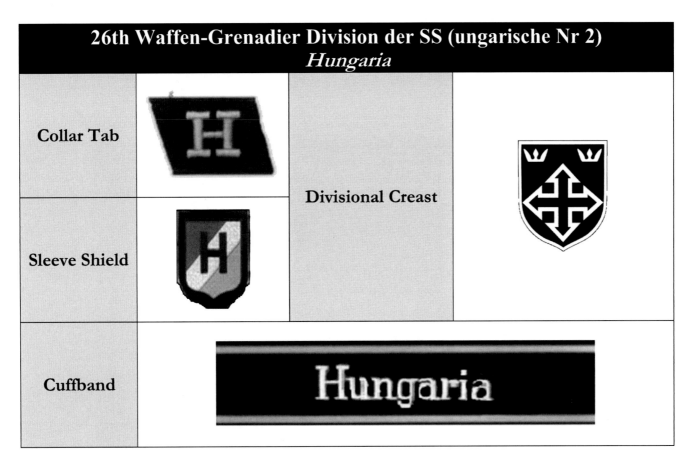	**Divisional Creast**	
Sleeve Shield			
Cuffband	Hungaria		

The 26th Waffen Division was formed as a sister unit to the 25th division, with both units formed and raised in Hungary. The 26th Waffen Division also recruited Romanians, which comprised approximately a third of the division's total number.

In December 1944, the 26th division had just begun forming in Budapest, when a retreat was ordered to avoid the encircling Soviet forces. As the 26th division evacuated, the Soviet forces began their siege of the Hungarian capitol which would eventually result in the capture of the city. The 26th division was able to escape, thereafter sent to Brno, Czechoslovakia before retreating into Austria.

Right: Staff officers of the 26th SS division in January 1945. The officer on the left is wearing the Hungarian "H" collar tab; the officer centered is József Grassy who commanded both the 25th and 26th Hungarian SS divisions (Federal German Archives)

Once in Austria, the 26th division linked up with the 25th Waffen Division and engaged British and American forces near Salzburg in April 1945. The division then retreated to Lake Attersee where it formally surrendered on May 4, 1945. The manpower of the 26th division at the time of its surrender numbered approximately 10,000 soldiers divided into three Grenadier Regiments as well as an artillery regiment, Panzer battalion, and Waffen-SS ski unit.

27th SS Freiwilligen-Panzergrenadier Division (flämische Nr 1) *Langemarck*

SS-Panzergrenadier Regiment 66	SS-Panzergrenadier Regiment 67	SS-Panzergrenadier Regiment 68

Waffen-Artillerie Regiment der SS 27

28th SS Freiwilligen-Panzergrenadier Division *Wallonien*

SS-Panzergrenadier Regiment 69	SS-Panzergrenadier Regiment 70	SS-Artillerie Regiment 28

29th Waffen-Grenadier Division der SS (russische Nr 1)

Waffen-Grenadier Regiment der SS 72	Waffen-Grenadier Regiment der SS 73	Waffen-Grenadier Regiment der SS 74

Waffen-Artillerie Regiment der SS 29

27th SS Freiwilligen-Panzergrenadier Division (flämische Nr 1)
Langemarck

Collar Tab	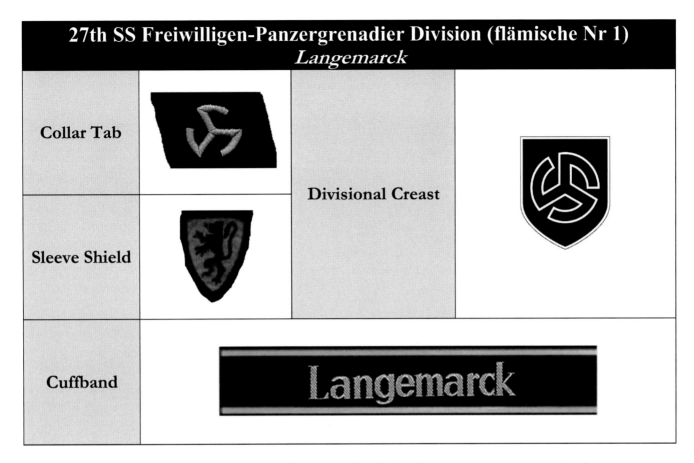	**Divisional Creast**
Sleeve Shield		
Cuffband		

Following the conquest of the Low Countries in the spring of 1940, the German occupation authorities began to sponsor local pro-Germanic organizations, among them a small armed SS unit comprised of foreign volunteers from the Flemish regions in France, the Netherlands, and Belgium. Originally known as the "Standarte Nordwest", this unit was created in late 1940 with training begun April 1941 at Hamburg.

By 1941, the Flemish SS unit had been renamed as the SS Freiwilligen Verband Flandern (Volunteer SS Unit Flanders), and was deployed in November 1941 near Novograd as part of Army Group North. By the end of that year, the unit was known informally simply as the SS Flanders Legion, and it participated in the siege of Leningrad as well as several other major battles with Soviet forces.

Right: A rare photograph of Flemish SS recruits, most likely taken in the spring of 1941. The unique training uniform includes the swastika armband (Private photograph)

In March 1943, the unit was removed from the front and sent to refit at Dębica. Two months later, now stationed in Bohemia, the Flanders Legion was expanded and then became the "SS Volunteer Sturmbrigade Langemarck". The brigade was then sent to fight in southern Russia and began a long retreat westward in the face of advancing Soviet forces. The Flemish SS brigade was upgraded as the 27th SS division in October 1944 while fighting in the Courland Pocket. In 1945, the 27th division was deployed to Mecklenburg and was then sent to fight the Red Army as part of the defense of Berlin. Reduced in strength, the division was re-designated as a Kampfgruppe in April 1945 and surrendered to Soviet forces on May 2, 1945.

28th SS Freiwilligen-Panzergrenadier Division
Wallonien

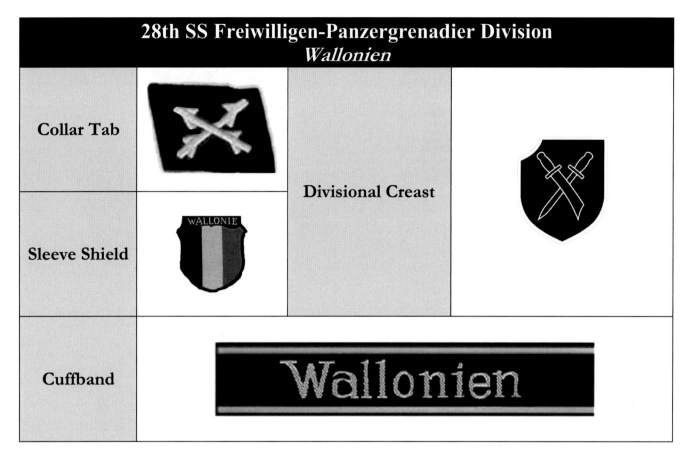

Collar Tab		
Sleeve Shield	**Divisional Creast**	
Cuffband	Wallonien	

The 28th SS division was the final product of several Belgium fascist military groups, beginning with the Walloon Free Corps, founded in 1940 by the leader of the Belgium Rexist Party, Léon Degrelle. In April 1941, the Walloon Free Corps was designated as part of the German Army, and thereafter became the 373rd (Wallonische) Infanterie Battalion.

While part of the German Army, the Wallonien battalion was assigned to anti-partisan duties in Belgium before transferring to combat duty on the Eastern Front. Considered undertrained and ill-equipped by their German Army counterparts, the Wallonien battalion nevertheless fought tenaciously against Soviet forces at the Donets River before being assigned to supply lines in the defense of the Caucasus.

Right: Léon Degrelle, the driving force behind the formation of a Belgium Waffen-SS unit. Degrelle rose to the rank of SS-Standartenführer and served as the final commander of the 28th SS division. After the war, he changed his name to José León Ramírez Reina and lived in Spain until his death in 1994. (National Archives)

In June 1943, the original Wallonien battalion was transferred to the control of the SS and upgraded to a brigade. Now known as the SS Volunteer Sturmbrigade Wallonien, this unit was sent back to the Eastern Front and posted to the Ukraine. That December, the Wallonien brigade fought alongside the 5th SS division Wiking as the Soviet Red Army launched the Dnieper–Carpathian Offensive with the aim being to liberate the Ukraine.

In January 1944, after withdrawing from the Ukraine, the Wallonien brigade was very nearly destroyed at the Battle of Narva, before retreating to Breslau in Poland along with the rest of the German forces. In October 1944, the unit was designated as the 28th SS division and thereafter fought against the Red Army in the vicinity of Berlin. After the collapse of Germany's capitol, the 28th SS division retreated to Lübeck and surrendered to British forces.

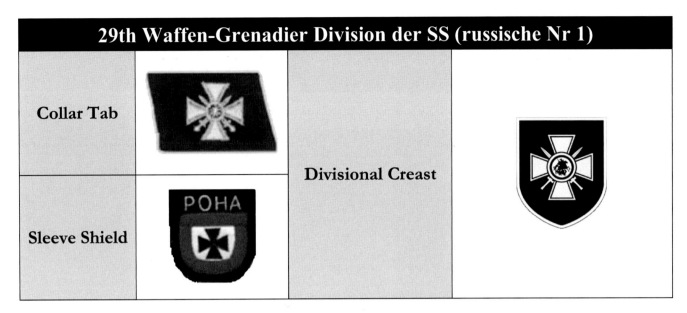

29th Waffen-Grenadier Division der SS (russische Nr 1)			
Collar Tab		**Divisional Creast**	
Sleeve Shield			

The origins of the 29th Waffen Divsiion may be traced to the Russian National Liberation Army (RONA), which was founded in 1941 as an auxiliary police unit under the command of Bronislav Kaminski, a Russian collaborator, who later became head of the Lokot Autonomy, an area of Russia just east of the Ukraine[xlii].

The forces under Kaminski first served as the militia for the Lokot Autonomy and originally numbered eight thousand soldiers in strength. In June 1943, Kaminski's forces were deployed as reserve troops in the Battle of Kursk, suffering heavy casualties and high desertion rates. Afterwards, the unit was sent to Belarus as a police security unit.

In March 1944, the Kaminski unit was renamed as the "Volksheer-Brigade Kaminski". During the summer of 1944, Kaminski and his men were engaged in a variety of anti-partisan operations and were known for brutality and atrocity. In June 1944, the unit was formally transferred to the operational control of the SS and renamed as the Waffen-Sturm-Brigade RONA. The unit then retreated westward, in the face of the Soviet military advance, and had reached Warsaw by August 1944.

Right: Bronislav Kaminski in 1943. He wears the makeshift uniform of the Russian National Liberation Army, which essentially was a German Army tunic with most of the insignia removed (Federal German Archives)

Kaminski and his men were then deployed to assist in suppressing the Warsaw city uprising (separate from the Ghetto uprising of 1943). On August 1st 1944, Kaminski was promoted to Waffen-Brigadeführer und Generalmajor der Waffen-SS, with his unit reconstituted as the 29th Waffen Division of the SS.

In Warsaw, the 29th SS division performed poorly and Kaminski himself was killed by partisans on August 28th, although some reports state that he was court-martialed and shot by the Germans for cowardice. The 29th division was thereafter stricken from the SS rolls with a new unit formed thereafter in Italy under the same numerical designation.

29th Waffen-Grenadier Division der SS (italienische Nr 1)

Waffen-Grenadier Regiment der SS 81

Waffen-Grenadier Regiment der SS 82 *Vendetta*

Waffen-Artillerie Regiment der SS 29

30th Waffen-Grenadier Division der SS (weissruthenische Nr 1)

Waffen-Grenadier Regiment der SS 75

Waffen-Grenadier Regiment der SS 76

Waffen-Grenadier Regiment der SS 77

Waffen-Artillerie Regiment der SS 30

31st SS Freiwilligen Grenadier Division *Böhmen-Mähren*

SS-Freiwilligen Grenadier Regiment 78

SS-Freiwilligen Grenadier Regiment 79

SS-Freiwilligen Grenadier Regiment 80

SS-Artillerie Regiment 31

29th Waffen-Grenadier Division der SS (italienische Nr 1)

Collar Tab			**Divisional Creast**	
Sleeve Insignia				
Cuffband	*Italien*			

An Italian SS unit was first proposed in September 1943 after the creation of the Italian Social Republic puppet state. Italian SS recruits were originally considered unorganized foreign volunteers and were grouped together at a recruit training camp in Münsingen, Germany. The Italian SS recruits were then formed into the "SS-Ausbildungsstab Italien" and issued unique collar insignia displaying the Italian Fasces crest[xliii] as well as an Italian SS cuffband.

By the end of 1943, the Italian SS was deemed combat ready and was deployed for anti-partisan duties in northern Italy. Shortly afterwards, the unit was renamed as the Italienische SS-Freiwilligen-Legion. In April 1944, the Italian SS had been renamed again as "1. Sturmbrigade Italienische Freiwilligen-Legion". The Italian SS brigade was thereafter deployed against American forces landing at Anzio, performing well in combat.

Right: An Italian SS officer in November 1944, wearing an Italian Army helmet along with red backed SS insignia.
(Federal German Archives)

The Italian SS next began a slow retreat northward as Allied forces advanced up the Italian peninsula towards Rome. In the September 1944, due to the division's exceptional performance in battle, Heinrich Himmler ordered that Italian SS members would be permitted to wear the standard SS Sig Runes on a red background. The Italian SS was then designated as a full division of the Waffen-SS and received designation as the 29th Waffen Grenadier Division. By October 1944, the division contained two Italian regiments (Waffen-Grenadier-Regiments 81 & 82) with the honor title "Vendetta" bestowed upon the 82nd regiment, although no cuff insignia was apparently authorized. In 1945, the 29th division was downgraded to a brigade, thereafter known as the Waffen-Grenadier-Brigade der SS (italienische Nr. 1). In May 1945, the unit surrendered to American forces along the Italian-Austrian border.

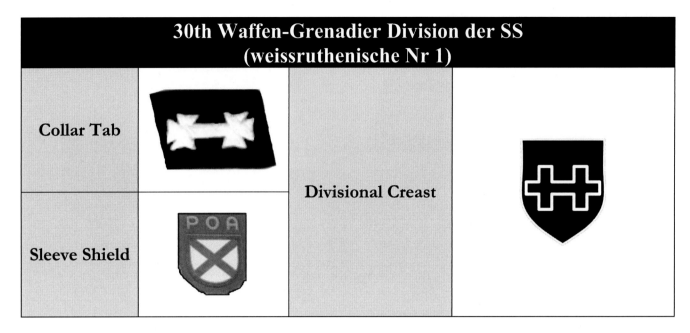

Collar Tab		**Divisional Creast**
Sleeve Shield		

The origins of the 30th Waffen Division may be traced to a Russian auxiliary police unit formed by German authorities in the summer of 1944. Known as the "Schutzmannschaft-Brigade Siegling", this unit was comprised of Belorussian collaborationist security forces, originally created by the German authorities in 1942 to provide security in western Russia.

Originally consisting of four under strength rifle regiments and an artillery battery, the Siegling Brigade was under the command of SS-Obersturmbannführer Hans Siegling, who had served extensively commanding auxiliary police forces since 1941. In August 1944, Siegling's command was declared a combat ready division as the 30th Waffen-Grenadier Division of the SS, although in terms of manpower the unit had barely enough personnel to man a full brigade.

The 30th division was next deployed to eastern France, in the vicinity of Mulhouse, where it was reorganized into three understrength infantry regiments as well as an artillery battery. The division also held a motorcycle reconnaissance unit, a reserve & replacement company, as well as supply, communications, and medical units.

In November 1944, the 30th division was assigned to fight French resistance fighters near Belfort. Combat performance was poor, and the division began to suffer from desertion, in particular from its ethnic Polish members. In October 1944 two battalions mutinied, murdering their German officers, and defected to Allied forces. Thereafter, the division was deemed unreliable by the German military and was assigned to fortification constructions in rear areas of combat zones.

In December 1944, the 30th division was transferred to a German training facility in Grafenwöhr. In January 1945 orders for disbandment were issued; the process was not completed until April, when the last remaining division members were transferred to the 25th and 38th SS divisions.

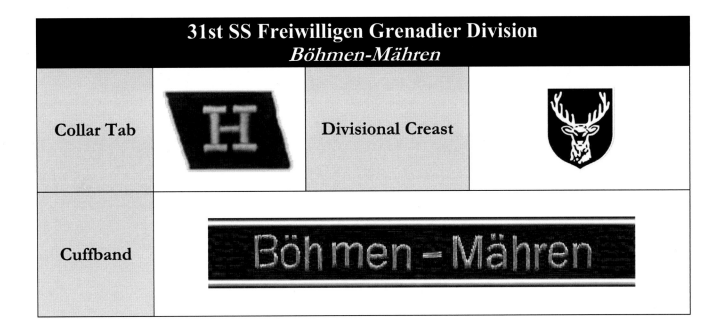

Collar Tab		**Divisional Creast**	
Cuffband			

31st SS Freiwilligen Grenadier Division
Böhmen-Mähren

The 31st SS division existed for less than a year and was recruited from ethnic Germans and Hungarians living in the Serbian border region of Bačka. The unit was first established in September 1944 as the "Battalion Batschka", later expanded into a regiment with two infantry battalions and an artillery company.

In November 1944 the unit was upgraded to a division in name only, with three under strength regiments and an artillery unit. The division was then deployed against Soviet forces who were advancing into Hungary from the east. Supporting divisional units included a signals battalion, supply troop, engineering unit, assault gun company, medical battalion, and a veterinary company. The division also briefly maintained a fusilier battalion, known as the SS Füsilier Battalion 31; however, this unit was almost immediately destroyed when pitted against attacking Red Army forces. It was thereafter replaced with a mixed Hungarian-German unit known as the Hungarian SS Grenadier Battalion "Szálasi".

For most of its existence, the 31st divisional commander was Gustav Lombard, a veteran of the 8th SS Cavalry Division. Lombard commanded the division from October 1944 to April 1945 and was awarded the Knight's Cross for bravery while fighting Red Army forces.

Right: Gustav Lombard in 1944, shortly after receipt of the Knight's Cross (Federal German Archives)

In January 1945, after suffering heavy losses in Hungary, the 31st division retreated into Austria and next was deployed to Silesia where it fought against Soviet forces in that area. In the spring of 1945 the division had retreated to Czechoslovakia where it surrendered to the Red Army at Hradec Králové in May 1945.

32nd SS Freiwilligen Grenadier Division
30 Januar

SS-Freiwilligen Panzergrenadier Regiment 86
Schill

SS-Freiwilligen Panzergrenadier Regiment 87
Kurmark

SS-Freiwilligen Artillerie Regiment 32

33rd Waffen-Grenadier Division der SS (französische Nr. 1)
Charlemagne

Waffen-Grenadier Regiment der SS 57
(*französisches Nr. 1*)

Waffen-Grenadier Regiment der SS 58
(*französisches Nr. 2*)

34th Waffen-Grenadier Division der SS
Landstorm Nederland

SS-Freiwilligen Panzergrenadier Regiment 83
(3rd Dutch)

SS-Freiwilligen Panzergrenadier Regiment 84
(4th Dutch)

SS-Artillerie Regiment 60

32nd SS Freiwilligen Grenadier Division
30 Januar

Collar Tab		**Divisional Creast**	
Cuffband			

The 32nd SS division was formed in January 1945 after Heinrich Himmler ordered a new division created, consolidated from under strength units or otherwise disbanded combat formations. The 32nd SS division further enrolled enlisted SS students from leadership and technical schools, and the division also made extensive use of the Waffen-SS reserves.

Formation of the division was tasked to SS-Standartenführer Johannes Mühlenkamp, a veteran SS officer since the 1930s with service in the SS-Verfügungstruppe, who had also commanded the SS Wiking Division. The 32nd division was to be considered a pure German unit and was granted the honor title "30 Januar", denoting Adolf Hitler's assumption to power on January 30th 1933.

The 32nd SS division was declared combat ready after only one month of training; the divisional command was then transferred to Knight's Cross recipient Joachim Richter. The division was then deployed along the Oder River and attached to the Fifth SS Mountain Corps. A month later, SS-Oberführer Adolf Ax was assigned as the division's third commander.

Right: Joachim Ritter, shown here in 1944, served as the 32nd SS division commander during its initial deployment in February 1945 (Federal German Archives)

At its greatest strength, the division held two grenadier regiments which were both issued honor titles ("Schill" and "Kurmark") although no cuffbands were ever manufactured. The division also incorporated an artillery regiment as well as engineer, pioneer, anti-aircraft, intelligence, and medical battalions.

In March 1945, the 32nd SS division was sent to Berlin, with leadership transferred to the division's final commander SS-Standartenführer Hans Kempin. Forming part of the Berlin Defense Area, the division fought against the onslaught of the Red Army and was completely destroyed at the Battle of Halbe, just outside of Berlin, in April 1945. Fearing summary execution by the Soviets, survivors of the division fled west to surrender to American forces at Tangermünde.

33rd Waffen-Grenadier Division der SS (französische Nr. 1)
Charlemagne

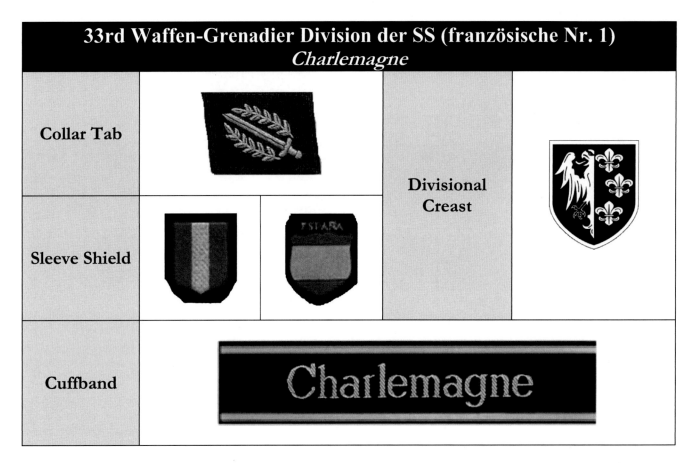

Collar Tab		
Sleeve Shield		**Divisional Creast**
Cuffband	Charlemagne	

The 33rd Waffen Division was originally proposed as a Hungarian unit, and was to be known by the designation "ungarische Nr 3". The first regiment was ordered for formation in December 1944, but the formation of this new division was quickly cancelled, and recruits absorbed into the 26th Waffen Division (2nd Hungarian).

The 33rd divisional numerical designation was then re-issued to a French unit, known as the 638th Infantry Regiment, which had served in the German Army since 1941. The French volunteer regiment had originally been known as the "Legion of French Volunteers against Bolshevism"; the unit was then designated as the 638th Infantry Regiment upon absorption into the German Army.

In 1943, the Waffen-SS formed a new unit from Vichy French volunteers, which was known as the Volunteer SS-Sturmbrigade France. This Sturmbrigade originally served as an anti-partisan unit in Russia before being deployed in combat and renamed as the Französische Brigade der SS. In late 1944, after suffering high casualties, the brigade was pulled from the front line and merged with the 638th Infantry Regiment, as the only other significant French unit in the German military.

The result was the creation of a new SS division of French volunteers, which also incorporated members of the German Navy, the National Socialist Motor Corps, as well members of the Vichy French Police, known as the Milice. In January 1945, this new French unit was declared as the Waffen-Grenadier-Brigade der SS "Charlemagne" (französische Nr.1). The next month the brigade was upgraded to a division and granted the numerical designation as the 33rd Waffen Division.

In the spring of 1945, the 33rd division was reduced to a single battalion after suffering heavy casualties fighting in Poland. Now known as the "Sturm Battalion Charlemagne", the unit was deployed to Berlin to defend the center of the city from Soviet attack. The battalion was involved in brutal house to house fighting and was one of the last German units in the city to surrender to Soviet forces on May 2nd.

34th Waffen-Grenadier Division der SS
Landstorm Nederland

Collar Tab		**Divisional Creast**
Sleeve Shield		
Cuffband	**Landstorm Nederland**	

The 34th Waffen Division was a sister unit to the 23rd volunteer division "Nederland", with both divisions recruiting Dutch SS volunteers from the Netherlands. The origins of the 34th division began in 1940, when a Dutch paramilitary police force was established by German authorities as the "Landwacht Niederlande". This organization primarily assisted in the enforcement of Nazi law, including Jewish arrests and round-ups for deportations.

In 1943, the Landwacht Niederlande was upgraded to a combat unit and declared as "SS-Grenadier Regiment 1", while also retaining its original name as an honor title. In October 1943, this title was changed to "Landstorm Nederland" and by this time the unit held a strength of 2,400 soldiers. The unit thereafter spent several months in training near the city of Hoogeveen.

Upon the Allied invasion of France, the Landstorm regiment was deployed to the Netherlands border, where it was subsequently attacked in September 1944 when British forces launched Operation Market Garden. The regiment fought near the town of Elst before withdrawing from the battle line on September 25th. In November 1943, after a brief period of rest and refit, the unit was upgraded to a brigade and renamed as the SS Volunteer Grenadier Brigade Landstorm Nederland. The unit was then deployed along the Waal River and was formally upgraded to a division in February 1945.

In the spring of 1945, the 34th division would fight advancing British forces at Zetten, before retreating to the town of Oosterbeek where it formally surrendered on May 5th. Some divisional members, knowing that they would be seen in the Netherlands as collaborators, fought on against Dutch resistance fighters in the city of Veenendaal. The last of the Landstorm Netherland surrendered to local authorities on May 9, 1945.

35th SS Polizei Grenadier Division

- SS und Polizei Grenadier Regiment 89
- SS und Polizei Grenadier Regiment 90
- SS und Polizei Grenadier Regiment 91
- SS und Polizei Artillerie Regiment 35

36th Waffen-Grenadier Division der SS
Dirlewanger

- Waffen-Grenadier Regiment der SS 72
- Waffen-Grenadier Regiment der SS 73

37th SS Freiwillingen-Kavallerie Division
Lützow

- SS Kavallerie Regiment 92
- SS Kavallerie Regiment 93
- SS Kavallerie Regiment 94
- SS-Artillerie Regiment 37

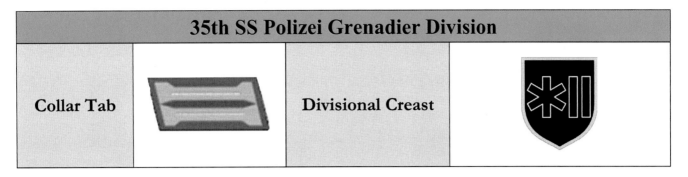

35th SS Polizei Grenadier Division			
Collar Tab		**Divisional Creast**	

The 35th SS-Police Division was formed in February of 1945 and was the second of only two Waffen-SS police formations (the other being the 4th Division Polizei). The 35th division was formed from various armed police formations, including what remained of the SS-Police regiments which had retreated from Russia in 1944.

The first commander of the division was Johannes Wirth, a Police Colonel in the Ordnungspolizei, as well as an SS-Oberführer in the Waffen-SS. The 35th division was initially organized into three under strength grenadier regiments.

The division further maintained an "SS and Police Artillery Regiment" (the only such combined SS-police battery ever established in the Waffen-SS) and also included various "Polizei Abteilung" commands, which were under strength battalions comprised of Panzerjäger, fusilier, pioneer, signals, and supply detachments.

Right: A solider of the 35th SS division. Note the Waffen-SS sleeve eagle on the left sleeve, which was worn in place of the Ordnungspolizei crest for police personnel serving in the Waffen-SS (Federal German Archives)

The 35th SS division was declared combat ready in March of 1945 and deployed north of Berlin to combat the Soviet encirclement of the city. The 35th SS division then became part of the German Ninth Army and engaged in heavy fighting in April of 1945. The most significant engagement was at the Battle of Seelow Heights, where the division suffered significant casualties attempting to stop the Soviet Red Army from advancing west towards Berlin.

During the Battle of Berlin, the second and last commander of the division, SS-Standartenführer and Police Colonel Ruediger Pipkorn, was killed in action on April 25th. The remnants of the 35th SS division were then incorporated into the 21st Panzer Division, with the 35th division thereafter ceasing to exist.

36th Waffen-Grenadier Division der SS
Dirlewanger

Collar Tab		**Divisional Creast**	

One of the most notorious Waffen-SS units ever created was the 36th Waffen Grenadier SS Division, a command which was known for rape, torture, murder and numerous other atrocities. This infamous unit began its existence in June 1940 as a paramilitary group called the "Wilddiebkommando Oranienburg". Originally classified as an "anti-poaching unit", its founder and only commander was Oskar Dirlewanger, who had joined the SS in 1938. Dirlewanger was a mercenary with service in World War I, the Freikorps, and the Spanish Civil War. He was also known as a fanatic and alcoholic.

By September 1940, Dirlewanger had recruited three hundred men (mostly from prisons and penal battalions) into his unit which was then renamed as the "Sonderkommando Dirlewanger". The unit was next placed under the command of the SS Concentration Camp service and was then again renamed as the "SS-Sonderbataillon Dirlewanger". Between 1940 and 1942, the unit served as a guard battalion near Lublin, Poland; during this time, Dirlewanger's men also raided homes and farms in the Polish countryside, with pillage, arson, and murder commonplace. The savagery of Dirlewanger's unit was so severe that complaints were filed by the Nazi authorities themselves, who petitioned Himmler to have the unit transferred to combat duty.

In February 1942, Dirlewanger's battalion was attached to the command of Erich von dem Bach-Zelewski, who was the SS and Police Leader in western Russia and also in charge of all anti-partisan actions in the occupied east[xliv]. Zelewski would later go on to crush the Warsaw City Uprising in 1944. He escaped any serious prosecution after the war, spent just over ten years in prison, and died in 1972.

**Oskar Dirlewanger in 1944
(Polish State Archives)**

In August 1942, Dirlewanger's command began to recruit local volunteers from Poland and Russia, as well as hardened German criminals who were offered a pardon to serve in the SS. Now at regimental strength, Dirlewanger's unit was renamed the "SS-Sonderregiment Dirlewanger" and classified as a combat formation of the Waffen-SS. Between November 1942 and December 1943, the unit was attached to Army Group Center and fought in combat against Soviet forces. Dirlewanger's unit suffered heavy losses, due to combat inexperience and general lack of discipline, and it was withdrawn from the front lines after taking 75% losses in a single engagement.

In 1944, the Dirlewanger unit returned to Poland where it was reformed with fresh recruits from the ranks of criminals, military delinquents, and anti-Communist volunteers. The command was then redesignated as an anti-partisan unit and spent the next several months conducting rape, murder, torture, and the indiscriminate massacre of civilians. In August of 1944, the command assisted with the suppression of the Warsaw Ghetto Uprising and in October 1944 was expanded to a brigade and renamed as the SS-Sonderbrigade Dirlewanger.

In December 1944, Dirlewanger's command was reorganized yet again as the "SS-Sturmbrigade Dirlewanger" and upgraded with two attached regiments (known simply as SS-Regiment 1 & SS-Regiment 2). Shortly thereafter, the unit was deployed to Czechoslovakia to assist in the suppression of a Slovakian uprising.

EVOLUTION OF THE DIRLEWANGER COMBAT FORMATIONS

Formation	Designation
June 1940	Wilddiebkommando Oranienburg
September 1940	SS-Sonderkommando Dirlewanger
December 1940	SS-Sonderbataillon Dirlewanger
August 1942	SS-Sonderregiment Dirlewanger
June 1944	Kampfgruppe Dirlewanger
August 1944	SS-Sonderbrigade Dirlewanger
December 1944	SS-Sturmbrigade Dirlewanger
February 1945	36th Waffen-Grenadier Division der SS "Dirlewanger"

Above (Left): Erich von dem Bach-Zelewski, the superior officer to Oskar Dirlewanger from 1942 to 1943. During this time, Dirlewanger's unit was assigned to Zelewski's "SS-Bandenkämpfverbände" (Bandit Combat Command) and committed some of its worsts acts of atrocities. Above (Right): One of the only known photographs showing the unique collar insignia used by Dirlewanger's SS troops (Images courtesy Polish State Archives)

In December 1944, Dirlewanger and his unit were deployed to Hungary to combat advancing Soviet forces, but quickly retreated into Slovakia after suffering heavy losses. The unit was next deployed north of the Oder River and in February 1945 formally expanded to a division.

Now known as the 36th Waffen-Grenadier Division, by the end of 1944 Dirlewanger's command held a strength of 4,000 men organized into two infantry regiments, a small tank unit, a fusilier and artillery battalion, as well as three regiments assigned from the German Army (the 1244th Volks Grenadier Regiment, 687th pioneer battalion and the 681st anti-tank detachment).

In April of 1945, the division was destroyed by the Soviet Army, after which Dirlewanger fled his command while munity and desertion ran rampant. By the end of April, the surviving division members retreated west towards American lines and surrendered to Allied forces on May 3rd. Dirlewanger would be captured a month later and died in his jail cell, reportedly of natural causes, although present day theories suggest he was beaten to death by Polish guards.

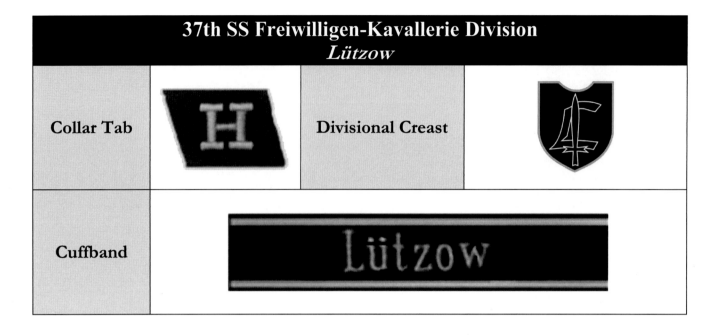

37th SS Freiwilligen-Kavallerie Division *Lützow*			
Collar Tab	H	**Divisional Creast**	
Cuffband	Lützow		

The 37th SS division was the last divisional cavalry unit fielded by the SS during the Second World War. The order to form the division was issued in February 1945, with cadre selected from the existing 8th and 22nd SS cavalry divisions.

The new division's rank and file consisted mainly of Hungarian volunteers, although the command was designated as a regular SS formation and not as a foreign volunteer unit. Even so, recruits wore the standard "H" insignia used by Hungarian SS personnel, instead of the standard SS runes. Waldemar Fegelein, the younger brother of SS career cavalry officer Hermann Fegelein, supervised the formation of the division which was declared combat ready in April 1945.

Right: Waldemar Fegelein, seen as an SS-Obersturmbannführer early in the Second World War. He would later serve as an SS-Oberführer and as the 37th Cavalry division commander, before being replaced by the more experienced Karl Gesele. (National Archives)

In addition to the three primary cavalry regiments, the division was allocated an artillery unit as well as a Panzerjäger anti-tank battalion. Only two of the cavalry regiments were ever fully formed, each with two battalions a piece. The division further maintained a small headquarters staff, as well as understrength engineering, medical, and communications battalions. The division also possessed its own indoctrination and basic training unit, known as "SS-Feldersatz-Bataillon 37".

In mid-April 1945, the 37th division was deployed to halt the Soviet invasion of Czechoslovakia and Austria. In May 1945, after retreating westward in the face of the Red Army advance, the division surrendered to American forces in central Austria.

38th SS Grenadier Division
Nibelungen

Collar Tab		**Divisional Creast**	
Cuffband	Nibelungen		

Subordinate Units

SS-Panzergrenadier Regiment 95	SS-Panzergrenadier Regiment 96	SS-Artillerie Regiment 38

The 38th SS division was the final combat division formed by the Waffen-SS during the Second World War. The unit was created in March 1945 by transferring SS personnel of the Bad Tölz SS officer candidate school into a new combat formation. The unit was organized by SS-Obersturmbannführer Richard Schulze[xlv] and was originally known as the SS-Division Junkerschule. In addition to the students and staff of Bad Tölz, the division also recruited from Himmler's SS-Begleitkommando, as well as border guards and various troops from the 6th, 7th, and 30th SS divisions. The division also contained a battalion of Hitler Youth as well as a small number of French volunteers.

Right: Richard Schultze (in later life known as Richard Schultze-Kossens), commander of the Bad Tölz SS officer candidate school, who served as the commander of the 38th SS division during its initial organization. He was later replaced by the more experienced Martin Stange, who had served as an artillery regimental commander in the 3rd SS division Totenkopf. (Image courtesy National Archives)

In April 1945, the division was granted its numerical designation as the 38th SS division, and further issued the honor title "Nibelungen", in reference to Richard Wagner's opera "Der Ring des Nibelungen"[xlvi]. Command of the division was the assigned to SS-Standartenführer Martin Stange.

The division was then deployed against American forces at the Danube River and retreated to Landshut, Germany after engaging the American 20th Armored Division. In late April 1945, the 38th SS division withdrew to Chiemsee in Bavaria. The division's final combat engagement was on May 4th 1945. Thereafter, the division formally surrendered to American forces on May 8, 1945.

SS war correspondents

To document the combat exploits of the Waffen-SS, each division was assigned a number of war correspondents who would travel with the division to the front lines, creating film and photography of the SS in battle. The very first SS war correspondent unit was created in January 1940, when a single military company was formed to act as an SS news agency and was known as the SS-Kriegsberichter-Kompanie.

The first mission of this new SS correspondence unit was to report on the pending invasion of France. The unit was led by SS-Captain Günther d'Alquen and recruited from staff writers of the SS weekly periodical newspaper "Das Schwarze Korps" (the Black Corps – first published in 1935).

Right: Günther d'Alquen, seen here as an SS-Standartenführer during the later years of the Second World War, was the first commander of the SS war correspondents. (Federal German Archives)

Technically, the war correspondence company was under the authority of the SS-Main Office but operated independently with significant editorial assistance from Reinhard Heydrich's secret police forces.

The early SS war correspondence company was divided into two platoons, the personnel of which were then cross assigned to one of the four main armed SS divisions. Following the invasion of the Soviet Union, the unit was renamed as the SS-Kriegsberichter-Abteilung (War Reporting Detachment) and expanded to three hundred personnel. By December 1943 the SS war correspondents numbered over one thousand and were recruited primarily from an SS journalism school in Berlin. By 1944, the SS correspondence section was renamed as the "SS-Standarte Kurt Eggers", in honor of a Schwarze Korps editor killed near Kharkov on August 13th 1943.

(Jan 1940 – Jul 1941)

(Sep 1941 – Nov 1943)

(Dec 1943 – May 1945)

The three cuffbands used by the SS War Correspondence Section.
For collar insignia, correspondence members wore the standard SS runes of the Waffen-SS

SS war correspondents were trained in front line combat film and photography, with many SS reporters risking their lives to provide close combat coverage of Waffen-SS engagements. Of interest is that there are no known SS correspondence records of war crimes and atrocities, with the few films of Einsatzgruppen actions recorded by the German Army. While films of Jewish ghettos were created by the German Propaganda Ministry, these reels were produced in a deceptive manner so as to portray Jews and other minorities as well treated. The SS strictly forbade the filming and photography of Concentration and Death Camp operations, although a handful of privately created photographs were produced and survive to the present day.

SS WAR CORRESPONDENCE REGIMENT "KURT EGGERS"

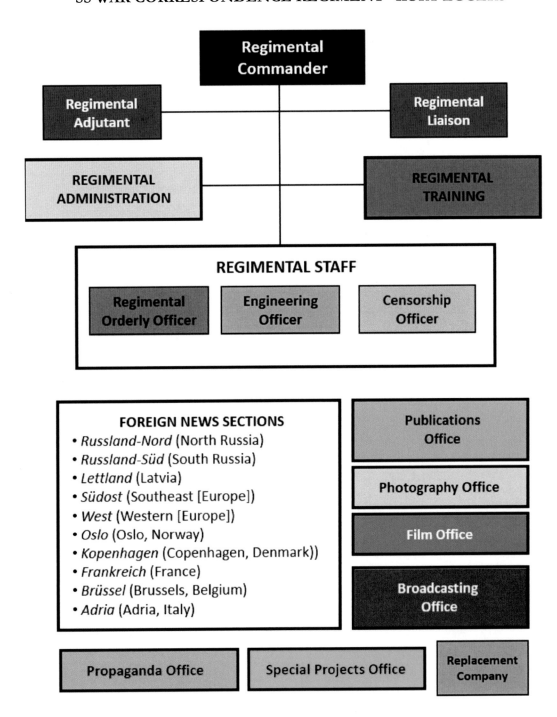

The SS foreign news offices were divided into several "Abschnitt", which covered major war theaters, and "Kommando" which were assigned to cities and countries where no active combat was occurring. The SS propaganda office maintained two "Propaganda Platoons" which were known as "SS-Kampfpropaganda Zug". The SS film office operated without sub-sections.

SS WAR CORRESPONDENCE SUB-OFFICES

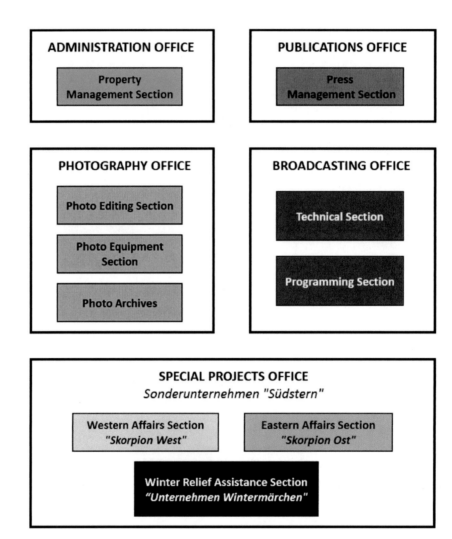

ADMINISTRATION OFFICE
- Property Management Section

PUBLICATIONS OFFICE
- Press Management Section

PHOTOGRAPHY OFFICE
- Photo Editing Section
- Photo Equipment Section
- Photo Archives

BROADCASTING OFFICE
- Technical Section
- Programming Section

SPECIAL PROJECTS OFFICE
Sonderunternehmen "Südstern"
- Western Affairs Section *"Skorpion West"*
- Eastern Affairs Section *"Skorpion Ost"*
- Winter Relief Assistance Section *"Unternehmen Wintermärchen"*

Waffen-SS weapons and equipment

The weapons and equipment of the Waffen-SS were, at least initially, above par to the common German soldier. Soldiers of the Waffen-SS were also trained in group tactics as well as individual assault, with a strong emphasis on combined arms. The Waffen-SS also was equipped primarily as a motorized force, with many of Germany's latest tanks and other heavy armaments issued to the Waffen-SS.

Left: A soldier of the Waffen-SS in Russia, taken in early 1943. Front line SS soldiers were initially issued some of the best weapons and equipment available. (Federal German Archives)

RIFLE WEAPONRY OF THE WAFFEN-SS

WEAPON		SERVICE YEARS	CARTRIDGE TYPE	ACTION TYPE
Karabiner 98k		1935-1945	7.92x57mm	Bolt Action
Gewehr 43			8x57mm	Gas Operated
Sturmgewehr 44		1943-1945	7.92x33mm	Gas Operated
Fallschirm-jägergewehr 42			7.92x57mm	Recoil Operated
Maschinen-gewehr 34		1934-1945	7.92x57mm	Recoil Operated
Maschinen-gewehr 42		1942-1945		Recoil Operated
Maschinen-pistole 34		1929-1940	9x25mm	Bolt Action
Maschinen-pistole 40		1940-1945	9x19mm	Bolt Action

Images graphical recreations based on original photographs courtesy Imperial War Museum

In addition to rifle weapons, there were two standard handguns which were widely used as sidearms by the SS. The Luger Parabellum 1908 was a standard field sidearm, firing a 7.65x21mm round under short recoil. The Walthar P38, firing a 9x19mm round, was the sidearm of choice for most SS officers and members of the security forces.

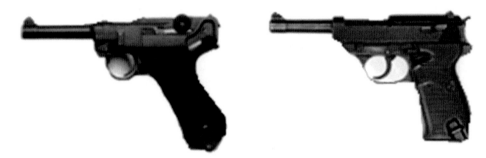

A comparison between the Luger handgun and the Walthar P38 (Graphical recreations)

The standard hand grenade for use by the Waffen-SS solider was the Stielhandgranate 24. At 21 ounces in weight, this grenade was thrown using a wooden attached stick and pulling a porcelain pull cord. The grenade had a blast power of 5 ounces TNT. A similar grenade was the Einhandgranate 39, modeled more after western designs, and thrown freely after activating an ignitor switch. The standard Waffen-SS rocket propelled grenade was the Raketenwerfer, firing an 88-millimeter shell casing at a distance of up to seven hundred and fifty yards.

Left: A comparison between the stick thrown Stielhandgranate and the freely thrown Einhandgranate
Below: The Raketenwerfet rocket propelled grenade, first issued in 1943

The standard mortars of the Waffen-SS were the Granatenwerfer 34 and 42. The pre-war Granatenwerfer 34 fired an eighty-millimeter shell casing at a range of 2,400 meters. The Granatenwerfer 42, which saw widespread issuance in 1943, greatly expanded this range to over six thousand meters and fired a more powerful one-hundred-and-twenty-millimeter shell.

Right: The Granatenwerfer 34, used both before and during the Second World War, was the standard mortar of the German armed forces

In the larger caliber range of field artillery, the Waffen-SS made use of the same artillery inventory as the regular German Army, with weapons ranging from small field guns to heavy howitzers. The most commonly employed artillery pieces were those within the 7.5 to 17 centimeter caliber range. By 1943, the standard artillery piece for most Waffen-SS artillery regiments was the 15 cm sFH (schweres-Feld-Haubitze) artillery battery.

Right: The 15 cm sFH artillery piece (Federal German Archives)

Waffen-SS artillery regiments contained four battalions totaling eight to ten batteries, each possessing between two to three artillery pieces each. The artillery regiment also maintained a forward observation company as well as a transport element.

SS tanks and vehicles

The Waffen-SS made use of the same tanks as the German Army, although SS tank crew training was considered far more aggressive, with emphasis on individual tank warfare and tactics rather than group blitzkrieg attacks. There were seven classes of tanks used by the Waffen-SS during the Second World War. The Panzer I & II series were used for training and also during the invasions of Poland and France. This class of tank was also used periodically on the Eastern Front as a light tank reserve, or for the purposes of reconnaissance.

The Panzer III and IV tanks were the most common tanks manufactured during the Second World War. This class of tank was used as a frontal assault weapon during the invasion of France and also as the mainstay tank during the battles of Kursk and Kharkov in 1943. The tank also saw extensive service in the German Army during the North African campaign, although the Waffen-SS was not active in that theater.

The Panthar and Tiger tanks were used as the heavy tanks of the Waffen-SS, and were also the first to be deployed along the Eastern Front in 1943, after prototype testing in Germany. These tanks also saw limited deployment to North Africa. The German heavy tank classes comprised the vanguard of several Eastern Front battles and were also present in France during the landings at Normandy and during the Battle of the Bulge. The Panthar tank was more numerously produced than the Tiger series, due to the latter's weight and more complex mechanics.

Left: A Waffen-SS tank crew in 1943 pauses for the camera in front of a Panzer IV tank in Russia (Federal German Archives)

Tank Destroyers were heavy anti-tank platforms, built on the chassis of a German tank, and were heavily employed by the Waffen-SS along the Eastern Front. The Jagdpanzer IV was the most commonly produced German tank destroyer of the Second World War with over five thousand manufactured. Considered the mainstay of the Waffen-SS anti-tank arsenal, the Jagdpanzer IV was built upon the chassis of the battle tested Panzer IV and made use of a 7.5-centimeter caliber gun which fired a seventy-millimeter tank shell.

The more advanced heavy classes of tank destroyers were prototyped in the last year of World War II and saw limited success along both the Eastern and Western front. Less than five hundred of the Jagdpanther were ever produced, while the heaviest tank destroyer class ever manufactured (the Jagdtiger) saw less than one hundred units deployed to the field.

TANKS OF THE WAFFEN-SS

TANK		SERVICE YEARS	CREW	ARMAMENT	ENGINE
Panzer I		1934 - 1945	2	7.92 mm MG-13 gun (2)	59 HP Krupp M 305 four-cylinder engine
Panzer II		1936 - 1945	3	2 cm cannon (KwK 30 L/55) w/7.92 mm MG-34 gun	138 HP 6-cyl petrol Maybach HL 62TRM
Panzer III		1939 - 1945	5	5 cm cannon (KwK 39 L/60) w/7.92 mm MG-34 gun (2-3)	296 HP 12-cylinder Maybach HL 120 TRM
Panzer IV				7.5 cm cannon (KwK 40) w/7.92 mm MG-34 gun (2)	
Panthar		1943 - 1945		7.5 cm cannon (KwK 42) w/7.92 mm MG-34 gun (2)	650 HP V-12 petrol Maybach HL230 P30
Tiger I		1942 - 1945		8.8 cm cannon (KwK 36 L/56) w/7.92 mm MG-34 gun (2)	690 HP V-12 petrol Maybach HL230
Tiger II		1944 - 1945		8.8 cm cannon (KwK 43 L/71) w/7.92 mm MG-34 gun (2)	

WAFFEN-SS TANK DESTROYERS

TANK DESTROYER		ARMOR CHASSIS	CREW	ARMAMENT	ENGINE
Panzerjäger I		Panzer I	3	47 mm cannon (P.U.V. vz. 36)	100 HP 6-cylinder Maybach (NL 38)
Jagdpanzer IV		Panzer IV	4	7.5 cm Pak 42 (L/70)	295 HP Maybach HL (120 TRM)
Jagdpanther		Panthar	5	8.8 cm Pak 43/3	690 HP Maybach V-12 petrol (HL230 P30)
Jagdtiger		Tiger II	6	12.8 cm PaK 44 L/55	

Images graphical recreations based on original photographs courtesy Imperial War Museum

Facing against the Waffen-SS tank arsenal were the enemy tank classes the Soviet made T-34, the British Churchill tank, and the American M4 Sherman. With the exception of the Churchill, which was more heavily armored than the German Tiger tank, German tanks generally outclassed their Allied counterparts. However, in the numbers of tanks deployed in battle (especially the T-34), combat superiority was firmly in the hands of the Allies and ultimately led to a German strategic defeat in the arms race of tank design and development.

In respect to anti-tank weaponry, the Waffen-SS made use of the same anti-tank guns as the German Army. Most anti-tank weapons were classified between the fifty and eight-eight-millimeter range. The most commonly employed anti-tank gun of the Waffen-SS was the 7.5 cm Pak 40. This gun fired a 75-millimeter shell and was an upgrade to the pre-war 5 cm Pak 38. The Pak 40 was upgraded in 1943 to the newer model 7.5 cm Pak 41.

Profile of the 7.5 cm Pak 40 (Imperial War Museum)

355

In addition to standard tank weaponry, the Waffen-SS also made use of armored cars. These vehicles were mainly used in reconnaissance roles and also for light armored attacks. Armored cars were also commonly deployed by the SS security services and were the vehicles of choice for the special action groups (Einsatzgruppen). The most commonly deployed armored car was the Sonderkraftfahrzeug, abbreviated as the "SdKfz" of which there were several classes. Heavier armored car classes included the Lastkraftwagen and Panzerspähwagen, of which there were the Gleisketten and Leichter classes respectively. The heaviest armored car was the Steyr and possessed the farthest range at 275 miles.

VEHICLE CLASS		SERVICE YEARS	CREW	ARMAMENT
SdKfz 7		1938 - 1945	12	Mounted Flak Gun
SdKfz 10			6	Mounted Anti-Tank Gun
SdKfz 251		1939 - 1945	12	7.92 mm MG-34 gun (2)
Gleisketten (SdKfz 4) Lastkraftwagen		1941 - 1945	4	7.92 mm MG-34 gun
Leichter Panzerspähwagen		1935 - 1945		7.92 mm MG-34 gun (2) w/20 mm cannon (KwK 30)
Steyr ADGZ		1942 - 1945	6	7.92 mm MG-34 gun (3) w/20 mm cannon (KwK 35)

Above: Armored car vehicles of the Waffen-SS (Graphical recreations based on original images courtesy Imperial War Museum)

In addition to armored cars, the Waffen-SS also utilized several of the same utility vehicles as the regular German military, with the SS troop trucks and staff cars drawn from the same military depots as the German Army. These same vehicles were also utilized by the SS Concentration Camp service, employed by the SS Einsatzgruppen, and further deployed by some General-SS headquarters and staff commands. This included the Mercedes-Benz 770, which was the standard command staff car for all senior SS leaders, including Heinrich Himmler.

VEHICLE		TYPE	MANUFACTUER
BMW R75		Motorcycle	Bayerische Motoren Werke (BMW)
Opel Blitz		3 ton truck	Adam Opel AG
Kübelwagen Type 82		4 door jeep	Volkswagen (VW)

Above: Utility vehicles of the Waffen-SS (Graphical recreations based on original images courtesy Imperial War Museum)

Late war insignia of the Waffen-SS

By 1943, the last insignia of the Waffen-SS had been issued, with little further changes until the end of the Second World War. During the latter half of the Second World War, the standard Waffen-SS uniform was the M43 tunic which was comprised of a heavier fabric than previous SS designs, which also displayed machine woven insignia.

Right: The M43 uniform design (Holocaust Memorial Museum)

The M43 uniform was olive colored, ranging from dark to light in shade, depending upon the quality of the fabric. By 1944, the M43 tunic was the standard uniform issued to all SS enlisted personnel. When the Concentration Camp service was absorbed into the Waffen-SS, most of the camps guards and staff were issued the M43 SS uniforms, although there were some veteran camp officers who chose to retain the light grey SS jackets used prior to 1943.

An area of uniform development which was heavily explored by the SS was that of camouflage clothing. In the 1930s the armed SS had experimented with camouflage uniform designs, with the first SS soldiers issued camouflage clothing in 1938. The SS further developed an entire range of camouflage rank insignia intended to be worn as subdued patches on the upper left sleeve of the camouflage uniform. Camouflage rank insignia was worn by SS commissioned and non-commissioned officers. Junior enlisted personnel wore no camouflage insignia.

Right: SS soldiers in full camouflage gear (Polish State Archives)

There were four primary camouflage patterns, each designed for the various terrain types in which the Waffen-SS engaged in battle. A desert camouflage uniform was never developed, since the Waffen-SS did not deploy to the North African theater during the course of World War II.

Below: SS camouflage insignia (Graphical recreations)

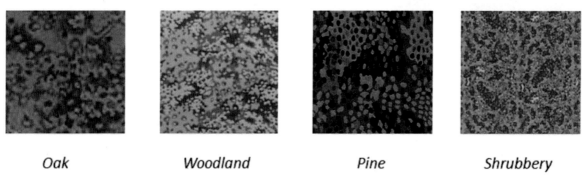

| Oak | Woodland | Pine | Shrubbery |

SS camouflage insignia was also used to denote rank on SS working uniforms, which consisted of a grey long sleeve shirt, work pants, and boots. This uniform was somewhat common within the Concentration Camp service but rare in the SS as a whole. SS winter uniforms had also developed by 1943 for use in the frozen wastes of Russia.

Alternate SS uniform items. Shown is the SS working uniform, battle goggles, and winter overcoat with fur SS cap
(Photos courtesy of Federal German Archives)

WAFFEN-SS CAMOUFLAGE INSIGNIA

RANK	CAMOUFLAGE INSIGNIA	RANK	CAMOUFLAGE INSIGNIA
SS-Unterscharführer		SS-Untersturmführer	
SS-Scharführer		SS-Obersturmführer	
SS-Oberscharführer		SS-Hauptsturmführer	
SS-Hauptscharführer		SS-Sturmbannführer	
		SS-Obersturmbannführer	
SS-Sturmscharführer		SS-Standartenführer	
		SS-Oberführer	

SS-Brigadeführer und Generalmajor der Waffen-SS	
SS-Gruppenführer und Generalleutnant der Waffen-SS	
SS-Obergruppenführer und General der Waffen-SS	
SS-Oberst-Gruppenführer und Generaloberst der Waffen-SS	

Throughout the Second World War, the Waffen-SS maintained a series of field post offices which served to liaison and coordinate with the German postal service in order to deliver mail and parcels to SS men at the front. Members of the SS postal service wore standard Waffen-SS insignia along with a postal service (Postschutz) cuffband.

SS postal service cuffband

To address disciplinary infractions committed by soldiers of the Waffen-SS, the SS maintained a courts martial system where SS men would be tried and sentenced depending upon the nature of their offense. Most Waffen-SS courts martial were conducted at the regimental level, with sentences ranging from extra duty, withholding of pay, or reduction in rank. More serious infractions were tried by division commanders and could result in imprisonment, dismissal from the SS, or death. The military justice system of the Waffen-SS was distinct and separate from the SS and Police Courts, maintained in Germany to deal with Allgemeine-SS men accused of violating SS code. In both cases, Himmler reserved the ultimate appeal rights, especially those involving capitol offenses.

To enforce discipline and assist with the carrying out of courts martial trials in the field, the Waffen-SS maintained a dedicated military police arm designated by a special uniform cuffband. The SS military police (SS-Feldgendarmerie) were organized into companies attached to Waffen-SS divisions. The SS military police also provided guards to the SS penal battalions of which two existed in Bohemia and Poland respectively.

SS military police cuffband

The last official insignia of the Waffen-SS ever created were badges designating a small number of technical qualifications. Several sleeve diamonds were created for wear by members of the SS Economics and Administration Main Office (WVHA) who were experts in agriculture, construction, and finance. An extremely rare sleeve diamond was also authorized for agriculture and race experts assigned to the Reich Commission for the Strengthening of German Nationhood (RKFDV).

SS Specialist sleeve diamonds for Finance, Construction, and Agriculture Experts.
The fourth badge denotes an SS Race and Agriculture Expert assigned to the RKFVD

A small number of SS insignia existed only on paper, or in the imagination of Allied military intelligence officers. Such was the case with a 1944 United States Army Intelligence report concerning officer insignia of the Waffen-SS. Referring to the rank of SS-Oberführer as "Senior Colonel", the Army speculated that such an insignia would consist of a double oak leaf collar patch accompanied by a three piped German Colonel's shoulder board (one more pip than the standard insignia for a regular German colonel). In reality, no such insignia existed since the Oberführer rank of the armed SS wore identical shoulder boards to the lower ranked SS-Standartenführer. (Right – source "Handbook on German military forces")

SENIOR COLONEL
Oberführer

Another insignia mentioned in SS uniform regulations, but which is unknown to have ever actually been issued, was the Führer Headquarters cuffband for SS staff personnel. Described as an SS version of the equivalent Army insignia, this cuffband was reportedly issued to SS personnel assigned directly to Adolf Hitler's personal military staff. An actual photograph of an SS officer wearing this cuffband has yet to be confirmed.

Führer Headquarters gothic scripted SS cuffband

In 1944, Adolf Hitler ordered the SS to begin procedures for promoting a Waffen-SS general to an SS rank equivalent of Field Marshal. In early conceptual designs, this rank was to be known as SS-Volksmarschall (People's Marshal) and denoted by field marshal shoulder boards along with special SS collar patches. The rank was never finalized, nor any officer approved for promotion to the position, although post war documentation has revealed that Sepp Dietrich may have been slated for the position.

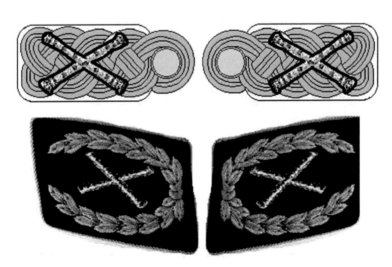

Conjectured insignia for SS-Volksmarschall, based on written descriptions of proposed insignia

CHAPTER SIX: THE SS DEATH'S HEAD UNITS

A branch of the SS most recognized for its oppression and terror were the SS Death's Head formations, responsible for the administration of the Nazi Concentration Camps. The SS Death's Head formations were originally formed as a single guard unit at Dachau Concentration Camp and eventually grew into a vast organization responsible for overseeing a network of concentration, labor, and extermination camps throughout occupied Europe. The Death's Head units also served as the basis for one of the more fanatical divisions of the Waffen-SS, the Totenkopf Division, which was known for ferocity in fighting and atrocities against both its enemies and civilians.

Establishing Concentration Camps

As a result of the February 1933 Reichstag Fire, Hitler's Nazi government passed the "Law for the Protection of People and State", which authorized arrests without warrant and arbitrary imprisonment of anyone considered a threat to the Nazi regime. By March of 1933, with the traditional German prisons filled to capacity, Hitler ordered the creation of extra-judicial detention centers to "concentrate" the enemies of the Reich. The concept of the "Konzentrationslager" (Concentration Camp) was established.

The first Nazi Concentration Camps were established in disused factories, abandoned farms, and the basements of city buildings. The Nazi storm troopers of the SA, who had been granted temporary police powers in the wake of the Reichstag Fire, were entrusted with running these early camps and were known for bullying and brutality, but not yet systematic cruelty. These early SA camps were also operated under poor administration and even worse leadership. Prisoner abuse was common, as was corruption and inefficiency from the SA camp commanders. With such a record, SS leaders began to petition Hitler for a transfer of the camp service to the authority of the SS. Hitler agreed and the first independently run SS concentration camp was then established outside of Munich, under Heinrich Himmler's authority as the Munich Police President.

Major Nazi Concentration Camps (1933)

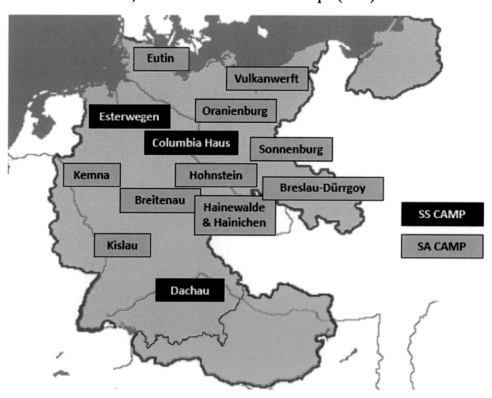

The SS concentration camp at Dachau was located near a small village and situated on the grounds of a former gunpowder factory. The camp was formally opened on March 22nd 1933. The first prisoners were transferred from nearby Stadelheim Prison, as well as Landsberg Fortress - ironically the same prison where Hitler had been imprisoned ten years earlier after his failed 1923 Nazi Putsch.

The first SS commander of the Dachau concentration camp was Hilmar Wäckerle, a veteran SS officer and also classmate of Heinrich Himmler's from their days together studying agriculture. Wäckerle's leadership of Dachau left much to be desired, and within just a few short weeks the camp was significantly corrupt and dilapidated. When the conditions at Dachau became public, local government officials demanded action from Nazi authorities. Himmler promptly dismissed Wäckerle from his post and began seeking a replacement.

SS guards at Dachau in the fall of 1933. At this point, guards were recruited from local SS units, were underpaid, and often went without adequate supplies, clothing, or weapons. (Bavarian State Archives)

The man which Himmler found to become the second commander of Dachau was Thedor Eicke. Eicke had been involved in Nazi activities since 1928 and had served in the SS since 1930. Eicke had also made many enemies in the SS and had briefly been detained in a mental asylum during the summer of 1933. Released and reinstated by Himmler, Eicke was ordered to reform Dachau and create a model prison camp for all other concentration camps to emulate.

Eicke's first task in reforming Dachau was to provide leadership and administration to what had previously been an unorganized ad hoc affair, with camp guards often unpaid and living in poverty. Guards at Dachau also lacked adequate supplies, weapons, and sometimes even proper clothing. Eicke, who was now promoted to SS-Oberführer, enacted his camp reforms by first organizing the Dachau camp guards and staff into the SS-Wachverbände. This small unit was not considered a separate branch of the SS, but was comprised of SS members recruited from the General-SS formations in and around Munich. Dachau was subordinated to the SS-Oberabschnitt (Senior District) South, which held little regard for Eicke's own authority.

Eicke promptly began petitioning to have his men declared independent, so that more funds could be made available in order to facilitate better supplies and conditions for Dachau personnel. A large number of the SS guards at Dachau were also known as "Versorgungsanwärter", a term which referred to older ex-military veterans entitled to disability and welfare benefits. A smaller number were the "dregs" of the SS, transferred into Eicke's Dachau because they were unwanted elsewhere. With incompetence and corruption rampant, Eicke began to purge many of the Dachau guards and instituted a new training program which stressed military discipline, obedience, and comradeship.

It was Eicke's philosophy towards the prisoners at Dachau which would eventually give the camp its well-deserved reputation of cruelty. Eicke developed a mindset which stated that prisoners were "sub-human", deserving no pity or remorse, and should be treated with utter contempt. Eicke did not advocate cruelty with no purpose, but rather systematic torment to degrade, demean, and ultimately destroy a man's spirit.

Eicke's goal of changing Dachau into a well-oiled machine of terror had succeeded by 1934, with the camp becoming one of the most feared institutions in Germany. Eicke next set his eyes on other concentration camps, with the camp at Esterwegen taken over by the SS in the summer of 1934. After the SS moved against the SA in the Night of the Long Knives, all SA concentration camps were ordered to be handed over to SS control.

By July 1934, all Concentration Camps in Germany were now under the authority of the SS. Thedor Eicke, who had been in charge of SA leader Ernst Röhm's execution, was promoted to the rank of SS-Gruppenführer and further appointed as "Inspekteur der Konzentrationslager und SS-Wachverbände" (Inspector of Concentration Camps and SS Watch Units). Eicke was allocated a small staff of SS personnel, with his new command technically subordinate to the SS Main Office. In practice, Eicke acted independently and reported directly to Himmler. By March of 1935, Eicke's office had taken over the administration of six major concentration camps. In an organizational oddity, which was not fully resolved until the outbreak of the Second World War, the guards assigned to the camps were drawn from the ranks of the General-SS, while actual staffs of the camps themselves were recruited and commanded separately.

DEVELOPMENT OF GERMAN CONCENTRATION CAMPS

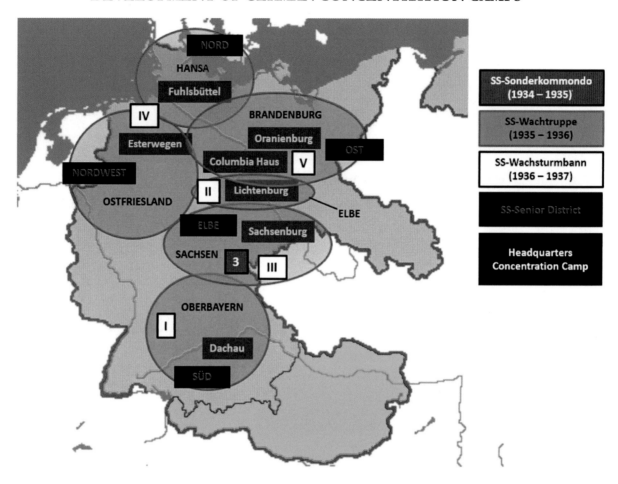

Concentration camp formations from 1935 to 1938. The "SS-Sonderkommondo" was an early unit of the SS-Verfügungstruppe, specifically recruited to guard the Sachsenburg Concentration Camp, and was not part of the regular concentration camp service

Under the original operational set-up of the Concentration Camps, Eicke and his tiny headquarters staff (numbering eleven officers and men in 1935) oversaw only the administration of the camps, while security was provided from the SS Watch Troops under the command of the regional SS leaders. Admittance and release from a Concentration Camp was also not a matter under Eicke's control, with this function reserved by the Gestapo. In April 1936, after nearly a year of petitions to Himmler, Eicke secured a major victory for his camp service when the guard troops were removed from the authority of local SS leaders and reformed into a new branch of the SS solely under Eicke's command. The new guard units, which collectively numbered over thirty-five hundred personnel, were declared as the SS-Totenkopfverbande (SS-TV) on April 1st 1936. The guard troops were organized into five guard battalions (Wachsturmbann), each headquartered at a major concentration camp.

Eicke's next task was to militarize the camp service and reform it along formal military lines. The guard battalions were divided into companies (known as "Centuries") and equipped with motorized military equipment. The camp service was nevertheless not an armed military force and its members were not exempt from conscription in the regular German military. Eicke encouraged his camp soldiers to serve their obligatory military duty in the Army, Navy, or Air Force, avoiding connections with the SS-Verfügungstruppe (the predecessor to the Waffen-SS), which was competing with the camp service for recruits.

CONCENTRATION CAMP COMMAND STRUCTURE
(1935)

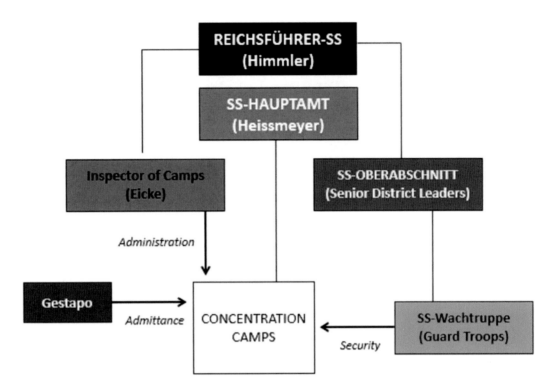

On July 1, 1937 the five guard battalions were collectively consolidated into three Death's Head Regiments (Totenkopfstandarten), responsible for guarding all Concentration Camps in Germany. A year later, after Austria was annexed into the German Reich, a fourth regiment was formed headquartered at the new Austrian Concentration Camp of Mauthausen. By 1939, a fifth camp guard regiment had been formed in East Prussia.

The camp guard troops were now designated as Nazi Party military formations but were still completely separate from the SS personnel who actually performed duties inside the Concentration Camps dealing with prisoner inmates. Such personnel of the "Camp Service Proper" were usually recruited for their harsh demeanor, violent backgrounds, and lack of any compassion, per Eicke's camp service philosophy. SS personnel serving within the camps were themselves organized in a paramilitary like manner, at the top of which was the Camp Commander (Kommandant) selected personally by Eicke and approved by Himmler for leadership at a given camp. By the spring of 1938, Thedor Eicke himself had adopted the title "Führer der SS-TV und Konzentrationslager", with the camp service now solidified into its final peacetime form.

In the fall of 1938, with the Totenkopfstandarten now at full strength, more defined regulations were promulgated concerning the military status of these Death's Head regiments. A supplementary reserve was established, comprised of SS men who were otherwise excused from general conscription, or had been unable to perform their draft service, and on August 17th 1938 a wartime mobilization plan was published for the Concentration Camp service.

While the personnel who served within the camps themselves were considered exempt from combat duty, the guard troops of the Totenkopfstandarten were to be mobilized to serve as reserves to the Army as well as to augment police forces. The task of guarding the concentration camps would then be taken over by reservists and older members of the General-SS (generally those above the age of 45). Ten thousand younger members of the General-SS would be drafted to become "Police Reserves" (Polizeiverstärkung) to maintain order and provide behind-the-lines security and garrison duty within Germany.

ORGANIZATION OF THE SS-TOTENKOPFVERBANDE
(1939)

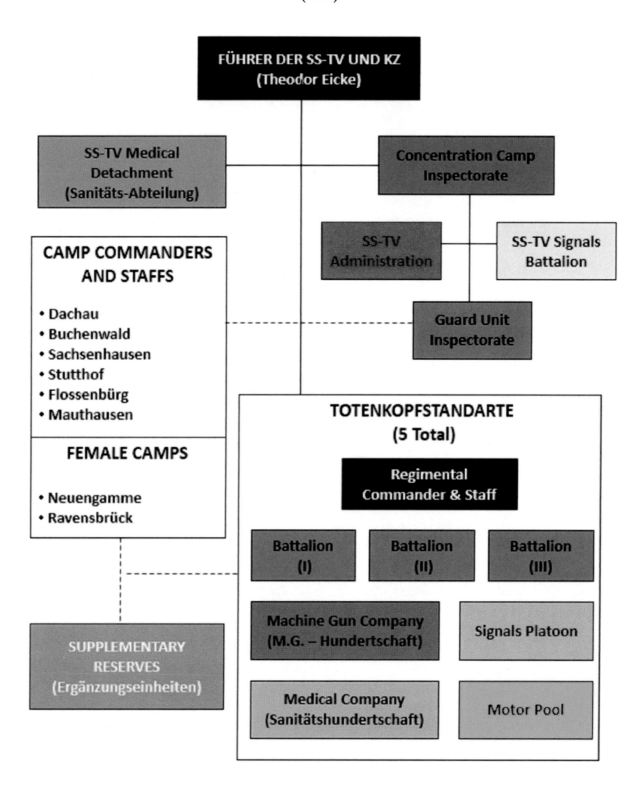

GERMAN CONCENTRATION CAMPS AND GUARD REGIMENTS
1939-1945

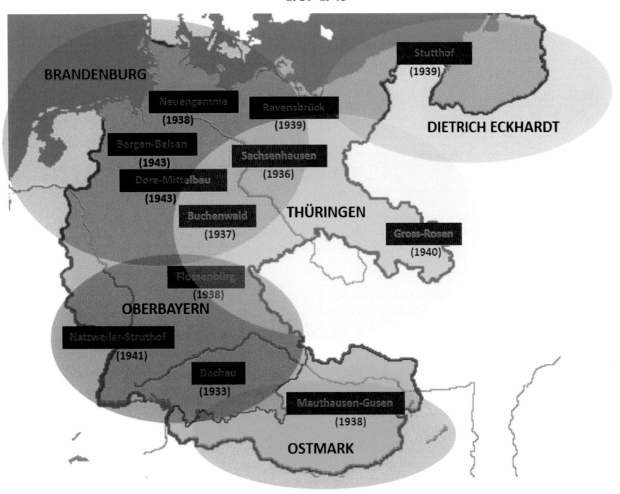

Above: All major camps in Germany were overseen by five guard regiments, which were separately formed and trained from the regular camps service. These regiment sized Totenkopfstandarte provided guard troops for all the Concentration Camps until 1940, when the camps were reorganized, and the guards incorporated directly into the camp staffs.

By the summer of 1939, designs on camp guards were that, in the event of war, the Totenkopfverbande would be mobilized as a reserve of the regular German Army. When Germany entered into war with Poland in September 1939, Eicke abandoned this original mobilization idea and announced plans to form his Concentration Camp service into a fully equipped military division. The result would change the organization of the camp service for the remainder of the Second World War.

Transforming for War

At the time of the Polish invasion, the Death's Head troops were not yet organized as fully equipped combat units. The only combat ready formation, known as the Heimwehr Danzig, was based in the city of Danzig and designated as a light infantry battalion. The Danzig formation comprised five hundred volunteers, formed into five rifle companies, an infantry unit, and two anti-tank formations. Led by Hans Friedemann Götze of the 4th SS-Totenkopfstandarte Ostmark, the Danzig unit was created in July 1939 as the "Wachsturmbann Eimann" and renamed as the "SS Sturmbann Goetze" the following month. Adopting its final name upon the outbreak of war, the Heimwehr Danzig assisted in securing the free city of Danzig from Polish forces and was disbanded on September 30th 1939.

In October 1939, the final stage of militarizing the Concentration Camp service was completed when Thedor Eicke formally founded the SS Death's Head Division. The Dachau Concentration Camp was cleared of all inmates and the camp turned into a military training facility. Recruits for the new division were drawn mainly from the Totenkopfverbände guard regiments, but also from the General-SS, the police, as well as a handful of cadre recruited from the SS-Verfügungstruppe. By February of 1940, the division was deemed battle ready and would shortly thereafter be deployed to France for the upcoming blitzkrieg attack.

Right: The commander of the Heimwehr Danzig, Hans Friedemann Götze (Polish State Archives)

To state that Eicke's new division was comprised entirely of Concentration Camp guards would be a misrepresentation, although a high percentage of the Totenkopf division was recruited from the camp guard regiments. More importantly was that Eicke's military division was now completely separate from the administration of the concentration camps, with Eicke himself having abandoned his passion and fervor for the camp service and instead would now be a division commander of the Waffen-SS. He was killed in 1943 while leading his forces on the Eastern Front.

The Totenkopfstandarte guard regiments, which Eicke had used as a recruiting ground for his military division, remained intact after 1940 but were now separated from their original role of providing guards to Concentration Camps. Camp guards were now to be incorporated directly into the Concentration Camp staffs, no longer as independent formations, but now referred to as "SS-Totenkopf–Wachsturmbanne". Each Wachsturmbanne held a compliment of approximately four hundred men, divided into companies of fifty to sixty SS soldiers. The companies were known as "camp garrisons" and referred to by company number and the name of the camp to which the guard battalion was assigned. An example being "4/SS-Sturmbann K.L. Dachau" signifying the fourth guard company of the Dachau Concentration Camp.

As with the predecessor Totenkopfstandarte, the war time guard battalions were designed for external camp security only, with the guards themselves prohibited from direct contact with camp inmates. The image of the "Concentration Camp guard", brutalizing and murdering prisoners, is more accurate with respect to the SS personnel who were full members of the camp service, meaning those who worked directly within the camp itself and interacted daily with the prisoners.

With the original Totenkopfstandarte no longer guarding concentration camps, these units were left to fill their original wartime purpose of police augmentation and military reserve duty. After the occupation of Poland, the Death's Head Regiments were deployed east to assist with security and anti-partisan duties. Sixteen Death's Head regiments were formed between 1937 and 1941 for these purposes.

ORIGINAL SS-TOTENKOPFSTANDARTE (SS DEATH'S HEAD REGIMENTS)

REGIMENT	ACTIVE	HONOR TITLE	WARTIME DUTIES
TK-S. 1	1937 – 1940	Oberbayern	Police and anti-partisan duties in Poland.
TK-S. 2	1937 - 1939	Brandenburg	Known for atrocities against Poles, Jews,
TK-S. 3		Thüringen	and other minority groups
TK-S. 4	1938 - 1941	Ostmark	Garrison duty in Prague
TK-S.5	1939 – 1941	Dietrich Eckhart	Garrison duty in Linz

Above: The first five Totenkopfstandarten were formed from the original concentration camp guard regiments, first established in 1937 from the camp guard battalions. By 1941, all of the Totenkopfstandarten had been reformed into SS Infantry Regiments

After the start of the Second World War, the Totenkopfstandarten were expanded with an additional eleven regiments formed by 1940, bringing the total number of active Totenkopfstandarten to sixteen.

WARTIME SS-TOTENKOPFSTANDARTE

REGIMENT	ACTIVE	WARTIME DUTIES
TK-S. 6	1939 – 1941	Garrison duty in Prague
TK-S. 7		Security duty in Drammen, Norway
TK-S. 8		Security duty in Kraków
TK-S. 9	1939 – 1940	Garrison duty in Brünn, Austria
TK-S. 10	1939 – 1941	Security duty in Kraków
TK-S. 11		Coastal defense in the Netherlands
TK-S. 12		Garrison duty in Posen
TK-S. 13	1939 – 1940	Garrison duty in Vienna
TK-S. 14	1940 – 1941	Security duty in Denmark and the Netherlands
TK-S. 15	1940	Garrison duty in Plock, Poland
TK-S. 16		Garrison duty in Prague

In January 1941, an announcement was made for a proposed 17th Death's Head Regiment, however one month later all of the remaining Totenkopfstandarte were ordered disbanded with their members transferred into a new series of SS Infantry Regiments. With the exception of the 9th and 12th SS Infantry Regiments, which were drawn from Death's Head troops previously garrisoned in Norway, all of the SS Infantry commands were formed from SS-Totenkopfstandarte bearing the same numeric designators.

THE SS INFANTRY REGIMENTS

REGIMENT (1941 – 1942)	UPGRADE/MERGER (1942)	FINAL DESIGNATION (1944)
SS-Infantry Regiment 1	3rd SS Panzer Division "Totenkopf"	
SS-Infantry Regiment 2		
SS-Infantry Regiment 3		
SS-Infantry Regiment 4	2nd SS Infantry Brigade	19th Waffen-Grenadier Division der SS
SS-Infantry Regiment 5		
SS-Infantry Regiment 6	6th SS Gebirgs Division "Nord"	
SS-Infantry Regiment 7		
SS-Infantry Regiment 8	1st SS Infantry Brigade	18th SS Freiwilligen-Panzergrenadier Division "Horst Wessel"
SS-Infantry Regiment 9	6th SS Gebirgs Division "Nord"	
SS-Infantry Regiment 10	1st SS Infantry Brigade	18th SS Freiwilligen-Panzergrenadier Division "Horst Wessel"
SS-Infantry Regiment 11	2nd SS Panzer Division "Das Reich"	
SS-Infantry Regiment 12	6th SS Gebirgs Division "Nord"	
SS-Infantry Regiment 13	Planned, but never formed	
SS-Infantry Regiment 14	2nd SS Infantry Brigade	19th Waffen-Grenadier Division der SS

Thedor Eicke – Commander of Concentration Camps

Theodor Eicke, a high school drop-out from a lower-class Bavarian family, enlisted in the First World War as a common infantry solider and later became a paymaster. In 1920, he briefly worked as a policeman, before being fired for political activities, and later found work as a factory foreman. He joined the Nazi Party and the SA in 1928, transferring to the SS in 1930. Under warrant for arrest for political violence, he fled Germany in 1932. A year later, Eicke returned from Italy, but was arrested and confined to a mental hospital. He was briefly expelled from the SS but reinstated in June of 1934 as Commander of Dachau. In June 1934, Eicke assisted with the execution of top SA leaders in the Night of the Long Knives and then became commander of all German Concentration Camps. In 1939, Eicke ordered the camp service formed as a military division; this became the 3rd SS Panzer Division "Totenkopf". On February 28, 1943, Eicke was killed in action during a reconnaissance flight during the opening hours of the Third Battle of Kharkov.

In September 1939, the SS formed a Death's Head cavalry regiment known as the "SS-Totenkopf-Reiter-Standarte". Comprised of volunteers from the General-SS Cavalry Regiments (Reiter-SS), this unit was later divided into two separate cavalry regiments (Reiter Standarte 1 & 2) and then reformed into the "SS-Kavallerie-Regimenter". In the fall of 1941, these commands were then merged into the SS Cavalry Brigade and upgraded to divisional status in 1942. The unit was then designated as the 8th SS Cavalry Division Florian Geyer and had no further connection with the SS Death's Head units.

To support manpower replacement for the Death's Head division, the SS maintained three reserve units known as the "SS-Totenkopf-Infanterie-Ersatz-Battalione" (Reserve SS Death's Head Battalions). The three replacement battalions, formed between 1939 and 1940, were predominately garrisoned in occupied Poland. In April of 1943 all three reserve battalions were reclassified as "SS-Panzergrenadier-Ausbildung-und-Ersatz-Bataillon", with the third battalion deployed that same month to participate in suppressing the Jewish Ghetto uprising of Warsaw.

An independent SS security unit was also formed for garrison duty in the Czech capital of Prague and was drawn from members of the 9th Totenkopfstandarte. The unit was designated as the "SS-Totenkopf-Wach-Bataillon Prag" and comprised just over two thousand men, some of which were deployed as guards to the Theresienstadt Ghetto. A larger garrison unit was also formed in Norway and was known as the "SS-Totenkopf-Standarte Kirkenes". This unit began as a company sized battalion, first known as the "SS-Sonderbataillon Reitz", and deployed to Norway for occupation duty on June 28th 1940. In July 1940, the command was re-designated as the "SS-Totenkopf-Bataillon Norwegen" and eventually rose to over one thousand members. After the summer of 1940, the command became known by its final name of "SS-Totenkopf Standarte K".

A final catch-all Death's Head unit was the "SS-Totenkopf-Rekreuten-Standarte" which was comprised of members of the original three SS-Totenkopfstandarten who had otherwise not transferred to either the SS Death's Head Division or some other Death's Head affiliated command. The unit was established in 1939 and disbanded a few months later. The remaining SS soldiers were then disbursed to the 6th, 7th, 14th, and 16th Totenkopfstandarten.

Service in the Camps

The SS men of the "Camp Service Proper", meaning those SS men who worked on either the Concentration Camp staff or were assigned to directly oversee camp inmates within the camp itself, were typically part of the Protective Custody Compound (Schutzhaftlager) and often personified the brutality of the Nazi camp system.

Internal camp personnel were recruited with harshness in mind. When Thedor Eicke was first forming the Concentration Camp service, he actively sought SS men with criminal backgrounds, including those who had served time in prison or who had been patients in mental institutions. The "Old Guard" of the camp service was comprised of brutal men who, even within the SS, were seen as uneducated thugs. Even the Death's Head guard units distanced themselves from their counterparts who worked within the camps, and preferred instead to show a closer association with the armed SS units of the SS-Verfügungstruppe.

Hanging torture, where prisoners were suspended by their wrists while forced to hang forward on their own body weight, was a favorite punishment used by SS camp guards. (Holocaust Memorial Museum)

The mid 1930s saw significant formalization of the camp service as a branch of the SS, to include the introduction of stricter regulations on the manner in which a Concentration Camp was to be operated. Far from the early SA camps, which had been seen as arbitrarily run and disorganized, the SS camps were regimented with every minute of a prisoner's day allocated, with severe consequences for non-compliance or disobedience.

Thedor Eicke's pattern of violence focused on draconian punishments, with every conceivable infraction covered by a specific consequence. Failing to stand at attention properly could earn a prisoner extra work hours, while working too slow or failing to follow an SS soldier's command warranted a more severe punishment. Technically, every punishment inflicted on a prisoner was to be annotated and recorded in camp records, while any infraction involving corporal punishment required the approval of the camp commander.

Left: "Shot while attempting escape" was a common excuse for the SS to murder camp inmates (Holocaust Memorial Museum)

In the early days of the Concentration Camps, some concern was raised over prisoner abuse and arbitrary killings, particularly from German families who would pressure authorities for explanations of a relative's sudden death within a Concentration Camp.

Prior to 1935, it was in fact illegal for an SS camp guard to unlawfully kill a prisoner; however, once Himmler became Chief of the German Police, the SS was removed from civil liability and further efforts in the area of prisoner rights were ignored and abandoned.

An inmate's work day in a Concentration Camp lasted between fourteen to sixteen hours, under constant verbal and physical abuse from both the SS overseers and prisoner inmate trustees known as Kapos. A standard meal consisted of ten ounces of bread, occasionally served with margarine or a thin slice of sausage. Meals were sometimes served with a watered-down version of coffee. Evening meals also included "soup" which was often dirty water combined with flecks of rice or meat.

One of the more grueling aspects of camp life was the "roll call" which, when used as a means of punishment, could last upwards of several hours. During roll call, prisoners were required to stand at perfect attention, arranged in formations based on "prisoner blocks" comprising a hundred prisoners from each barracks. Should any prisoner have died during the night, the body was required to be present at roll call the next morning, supported in a standing position by two other prisoners.

Evening roll call would often be followed by a "punishment hour", in which prisoners accused of disciplinary infractions would be beaten or otherwise abused in front of the entire camp. For more severe infractions, prisoners would be assigned to either a "punishment battalion", for extra hard labor in excess of 18-20 hours per day, or to the "punishment block" which was a barracks reserved for torture and executions.

Order and discipline in the camp was entrusted to SS protective compound personnel who held special titles in addition to their SS ranks. Prisoner trustees also held designations, with authority ranging from overseeing a block of prisoners to a chief trustee of the entire camp who assisted the camp commander. Special female ranks also existed in concentration camps with a female guard contingent.

CONCENTRATION CAMP POSITIONAL TITLES

SS PERSONNEL	PRISONER TRUSTEES		FEMALE AUXILIARIES	
	CAMP	WORK CREW		CAMP
Kommandant (Commander)			Chef Oberaufseherin (Chief Senior Guard)	
			Oberaufseherin (Senior Guard)	
Lagerführer (Camp Leader)	Lagerältester (Camp Senior)	Vorarbeiter (Foreman)	Erstaufseherin (First Guard)	Lagerführerin (Camp Leader)
Rapportführer (Report Leader)		Oberkapo (Senior Overseer)	Arbeitsdienstführerin (Work Team Leader)	Rapportführerin (Camp Leader)
Blockführer (Block Leader)	Blockältester (Barracks Senior)	Kapo (Overseer)	Kommandoführerin (Commando Leader)	Blockführerin (Block Leader)
	Stubenältester (Room Senior)			

The camp system of prisoner trustees fostered brutality amongst the inmates, with most of the trustees recruited from the prisoner classification "habitual criminal" and thereby more prone to violence. Trustees would often behave even more brutal towards prisoners than the SS, in an effort to gain favor with the German camp authorities. The SS camp administration would frequently encourage inmate brutality, but also punish trustees who did not perform to expectations. The worst punishment of all was to be stripped of the trustee status and returned to the barracks as a common prisoner. Such a course was tantamount to a death sentence, since other prisoners would show little mercy to a fellow inmate who had collaborated with the SS.

The theft of clothing and other personal items was also dealt with harshly by the prisoner population, in particular the theft of shoes or eating utensils. To steal another prisoner's shoes practically guaranteed their death, either by exposure or murder from the SS for violation of camp uniform regulations. Stealing food was also a serious offense, with internal camp justice (usually in the form of beatings) quickly meted out by other prisoners against the guilty.

Living conditions within Concentration Camps were harsh, with a vast majority of prisoners dying from disease as well as starvation and intentional abuse. Camp barracks were made from wood and were often drafty with little to no sanitation. Prisoners slept three to five inmates in one bunk with little to no personal space.

Concentration camp barracks in 1945 (Holocaust Memorial Museum)

Each morning before roll call, SS men and Kapo prisoners would conduct a "bed inspection" in which prisoners were required to clean their bunks and arrange stripped blankets so that the various stripes on each blanket were perfectly symmetrical with every other blanket in the entire barracks. A nearly impossible task to perform perfectly, failing a bed inspection was frequently used as a means to inflict severe punishments on inmates.

Within the more established Concentration Camps of Germany and Austria, a prisoner was eligible for punishment only after being put on report by a member of the SS and then only once the disciplinary infraction had been reviewed by an SS officer. In the 1930s, the SS in fact followed this procedure strictly; however, once World War II began, punishments within camps became more frequent with a lax in formal reporting procedures. The most common form of punishment for routine infractions was extra work hours or being forced to stand at attention for long periods of time. Another common punishment was the "hanging torture" in which prisoners would be suspended from their wrists with the arms pulled behind the back. This caused extreme pain, dislocation of the shoulders, and quite often permanent disability. Prisoner beatings were also very common, usually by administering dozens of strikes on the bare buttocks with a wooden cane.

SS men serving in the Concentration Camps were well known for sadism and cruelty, with this attitude leading to many innovative punishments and tortures, often inflicted solely for the amusement of the perpetrators. In Dachau, where arrested priests were housed together in Block 26, reports surfaced of crucifixions and other depraved acts of cruelty against clergy. When similar reports surfaced at Buchenwald, the SS conducted an investigation and in fact demoted an SS Sergeant who had been identified as having crucified two priests[xlvii].

Right: SS men beat a camp inmate (Polish State Archives)

Random shootings and summary executions, especially in smaller and lesser known camps, were a common threat to prisoners. In the concentration camp of Płaszów, SS officer Amon Göth would routinely shoot prisoners with a high-powered rifle from the balcony of his house. Göth was also known for roaming the camp during the day, shooting prisoners at random, and sometimes executing large numbers from barracks or work groups which had violated a camp regulation or had displeased Göth in some other way.

The presence of death within concentration camps was so common that every camp contained a dedicated morgue and crematorium. Duty in the camp morgue was ironically a choice assignment amongst the inmates, given that when a prisoner died, what little possessions on the body were distributed amongst the morgue attendants. On any given day within a Concentration Camp, the camp morgue would usually receive dozens of bodies for cremation. Ashes were unceremoniously dumped into nearby landfills or rivers. Among the dead would be those who had perished during the night hours, prisoners summarily executed by the SS, or those who had suffered more grueling fates such as starvation torture or death by denial of water and dehydration[xlviii].

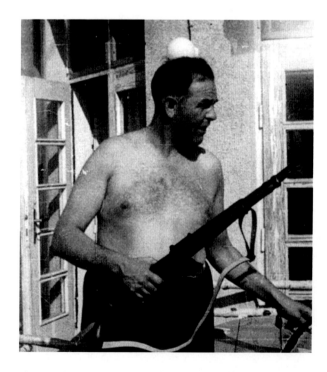

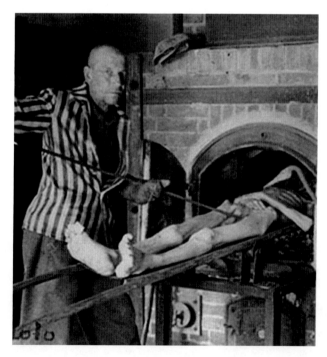

Above Left: SS-Captain Amon Göth. Above Right: A camp inmate prepares to cremate a body (Polish & Bavarian State Archives)

Suicide amongst camp inmates was also common, either by falling into an electrical fence or by crossing the camp perimeter line and being killed by SS men in guard towers. Crossing the fence line was often used by the SS as a means to kill prisoners, mainly by taking a prisoner's cap, throwing the garment across the perimeter line, and then ordering the inmate to retrieve it. Refusing to do so would entail the inmate being killed by the SS for refusing to obey orders, while crossing the line meant death from the guard tower.

A prisoner commits suicide on the camp electrical fence (Holocaust Memorial Museum)

After the close of the Second World War, many captured SS camp men claimed that they had performed barbaric and sadistic acts only under orders and also stated that failure to follow such orders would have bought criminal charges, imprisonment, and possibly even a death sentence by an SS court. In reality, the SS never recorded a single instance of a camp service member prosecuted for refusing to carry out acts of murder and torture.

Indeed, the SS judicial system was known for the reverse, with several cases of SS men punished for conducting unauthorized inmate killings and other acts of extreme depravation even beyond the norms of SS cruelty. The often used phrase "I was only following orders" was therefore a weak defense for the more notorious of the SS assigned in the Concentration Camps.

Corruption charges were also a common occurrence amongst the SS camp service. Towards the end of the war, when large amounts of Jewish property, money, and other valuables were being collected at extermination centers, SS members were found to be rampantly stealing confiscated money and valuables. The SS launched several investigations, and several SS personnel were prosecuted by Nazi authorities.

NOTABLE CONCENTRATION CAMP OFFICERS
ATTACHED TO SIGNIFICANT CAMPS

NAME AND RANK	PHOTOGRAPH	CAMP SERVICE	WAFFEN-SS SERVICE
Richard Baer SS-Sturmbannführer		Dachau, Neuengamme, Auschwitz	Totenkopf Division
Karl-Otto Koch SS-Standartenführer		Dachau, Sachsenhausen, Buchenwald	None
Josef Kramer SS-Hauptsturmführer		Dachau, Sachsenhausen, Mauthausen, Auschwitz, Bergen-Belsen	
Max Pauly SS-Obersturmbannführer		Neuengamme, Stutthof	Reserve officer
Franz Ziereis SS-Standartenführer		Mauthausen	

Images courtesy Holocaust Memorial Museum

Concentration Camp uniforms

The standard blue and grey stripped Concentration Camp uniform, which has since become an integral part of Nazi concentration camp imagery, was first invented at Dachau in 1933. The pattern of a stripped prison uniform had been common throughout Europe, dating from the mid-19th century and it is unclear who in the SS first proposed the design for use in concentration camps. The uniforms themselves were comprised of a course fabric, offering little protection from the elements, and worn with a cap, trousers, and wooden clog like shoes. Most prisoners wore an identification badge on their left breast, above which was a prisoner number. Variations of the camp uniform included a wool parka, intended to be worn in the winter months, and then only by prisoner trustees. A long "frock type" shirt, which extended downwards to the knees, was also common for use in camp workshops.

Right: A standard Concentration Camp prison uniform for a Jewish Anti-Social inmate. The prisoner number is displayed above the breast identification badge (Graphical recreation from original photographs courtesy of Holocaust Memorial Museum)

Trustee prisoners, known as "Kapos", were issued armbands to denote their status, as well as carrying whips and truncheons. Kapos were entrusted with order and discipline and often behaved with more brutality than their SS overseers. In camps which only housed Jews, a Star of David was also displayed on the Kapo insignia.

Armband for a regular Kapo and a Jewish "Oberkapo" (Senior Overseer). Kapos typically wore wool blue parka coats and were issued a whip to enforce discipline (Holocaust Memorial Museum)

Each Concentration Camp inmate was required to display a triangular badge identifying the crime for which they had been interned at the Concentration Camp. If the inmate was also Jewish, a second triangle was worn indicative of a Star of David. Jewish inmates were specifically singled out for abuse, torture, and executions. For those who were repeat offenders, with more than one stay in a Concentration Camp, a colored bar was worn above the standard identification badge. Circular badges were also issued to those prisoners assigned to a penal battalion. Another type of circular badge was issued to those prisoners who were deemed escape risks.

Former members of the German armed forces, who had been imprisoned for defeatism, desertion, or other disloyal activities, wore a red triangle which was also the standard insignia for enemy prisoners of war. Further special badges existed for Jewish inmates considered "race defilers", which meant prisoners who had been arrested for engaging in sexual relations with an Aryan, which was considered the ultimate offense against the German race. Jewish prisoners so marked could expect the most vicious abuse from their SS captors.

Another type of Concentration Camp insignia pertained to those inmates of major camps located outside of Germany. Such prisoners would display an embroidered letter within their camp badge to identify nationality.

CONCENTRATION CAMP INMATE IDENTIFICATION BADGES

CATEGORY	INSIGNIA	INSIGNIA FOR JEWS
Political Prisoners		
Habitual Criminals		
Forced Laborers		
Jehovah's Witness		
Homosexuals		
Anti-Socials		
Gypsy-Roma		

Graphical recreation from original photographs courtesy of Holocaust Memorial Museum

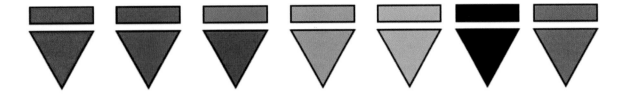

Repeat offender identification badges included a colored stripe above the standard prisoner triangle

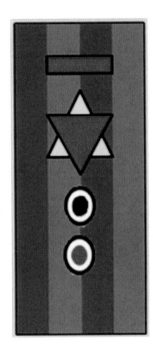

Left: Pattern of display for concentration camp uniforms. The example shown displays a repeat offender Jewish political prisoner assigned to a penal battalion and considered an escape risk.

Above: A red triangle indicated Concentration Camp inmates who were former members of the German armed forces; this insignia was also used by some prisoners-of-war. The black and yellow Star of David was issued to Jewish "race defilers", which implied having had sexual relations with an Aryan. A black triangle front indicated a male defiler while a yellow front was worn by female inmates.

Graphical recreation from original photographs courtesy of Holocaust Memorial Museum

CONCENTRATION CAMP NATIONALITY DESIGNATORS

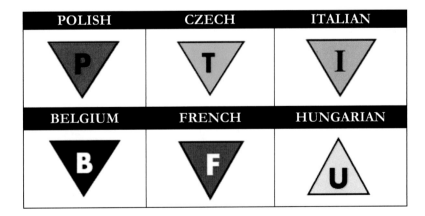

Graphical recreation from original photographs courtesy of Holocaust Memorial Museum

A special Concentration Camp insignia (see right), which appears to have been used only within German camps, was an embroidered "S" worn on the camp badge to indicate those prisoners considered a security risk.

Another unique insignia from Auschwitz, for those prisoners assigned to the I.G. Farben complex at Monowitz, was a horizontal yellow stripe in place of a standard camp badge. In camps intended solely for Jews, badges were not typically worn. Camp inmates who wore civilian clothing were required to paint a large white "X" on their backs to distinguish their status as prisoners.

In addition to concentration camp uniforms, the Nazi practice of registering Concentration Camp inmates with numbers was integrated into a broader philosophy of stripping prisoners of their identities and reducing them to objects devoid of human rights and dignity. During an inmate's stay in a Concentration Camp, they were to be referred to only by their prisoner number and never by name. Within the major Concentration Camps of Germany and Austria, prisoners were indexed numerically in chronological order based upon arrival date in the camp. A prisoner's number was sewn above their concentration camp badge, which was worn on the upper left breast of the inmate uniform.

The first prisoner at Dachau was Claus Bastian, a twenty-four year old law student from Munich, Bavaria. Bastian arrived at Dachau as part of a transfer of two hundred Communists from the Landsberg Prison on March 22nd 1933. Bastain was later released from the camp in September 1933 and went on to become a successful lawyer living in post war Germany.

Many of the camps established after Dachau also had their first inmates transferred from other facilities. For instance, when Buchenwald opened, one hundred fifty political prisoners were transferred from Gestapo prisons while Mauthausen held a prisoner population of one thousand one hundred on its first day, transferred from various police installations throughout Austria.

The first female prisoners at Ravensbrück were nine hundred women transferred from the Lichtenburg concentration camp in May 1939. Two dozen of these inmates were later transferred to Mauthausen as the first female prisoners of that camp.

In the occupied territories, registration and numerical assignment of prisoner numbers was less enforced, with some of the smaller concentration and labor camps ignoring this practice all together. Death camps, such as Sobibor and Treblinka, rarely assigned prisoner numbers to new arrivals, since most of the persons arriving in these camps were immediately killed.

The only camp to tattoo prisoner numbers was Auschwitz, a practice which began in 1941 after using a standard numerical registration in the same manner as the regular Concentration Camps in Germany. The first prisoners at Auschwitz were thirty common criminals who were transferred from Sachsenhausen on May 20th 1940. Auschwitz prisoner #1 was Bruno Brodniewicz, a German of Polish descent. Prisoner #31, the first processed inmate of Auschwitz, was Polish political prisoner Stanislaw Ryniak. Numerical registration of male inmates continued until 1945 with such numbers issued as part of the regular series of Auschwitz Concentration Camp prisoner numbers.

AUSCHWITZ CONCENTRATION CAMP INMATE NUMBERING SYSTEM

SERIES	PREFIX	INSTITUTED	HIGHEST NUMBER
Regular (Male)		May 1940	150,000+
Regular (Female)		March 1942	100,000+
Jewish Inmates	A	May 1944	25,378
	B	November 1944	< 10,000
Soviet Prisoners of War	AU	November 1941	12,000+
Reeducation Inmates	EH	Circa 1942	Unknown
Gypsy-Roma	Z	February 1943	c. 23,000

The tattooing of Auschwitz inmates began in late 1941 after 12,000 Soviet prisoners-of-war were transferred to Auschwitz from Stalag #308 in Neuhammer (Świętoszów), in eastern Poland. The original method to identify Soviet prisoners was by the letters "SU" written in oil paint on the Soviet soldier's uniform. Three hundred Soviet prisoners deemed "fanatical Communists", were selected for tattooing in November 1941, with the letter "AU" (Auschwitz) tattooed on their arm followed by a prisoner number. While this was the first use of tattoo numbers at Auschwitz, the practice did not expand to the regular camp population until the following spring.

Widespread use of prisoner tattooing at Auschwitz began in the spring of 1942, mainly as a means to identify dead bodies. By 1944, a standard prisoner identification tattoo series was in existence. Ethnic Germans, reeducation prisoners, and political prisoners registered at Auschwitz were not ordinarily tattooed and continued to wear prisoner numbers as patches on their uniforms. New arrivals selected for immediate extermination were never registered.

The wartime Concentration Camps

In September 1939, upon the outbreak of the Second World War, the headquarters of the SS Concentration Camp service was located at the Sachsenhausen Concentration Camp and employed approximately fifty full time SS members overseeing the administration of all camps in Germany. Thedor Eicke had by this time begun forming the Totenkopf division, and therefore was no longer involved in Concentration Camp affairs. The day to day running of the camp service had now fallen to Eicke's Chief of Staff - Richard Glücks. In November of 1939, Thedor Eicke formally assumed command of the Totenkopf division and Richard Glücks was named as the new Inspector of Concentration Camps. Glücks expanded the Inspectorate somewhat to include doubling the staff to one hundred persons.

CONCENTRATION CAMP INSPECTORATE (1939)

INSPECTOR OF CAMPS
(Theodor Eicke)

Chief of the Military Staff (Richard Glücks)

Political Department (Arthur Liebehenschel)

Administration Department (Anton Kaindl)

Medical Department (Karl Genzken)

Glücks' authority as Concentration Camp Inspector was short lived and was far less prestigious than Eicke's. By the start of 1940, all of the original Death's Head regiments were now considered military formations and had been removed from the Concentration Camp service. The task of guarding camp prisoners was now left to the smaller SS guard battalions known as the SS-Totenkopf–Wachsturmbanne. These units were far less trained than the guard regiments of the 1930s and were comprised mostly of older man unfit for general military service.

Right: Richard Glücks, who served for nine months as Inspector of Concentration Camps before becoming a Department Chief in the WVHA (Federal German Archives)

Compared to Eicke, Glücks was also seen as less competent and lacking in leadership qualities. Eicke had been known as a forceful and ruthless SS officer, a trait Glücks did not share, with many in the camp service lacking respect for him and often bypassing him in their reports of camp activities to the SS leadership.

In August of 1940, Himmler ordered the office of Concentration Camp Inspector disbanded, with the administration of all Concentration Camps thereafter transferred to the authority of Department D of the SS Economics and Administration Main Office (known as the WVHA). Glücks then became a Department Chief in the WVHA, now subordinate to Oswald Pohl.

Due to Pohl's interest in the concentration camps for their slave labor potential, Glücks' authority was diminished even further. Glücks was also not consulted regarding the Jewish extermination programs but was merely informed which camps would be utilized and ordered to provide the appropriate staff. By 1944, Glücks had come to be seen as completely incompetent by both his seniors and subordinates and had also become a severe alcoholic. Glücks is generally believed to have committed suicide, along with this wife, in May of 1945.

One main difference between Glücks and Eicke was the scale of the Concentration Camp system which they commanded. As Germany began to overrun and conquer new territories, the necessity quickly arose to establish new concentration camps in subjugated countries. Poland contained the largest number of such camps established outside of Germany, while France and Norway contained several major camps as well.

CONCENTRATION CAMP TYPES AND CLASSIFICATIONS

CAMP DESIGNATION	ABBREVIATION	DEFINITION	EXAMPLE
Konzentrationslager	KZ	Concentration Camp	Dachau
KZ-Außenlager	KZ-A	Sub-Camp	Trzebinia
Arbeitslager	AL	Labor Camp	Płaszów
Vernichtungslager	VL	Extermination Camp	Sobibor

Concentration Camps in occupied countries were governed by the same regulations as camps in Germany, were staffed by regular camp service officers, and were eligible for presentation of a uniform cuffband denoting the camp's name. In Poland, there were originally four such camps; however, this number grew as the war continued.

In contrast to concentration camps was the Nazi labor camp system, first established in 1941, and by 1943 had become a vast network of thousands of small camps across Europe run by both the German military and the SS. Labor camps were established in a variety of locations, some very isolated, while others were created within major cities. Prisoner populations could range from just under a dozen inmates to well over a thousand. SS labor camps were known for excessive brutality and cruelty, due in large part that the labor camps were not under the same administrative requirements as a formal concentration camp. Local commanders were therefore permitted a broad latitude in the manner in which the labor camp operated. The Płaszów Labor Camp, commanded by SS-Hauptsturmführer Amon Göth, was located just outside of Krakow and was known as one of the most brutal German labor camps ever established. The camp at Stary Dzików, located in eastern Poland, held a similar nefarious reputation. Stary Dzików was commanded by the notorious SS anti-partisan commander Oskar Dirlewanger, and SS guards were known to strip Jewish women, before beating and raping them, then injecting strychnine to cause a causing a torturous death.

The designation of "Hauptlager" referenced a Concentration Camp which was established entirely within the confines of a major city. Only one such camp is known to have existed and was referred to as the "Warsaw Concentration Camp". This concentration camp was a collection of camps within the city of Warsaw; the first was in the Warsaw district of Koło, while a "reeducation camp" (Arbeitserziehungslager) was established in the neighborhood of Gęsiówka. Satellite camps in Warsaw were established on Nowolipie Street, Bonifraterska Street near Muranowski Square, and in a jail located on Pawia Street (known as the Pawiak Sub-Camp). In the 1990s, a tunnel beneath the Warsaw Zachodnia train station was claimed by Polish authorities to be the sixth of the Warsaw Concentration Camps and a gas chamber during World War II. The validity of these claims was disputed given that there were no German records or witnesses to a gas chamber in Warsaw during the Second World War.

CONCENTRATION CAMP ORGANIZATION
(1943)

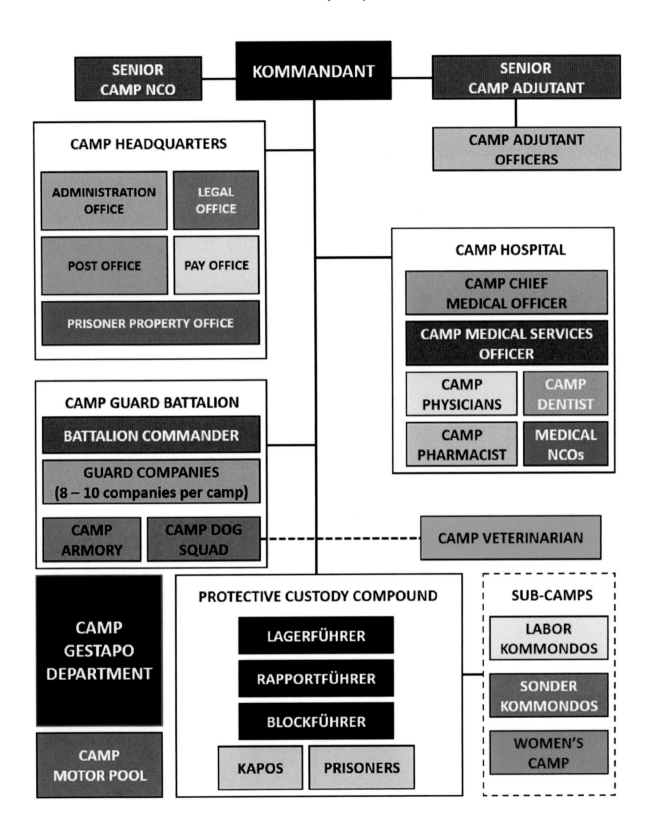

MAJOR NAZI CONCENTRATION CAMPS OF EUROPE

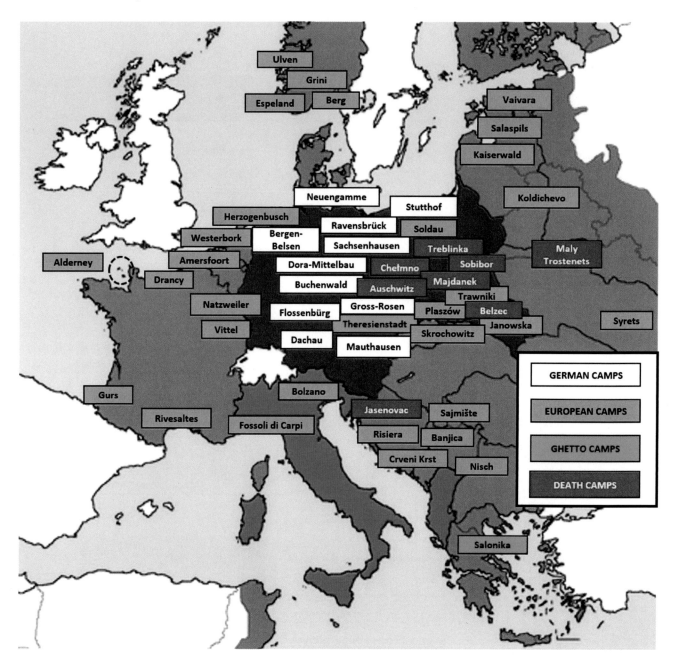

Smaller concentration camps, labor camps, and sub-camps are not shown on the above map due to scale

At the height of the Second World War, there were three main types of Concentration Camps operated by the SS. The Concentration Camps in Germany and Austria dealt with political prisoners, while camps in Poland were involved in Jewish slave labor and extermination measures. Camps in occupied territories served as labor camps, internment centers for enemies of the Reich, as well as transit camps to the larger more well-established camps. All major camps also had a network of dozens of smaller sub-camps.

The concentration camp at Trawniki bears special mention, for it was here that the SS trained an auxiliary corps of camp guards comprised mostly of former Russian prisoners-of-war as well as volunteers from the Baltic countries and the Ukraine. Established in August of 1943, and known as the "SS-Ausbildungslager Trawniki", the guards trained at Trawniki wore all black uniforms with a simple generic rank system. Trawniki guards were mainly deployed as perimeter guards in concentration camps, as well as within ghettos, and were often seen as unreliable by the SS with questionable loyalty.

Trawniki personnel were deemed unfit for combat and, in one of the few engagements of Trawniki men during the Warsaw Ghetto Uprising, a squad of Trawniki riflemen fired blindly towards resistance fighters and nearly killed several German soldiers in the process. Desertions of Trawniki men were also reported at Auschwitz and, during the Sobibor revolt, Trawniki guards fled under attack from escaping Jewish prisoners.

Right: An auxiliary camp guard at Trawniki (Polish State Archives)

In certain cases where a labor camp had become significantly important, the SS would upgrade the labor camp to the status of a formal concentration camp. Two examples of an upgraded labor camp occurred at Płaszów and Soldau in Poland. Ironically, the administrative shift between a labor and concentration camp was in fact often welcomed by the prisoners, since concentration camps were known for slightly better treatment of inmates, with far less brutality than that found within a labor camp.

Attached to every major concentration camp was also a network of smaller sub-camps (KZ-Außenlager) which were outwardly indistinguishable from labor camps, yet commanded by a camp leader (Lagerführer) and directed by the same regulations employed by the regular concentration camps. During the Second World, the SS operated nearly one thousand sub-camps, the largest of which were situated around the major concentration camps in Germany. Some sub-camps were relatively small, with no more than a few dozen inmates, while others were vast and encompassed thousands of prisoners.

If a sub-camp became important enough, the facility would be upgraded to a full Concentration Camp with a designated Kommandant, along with a larger guard battalion and administrative staff. Two of the most significant examples of an upgraded sub-camp were Gross-Rosen, originally a sub-camp of Sachsenhausen, and Dora-Mittelbau[xlix], which had been founded in 1943 as "Arbeitslager Dora", attached as a sub-camp to Buchenwald. In both cases, once designated as a Concentration Camp, the two facilities began to administer sub-camps of their own.

A unique series of sub-camps, as well as the only camps of the Nazi concentration camp system to be established within British territory, were the camps at Alderney located on the British Channel Islands.

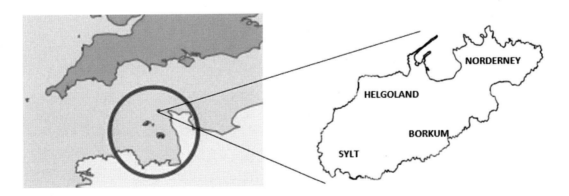

Above: The Alderney camp system with major and minor sub-camps indicated

GERMAN CONCENTRATION CAMP SUB-CAMP SYSTEM

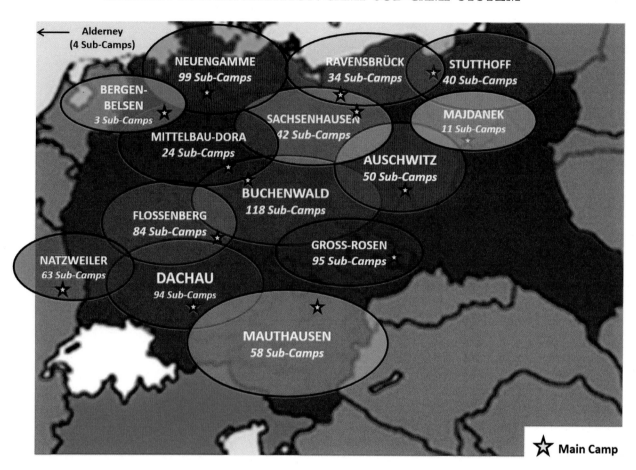

The Alderney camps were administratively designated as sub-camps of Neuengamme Concentration Camp; the SS operated four camps at Alderney which held a combined prisoner population of over six thousand. The camps were operated from 1942 to 1944 and were under the overall command of SS-Hauptsturmführer Maximilian List. The sub-camps of Norderney and Sylt were forced labor compounds, the latter of which was a smaller camp exclusively for Jews. Borkum and Helgoland (the largest sub-camp) were considered "Hilfswilligelager" (volunteer labor camps) which housed workers of mostly Eastern European origin who constructed and maintained the island's defensive structures.

One of the more famous sub-camps was at Brünnlitz, in Czechoslovakia, known as the Brünnlitz Labor Camp and considered a sub-camp of Gross Rosen. It was here that the German industrialist Oskar Schindler transported over twelve hundred Jews from the labor camp at Płaszów, in order to avoid their being transported to Auschwitz and exterminated. The Brünnlitz Labor Camp possessed a guard battalion of approximately one hundred SS personnel under the command of SS-Obersturmführer Josef Leipold. However, from the day the camp opened in October 1944, Oskar Schindler forbade the SS from harassing or even interacting with the Jewish prisoners. Through his actions, the Jewish workers at Brünnlitz survived the war, although Schindler himself went bankrupt using the last of his wealth to purchase arms and ammunition, ensuring that his factory in fact never produced actual armaments which could be used to prolong the war.

By 1942, the entire concentration camp service was now administratively part of the Waffen-SS, while the camps themselves were organized similarly to a military regiment with administrative staff, guard battalions, and internal camp personnel working collectively under the authority of the camp commandant. Every formal concentration camp also maintained an office of the Gestapo which served the original purpose of "protective custody", mainly deciding who would be imprisoned and released from the camp, as well as ensuring camp security against any resistance or underground activities of the prisoners. During World War II, Gestapo personnel assigned to concentration camps wore either uniforms of the SS security police or the Waffen-SS

A unique series of Concentration Camps were established in Norway in late 1940 and were known as "Häftingslager" (Detainee Camps). The German Army also operated a number of labor and prison camps in Norway for Soviet prisoners-of-war; these prisoner camps were collectively known as Stammlager. The SS run concentration camps in Norway were considerably smaller than those in other countries, with most camps holding a prisoner population of six hundred to one thousand. The SS made use of the Totenkopfverbände to administer and command the Norwegian camps; however, most of the camp security was provided by the German Police as well as Norwegian collaborators.

NORWEGIAN CONCENTRATION CAMPS

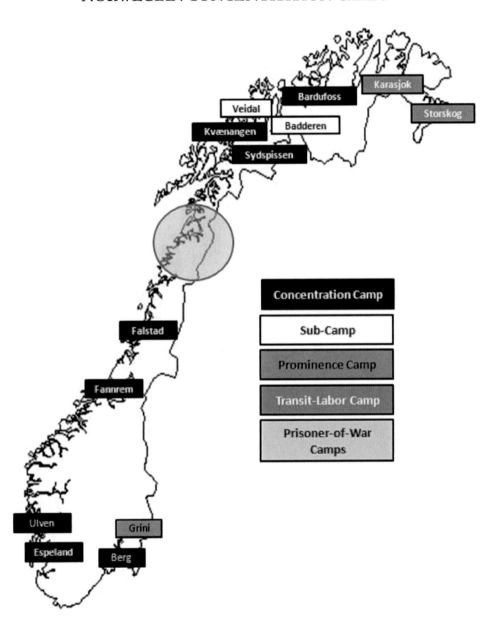

In addition to the standard SS run camps in Norway, the German Army operated twenty-eight prisoner-of-war camps, of which three of were jointly run by the SS. The Gestapo further maintained three security camps in the Finnmark towns of Kirkenes, Elvenes, and Sandnes which were used to imprison Norwegian teachers.

Within Norway, the SS also established "prominence camps" (Geisellager) for noteworthy Norwegians who were held as hostages. The Prominence Camp at Grini was one of the larger concentration camps in Norway and held a total of 19,247 prisoners. The SS also operated several transit camps (Durchgangslager) used to deport Norwegians to either forced labor locations or to concentration camps within Germany. Jewish deportations also occurred from Norway but numbered less than eight hundred. The Gestapo in Norway further maintained a prison system, separate from the concentration camps, which housed political prisoners in pre-existing Norwegian jails. These facilities were collectively known as "Security and Internment Prisons" and were under the operational authority of the SS Security Police.

Right: Hans Hüttig, a veteran camp officer of Buchenwald, Sachsenhausen, and Flossenbürg, was assigned by the SS to construct several concentration camps in Norway. (National Archives)

Within Czechoslovakia, the camp at Theresienstadt held the unique classification as a combined ghetto-concentration camp. Outwardly, Theresienstadt appeared as a Jewish ghetto, complete with a Judenrat administration and Jewish police, yet administratively was run identically to a concentration camp. Theresienstadt further served not only as a concentration camp, but also as a transit camp, as well as a prominence camp for high profile Jewish personalities.

The propaganda value of the camp was immense, with the SS going to great lengths to display Theresienstadt as a comfortable place to live. Internally, torture and murder were common as were mass deportations to extermination facilities. Three SS officers (Siegfried Seidl, Anton Burger, and Karl Rahm) served as Commandant of Theresienstadt during the four years of the ghetto's existence. All were recruited based on past experiences dealing with Jewish internees, as well as a reputation for cruelty and brutality.

Theresienstadt was closed on May 5th 1945, with the last of the SS staff evacuated, leaving all remaining prisoners behind in the custody of the International Red Cross. Karl Rahm was captured a few weeks later and extradited in 1947 to Czechoslovakia, where he was executed. Siegfried Seidl was tried by an Austrian court and also executed that same year. Anton Burger, who was considered the most sadistic of the three commanders, was sentenced to death by a Czech court but escaped from confinement and fled to Germany. He lived the rest of his life under the assumed name Wilhelm Bauer and died on Christmas Day in 1991.

Left: Karl Rahm (Holocaust Memorial Museum)

The term "Concentration Camp" was also used in the vernacular to describe any forced labor camp set up by the German armed forces. Non-SS camps, administered by the regular German military, included slave labor centers for Germany's V-2 rocket development program, as well as various armaments industries under contract with the German government. Where the SS did not directly control such camps, the installations were often under the authority of the Reich Office for the General Plenipotentiary for Labor, headed by Fritz Sauckel. Sauckel was later executed for war crimes.

The SS was often called upon to provide forced labor for German government industrial projects, using prisoners from pre-existing concentration camp as labor fodder. Such projects would often be established within military prison camps, frequently referred to in the vernacular as concentration camps. One such German Army installation was the Berga Concentration Camp, located in the German state of Thuringia. Utilizing prisoners from Buchenwald, as well as Jewish-American prisoners-of-war, the Berga camp was overseen by a detachment of German Army reservists headed by Sergeant Erwin Metz. Prisoners at the camp were forced to dig a total of seventeen mining tunnels for coal, and other valuable ores, working in the most brutal of conditions, with little food and no medical care.

One area of incarceration, over which the SS was never able to gain control, were the traditional prisons of Germany. Under the original pre-Nazi penal code of Germany, standard felony crimes such as burglary, robbery, arson, and murder carried prison sentences to be enforced by various penal institutions run by the individual state governments of Germany. Known either by the term "Gefängnis" or "Zuchthaus", traditional German prisons were run by state officials known as "Governors", with guards and other staff wearing unique uniforms specific to each particular prison.

For habitual offenders of felonious crimes, a law in 1933 (the Law against Dangerous Habitual Criminals) allowed for the transfer of such persons to a Concentration Camp. If deemed an extreme risk to national security, the SS was also authorized to execute the offender. Such was the case of the Sass brothers (see right – Bavarian State Archives), Erich and Franz Sass, who were notorious bank and jewel robbers, sentenced to twelve years in prison by a Berlin court. Under order of Heinrich Himmler, the two bank robbers were transferred to Sachsenhausen Concentration Camp and summarily executed by firing squad.

The Nazi death camp system

The SS Death's Head service has historically been the most outward sign of the Holocaust, in that the majority of wholescale extermination was carried out by those SS concentration camp members stationed in permanent killing facilities. Taking lessons from the field extermination measures of the Einsatzgruppen and acting under extermination directives codified in the 1942 Wannsee conference, the SS would create a systematic bureaucracy of genocide.

There were three types of Death Camps which the SS operated between 1941 and 1944. The first were death camps run directly by the SS Security Police, of which there were two such camps in existence, at Chełmno in Poland and Maly Trostenets near Minsk in the Soviet Union. The second type of death camp, those administered under Operation Reinhard, were all located in Poland near small towns and villages. The final type of death camp were facilities in which the SS established killing centers within previously established Concentration Camps (Auschwitz and Majdanek). In these cases, extermination took place side by side with routine concentration camp operations.

SS EXTERMINATION CAMPS

CAMP	TYPE	OPERATIONAL	VICTIMS
Auschwitz	Combined Concentration-Death Camp	May 1940 – Jan 1945	1.1 million
Majdanek		Oct 1941 – Jul 1944	78,000
Belzec	Operation Reinhard Death Camp	Mar 1942 – June 1943	550,000
Chełmno	Security Police Death Camp	Dec 1941 - March 1943	300,000
		Apr 1944 – Jan 1945	
Maly Trostenets		Jul 1942 – Oct 1943	65,000
Sobibor	Operation Reinhard Death Camp	Mar 1942 – Oct 1943	225,000
Treblinka		July 1942 – Oct 1943	900,000

In addition to the above facilities, the SS also established a "Treblinka Labor Camp", which was a forty acre quarry and forest lumber yard which operated from late 1941 to early 1944. Often referred to as "Treblinka I" to differentiate from the similarly named death camp, the Treblinka labor compound was commanded by Sturmbannführer Theodor van Eupen and collectively housed just under two thousand prisoners.

The SS death camps run by the Totenkopfverbände were established and operated under the same guidelines as regular concentration camps, complete with a Kommandant, an SS administrative staff, internal camp SS personnel, as well as an assigned guard battalion. Within the Operation Reinhard camps, guards were typically Baltic or Ukrainian volunteers recruited from the Trawniki training center. The camps run by the SS Security Police were less formal, although still retained camp titles such as Kommandant for the camp commander.

The killing centers of Operation Reinhard maintained only a small number of inmates (usually less than a few hundred) to help support the logistics and administration of genocide, to include sorting through victim belongings, maintaining certain camp industries, as well as assisting in the gassing process and the disposal of bodies. Auschwitz and Majdanek, which were regular concentration camps as well as killing centers, used the pesticide gas "Zyklon-B" to kill victims, while the Operation Reinhard camps used carbon monoxide chambers similar to those of the T4 euthanasia program. In camps housing a normal inmate population, SS members and prisoners who worked in the gas chambers were segregated from the rest of the camp. At Auschwitz, this directive was taken very seriously, but the camp at Majdanek was known to conduct gas operations in an unsecured location often within sight of the regular camp prisoner population.

The gas chamber at Majdanek, located near to the center of the camp (Polish State Archives)

Within the killing facilities of the Operation Reinhard camps, prisoners were divided into a general labor force, as well as the "Sonderkommandos" who helped run the gassing facilities. Death camps also had a system of prisoner trustees (Kapos) who assisted the SS in maintaining camp order. As with regular camps, each death camp was overseen by an SS commander who maintained an adjutant and a small headquarters staff. Internal camp order was overseen by several SS-Blockführer who reported to the Rapportführer, usually a senior SS non-commissioned officer.

Right: Gustav Wagner, Rapportführer of Sobibor (Federal German Archives)

All SS men assigned to the Operation Reinhard camps were required to take an oath of secrecy and were usually selected based on past history with the T4 euthanasia program, as well as a willingness to commit genocide and brutality. Life for inmates in Operation Reinhard camps was also a daily struggle for survival, given that the SS had a standing policy to exterminate all Jews interned within death camps, including those selected for special duties who would normally be killed after a few weeks and replaced with new camp arrivals.

In Treblinka, with a standing prisoner population of several hundred, only sixty seven inmates survived the war. Belzec and Sobibor experienced similar numbers, with just over fifty survivors at each camp from the hundreds which were interned.

SS DEATH CAMP COMMANDERS

Name	Death Camp Assignment	Photograph	Biography
Irmfried Eberl (Obersturmführer)	Chełmno & Treblinka		A veteran of the T4 euthanasia program, Eberl joined the SS in 1940 and served at Chełmno before appointment as Treblinka's first commander. He served less than a month and was relieved for incompetence after allowing piles of bodies to accumulate in the camp and stealing property from the camp stores. He was released from active SS service in 1944 and joined the Army. After the war, he was arrested in 1948 but committed suicide before standing trial for war crimes.
Kurt Franz (Untersturmführer)	Belzec & Treblinka		A former Army cook, Franz joined the SS in 1937 and became a guard at Buchenwald before assisting with the T4 program. In 1942, he was posted to Belzec and shortly thereafter transferred to Treblinka as deputy commandant. Known for torturing prisoners and training his personal dog to attack inmates, Franz took over command of Treblinka in 1943. When the camp closed later that year, Franz was sent to Italy to fight partisans. He survived the war and was arrested in 1959. Sentenced to life imprisonment in 1969, he was released in 1993 and died in 1998.
Gottlieb Hering (Hauptsturmführer)	Belzec		Born in 1887, Hering joined the German Army in 1907 and the police in 1912. During World War I, he was recalled to duty as a machine gunner. During the 1920s and early 30s, Hering was a police detective and was a known anti-Nazi. Hering later joined the Criminal Police (Kripo) and was recruited for euthanasia duties in 1940. Augmenting to the full time SS, he became the Prague SD commander in 1942 and was posted to command Belzec later that year. In 1944, he was sent to Italy to fight partisans and died of medical complications in October of 1945.

Name	Death Camp Assignment	Photograph	Biography
Franz Reichleitner (Hauptsturmführer)	Sobibor		Austrian born Reichleitner joined the SS in 1937 and became a Gestapo officer in Linz before transferring to assist in the T4 program. In 1942 he was transferred to Poland and took command of the Sobibor extermination camp. Away from the camp on leave during a major prisoner revolt, the camp was closed in October 1943 and Reichleitner was transferred to Italy for anti-partisan duties. He was killed in action during a partisan attack in January of 1944.
Franz Stangl (Hauptsturmführer)	Sobibor & Treblinka		An Austrian Nazi Party member since 1931, Stangl joined the SS in 1938 and worked as a criminal detective and Gestapo agent. He then joined the T4 program and commanded a euthanasia center. In March 1942, he was assigned to construct the camp at Sobibor and became its first commander. He was then sent to Treblinka and in 1944, he was transferred to Italy and ended the war on the Austrian border. Escaping first to Syria and then Brazil, Stangel was arrested in 1967 and extradited to West Germany. He was sentenced to life imprisonment and died in 1971.
Richard Thomalla (Hauptsturmführer)	Belzec & Treblinka		Thomalla joined the SS in the early 1930s, and by 1935 was serving in the SS Security Police. In 1941, Thomalla designed and oversaw construction of Belzec, after which he supervised building Treblinka, which he also commanded. In 1944, he was transferred to combat duty and was captured by Russian forces in 1945. He was summarily executed on May 12, 1945.
Christian Wirth (Sturmbannführer)	Chełmno, Belzec, & Treblinka		A member of the Nazi Party since 1923, Wirth was a World War I veteran and police officer who joined the SA in 1933. In 1939, he transferred to the SS and oversaw administration of the T4 euthanasia program. In 1941, he opened Chełmno and was appointed administrator of Operation Reinhard in 1942. He further commanded Belzec and Treblinika before reassignment to Italy in 1944. Briefly serving as a labor camp commander, Wirth was next sent to Yugoslavia where he was killed in action in May 1944.

The combined concentration-death camp at Majdanek maintained gas chambers which killed close to eighty thousand victims, a small number compared to other camps. Majdanek was also run with indifference, bordering on incompetence, with two of the commanders (Koch and Florstedt) executed by the SS for corruption, dereliction of duty, and (in Koch's case) murder. After all four of Majdanek's consecutive commanders had been relieved, Arthur Liebehenschel, the Auschwitz commander in 1944, became Majdanek's last commandant until the camp was liberated in the summer 1944. Liebehenschel was executed in 1948.

MAJDANEK CAMP COMMANDERS (1941 – 1944)

SS Officer		Assignment Dates	Post War Fate
SS-Standartenführer Karl-Otto Koch		Sep 1941 - Aug 1942	Executed by Nazi authorities in April 1945
SS-Obersturmbannführer Max Koegel		Aug 1942 - Nov 1942	Captured by Allies in 1946. Committed suicide before trial
SS-Standartenführer Hermann Florstedt		Nov 1942 - Oct 1943	Executed by Nazi authorities in April 1945
SS-Obersturmbannführer Martin Weiss		Nov 1943 - May 1944	Executed for war crimes in May 1946

Images courtesy of National Archives and Holocaust Memorial Museum

The first indications that the Nazi genocide program was coming to an end began when Operation Reinhard was formally cancelled on October 19th 1943. The camp at Belzec had already shut down, while Sobibor was closed mid October 1943 after a major prisoner revolt and escape. The camp at Treblinka closed in November 1943, while Majdanek ceased gassing operations the following summer. Auschwitz was the last major death camp to close its gas chambers in November 1944. The camp at Chełmno, which had closed in the spring of 1943, was reopened the following year with the last killings taking place at the end of 1944. The camp was evacuated with all remaining Jewish prisoners shot in January 1945.

All of the Operation Reinhard camps were dismantled upon closing, with trees and grass planted over the camp locations to remove all evidence of genocide. The SS personnel of Operation Reinhard, whose primary duty had been systematic extermination of Jews, were now seen as a liability to the SS. By 1944, most of the Operation Reinhard camp officers and soldiers had been reassigned to anti-partisan duties, either along the Eastern Front or in Italy. As this was considered one of the more dangerous assignments, several SS members from the Operation Reinhard camps were killed in action before the end of the war in 1945. It is today widely believed by historians that the SS intentionally posted these men to dangerous assignments, hoping they would be killed in order to ensure their silence.

Auschwitz – Factory of Death

The most notorious concentration camp ever operated by Nazi Germany was first opened in May of 1940 and situated in an abandoned Polish cavalry barracks on the outskirts of the small Polish town of Oswiecim. Originally intended as a concentration camp for Polish political prisoners, a second camp (known as Birkenau) was opened in 1941 as a Russian prisoner-of-war facility. By 1942, the potential of Auschwitz as a slave labor center in occupied Poland had been realized, with the first major Auschwitz sub-camp (Monowitz) opened that October. By the end of 1942 the three main camps of Auschwitz, Birkenau, and Monowitz had been combined into the "Auschwitz Camp Complex" and were thereafter respectively known as Auschwitz I, II, and III.

The association of Auschwitz with Jewish exterminations began in mid-1942 under directives from the Wannsee Conference. Auschwitz was chosen to perform gassing operations as part of the Final Solution genocide program and, while still maintaining status as a regular concentration camp, Auschwitz II (Birkenau) constructed an independent gassing complex where over one million victims would be killed in the course of the next two and a half years.

The camp complex at Auschwitz was situated at the junction of two major rivers in southwest Poland. The Auschwitz main camp housed political prisoners, with a population of just under eleven thousand in 1943, while Auschwitz III (known as Monowitz or "Buna") was a satellite camp intended to house a labor force for the I.G. Farben factory industries. Monowitz camp held a wartime population of over ten thousand, with an additional twenty five thousand from other camps forced to work in the factories as well. Conditions were brutal and over two thirds of these factory workers would die by 1944.

Rudolf Hoess (also spelled Höß or Höss) served as the commander of the Auschwitz Camp Complex from 1940 to 1943 and again from 1944 to the camp's evacuation in 1945 (Holocaust Memorial Museum)

Auschwitz-Birkenau, the largest and most well-known Auschwitz camp, housed gas chamber extermination facilities as well as a camp population of over two hundred thousand. Over twenty thousand were interned Gypsy-Roma families, ninety percent of which would be systematically killed by the SS. For eighteen months, between early 1943 and late 1944, Auschwitz experienced its highest numbers of exterminations, even surpassing the dedicated death camp of Treblinka as the largest killing center in Nazi occupied Europe. Meanwhile, thousands of prisoners continued to live and work within the Auschwitz camp itself, performing various slave labor tasks for both the SS and German industry. Auschwitz was evacuated in January 1945 as the Red Army moved into Poland and liberated a week later by Soviet forces. Many of those held responsible for Auschwitz's operation were later put on trial and executed, including the camp commander Rudolf Höss who was hanged on the grounds of the Auschwitz main camp on April 16th 1947.

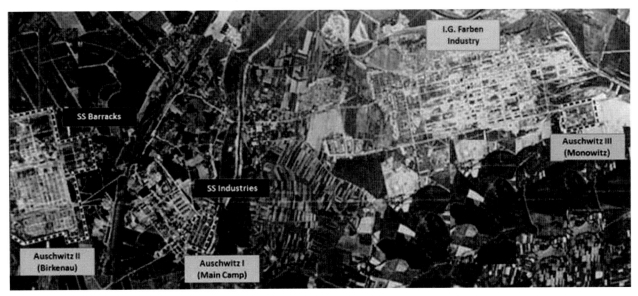

Aerial view of the Auschwitz camp complex (Holocaust Memorial Museum)

At the main camp of Auschwitz I, prisoners were organized into barracks blocks along the same lines as Concentration Camps in Germany. One SS soldier served as an SS-Blockführer for each barracks while a single Rapportführer oversaw all barracks and reported to the SS officer-in-charge, known as the Schutzhaftlagerführer (Protective Custody Camp Commander). Auschwitz I further maintained its own crematorium (Crematorium #1) which was used as a makeshift gas chamber prior to the establishment of the more permanent killing facilities at Auschwitz-Birkenau. The main camp of Auschwitz also had several special barracks blocks, the most infamous of which was Block 11, used for prisoner punishments as well as early gassings, as well as Block 10 which was used for medical experiments. Beginning in 1942, the main camp at Auschwitz was allocated a full commander (Lagerführer) in addition to the Protective Custody Compound Commander[1]. Both individuals reported to the Auschwitz Commandant who oversaw all three camps of the Auschwitz camp complex.

Aerial view of the Auschwitz main camp (Polish State Archives)

Auschwitz-Monowitz (commonly known as Auschwitz III or "Buna") was a relatively small camp in comparison to the remainder of the Auschwitz camp complex. Monowitz was originally a sub-camp and existed primarily to serve the slave labor needs of the nearby I.G. Farben industrial complex. Throughout the camp's existence, only one SS officer served as Camp Commander, this being SS-Hauptsturmführer Heinrich Schwarz. Records of the SS enlisted personnel are fragmentary, however SS-Oberscharführer Richard Stolten is listed as having served as Rapportführer of Monowitz.

Left: SS-Hauptsturmführer Heinrich Schwarz (National Archives)

It is by far Auschwitz-Birkenau (Auschwitz II) which is the most well-known camp of the Auschwitz complex. From 1941 to 1944, Birkenau had its own camp commander and staff, although after 1944 the camp was run directly by Rudolf Höss who also served as Commandant of the entire Auschwitz complex.

AUSCHWITZ-BIRKENAU GENERAL LAYOUT

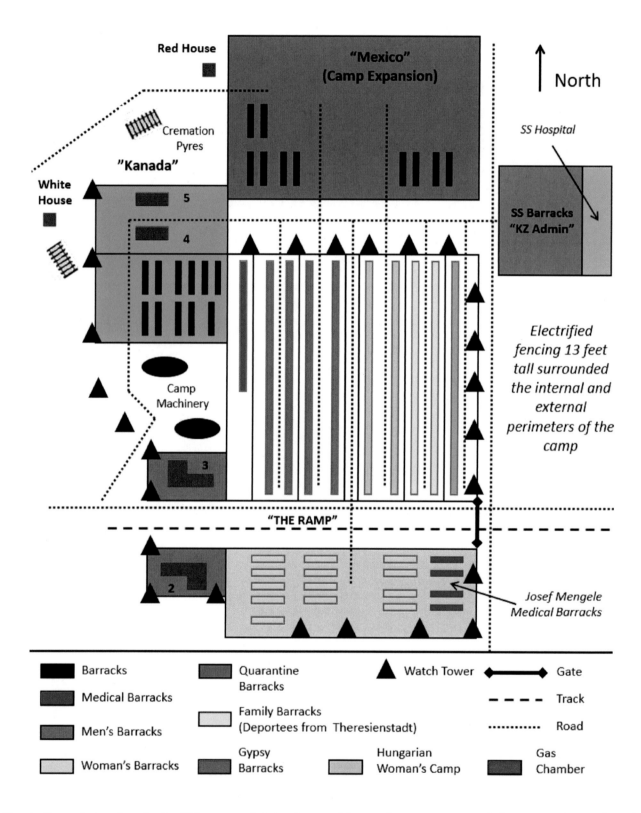

Due to its vast size, Auschwitz-Birkenau maintained several internal camp compounds (known as Stammlager) each with its own Lagerführer, Rapportführer, and various Blockführer.

The Men's Camp of Auschwitz-Birkenau contained the majority of the Auschwitz prisoner population and supplied inmates for use in slave labor projects at the nearby SS industrial complex. A Men's Quarantine Camp also existed, which was a smaller prisoner block, housing male inmates immediately upon arrival at Auschwitz. Newly arrived prisoners stayed in the quarantine camp for several days in order to screen for infectious or contagious disease[li].

Birkenau also maintained a large compound for female inmates in the southern section of the camp, opposite and separated from the main camp by "the Ramp", where arriving trains would deposit Auschwitz prisoners. The women's camp was overseen almost entirely by female SS auxiliaries who answered to the main camp administration through a liaison desk manned by an SS non-commissioned officer[lii]. A separate female camp compound, located within the heart of Auschwitz-Birkenau, was established in 1944 specifically to house the overflow of female inmates arriving on transports from Hungary.

PROMINENT AUSCHWITZ FEMALE SS-AUXILIARIES

Name	Position	Photograph	Post War Fate
Margot Dreschel	Female Camp Leader		Executed June 1945 (37 years old)
Irma Grese	Female Camp Guard		Executed December 1945 (22 years old)
Johanna Langefeld	Female Camp Leader		Aged 45 when Auschwitz was liberated; arrested and escaped from Polish custody. Died in Augsburg, Germany in 1974
Maria Mandel	Female Report Leader		Executed January 1948 (36 years old)
Elisabeth Volkenrath			Executed December 1945 (26 years old)

Images courtesy Polish State Archives

One of the more tragic stories of Auschwitz-Birkenau relates to the internment of entire families of Gypsy-Roma, who were considered an undesirable ethnic group under Nazi racial policy. The first transports of Gypsies began arriving at Auschwitz in 1943. On August 2nd 1944 the Gypsy area of the camp was closed down and all of the inhabitants murdered; in all, twenty five thousand Gypsies perished at Auschwitz.

Other internal camps at Auschwitz-Birkenau included the Auschwitz family camp, first opened in 1943 to house incoming deportees from the Theresienstadt Ghetto in Czechoslovakia. Families were permitted to live together; however, the family camp was periodically purged of ill or unfit inmates who were sent to the gas chambers and exterminated. Medical facilities for families included a camp hospital, located outside the wire of Auschwitz-Birkenau, as well as an internal medical barracks existing for sick or infirmed inmates. Reporting to the medical barracks was often a death sentence, since the assigned SS medical personnel would routinely kill patients with lethal injections of poison to the heart. Separate from the medical barracks was an experimentation block, overseen by the infamous Doctor Josef Mengele, who oversaw experiments on camp inmates to include twin children. Twins who died under Mengele's care were often autopsied alongside their sibling, who would be murdered upon the first twin's death for comparative dissection biopsies.

Special facilities at Auschwitz included the "Kanada" compound, named after the North American nation of Canada which was seen as housing great treasures and riches. The Kanada Compound was an area of great wealth in that it was here that all of the money and valuables belonging to gas chamber victims were collected and sorted. The Kanada Compound maintained its own prisoner work force of approximately seventy five to one hundred inmates, assigned to sort through the luggage and other personal belongings of those arriving at Auschwitz and further segregate valuables such as jewelry and currency.

Right: Workers at the Kanada compound sort through suitcases of recent arrivals at Auschwitz (Holocaust Memorial Museum)

Kanada workers had access to regular clothing, food, and other commodities making a high survival rate for those who were assigned to this duty. Kanada workers were also better treated than most inmates by the SS, with fewer summary executions and random liquidations as compared to the rest of the Auschwitz camp complex.

Left: The Auschwitz ramp, where prisoners were selected for either work or extermination upon arrival at Birkenau (Polish State Archives)

One of the more well-known inmates assigned to Kanada was Rudolf Vrba, a Slovakian Jew who later escaped from Auschwitz along with another inmate named Alfréd Wetzler. Vrba worked both as an inmate administrator, as well as being part of the "Railway Brigade" which unloaded passengers from incoming freight cars at "the Ramp" which was the main railway platform of Auschwitz-Birkenau. Although brutality did occur (Vrba himself was once nearly beaten to death by an SS soldier), some of the SS assigned to Kanada were known for thier humane treatment of the Jewish inmates, although SS corruption and greed for the wealth stored at Kanada played a large part in this attitude.

Located across a main road from the Auschwitz-Birkenau camp was the Auschwitz SS barracks, home to several hundred members of the SS who worked and lived at the camp performing a variety of functions and duties. After 1943, SS members at Auschwitz were considered "deployed" and were not permitted to bring families to the camp. The Camp Commander was an exception who lived with his wife and children at a house approximately a half mile from the main camp.

A posting at Auschwitz was considered a choice assignment in the SS, due to the extensive facilities not available in other concentration camps. The Auschwitz administrative complex, which contained the camp management buildings, also possessed a movie theater, sports club, shooting range, as well as comfortable barracks, barber shop, restaurant, and mess hall. Many of the employees of these facilities were themselves camp inmates designated as prisoner trustees. In 1943, the SS also opened a recreation lodge at Solahuette, located several miles away from Auschwitz, in which SS members could enjoy days off and relax away from the shadow of living in a concentration camp[liii]. The SS barracks at Auschwitz were evacuated in January 1945, with some prisoners who raided the complex for food shot and killed by retreating SS guards.

Of all the facilities at Auschwitz, it is the extermination areas which are perhaps best known to history. When the Auschwitz camp was first ordered opened on January 25, 1940, extermination was not its intended purpose. Originally, the camp was chosen as a concentration camp for political prisoners, and would use an abandoned Polish cavalry barracks, near the town of Oswiecim, Poland, for its facilities. The name of the camp "Auschwitz" was a Germanized version of the nearby town name of Oswiecim.

The main Auschwitz camp was constructed in May 1940, when prisoners from the Sachsenhausen Concentration Camp converted the original Polish barracks into Concentration Camp offices, storerooms, and prisoner barracks. In March 1941, Heinrich Himmler inspected Auschwitz and ordered an expansion of the camp. The original camp would continue to hold Polish political prisoners and criminals, while Auschwitz II, also to be known as "Birkenau", would be constructed for an expected 30,000 prisoners of war. Himmler also ordered the construction of a third facility at the nearby village of Dwory, in order to host an industrial complex of the German manufactory firm I.G. Farben. This camp would become Auschwitz III, or "Monowitz".

The first gassing operation at Auschwitz took place on September 3, 1941 when six hundred Soviet prisoners of war were sealed inside a room at Block 11 and gassed with a cyanide pesticide known as Zyklon-B. The first organized extermination of Jews took place on February 15, 1942 when a transport of German Jews from Upper Silesia were gassed in an above ground facility known as the "Little Red House". A second brick facility, known as the "White House" was built a few weeks later.

Above (left): The only known photograph of early gassing operations near the Red House, also known as "Bunker I". This photograph was taken by a Jewish prisoner assigned to dispose of the bodies after gassing. The photograph on the right shows an outdoor cremation pit at Auschwitz in early 1943 (Holocaust Memorial Museum)

By 1944, there were four permanent gas chambers established at Auschwitz, of which Crematorium #2 & 3 were the largest, consisting of a two-story building with a basement undressing room and gas chamber.

Right: Crematorium and gas chamber building at Auschwitz (Holocaust Memorial Museum)

The main floor of the gas chamber was used for valuable collections and burning of bodies, while the upper floor was the living quarters for the Jewish inmates who were forced to assist in the extermination process. These special teams of prisoners, known as the Sonderkommandos, were assigned under threat of death to aid the SS in the processing of extermination victims to the gas chambers, although it was always the SS who initiated the actual gassing. The Sonderkommando were permitted a better quality of life than other inmates but were themselves killed after about four months of service. The duty of the succeeding Sonderkommando would always be to dispose of the bodies of the previous.

AUSCHWITZ GAS CHAMBER AND CREMATORIUM LAYOUT

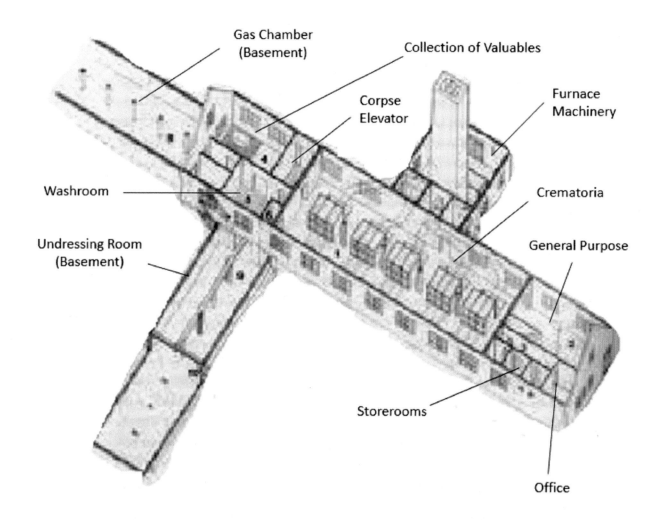

Graphical recreation based on original diagram courtesy of Holocaust Memorial Museum

In each gas chamber there were between four to six SS personnel overseeing as many as eighty-five prisoners. A head SS non-commissioned officer, with a small staff of his own, oversaw all four gas chambers and reported to the camp commandant. The gas chamber installations within Auschwitz were administratively considered separate from the main camp of Birkenau and were staffed by a select group of SS personnel who had signed oaths of secrecy and had agreed to work in the extermination program. Guard and watchtower personnel at the perimeter of the gas chamber complexes were not permitted inside the facility, except in the event of security emergencies or prisoner uprisings.

AUSCHWITZ CREMATORIUM ORGANIZATION

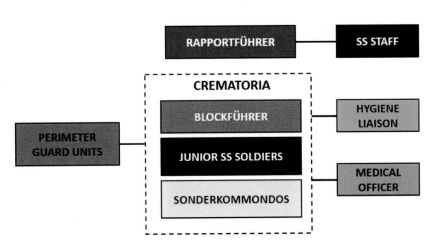

The Blockführer of the Crematorium typically performed the actual gassing of victims, while the Auschwitz Hygiene Institute delivered the poison gas Zyklon-B to the crematorium, normally in a van disguised as a Red Cross ambulance. As a rotating duty, Auschwitz medical officers were required to select prisoners for extermination and then witness the gassing operation in order to certify the victims' deaths. At peak operational capacity, the crematorium at Auschwitz was rated to process approximately 4,500 victims a day. The below ground gas chambers of Crematorium 2 & 3 possessed larger industrial furnaces than the above ground facilities of Crematoria 4 & 5. When these facilities were overburdened, bodies were burnt in outdoor cremation pits containing railway tiers drenched in gasoline.

CREMATORIUM	GAS CHAMBER	FIRST OPERATED		CAPACITY
Crematorium I	Crematorium I was located at Auschwitz I and was first operational in August 1940			
Crematorium II	Below Ground	31 March 1943		60 an hour
Crematorium III		25 June 1943		(1440 per day)
Crematorium IV	Above Ground	22 March 1943		32 an hour
Crematorium V		4 April 1943		(768 per day)

Between 1943 and 1945, six SS non-commissioned officers were posted as Rapportführer to the Auschwitz gas chambers, and thus were in charge of the day to day operation of all crematorium and gas chambers. The most notorious was Eric Muhsfeld who was described in his mannerism by Doctor Miklós Nyiszli, a Jewish pathologist who worked with Doctor Josef Mengele and further lived on site at one of the Auschwitz crematoria.

Right: An Auschwitz camp survivor's drawing of Eric Muhsfeld, as compared to Muhsfeld's prisoner photograph in 1947 (Holocaust Memorial Museum)

Muhsfeld would be executed for war crimes in 1948. Other SS soldiers assigned to the gas chambers included Hauptscharführer Otto Moll as well as the SS-Sergeants Hirsch, Steinberg, Buch, and SS-Scharführer Voss.

The last wave of Jewish transports arrived at Auschwitz in June 1944 and ushered in a period between July and November 1944 where over 600,000 would perish in the gas chambers. Most of the victims were from Hungary, leading the Hungarian government to suspend transporting Jews to death camps as a result. The Germans would respond by invading and occupying Hungary in October 1944. That same month, on October 7, 1944, members of the Jewish Sonderkommandos revolted and destroyed Crematorium #4. After several SS guards were killed, the Auschwitz guard battalion entered the crematorium compound and suppressed the uprising.

Right: Karl Friedrich Höcker, who served as Camp Adjutant of Auschwitz through most of the facility's existence. He became known in later years for creating a photo album at Auschwitz, revealing a previously unseen insight into the camp's inner workings. He died in 2000. (Image courtesy Holocaust Memorial Museum)

The following month, on November 25th 1944, Heinrich Himmler ordered the cessation of all killing operations at Auschwitz and the dismantling of the gas chambers. Two months later, on January 18, 1945, a general evacuation of Auschwitz was ordered. Sixty thousand prisoners were herded from the camp by SS guards on a death march where stragglers were shot down without hesitation.

Some fifteen thousand would die during the Auschwitz evacuation, while thousands more perished after reaching their destinations in concentration camps within Germany. On January 27, 1945, the Soviet Red Army liberated Auschwitz and found seven thousand prisoners remaining alive in the camp, having been abandoned by the SS.

Concentration Camp medical personnel

An infamous connection to which Nazi Concentration Camps are often associated is human medical experimentation. Decades after the close of the Second World War, there are still living survivors of Nazi medical experiments, some of whom were only children when these inhumane treatments occurred. The SS doctors assigned to the Concentration Camps bear a significant amount of guilt for medical war crimes and crimes against humanity.

There were two types of SS doctors who served in Germany's Concentration Camps. The first were the garrison physicians who served as regular members of the SS Concentration Camp service and were members of the Death's Head (Totenkopf) service. Garrison physicians were more concerned with the upkeep of SS health care rather than inmates, although many of these SS doctors also conducted medical experiments on Concentration Camp inmates.

The boarder category of SS doctors were the camp staff physicians. These SS doctors were assigned to the Concentration Camps from other branches of the SS and were not considered regular Concentration Camp personnel. Such doctors were assigned to provide limited health care to camp inmates, but also to make use of their time performing human experimentation. In the extermination camps, the SS doctors were also tasked with segregating Jews and selecting from arriving trains those who would live and die. In Auschwitz, a system of using two lines was perfected to a science, where one line on the right would be taken to the Concentration Camp while those on the left would be gassed to death.

A smaller segment of Concentration Camp doctors were non-SS civilians, contracted to perform certain specific experiments on camp inmates. One of the more infamous such doctors was Carl Clauberg (right – Holocaust Memorial Museum) who operated a female clinic out of Auschwitz where he forcibly sterilized women and often removed uteruses without anesthetic. Clauberg was sentenced after the war to twenty five years in prison by the Soviet Union, but was released in 1955 as part of a prisoner exchange. Re-arrested in West Germany that same year, he died of a heart attack in 1957 before legal proceedings against him could begin.

In addition to the doctors who performed medical experiments on Concentration Camp inmates, the SS also made use of medical orderlies, many of whom were more sadistic than their superiors. Such was the case of Josef Klehr, a medical orderly at Auschwitz, who was in charge of the prisoner infirmary. Klehr was a mid-level SS sergeant, yet often wore a white lab coat and proclaimed himself a doctor. Klehr's main activity was to select the sicker inmates for "examination" in his office. Klehr would then order the prisoner to lay down on a table and then kill his victim with an injection of phenol to the heart.

CONCENTRATION CAMP MEDICAL EXPERIMENTS

Camp	Experiment	Participating doctors
Auschwitz	Vivisections of patients	Josef Mengele
	Comparative experimentation of twin children	
	Injecting chemicals and drugs into blood and organs	Helmuth Vetter
	Forced exposure to radiation and x-rays	Viktor Brack
	Electrocution and shock therapy experiments	Hans Wilhelm König
	Surgical removal of women's breasts	
	Surgical removal of organs without anesthetic	
	High doses of barbiturates and morphine	
	Male and female forced sterilization and castration	Carl Clauberg
		Horst Schumann
	Intentional injection of typhus and hepatitis into inmates	Kurt Gutzeit
	Exposing muscles to chemicals, electricity, and pathogens	
	Surgical removal of the gallbladder	
	Intentional infection of Noma	Berthhold Epstien
	Surgical removal of a prisoner's liver	Arnold Dohmen
Buchenwald	Live skinning of inmates with tattoos	
	Forced apomorphine injections	
	Amputations of healthy limbs	
	Injection of infectious diseases to include yellow fever, smallpox, paratyphoid fever, cholera, and tuberculosis	Siegfried Handloser
	Vivisection and medical torture of homosexuals	
	Forced injections of luminal, pervitin (a type of methamphetamine), evapium sodium, and chloral hydrate	Waldemar Hoven
	Spraying poison and acid on open wounds	
	Deliberate infection of prisoners with typhus	Arthur Dietzsch
Dachau	Hypothermia freezing experiments	Karl Brandt
		Erwin Gohrbandt
	High altitude experiments followed by brain dissecting	Sigmund Rascher
	Forced infection of malaria	Klaus Schilling
Mauthausen	Infection of prisoners with various deadly diseases then experimentation with drugs to gauge effective treatments	
Ravensbruck	Deliberate infection of prisoners with gangrene	Karl Gebhart
	Surgical removal of bones without anesthetic	
	Forced sterilization of woman and genital mutilation	Hermann Stieve
Neuengamme	Deliberate infection of prisoners with tuberculosis	
Sachsenhausen	Bacteriological warfare experiments	Joachim Mrugowsky
	Experiments with "poison bullets" - shooting prisoners with bullets laced with cyanide or filled with poison	
Various Camps	Forced starvation of prisoners	Heinrich Berning

Specific doctors are listed when known. Many experiments were carried out by teams of physicians as well as jointly between the SS and the German armed forces.

Without a doubt, the most infamous doctor at Auschwitz was Josef Mengele, who held both a medical degree and a PhD in anthropology[liv]. Mengele began his SS career in 1938 as a reservist and was then transferred to combat duty in 1941. He served as a combat medic and was awarded decorations for bravery before being wounded and transferred to Auschwitz Concentration Camp as a staff physician. Mengele's primary area of medical experimentation at Auschwitz was on twin children where the SS doctor would often infect one twin with an infectious disease, wait for them to die, then murder the counterpart twin for a comparative autopsy. Mengele further performed experiments involving injecting dye into the eyes, human vivisections, as well as various other medical procedures usually to the fatal agony of his victims.

**Josef Mengele in 1941
(Holocaust Memorial Museum)**

The SS medical corps further contained specialists such as pharmacists and dentists, both of whom were routinely assigned to the Concentration Camp service. Victor Capesius, a Romanian Army veteran who had joined the SS in 1940, served at Dachau before becoming the Auschwitz chief pharmacist from 1943 to 1945. Arrested in 1959, he was sentenced to prison, released in 1969, and died in 1985. Another notable Auschwitz medical specialist was SS-Obersturmbannführer Willi Schatz, who served as the Auschwitz camp dentist. Schatz was briefly arrested in 1946 but was released due to lack of evidence.

Left: Victor Capesius (Polish State Archives)

The SS also made use of prisoners with medical degrees and recruited Jewish doctors to assist in medical experimentation when needed. One of the more famous cases was Miklós Nyiszli, who was a Hungarian Jewish doctor sent to Auschwitz in 1944. Nyiszli served for eight months on the medical staff of Josef Mengele and also served as the Auschwitz chief pathologist. Nyiszli would often perform autopsies of Mengele's victims and later claimed he was respected by Mengele and would engage in professional conversations and even arguments with the SS doctor. Nyiszli survived the Second World War and died in 1956.

One of the more sinister SS medical organizations was the "Auschwitz Hygiene Institute", itself subordinated to the "Central Hygiene Institute of the Waffen-SS" which was a branch of the SS Central Hygiene Office in Berlin. The stated purpose of the Hygiene Institute was to conduct research in contagious disease prevention and develop better sanitation methods for the German armed forces.

Auschwitz Hygiene Institute organization

CENTRAL HYGIENE OFFICE
(Rajsko)

Bacteriological Studies

Chemical Studies

Biological Studies

Histological Studies

Serological Laboratory #1

Serological Laboratory #2

Serological Laboratory #3

Wassermann Test Laboratory

General Experimentation Laboratory

Bacteria Laboratory

Production Section

Climatological Section

The Auschwitz Hygiene Institute was involved mainly in research and development, both of which were heavily associated with human experimentation. The Auschwitz camp had originally contained the headquarters of the Hygiene Institute, but this agency was moved to the nearby village of Rajsko in 1943. In addition to the Institute's laboratories on site at Rajsko, the majority of human experimentation took place in Block 20 of the Birkenau (Auschwitz II) camp. The Hygiene Institute also oversaw the requisition and use of poison gas and directed the "Desinfektionskommando" (Disinfection Squads) who were in charge of transporting the cyanide based gas Zyklon-B to the gas chambers. The SS officer in charge of actually procuring Zyklon-B for Auschwitz was SS-Obersturmbannführer Karl Möckel, who served as the Auschwitz Administration and Supply officer. After the war, he was tried and executed in 1948.

Karl Möckel
(Holocaust Memorial Museum)

Zyklon-B is a hydrogen cyanide compound first invented in 1922 as a commercial pesticide; the man most directly responsible for Zyklon-B's creation was Bruno Tesch, a commercial chemist and business industrialist. By the start of the Second World War, Zyklon-B was contracted for sale to the German military and was used to fumigate empty buildings and barracks in order to kill lice and rats and other disease carrying vermin.

In September 1941, SS Captain Karl Fritzsch came up with the idea to use Zyklon-B to kill people after an SS guard inhaled a very small quantity of the pesticide and became ill. After using the gas in an experiment to kill six hundred Soviet prisoners, Zyklon-B became the primary means of extermination at Auschwitz in comparison to carbon monoxide poisoning used at other camps.

Auschwitz would eventually purchase nearly twenty-four tons of Zyklon-B through Bruno Tesch's company "Tesch & Stabenow" (often shortened to "Testa"). Zyklon-B was also adopted for extermination in the camp of Majdanek. In its original purpose of fumigation, Zyklon-B was also used at Dachau, Buchenwald, and Mauthausen[lv]. The SS Hygiene Institute was the main liaison for the purchasing of Zyklon-B from its manufacturers.

Left: A canister of Zyklon-B with crystalline pellets (Holocaust Memorial Museum)

Death by Zyklon-B was reported to be horrific, with victims coughing out their lungs and drowning in their blood after exposure to cyanide gas. Reports of mass gassings indicate victims clawed and scratched upon the dead to form pyramids of bodies in an attempt to reach fresh air at the roof of the gas chamber. Special prisoner teams of Sonderkommandos were then required to enter the gas chambers and pull apart the dead bodies for cremation. Bruno Tesch was later tried and executed for war crimes as was the head of the SS Hygiene Division, SS-Oberführer Dr. Joachim Mrugowsky.

While the majority of SS doctors whole headedly participated in human experimentation, there were some notable exceptions. Kurt Gerstein, who did not hold a medical degree but was educated in both mining and chemistry, was assigned by the SS to develop more efficient gassing methods on human subjects. While Gerstein apparently complied, he is also believed to have leaked information regarding extermination to a Swiss diplomat and to officials of the Vatican in Rome. Gerstein was later arrested for war crimes but then was found dead in his cell. While ruled a suicide by Allied authorities, modern day analysis strongly suggests Gerstein was beaten to death either by guards or other prisoners.

Another case was that of Hans Münch, a doctor who had maintained a practice in a small Bavarian town before World War II. Münch joined the SS in 1942 and was assigned to the SS Hygiene Institute as a staff physician posted to Auschwitz. Münch worked primarily in the SS laboratories at Rajsko, during which time he was reprimanded by his superiors for appearing too soft and compassionate towards Jewish inmates. Münch further refused to participate in gas chamber selections, although he did certify deaths as a result of gassing actions – something every doctor in Auschwitz was required to do. After the war, Münch was arrested for war crimes but found not guilty after several former prisoners testified that Münch had protected inmates and had engaged in meaningless experiments in order to save Jews from actual human experimentation.

Above: The exception to the rule - Kurt Gerstein and Hans Münch, both of whom opposed extermination actions at Auschwitz (Holocaust Memorial Museum)

It is of note that most of the doctors who participated in the more brutal experimentation and extermination actions were not in fact members of the Concentration Camp service. Josef Mengele, for instance, was a reserve line officer of the Waffen-SS, as were several other notorious SS doctors. This disparity was not the result of any moral reasons, but rather that Death's Head service camp doctors were mainly in charge of the medical needs of SS personnel, rather than the inmates. Doctors who were full members of the Concentration Camp service were entitled to display a Death's Head insignia with an "S" rune, denoting sanitation-medical duties. (see right)

Evacuation and Liberation

By the fall of 1944, the SS leadership was acutely aware that the Second World War was coming to an end and thereafter began a somewhat frantic effort to distance the SS from the horrors of the concentration camps. One of the primary aims in this regard was to create a false perception that the camps had served as legitimate facilities for internees and refugees. Nowhere was this mentality more evident than at the camp of Bergen-Belsen. The SS had acquired the camp, which had been a former Army prisoner-of-war center, in 1943 with the designation of a "Zivilinterniertenlager" (civilian internment camp) rather than a concentration camp. In the summer of 1943, the camp was designated as an "Aufenthaltslager" (holding camp) which under international law permitted the camp to house foreign refugees. In the fall of 1944 Bergen-Belsen received its final designation as an "Erholungslager" which stated that the camp was a recovery center for injured or ill prisoners from other facilities.

The reference to concentration camps by these alternate titles lay in the German wish to conceal the true nature of the camps, especially as the facilities came under danger of Allied and Soviet liberation. In Bergen-Belsen there was less brutality than in other camps, and by the end of 1944 roll calls and work labor details had been discontinued. Nevertheless, with disease and starvation running rampant, by the time of its liberation Bergen-Belsen was overrun with dead bodies.

The first major Nazi camps to be liberated were in Poland, with these facilities falling to the advance of the Soviet Red Army beginning in November 1944. Knowing full well the fate of SS members captured by Soviet forces, camp authorities in Poland ordered a general evacuation of all camps in January 1945. All inmates were to be moved west into Germany with any person unfit for travel to be shot. As prisoners were then evacuated from the camps, separate orders were issued to SS combat formations to move in and execute any sick or ill who remained behind. These orders were sometimes ignored, as in Auschwitz where several thousand inmates were abandoned while the SS unit assigned to exterminate the indigent never arrived to carry out the killings. The reason for this inaction was that the SS membership were fully aware that the Second World War was lost, and few SS soldiers wished to participate in atrocities with final capitulation so near.

Camp evacuations also occurred in the west, but to a far less frantic degree. As Allied forces liberated France and the Low Countries, surviving populations of labor and transit camps were either moved east into Germany or abandoned on site to be liberated by the Allies. Simultaneously, as prisoners from the eastern camps began to arrive in Germany, the already overcrowded facilities became overburdened resulting in starvation, disease, and death. Unlike the eastern camps, of which some had large scale body disposal facilities, the camps in Germany were unable to cope with the large numbers of the dead. As a result, some camps in central Germany literally became piled high with corpses while emaciated prisoners wandered about the bodies.

Above: Concentration Camp inmates march west from Poland into Germany. During these death marches, SS guards immediately shot down any stragglers or those who fell out of line. Below: Bodies at Bergen-Belsen (left) and piles of clothing taken from extermination victims, discovered upon liberation of Auschwitz (Holocaust Memorial Museum)

407

Once Allied and Soviet forces entered Germany, Heinrich Himmler ordered all remaining camp inmates evacuated either to undetermined regions in Northern Germany or executed on site by the SS. At this late stage of the war, many in the camp service leadership advocated simply abandoning the concentration camps or transferring control to the Red Cross under the status of refugee camps. Himmler refused this suggestion and ordered additional forced marches which caused thousands of camp inmates to perish.

Early liberation reports from the Soviet Union announced horrific camp conditions to the world, including heaps of unburied corpses, confiscated valuables from extermination victims, as well as torture chambers and brutal abuse at the hands of the SS. These reports were initially dismissed in the west as propaganda, but when the first major camps in Germany were liberated by the Allies, the truth quickly became known. Among mounds of dead bodies, the Allied soldiers discovered shoes and clothing of camp victims as well as gold teeth and prosthetic limbs taken from the dead. With the full scope of the concentration camps now exposed, efforts turned to both justice and revenge.

MAJOR CONCENTRATION CAMP LIBERATIONS

Concentration Camp	Evacuated by SS	Liberation	Liberating Force
Majdanek	20 Jul 1944	24 Jul 1944	Soviet Army
Natzweiler	29 Sep 1944	23 Nov 1944	U.S. Army
Auschwitz	17 Jan 1945	27 Jan 1945	Soviet Army
Gross-Rosen	1 Feb 1945	14 Feb 1945	Soviet Army
Buchenwald	6 Apr 1945	11 Apr 1945	U.S. Army
Dora-Mittelbau	6 Apr 1945	11 Apr 1945	U.S. Army
Westerbork		12 Apr 1945	Canadian Army
Bergen-Belsen		15 Apr 1945	British Army
Sachsenhausen	20 Apr 1945	22 Apr 1945	Soviet Army
Flossenbürg	20 Apr 1945	23 Apr 1945	U.S. Army
Dachau	26 Apr 1945	29 Apr 1945	U.S. Army
Ravensbrück	25 Apr 1945	30 Apr 1945	Soviet Army
Neuengamme	26 Apr 1945	2 May 1945	British Army
Mauthausen		5 May 1945	U.S. Army
Theresienstadt	5 May 1945	8 May 1945	Soviet Army
Stutthof	25 Jan 1945 (Land) / 20 Apr 1945 (Sea)	9 May 1945	Soviet Army

The "Operation Reinhard" death camps of Sobibor, Belzec, and Treblinka had all been closed and destroyed in late 1943, prior to the liberation of Poland. Soviet and Allied forces also liberated dozens of labor and sub-camps in France, Italy, Poland, and finally Germany. Few camps offered armed resistance, while some camps even maintained a small SS staff to the very end in order to coordinate a formal surrender to Allied forces.

Following the liberation of the major concentration camps, both the Allies and the Soviets attempted to design a justice system in order to deal with captured SS camp personnel. The first legal measures taken against SS concentration camp staff occurred in 1944 when the Red Army moved into Eastern Europe. SS men who fell into Soviet hands were either subject to summary execution or appearance before ad hoc military tribunals. Upon liberation of the first major concentration camp at Majdanek, the Soviets established the "Soviet-Polish Special Criminal Court" which thereafter held authority to try suspected Nazi war criminals in liberated Poland. In the west, following the liberation of such major camps at Buchenwald, Bergen-Belsen, and Dachau, tension and anger ran high amongst Allied soldiers. Troops entering these facilities were typically confronted with thousands of rotting bodies, half dead prisoners, and in some cases a handful of remaining SS personnel. Although under orders to treat SS personnel as standard prisoners-of-war, some Allied soldiers showed little restraint in enacting swift justice.

The camp at Dachau was first encountered by Americans troops of H Company, 22nd Infantry Regiment, on April 29th 1945. After a brief standoff with SS guards who were still manning watch towers, the camp was surrendered by the highest ranking SS officer – Untersturmführer Heinrich Wicker, who had remained at the camp with approximately five hundred SS personnel in order to facilitate a peaceful surrender to the Allies. The main occupying American force at Dachau consisted of several hundred American troops who were part of 157th Infantry Regiment, 45th Infantry Division. Having already encountered boxcars full of dead bodies, and after seeing conditions within the Dachau camp itself, the American soldiers began to engage in reprisals against the surrendering SS. Nearly two dozen SS men were marched into a secure area of the camp near a coal yard and machine gunned. Additional members of the SS, who had been manning watch towers, were shot in the head with pistols while still others were attacked and killed by former inmates who had been given weapons by American forces.

Heinrich Wicker surrendered Dachau to Allied forces in April 1945. He was later shot and killed by American soldiers (Bavarian State Archives)

The ranking American in Dachau, Lieutenant Colonel Felix L. Sparks, reportedly allowed both American troops and inmates to kill Germans under the guise that German prisoners were attempting to escape. Nearly fifty SS and German Army personnel were killed in these reprisal measures. When word of the Dachau killings reached the upper echelons of the U.S. Army, a Judge Advocate General report entitled "American Army Investigation of Alleged Mistreatment of German Guards at Dachau" specified that at least twenty two United States Army personnel had engaged in the unlawful execution of German prisoners-of-war. Court martial papers were prepared, ranging from American soldiers on the scene to Lieutenant Colonel Sparks himself, who was charged with negligence and dereliction of duty. Before any legal action could be initiated, however, the newly appointed American occupation commander of Bavaria, General George S. Patton, dismissed all charges and ordered the matter dropped.

Similar stories emerged in other camps of retaliation against SS personnel after liberation. In Buchenwald, which had been liberated by soldiers of the U.S. 80th Infantry Division, reports surfaced of American soldiers giving hand weapons to camp inmates and allowing SS soldiers to be beaten to death. Upon Germany's general surrender in May 1945, directives were issued by the Allied Expeditionary Force that acts of vengeance and retaliation against German prisoners would be met with stern repercussions. Special prisoner-of-war camps for SS personnel were then established, leading to better accountability and less acts of vigilante justice.

Left: An American soldier is confronted with dozens of unburied corpses at Buchenwald (Holocaust Memorial Museum)

Some groups of former camp inmates, especially in Italy, the Balkans, and Eastern Europe, paid little heed to formal Allied directives and continued to hunt down and murder any person suspected of being a former SS member. Some of these activities continued well into the 1950s.

A further repercussion of the camp liberations was the undeniable knowledge to the German public that the Nazi regime had been involved in unspeakable atrocities. Allied authorities, to ensure that this knowledge was widespread, ordered German civilians from towns bordering Concentration Camps be taken under armed guard and forced to view the desolation within the camps. In many cases, German civilians reacted with horror, claiming no knowledge of what occurred behind the barbed wire of the SS run concentration camps, and proclaimed that these atrocities were completely unknown to the German public. In response, the Allies forced the Germans to clean the camps of dead bodies and formed civilians into burial details.

Above: Photos taken of German civilians being forced to view Concentration Camps. From left to right, a town mayor is shown a pile of bodies. German civilians view piles of corpses. A German couple buries a victim (Holocaust Memorial Museum)

After the initial shock and horror of the camps had passed, both Allied and Soviet authorities began to form legal tribunals to deal with the prosecution of SS personnel who had served within the camps. Female SS auxiliaries were also a target for justice as were some prisoner trustees who, by some accounts, had acted with even more viciousness than the Germans.

The top commanders of the SS Economics and Administration Main Office, which had overseen the entire Concentration Camp system, faced trial at Nuremberg between January 1947 and August 1948. Oswald Pohl and the top commanders of the WVHA, who were all responsible for administration of the Concentration Camp system during the Second World War, were charged with crimes against humanity, the use of slave labor, as well as participating in a genocide program. Of eighteen defendants, fifteen were convicted with two death sentences. Oswald Pohl, head of the WVHA, was the only defendant who was actually executed.

For the staff of specific concentration camps, the Allied authorities established military tribunals which had the power to pass death sentences. This differed in eastern countries which, now under Soviet control, were empowered to form civilian courts in order to try former SS concentration camp members. By the end of 1948, all of the major concentration camp trials had been concluded. Local Polish courts continued to try suspected camp guards into the 1950s, while Soviet authorities prosecuted some suspected Ukrainian collaborators as late as 1964. Thereafter, accused SS camp personnel faced justice through the West German penal system which, after a referendum in the 1960s, had abolished the death penalty. The last major concentration camp trial of the 20th century took place in 1981.

In total, between 1944 and 1981, there were over forty independent trials of Concentration Camp personnel. The very first, held at Majdanek by Soviet forces, was conducted in the fall of 1944 while the Second World War was still ongoing. The first major trial in the west, conducted by a British military tribunal, was the Belsen Trial in September 1945. Thirty-one former SS, one female auxiliary, and thirteen prisoner trustees assigned to Bergen-Belsen were convicted, including eleven death sentences, among them camp commandant Josef Kramer who was subsequently executed.

The U.S. Army conducted a series of trials, collectively known as the Dachau Trials, between 1945 and 1947. The trials were held at Dachau Concentration Camp, ironically now imprisoning former SS members, and dealt with crimes at such camps as Dachau, Buchenwald, Mauthausen, and Flossenbürg Concentration Camps. Simultaneously, the British Army conducted seven separate trials of Ravensbrück camp personnel between 1946 and 1948.

In the east, the first legal body established to try former SS for war crimes was the Soviet-Polish Special Criminal Court, which tried former camp personnel of Chełmno in October 1945. This was followed by a trial of Stutthof personnel in 1946, after which the Soviets turned over legal jurisdiction of war crimes to the new communist Polish government. Poland then established the Supreme National Tribunal of Poland as well as the Special Polish Criminal Court. These bodies oversaw some of the most important trials in the east, such as the trials of Amon Göth, Auschwitz commander Rudolf Höss, as well as a general trial in 1947 of former Auschwitz camp personnel. These included Arthur Liebehenschel, who was charged with war crimes, as well as forty former SS and female auxiliary personnel. Twenty-three were sentenced to death and executed, seventeen sentenced to terms of imprisonment, and one acquittal[lvi].

Elsewhere, in April 1947, Karl Rahm, the former commandant of Theresienstadt, was put on trial by a Czechoslovakian District Court, along with several members of his staff. Rahm was found guilty of war crimes and crimes against humanity, and executed on April 30, 1947. Over a decade later, the Soviet government would begin the Trawniki Prosecutions, which was a five year period between 1960 and 1965 when Soviet authorities prosecuted several Ukrainians who had served as concentration camp guards.

Beginning in 1950, the West German government began to try former members of the SS who had served in the camps, beginning with Erich Bauer, who had operated the gassing facilities at Sobibor and was referred to as "Gasmeister" by the inmates. Bauer was tried and sentenced to death, but his term was later commuted to life imprisonment and he died in 1980.

In the 1960s, the West German district courts held over eight trials of former camp personnel, the most important of which was the Treblinka trial[lvii], held from October 1964 to September 1965, as well as the Frankfurt Auschwitz Trial held between 1963 to 1965, focusing on twenty-two former SS staff members and guards of Auschwitz. Twenty were convicted (two of these appealed) with the court handing down numerous sentences of life imprisonment. A much smaller trial, known as the Second Frankfurt-Auschwitz Trial, was held in September 1977 when two SS soldiers assigned to the Auschwitz sub-camp of Lagischa were accused of organizing a death march in 1945. The last major trial in West Germany was the Majdanek Trial[lviii], lasting for nearly six years between 1975 to 1981, when sixteen SS and female auxiliaries were charged with war crimes. One defendant died of natural causes during the trial, while eight were convicted and sentenced to various prison terms between 3 to 12 years.

In the last years of the twentieth century, a handful of lesser known trials occurred against persons accused of collaborating with the Nazi occupation forces by serving as guards in concentration camps. One of the more sensational cases pertained to John Demjanjuk, who was an American citizen of Ukrainian origin, and was accused in the early 1980s of serving as a Treblinka concentration camp guard known as "Ivan the Terrible". In 1986, he was deported to Israel where he was convicted of war crimes and sentenced to death.

Left: John Demjanjuk in 1944 as compared to during his trial (Polish State Archives)

The conviction was overturned in 1993 on the basis of mistaken identity. Demjanjuk returned to the United States and was indicted again in 2001. After a lengthy extradition battle, he was sent to Germany to stand trial in 2009 and was convicted of war crimes in 2011. Demjanjuk died in 2012 while his case was undergoing appeal.

By the first decade of the twenty first century, very few SS members were still living who had served in Concentration Camps. However, for those still alive, efforts of prosecution were still underway. As of 2018, the German government still held over one thousand active case files on former SS members who had served in Concentration Camps. A report generated in 2010 also estimated that, of the nearly seven thousand SS who had served at Auschwitz, only forty-nine had ever been successfully prosecuted.

In 2013, the German government sought prosecution against thirty former Auschwitz SS guards. A number of the defendants, all of whom were in their late 80s and early 90s, were deemed too frail or infirmed to stand trial. The most famous of these was Oskar Gröning, who had served as both a guard and currency clerk at Auschwitz, and had spoken openly for many years about his time at Auschwitz and how he had opposed the atrocities there.

Right: Oskar Gröning in 1944 as compared to a current photograph from 2013 (Federal German Archives)

Gröning was subsequently convicted of accessory to the murder of three hundred thousand Jews and sentenced to four years in prison. He died in 2018 before his sentence could begin.

Concentration Camp SS uniforms and insignia

The SS men who served in the Nazi Concentration Camps were undoubtedly one of the more visible faces of Nazi terror and oppression. Those assigned to the camps were accountable only to themselves and were the only branch of the SS which displayed the Death's Head emblem as a unique unit insignia. The Concentration Camp service would ultimately develop a unique series of insignia which evolved from the 1930s and into the Second World War.

Right: Concentration camp guards in 1934 (Bavarian State Archives)

The earliest SS concentration camp guards wore uniforms and insignia of their General-SS units, with no specific badges to denote camp affiliation. Such personnel were typically outfitted in the brown storm trooper SS shirt, with the addition of a grey parka coat worn with a chest-shoulder strap. When Theodor Eicke, himself a First World War veteran, took over Dachau Concentration Camp he ordered the issuance of special SS headgear to denote camp affiliation. This headgear, known as the SS-Mütze, was an SS cap designed after the Imperial German Army headgear used throughout World War I.

Eicke's Concentration Camp used the SS-Mütze until 1934, after which time the camp service adopted the black SS uniform and traditional black cap as a standard attire.

Left: The SS-Mütze used in the early days of the Concentration Camp service (Holocaust Memorial Museum)

The first specific Concentration Camp insignia was adopted in late 1933 when certain members of the Dachau camp staff began displaying a collar patch with an aluminum embroidered Death's Head emblem. After the Night of the Long Knives in 1934, Thedor Eicke issued standardized uniform regulations which specified that SS members assigned to the Dachau Concentration Camp would display an embroidered "D" as their unit insignia, while the camp guards would wear a silver death's head emblem above a Guard Company number.

In 1935, the guard companies were placed under the command of five Wachtruppe, which were geographical areas encompassing several concentration camps. Under the Wachtruppe system, camp guards were issued cuffbands displaying the Wachtruppe name, while the guard companies also wore an early pattern Death's Head patch with guard company number. The staff of Dachau continued to wear a silver "D", while the staffs of other camps adopted a machine cut Death's Head insignia which would eventually become the standard unit insignia for the entire Concentration Camp service.

The earliest insignia used by Concentration Camp guards until 1935

412

By 1935, there were approximately twenty numbered guard units through Nazi Germany's original camp system; these units displayed a death's head emblem with company numeral. The unnumbered death's head patch was used by the staffs of Concentration Camps which were not otherwise designated a special insignia.

Right: Camp insignia examples in 1935 (Graphical recreations)

In 1936, the Wachtruppe were reconsolidated and the camp guard companies were placed under the command of larger guard battalions, which in turn displayed a death's head emblem with a roman battalion numeral. There were five battalions in all, with each battalion containing approximately five companies, for a total of twenty-five companies in all disbursed throughout all of Germany's Concentration Camps. Upon the formation of the guard battalions (Wachsturmbann), the guard companies were renamed as "Hundertschaften" and issued similar patches with Arabic numerals.

Above: Concentration camp guard battalion insignia. Below: Guard company insignia issued in 1937

After 1936, all Concentration Camp personnel began wearing a brown duty uniform, which was later adapted as a working uniform for the entire Allgemeine-SS. All SS personnel who performed regular duties within Concentration Camps were required to wear the duty uniform when not engaged in ceremonial functions. The black SS uniform was thereafter worn only by guards performing sentry duty at the front camp gates, or for SS parades and other ceremonial events.

Right: The brown duty uniform of the SS, first invented for the camp service in 1936. Shown here is a member of the Allgemeine-SS senior district "Donau". After circulation in the camp service, the duty uniform was issued throughout the entire Allgemeine-SS (Photograph courtesy Federal German Archives)

On April 1st 1936, following the declaration of the Concentration Camp service as an independent branch of the SS, Thedor Eicke ordered the creation of a special insignia to be worn by the staff of the Concentration Camp Inspectorate. Borrowing a cuffband from the SS-Verfügungstruppe, an insignia bearing the word "SS-Inspection" was used by Eicke's staff until 1937[lix]. This cuffband was then replaced with an updated version reading "Totenkopfverbände" which was issued until 1942.

Concentration Camp Inspectorate cuffband used from 1937 to 1942

By 1938, a collar insignia of a plain death's head emblem was designated for members of Eicke's staff, all Concentration Camp commanders, as well as officers assigned to the various guard companies[lx]. For SS members assigned to individual Concentration Camp staffs, an embroidered "K" was worn.

Above: Unit insignia for Concentration Camp staff members. From left to right is the generic Death's Head patch used by Camp Inspectorate staff, senior camp officials, and guard company officers. The "K" insignia was used until 1937 by junior camp staff members. The later pattern Death's Head "K" emblem was used until 1941 by all camp staff members.

The insignia used by the staff members of Dachau Concentration Camp was unique, given the significance of Dachau as the first Concentration Camp managed entirely by the SS. Dachau would also host a variety of SS installations, including an administration school, military training complex, as well as several industry and construction complexes run by separate branches of the SS.

Additional Dachau insignia included special insignia for the Dachau economics office (SS-Wirtschaftsbetriebe) and clothing depot (SS-Bekleidungslager), as well as a special cuffband issued to Dachau training students. Prior to 1935, the Dachau camp staff was operationally subordinate to the General-SS commander (Oberabschnitt Führer) of SS Group South. Most camp personnel wore the "Group South" cuffband during this time.

Right: A Dachau guard in 1934, wearing the distinctive "D" collar insignia (Bavarian State Archives)

Photographic evidence reveals that the "D" unit insignia for Dachau fell into disuse by 1937 and was replaced by the generic Concentration Camp Death's Head patch. No other camp apart from Dachau was authorized cuffbands during the 1930s, with the sole exception of Buchenwald. In 1938, a training school opened in an annex near Buchenwald with students and staff authorized a special cuffband to denote assignment on training duties.

SPECIAL CAMP INSIGNIA (1935 – 1941)

PERSONNEL	COLLAR INSIGNIA	CUFFBAND
Dachau camp staff	D	Dachau
Dachau training staff	꞉⇒	kdtr.U.L.Dachau
Training students		SS-Übungslager Dachau
Dachau Economics Office		W.B.Dachau
Dachau Clothing Depot		
Buchenwald training (staff and students)	☠	SS-Übungslager Buchenwald

Images graphical recreations based on original insignia samples, courtesy Bavarian State Archives

Separate from the concentration camp staffs were the guard battalions and regiments which maintained their own series of insignia. When the original Wachtruppen were formed into larger guard battalions, battalion staff members wore a plain death's head insignia while guard company members continued to wear Death's Head patches displaying the guard company numeral. The honor title cuffbands used by the original Wachtruppen were also carried over to the guard battalions. After Thedor Eicke ordered the reconsolidation of all Concentration Camp guard units into military styled regiments, the last major insignia series of the Totenkopfverbände was issued based on patterns used by the armed SS. The insignia pertained to guard units only, while the internal camp staff insignia remained unchanged.

The first Totenkopfstandarte was based in Munich and encompassed some of the more prominent camps in Germany, most notably Dachau. Insignia regulations specified that all regimental and battalion staff members would display a Death's Head emblem with the numeral "1", while the individual guard companies (now known as "Centuries") would continue to wear the company numeral beneath the Death's Head emblem. On the field and duty uniforms, a numbered shoulder strap would also be worn.

The second and third guard regiments were issued insignia along similar lines; however regimental and battalion staff displayed a generic Death's Head unit patch without a regimental number (this number was still displayed on the duty uniform shoulder straps). After Germany annexed Austria in 1938, a fourth guard regiment was established based at Mauthausen. The use of numbered Death's Head insignia for guard companies was then discontinued and a generic Death's Head insignia was worn by all ranks. The fifth and final guard regiment, based in East Prussia, further eliminated the display of the regimental number on the uniform shoulder straps.

GUARD BATTALION HONOR TITLES AND CUFFBANDS (1937)

Guard Battalion	Cuffband
SS-Totenkopfsturmbann I (Oberbayern)	Oberbayern
SS-Totenkopfsturmbann II (Elbe)	Elbe
SS-Totenkopfsturmbann III (Sachsen)	Sachsen
SS-Totenkopfsturmbann IV (Ostfriesland)	Ostfriesland
SS-Totenkopfsturmbann V (Brandenburg)	Brandenburg

CONCENTRATION CAMP REGIMENTAL INSIGNIA (1939)

Guard Regiment	Collar Patch	Cuffband	Shoulder Strap
SS-Totenkopfstandarte 1 (Oberbayern)	(skull / 1)	Oberbayern	1
SS-Totenkopfstandarte 2 (Brandenburg)		Brandenburg	2
SS-Totenkopfstandarte 3 (Thüringen)	(skull)	Thüringen	3
SS-Totenkopfstandarte 4 (Ostmark)		Ostmark	4
SS-Totenkopfstandarte 5 (Dietrich Eckhardt)		Dietrich Eckart	

Subordinate to both the guard battalion and regiments, were the Concentration Camp guard companies, all of which maintained their own unique series of insignia. The guard companies of the Concentration Camp service were originally recruited from local Allgemeine-SS personnel and assigned as "Wachkompanie" attached to five "Wachtruppen" across Germany. By 1935, there were approximately twenty guard companies in Germany; these were then attached to five guard battalions. By 1936, guard companies were displaying a number beneath the Death's Head emblem – numbers ranged sequentially without regards to individual battalions (for instance, the second company of the second battalion would display a "7" as the seventh guard company in all).

Right: An officer of the twentieth guard company in 1940 (National Archives)

With the establishment of the larger guard regiments, each regiment contained approximately twenty-five guard companies, with collar patches ranging from one to twenty-five in each regiment. Insignia was specific to each regiment, meaning that the ninth company of the second regiment would display a "9", the same as the ninth company of the first regiment, even though the second regiment's ninth company was the thirty fourth in all.

The use of guard company numerals on the Death's Head patch was formally discontinued in 1941; however, some SS members continued to display the numbered Death's Head patch as late as 1944. There were also sporadic appearances of the numbered death's head insignia within the Totenkopf Waffen-SS division, most often to denote infantry company affiliation. This usage was unofficial, and the SS members displaying this insignia had often obtained the collar patches from surplus insignia stock.

Wartime Concentration Camp insignia

When the Second World War began, the city of Danzig was an autonomous entity governed by the League of Nations. In the summer of 1939, a pro-German element in the Danzig Senate had requested German troops to form a self-defense force in the event of the outbreak of war. Using the 3rd battalion of the 4th SS Death's Head regiment as a cadre, Thedor Eicke created the SS Home Guard of Danzig, otherwise known as the SS-Heimwehr Danzig. The unit wore standard Death's Head collar insignia with a unique cuffband.

SS Danzig Home Guard cuffband

In July 1939, the SS Danzig Home Guard oversaw the creation of a police auxiliary force known as the "SS-Wachsturmbann Eimann". This unit was formed from Danzig policeman and consisted of four infantry companies supported by a motorized transport squad. No special insignia was created, and most members wore either Danzig green police uniforms or surplus black SS jackets.

With respect to the regular Concentration Camp guards and staffs in Germany, by the time war had broken out in 1939, the black SS uniform had been discontinued. Camp guards and staffs were now issued a grey field jacket which was worn either with a closed collar or open with a brown shirt and tie. Collar insignia remained unchanged, while shoulder rank was now denoted by the same military-like boards as in the armed SS.

417

The closed collar version of the Concentration Camp uniform originally displayed the Death's Head insignia tilted on its side, but this was quickly changed to display the Death's Head vertical against the jacket. By a directive of early 1940, all numbers and symbols were eliminated from the Death's Head unit badge and all members of the Concentration Camp service thereafter wore a generic Death's Head insignia. By the end of 1940, all Death's Head guard regiments had been deployed as military units with the task of guarding Concentration Camps transferred to internal camp guards which were known as Wachsturmbanne. These guard units displayed the same generic Death's Head unit patch which was now in use by the entire SS-Totenkopfverbände.

Right: Two members of the camp service wearing both the open and closed collar versions of the 1938 duty uniform (Bavarian State Archives)
Left: The generic Death's head insignia used by the entire Concentration Camp service after 1941 (Graphical recreation)

In 1941, the entire camp service was transferred to the authority of the SS Economics and Administration Main Office (WVHA), with camp personnel now considered members of the Waffen-SS. The camp service was thereafter listed as a branch of the armed SS with light brown piping (Waffenfarbe) worn on shoulder boards to denote camp affiliation. An effort was further made to issue cuffbands for each regular Concentration Camp, in the same manner as a regiment or division of the Waffen-SS. By the end of the Second World War, there were twenty-three formal camps listed as entitled to a military cuffband. In practice, only four of these camps ever appeared to have actually been issued specific insignia.

CONCENTRATION CAMP CUFFBANDS (1941 – 1945)

CAMP	CUFFBAND
Dachau Concentration Camp	DACHAU
Buchenwald Concentration Camp	Buchenwald
Ravensbruck Concentration Camp	Ravensbrück
Auschwitz Concentration Camp	Auschwitz
Auschwitz Training Command	ϟϟ-Übungslager Auschwitz

By 1943, the Totenkopfverbände had effectively ceased to exist as a separate branch of the SS. All Concentration Camp senior officers were now considered members of the Economics and Administration Main Office, while camp guards and staff were considered part of the Waffen-SS. Uniforms provided to SS camp personnel were now standard Waffen-SS issue, although cut from a heavier olive fabric and issued with machine press insignia. The "old guard" of the camp service, referring to those SS members who had served in the camps during the 1930s, would frequently retain original uniforms and insignia, with photographic evidence revealing camp service personnel simultaneously displaying different uniform materials and wearing outdated insignia.

Right: A concentration camp guard in 1943 (Federal German Archives)

During the Second World War, the Concentration Camp service issued one camp specific sleeve diamond, originally intended for enlisted SS members of a Concentration Camp commander's personal staff, and later worn by all senior camp officers who were ranked SS-Standartenführer or above.

Left: Two versions of the Death's Head Sleeve Diamond. The checkered border, denoting the enlisted command staff diamond, was used between 1936 and 1938. The silver bordered insignia was worn by all camp officers ranked Standartenführer or above after 1940 (Insignia images graphical recreation)

A Death's Head cuffband (see below) was originally created in 1938, as an alternate insignia for use by the First Death's Head Guard Regiment "Oberbayern". Discontinued in 1940, the Death's Head cuffband returned a year later after the camp service had been absorbed by the Economics and Administration Main Office. The cuffband was now displayed by senior camp officers ranked SS-Standartenführer and above. The cuffband was further used informally by certain companies within the Totenkopf division.

One of the rarest insignias of the Concentration Camp service was the Camp Guard Replacement cuffband (below left), first issued in 1943 and intended for reservists who were called up to serve as Concentration Camp guards. An even rarer insignia, and the last formal insignia issued by the SS Concentration Camp service, was a tri-swastika collar patch intended for the Auxiliary-SS (below right), who were non-SS personnel conscripted to serve as camp guards.

CHAPTER SEVEN: THE GERMANIC-SS

One of the least studied aspects of the SS relates to the collaborationist groups which arose in Western Europe between 1941 and 1944. Collectively referred to as the "Germanic-SS" (Germanische-SS), these organizations were created by decree of Heinrich Himmler as an attempt to form a broader version of the Allgemeine-SS throughout occupied Western Europe.

Himmler's ultimate goal was for the Germanic-SS to be the starting point for a western SS nation, in much the same way that plans existed to establish an SS state in the conquered eastern lands of the Soviet Union. Himmler foresaw a future in which the western countries of France, Belgium, and the Netherlands would return to their status as independent nations, yet as puppets of Nazi Germany. SS groups in these countries would form a power base, and thereafter create a type of SS confederation over which Himmler would oversee as one single racial community.

Despite Himmler's grand vision, the Germanic-SS was doomed to failure even before the group was originally formed. Senior Nazi leaders, Hitler among them, saw no reason for Germany to give up conquered western territories, but rather held the ultimate aim of incorporating the countries of old Europe into the Greater German Reich. National identity was something Hitler and others wanted to avoid rather than foster. The practical side of the Second World War also made the Germanic-SS a failed endeavor since, by the time local SS groups began emerging in occupied countries, the military situation for Germany had become disastrous. Instead of home guard SS units, the Nazi leadership far preferred able-bodied men to enlist in the foreign legions and divisions of the Waffen-SS. This relegated what remained of the Germanic-SS to those unfit for military service and then only in very small numbers.

In practical terms, Germanic-SS groups existed more on paper than in reality and were furthermore looked down upon by the citizens of their own countries. Local SS members were often seen as the lowest form of collaborator and there were harsh reprisals against all such persons once liberation had come at the hands of the Allies.

Forming the Germanic-SS

There would eventually exist five national SS groups collectively known as the Germanic-SS. The first such group was formed in the Netherlands, which had the largest local National Socialist population of all the western European nations. The original idea for the Netherlands SS was proposed by Hans Albin Rauter, who had been appointed by Heinrich Himmler as commander of the Dutch Police and was also a General in the Waffen-SS.

Together with the support of Dutch Nazi leader Anton Mussert, the "Netherlands General SS" (Algemeene SS in Nederland) was proposed to Arthur Seyss-Inquart, the Reich Commissioner of the Netherlands, in August 1940. The group was approved and established on September 11th 1940 and declared an extension of the Dutch Nazi Party, which was known as the "Nationaal-Socialistische Beweging" or NSB.

The original Netherlands SS was nominally independent from the SS in Germany, and was at first known as "Department IX" of the NSB headquarters (Nederlandsche SS im Hoofdafdeeling IX van de N.S.B.). The group was placed under the command of Johannes Hendrik Feldmeijer, while SS-Standartenführer Richard Jungclaus was appointed as a German SS advisor. The first members of the Dutch SS were recruited from the "SS-Standarte Westland" which was a small military formation which would eventually become the 23rd Volunteer SS Panzer Division Nederland.

Hans Rauter and Anton Mussert. Together, the two would form the foundation of the Germanic-SS in the Netherlands. (Images courtesy National Archives and Federal German Archives)

SS GERMANIC AFFAIRS OFFICE
(SS HAUPTAMT)

AMTSGRUPPE D
(Germanic Affairs)

AMT D II
(Germanic-SS Operations)
SS-Obersturmbannführer
Max Kopischke

Germanic-SS Political
Leadership School
SS-Sturmbannführer
Dr. Peter Paulsen

Known in its full title as the
Germanische Schutzstaffel
Haus Germanien Hildesheim
Politische Führerschule

Abteilung 1A
(Germanic-SS in Germany)
SS-Untersturmführer
Johannes Gustke

Referent Flanders
Referent Holland
Referent Switzerland
Referent Denmark

Abteilung 1B
(Germanic-SS Abroad)

Referent Flanders
Referent Holland
Referent Switzerland
Referent Denmark

Swiss SS Section
(Proposed)

Swiss-SS within Germany
Swiss-SS within Switzerland

The Germanic Affairs office was attached to the SS Main office (SS-Hauptamt) in Berlin and served as a command hub for all Germanic-SS groups in Western Europe. A notable exception to the office's control was Norway, which maintained its own independent command for the Norwegian Germanic-SS

ORGANIZATION OF THE NETHERLANDS-SS

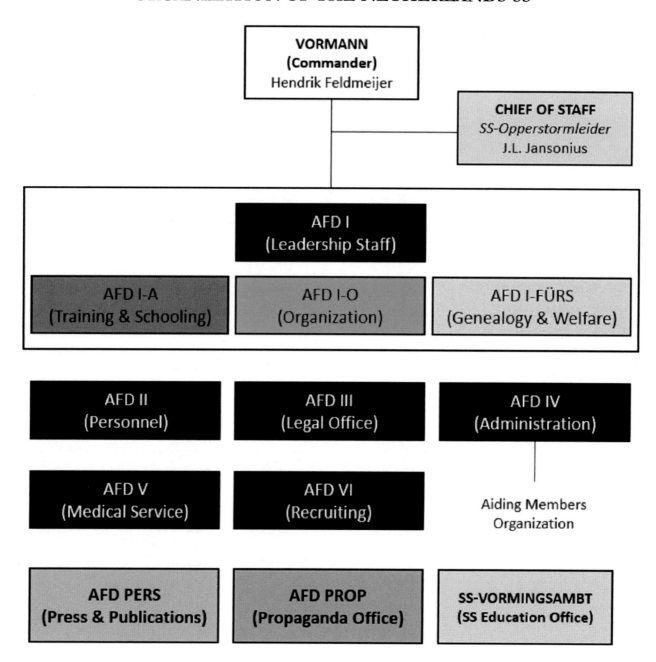

The first parade of the Netherlands SS took place in The Hague on January 11th 1941. By February, the group had six hundred members; that number would rise to eight hundred by the end of the summer. On November 1st 1942, the formal name of the Dutch SS was changed to "Germaansche SS in Nederland". The group now answered to the SS in Germany, rather than Dutch authorities, through the Office of the Germanic-SS which was a special section of the SS headquarters in Berlin.

The Netherlands-SS became the largest of the Germanic-SS formations and thus served as a template for all other national groups to follow. Structurally, the Germanic-SS was to mirror the Allgemeine-SS in Germany, would be issued black surplus General-SS uniforms, and maintain a rank system parallel to the ranks of the regular SS. Germanic-SS personnel, unlike their foreign Waffen-SS counterparts, were also permitted to use the "SS" prefix before their ranks with the highest obtainable rank equivalent to SS-Obergruppenführer. In the Netherlands, a special rank known as "Vormann" was created solely for the Dutch SS Commander.

Henk Feldmeijer – Chief Collaborationist of the SS

Johannes Hendrik Feldmeijer was a Dutch political activist born in 1910. Feldmeijer joined the National Socialist Movement in the Netherlands (NSB) in 1932 and in 1937 he founded "Der Vaderen Erfdeel" which was a racial organization dedicated to researching Dutch culture.

In 1938, Feldmeijer became a German spy, making several trips to Berlin and advising the German government on various aspects of the Dutch state. He was imprisoned by Dutch authorities in 1940, but liberated by invading German forces later that year. In September of 1940, Feldmeijer helped form the Nederlandsche-SS (Netherlands SS), the first of several Germanic-SS organizations. In addition to serving as head of the Netherlands SS, Feldmeijer twice served in combat as a Waffen-SS foreign volunteer. Returning home in 1943, he became involved with suppressing resistance and assisted police with round-ups, arrests, and executions. On February 22nd 1945, Feldmeijer was killed when his car was strafed by an attacking Allied aircraft

NETHERLANDS-SS DEPARTMENT VII

AFD VIII-A *Vorming* (Academic Office)	AFD VIII-B *SS-Ras- en Sibbeambt* (Race & Research)	AFD VIII-C *Soldaat en Sibbe* (Soldier Geneology)

FOTO- EN FILMDIENST (Photo & Film Office)	TAMBOER- EN PIJPERKORPS (Drum & Fife Corps)

HOOFDREDACTEUR "STORM" (Publication Direction for the newspaper "The Storm")	HOOFDREDACTEUR "HAMER" (Publication Direction for the newspaper "The Hammer")

In 1943, the Netherlands-SS headquarters created the SS Education Office, which was designated as "Department VII" and maintained authority over racial and ideological training. This was followed by the creation of a "Department VIII" which combined the functions of several previously established offices.

The "Aiding Members Organization" was formed in 1941 to solicit donation funds from Dutch citizens who were otherwise not full members of the Netherlands SS. An aiding member could donate any amount of funds they wished, after which they would be referred to as a "Fördernde Mitglieder" (F.M.) and be issued a special lapel pin for wear on civilian clothes.

Donations of the Aiding Members was at first under the authority of the Netherlands-SS administration office; however, by 1943 a separate organization had been formed known as the "Instituut der Begunstigende Leden der Germaansche SS in Nederland" often shortened to "Begunstigende Leden" or simply "B.L". The intent of the Netherlands-SS leadership was to eventually evolve the B.L. into a reserve force of the regular Dutch SS. The B.L. eventually reached a membership of four thousand by 1944, but was never converted into a paramilitary force and remained a financial assistance group.

GERMANIC-SS REGIMENTS IN THE NETHERLANDS

SS REGIMENT	REGIMENTAL TITLE	HEADQUARTERS	NSB DISTRICT
1. SS-Standaard	Groningen	Kraneweg 19	Friesland, Groningen & Drenthe
2. SS-Standaard	Arnheim	Sw. de Laandasstraat	Overijssel & Gelderland
3. SS-Standaard	Amsterdam	Koningslaan 12	North Holland & Utrecht
4. SS-Standaard	Den Haag	Groenhovenstraat 12	South Holland & Zeeland
5. SS-Standaard	Eindhoven	Ten Hagestraat 1	North Brabant & Limburg

A final office of the Netherlands-SS, founded in the last days of German occupation in 1944, was the "Germaansche Werkgemeenschap Nederland" (German Research Association) which was an independent office conducting Aryan racial research. Throughout the German occupation, the Netherlands-SS also maintained a group known as the "SS-Politie-Standard" (SS Police Regiment) which consisted of Dutch police officers who were also members of the Netherlands-SS. The police regiment was commanded directly by the Higher SS and Police Leader of the Netherlands and its members wore standard Dutch police uniforms and insignia.

Expanding the Germanic-SS

While the Germanic-SS in the Netherlands met with a resounding success, at least initially, exactly the opposite befell attempts to establish a similar group in Belgium. When Germany occupied Belgium in the spring of 1940, the country was both ideologically and racially divided between the Flemish in the north (who supported the Germans) and the Wallonia population in the south who held sympathies towards France. Belgium also contained several conflicting pro-Nazi movements, all of which were now attempting to curry favor with the new Nazi regime.

The oldest and most significant nationalist party in Belgium was the Frontpartij (Front Party) which in the mid-1930s was absorbed into the "Vlaamsche Nationaal Verbond" or VNV. Both of the aforementioned groups were supported by the veteran's organization "Vlaamsche Oud Strijders" (VOS) and were in competition with the Verdinaso, also known as the "Green Shirts". In 1935, a new Belgium National Socialist movement was founded known as "DeVlag" (the Flag) and it was this group which eventually won the power struggle as the dominant pro-Nazi organization in Belgium. The VNV became a counterpart organization to the Flag, and was outwardly recognized as the officially sponsored Belgium Nazi Party.

Himmler ordered the establishment of a local SS group in Belgium in the fall of 1940. The Flag organization was tasked with initial recruitment; however, Himmler then declared that the Belgium SS would be controlled directly by Germany and not local Belgium Nazis. Richard Jungclaus, who had served as the SS advisor in the Netherlands, was appointed as the administrator of the Belgium SS, with this group to be operationally controlled by the Higher SS and Police Leader of Belgium.

In September 1941, recruitment for the Belgium SS began in Antwerp and Ghent, with just under two hundred members enlisting. The Belgium SS was initially known as the "Algemeene SS Vlaanderen", frequently shortened to the "Vlaamsche-SS". The organization held a small headquarters staff, and on September 1st 1941 all Flemish SS men were grouped into the First Flemish SS Regiment, which was the only major Belgium Germanic-SS unit ever formed. The Belgium SS also formed a reserve force, first known simply as the "SS militia" and later becoming the "Vlaanderen Korps" (Flemish Corps). The Flemish Corps was open to members aged thirty-five years or older who did not otherwise fulfill the requirements of the regular Belgium SS. The Flemish Corps appears to have been a repository for inactive SS members and had no further internal organization.

Like the Netherlands, the Belgium SS maintained an Aiding Members Society and furthermore operated a small training department which ran an SS school known as the "SS-Ausbildungslager Schoten" in Antwerp. By 1943, the operation of the school had been taken over entirely by the regular SS in Germany. The German authorities also appointed several leaders of the Belgium SS, most of which did not serve long in their positions but rather transferred to serve in the foreign divisions of the Waffen-SS. Thus, with weak leadership and a growing need for Belgians to serve in combat, membership in the Belgium-SS began to decline. In 1944, with just over a thousand registered members, only five hundred were serving on active duties, with the majority of these later transferred to duties in other organizations or sent to Germany as foreign workers. A brief attempt to bolster SS membership through a youth group (known as the NSJV) also met with failure.

In May 1944, the Belgium SS membership was merged with the political group DeVlag. A new group was then formed, known as the Sicherheitskorps (Security Corps), which served as an auxiliary police force until the liberation of Belgium by Allied forces in the fall of 1944. The relative failure of the Belgium SS was slightly compensated by the formation of another SS group in Norway, which would grow to become the second largest of the Germanic-SS groups.

When Germany occupied Norway in April 1940, a strong pro-Nazi political party was ready to seize power. Led by Vidkun Quisling, the Norway National Union (also known as the NS) held a membership of over fifty thousand, as well as maintaining a storm trooper paramilitary group called the Hird. Expecting the Germans to install him as leader of Norway, Quisling was incensed when his country was placed under occupation and subjugated to the rule of a Reich Commissioner. The German commissioner Josef Terboven was also hostile to Quisling and saw him as a potential radical and enemy to Germany.

ORGANIZATION OF THE NORWEGIAN-SS (1943)

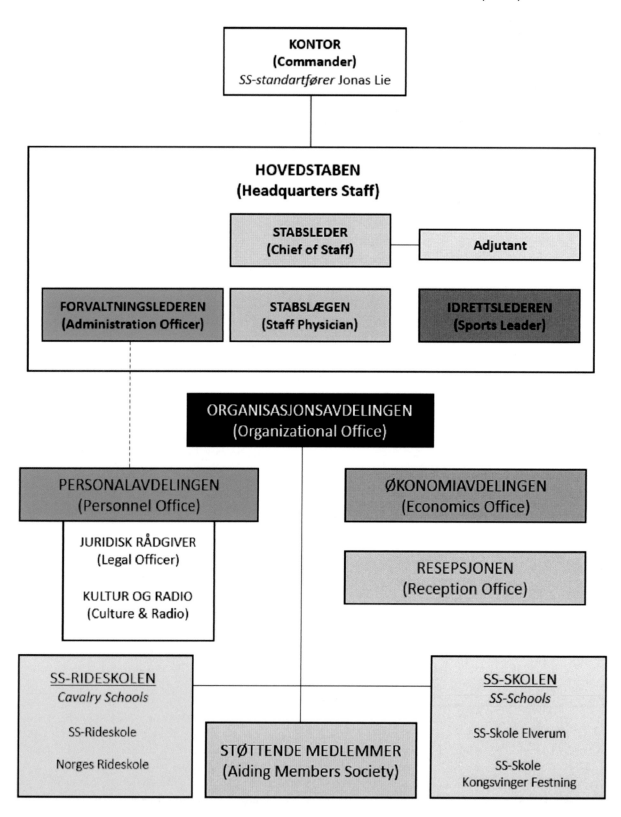

GERMANIC-SS UNITS IN NORWAY

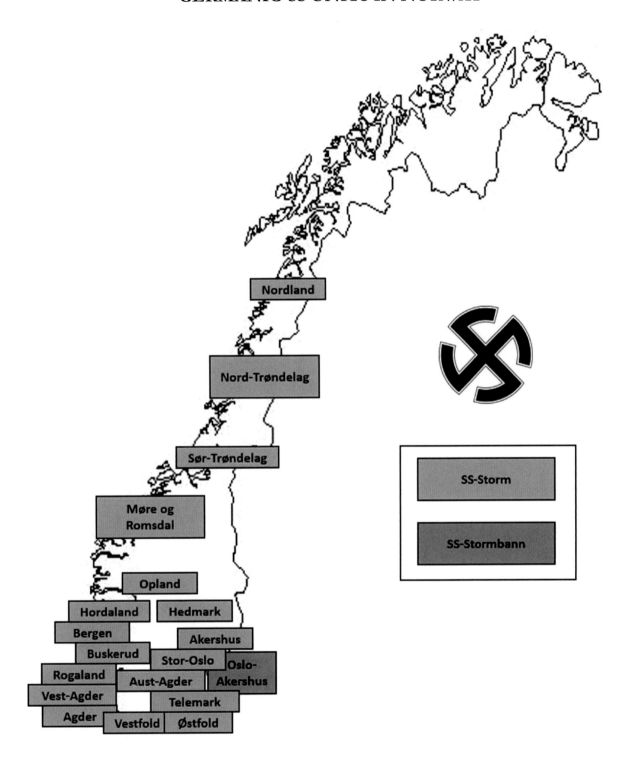

In addition to a headquarters in Oslo, the Germanic-SS in Norway (Germanske SS Norge) was organized into company sized units (SS-Stormer), mainly in the southern part of the country. Battalion sized formations, containing upwards of four companies, were authorized; however, only one was ever formed, known as the "SS-Stormbann Oslo-Akerhus". This battalion was also referred to as a "Fylking". Regiment sized formations, known as "SS-Standart" were proposed but none were ever created.

When the Norwegian SS was first formed, this act was done without Quisling's consent. Instead, the Germans appointed the Chief of the Norwegian Police (Jonas Lie) as commander of this new group, which was then named the "Norges SS" in May 1941. Recruits in the Norges SS were transferred directly from the Norwegian Hird storm troopers.

The SS recruits were first sent to a hastily established SS school at Elerum, while Jonas Lie set about establishing a headquarters staff in the Norwegian capitol of Oslo. Quisling continued to vehemently oppose the existence of the SS group, but this would change following his appointment as Minister President of Norway in February 1942, after which time he gradually lent support to the SS organization. On July 21st 1942, Quisling fully endorsed the Norwegian SS, which then formally changed its name to the "Germanske SS Norge".

Rivals in Norway: Josef Terboven and Vidkun Quisling (Federal German Archives)

Norwegian	German	Equivalent
Rode	Rotte	Team
Lag	Schar	Squad
Tropp	Trupp	Platoon
Storm	Sturm	Company
Fylking	Sturmbann	Battalion
Stormbann		
Standart		Regiment

The Norwegian SS eventually held a membership of 1,247 organized into a headquarters, several departments, as well as local units situated mainly in the southern regions of Norway.

Left: Norwegian-SS unit titles and comparisons

The tide of World War II would bring an end to the Norwegian-SS, and by 1944 the war situation against the Soviet Union required most able-bodied Norwegians to transfer to active combat. By 1945, nearly all members of the Norwegian-SS were serving in units of the Waffen-SS and the group thereafter existed effectively only on paper.

The last major Germanic-SS group to be formed was in Denmark, a country which had been permitted relatively autonomous rule under Nazi occupation, both with an independent government and reigning Danish king. Between the initial German invasion of 1940 and the year 1943, Denmark existed in a grey zone between occupied country and protectorate, overseen by a Reich Plenipotentiary in the person of SS-General Dr. Werner Best.

Left: Knud Martinsen, the first commander of the Schalburg Corps – previously known as the Danish Free Corps of the SS (National Archives)

While Denmark did possess a local Nazi Party (known as the DNSAP), it was not until August 1943 in which this group was granted any sort of substantial power by the German authorities. In that month, due to increased unrest amongst the Danish people who were becoming openly critical of the Nazi regime, the Germans tightened their grip on Denmark and granted the Danish Nazis more control over the government. At the same time, Heinrich Himmler ordered the formation of a Danish branch of the SS, but also indicated that this group was to be controlled directly by Germany and not the Danish Nazi Party[lxi].

The Danish Free Corps, which had been a formation of the Waffen-SS since June 1941, was used as the primary recruiting pool for members of the new Danish SS. Formed in February 1942 simply as the "Germanic Corps", the name of the Danish SS was quickly changed to avoid confusion with the Third Germanic Corps of the Waffen-SS. On March 30th 1943, the Danish SS was re-designated as the "Schalburg Corps", named in honor of Christian Frederik von Schalburg who had commanded the Danish Free Corps and had been killed in action while serving in Russia.

SCHALBURG CORPS ORGANIZATION (1943)

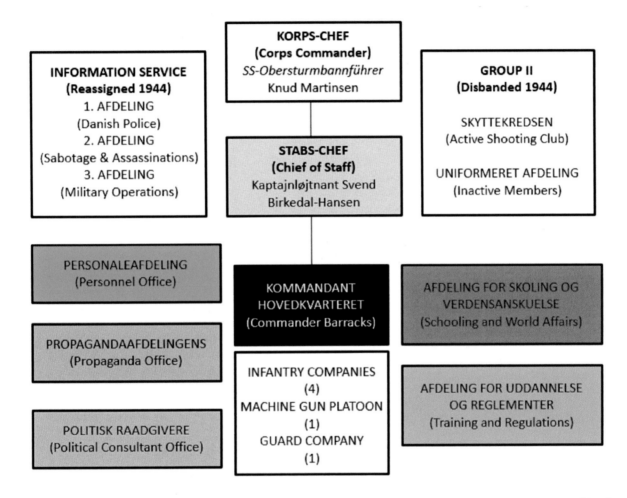

The Schalburg Corps was unique amongst the Germanic-SS formations, in that the unit was organized in the same manner as an armed SS unit of the Waffen-SS. SS-Obersturmbannführer Knud Martinsen was the Schalburg Corp's chief organizer and first commander, while the corps itself was formed with three infantry companies and a machine gun unit.

From the onset, the Schalburg Corps was clearly intended for use as a military formation. By the end of 1943, the Schalburg Corps had been divided into two components (or Groups), with Group I considered an active military formation for use in training Danish recruits of the Waffen-SS. Group II was considered a home guard formation intended for older Danes and those ineligible for military service; Group II was itself divided into both an active and inactive component. Both groups answered to the Schalburg Corps headquarters which maintained offices for administration, finance, supply, and training.

The Schalburg Corps was also the only Germanic-SS unit to create a dedicated intelligence service, this being the Efterretningstjenesten (Information Service) abbreviated as the ET. The ET was modeled after the secret police in Nazi Germany and held sections for intelligence, sabotage, assassinations, and police operations. The Schalburg Corps controlled the ET until April 1944, after which the group was transferred directly to the command of the Higher SS and Police Leader of Denmark and re-designated as a foreign auxiliary of the Sicherheitsdienst.

In late 1944, the Nazi authorities created a second Germanic-SS group in Denmark, separate from the Schalburg Corps, and known as the "Germanische SS Dänemark". This new organization was controlled directly by the Waffen-SS and served as a health and welfare organization for wounded Danish members of armed SS foreign volunteer units. The unit was divided into districts by which aide was disbursed.

GERMANIC-SS DISTRICTS IN DENMARK

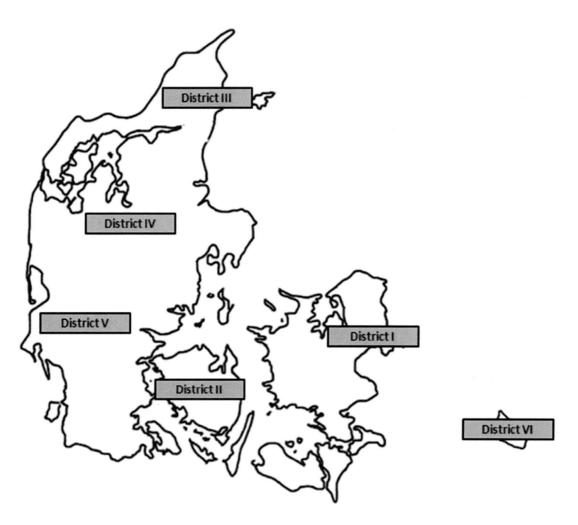

During the final year of its existence, the Schalburg Corps established a one hundred man guard company which was used for homeland defense as well as prospective concentration camp duties[lxii]. By the end of 1944, Group II of the Schalburg Corps had been revamped into the "People's League", which was now considered a formation of the Luftwaffe and thereafter became known as the "Grey Corps". By mid-1944, the Schalburg Corps possessed approximately one thousand members and had increased its organization to include four infantry companies. The corps was unique in that its members retained Danish Army ranks and also the corps had no geographical divisions but existed primarily as a single armed regiment headquartered at the Ringsted barracks in Copenhagen. The "Schalburg-Skolen Høvelte pr. Birkerød" was the primary training academy for the Schalburg Corps, at which most prospective corps members were required to complete a six-week indoctrination course. If a member had served on the eastern front, initial training was waived.

At the end of 1944, the Schalburg Corps was re-designated as a foreign SS training battalion with the name changed to the "SS-Uddannelsesbatallion Sjælland" (Training Battalion Seeland). Another group, which had emerged apparently as a penal battalion for those who had violated discipline within the Schalburg Corps, was the SS-Sonderkommando Dänemark. Little is known of this command, with the exception that undercover SS members were tasked to encourage Schalburg Corps members to make disloyal statements regarding Germany, thus leading to an arrest for defeatism. The Schalburg Corps was formally disbanded on February 28th 1945.

COMPARATIVE RANKS OF THE GERMANIC-SS

SS Rank	Netherlands Belgium	Norway	Denmark
SS-Anwarter	SS-Maat		
SS-Mann	SS-Man	SS-mann	Schalburgmand
SS-Sturmmann	SS-Stormman	SS-stormmann	Tropsfører
SS-Rottenführer	SS-Rottenleider	SS-rodefører	
SS-Unterscharführer	SS-Onderschaarleider	SS-nestlagfører	Obertropsfører
SS-Scharführer	SS-Schaarleider	SS-lagfører	Vagtmester
SS-Oberscharführer	SS-Opperschaarleider	SS-nesttroppfører	Obervagtmester
SS-Hauptscharführer	SS-Hoofdschaarleider	SS-troppfører	Stabsvagtmester
SS-Sturmscharführer			Fændrik
SS-Untersturmführer	SS-Onderstormleider	SS-neststormfører	Løjtnant
SS-Obersturmführer	SS-Opperstormleider	SS-stormfører	Overløjtnant
SS-Hauptsturmführer	SS-Hoofdstormleider	SS-høvedsmann	Kaptajn
SS-Sturmbannführer	SS-Stormbanleider	SS-stormbannfører	Major
SS-Obersturmbannführer	SS-Opperstormbanleider	SS-neststandartfører	Oberstløjtnant
SS-Standartenführer	SS-Standaardleider	SS-standartfører	Oberst
SS-Oberführer	SS-Opperleider	SS-nestbrigadefører	
SS-Brigadeführer	SS-Brigadeleider	SS-brigadefører	
SS-Gruppenführer	SS-Groepsleider	Stabsleder	
SS-Obergruppenführer	SS-Oppergroepsleider		

A unique Germanic-SS group, proposed but never completely formed, was the Germanic-SS in Switzerland. Nazi sentiments had existed in Switzerland since the early 1930s, although a wide spread movement in support of German unification never developed. Unlike other Germanic regions, such as Austria and the Sudetenland, Switzerland had a mixture of both German and French culture giving the Swiss a unique background, in addition to that nation's long standing stance of neutrality in Europe.

In Adolf Hitler's view of foreign policy, Switzerland was an annoyance to German expansion and an invasion plan had been ordered in 1940. Prepared as "Operation Tannenbaum", Hitler's military strategists foresaw great difficulties in the conquest of Switzerland due to the high alpine terrain and the fierce determination of Swiss defenders in the face of invasion. The plan to attack Switzerland was put on hold for four years and finally abandoned completely in 1944.

Switzerland's small Nazi Party, known as the "National Movement of Switzerland", had grown to a size of four thousand members by the end of 1940, at which time the group was banned by Swiss authorities yet continued to operate in underground cells. At the same time, Heinrich Himmler began investigating the possibility of a Swiss branch of the SS, yet it would be two more years before this aim was only partially realized.

In the fall of 1941, Himmler tasked Franz Riedweg, a Swiss volunteer of the Waffen-SS, to form an SS branch in Switzerland. Riedweg had served in the SS since 1938, first in the SS Main Office of Personnel and later as a volunteer in the Waffen-SS. Having known Riedweg personally, Himmler considered him a prime candidate to form a Swiss branch of the SS.

Left: Franz Riedweg (Federal German Archives)

By 1942, Riedweg had recruited approximately two hundred Swiss citizens to form an SS group which was then declared as the "Germanische SS Schweiz" (Germanic SS in Switzerland). In its early stages of organization, the group had no central headquarters, nor were any of its members considered regular SS personnel. By 1943, membership had risen to five hundred, with the group controlled directly by the Germanic-SS office in Germany. Riedweg himself was not in Switzerland during this period, having returned to fight at the front as a member of the Waffen-SS, thus leaving the running of the Swiss SS to subordinates.

In 1944, the "Schweizer Sportbund" was founded, which Riedweg hoped would serve as the nucleus for a Swiss SS combat unit. With the war now undeniably turning against Germany, Riedweg foresaw the possibility of the Swiss SS becoming a guerilla unit, possibly sent to Germany to fight in mountainous terrain against Allied occupation forces. The war ended before any serious consideration could be given to this idea. In 1945, Riedweg was captured by the British but was not extradited to Switzerland, which had sentenced him in absentia to sixteen years in prison for treason. He lived the rest of his life in Germany and died 2005 in Munich.

The Germanic-SS in Germany

A parallel organization to the Germanic-SS groups in occupied Europe was the "Germanic-SS in the Reich" which was administrated as sub-department of the SS Main Office. The Germanic-SS in Germany was considerably different from its counterparts abroad and was intended to oversee special groups of foreign workers who were brought to Germany under the authority of the SS. Foreign workers were recruited from all of the countries which maintained their own official Germanic-SS groups, as well as from Switzerland. Workers brought to Germany were then organized into "Germanic Battalions" (Germanische Sturmbanne) which were administratively assigned to senior districts of the Allgemeine-SS. In theory, every senior district of the SS was to be attached a Germanic Battalion, yet only seven such units were ever established. The battalions were commanded by a Sonderstäbe (Special Staff) which was attached to the office of an SS-Oberabschnitt. Each Special Staff also had the option of establishing Outstations (Aussenstellen) of which only one was ever actually formed.

GERMANIC-SS UNITS WITHIN GERMANY

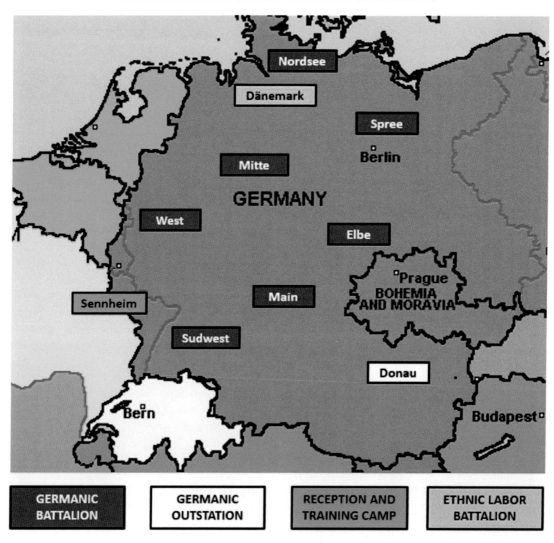

| GERMANIC BATTALION | GERMANIC OUTSTATION | RECEPTION AND TRAINING CAMP | ETHNIC LABOR BATTALION |

Foreign workers recruited under the Germanic-SS program were first sent to a reception and training camp, the largest of which was at Sennheim in France, itself a sub-camp of the Natzweiler-Struthof concentration camp. Germanic-SS recruits were housed in separate facilities and provided with decent food as well as a standard uniform consisting of black trousers, work boots, and a khaki colored shirt. Upon completion of basic training, the foreign workers were assigned to a battalion of the Germanic-SS and typically wore grey Waffen-SS tunics with no insignia.

In mid-1942, the SS established the first and only "ethnic labor battalion" in Hamburg, which was formed from Danish dock workers and was considered separate from the other units of the Germanic-SS in Germany. Known as the "Denmark Germanic Battalion" (often abbreviated as the GSD), this organization existed as a miniature version of the Germanic-SS in Denmark, complete with SS uniforms and titles. The ultimate aim of the Denmark Germanic Battalion was never made clear, even to the Germans themselves. Recruits in Hamburg were first sent to Sennheim, where they attended a special school known as the "SS-Ausbildungslager", which provided six weeks of military training as well as ideological instruction on pan-Germanic ideals throughout Europe. The SS recruit was then technically to serve in the Waffen-SS, but very few ever did, instead returning to war essential duties in Hamburg.

The Denmark Germanic Battalion was administered from the SS Main Office, and from the beginning was unpopular with both the Germans and the Danish. In 1943, the Danish Nazi Party formally requested the group be disbanded to which the Germans complied with little hesitation.

The end of the Germanic-SS

All Germanic-SS groups in occupied countries typically met with a hasty end once Allied troops began liberating conquered western nations from the Germans. In the Netherlands, which had seen the birth of the Germanic-SS and had hosted the largest of all the Germanic-SS groups, British forces entered the country in September 1944 and slowly began to liberate the population. The Germans maintained a military presence until the end of the war, although most German resistance had been suppressed by the start of 1945.

COUNTRY	MEMBERSHIP
Belgium	505
Denmark	< 1,000
Netherlands	6,127
Norway	1,247
Switzerland	< 500

Membership of the Germanic-SS in 1944

The Flemish-SS in Belgium underwent a similar fate when Allied forces entered that country in the fall of 1944. With British forces rapidly advancing towards Brussels and Antwerp, the Flemish-SS literally fled, disbanded its headquarters, and its members were ordered to integrate into German combat units. By the end of 1944, the Belgium branch of the Germanic-SS had ceased to exist.

Left: A member of the Germanic-SS smiles for the camera in 1944. Less than a year later, former members of the Germanic-SS would be branded as the vilest form of traitors by their respective home countries. (Federal German Archives)

The Schalburg Corps was the only Germanic-SS group which was formally disbanded by the Germans themselves, having been disestablished in February 1945. In Norway, the end of the Germanic-SS began in September of 1944 when German trust in the puppet Nazi government began to wane. In January 1945, Himmler dismissed Jonas Lie, the Norwegian-SS Chief of Staff, and replaced him with Leif Schjøren. Three months later, Himmler fired this new Chief of Staff as well, and placed the entire Norwegian SS under direct German control. The last commander was SS-Hauptsturmführer Olaf Lindvig who ran the group until the last German forces in Norway surrendered to the Allies on May 7th 1945.

In the wake of liberation, Germanic-SS members were branded as traitors by their countries and subject to harsh prosecution and penalties. In Norway, the Nazi puppet Vidkun Quisling was executed in October 1945 while Jonas Lie died of a heart attack before trial. Dutch SS commander Hendrik Feldmeijer ended the Second World War on a sinister note by establishing "SS-Sonderkommando-Feldmeijer", which was responsible for suppressing resistance and executing dissidents. Feldmeijer himself was killed by Allied aircraft in February 1945.

After the end of the Second World War, the general membership of the Flemish-SS in Belgium was arrested by Allied authorities, tried by local courts, while many more were killed by vigilante groups. In all, some 56,000 collaborators were prosecuted in the Netherlands with nearly three hundred executed. Belgium authorities were also known to prosecute foreign volunteers of the Waffen-SS. Léon Degrelle, who had been a key figure in recruiting Walloon volunteers into the armed SS, received a death sentence although he escaped to Norway, then Spain, and lived the rest of his life in exile.

Germanic-SS uniforms and insignia

Based on the black tunics of the Allgemeine-SS in Germany, surviving examples of Germanic-SS uniforms are today extremely rare. Seen as a sign of collaboration, most Germanic-SS uniforms were destroyed by their owners at the end of the Second World War, with little post-war research existing concerning these SS clothing articles.

Germanic-SS uniforms were independently designed by each respective national group, with only basic guidelines issued from the SS in Germany. Germanic-SS uniforms were to use the same collar tab rank system as in Germany, with national insignia worn in the place of the red swastika armband and headgear eagle crest.

Above: The four uniforms of the Germanic-SS. From left to right is shown the Netherlands-SS, Flemish-SS (Belgium), Norwegian-SS, and the Dutch Schalburg Corps. (Images courtesy of Federal German Archives) Below: Germanic-SS cap and collar insignia

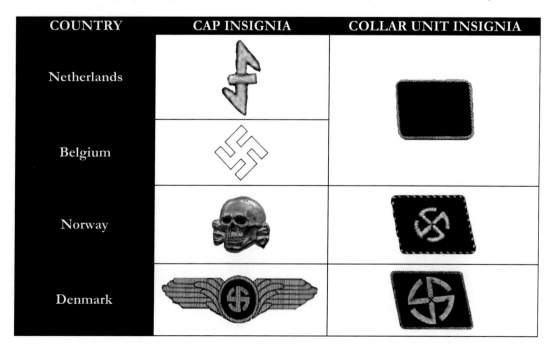

COUNTRY	CAP INSIGNIA	COLLAR UNIT INSIGNIA
Netherlands		
Belgium		
Norway		
Denmark		

Members of the Flemish-SS and the Schalburg Corps wore khaki brown undershirts, while the SS in the Netherlands wore black[lxiii]. The Norwegian-SS was the only group to routinely wear white shirts beneath the black tunic. Norway and Denmark developed national unit insignia, for wear on the left collar patch, while in the Netherlands and Denmark a blank collar tab was displayed. For a brief period in 1944, the "Danish Schalburg Corps Information Service" wore a distinctive collar badge in lieu of national insignia (see right – graphical recreation).

With the exception of Norway, which wore a peaked black mountain SS cap, the Germanic-SS utilized standard SS headgear with black chinstraps for SS solders and silver cords for officers. The Nazi national eagle, present on the front of all SS headgear, was replaced by a unique emblem for each branch of the Germanic-SS. The death's head cap pin was standardized with the SS in Germany.

Germanic-SS rank insignia was identical to the SS in Germany, although modified SS rank titles were used in each respective country. Denmark was the only nation to utilize non-SS ranks for its Germanic-SS members, choosing instead to bestow rank titles standard with the Danish Army.

Sleeve and cuffband insignia placement for the Germanic-SS. From left to right is shown insignia for the Netherlands-SS, Flemish (Belgium-SS), Norwegian-SS, and the Dutch Schalburg Corps (Insignia images graphical recreations)

All branches of the Germanic-SS maintained unique unit insignia, to include sleeve insignia, cuffbands, and collar unit insignia. Both Norway and Denmark displayed a wheeled swastika unit insignia, while the Flemish SS maintained a blank collar tab for all personnel. In the Netherlands, this same blank collar insignia was issued to headquarters personnel. The Germanic-SS in the Netherlands was the only national SS group to display individual regimental collar insignia with five regimental numbers authorized.

SS-regiment insignia displayed by the Netherlands branch of the Germanic-SS (Graphical recreations)

The Norwegian-SS was the only branch of the Germanic-SS to display a national eagle shoulder crest while the Schalburg Corps of Denmark displayed a colored crest which also appeared on all Schalburg Corps flags. Netherlands-SS members displayed a triangular crest which was bordered in gold if the SS member served as an SS Department Chief.

The Germanic-SS issued two versions of an SS runes sleeve diamond, both intended to be worn on the upper sleeve of the black SS tunic. The aluminum braided sleeve diamond was worn by the enlisted Flemish-SS, as well as by the entire Germanic-SS in Norway. An SS sleeve diamond bordered in silver was worn by all members of the Netherlands-SS as well as Flemish SS officers.

Above left: Sleeve diamond insignia of the Germanic-SS.
Right: Netherlands-SS patches for regular members and department chiefs

The solid silver SS sleeve diamond was also worn occasionally by the Norwegian SS Chief of Staff. The commanders of both the Netherlands and Norwegian branches of the Germanic-SS were entitled to display unique insignia on both collars.

Netherlands

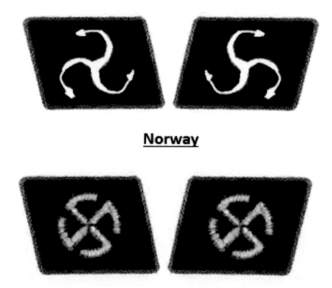

Norway

Commander's insignia for the Netherlands and Norwegian branches of the Germanic-SS

CUFFBANDS OF THE GERMANIC-SS

CUFFBAND	DESCRIPTION
	Worn by all members of the Netherlands-SS
SS-Vlaanderen	Worn by all regular members of the Flemish-SS in Belgium
Vlaanderen-Korps	Worn by members of the Belgium-SS Reserve (known as the "Flemish Corps")
Germanske SS Norge	Worn by all members of the Norwegian-SS
Schalburg	Worn by all members of the Schalburg Corps except for those issued honor cuffbands
Skjalm Hvide	
Absalon	
Herluf Trolle	Company honor cuffbands of the Schalburg Corps. The cuffbands were named after popular Flemish religious and folk heroes.
Olaf Rye	
Cæssøe	

Cuffbands of the Germanic-SS were worn on the lower left sleeve of the black SS uniform in the same manner as the regular SS in Germany. With the exception of the Schalburg Corps, which was the only Germanic-SS group to issue honor cuffbands for individual SS companies, the Germanic-SS cuffbands were generic and worn by all members of the particular national SS organization.

Right: A Schalburg Corps officer wears the Danish khaki tunic (Federal German Archives)

The Schalburg Corps in Denmark was also the only Germanic-SS organization to adopt a field uniform similar to the grey tunic used by the Waffen-SS. The Schalburg field jacket was designed after the khaki service uniform of the Danish Army and displayed SS insignia in the same manner as the regular black SS service jacket. All collar insignia was worn with white piping, while non-commissioned officers wore a thick collar braid in the same manner as senior enlisted personnel of the Waffen-SS[lxiv].

BIBLIOGRAPHY AND ENDNOTES

Cited sources

Allen, M. (2002). The Business of Genocide: The SS, Slave Labor, and the Concentration Camps. Chapel Hill, North Carolina: University of North Carolina Press

Bishop, C. (2005). Hitler's Foreign Divisions: Foreign Volunteers in the Waffen-SS. London: Amber Books

Butler, R. (2001). SS-Leibstandarte: The History of the First SS Division. Zenith Press

Calic, E. (1985). Reinhard Heydrich: The Chilling Story of the Man Who Masterminded the Nazi Death Camps. New York: William Morrow & Company

Cecil, R. (1972). The Myth of the Master Race: Alfred Rosenberg and Nazi Ideology. New York: Dodd, Mead

Cook, S. & Bender J. (1994). Leibstandarte SS Adolf Hitler: Uniforms, Organization, & History. San Jose, California: R. James Bender Publishing

Hayes, A. (1996). SS Uniforms, Insignia, & Accoutrements. Atglen, Pennsylvania: Schiffer Military History

Hayes, A., & Maguire, J. (1997). Uniforms of the Third Reich: A Study in Photographs. Atglen, Pennsylvania: Schiffer Military History.

Höss, R. (1996). Death Dealer: The Memoirs of the SS Kommandant at Auschwitz. New York: Da Capo Press.

Koehl, Robert (2004). The SS: A History 1919–45. Stroud: Tempus Publishing

Knížek, A., Burian, M., Rajlich, J., & Stehlík, E. (2002). Assassination: Operation Anthropoid (1941 - 1942). Prague: Czech Republic Ministry of Defense.

Krawczyk, W., & Lukacs, P. (2001). Waffen-SS Uniforms and Insignia. Ramsbury, Marlborough: Crowood Press.

Lehrer, S. (2000). Wannsee House and the Holocaust. Jefferson, North Carolina: McFarlan Press

Lumsden, R. (1997). Himmler's Black Order: A History of the SS (1923-45). Gloucestershire, England: Sutton Publishing.

Lumsden, R. (2001). Medals and Decorations of Hitler's Germany. Osceola, Wisconsin: MBI Publishing Company.

MacLean, F. L. (1999). The Camp Men: The SS Officers who ran the Nazi Concentration Camp system. Atglen, Pennsylvania: Schiffer Military History.

MacLean, F. L. (1999). The Field Men: The SS Officers who led the Einsatzkommandos - the Nazi Mobile Killing Units. Atglen, Pennsylvania: Schiffer Military History.

Månsson, M. (2001). Reichsführer-SS: A Photographic Chronicle of Heinrich Himmler. Atglen, Pennsylvania: Schiffer Military History.

McDonnell, L. (1999). Insignia of World War II. London, England: Amber Books.

Mollo, A., & Taylor, H. (1997). Uniforms of the SS (Collected Edition, Volumes 1 - 6). London, England: Windrow & Greene.

Nyiszli, M. (2011). Auschwitz: A Doctor's Eyewitness Account. Arcade Publishing.

Padfield, P. (1991). Himmler: Reichsführer-SS. Henry Holt & Company Publishing

Scheibert, H. (1990). Panzer: A Pictorial Documentation. Atglen, PA: Schiffer Publishing, Ltd.

Schellenberg, W. (2000). The Labyrinth. De Capo Press.

Schutzstaffel der NSDAP. (1942). SS Officers List. Berlin, Germany: Schiffer Military Publishing.

Swift, M., & Sharpe, M. (2001). Historical Maps of World War II Europe. London, England: PRC Publishing.

United States Holocaust Memorial Museum. (1996). Historical Atlas of the Holocaust. New York, New York: Macmillan Publishing.

Time Life. (1988). The Third Reich – The SS. Alexandria, Virginia: Time Incorporated

United States War Department. (1945). Handbook on German Military Forces. Washington, DC: United States Government Printing Office.

Vrba, R. (1997). I Cannot Forgive. Regent College Publishing.

Williamson, G. (1995). Loyalty is my Honor: Personal Accounts from the Waffen-SS. Osceola, Wisconsin: Motorbooks International.

Williamson, G. (1994). The SS: Hitler's Instrument of Terror. Osceola, Wisconsin: Motorbooks International.

Yerger, M. C. (1997). Allgemeine-SS: The Commands, Units, and Leaders of the General SS. Atglen, Pennsylvania: Schiffer Military History.

Primary Document Sources

SS Officer Personnel Records, National Archives & Records Administration (College Park, Maryland), Publication T354. 799 rolls. (GG 27, 75, 79, 95 and T176/rolls 19 & 24)

Office of Strategic Services (OSS). (1945). Organization of the RSHA. Washington, DC: German Section, OSS.

Operational Reports of the SS-Einsatzgruppen, Reich Central Security Office (1942)

"Report on the Destruction of the Warsaw Ghetto", SS and Police Leader Jürgen Stroop (1943)

Trial of the Major War Criminals before the International Military Tribunal at Nuremberg (1946) Testimony of Witnesses Dr. Ernst Kaltenbrunner, Otto Ohlendorf, Walter Schellenberg, & Rudolf Höss

Image Sources

Bavarian State Archives, Schönfeldstr. 5, 80539 München, Germany

Federal German Archives, Potsdamer Straße 1, 56075 Koblenz, Germany

Imperial War Museums, IWM London, Lambeth Road, London SE1 6HZ

National Archives & Records Administration, 8601 Adelphi Rd, College Park, MD 20740

State Archives of Poland, ul.Rakowiecka 2D, 02-517 Warsaw, Poland

United States Holocaust Memorial Museum, 100 Raoul Wallenberg Place, SW, Wash, DC 20024-2126

The author also thanks the donation of privately-owned photographs which appear on the following pages: 27, 161, 221, 313, 328, and 331

All graphical images of insignia, badges, and other SS accoutrements are recreations based on original photographs and source material from the references listed above. In cases of rare insignia items which have not been photographed, images have been recreated from written descriptions

Map Sources

Bundeswehr Military History Museum, Olbrichtpl. 2, 01099 Dresden, Germany

U.S. Army Center of Military History, 102 4th Avenue, Building 35, Fort McNair, DC 20319-5060

Virginia Tech Center for Judiac Studies, 295 West Campus Drive, Blacksburg, VA 24061

Interview Source Material

Dr. Rudolf Vrba (Interview conducted April 2001)

Eva Mozes Kor (Interview conducted June 2011)

Endnotes

[i] By 1929, this rank had been slightly modified to the much more familiar term "Reichsführer-SS"

[ii] The rumor of Reinhard Heydrich's Jewish heritage originates from the second husband of Heydrich's paternal grandmother, who remarried a man named "Süß" (a Jewish sounding name) after Heydrich's father Bruno had been born. The Herr Süß of the second marriage was not in fact Jewish, but even simply having a relative with a Jewish sounding name was enough for the circumstances to be used against Heydrich by his enemies both within the SS and the Nazi Party.

[iii] Known as the "SS Heimwehr Danzig", this unit was disbanded in October 1939.

[iv] Fromm himself was executed for dereliction of duty on March 12, 1945.

[v] Two hundred eighty-two thousand from Germany and one hundred seventeen thousand from Austria.

[vi] In August of 1941, Adolf Hitler was shouted down and jeered by a crowd in Hof, Bavaria.

[vii] 95,600 in Latvia, 155,000 in Lithuania, and 4,560 in Estonia.

[viii] The three commandants of Theresienstadt were respectively Siegfried Seidl, Anton Burger, and Karl Rahm.

[ix] In film portrayals of the Wannsee Conference ("The Wannsee Conference" in 1984 and "Conspiracy" in 2001) Klopfer is portrayed as a crass Nazi, with "Conspiracy" further portraying him as morbidly obese. In reality, Klopfer was said to be a quiet and polite man, with reserved views regarding the Jewish extermination measures proposed at Wannsee.

[x] Johannes Klein, reportedly a large and bulky man, was serving temporarily as Heydrich's driver on the day of the assassination attempt. After Heydrich's death, Klein was commissioned as an SS officer and taught driving instruction courses at a school for SS troops of motorized units.

xi Heydrich's grave originally consisted of a wooden marker before a stone memorial was constructed several weeks later. Originally, the grave was overseen by an honor guard, but this was discontinued in 1945 as the Soviet Army approached Berlin. After the close of World War II, Heydrich's memorial was destroyed by the Soviets and today is an unmarked plot in the rear of the Invalidenfriedhof cemetery.

xii The German 9th Army was the overall command for suppressing the Warsaw Uprising. The primary SS unit which participated in the fighting, under the command of Erich von dem Bach-Zelewski, was the "Korpsgruppe Bach" which consisted of "Kampfgruppe Reinefarth" and "Sturmgruppe Dirlewanger".

xiii The Office of Strategic Services (OSS) was the predecessor organization to the Central Intelligence Agency (CIA) and during World War II the American competitor to Nazi military intelligence (the Abwehr) as well as the SS foreign intelligence service of the Ausland-SD.

xiv The Katyn Forest massacre in Poland, in which 22,000 Polish military officers, political officials, landowners, and clergy were all executed, was originally blamed upon the Germans by the Soviet Union. It was not until 1990 that the Russian Federation acknowledged that the act had been committed by Soviet security forces and not until 2010 that the massacre was proven to have been ordered personally by Soviet leader Joseph Stalin.

xv Matthias Graf, a junior SD officer, was acquitted on all charges except for SS membership.

xvi Soviet authorities had also sentenced Dietrich to death in absentia, but due to the onset of the Cold War, the former SS-General was never extradited and instead retired to private life in West Germany.

xvii "The Odessa File" was a bestselling novel, later made into a motion picture, detailing the supposed activities of this secretive organization.

xviii The formal name for this group was the "Ministerium für Staatssicherheit" (State Security Service) abbreviated as the MfS. The agency was known in the vernacular as the "Staatssicherheitsdienst", or SSD, and commonly referred to as the Stasi.

xix During the Second World War, service in the Reich Labor Service was often waived.

xx The higher enlisted rank of SS-Sturmscharführer was only utilized in the Waffen-SS, where promotions were issued at the divisional level.

xxi Refer to Chapter 3, page 97 for the wartime organization of the WVHA

xxii It is unknown if a cuffband for the short-lived SS-Oberabschnitt Lothringen-Saarpfalz was ever created. The cuffband image for the Westmark senior district is a conjectural design based upon written descriptions.

xxiii The 24th SS Cavalry Regiment was never designated a headquarters unit. In addition, the 9th SS Cavalry District (Reiterabschnit IX) reportedly possessed no subordinate SS cavalry regiments. Several cavalry regiments were also directly attached to SS Senior Districts without an intermediary command. After 1938, all cavalry regiments were declared subordinate to the commanders of the SS-Oberabschnitt, after which time the SS-Cavalry Districts were disbanded.

xxiv Prior to 1939, all members of the 3rd transport company in Berlin displayed the collar insignia "Ost".

xxv Dietrich's headquarters detachment (the Stabswache) was separate from a pre-SS group of the same name.

xxvi In early 1933, the unit was also briefly based at the Berlin Alexander barracks.

xxvii These units were initially known as the 13th, 14th, and 15th SS Regiments.

xxviii The Berlin based replacement unit was also designed as "(mot)" indicating the battalion was motorized.

xxix A small number of Swiss SS volunteers served as SS war correspondents.

xxx The 22nd, 25th, 26th, 31st, and 37th SS divisions were raised from either ethnic Hungarians or Hungarian citizens.

xxxi The same collar insignia was issued to Norwegian SS volunteers later that year.

xxxii The primary divisions of the Waffen-SS maintained recruiting depots first established by the SS-VT (See page 247).

xxxiii By 1943, the Waffen-SS had also formed administrative command areas throughout Germany and occupied territories. These areas were commanded by officers known as "Befehlshaber der Waffen-SS" who was responsible for administrative matters within their region of responsibility. Operational combat forces were separate and answered to their own direct chain of command.

xxxiv The head of the SS Pharmacy Corps, ranked as an SS-Gruppenführer, held the special staff rank of "SS-Chefapotkeker".

xxxv The Waffen-SS squad unit (known as a "Gruppe") created an oddity in precedence due to the rank of SS-Gruppenführer as one of the SS general officer ranks. An apocryphal story of the Second World War states that Sepp Dietrich, inspecting the front lines in 1942, stopped an SS soldier and asked his position, to which the soldier responded: "Gruppenführer, Herr Gruppenführer!"

xxxvi Peiper was released in 1956 but was murdered in his home, presumably by French communists, in 1976.

xxxvii These SS forces were collectively referred to as the "Begleit-Bataillon Reichsführer-SS" and the "Führer-Begleit-Kompanie".

xxxviii There were forty Waffen-SS divisions, but two of these (the 23rd and 29th) were formed twice after an initial disbandment and later reforming of the divisions under the same numerical designator but with different personnel.

xxxix In the 1977 classic war film "A Bridge Too Far", Heinz Harmel is portrayed by actor Hardy Krüger. Harmel, still living when the film was produced, did not approve the use of his real name, thus the film character is referred to as "Karl Ludwig".

xl When reports reached Heinrich Himmler that foreign volunteers were wearing SS runes collar insignia, the Reichsführer-SS reportedly became very angry and issued a command order to the entire Waffen-SS specifying that foreign volunteers were strictly prohibited from wearing the SS runes used by the regular German SS and should instead wear unique national collar insignias.

xli The cuffband for this division was spelled slightly differently from the division name, printed in a script which read "Maria Theresa".

xlii The Lokot Autonomy was a semi-autonomous region in Russia, which the Germans had established as a test case for a Russian puppet government should German forces succeed in conquering Moscow and forcing a Soviet surrender. The Lokot Autonomy was also seen as a prelude to the establishment of the "Reichskommissariat Moskowien" to govern central Russia. The Autonomy existed for just over a year, from July 1942 to August 1943, under Russian collaborator Bronislav Kaminski as its head of state.

xliii Refer to pages 257-258 for Italian volunteer and conscript SS insignia. Italian SS conscripts were drafted from the Italian Army and originally wore a sideways Fasces collar patch, in contrast to Italian SS volunteers who wore this insignia vertically. By 1944, conscripts were also wearing a unique trident collar patch. SS conscripts were considered separate from the Italian SS volunteers, which were eventually formed into the 29th SS division and authorized a unique red SS collar insignia. However, by the end of 1944, mainly due to insignia supply shortages, most Italian SS members were simply wearing the same standard black backed SS runes as used by the regular SS.

xliv This command was known as the SS-Bandenkämpfverbände.

xlv Known in later life as Richard Schulze-Kossens.

xlvi The Nibelungen division is perhaps best-known outside of World War II history due to its appearance in the 1967 film "Night of the Generals", staring several famous actors of the time. In the film, the Nibelungen division is depicted as an Army division, later converted to an SS unit, which participates in the suppression of both the Warsaw City Uprising and the 1944 Hitler bomb plot. In reality, no SS units were ever formed entirely from German Army divisions, although several German Army officers did transfer to the Waffen-SS during the course of the war.

xlvii SS-Hauptscharführer Walter Sommer (1915 – 1988), known as the "Hangman of Buchenwald".

xlviii A common torture by the SS consisted of force feeding a prisoner extremely salty food (often herring), then placing the victim within a hot dry cell with no access to water and then allowing the victim to die of thirst.

xlix Also known interchangeably as "Mittelbau-Dora".

l Protective custody compound commanders of Auschwitz I included SS-Obersturmführer Heinrich Josten and SS-Sturmbannführer Franz Xavier Kraus. During its existence, four senior SS-NCOs would service as Rapportführer. The Auschwitz main camp also maintained between seven to ten Blockführer, as well as a "Death Block Leader" who supervised the punishment barracks, known as Block 11. Leaders of Block 11 included SS-Unterscharführers Kurt Muller, Otto Latch, and Bruno Schläge.

li SS-Oberscharführer Karl Czapla is known to have served as the Rapportführer for the men's quarantine barracks at Birkenau.

lii SS-Unterscharführer Richard Perschel is known to have once occupied this position.

liii In 2007, a photo album belonging to Auschwitz adjutant Karl-Friedrich Höcker was discovered containing several pictures taken at Solahuette including photographs of several senior camp officers.

liv Contrary to what is often reported, Josef Mengele was not the Chief Medical Officer of Auschwitz. Mengele was assigned to Auschwitz as a staff physician and answered to the office of the Auschwitz Garrison Physician, headed by SS-Sturmbannführer Eduard Wirths. Wirths was a veteran concentration camp doctor, assigned to Auschwitz primarily to study the spread of typhus. He committed suicide in 1945.

lv Zyklon-B, being used for its original purpose of fumigation, is a point often cited by Holocaust deniers to claim that the gas was never actually used to kill people. However, due to the large amounts of Zyklon-B shipped to Auschwitz, nearly ten times the amount sent to other camps, it is well established that Auschwitz was utilizing this gas as its primary means of extermination.

lvi The sole acquittal at the Auschwitz trial was Hans Münch.

lvii During the Treblinka trial, eleven former SS members, including deputy Treblinka commandant Kurt Franz, were charged with war crimes. One defendant died before trial while all of the remaining defendants were convicted, with four receiving the maximum penalty of life in prison.

lviii Unrelated to the Soviet trial of the same name in 1944.

lix See page 241.

lx Most guard company officers continued to wear numbered Death's Head insignia even after this directive was issued.

lxi During the German occupation, the Danish Nazi Party operated a large paramilitary force known as the Storm Afdelingen. The group was abbreviated as SA and was modeled directly after the Nazi storm troopers.

lxii It is unknown if any members of the guard company actually served as camp guards.

lxiii Photographic evidence indicates senior members of the Flemish-SS wore white undershirts.

lxiv Danish SS soldiers holding the rank of Fændrik (the equivalent of Sturmscharführer in the Waffen-SS) were further entitled to wear white sleeve cuffs (known as Tresse or "double pistons") to denote status as a First Sergeant or Sergeant Major. Headgear for the khaki service uniform consisted of a Danish Army field cap, worn with two buttons and cockade. A khaki field helmet, with a circular swastika on the right side, was also worn during combat conditions.

INDEX

Comparison of SS ranks

ORIGINAL	ALLGEMEINE	WAFFEN	TRAINING	SPECIAL
	Bewerber			
Anwärter				
Mann		Schütze¹		
		Oberschütze¹		
	Sturmmann			
	Rottenführer		Unterführer-Anwärter	
Scharführer	Unterscharführer		Unterführer | Junker	
	Scharführer		Oberjunker	Sonderführer
Truppführer	Oberscharführer		Standartenjunker	
Obertruppführer	Hauptscharführer		Standartenoberjunker	Stabsscharführer
Haupttruppführer		Sturmscharführer		
(Staffel)Führer | Sturmführer	Untersturmführer			Fachführer
	Obersturmführer			
Sturmhauptführer	Hauptsturmführer			
	Sturmbannführer			
	Obersturmbannführer			
Standartenführer (I/II)	Standartenführer			
Gauführer	Oberführer			
	Brigadeführer	Generalmajor der Waffen-SS		
	Gruppenführer	Generalleutnant der Waffen-SS		
	Obergruppenführer	General der Waffen-SS		
	Oberst-Gruppenführer	Generaloberst der Waffen-SS		
Reichsführer-SS				*Volksmarschall²*
Oberste Führer der Schutzstaffel				

¹ Known by additional titles, depending upon the career field of holder
² Proposed rank which was never introduced or created

COMING SUMMER 2019

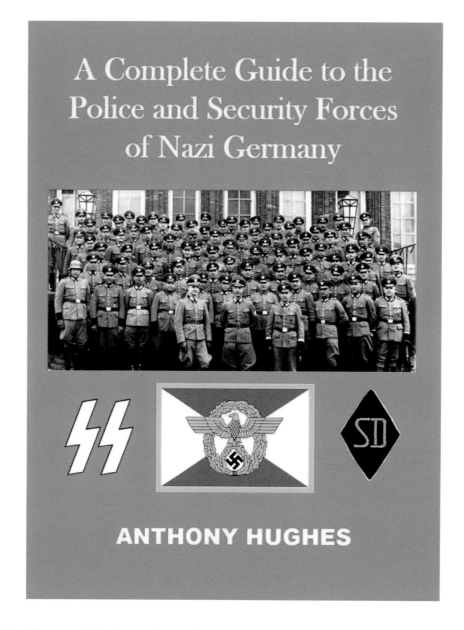

The German police forces of the Second World War were seen as virtually one and the same with the SS. Between 1936 and 1945, most senior German Police personnel also held SS rank, and by 1943 the police were commanded nearly entirely by SS officers. The SS also maintained control over several SS-Police regiments, manned and staffed by the German police, while the Nazi Secret Police, including the much feared and well-known Gestapo, was itself a police agency answering to the German Interior Ministry. While never actually part of the SS, the secret police forces were virtually synonymous and led entirely by SS personnel.

"A Complete Guide to the Police and Security Forces of Nazi Germany" tells the story of the German police; of how this organization, which had once opposed the Nazis, eventually became one of the most critical elements of the Nazi state and the SS. Told also is the story of the SD, the Nazi intelligence service, as well as detailed descriptions of the SS and Police Leaders – powerful men appointed by Heinrich Himmler who commanded every aspect of the SS and police within the Greater German Reich.

Made in the USA
Middletown, DE
27 April 2020